MOON HANDBOOKS®

BUENOS AIRES

SECOND EDITION

WAYNE BERNHARDSON

AVALON TRAVEL

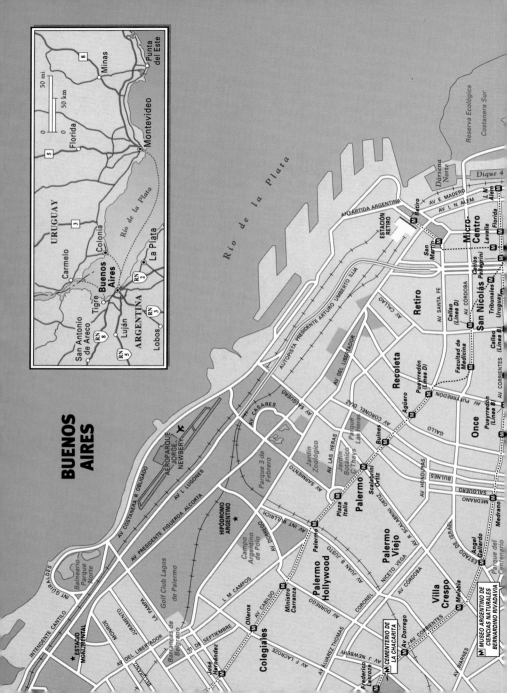

Lago de
los Patos

Lago de
los Coipos

AV INT HERNAN M GIRALT

Dique 3   Dique 2   Dique 1

Plaza de
Mayo

AV INGENIERO HUERGO

AV PASEO COLÓN

AV DON PEDRO DE MENDOZA

AUTOPISTA LA PLATA

AV ALMIRANTE BROWN

AV ESPAÑA

SARGENTO PONCE

La
Boca

Plaza
Lezama

AV REGIMIENTO DE PATRICIOS

AV MONTES DE OCA

AUTOPISTA 9 DE JULIO

San Telmo

AV GENERAL B MITRE

GENERAL BELGRANO

AV HIPÓLITO YRIGOYEN

Riachuelo

BRANDSEN

SUÁREZ

DR R CARRILLO

VIEYTES

Barracas

SUÁREZ

IRIARTE

OSVALDO CRUZ

PEDRO DE LUJÁN

AV GALICIA

Plaza
España

Constitución

ESTACIÓN
CONSTITUCIÓN

AV VÉLEZ SARSFIELD

Monserrat

AV ENTRE RÍOS

Independencia
(Línea E)

San
José

Entre
Ríos

Pichincha

BRASIL

AV CASEROS

COLONIA

CLUB HURACÁN

Nueva
Pompeya

San Cristóbal

AV JUJUY

Balvanera

AV BELGRANO

Boedo

General
Urquiza

Jujuy

Boedo

DEÁN FUNES

Parque
Patricios

Parque de los
Patricios

USPALLATA

AV CHICLANA

AV ALMAFUERTE

AV SÁENZ

Almagro

Plaza
Miserere

AV BOEDO

AV JUJUY

VENEZUELA

DE JANEIRO

Río de
Janeiro

AV LA PLATA

AUTOPISTA 25 DE MAYO

AV JUAN DE GARAY

AV COBO

AV PERITO MORENO

Parque
Rivadavia

AV INDEPENDENCIA

Av La
Plata

José M
Moreno

AV JOSÉ M MORENO

AV DE VEDIA

DR DÍAZ VÉLEZ

AV CAMPICHUELO

ACOYTE

Caballito

Primera
Junta

Emilio
Mitre

Parque
Chacabuco

AV DE LA CRUZ

San Lorenzo
de Almagro

AV ROCA

AV 27 DE FEBRERO

GENERAL J J VALLE

Parque
Julio A
Roca

DE PUEYRREDÓN

NEUQUÉN

AV GALLARDO

AV RIVADAVIA

AV EVA PERÓN

AV DIRECTORIO

EMILIO MITRE

Medalla
Milagros

AV BOYACÁ

CASTAÑARES

VARELA

LACARRA

MARIANO ACOSTA

Parque
de la
Ciudad

AV FERNÁNDEZ DE LA CRUZ

AV GENERAL FERNÁNDEZ DE LA CRUZ

AV INTI HUASI

AV RABANAL

0.5 mi

0   0.5 km

© AVALON TRAVEL PUBLISHING, INC.

PALERMO

Río de la Plata

CLUB DE
PESCADORES

Punta
Carrasco

ASOCIACIÓN
ARGENTINA DE
GOLF

NUEVO
CIRCUITO
K D T

COSTA SALGUERO
GOLF CENTER

AV. PRESIDENTE RAMON S CASTILLO

Dársena F

AV. CASARES

SALGUERO TENNIS/
PADDLE/SQUASH

PASEO
ALCORTA

JERÓNIMO SALGUERO

CANVIA

AUTOPISTA PRESIDENTE A U ILLIA

MUSEO DE ARTE
LATINOAMERICANO
DE BUENOS AIRES

SAN MARTIN
DE TOURS

JUEZ TEDIN

MUSEO DE MOTIVOS
ARGENTINOS JOSÉ HERNÁNDEZ

Plaza Grand
Bourg

INSTITUTO NACIONAL
SANMARTINIANO

Plaza Naciones
Unidas

HOSPITAL MUNICIPAL
JUAN FERNÁNDEZ

Plaza
República
de Chile

AV. PTE FIGUEROA ALCORTA

Recoleta

MUSEO NACIONAL DE
ARTE DECORATIVO

AUTOMÓVIL CLUB
ARGENTINA

AV. DEL LIBERTADOR

AV. GENERAL LAS HERAS

HOSPITAL
RIVADAVIA

PEÑA

AV. PUEYRREDÓN

FRENCH

AGÜERO

HAEDO

LAPURIDA

VICENTE LÓPEZ

GUIDO

JUNCAL

AV. PUEYRREDÓN

LARREA

AZCUÉNAGA

PTE J E URBIRU

AYACUCHO

ARENALES

RODRIGUEZ PEÑA

0   500 yds

0   500 m

Pueyrredón

ECUADOR

AV. CALLAO

AV. PUEYRREDÓN

AV. SANTE FE

MONTEVIDEO

Gurruchaga
1946

CONTENTS

Discover Buenos Aires

Explore Buenos Aires

Excursions from Buenos Aires

Know Buenos Aires

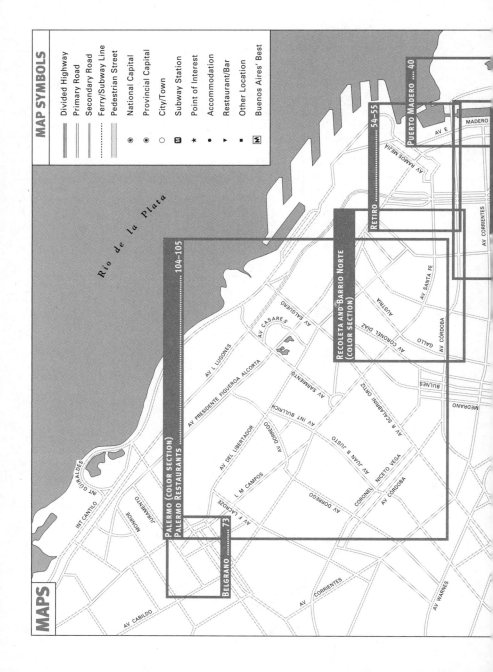

MAPS

MAP SYMBOLS

▤	Divided Highway
	Primary Road
	Secondary Road
	Ferry/Subway Line
⋯⋯	Pedestrian Street
✲	National Capital
◉	Provincial Capital
○	City/Town
Ⓜ	Subway Station
★	Point of Interest
●	Accommodation
▶	Restaurant/Bar
■	Other Location
ⓜ	Buenos Aires' Best

Río de la Plata

PALERMO (COLOR SECTION)
PALERMO RESTAURANTS 104–105

BELGRANO 73

RECOLETA AND BARRIO NORTE
(COLOR SECTION)

RETIRO 54–55

PUERTO MADERO 40

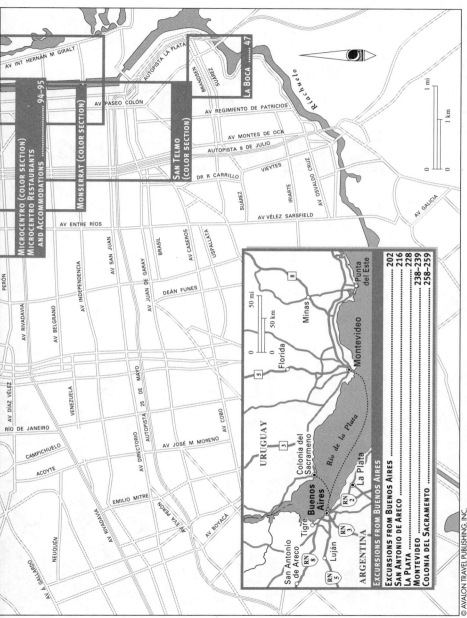

MICROCENTRO (COLOR SECTION)
MICROCENTRO RESTAURANTS
AND ACCOMMODATIONS 94–95

MONSERRAT (COLOR SECTION)

SAN TELMO
(COLOR SECTION)

LA BOCA 47

AV INT HERNÁN M GIRALT

AUTOPISTA LA PLATA

BRANDSEN

SUÁREZ

AV PASEO COLÓN

AV REGIMIENTO DE PATRICIOS

AV MONTES DE OCA

AUTOPISTA 9 DE JULIO

DR R CARRILLO

VIEYTES

SUÁREZ

IRIARTE

AV OSVALDO CRUZ

AV VÉLEZ SARSFIELD

AV GALICIA

AV ENTRE RÍOS

PERÓN

AV SAN JUAN

BRASIL

AV CASEROS

USPALLATA

AV RIVADAVIA

AV BELGRANO

AV INDEPENDENCIA

AV JUAN DE GARAY

DEÁN FUNES

RÍO DE JANEIRO

VENEZUELA

AUTOPISTA 25 DE MAYO

AV COBO

AV JOSÉ M MORENO

AV DIRECTORIO

RÍO DÍAZ VÉLEZ

CAMPICHUELO

ACOYTE

EMILIO MITRE

AV EVA PERÓN

AV RIVADAVIA

AV BOYACÁ

NEUQUÉN

AV A GALLARDO

Riachuelo

URUGUAY

Colonia del
Sacramento

Río de la Plata

Montevideo

Minas

Florida

Punta
del Este

8

5

3

50 mi
0
0   50 km

ARGENTINA

Buenos
Aires

Tigre

Luján

San Antonio
de Areco

RN
8

RN
5

RN
3

RN
2

La Plata

EXCURSIONS FROM BUENOS AIRES

EXCURSIONS FROM BUENOS AIRES 202
SAN ANTONIO DE ARECO 216
LA PLATA 228
MONTEVIDEO 238–239
COLONIA DEL SACRAMENTO 258–259

1 mi

1 km

0

0

© AVALON TRAVEL PUBLISHING, INC.

Discover
Buenos Aires

Famous for the melancholy melodies and intricate moves of the tango, cosmopolitan Buenos Aires has long enjoyed a reputation as the "Paris of the South," because of its broad avenues, colossal monuments, and mansard-capped mansions. With its New World vigor, though, it's at least as accurate to call Argentina's capital, the first Latin American metropolis to exceed a million inhabitants, the "New York of the South."

Despite Buenos Aires's cosmopolitan outlook, many of its inhabitants, known as *porteños* (port residents), still identify strongly with their own *barrios* (neighborhoods) in what was, before massive post-independence immigration and rocketing prosperity, the Gran Aldea (Great Village). Like New Yorkers, they are often assertive to the point of brashness, and their characteristic accent sets them apart from the peoples of Argentina's other provinces. Like New York, Buenos Aires never sleeps, with its cinemas, theaters, and bars and discos open until daybreak.

Every *Baires* neighborhood has a distinctive personality. The compact, densely built Microcentro boasts the major shopping and theater districts, as well as the capital's Wall Street—"La City." Immediately south, in Monserrat, the Avenida de Mayo is the city's civic axis—the site of spectacle and debacle in Argentina's tumultuous contemporary politics. Monserrat gives way to San Telmo's cobbled colonial streets, with their tango bars and famous Plaza Dorrego flea market. Farther south is the working-class outpost of La Boca, also an artists' colony known for the Caminito, its colorful curving pedestrian mall.

Northern neighborhoods like Retiro and Recoleta are elegant and even opulent—so much so that affluent Argentines often elect to spend eternity at the Cementerio de la Recoleta, one of the world's most exclusive graveyards. Beyond Recoleta, the parks of Palermo were once the dominion of 19th-century despot Juan Manuel de Rosas, but much of the barrio has become a middle- to upper-middle-class area with the city's finest dining and wildest night life. North of Palermo, woodsy Belgrano fancies itself not just a suburb or a separate city, but a republic in itself—and it was in fact briefly Argentina's capital.

For some visitors, Buenos Aires alone is enough, but it's also the port of entry to some remarkable excursions. The delta of the Río de la Plata, which empties into the South Atlantic here, is a wonderland of narrow channels through wildlife-rich gallery forest; to the west, the gaucho homeland of the flat green pampas stretches beyond the horizon. Only a short sail across the river, neighboring Uruguay can boast the UNESCO World Heritage Site of Colonia, a distinctive capital city in Montevideo, and the world-class beach resort of Punta del Este.

By jet, Buenos Aires is only eight hours from Miami, ten hours from New York, or 15 hours from Los Angeles—close enough for short-term visitors focused on special interests. Since Argentine standard time is only two hours ahead of New York and three hours behind Western Europe, jet lag is only a minor

issue. Even to those with devalued U.S. dollars, it remains affordable—even cheap.

For much of the 20th century, Buenos Aires underwent a
steady decline, interrupted by spectacular growth spurts and
even more spectacular economic and political calamities, including one of the most brutal and arbitrary military dictatorships on a continent that was infamous for them. Yet somehow,
like its melancholy traditional music and dance—the tango—
Buenos Aires has managed to retain a certain stability by way
of an identity mystique that sets it apart from both Europe and
North America.

Unlike some Latin American mega-cities, Buenos Aires has a broad-based, modern travel and transportation infrastructure, with contemporary accommodations, restaurants, and other services eager to deal with overseas visitors. The devaluation-fueled demand of the last few years, though, has put pressure on the best accommodations and, unless you're flexible with respect to hotel needs, reservations are advisable and may even be essential.

Likewise, for visitors traveling elsewhere in Argentina, peak season demand has tested airline capacity in particular, and even long-distance bus tickets may be harder to come by at peak travel times, such as Christmas and Easter. If your time is limited, advance planning may be crucial. Another factor to consider, for those interested in museums and galleries, is that many of them close in the summer months of January and February. For further tips, see the author's *Moon Handbooks Argentina,* which covers the entire country.

WHEN TO GO

Buenos Aires's urban appeal is largely independent of the seasons, but some visitors—and many Argentines for that matter—would rather avoid the capital's hot, sticky summer; business travelers should avoid January and February if at all possible, since many potential contacts will be on vacation. Activities like the theater and special events, most notably the increasingly popular Festival del Tango, resume in March as *porteños* return from summer holidays. The spring months of September, October, and November may be the most comfortable, but the relatively mild winter sees some stretches of warm, brilliant weather.

For most of this book's suggested excursions, weather will not be a factor either. The summer months of January and February, though, can be uncomfortably crowded at Uruguayan beach resorts like Punta del Este.

WHAT TO TAKE

A good rule of thumb is to bring appropriately seasonal clothing for comparable northern hemisphere latitudes. Buenos Aires's climate is mild in spring and autumn, hot and humid in summer, and cool but not cold in winter—though humidity and winter winds can make it feel colder than absolute temperatures might suggest (though frost is almost unheard of). For summer, then, light cottons are the rule, while a sweater and perhaps a light jacket suffice for the shoulder seasons. A warm but not polar-strength jacket and rain gear are advisable for winter.

Much depends, of course, on what sort of activities you will be undertaking—for opera at the Teatro Colón, for instance, formal clothing is obligatory. Likewise, individuals conducting business in the capital will dress as they would in New York or London, with suit and tie for men and similarly appropriate clothing for women. A compact umbrella is a good idea at any time of year.

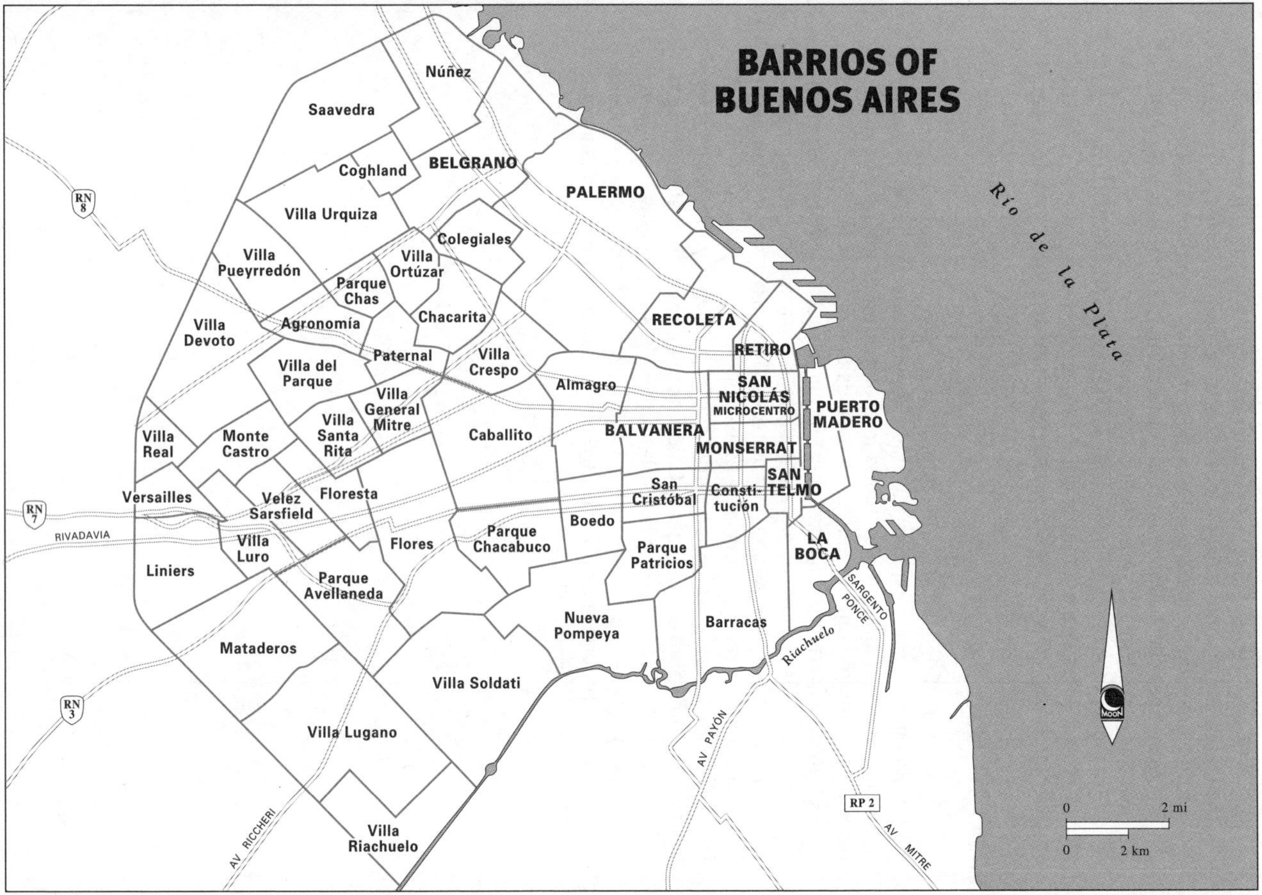

BARRIOS OF BUENOS AIRES

Río de la Plata

2 mi

2 km

0

0

RETIRO

PUERTO MADERO

SAN NICOLÁS
MICROCENTRO

MONSERRAT

SAN TELMO

Consti-
tución

LA
BOCA

SARGENTO
PONCE

Barracas

Riachuelo

RP 2

AV. MITRE

AV PAYÓN

RECOLETA

BALVANERA

San
Cristóbal

Parque
Patricios

Boedo

Nueva
Pompeya

PALERMO

Almagro

Parque
Chacabuco

Villa Soldati

Núñez

BELGRANO

Colegiales

Chacarita

Villa
Crespo

Caballito

Flores

Parque
Avellaneda

Villa Lugano

Villa
Riachuelo

AV. RICHIERI

Saavedra

Coghland

Villa Urquiza

Villa
Ortúzar

Parque
Chas

Paternal

Villa
General
Mitre

Villa
Santa
Rita

Villa
Floresta

Villa
Luro

Mataderos

Villa
Pueyrredón

Agronomía

Villa del
Parque

Velez
Sarsfield

Villa
Devoto

Monte
Castro

Villa
Real

Versailles

Liniers

RN
8

RN
7

RIVADAVIA

RN
3

Gran Buenos Aires (Greater Buenos Aires) is a sprawling megalopolis that takes in large parts of surrounding Buenos Aires province. Even without those suburbs, it's a large, densely populated city, but its barrios give it a cozier feel, even in areas like the downtown financial district.

Formally known as the Ciudad Autónoma de Buenos Aires (Autonomous City of Buenos Aires), the Capital Federal (Federal Capital) of Buenos Aires lies within the boundaries formed by the Río de la Plata, its tributary the Riachuelo, and the ring roads of Avenida General Paz and Avenida 27 de Febrero.

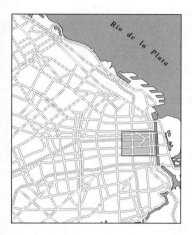

MONSERRAT

In B.A.'s oldest barrio, the historic center is the **Plaza de Mayo,** the locus of Spanish colonial power and site of major public buildings like the **Casa Rosada** presidential palace and the **Catedral Metropolitana** (which is the reason the barrio also goes by the name **Catedral al Sur,** South of the Cathedral). Except for vestiges of the Cabildo, those colonial buildings are long gone from the plaza itself, but others survive nearby. The original grid stretches in all directions except where modern thoroughfares, such as the east-west Avenida de Mayo and the broad north-south Avenida 9 de Julio, have obliterated narrow colonial streets.

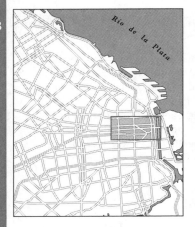

MICROCENTRO

Formally known as **San Nicolás,** the area bounded by Avenida Córdoba on the north, Avenida Eduardo Madero on the east, Avenida Rivadavia on the south, and Avenida Callao on the west encompasses much of the city's traditional financial, commercial, and entertainment center. The area between Avenida 9 de Julio and the riverfront, immediately north of the Plaza de Mayo, is commonly called the Microcentro or the Catedral al Norte.

For many visitors, one of Microcentro's highlights is the pedestrian **Calle Florida,** once the city's most fashionable shopping district and still home to the **Galerías Pacífico,** the most impressive of several historic buildings recycled into modish shopping malls. The cultural bellwether, though, is the landmark **Teatro Colón,** while Avenida Corrientes is the axis of an attenuated but recovering theater district.

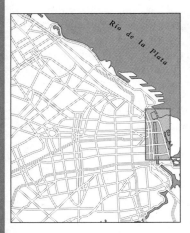

PUERTO MADERO

East of Monserrat, the Microcentro, and San Telmo, stretching north-south along the river, redeveloped Puerto Madero is the city's newest barrio. Its chic recycled warehouses and high-rise luxury flats give it a gated-community air of exclusivity, but it's also the city's largest open space, drawing people from around the city to its scenic yacht basin, waterside esplanades, and ecological reserve—a onetime landfill that went wild with volunteer flora and fauna. Thanks to the fact it's not en route to anywhere else, it's also one of the city's quietest neighborhoods. At the same time, there's a palpable sense of history in Puerto Madero's former granaries and rectangular basins, and especially in its ambitious immigration museum.

SAN TELMO

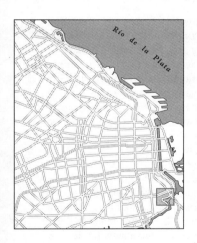

Tourist-friendly San Telmo, with its narrow colonial streets, antique shops, and street fairs, is a favorite barrio among Argentines and foreigners alike. Six blocks south of the Plaza de Mayo, bounded by Chile on the north, Piedras to the west, Puerto Madero to the east, and Avenida Brasil, Parque Lezama, and Avenida Caseros to the south, it's one of the city's best neighborhoods for walkers—especially on Sunday, when most of Calle Defensa is closed to motor vehicles.

Until the yellow fever outbreaks of the 19th century, San Telmo was a prestigious address; today, it's a Bohemian blend of the colonial barrio, peopled with artists and musicians, plus a scattering of old-money families and more than a scattering of *conventillos* (tenements) abandoned by old money. Its number-one attraction is Plaza Dorrego's Sunday flea market, the **Feria de San Pedro Telmo;** it's also a key entertainment district that's home to many tango floor shows and other activities.

LA BOCA

Southeast of San Telmo, along the Riachuelo, the immigrant working-class barrio of La Boca has never been prosperous, but it has a colorful history and an extravagantly colorful vernacular architecture along its **Caminito** pedestrian mall. It also has a palpable sense of community, symbolized by its solidarity with the local soccer team and the presence of institutions like the **Catalinas Sur** theater company. Thanks to the legacy of painter Benito Quinquela Martín, it's also an artists' colony with museums and galleries.

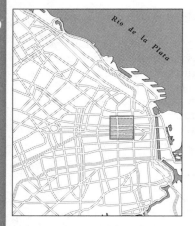

BALVANERA

West of Monserrat and San Nicolás, rarely mentioned by its official name, Balvanera subsumes several smaller neighborhoods with scattered points of interest: the bustling but vaguely defined area commonly known as **Congreso** (home to the imposing headquarters of the Argentine legislature) overlaps the barrios of Monserrat and San Nicolás, while **Once** (the conspicuously Jewish garment district) and the **Abasto** (which gave the city tango legend Carlos Gardel) have their own distinct identities.

One of the city's most distinctive landmarks is the **Palacio de las Aguas Corrientes,** the former city waterworks just west of San Nicolás on Avenida Córdoba. The recycled **Mercado del Abasto,** a onetime wholesale produce market that's now a shopping mall, has helped revive the neighborhood.

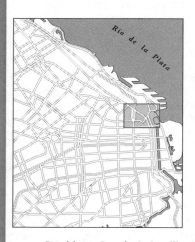

RETIRO

Marking a transition to the northern and northwestern upper-middle-class residential barrios, the area surrounding **Plaza San Martín** was once home to the city's most extravagant mansions. While much of it's still elegant, many of those buildings have passed into the hands of the federal government, foreign embassies, and luxury hotels. There are also key art museums and especially galleries here.

Retiro commonly refers to the area surrounding the Plaza San Martín, but it includes all the terrain north of Avenida Córdoba, also bounded by Uruguay, Montevideo, Avenida Presidente Ramón S. Castillo, San Martín, and Avenida Eduardo Madero. Parts of the barrio, beyond the train and bus stations to the northeast, are desperate slums.

Retiro also overlaps the sector known as Barrio Norte, which is closely identified with Recoleta and extends into Palermo by some accounts.

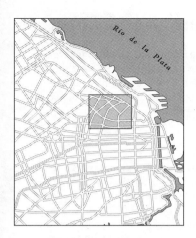

RECOLETA AND BARRIO NORTE

Immediately northwest of Retiro, Recoleta is the one barrio that retains an almost undiminished air of elegance, especially in and around its legendary necropolis, the **Cementerio de la Recoleta** (Recoleta Cemetery). In one of the city's most touristed barrios, the line between vigorous excess and serene but opulent eternity is a thin one.

In everyday usage, Recoleta refers to the area in and around the celebrated Cementerio de la Recoleta. Formally, it's a sprawling barrio that includes all the territory bounded by Montevideo, Avenida Córdoba, Mario Bravo, Avenida Coronel Díaz, Avenida General Las Heras, Tagle, the Belgrano railway line, and the new northbound Autopista Illía to the eastward prolongation of Montevideo.

Recoleta also encompasses large parts of Barrio Norte, a mostly residential area of vague boundaries that extends westward from Retiro and north into Palermo. Neither a formal barrio nor even a state of mind, Barrio Norte is more a real estate concept, but one which is widely accepted by both its residents and those of other parts of the capital.

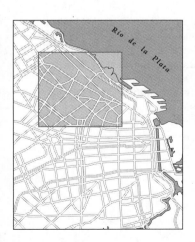

PALERMO

Beyond Recoleta, the northbound arteries of Avenida Santa Fe, Avenida Las Heras, and Avenida del Libertador lead to Palermo, the city's largest and arguably most diverse barrio; its wooded parks were once the country estate of dictator Juan Manuel de Rosas. Those open spaces still draw large numbers of *porteño* picnickers and recreationists, but the barrio is also ground zero for an explosion of gourmet restaurants, bars and other entertainment locales, and design and fashion shops.

One of the city's most rapidly changing areas, Palermo subdivides into several smaller but distinct units: the embassy row of **Palermo Chico** between Avenida del Libertador and the river; the vibrant residential and nightlife zone of **Palermo Viejo** across Avenida Santa Fe, which further subdivides into

Palermo Soho and Palermo Hollywood; and Las Cañitas, on the border with Belgrano.

Formally, Palermo's boundaries zigzag along La Pampa, Avenida Figueroa Alcorta, Avenida Valentín Alsina, Zabala, Avenida Cabildo, Jorge Newbery, Cramer, Avenida Dorrego, Avenida Córdoba, Mario Bravo, Avenida Coronel Díaz, Avenida Las Heras, Tagle, the tracks of the Ferrocarril Belgrano, Salguero, and the Avenida Costanera Rafael Obligado.

BELGRANO

Once a separate city, Belgrano prizes its distinct residential identity, but its leafy streets also host an assortment of museums, most notably those of sculptor Rogelio Yrurtia and novelist Enrique Larreta, and other cultural resources. With the recent extension of the Subte beneath Avenida Cabildo, to Congreso de Tucumán on the border with Núñez, the barrio's sights are more accessible than ever.

Belgrano subdivides into three distinct areas: the wooded residential area of **Belgrano R**, west of Avenida Cabildo (the *R* stands not for residential, but for the city of Rosario, the ultimate destination of the area's rail line); **Barrancas de Belgrano,** between Avenida Cabildo and the tracks of the Ferrocarril Mitre commuter line to Tigre; and **Bajo Belgrano,** alternatively known as **Belgrano Chico,** between the tracks and the Río de la Plata.

Belgrano is bordered on the south by Palermo, on the west by Colegiales and Villa Ortúzar, on the north by Coghland and Núñez, and on the east by the Río de la Plata. The actual line zigzags among many streets, but the approximate border with Palermo runs along La Pampa, Avenida Valentín Alsina, and Zabala. The major thoroughfares are Avenida Cabildo, the northward extension of Avenida Santa Fe; Avenida Luis María Campos; and Avenida del Libertador.

OUTER BARRIOS

Further outlying barrios have scattered points of tourist interest, including museums, parks, and *ferias* (street fairs). Among them are the southerly working-class barrios of **Barracas, Parque Patricios,** and **Nueva Pompeya;** middle-class **Caballito,** in what was once the city's periphery but is now its precise geographical center; the far western **Mataderos,** where the countryside still has its urban outpost; and the northern barrios of **Núñez** and **Saavedra.**

In a city with so many highlights, it's truly hard to choose the best, but most visitors will agree with at least some of the following. These suggestions assume a Saturday-morning arrival in Buenos Aires, but they can be mixed and matched at your convenience.

DAY 1

After settling into your hotel, visit Ground Zero: the Plaza de Mayo, with its historic sites, including the Casa Rosada presidential palace, the colonial Cabildo, and the Catedral Metropolitana. Take a breather for coffee or a light lunch at the Café Tortoni before visiting the underrated Museo de la Ciudad and the Manzana de las Luces.

Since it was a long flight, you may enjoy a nap before considering the theater (for an eye-opening perspective on Argentine history, consider Teatro Catalinas Sur, in the working-class barrio of La Boca), and go slumming for steaks at nearby El Obrero afterwards.

DAY 2

Enjoy a leisurely Sunday brunch at Recoleta's La Biela, then make the short walk to the Cementerio de la Recoleta, where former La Biela clients are spending eternity. After a stroll among its historic crypts, grab a cross-town cab to Plaza Dorrego's Feria de San Pedro Telmo, the capital's one can't-miss market, for antiques and street performers, including mimes and highly skilled *tangueros*.

After lunch overlooking Plaza Dorrego, or a few blocks away at the ageless Bar El Federal, take a bus or cab to the brightly painted houses along the Caminito pedestrian mall, a tourist trap that retains elements of integrity in the working-class barrio of La Boca.

© WAYNE BERNHARDSON

Plaza de Mayo and Casa Rosada

© WAYNE BERNHARDSON

Sunday morning at La Biela, Recoleta

Any time after about 9 P.M., you can enjoy B.A.'s best beef at Cabaña Las Lilas, on the Puerto Madero waterfront. While this may be early for *porteños,* Puerto Madero restaurants are more accustomed to serving as early as 7 P.M., and you may be able to catch a floor show at one of the flashier *tanguerías;* they also serve dinner, but their food can't match Las Lilas.

DAY 3

Many museums and other attractions are closed Mondays, so this makes a good day for excursions to the "gaucho capital" of San Antonio de Areco or Uruguay's UNESCO World Heritage Site of Colonia, only an hour away by high-speed catamaran. There are plenty of good options for sightseeing, dining, and shopping at both destinations.

On your return, enjoy a drink at a fashionable Barrio Norte bar like Milión or Gran Bar Danzón, which also have fine restaurant menus. Many other restaurants are closed Mondays, so consider a traditional *fugazza* (pizza with mozzarella, ham, and sweet onions) at Güerrín,

on Avenida Corrientes. For dessert, walk a few blocks west to Cadore, the author's nominee for B.A.'s best ice creamery.

DAY 4

This high-culture day includes visits to the legendary Teatro Colón, the Southern Hemisphere's first great opera house, and the modern Latin American art collection at Palermo's state-of-the-art Museo de Arte Latinomericano de Buenos Aires (MALBA). For a view of recent Argentine history through partisan eyes, visit the not-so-distant Museo Eva Perón before taking a breather at Parque Tres de Febrero, the city's largest open space. Its Parque Japonés (Japanese Garden) and Rosedal (Rose Garden) are islands of calm in a city of noise.

After sunset, take a leisurely walk from Plaza Cortázar through the "gourmet ghetto" of Palermo Viejo before deciding on any of dozens of creative restaurants for dinner—one of the best is Palermo Hollywood's Olsen, across Avenida Juan B. Justo, with its improbable Scandinavian/ Patagonian menu, creative vodka-based drinks, and Nordic garden.

At the end of the business week, there may be time to relax and enjoy the capital's cultural and entertainment offerings before resuming work or continuing the trip on Monday. Some of these are typical tourist activities, while others are less routine, but all of them are worthwhile.

DAY 1

As Friday's labors end, unwind with coffee or a cocktail at the landmark **Café Tortoni,** where tourists and locals alike gather around its marble tables; consider a tango music or dance show, or other live entertainment, at the **Tortoni's Sala Alfonsina Storni.** Any time after about 9 P.M., you and your contacts can enjoy B.A.'s best beef at Puerto Madero's **Cabaña Las Lilas.** If you dine early, some of the flashier *tanguerías* have late-night floor shows; they also serve dinner, but their generic meals are no match for the succulent steaks from Las Lilas's own Luján *estancia.*

DAY 2

For a change of pace from urban turmoil, consider any of several possible excursions: the fascinating historic and natural environment of the Paraná delta's **Isla Martín García,** a Día de Campo (day in the country) at an *estancia* or the "gaucho capital" of **San Antonio de Areco,** or Uruguay's placid UNESCO World Heritage Site of **Colonia del Sacramento.** On returning to the city, have a drink at a hip Barrio Norte bar like **Gran Bar Danzón** or the terrace at **Milión.**

For a further antidote to the conventional business world, try to appreciate the working-class immigrant perspective on Argentine history at La

San Telmo's classic Bar El Federal makes some of B.A.'s best ravioli.

© WAYNE BERNHARDSON

Sunday shoppers at Plaza Dorrego's Feria de San Pedro Telmo

Boca's wildly visual Teatro Catalinas Sur, where a lack of Spanish is no impediment to getting the message. For a post-theater dinner, nearby no-frills El Obrero is the anti–Las Lilas in style, but its beef's not that far behind.

DAY 3

For a leisurely Sunday brunch, retreat to the boreal forest landscaping of Palermo Hollywood's Olsen. Then do the tourist sights: Plaza Dorrego's Feria de San Pedro Telmo, the capital's one can't-miss market, for its antiques, mimes and *tangueros,* and the brightly painted houses along La Boca's Caminito pedestrian mall, a tourist trap that retains an element of integrity. Have lunch overlooking Plaza Dorrego, or a few blocks away at the ageless Bar El Federal, where there's refreshing hard cider on tap.

Following lunch, stroll through the world-famous Cementerio de la Recoleta, where the rich and famous flaunt their status in death as in life; many were clients of the nearby Café La Biela, an ideal stop for coffee and dessert. Spend the rest of the afternoon in Palermo's Parque Tres de Febrero, the city's largest open space, whose Parque Japonés (Japanese Garden) and Rosedal (Rose Garden) are islands of calm. After sunset, take a leisurely walk through Palermo Viejo's "gourmet ghetto" before deciding on any of dozens of creative restaurants for dinner—try the industrially cool Bar Uriarte or the more casual Lelé de Troya.

Buenos Aires has a vital art scene, and the galleries, museums, and public art to prove it. It may have been slow to establish its identity—one critic says the colonial period lasted into the 20th century—but Argentine painters and sculptors have made an impact on the global art market.

Its Francophile mansions, with their conspicuous mansards, have given Buenos Aires its misleading "Paris of the South" nickname, but in reality the city is far more diverse. Many Spanish colonial or colonial-style buildings still survive, and vernacular styles range from "sausage houses" with narrow frontages on deep lots to the brightly painted metal-clad structures of La Boca. Many contemporary buildings are less distinguished, but a handful truly stand out.

DAY 1

After settling into your accommodations, orient yourself by visiting the Plaza de Mayo, with its historic sites, including the Casa Rosada presidential palace, the colonial Cabildo, and the neoclassical Catedral Metropolitana. Take a breather for coffee or a light lunch at the landmark Café Tortoni before visiting the underrated

Puente de la Mujer, by Spanish architect Santiago Calatrava, Puerto Madero

Museo de la Ciudad and the Manzana de las Luces. For an underground perspective on the colonial city, take a guided tour of the restored tunnels at San Telmo's El Zanjón (weekdays only); if it's a weekend, visit the nearby Museo de Arte Moderno.

Late afternoon is a good time to stroll the Puerto Madero waterfront and appreciate how builders have recycled former granaries and mills into upmarket lofts, restaurants, and hotels; the Hyatt Hotel and architect Santiago Calatrava's Puente de la Mujer, a pedestrian bridge that swings open to allow yachts to pass, are modern design infusions.

As long as you're exploring Puerto Madero, consider testing B.A.'s best beef at Cabaña Las Lilas, which has outdoor seating looking onto the yacht basin. Dining early would leave time for a flashy *tanguería* floor show or a more authentic alternative, such as live music or song at San Telmo's Torquato Tasso.

DAY 2

Take a leisurely breakfast or brunch in the shade of the *gomero* at Recoleta's La Biela, then cross the plaza to the Cementerio de la Recoleta, where Argentina's elite have built crypts to match their mansions (and many former La Biela clients are spending eternity).

After a stroll among its extravagant tombs, cross Avenida del Libertador to the **Museo Nacional de Bellas Artes**, the traditional repository of the best Argentine art. Recrossing the avenue, walk the surrounding Recoleta streets, where the "Paris of the South" comes closest to reality. Head toward Retiro, where galleries like **Ruth Benzacar** display the latest in Argentine art. Don't forget to lift your eyes to the **Edificio Kavanagh**, the deco landmark apartment building that was B.A.'s first skyscraper.

After lunch, depending on the day, backtrack to Palermo's **Museo de Arte Latinoamericano de Buenos Aires**, as distinguished for its contemporary design as for its regional art collections. If it's not open, try the other extreme and take a bus or cab to the exuberantly painted tenements along La Boca's **Caminito** pedestrian mall, a tourist trap that retains more than an element of integrity. The contemporary **Fundación Proa** and the **Museo Benito Quinquela Martín**, housing the works of a late barrio painter, both lend La Boca an artistic edge.

DAY 3

For an unconventional excursion, ride the Subte to Belgrano, stopping en route at stations like **Facultad de Medicina** and **Plaza Italia** to view their elaborate wall and floor murals. Detraining at Juramento, walk past landmarks like the museum/house of Hispanophile novelist **Enrique Larreta**, with its elaborate gardens, and the

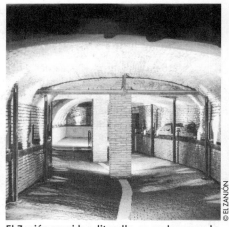

El Zanjón provides, literally, an underground tour of San Telmo

dome of the **Iglesia la Redonda**. The real gem, though, is the **Museo Rogelio Yrurtia**, boasting the works of a sculptor whose monumental works challenged the equestrian-statue paradigm of *porteño* public art.

On the way back, detrain at Plaza Italia for a stroll through landscape architect Carlos Thays's **Jardín Botánico**, whose layout set a standard for public parks not just in Buenos Aires but throughout the country. Nearby Palermo Soho boasts dozens of stylishly recycled "sausage houses" that have become restaurants, bars, and shops (many focusing on art, design, and fashion).

© EL ZANJÓN

Ever since Pedro de Mendoza stepped out of his ship and onto the Río de la Plata's *barrancas* in the 16th century, Buenos Aires was destined to be a larger-than-life place, even as it languished during colonial times. Some of the uprisings that led to the Latin American independence movement started here, on the periphery, and their imprint is still palpable. The tumultuous 19th century, dominated by caudillos like Juan Manuel de Rosas, and the chaotic 20th century legacy of Juan and Evita Perón, and their successors, are no less apparent.

DAY 1

After settling into your accommodations, visit the Plaza de Mayo, where Perón and Evita played to their partisans from the balcony of the Casa Rosada presidential palace, naval planes strafed the Economy Ministry in a 1955 coup that drove Perón from power, and the Madres de la Plaza de Mayo began their eloquently silent marches against the Dirty War dictatorship of 1976–1983.

Not so far away, across Paseo Colón, the university Facultad de Ingeniería (once the Fundación Eva Perón) and the CGT labor union headquarters were loci of Peronist power. In 1952, weeping working-class Argentines lined both sides of Avenida de Mayo from the Casa Rosada as Evita's casket proceeded west to the Congreso Nacional, where it lay in state.

Buenos Aires has an earlier history, though, in the remains of the nearby colonial Cabildo (town council) and the narrow streets of Monserrat and San Telmo. Here, south of the Plaza, the Manzana de las Luces was the colonial city's "block of enlightenment" and, from the low roofs along the street, the *porteño* resistance poured boiling oil and water on British invaders in the early 19th century. The Museo de la Ciudad and the restored drainage tunnels at El Zanjón (weekdays only) reveal everyday aspects of *porteño* life even as epic events overshadowed them.

DAY 2

Part of Argentine history is small things writ large, such as the individual stories of the millions of European immigrants who arrived at the docks of Puerto Madero's Hotel de Inmigrantes,

© WAYNE BERNHARDSON

Now a museum, Puerto Madero's former Hotel de Inmigrantes was the first stop for new arrivals from Europe in the early 20th century.

Buenos Aires's Ellis Island, from the late 19th century. A walk south along the port's fashionably recycled *diques* (boat basins), storehouses, and granaries, with their cranes still standing but now inert, recalls that era when Argentina boomed with wheat, wool, and beef exports. Many of these granaries have become stylish restaurants, but the only one truly worth the price is **Cabaña Las Lilas,** widely considered to have B.A.'s best beef.

To see where many of those immigrants ended up, and how they still live, take a bus or cab to the brightly painted houses along the **Caminito** pedestrian mall, a tourist trap that retains elements of proletarian integrity in La Boca. These were the people who idolized the Peróns and filled the La Bombonera soccer stadium for working-class hero Diego Maradona.

Another symbol of solidarity is the barrio's **Teatro Catalinas Sur,** which brings the immigrant experience vividly alive—no Spanish necessary. For a post-theater meal, nearby **El Obrero** (The Worker) draws international celebrities without making any concessions to fashion.

Argentine politics in her life, and her grave is a frequent pilgrimage site. Her former apartment is on chic **Calle Posadas;** to get a better grasp of Evita worship, though, visit nearby Palermo's **Museo Eva Perón.**

Have lunch at any of dozens of stylish restaurants in Palermo Viejo, a mostly residential area that was home to literary great Jorge Luis Borges and the place where revolutionary Ernesto "Che" Guevara started his legendary *Motorcycle Diaries* ride across South America. For lunch, try the bistro café **Bella Italia,** east of the Jardín Botánico.

Across Avenida del Libertador, in **Parque Tres de Febrero,** the city's greatest open space, sites such as the **Parque Japonés** (Japanese Garden) and **Rosedal** (Rose Garden) are islands of calm, but it all belonged to 19th-century dictator Juan Manuel de Rosas, who claimed the gauchos as his allies but exploited them ruthlessly. Later landowners conspicuously co-opted the gaucho instead, as is evident in the nearby **Museo de Motivos Argentinos José Hernández.**

DAY 3

In Francophile Recoleta, visitors can see how the affluent and influential sector of *porteño* society lives—and dies. After breakfast or brunch at **Café La Biela,** cross to the **Cementerio de la Recoleta,** where former La Biela clients are spending eternity—many tombs here are worth more than most city apartments. Though not an elite figure, Evita Perón shoved her way into Recoleta as she did into the upper echelons of

DAY 4

To understand Buenos Aires and its hinterland, it's not enough to stay within the city limits. The gaucho tradition thrives, in an attenuated version, in the pampas town of **San Antonio de Areco,** a potential UNESCO World Heritage Site that's home to a remarkable density of gifted silversmiths. San Antonio is doable as a day trip but better as an overnight, preferably at one of the area's historic *estancias* (ranches).

There's a tango tsunami, and its epicenter is still Buenos Aires. *Porteño* theater professionals and tango teachers may be going as far afield as Europe, North America, and Japan, but thousands of foreigners are coming to Buenos Aires to watch the dancers, listen to the music, study with the finest instructors, and do their best to emulate them. There's a tension between the "authenticity" of the *milonga* and the flashiness of the floor show "for export," but both have something to offer to discriminating visitors.

DAY 1

The starting point for any visit to Buenos Aires has to be the Plaza de Mayo, where the historic Avenida de Mayo is the spinal cord of public life and the Café Tortoni recalls the early 20th-century era when tango became a global phenomenon. In the same building, the Academia Nacional del Tango has an upstairs museum, but for a living museum, visit the Confitería Ideal—the site of afternoon *milongas* and tango

Tango legend Carlos Gardel's tomb is the most visited at the Cementerio de la Chacarita.

lessons—whose aging facilities evoke tango's underlying nostalgia.

South of the Plaza de Mayo, it's a matter for argument whether San Telmo or La Boca had more to do with tango's origins, but the history is here—the narrow colonial streets were part of the *arrabales* (outskirts) where the tango supposedly arose out of Afro-Argentine dance and music, transformed by the input of later European immigrants. Sunday dancers pass the hat on San Telmo's Plaza Dorrego, while others stride through La Boca's sidewalk cafés daily.

As night falls, consider a tango concert or floor show at the Tortoni's Sala Alfonsina Storni or a concert at San Telmo's Centro Cultural Torquato Tasso, followed by dinner at the classic neighborhood grill 1880.

DAY 2

After breakfast, take the Subte to Estación Federico Lacroze and the Cementerio de la Chacarita, to visit the grave of Carlos Gardel and other tango legends, including musicians Aníbal Troilo and Osvaldo Pugliese. On the way back, detrain at Estación Carlos Gardel for the historic Abasto tango district, where Gardel grew up and where the recycled landmark Mercado del Abasto still stands (the exterior is more pleasing than the interior). Continue the pilgrimage to the nearby Museo Casa Carlos Gardel, the great singer's boyhood home.

In the evening, consider a tango floor show, such as El Querandí or the Esquina Carlos Gardel

—venues like these have harsh purist critics, but their musicians, singers, and dancers still manage to communicate history and emotion.

DAY 3

Morning may be slow for dancing, but it's a good time for shopping for tango CDs at shops, such as Zivals, on Avenida Corrientes, and other music stores. After lunch, think about attending a *milonga*, at least as a spectator, to appreciate how it contrasts with tango as spectacle (there are numerous afternoon *milongas,* but many also take place late at night).

For dinner, try Palermo's Loco Berretín, also a wine bar whose unembellished floor shows more closely resemble *milongas* than they do the spectacles of Monserrat, San Telmo, and Barracas. At an earlier hour, they also offer lessons and, on occasion, the shows themselves become more participatory.

Palermo Viejo's Loco Berretín is a restaurant and wine bar presenting a vision of tango that's closer to the *milonga* than a glitzy floor show.

Explore
Buenos Aires

Sights

For sightseers, Buenos Aires is a paradise of diversity. Like New York City, it's a city of barrios—48 of them, officially—but even that designation can be misleading. Many barrios consist of even smaller neighborhoods with distinct identities and some, such as Barrio Norte (more a real estate term or a state of mind for its mostly upper-class residents), overlap official barrios.

For much of the 20th century, the Plaza de Mayo and surrounding Monserrat were the nerve center of Argentine politics, the site of spectacle for the Peróns and their successors. The colonial quarter of San Telmo is the home of the tango, while the working-class La Boca neighborhood fuses its passion for soccer with a conspicuous commitment to the arts.

Downtown Buenos Aires, the Microcentro, is the city's traditional business, shopping, and theater district, with many museums and landmark buildings. To the north, the mansions of Retiro and chic Recoleta are home to the *porteño* elite and some of the city's best and newest museums. For wide-open spaces, *porteños* visit the parks of Palermo, an area with its own share of museums and monuments.

On weekends, Buenos Aires's municipal tourist office offers free theme-oriented walking tours of many neighborhoods; some, but not all, have English-speaking guides. For each week's offerings, check the Friday "getOut!" section of the *Buenos Aires Herald* or the entertainment section of *Clarín*. In case of rain, tours are canceled.

Buenos Aires's Best

Look for  to find the sights you can't miss.

Best Chance to See History in the Making: Buenos Aires's **Plaza de Mayo** is ground zero for Argentine public life (page 26).

Best Cultural Bulwark: Through a century of political turmoil, the **Teatro Colón,** South America's most important performing arts venue, has retained its style and dignity (page 36).

Best Nature-Oriented Activity: In what was once a rubbish tip, the spontaneously lush woodlands and marshy wetlands of Puerto Madero's **Reserva Ecológica Costanera Sur** are ideal for birders: *Real* pink flamingos, black-necked swans, coots, and countless other species make a walk through this oasis of calm unique in an often cacophonous city (page 41).

Best Street Market: Sunday is the day that antiques vendors and spirited street performers clog San Telmo's **Plaza Dorrego** and surrounding streets (page 46).

Top Post-Mortem Status Symbol: For the quick, the barrio of Recoleta is the capital's prestige address, but for the dead, a tomb at its **Cementerio de la Recoleta** is even more exclusive (page 59).

Best Contribution to the Arts: For decades, even during dictatorships, Argentina has had a thriving modern art scene, but businessman Eduardo Constantini's **Museo de Arte Latinoamericano de Buenos Aires (MALBA)** has given it a new focal point (page 67).

Most Elusive Museum: Promoted by Eva Perón's partisans, the **Museo Eva Perón**—Argentina's first museum dedicated to a woman—is as notable for what it omits as for what it includes (page 69).

Best Landscaping: Once it was dictator Juan Manuel de Rosas's private estate, but French landscape architect Charles Thays made Palermo's sprawling **Parque Tres de Febrero** a place for the people. Within the park, rehabbed Plaza Alemania comes closest to Thays's original vision (page 70).

Best Plan B, Post-Mortem Division: Having failed to qualify for Recoleta, many of Argentina's most illustrious and/or notorious figures repose at the capital's more egalitarian **Cementerio de la Chacarita** (page 75).

Most Underrated Museum: In the decidedly untouristed barrio of Caballito, the improving **Museo Argentino de Ciencias Naturales Bernardino Rivadavia** has never achieved the grandeur to which its original plans aspired, but the exhibits within this still handsome building shed light on the impressive Argentine dinosaur discoveries of recent decades (page 78).

© WAYNE BERNHARDSON

Cementerio de la Recoleta is Buenos Aires's world-famous necropolis.

Monserrat

Buenos Aires's oldest barrio takes its name from the Catalonian Nuestra Señora de Monserrat, a sacred image that was hidden in the mountains near Barcelona to protect it from Muslim invaders. Found after a century of weathering, the darkened Madonna resonated with Buenos Aires's black slave population, who feted her every September 8. Monserrat was also known as Barrio del Tambor for the drums Afro-Argentines played during Carnaval.

Monserrat encompasses substantial parts of the Congreso neighborhood, which also overlaps the barrios of San Nicolás and Balvanera. Monserrat's precise southern border with San Telmo is a more subtle transition—some businesses technically within Monserrat's limits vocally proclaim they're part of tourist-friendly San Telmo.

Most major Argentine institutions surround the Plaza de Mayo, which has undergone significant transformations since its colonial ori-

gins to reach its present status as the city's civic heart. Its present name derives from the date of the May Revolution of 1810, but its fame comes from the massive and spectacular demonstrations that have taken place here in support and protest of the Peróns, the Falklands/Malvinas War, and other political causes.

◤ PLAZA DE MAYO

In 1580, Juan de Garay reestablished Pedro de Mendoza's failed settlement on what is now the **Plaza de Mayo.** Garay platted the rectangular Plaza del Fuerte (Fortress Plaza), which became the Plaza del Mercado (Market Plaza) and then the Plaza de la Victoria (Victory Plaza), following victory over British invaders in 1806 and 1807. Colloquially known as the Plaza de Protestas for its frequent, large, and contentious political demonstrations, the Plaza de Mayo has often held center-stage in Argentine history. Juan and Eva Perón used it for spectacle, convoking hundreds of thousands of the fervent *descamisados* (shirtless ones) who comprised their underclass disciples.

Internationally, though, the plaza became notorious for some of its smallest gatherings ever. During the late 1970s, a handful of Argentine mothers marched silently every Thursday afternoon to demand the return of their adult children kidnapped by the armed forces and paramilitary gangs. Most of the *desaparecidos* (disappeared) died at the hands of their captors but, in the absence of a complete accounting, the Madres de la Plaza de Mayo still parade every Thursday at 3:30 P.M. around the **Pirámide de Mayo,** the plaza's small central obelisk. Nobel Prize winner V.S. Naipaul chronicled the mothers' bravery while making caustic comments on Argentine society in his long essay *The Return of Eva Perón.*

Ironically, emotional throngs cheered the 1976–1983 dictatorship here following Argentina's April 1982 occupation of the British-

© WAYNE BERNHARDSON

Though often covered with graffiti, the Spanish Renaissance Banco de Boston is one of Monserrat's most handsome buildings.

ruled Falkland Islands, which Argentina still claims as the Malvinas. As the war went badly, though, the crowds turned on General Leopoldo Galtieri's de facto regime and the military collapse brought a quick return to constitutional government.

Following Argentina's 2001 economic meltdown, the Plaza de Mayo witnessed major protests and a police riot that killed several demonstrators; this brought about the resignation of President Fernando De la Rúa, an indecisive leader who was undercut by the opposition Peronists. Since then, occasionally heated demonstrations have taken place by leftist groups who deplore the so-called free-market capitalism ostensibly imposed by the International Monetary Fund (IMF) and other lending agencies and by bank depositors outraged at the *corralito* that limits access to their savings. Most recently, the protestors have been family members and activists seeking a culprit—or scapegoat—for the tragic December 2004 fire that killed nearly 200 people at a rock concert in the neighborhood of Once.

Café Tortoni

AVENIDA DE MAYO 825, TEL. 011/4342-4328
OPEN DAILY 7 A.M.–2 A.M.
WWW.CAFETORTONI.COM.AR

One of B.A.'s most fiercely if quietly traditional places, Tortoni's made no concessions to the 21st century and only a few to the 20th: Upholstered chairs and marble tables stand among sturdy columns beneath a ceiling punctuated by *vitraux;* the wallpaper looks original between the dark-stained wooden trim; and the walls are decorated with pictures, portraits, and *filete,* the traditional calligraphy of *porteño* sign-painters.

Among the patrons acknowledged on the walls are tango singer Carlos Gardel, La Boca painter Benito Quinquela Martín, dramatists Luigi Pirandello and Federico García Lorca, and pianist Arthur Rubinstein; more recently, the Tortoni has hosted King Juan Carlos I of Spain and Hillary Rodham Clinton. Almost everybody who visits the city should join them.

Casa Rosada (Casa De Gobierno Nacional)

HIPÓLITO YRIGOYEN 219, TEL. 011/4344-3804
OPEN WEEKDAYS 10 A.M.–6 P.M., SUN. 2–6 P.M.
WWW.MUSEO.GOV.AR

For better or worse, the presidential palace, which faces the Plaza de Mayo, has been the site of political spectacle. It's the place where Juan and Evita Perón summoned the cheering masses who later jeered the ruthless military dictatorship after the 1982 Falklands War; as recently as December 2001, it witnessed the shooting of demonstrators by federal police under the De la Rúa administration. Culturally speaking, one of its lowest points must have been pop singer Madonna's balcony appearance in director Alan Parker's film version of the stage musical *Evita* (an event that enraged diehard Peronists).

The Casa Rosada owes its distinctive pink hue to President Domingo F. Sarmiento, who proposed the blend of Federalist red and Unitarist white to symbolize reconciliation between the two violently opposed factions of 19th-century Argentine politics. It was not originally a single building; in 1884, Italian architect Francesco Tamburini (who later worked on the Teatro Colón) merged the original Casa de Gobierno with the Correo Central (Central Post Office) to create the present, slightly asymmetrical structure. On the east side, facing Parque Colón, pedestrians can view the excavated ruins of the colonial **Fuerte Viejo** (old fortress) and early customs headquarters (buried beneath landfill during 1890s port improvements).

In the basement, entered from the south side on Hipólito Yrigoyen, its museum contains memorabilia from Argentine presidents, a 17,000-volume library, an archive, and newspaper and magazine collections; unfortunately, its charter prohibits inclusion of recent, more controversial items. Visitors can stroll among the colonial catacombs, which are also visible from the pedestrian mall outside.

Museum admission is free; free guided tours take place at 11 A.M. and 4 P.M. weekdays, at 3 and 4:30 P.M. Sunday. Guided tours of the

WALKING TOUR: MONSERRAT

Monserrat is Buenos Aires's oldest neighborhood, but its Plaza de Mayo is the flashpoint of modern Argentine history. The barrio's axis is the **Avenida de Mayo,** the city's first major boulevard, which links the **Casa Rosada** presidential palace (built 1873–1898) with the **Congreso Nacional** (National Congress, 1906). Running perpendicular to Avenida de Mayo, Avenida 9 de Julio splits Monserrat in half.

At the Plaza de Mayo's northwest corner, the imposing **Catedral Metropolitana** (1827) gives the barrio its alternate name. At the southwest corner, the Avenida de Mayo's construction required demolishing part of the colonial **Cabildo de Buenos Aires** (1725–1765), but a representative segment of the original building remains.

At the northeast corner, designed by renowned architect Alejandro Bustillo, the **Banco de la Nación** (1939) occupies the original site of the Teatro Colón, the opera house that moved to Plaza Lavalle early in the 20th century; if the economy were as solid as this state-run bank's neoclassical construction, Argentina would still be a global economic power.

Across the Plaza de Mayo, immediately south of the Casa Rosada, the marble facade of the **Ministerio de Economía** (Economy Ministry) still bears marks from the navy planes that strafed these and other public buildings in the 1955 Revolución Libertadora that sent Juan Domingo Perón into exile. Across Avenida Paseo Colón, generations of military coup-mongers plotted against constitutional governments in the **Edificio Libertador** before belatedly realizing they were no more capable of governing than the civilians they overthrew.

After 1894, as the Avenida de Mayo obliterated several city blocks to become Buenos Aires's first boulevard at 30 meters wide, it experienced a major building boom, but several landmarks survive. First among them, without a doubt, is the **Café Tortoni** (Avenida de Mayo 825), a *porteño* institution since 1858 (the original entrance was on Rivadavia, on the building's north side).

Reopened in 1994 after nearly being destroyed by fire in 1979, the **Teatro Avenida** (Avenida de Mayo 1222) is second only to Teatro Colón as a classical-music and dance venue. Dating from 1907, **Hotel Chile** (Avenida de Mayo 1295) is a prime example of the early-20th-century art nouveau architecture that was fashionable here.

carved doorway, Monserrat

© WAYNE BERNHARDSON

The avenue's most literal landmark is Mario Palanti's marvelously detailed **Pasaje Barolo** (1923), a recently restored office building topped by a high-powered rotating semaphore visible from Montevideo's Palacio Salvo (the work of the same architect). In 1923, when Argentine heavyweight Luis Angel Firpo fought Jack Dempsey in New York, the Barolo erroneously announced a Firpo victory with a green light from the tower; director Russell Mulcahy shot parts of the ill-fated 1986 sequel to *Highlander* in the building.

At the west end of the avenue, the **Plaza del Congreso** (officially Plaza de los Dos Congresos, 1904), another frequent site for political demonstrations, faces the **Congreso Nacional** (1908), home to Argentina's notoriously dysfunctional national legislature. The plaza itself houses the **Monumento a los Dos Congresos,** commemorating the meetings in Buenos Aires (1813) and Tucumán (1816) that achieved the country's independence. Two Belgians, sculptor Jules Lagae and architect Eugene D'Huique, created the monument, which reflects Argentina's geography: The eastern fountain symbolizes the Atlantic Ocean, and the granite stairways signify the Andes mountains that form Argentina's western border with Chile.

South of the Plaza de Mayo, nearly all Monserrat's major landmarks are colonial, though most have undergone major modifications. The most significant attraction is the **Manzana de las Luces:** several ecclesiastical and educational institutions that occupy an entire block bounded by Alsina, Bolívar, Moreno, and Perú. Two blocks west, the **Iglesia San Juan Bautista** (Alsina and Piedras) was one of B.A.'s elite churches in the 18th century.

At opposite corners of Alsina and Defensa are the **Capilla San Roque** (1759), a colonial chapel, and the **Farmacia La Estrella** (1900), a classic apothecary with magnificent woodwork and health-themed ceiling murals. The Farmacia's exterior windows display materials from the **Museo de la Ciudad,** upstairs in the same building.

A block to the south, the **Museo Etnográfico Juan B. Ambrosetti** (Moreno 350) has become one of the country's top anthropological museums. The **Museo Nacional del Grabado** (Defensa 372) occupies the **Casa de la Defensa,** which played a key role in repelling the British occupations of 1806 and 1807.

Half a block south, at the corner of Avenida Belgrano, the 18th-century **Iglesia y Convento de Santo Domingo** shares grounds with the **Instituto Nacional Belgraniano,** a patriotic research institute that contains the tomb of General Manuel Belgrano, designer of the Argentine flag.

Two blocks south, at the corner of Defensa and México, the erstwhile **Casa de la Moneda** (National Mint, 1877) now houses the army's **Instituto de Estudios Históricos del Ejército** (Army Institute of Historical Studies). This handsome 10,000-square meter building, though, is projected to become a contemporary science museum with emphasis on astronomy, robotics, information technology, electronics, environment, and biotechnology, as well as Argentine history and geography.

Two blocks west, dating from 1901, the former **Biblioteca Nacional** (National Library, México 564) first housed the national lottery; after the library moved to Recoleta in 1992, this neoclassical building became the **Centro Nacional de la Música** (National Music Center).

Casa Rosada itself take place at noon and 4 P.M. weekdays. These are also free, but make reservations at the museum at least two hours ahead of time, and show identification.

Catedral Metropolitana
AVENIDA RIVADAVIA AND SAN MARTÍN
At the Plaza de Mayo's northwest corner, the capital's cathedral occupies the site of the original colonial church designated by Juan de Garay in 1580. It opened in 1836 in its present form; on the pediment above its Hellenic columns, Joseph Dubourdieu's symbolic bas-reliefs (1862) equate the biblical reconciliation of Joseph and his brothers with the results of the battle of Pavón, in which Bartolomé Mitre's Buenos Aires forces defeated Santa Fe province caudillo Justo José Urquiza.

Even more significant for Argentines, a separate chapel contains the **Mausoleo del General José de San Martín,** the burial site of the country's independence hero. Disillusioned with the country's post-independence turmoil, San Martín suffered self-exile in France until his death in 1850; his remains returned to Argentina in 1880, after President Nicolás Avellaneda ordered construction of this elaborate tomb, marked by an eternal flame outside the cathedral's easternmost entrance.

Iglesia y Convento de Santo Domingo
AVENIDA BELGRANO AND DEFENSA
In 1601, shortly after the Dominican order arrived in Buenos Aires, it acquired a large block of land stretching from present day Avenida Belgrano and Defensa to the riverfront, which it used for vegetable gardens, livestock corrals, and a primitive chapel and convent. In 1751, the Dominicans finally laid the cornerstone for the present church and convent, but the second of its twin towers went uncompleted until 1858. Its altars and artwork date from the 17th and 19th centuries.

Santo Domingo (also known as the Iglesia de Nuestra Señora del Rosario) witnessed some of Argentine history's most dramatic events. It still contains banners captured by Viceroy Santiago de Liniers from the High-landers Regiment No. 71 during the initial British invasion (1806), and its facade and left-side tower still show combat damage from the following year's British occupation. After the independence wars, General Manuel Belgrano donated flags of the defeated Royalists to the collection.

On the east side, near the church entrance, an eternal flame burns near sculptor Héctor Ximenes's **Mausoleo de Belgrano** (1903), the burial site of Argentina's second-greatest hero, Belgrano; by most accounts, Belgrano was an indifferent soldier, but he did design the Argentine flag.

Following independence, President Bernardino Rivadavia secularized the church, turning the main building into a natural history museum and one of its towers into an astronomical observatory. In 1955, during the overthrow of Juan Perón, anti-clerical Peronists set it afire.

Manzana de las Luces
PERÚ 272, TEL. 011/4331-5934
OPEN MON.–FRI. 3 P.M., WEEKENDS 3, 4:30, AND 6 P.M. (TOURS)
WWW.MANZANA.FWD.COM.AR
Ever since the mid-17th century, when the Jesuit order established itself on the block bounded by the present-day streets of Bolívar, Moreno, Perú, and Alsina, Monserrat has been a hub of the capital's intellectual life. While the Jesuits were perhaps the most intellectual of all monastic orders, they were also the most commercial, and architect Juan Bautista Ronoli designed the five buildings of the **Procuraduría** (two of which survive, fronting on Alsina) to store products from their widespread missions.

The Jesuit structures, which also housed missionized indigenous people who came to Buenos Aires from the provinces, contained a number of defensive tunnels; the tunnels were rediscovered in 1912 and are now open to the public. After the Jesuits' expulsion from the Americas in 1767, the buildings served as the Protomedicato, which regulated the city's doctors. Following independence, they housed at various times the Biblioteca Pública (Public Library, 1812);

the Cámara Legislativa (Provincial Legislature, 1821); the Universidad de Buenos Aires (1821); the Academia de Medicina (Medical Academy, 1822); the Sociedad Literaria (Literary Society, 1822); the Banco de la Provincia de Buenos Aires (Buenos Aires Provincial Bank, 1822); the Museo Público de Buenos Aires (Public Museum, 1823); the Congreso Nacional (1824); the Museo de Historia Natural (1854); the Departamento de Ciencias Exactas (Department of Exact Sciences, 1865); the Facultad de Ciencias Exactas, Físicas, y Naturales (Faculty of Exact, Physical, and Natural Sciences, 1881); and others. After 1974, the Comisión Nacional de la Manzana de Las Luces attempted to salvage the historical buildings for cultural purposes, opening the tunnels to the public and restoring part of the "Universidad" lettering along the facade on the Perú side.

In 1722, a new **Iglesia San Ignacio** replaced its deteriorating namesake, which was begun in 1661 and finished in 1675. After the Jesuits' expulsion in 1767, the new building briefly served as the cathedral while the permanent cathedral underwent repairs; following an invitation from dictator Juan Manuel de Rosas, the Jesuits returned in 1836. In 1955, at Juan Perón's instigation, mobs trashed the building, which is currently undergoing an exterior restoration.

The church has one common wall with the Colegio Nacional de Buenos Aires (1908), the country's most prestigious and competitive secondary school, taught by top university faculty. Another notable feature is the re-created **Sala de Representantes,** the province's first legislature.

The **Instituto de Investigaciones Históricas de la Manzana de las Luces Doctor Jorge E. Garrido** charges US$1 pp for guided tours.

Museo de la Ciudad

DEFENSA 219, TEL. 011/4343-2123
OPEN WEEKDAYS 11 A.M.–7 P.M., SUN. 3–7 P.M.
In the same building as the remarkable Farmacia La Estrella, the city museum specializes in themes dealing with the city proper and elements of everyday life, including architecture, furniture, floor tiles, and postcards; the pharmacy's exterior windows have been turned into display cases. Though most of its displays are upstairs, above the pharmacy, there is also a ground-level exhibition room on the Defensa side. It features rotating programs on topics such as tango legend Julio Sosa (second only to Carlos Gardel among tango singers) and doors salvaged from buildings long ago demolished.

Actress Niní Marshall once resided here. Museum admission costs US$.35 except Wednesday, when it's free; it closes the entire month of February.

Microcentro

One of the Microcentro's foci is the pedestrian **Calle Florida,** which runs north from Rivadavia and crosses Avenida Córdoba into Retiro. Florida first became a *peatonal* (pedestrian walk) in the early 20th century, but for only a few hours each day. When it was completely closed to automobile traffic, it became the city's smartest shopping area, sporting stores like the former Harrod's (1913), a subsidiary of the famous London retailer that became legally separate in the 1960s and closed in the late 1990s. Though the seven-story building boasted 47,000 square meters of floor space,

by the time it closed, it was operating only at street level.

As a shopping district, Florida is less fashionable than it once was, with one major exception: the restored **Galerías Pacífico,** an architectural and historical landmark that occupies most of a city block.

East-west **Avenida Corrientes,** the traditional center of *porteño* nightlife, has taken a back seat to trendier areas like Puerto Madero and Palermo; several cinemas have closed and, while some traditional cafés and restaurants have survived beneath gaudy

WALKING TOUR: MICROCENTRO

Traditionally, the Microcentro is the city's main shopping and entertainment district and, if all goes well, it may start to regain that status. Presently being widened to accommodate theater-district pedestrians, east-west Avenida Corrientes is the main thoroughfare, while north-south Calle Florida is a shoppers' Mecca. Both main streets and many side streets, though, abound with historical landmarks.

Originally a private residence, dating from 1910, the headquarters of the **Sociedad Rural Argentina** (Florida 460) houses an organization that has voiced the interests of large-scale landowners—many Argentines would say "the oligarchy"—since 1866.

During the invasions of 1806 and 1807, British forces occupied the **Monasterio de Santa Catalina de Siena** (1745; San Martín and Viamonte), the city's first women's convent. The Asociación Cristiana Femenina de Buenos Aires (YWCA, Tucumán 846) occupies the **Solar Natal de Borges,** the birthplace of Jorge Luis Borges, Argentina's most internationally famous literary figure.

At the foot of Corrientes, occupying an entire block bounded by Avenida Leandro N. Alem, Bouchard, and Sarmiento, the **Correo Central** (central post office, 1928) is a beaux arts landmark whose original architect, Norberto Maillart, based his design on New York City's General Post Office. After Maillart's departure, the Ministerio de Obras Públicas (Public Works Ministry) changed the plans to incorporate a Francophile mansard.

To the south, with its concentration of banks and exchange houses between Avenida Rivadavia and Avenida Corrientes, Calle San Martín is the main axis of the financial district, colloquially known as **La City.** Directly west of the post office, dating from 1916, architect Alejandro Christopherson's **Bolsa de Comercio de Buenos Aires** (Stock Exchange, 25 de Mayo 375) is one of the key institutions. Other oligarchs include the financial and commercial house of **Bunge y Born,** with headquarters at 25 de Mayo 501.

Half a block east of the stock exchange, the **Archivo y Museo Histórico del Banco de la Provincia de Buenos Aires Dr. Arturo Jáuretche** (Sarmiento 364) occupies part of the provincial bank's contemporary headquarters (1980). Argentina's central bank, the Italianate **Banco Central de la República Argentina** (San Martín 265) has an identical facade at Reconquista 266. The Reconquista entrance offers access to its **Museo Numismático Dr. José E. Uriburu,** a museum that illuminates Argentina's volatile economic history.

At La City's end of Calle Florida, to express their *bronca* after the events of late 2001 and early 2002, angry bank depositors painted, scrawled, and scratched graffiti on the corrugated aluminum that covered the windows of financial institutions. Even sturdy, secure buildings, such as the elegant Spanish Renaissance **Banco de Boston** (1924), at the intersection with the diagonal Roque Sáenz Peña, suffered defacement from *corralito* protestors. In 1936, Jorge Fioravanti (1896–1977) sculpted the statue of Sáenz Peña, the Argentine president who initiated universal male suffrage during his term (1910–1913), on a small triangular plaza opposite the bank's entrance.

Immediately southeast, dating from 1926, the **Edificio Menéndez-Behety** (Roque Sáenz Peña 543) was the Buenos Aires command center for multinational wool merchants who, in Patagonia and Tierra del Fuego, were more powerful than the Argentine and Chilean governments under which they operated.

Not all La City landmarks reflect lucre. Built in 1779 by Jesuit architect Andrés Blanqui and remodeled 1889–1900 by Italian Antonio Buschiazzo, **Basílica Nuestra Señora de la Merced**

(Reconquista 207) is undergoing a restoration that, with luck, will be completed before the end of its third century. Half a block north, the adjacent **Convento de la Merced** (Reconquista 269) offers sanctuary from the financial district's bustle; parts of it are open to the public as an art space, a small theater, offices, and a Sunday crafts and antiques market. Three blocks west of Banco de Boston, dating from 1788, the **Parroquia San Miguel Arcángel** (Mitre 866) is a national historical monument.

A handful of other monuments and museums have nothing to do with finance. The **Museo Mitre** (San Martín 366) was the home of soldier, president, and journalist Bartolomé Mitre; the **Museo de la Policía Federal** is across the street at San Martín 353.

At the intersection of Avenida 9 de Julio and Corrientes, rising above the oval Plaza de la República, the 67.5-meter **Obelisco** (Obelisk, 1936) is a city symbol erected for the 400th anniversary of Pedro de Mendoza's initial encampment along the Río de la Plata. There are 206 steps to the top, but the structure is rarely open.

Five blocks west of the Obelisco, the **Teatro General San Martín (Avenida Corrientes 1560)** is the capital's only notable cultural facility from the second half of the 20th century. Its facade is unimpressively modern, even drab, but its facilities—three theaters, a repertory cinema, and exhibition halls, including a branch of San Telmo's Museo de Arte Moderno—are first-rate.

Three blocks south of the theater, Congreso's colonial **Iglesia Nuestra Señora de la Piedad** (Mitre 1502) dates from 1769.

From the Obelisco, the diagonal Roque Sáenz Peña is now a pedestrian mall ending at **Plaza Lavalle,** which stretches north three woodsy blocks along Talcahuano and Libertad between Lavalle and Avenida Córdoba. Occupying an entire block fronting on Talcahuano, the **Palacio de Justicia** (commonly known as Tribunales or Law Courts, 1904) has lent its colloquial name to the neighborhood. Every Monday, at 9:53 A.M., the capital's Jewish community gathers to observe a moment of silence to protest judicial inaction on the bombing of the Asociación Mutualista Israelita Argentina (AMIA), which took place July 18, 1994. Since 2002, it has been the site of protests against judicial decisions favoring the reviled *corralito* banking restrictions.

Among several important areas west of Avenida 9 de Julio, Tribunales is also home to several major landmarks, including the **Congreso,** which overlaps the barrios of Balvanera and Monserrat.

Across the plaza from the Tribunales, dating from 1907, the kaleidoscopic confines of the **Conventillo de las Artes** (Libertad 543) were once law offices but are now home to a motley assortment of artists and writers. In its present state, the Conventillo contrasts dramatically with Italian-born architect Carlo Morra's sober neoclassical **Escuela Presidente Roca** (Libertad 581), a 1902 building three doors north, distinguished by massive granite columns quarried at Tandil. (Morra designed some 25 Argentine schools in similar styles.) It's an even more dramatic contrast with the stately **Teatro Colón** (Libertad 621).

At Plaza Lavalle's north end, fronting on Libertad and protected by bulky concrete planter boxes, architect Alejandro Enquín's **Templo de la Congregación Israelita** (1932) is home to a conservative congregation and is the capital's largest synagogue; it also holds the **Museo Judío de Buenos Aires Dr. Salvador Kibrick,** which deals with Jewish history both within and beyond Argentina. Do not photograph this or any other Jewish community site without express permission from that site.

illuminated signs, others seem to be hanging on by a thread. This may change, though, as authorities have begun a project to widen Corrientes's sidewalks, between Avenida 9 de Julio and Callao, by 1.5 meters on each side of the street, to make the traditional theater district more pedestrian friendly.

At the same time, though, the cinema district along the Lavalle pedestrian mall, which crosses Florida one block north of Corrientes, has experienced an unfortunate diversification. While movie multiplexes have taken up some of the slack, other cinemas have become bingo parlors, evangelical churches blaring amplified hymns, and raucous video arcades.

Named for Argentina's independence day, the broad **Avenida 9 de Julio** separates the Microcentro from the rest of the barrio—literally so, as only a world-class sprinter could safely cross its 16 lanes of seemingly suicidal drivers fudging the green lights. Fortunately for pedestrians, there are several traffic islands, as well as subterranean passageways, to help reduce exposure to high-speed traffic.

© WAYNE BERNHARDSON

The Argentine flag waves across from the landmark Obelisco, on Avenida 9 de Julio.

Archivo y Museo Histórico del Banco de la Provincia de Buenos Aires Dr. Arturo Jáuretche

SARMIENTO 362, TEL. 011/4331–1775, 011/4331-7943
OPEN WEEKDAYS 10 A.M.–6 P.M.
WWW.BAPRO.COM.AR/MUSEO

Before Argentina existed as a true country (until the 1880s' federalization of Buenos Aires), it was really a loose confederation of provinces, some governed by ruthless warlords), the provincial bank was its main financial institution. It held that status until 1891 and issued the first Argentine and Uruguayan banknotes.

The museum provides an even longer-term perspective, covering Argentine economic and monetary history since viceregal times. Its displays include banknotes, coins, and medallions that offer insights on topics that include early economic geography, the financial mechanisms and consequences of independence (including controversial loans from the British Baring Brothers house), counterfeiting, and the 1980s hyperinflation.

The first of its kind in the country, the Museo Jáuretche has operated since 1904, but its current facilities are the best it's ever had. Admission is free; guided tours are available by appointment.

Galerías Pacífico

FLORIDA AND AVENIDA CÓRDOBA
WWW.GALERIASPACIFICO.COM.AR

As Calle Florida became an elegant shopping district in the late 19th century, Francisco Seeber and Emilio Bunge were the main shareholders in the proposed Bon Marché Argentino, inspired by Milan's Galleria Vittorio Emmanuelle II. Unfortunately for Seeber and Bunge, their French investors backed out during the early 1890s' global recession. Seeber resurrected the project by 1894 as the Galería Florida, housing a variety of shops and other businesses.

At one time or another, the distinctive building, divided into four discrete sectors by perpendicular galleries with a central cupola and a glass ceiling, held the Museo de

Bellas Artes (Fine Arts Museum) and the Academia Nacional de Bellas Artes (National Fine Arts Academy), artists' studios, and even government offices. One of its era's tallest and broadest buildings, with a double basement and four upper stories, it covered an entire city block bounded by Florida, Avenida Córdoba, San Martín, and Viamonte.

In 1908, though, the British-run Ferrocarril de Buenos Aires al Pacífico, which operated the railroad that ran from the capital to the western city of Mendoza, acquired the sector fronting on Córdoba for its business offices; within two years, it controlled the rest of the building. In 1948, when Juan Perón nationalized the railroads to create Ferrocarriles Argentinos, it passed into state control.

During a 1945 remodel, Argentine artists gave the cupola its most dramatic feature: some 450 square meters of murals, including Lino Spilimbergo's *El Dominio de las Fuerzas Naturales* (The Dominion of Natural Forces), Demetrio Urruchúa's *La Fraternidad* (Brotherhood), Juan Carlos Castagnino's *La Vida Doméstica* (Domestic Life), Manuel Colmeiro's *La Pareja Humana* (The Human Couple), and Antonio Berni's *El Amor* (Love). Linked to famous Mexican muralist David Alfaro Siqueiros through Spilimbergo, all belonged to the socially conscious Nuevo Realismo (New Realism) movement; the murals have twice been restored, in 1968 under Berni's direction and then again by an Argentine-Mexican group in 1991.

For most of the 1980s, though, the Galerías languished through economic disorder until, in 1992, the murals became a highlight of the building's transformation into one of the capital's most fashionable shopping centers—finally achieving its original purpose. Well worth a visit even for anti-shoppers, the tastefully modernized Galerías offers guided tours Wednesdays at 6:30 P.M. from the street-level information desk. On the basement level, it has a high-quality food court and, in addition, the city's best public toilets.

Museo Judío de Buenos Aires Dr. Salvador Kibrick

LIBERTAD 769, TEL. 011/4123 0102

Alongside Plaza Lavalle's imposing synagogue, and named for its founder, the Jewish museum contains a small but impressive collection of medieval Judaica, along with documents, photographs, and recordings dealing with the Jewish presence in Argentina. There is also a gallery of Jewish Argentine and Jewish-themed art.

Buenos Aires's Jewish community became prominent after 1862, with the founding of its first synagogue. The major impetus toward immigration came with the German-born Baron Maurice Hirsch's project to resettle persecuted Russian Jews in the Argentine countryside in the 1890s, and his achievements attract considerable coverage here.

Guided tours of the Museo Judío, in Spanish, English, and Hebrew, include a visit to the adjacent synagogue, reached by an interior door. Admission costs US$5 pp, and identification is obligatory; knock loudly. Male visitors to the temple, even non-Jews, must wear a yarmulke (which is provided).

As of mid-2005, the museum was closed for repairs.

Museo Mitre

SAN MARTÍN 366, TEL. 011/4394-8240
OPEN WEEKDAYS 12:30–6:30 P.M.
WWW.MUSEOMITRE.GOV.AR

Bartolomé Mitre (1821–1906), Argentina's first president under its 1853 Constitution, spent a good part of his 1862–1868 term fighting Paraguayan dictator Francisco Solano López in the War of the Triple Alliance, which pitted a seemingly overmatched Paraguay against Argentina, Brazil, and Uruguay. Also a serious historian and pioneer journalist, Mitre founded the daily *La Nación*, a *porteño* institution for well over a century.

Mitre rented the building that now houses the museum, a late 18th-century structure with several patios, before receiving it as a gift from the city upon completing his term. He lived there the rest of his life with his family;

to what was originally a single story building, he added an upper floor with a bedroom, bathroom, and private office. A side door led to *La Nación* offices.

Museum exhibits cover Mitre's military and civilian careers, and there's an 80,000-volume research library that includes original documents from such figures as independence heroes José de San Martín and Manuel Belgrano. Admission costs US$.50.

Museo Numismático Dr. José E. Uriburu

RECONQUISTA 266, TEL. 011/4393-0021
OPEN WEEKDAYS 10 A.M.–3 P.M.

If the Banco Central could manage the country's monetary policy as well as it has organized this museum, which tells the story of Argentine currency from colonial times to the chaotic present, Argentina might not experience dire economic straits so often. Its most unusual exhibit consists of coins minted in Buenos Aires and postage stamps printed for Romanian engineer and adventurer Julio Popper, who attempted to establish his own empire on the island of Tierra del Fuego in the 1880s. A historical display of provincial bonds is a reminder that "funny money" has a long history in Argentina.

The Museo Numismático charges no admission, but the federal police guarding the gate demand identification from those ascending to the first-floor museum.

Teatro Colón

CERRITO 618, TEL. 011/4378-7100
OPEN MON.–SAT. 9 A.M., 10:30 A.M., 11 A.M., NOON, 1 P.M., 2:30 P.M., 3 P.M., AND 4 P.M. (TOURS)
WWW.TEATROCOLON.ORG.AR

Arguably the continent's most important performing-arts center, the ornate Teatro Colón (1908) is approaching its centenary after weathering Argentina's acute economic crisis of 2002. While the weak peso still makes paying for top-tier international opera, ballet, and symphonic performers difficult, it still manages to present top-flight local talent in those and other performance media, and it's under-

going a major rehab in preparation for its centennial celebrations.

Argentine lyric theater dates from the early 19th century, immediately after the May Revolution of 1810, and its first European artists arrived in the 1820s. In 1825, Rossini's *Barber of Seville* was the first opera ever staged in the country, but artistic development stagnated under the Rosas dictatorship.

The original Teatro Colón, facing the Plaza de Mayo, seated almost 2,500 people and opened with Verdi's *La Traviata* in 1857. As the original theater became the Banco Nacional (later the still-existent Banco de la Nación), the city chose one of the country's first railway station sites, on Plaza Lavalle's west side, for the new facility. Architect Francesco Tamburini was responsible for the original Italian Renaissance design, but his countryman Víctor Meano took charge of the project upon Tamburini's death.

Occupying a lot of more than 8,000 square meters, boasting nearly 38,000 meters of floor space on seven levels, the new Colón opened with Verdi's *Aida*. Seating 2,478 patrons with standing room for another 700, it's one of the country's most ornate buildings with its **Gran Hall,** outfitted with Verona and Carrara marble; a **Salón de los Bustos** studded with busts of famous figures, like Beethoven, Bizet, Gounod, Mozart, Rossini, Verdi, and Wagner; and a **Salón Dorado** (Golden Salon) modeled on palaces like Paris's Versailles and Vienna's Schoenbrunn. In 1961, Raúl Soldi replaced Marcel Jambon's earlier cupola murals with paintings of singers, dancers, and actors; Soldi's canvases cover 318 square meters of wall space.

The main theater follows lines of French and Italian classics with world-class acoustics; its stage is 35.25 meters wide, 34.5 meters deep, and 48 meters high. A rotating disc simplifies scene changes. The orchestra accommodates up to 120 musicians. The seating ranges from comfortably upholstered rows to luxury boxes (including a presidential box with its own Casa Rosada phone line, and a separate exit to Tucumán). Presidential command performances take place on the winter patriotic holidays of May 25 and July 9.

Since the Colón's opening, its performers have been a who's who of classic music: the composers Richard Strauss, Igor Stravinsky, Camille Saint-Saëns, Manuel de Falla, and Aaron Copland; conductors Otto Klemperer, Wilhelm Furtwängler, Herbert von Karajan, Arturo Toscanini, and Zubin Mehta; singers Enrico Caruso, Lily Pons, Ezio Pinza, María Callas, José Carreras, Frederika von Stade, Kiri Te Kanawa, Plácido Domingo, and Luciano Pavarotti; dancers Anna Pavlova, Vaslav Nijinsky, Rudolf Nureyev, Margot Fonteyn, and Mikhail Barishnikov; and choreographer George Balanchine.

Foreign dance companies on the Colón's stage have included the Ballet de Montecarlo, London's Festival Ballet, the Opera Privée de París, the Ballet de la Opera de París, and the Ballet de la Opera de Berlín; orchestras have included the New York Philharmonic, the London Philharmonic, and the Washington Philharmonic. Soloists have included Arthur Rubinstein, Pablo Casals, Yehudi Menuhim, Mstislav Rostropovich, Isaac Stern, Itzhak Perlman, Yo-Yo Ma, Andrés Segovia, and Anne Sofie Mutter. At times, though, the administration has let its hair down to accommodate performers like politically conscious folksinger Mercedes Sosa, the *porteño* rhythm-and-blues unit Memphis La Blusera, and rock guitarist-songwriter Luis Alberto Spinetta.

In a season that runs mostly from May to November, the Colón presents some 200 events each year. About half are opera; the remainder comprise about 65 orchestra concerts and 35 ballet performances. The building fills an entire block bounded by Tucumán, Viamonte, and Cerrito (Avenida 9 de Julio); the ticket office is open 10 A.M.–8 P.M. Thursday–Saturday, 10 A.M.–5 P.M. Sunday, and 5 P.M. until the beginning of the performance (if there is one) Monday. Although the main entrance is on Libertad, tours enter from the Viamonte side.

For tour reservations, always available in Spanish and English and sometimes available in French, German, and Portuguese, contact the Colón (Viamonte 1168, tel. 011/4378-7132, visitas@teatrocolon.org.ar). Admission costs US$2.50 for non-resident adults, and US$.70 for children up to age 17; tours last 50 minutes and take you behind the scenes for glimpses of sculptors, seamsters, set-builders, wigmakers, and the like.

Puerto Madero

Born in controversy and corruption in the 19th century and designated a separate barrio in 1991, modern Puerto Madero is an attempt to reclaim the riverfront, which languished off-limits during the military dictatorship of 1976–1983. Comparable to Baltimore's Inner Harbor and London's Docklands, it partly represents the political and economic excesses of the 1990s Carlos Menem presidency, when speculative privatization was rampant in Argentina.

At the same time, according to journalist Andrew Graham-Yooll, it also marks the beginning of a time when Argentines began to value their material past. Developers have recycled several handsome brick warehouses around its four large *diques* (basins, one of which has become a yacht harbor) into stylish lofts, offices, restaurants, bars, and cinemas, and other investors have followed their example. One measure of its success is that director Fabián Bielinsky used the pedestrian promenade for a uniquely entertaining chase scene in his con-man film *Nine Queens*.

Built on landfill east of the river's *barrancas,* what is now Puerto Madero expanded during the dictatorship as the military dumped debris from its massive public works projects east and southeast of the *diques.* Ironically enough, as plants and animals colonized this expanse of rubble and rubbish, it became the **Reserva Ecológica Costanera Sur,** now a popular destination for Sunday outings.

UNDERGROUND CULTURE

In his short story "Text in a Notebook," Julio Cortázar imagines a society of pallid people who never leave the Subte system—"their existence and their circulation like leukocytes." Filmmaker Gustavo Mosquera went even farther in his 1996 movie *Moebius,* which depicts a Subte train and its passengers in an endless loop beneath the city.

In reality, there is an underground culture in the city's subways, but nothing quite so enigmatic as Cortázar and Mosquera concocted. Beginning in the 1930s, builders embellished Subte stations with tiled ceramic murals; more recently, the private operator Metrovías has begun to restore some of these faded glories and, at the same, commission new ones and even construct mini-museums with rotating or permanent art and history exhibits at newer stations.

The Subte provides a means to see both classic and contemporary Argentine art on the move. Visitors can use the following details to orient themselves to this artistic legacy.

Línea A
Buenos Aires's oldest subway line, originally the Compañía de Tranvías Anglo Argentina (Anglo-Argentine Tramway Company) or Línea Anglo (Anglo Line) is its least decorated, though its classic wooden cars are works of art in their own right. Nevertheless, the *vidrieras* (display cases) at Estación Perú and Estación Congreso often hold items of historical interest. The walls of the passageways linking Línea A and Línea C contain Hermenegildo Sábat's three-part *Músicos de Buenos Aires* (2000) and also cartoonist Horacio Altuna's *Gente de Buenos Aires* (People of Buenos Aires, 2002).

Línea B
While it has some of the system's newest and most comfortable cars, Línea B is also short on decoration. The Abasto district's remodeled Estación Carlos Gardel, though, features a ceramic mural of an *orquesta típica* (typical orchestra), on its northern platform. More contemporary works include Carlos Páez Vilaró's *Homenaje a Buenos Aires* (Homage to Buenos Aires) and *Mi Querida Buenos Aires* (My Dear Buenos Aires, after a popular tango) and Andrés Compagnucci's *Gardel por Tres* (Gardel Times Three) and *Abasto,* depicting the old but since rehabilitated market building.

In late 2003, Metrovías re-inaugurated Estación Uruguay with a cinema-themed display that includes film posters and even its own Hollywood-like Walk of Fame, with aging stars, such as Alfredo Alcón and Mirtha Legrand, and newcomers, such as Gastón Pauls and Cecilia Dopazo.

Línea C
Imported Spanish tiles adorn the so-called Línea de los Españoles (Spanish Line) opened in 1934 with Iberian scenes, but more recent additions provide some balance. The most venerable pieces are a series of ceramic *Paisajes de España,* depicting landscapes from Lérida, Segovia, Sevilla, and other locales at Estación Avenida de Mayo, Estación Independencia, Estación Lavalle, and Estación Moreno. Martín Noel and Manuel Escasany were among the Argentine artists involved in the project.

The line is also notable for its Moorish masonry and elegant friezes, such as the ceramic coats of arms at Estación San Juan, the decorative dragon at Estación Moreno, and the Arabic script, also at Estación Moreno, of the aphorism "There is no greater victor than God."

More recent works are more self-consciously Argentine, such as Rodolfo Medina's *La Gesta Sanmartiniana* (1969), a series of eight narrative murals in polychrome cement on the achievements of national icon General José de San Martín. Appropriately enough, it covers the walls of the general's namesake station, which also includes a recent mural by Luis Benedit.

Since 1998, reproductions of three of *gauchesco* caricaturist Florencio Molina Campos's paintings have lined the western platform of Estación Constitución: *El de Laj Once y Sais,* depicting gauchos awaiting a train; *Pa' Nuevos Horizontes,* showing a gaucho family on a horsecart loaded with personal belongings, bound for a new *estancia* (ranch); and *Beyaquiando Juerte,* a gaucho breaking a new mount. Molina Campos titled these pieces in the gaucho dialect.

Renovated Estación Retiro includes three murals by painter Fernando Allievi, also dating from 1998: *Historia de Sábado* (Saturday Story), a family on a city outing; *Las Primeras Luces* (First Light), a bedraggled shoeshine boy and his dog at daybreak; and the surrealistic *Las Máscaras* (The Masks).

Línea D

In contrast to Línea C's Iberian-themed murals, most of Línea D's are more strictly nationalist, dealing with Argentine landscapes, legends, traditions, and native customs interpreted by artists like Léonie Matthis de Villar, Rodolfo Franco, and Alfredo Guido. The line opened in 1937, so this change of focus may reflect events of the Spanish Civil War and the military regime then ruling Argentina. The thematic exception is Estación Palermo, whose ceramic vestibule mural resembles those of Línea C's *Paisajes de España.*

On Estación Catedral's north platform, *Buenos Aires 1936* reflects the modern city's construction, with its subways and skyscrapers. In the same station, the ceramic *Buenos Aires en 1830* recalls early republican times.

Ceramic murals at Estación Facultad de Medicina offer insight into provincial cities with *Rosario 1836, Santa Fe 1836,* and *Rosario 1938.* Estación Agüero's *Camino a Córdoba del Tucumán* suggests the rigors of 19th-century travel between provincial capitals.

Estación Bulnes's *Las Leyendas del País de la Selva* (Legends of the Forests) has a folkloric focus, while *Arqueología Diaguita* portrays northwestern Argentina's archaeological heritage. Estación Scalabrini Ortiz's *Evocaciones de Salta* depicts the far northwestern province.

Among this line's best works is Estación Plaza Italia's *La Descarga de los Convoyes,* a series of port scenes based on sketches by Benito Quinquela Martín, which cover the platforms themselves.

The spacious, well-lighted new stations on the Línea D extension—José Hernández, Juramento, and Congreso de Tucumán—all feature custom-made display cases with rotating exhibits of historical and cultural artifacts and artwork, such as sculptures. Estación José Hernández features several 1997 reproductions of Raúl Soldi murals originally created elsewhere in the city: *La Música* (Music), *El Ensayo* (The Rehearsal), *Los Amantes* (The Lovers), and *En el Jardín* (In the Garden). Estación Juramento displays a reproduction of Cándido López's 19th-century *Batalla de Curupaytí.*

Línea E

Opened in 1944, Línea E reflects even more nationalistic times, coinciding with the rise of Juan and Evita Perón. Estación San José is the only station to celebrate the country's scenic treasures, *Las Cataratas del Iguazú* (Iguazú Falls) and *Los Lagos del Sur* (The Southern Lake District).

Estación Entre Ríos, though, glorifies *La Conquista del Desierto,* General Julio Argentino Roca's 19th-century genocide against the Patagonian Mapuche and their allies, and the *Fundación de Pueblos en la Pampa,* the founding of the towns that displaced the indigenes.

Estación Jujuy represents its namesake province and people in *Jujuy, Sus Riquezas Naturales* (Jujuy's Natural Riches) and *Los Gauchos Norteños* (The Northern Gauchos). Estación General Urquiza celebrates the defeat of the dictator Rosas in a reproduction of Cándido López's *La Batalla de Caseros* and *La Entrada Triunfal del General Urquiza en Buenos Aires* (General Urquiza's Triumphant Entry into Buenos Aires).

Estación Boedo, by contrast, contains more everyday scenes like *Boedo a Mediados del Siglo XIX,* showing the barrio's mid-19th century economic activities. It also contains the ceramic lunette *Niños Jugando* (Children at Play). Estación Medalla Milagrosa contains surrealistic 2001 murals by Santiago García Sáenz.

Museo de la Inmigración

AVENIDA ANTÁRTIDA 1355,
TEL. 011/4317-0285
OPEN 10 A.M.–5 P.M. WEEKDAYS,
11 A.M.–6 P.M. WEEKENDS
WWW.MININTERIOR.GOV.AR/
MIGRACIONES/MUSEO/
INDEX.HTML

Toward the barrio's north end, the Hotel de Inmigrantes was Argentina's Ellis Island for European immigrants. From 1911 until 1953, arrivals from the Old World could spend five nights in the building before heading into the great Argentine unknown. By all accounts, it was an exemplary facility.

Recently reopened to the public as the Museo de la Inmigración, it's still a work in progress, but is off to a good start with displays of sample family histories and panels showing the evolution of Argentine immigration and the treatment of new arrivals. At present, the only areas open to the public are the reception and the dining room, where visitors can search a computer database for information on the 3.7 million immigrants from 60 countries who have arrived by boat since 1882. The upstairs accommodations—actually large dormitories—are due to undergo restoration.

Museum admission is free of charge. It's possible to research genealogies online at the museum.

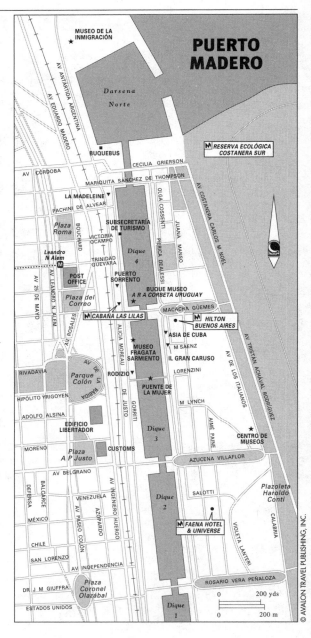

PUERTO MADERO

© AVALON TRAVEL PUBLISHING, INC.

© WAYNE BERNHARDSON

The modern B.A. skyline rises behind Puerto Madero's Dique No. 3.

Reserva Ecológica Costanera Sur

AVENIDA TRISTÁN ACHÁVAL RODRÍGUEZ 1550,
TEL. 011/4893-1597
OPEN TUES.–SUN. 8 A.M.– 7 P.M.

Plans to create a satellite city on landfill east of Puerto Madero were part of the military dictatorship's Proceso, but the 1982 Falklands fiasco short-circuited their projects to transform the city and the country. While things were on hold, volunteer trees, shrubs, and grasses colonized the area and, ironically, turned it into a lush wildlife habitat that's become a major recreational resource for *porteños*.

A few years after the return to representative government, lobbying from the Fundación Vida Silvestre, the Fundación Amigos de la Tierra, and the Asociación Ornitológica del Plata persuaded the city government to declare the area a nature reserve. It now offers hiking and bicycle trails and ample habitat for migratory wildfowl, such as black-necked swans, coots, and flamingos, permanent residents, such as black-crowned night herons and parakeets, and reptiles like river turtles. It has also become a cruising area for the capital's homosexuals.

At the foot of Avenida Belgrano, the Reserva Ecológica Costanera Sur offers guided tours weekends and holidays at 10:30 A.M. and 3:30 P.M. There are also moonlight tours at 8:30 P.M. on designated Fridays—by reservation only on the previous Monday.

There is also a convenient entrance at the north end of Avenida de los Italianos, where Bici Bus (a mobile bike shop) rents bicycles (US$1.75 per hour) from 8 A.M.–7 P.M. weekends and holidays only. It's possible to ride around the reserve in a little over an hour, but that's pushing it.

WALKING TOUR: PUERTO MADERO

Over the past decade-plus, the Puerto Madero docklands have undergone a transformation from abandonment to fashionability, becoming one of the city's most popular neighborhoods for Porteños and foreigners alike. Sequentially numbered from south to north, its four rectangular *diques* (basins) stretch from La Boca in the south to Retiro in the north.

Dique No. 3 holds the 450-berth yacht harbor; its **Buque Museo *Fragata A.R.A. Presidente Sarmiento*** is a national historical monument. The newest feature along the basins is Spanish architect Santiago Calatrava's modernistic **Puente de la Mujer,** a modernistic pedestrian bridge whose harp-like suspension section rotates to allow vessels to pass between Dique No. 3 and Dique No. 2. Recently moved to the northernmost Dique No. 4, the **Buque Museo A.R.A. Corbeta Uruguay** (1874) rescued Norwegian explorers Carl Skottsberg and Otto Nordenskjöld from Antarctica in 1903.

Several original cranes remain in place along the west side of the basins, where British engineers designed the handsome but practical red brick *depósitos* (warehouses), now recycled into some of the barrio's bars, restaurants, and entertainment venues, as well as apartments and offices. Work on the east-side buildings has been slower to progress, but it does include a pair of landmark luxury hotels and a scattering of high-rise luxury apartments.

Trending northwest to southeast, the **Avenida de los Italianos** features a broad esplanade that overlooks the Reserva Ecológica and is a favorite destination for weekend strollers, joggers, and cyclists. The city's **Centro de Museos** (Avenida de los Italianos 851, tel. 011/4516-0941, open 2–6 P.M. Tues.–Fri. and noon–6 P.M. weekends) has some exceptional special exhibitions, such as 2005's program on Buenos Aires's bus service, which includes some of the city's earliest *colectivos.*

Historically, the Puerto Madero area is where immigrants arrived, and the developing **Museo de la Inmigración,** north of the Buquebus ferry port, is an essential stop for appreciating the scale and significance of the European invasion.

Puerto Madero's handsome brick *depósitos* (warehouses) have been recycled into lofts and restaurants.

San Telmo

Once an elite residential area, San Telmo faded in the 1870s after a devastating yellow fever epidemic drove moneyed families to higher ground in northern barrios like Palermo and Belgrano. Like La Boca, to the south, it became an area where impoverished immigrant families could establish a foothold in its *conventillos,* abandoned mansions where large groups crowded into small spaces—often single rooms. Today, it's a mixed neighborhood where *conventillos* still exist, but young professionals have also recycled crumbling apartment buildings and even industrial sites into stylish lofts.

San Telmo is the barrio most closely identified with tango—at least the tango of high-priced floor shows and professional dancers. Otherwise, its nightlife is less impressive than that of other areas, such as Palermo, in part because some *porteños* perceive picturesque San Telmo as crime-ridden. Nevertheless, improvements are taking place, with increasing numbers of sidewalk cafés, wine bars, and restaurants popping up.

San Telmo's heart, though, is **Plaza Dorrego** (Defensa and Humberto Primo), site of the hectic weekend flea market; it's a more leisurely place during the week, when shaded tables replace the crowded stalls and it's easier to enjoy lunch. Antique shops line both sides of Defensa, north and south from the plaza.

Museo Histórico Nacional
DEFENSA 1600, TEL. 011/4307-1182
OPEN TUES.–FRI. 11 A.M.–5 P.M., SAT. NOON–6 P.M., SUN. 11 A.M.–6 P.M.

From the permanent exhibits at Parque Lezama's national history museum, it's hard to tell that Argentina lived through the 20th century, let alone made it to the 21st. Mostly chronological, it offers a token account of pre-Columbian Argentina and a brief description of the founding of Spanish cities; its most vivid exhibits are meticulous 19th-century illustrations of Buenos Aires and the surrounding pampas by Royal Navy purser Emeric Essex Vidal.

The museum offers a perfunctory narrative of independence and the 19th century caudillos (provincial warlords), plus a substantial if stereotypical nod to the gaucho. Its nadir is a chauvinistic account of the so-called Conquista del Desierto (Conquest of the Desert), which expanded the country's territory on the Patagonian frontier at the expense of the indigenous population in the late 19th century.

One entire salon extols the maturation of iconic independence hero José de San Martín, but a superficial narrative of the conservative 19th century republic—consisting mostly of presidential portraits—ends abruptly with the deposed Hipólito Yrigoyen, victim of the country's first modern military coup in 1930. There's nothing whatsoever on Juan Domingo Perón, his equally charismatic wife Evita, the 1970s' Dirty War, the 1980s' democratic restoration, or the 1990s' abortive boom.

Despite its shortcomings as a museum, the

The onion domes of San Telmo's Iglesia Ortodoxa Rusa face Parque Lezama.

© WAYNE BERNHARDSON

WALKING TOUR: SAN TELMO

South of Monserrat, San Telmo is the most colonial of all Buenos Aires's barrios. Although the Spanish Laws of the Indies dictated city plans with rectangular blocks of equal size, in practice things were not quite so regular here. North-south **Calle Balcarce,** for instance, doglegs several times between Chile and Estados Unidos, crossing the cobblestone alleyways of **Pasaje San Lorenzo** and **Pasaje Giuffra.**

This area's quirkiest landmark is the **Casa Mínima** (Pasaje San Lorenzo 380), a *casa chorizo* (sausage house) whose width is barely greater than an average adult male's armspread; it is now open for visits through nearby **El Zanjón** (Defensa 755).

Befitting its artists' colony reputation, San Telmo is home to a large and growing number of murals, usually collective efforts. One notable piece, at Avenida Independencia and Bolívar, depicts the Afro-Argentine **Carnaval.** Two blocks east, at Independencia and Balcarce, the restored mural *Tango* covers the walls behind the **Plazoleta Leonel Rivera.** Six blocks south, at the corner of Avenida Juan de Garay and Avenida Paseo Colón, the stylized *Educación y Esclavitud* (Education and Slavery) tackles Argentina's authoritarian political heritage.

To the east, where Avenida Paseo Colón narrows toward La Boca at the elliptical **Plaza Coronel Olazábal,** Rogelio Yrurtia's monumental *Canto al Trabajo* (Ode to Labor) may be the city's finest public sculpture. Unfortunately, a metal fence intended to dissuade vandalism blunts the impact of this tribute to hard-working pioneers, a welcome antidote to many of the pompously heroic monuments elsewhere in the city.

On the plaza's east side, the Universidad de Buenos Aires's neoclassic **Facultad de Ingeniería** originally housed the Fundación Eva Perón, established by Evita herself to aid the poor—and her own political ambitions. Immediately behind it, infamous for corruption, the controversial **Confederación General de Trabajo** (CGT, General Labor Confederation, Azopardo 802) is a traditional source of Peronist power.

Buenos Aires has many immigrant communities, but one of the unlikeliest must be the Scandinavians, who nonetheless have left a mark in San Telmo. The Danish architects Rönnow and Bisgaard designed the distinctive red brick, neo-Gothic **Dansk Kirke** (Danish Lutheran Church, Carlos Calvo 257), dating from 1931; its interior is known for its chandeliers. Five blocks southeast, dating from 1944, the comparable **Svenska Kyrkan** (Swedish Lutheran Church, Azopardo 1428) looks as if it were airlifted intact from Stockholm.

One block west of the Danish church, the **Antigua Tasca de Cuchilleros** (Carlos Calvo 319) is an intriguing colonial house that holds a bad restaurant—look but don't eat. To the west, the unassuming *ochava* (corner entrance) at the 1897 **Mercado San Telmo** (Carlos Calvo and Bolívar) opens into a roomy market where barrio residents shop for produce, but it's also become a crafts outlet.

Half a block east of Plaza Dorrego, the **Museo Penitenciario Nacional** (Humberto Primo 378) was originally a convent of the colonial **Iglesia Nuestra Señora de Belén** (1750); it became a women's prison after independence. Across the street, the 1858 **Protomedicato** (Humberto Primo 343) was the capital's first medical school.

San Telmo has always been a neighborhood where the upwardly and downwardly mobile mix. The 1880 **Pasaje de la Defensa** (Defensa 1179) originally belonged to a single wealthy family but later housed upwards of 30 families before being turned into a shopping gallery. The **Galería del Viejo Hotel** (Balcarce 1053) is a similar cluster of workshops, studios, shops, and a bar/restaurant around a courtyard; until its present incarnation around 1980, though, it served at various times as a hotel, hospital (during the yellow fever epidemic), *conventillo*, and even an *albergue transitorio* (a by-the-hour hotel). Nearby, the former **Patronato de la Infancia** (Balcarce 1170) was a *conventillo* until early 2003, when city authorities cleared out squatters.

Across Avenida San Juan are two more significant museums: the **Museo de Arte Moderno** (Avenida San Juan 350), in a cavernous recycled warehouse, and the **Museo del Cine,** (Defensa 1220), the cinema museum. One of the more unsettling sights, on Paseo Colón beneath the Autopista 25 de Mayo (the freeway to Ezeiza), the so-called **Club Atlético** is a grisly archaeological dig, whose basement cells belonged to a building used as a torture center during the military dictatorship of 1976–1983 before being demolished to build the *autopista.*

At the corner of Defensa and Avenida Brasil, a graffiti-covered statue of Pedro de Mendoza guards the entrance to **Parque Lezama,** where Mendoza ostensibly founded the city in 1536. This is also the site of the **Museo Histórico Nacional,** the national history museum. Across from the park, architect Alejandro Christopherson designed the turquoise-colored onion domes and stained-glass windows of the 1904 **Iglesia Apostólica Ortodoxa Rusa** (Russian Orthodox Apostolic Church, Avenida Brasil 315), built with materials imported from St. Petersburg.

Adjacent southern barrios, such as Constitución and Barracas, have fewer conspicuous points of interest. Just to the west of San Telmo, across Avenida 9 de Julio, **Plaza Constitución** is a mess of a hub for city buses. The bus stops are due to move beneath the nearby freeway, allowing authorities to redevelop the plaza as open space. **Estación Constitución,** the station for the former Ferrocarril Roca rail line that now serves mostly southern suburban destinations, has undergone a badly needed facelift but still needs work.

To the southwest, the 1915 **Edificio Crítica** (Salta and Echagüe), now the home of the Fundación Cinemática Argentina (Argentine Cinema Foundation), housed one of the capital's important early newspapers. The **Centro Cultural del Sur** (Avenida Caseros 1750) occupies a colonial-style house that was once a plant nursery and today hosts major tango and other cultural events. The adjacent **Jardín Botánico del Sur** is not a true botanical garden, but it has merged with Plaza España to form a large green and shady area.

The portrait of a youthful, vigorous Eva Perón is still a feature of the San Telmo headquarters of the Confederación General de Trabajo, the Peronist trade union.

building itself is a well-kept landmark whose subterranean gallery hosts special exhibits, and on occasion there are weekend concerts. Admission costs US$.65; there are guided tours at 3:30 P.M. Saturday and Sunday. Summer hours are greatly reduced: 3–5 P.M. weekdays only.

Parque Lezama

The rumored (if improbable) site of Pedro de Mendoza's founding of the city, famed landscape architect Carlos Thays's Parque Lezama is an irregular quadrilateral on the banks above the old river course, which has long been covered by landfill. Shaded by mature palms and other exotic trees and studded with monuments, it's the place where aging *porteños* play chess, working-class families have weekend picnics, and a Sunday crafts fair stretches north along Calle Defensa to Avenida San Juan. The park appears better-maintained than in recent years, despite its severe feral cat problem—a dilemma it shares with many other city parks.

Sights

On the capital's southern edge in colonial times, the property came into the hands of Carlos Ridgley Horne and then Gregorio Lezama, whose widow sold it to the city in 1884. Horne built the Italianate mansion (1846), which is now the **Museo Histórico Nacional,** the national history museum; at the park's northwest entrance, Juan Carlos Oliva Navarro sculpted the graffiti-covered *Monumento a Don Pedro Mendoza* (1937) to mark the 400th anniversary of Buenos Aires's founding—a year too late.

Plaza Dorrego

DEFENSA AND HUMBERTO PRIMO

Six days a week, Plaza Dorrego is a shaded, nearly silent square where *porteños* sip *cortados* (espresso with milk) and nibble lunches from nearby cafés. On weekends, though, when municipal authorities close Calle Defensa between Avenida San Juan and Avenida Independencia, it swarms with Argentine and foreign visitors who stroll among dozens of antiques stalls at the **Feria de San Telmo** (formally Feria de San Pedro Telmo), the most famous and colorful of the capital's numerous street fairs. Items range from antique soda siphons to brightly painted *filete* plaques displaying *piropos* (aphorisms), oversized early radios, and many other items.

The plaza and surrounding side streets fill with street performers, like the ponytailed Pedro Benavente, known as El Indio, a smooth *tanguero* (dancer) who with various female partners entrances locals and tourists alike— even though his boom box provides the music. Up and down Defensa there are also live tango musicians and other dancers, not to mention puppet theaters, hurdy-gurdy men with parrots, and a glut of *estatuas vivas* (living statues or costumed mimes), some of whom are remarkably original and others of whom are trite. The author's favorite performers, though, are the trio who (for a small donation) will jabber in *cocoliche,* the Italian-Spanish pidgin that has influenced the Argentine language since the late 19th century.

The Feria de San Telmo takes place every Sunday, starting around 9–10 A.M. and continuing into late afternoon. Even with all the antiques

and crafts stands, there's room to enjoy lunch and the show from the sidewalk cafés surrounding the plaza and balconies overlooking it.

El Zanjón

DEFENSA 755, TEL. 011/4361-3002
OPEN WEEKDAYS 10 A.M.–6 P.M. (TOURS)
WWW.ELZANJON.COM.AR

In 1986, when businessman Jorge Eckstein bought the Italianate building at Defensa 755 with the idea of recycling it for a music and events center, he had no idea that workers would stumble upon a labyrinth of tunnels that encased the Tercero del Sur, a Río de la Plata tributary, in late colonial times. Calling in urban archaeologist Jorge Schávelzon to supervise salvage and restoration, Eckstein worked around the remaining structures, including cisterns, wells, and even some houses, unobtrusively reinforcing them with concrete and other materials when necessary.

Visitors to El Zanjón can now tour these tunnels, which were filled with rubble during the yellow fever scare of the 1870s, and view the numerous colonial and republican artifacts, including tools and ceramics, that Schávelzon salvaged and organized. Despite its relatively recent exterior, the building itself has three impressive colonial patios and sits atop one of the city's oldest land grants, from city founder Juan de Garay himself. The tunnels run beneath neighboring buildings and, pending mutual agreement, the restoration may be extended.

Expertly led, hour-long guided tours of El Zanjón, in Spanish or English, cost US$7 pp— expensive by current standards—but this is a private initiative and an almost unique sight. To make it even more appealing, tours include a visit to the famous **Casa Mínima** (San Lorenzo 380), an unoccupied "sausage house" that was ostensibly a slaveholder's gift to his former chattel (there is no documentary evidence to prove, or disprove, this legend). The narrow house entrance opens onto a slightly wider patio where the former kitchen sits, while a wall-hugging staircase leads to an even narrower bedroom, which has a street-side balcony directly above the exterior doorway.

La Boca

On the west bank of the twisting Riachuelo, which separates the capital from Buenos Aires province, the working-class barrio of La Boca owes its origins to mid-19th century French Basque and Genovese immigrants who worked in packing plants and warehouses during the beef-export boom. Perhaps more than any other neighborhood in the city, it remains a community symbolized by fervent—most would say fanatical—identification with the

Boca Juniors soccer team (the team's nickname Xeneizes, by the way, comes from the Genovese dialect).

La Boca is, in a literal sense, the city's most colorful neighborhood, thanks to the brightly painted houses with corrugated zinc siding that line the pedestrian **Caminito** and other streets. Initially, these bright colors came from marine paints salvaged from ships in the harbor. The colors are inviting, but the poorly insulated

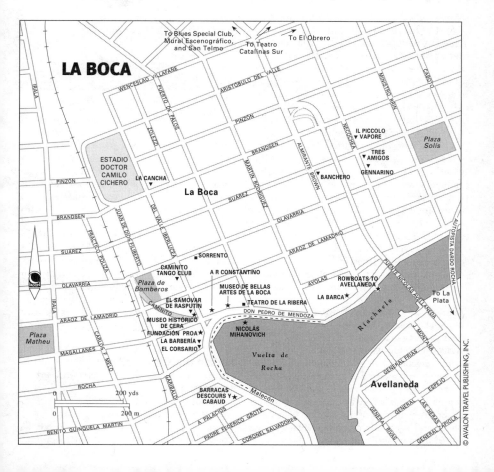

Sights

buildings can be unbearably hot in summer and frigid in winter.

Porteños may still claim that the barrio is dangerous, but anyone with basic street smarts should be able to visit without incident. There is, however, far more graffiti on the walls than in past years and more dog droppings on the sidewalks—perhaps signs of a declining sense of community. Some locals blame the police, who they say view the job not as a vocation but rather as a last-chance option. For this reason, some visitors prefer guided tours, which often start at the Caminito.

Museo de Bellas Artes de La Boca Benito Quinquela Martín

PEDRO DE MENDOZA 1835, TEL: 011/4301-1080
OPEN DAILY EXCEPT MON., 10 A.M.–5:45 P.M.

Boca's very own artist-in-residence, Benito Quinquela Martín (1890–1977), was an orphan who became a son of his barrio, living and painting in the building that is now a homage to his life and work promoting the community. His well-lighted studio displays a collection of his oils of working-class life (Quinquela himself was a stevedore before devoting himself to painting). There's also a collection of brightly painted bowsprits that reflects the barrio's maritime orientation and a selection of works by other notable Argentine painters, including Antonio Berni, Raquel Forner, Eduardo Sívori, and Lino Spilimbergo.

The Museo de Bellas Artes shares a street-level entrance with the Escuela Pedro de Mendoza, an elementary school. There's no obligatory admission charge, but donations are appropriate.

Museo de la Pasión Boquense

BRANDSEN 805, TEL. 011/4362-1100
OPEN DAILY 10 A.M.–7 P.M.
WWW.MUSEOBOQUENSE.COM

In the catacombs of La Bombonera, Boca's newest museum is a thunderous interactive homage to the barrio's passion for soccer and its role in the community. Professionally organized, this state-of-the-art facility's 1,800 square meters include photographs of almost every individual who ever played for the team, ranging from single-match

Caminito, La Boca

© WAYNE BERNHARDSON

nobodies to Roberto Morizo, who played in 426 matches. The museum also includes roster cards, trophies, and even a photograph of Eva Perón in a blue-and-gold jersey. Boca's ultimate icon and idol, though, remains retired striker Diego Maradona, whose adoring fans seem oblivious to his drug problems and other erratic behavior.

Interactive video timelines attempt to integrate local, national, and international events—even the Dirty War that the military dictatorship waged as Argentina hosted the 1978 World Cup—with those in the sporting world. In the end, though, non-soccer fans will find it dull except for its depiction of the barrio.

The Museo de la Pasión Boquense charges US$2.60 pp admission, or US$4.20 pp with a guided stadium tour. Hours may change on game days.

Museo Histórico de Cera

DEL VALLE IBERLUCEA 1261, TEL. 011/4301-1497
OPEN WEEKDAYS 10 A.M.–8 P.M.,
WEEKENDS 10 A.M.–9 P.M.
WWW.MUSEODECERA.COM.AR

The only one of its kind in the country, La Boca's historical wax museum re-creates

WALKING TOUR: LA BOCA

Thanks to the late Benito Quinquela Martín, a barrio resident who sympathetically portrayed its hard-working inhabitants in his oils, La Boca is an artists' colony as well as a thriving working-class neighborhood. Its gateway is Avenida Almirante Brown, at the southeast corner of Parque Lezama, where the *Mural Escenográfico Parque Lezama,* a three-dimensional mural erected by the barrio's Catalinas del Sur theater group, depicts community life through colorful caricatures. Three blocks southeast, the **Casa de Almirante Brown,** also known as the Casa Amarilla (Yellow House) replicates the country house of the Argentine navy's Irish founder.

Only a block east of Avenida Almirante Brown, the parallel **Calle Necochea** houses a cluster of gaudy and raucous cantinas that were once brothels, but this area's tourist appeal is declining. From the foot of the avenue, where it intersects Avenida Pedro de Mendoza at the Riachuelo, the remaining massive girders of the former **Puente Nicolás Avellaneda** (1940), towering above the river, are a civil-engineering landmark; the current namesake bridge parallel to the girders is an unremarkable concrete construction leading into the capital's major industrial suburb. To avoid climbing the massive structure, especially in the summer heat, most pedestrians hire rowboats for the short crossing to Avellaneda.

The starting point for most visits to the barrio remains the cobbled, curving **Caminito,** once the terminus of a rail line and now a pedestrian mall where artists display their watercolors (there are more artists there on weekends than on weekdays). Taking its name from a popular tango, the Caminito may once again sing with the sound of the rails—a new tourist train to the **Plaza de Bomberos** (Firemen's Plaza) is due to connect to Puerto Madero.

On either side of the Caminito, along Avenida Pedro de Mendoza, several landmarks lend character to the neighborhood. Immediately east, high-relief sculptures stand out above the display window of the ship chandler A.R. Constantino. Across the avenue, at permanent anchor, the former ferry *Nicolás Mihanovich,* which linked Buenos Aires to Uruguay, now houses a cultural center and crafts market.

A short distance east stands the **Museo de Bellas Artes de La Boca,** in Quinquela Martín's former studio; one block farther east, the former restaurant **La Barca** retains a batch of Vicente Walter's well-preserved bas reliefs on nautical themes.

Immediately south of the Caminito, also fronting on Avenida Pedro de Mendoza, the **Fundación Proa** is one of the capital's best galleries for abstract and figurative art. Beyond several sidewalk cafés, colorfully decorated with *filete* signboards, the **Barracas Descours y Cabaud** (1902) is a former warehouse.

For residents, though, the barrio's key landmark is the **Estadio Doctor Camilo Cichero,** better known by its nickname **La Bombonera** (at Brandsen and Del Valle Iberlucea); murals of barrio life cover the walls along the Brandsen side of the stadium. It's now home to the appropriately named **Museo de la Pasión Boquense** (Museum of Boca's Passion), which integrates the soccer team's history with its role in the community.

Numerous *colectivos* (city buses) from throughout the city either pass through or end their routes at La Boca, most notably the No. 86 from Congreso, but also No. 29 (from Belgrano and Palermo), No. 33 (from Retiro), No. 64 (from Belgrano, Palermo, and Congreso), and No. 152 (from Belgrano, Palermo, and Retiro).

events, scenes, and significant figures in Argentine history. Among its themes are the founding of the city, the gaucho, the tango, and even the Afro-Argentine dance *candombe;* the latter serves as an open acknowledgement of the capital's once-substantial black community. In addition to historical and political figures, like Pedro de Mendoza, Juan Manuel de Rosas, and Guillermo Brown, there are representations of indigenous leaders, such as Calfucurá and Ceferino Namuncurá, and of cultural icons, like Carlos Gardel and Juan de Dios Filiberto (composer of the tango *Caminito*), and the artist Quinquela Martín.

Occupying a century-old Italian Renaissance residence, the Museo de Cera charges US$1.65 admission.

Balvanera

West of Avenida Callao, between Avenida Córdoba and Avenida Independencia, Balvanera's most obvious sights are major public buildings, like the **Congreso Nacional,** which faces the Plaza del Congreso from Avenida Entre Ríos, and architectural landmarks, like the sadly neglected **Confitería del Molino,** a national monument at the corner of Avenida Callao and Avenida Rivadavia. In contrast to this neglect is the magnificently preserved **Palacio de las Aguas**

The Palacio de las Aguas Corrientes, the former city waterworks also known as Obras Sanitarias, is one of the capital's most striking buildings.

Corrientes, the former city waterworks, which fills an entire block at the north end of the barrio.

Once, roughly bounded by Avenida Córdoba, Junín, Avenida Rivadavia, and Avenida Pueyrredón, is the city's garment district; it takes its colloquial name from the **Estación 11 de Septiembre,** the westbound Ferrocarril Sarmiento station that has both commuter rail service and a few remaining long-distance trains. It is one of the most densely populated parts of town, with little green space, but its **Plaza Miserere,** alongside the station, and **Plaza 1° de Mayo** are undergoing renovation.

Ethnically, Once is the capital's most conspicuously Jewish neighborhood, where men and boys in yarmulkes and Orthodox Jews wearing plain suits and long beards are common sights, especially east of Pueyrredón between Córdoba and Corrientes. There are several Jewish schools, noteworthy for the heavy concrete security posts outside them: Once saw the notorious 1994 bombing of the **Asociación Mutualista Israelita Argentina** (AMIA, Pasteur 633, between Viamonte and Tucumán). Investigation of this terrorist act, which killed 87 people, has been a chaotic bungle, despite suspected links to Iran and the Buenos Aires provincial police.

Mercado del Abasto
CORRIENTES 3247

Until 1893, the area bounded by Avenida Corrientes, Anchorena, Agüero, and Lavalle was a sprawling open-air market for wholesale fruits,

© WAYNE BERNHARDSON

Balvanera's Congreso Nacional is home to Argentina's bicameral legislature.

vegetables, and meats. In that year, though, the Italian Devoto family's construction of the Mercado de Abasto made room for merchants displaced by mayor Torcuato de Alvear's ambitious transformation of the city's civic axis along the newly created Avenida de Mayo.

Rebuilt in 1934 by Italian architect José Luis Delpini, under the auspices of the Bunge & Born conglomerate, the cavernous Abasto served its purpose until the 1970s, when the military dictatorship moved its functions to the new and far larger (if clearly misnamed) Mercado Central in La Matanza, beyond the city limits in Buenos Aires province.

In 1998, after nearly two decades of neglect, the Mercado del Abasto reopened as a four-story shopping center with 120,000 square meters of display space, 186 shops, 12 cinemas, parking, and a food court (with a kosher McDonalds!). Part of a project for rejuvenating the neighborhood, sponsored by U.S.-Hungarian financier George Soros (who has since bowed out of Argentina), this adaptive reuse saved a magnificent building from demolition. Unfortunately, it's notoriously noisy and less appealing than com-petitors like the Galerías Pacífico and Patio Bullrich; the restored exterior is all that's worth seeing.

One unique feature is its children's museum, the **Museo de Niños Abasto** (tel. 011/4861-2325, www.museoabasto.org.ar), which amuses and presumably educates the children when they tire of toy shopping. Hours are 1–8 P.M. daily except Monday; admission costs US$2.25 pp, but there are package fees for families with children (comprising most of the museum's patrons).

Palacio de las Aguas Corrientes (Obras Sanitarias)
RIOBAMBA 750, TEL. 011/6319-1104 (MUSEUM)
OPEN WEEKDAYS 9 A.M.–NOON (MUSEUM)
Arguably the capital's most photogenic building, the former city waterworks (1894) glistens with 170,000 rust-colored tiles and 130,000 enameled bricks imported from Britain, crowned by a Parisian mansard. Filling an entire city block bounded by Avenida Córdoba, Riobamba, Viamonte, and Ayacucho, the extravagant exterior of the building popularly known as Obras Sanitarias (Water Works) disguises a far more utilitarian interior of 12

© WAYNE BERNHARDSON

In summer, kids scale the fences to cool off in the fountains of the Plaza del Congreso.

metallic tanks that held more than 60 million liters of the growing city's drinking water. There were similar, though less conspicuously lavish, structures in the barrios of Caballito and Villa Devoto.

Swedish architect Karl Nystromer conceived the building, whose tanks became superfluous as engineers developed a series of subterranean tunnels for shifting water through the city. Since its 1990s privatization as part of Aguas Argentinas, the building has housed offices and the small but interesting **Museo del Patrimonio Aguas Argentinas.**

The museum, which offers excellent guided tours in Spanish only, displays an astonishing assortment of antique plumbing fixtures ranging from taps, tubs, pipes, and sinks to bidets and urinals, many of them imported, all of them needing approval from what was then a state-run bureaucracy. The old storage tanks now hold the archives of city maps and plans that were created in conjunction with the waterworks.

While the Palacio's street address is Riobamba 750, the museum entrance is on the Córdoba side; follow the arrows to the elevator, which takes you to the first floor.

Palacio del Congreso Nacional

AVENIDA RIVADAVIA AND AVENIDA CALLAO
WWW.CONGRESO.GOV.AR

Balvanera's largest landmark, the neoclassical Congreso Nacional, is the Congreso neighborhood's centerpiece. One of the last major public works projects undertaken before Francophile architecture became the norm, the Italianate building faces the Plaza del Congreso and, in the distance, the Casa Rosada.

Argentines typically view their legislators with skeptical and even cynical eyes, and the Congreso gave them good reason from the start. The progressive if authoritarian mayor Torcuato de Alvear chose the site in 1888, after the city's designation as federal capital, but in 1895 the Italian Vittorio Meano won a controversial design competition (decades later, his rival Alejandro Christopherson wrote that Meano did not prepare the sketches submitted for the competition). The project went far over budget, launching a major congressional investigation, and Meano died mysteriously, shot by his maid in 1904. The building was functional by 1906, but not until 1946 were the final touches applied.

CABALLITO AND VICINITY

Now precisely in the center of the federal capital, but still well off the tourist circuit, the middle-class barrio of Caballito once lay on the city's western fringes. It takes its name (little horse) from the design of a weathervane placed by Italian immigrant Nicolás Vila on the roof of his *pulpería* (general store) at Avenida Rivadavia and Cucha Cucha; Vila's establishment was a landmark in an area of country-style houses with large gardens.

Today, sculptor Luis Perlotti's replica of Vila's weathervane sits atop a flagpole at **Plazoleta Primera Junta,** now the terminus of the Subte's Línea B. Immigration and the Subte have transformed Caballito into a residential barrio for downtown workers, with notable open spaces. One of those open spaces, **Parque Rivadavia,** was formerly the *quinta* (country estate) of Ambrosio Lezica, cofounder of the influential *porteño* daily *La Nación*.

In the vicinity of Parque Rivadavia are several significant buildings, such as the **Liceo de Señoritas** (Avenida Rivadavia 4950), immediately to the north. Across the street, the restored Romanesque **Parroquia Nuestra Señora de Caacupé** (Rivadavia 4879) was once part of a convent; it is particularly precious to Paraguayans, to whom the Virgin of Caacupé is their patron saint. Especially appealing in the late afternoon light, it holds an image of the saint that, legend says, was carved by an indigenous man who pledged to do so if he escaped his enemies. Down the block, dating from 1910, the rococo **Club Italiano** (Rivadavia 4731) sports a mansard dome and an ornate ballroom with parquet floors.

Caballito is also the site of Buenos Aires's last operating tramway, the **Tranvía Histórica,** which operates weekends only from the corner of Avenida Rivadavia and Emilio Mitre (the car itself had to be imported from Portugal since all other city tramlines have been torn up and the cars scrapped). North of the suburban Ferrocarril Sarmiento's railroad tracks, the **Museo de Esculturas Luis Perlotti** is a small but outstanding art museum.

On Caballito's northern edge, the nearly circular **Parque Centenario** is known for its exceptional natural sciences museum, **Museo Argentino de Ciencias Naturales Bernardino Rivadavia,** its **Observatorio Astronómico,** and its open spaces.

The Congreso's 80-meter-high bronze cupola still bears marks from the military coup of 1930 against Hipólito Yrigoyen. Presidents who have died in office, such as Perón, have lain in state here, as did Perón's wife Evita.

Phone at least an hour ahead for guided tours of the upper house Senado (Hipólito Yrigoyen 1849, tel. 011/4959-3000, Ext. 3855). Tours take place weekdays at 11 A.M., 5 P.M., and 6 P.M. in Spanish; the 11 A.M. tour can accommodate English and French speakers. There's a separate 4 P.M. tour for English speakers.

Spanish-only visits to the lower Cámara de Diputados (Avenida Rivadavia 1864, tel. 011/6310-7532) take place Monday, Tuesday, Thursday, and Friday at 10 A.M., noon, and 4 and 6 P.M. The congressional website has separate entries for each house.

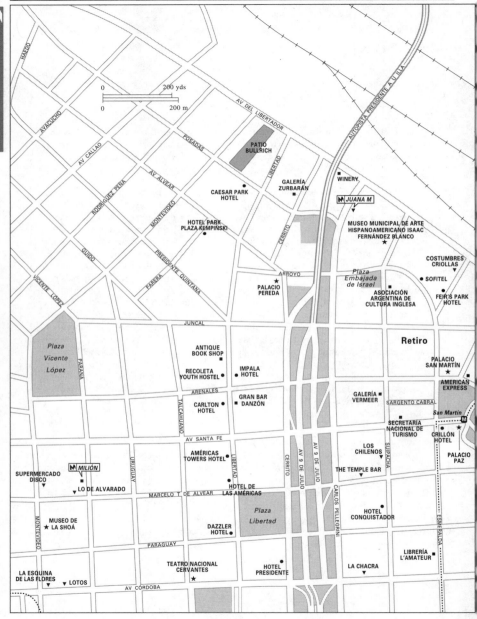

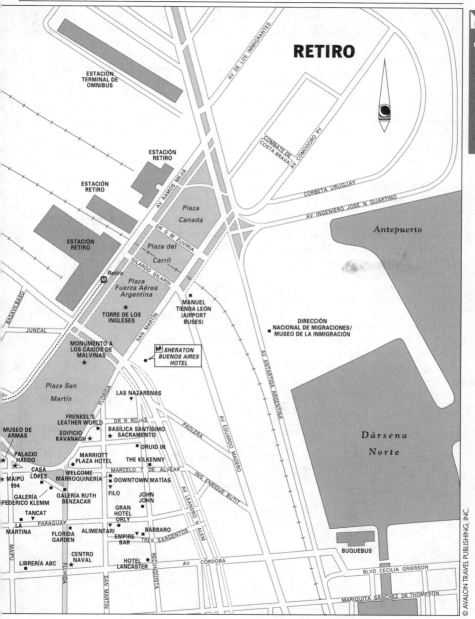

RETIRO

ESTACIÓN TERMINAL DE OMNIBUS

ESTACIÓN RETIRO

ESTACIÓN RETIRO

ESTACIÓN RETIRO

AV DE LOS IMMIGRANTES

COMBATE DE COSTA BRAVA

AV COMODORO PY

CORBETA URUGUAY

AV INGENIERO JOSE N QUARTINO

Antepuerto

AV RAMOS MEJIA

Plaza Canadá

DR G M ZUVIRIA

Plaza del Carril

GILARDO GILARDI

Retiro M

Plaza Fuerza Aérea Argentina

★ TORRE DE LOS INGLESES

SAN MARTIN

MANUEL TIENDA LEÓN (AIRPORT BUSES)

DIRECCIÓN NACIONAL DE MIGRACIONES/ MUSEO DE LA INMIGRACIÓN

P ASAVILBASO

JUNCAL

MONUMENTO A LOS CAIDOS DE MALVINAS ★

M SHERATON BUENOS AIRES HOTEL

AV ANTARTIDA ARGENTINA

Plaza San Martín

LAS NAZARENAS ▼

FLORIDA

FRENKEL'S LEATHER WORLD

DR R ROJAS

MUSEO DE ARMAS

EDIFICIO KAVANAGH ★

BASÍLICA SANTÍSIMO ★ SACRAMENTO

DRUID IN

PAOLERA

AV EDUARDO MADERO

Dársena Norte

PALACIO HAEDO ★

MARRIOTT PLAZA HOTEL

THE KILKENNY

CASA LÓPEZ

WELCOME MARROQUINERÍA

MARCELO T DE ALVEAR

★ MAIPÚ 994

DOWNTOWN MATÍAS

ING ENRIQUE BUTH

GALERÍA FEDERICO KLEMM

GALERÍA RUTH BENZACAR

FILO

JOHN JOHN

AV LEANDRO N ALEM

TANCAT ▼

GRAN HOTEL ORLY ▼

LA MARTINA ▼

PARAGUAY

ALIMENTARI

BÁRBARO

FLORIDA GARDEN

EMPIRE ▼ BAR

TRES SARGENTOS

MAIPU

LIBRERÍA ABC

CENTRO NAVAL ★

HOTEL LANCASTER ●

RECONQUISTA

AV CÓRDOBA

BUQUEBUS

BLVD CECILIA GRIERSON

FLORIDA

SAN MARTIN

MARIQUITA SÁNCHEZ DE THOMPSON

Retiro

Well north of Juan de Garay's refounded Buenos Aires of 1580, Retiro (literally, a retreat) was home to an isolated monastery in the 17th century. The name Retiro, though, does not appear formally until 1691, when Spanish Governor Agustín de Robles built a house on the *barranca* (terrace), where Plaza San Martín now sits, above the river. For a time, Retiro became a zone of *quintas* (country houses), but by 1862 the erection of General San Martín's equestrian statue marked its definitive urbanization. Beginning in the late 19th century, the surrounding streets became the city's most elite residential area.

Museo de la Shoá
MONTEVIDEO 919, TEL. 011/4811-3537
OPEN MON.–THURS. 11 A.M.–7 P.M.,
FRI. 10 A.M.–5 P.M.
WWW.FMH.ORG.AR
Opened in October 2001, Buenos Aires's Holocaust museum is a truly professional endeavor with both permanent collections and rotating exhibits on such topics as the Warsaw ghetto, the Danish resistance to deportation of the Jews, and the 60th anniversary of the liberation of Auschwitz. Its bright explanatory panels, illustrated with photographs and documents, intertwine European events with those in Argentina; its Sala de la Memoria (Memorial Hall) evokes the memory of Argentine Jews who died in the European carnage.

Admission costs US$.35. Note that even when the museum is open, the sturdy metal door is closed for security purposes, and the friendly but muscular young men at the entrance are a further deterrent to potential malefactors.

Museo Municipal de Arte Hispanoamericano Isaac Fernández Blanco
SUIPACHA 1422, TEL. 011/4327-0272
OPEN TUES.–SUN. 2–7 P.M., HOLIDAYS 3–7 P.M.
WWW.MUSEOS.BUENOSAIRES.GOV.AR
Housing the extensive colonial and independence-era art collections of its namesake founder, the municipal art museum contains an impressive array of Spanish- and Portuguese-American religious painting and statuary, as well as exquisite silverwork and furniture. It occupies the Pa-

Densely built Retiro lies mostly west of Avenida del Libertador and north of Plaza San Martín.

lacio Noel, an impressive neocolonial residence built for city mayor Carlos Noel by his brother Martín in 1921—with its nods to Andalucía, Arequipa (Perú), and especially Lima for its balconies, the building was an overdue antidote to the fashionable Francophile architecture of the time, especially in this neighborhood.

Admission costs US$.35 except Thursday, when it's free. There are guided tours at 4 P.M. Saturday and Sunday, and occasional concerts and other cultural events. It sometimes closes during the summer months of January and February.

Palacio San Martín
ARENALES 761, TEL. 011/4819-8092
OPEN THURS. 11 A.M., FRI. 3, 4, AND 5 P.M. (TOURS)
Mercedes Castellano de Anchorena, matriarch of one of Argentina's most powerful families, ordered the construction of the three interconnected beaux arts residences that constitute the Palacio San Martín. Designed by renowned architect Alejandro Christopherson and finished in 1912, the three houses share imposing gates and a common circular courtyard, but each

has its own separate entrance, marble staircases and balustrades, elaborate stained-glass windows, immense dining rooms (still used for state functions), and other elements of Parisian-style opulence. The satellite plaza immediately south of the palace was, de facto at least, the Anchorena family's private garden.

Sold to the foreign ministry for 1.5 million pesos in 1936, the building has served diplomatic purposes ever since; however, due to construction of the new high-rise *cancillería* (chancellery) across Esmeralda immediately to the west, it no longer houses permanent offices. Now open to the public, it provides an unmatched opportunity to grasp the Argentine oligarchy's lifestyle. It also holds a small museum of pre-Columbian antiquities from northwestern Argentina and works by famous Latin American artists, including the Argentine Antonio Berni, Uruguayan Pedro Figari, and Chilean Roberto Matta. One of its gardens holds a chunk of the Berlin Wall.

When not needed for official functions, the Palacio San Martín is open for free guided tours in both Spanish and English.

Recoleta and Barrio Norte

Once a bucolic outlier of the capital, Recoleta urbanized rapidly after the 1870s yellow fever outbreaks, when upper-class *porteños* concluded that low-lying San Telmo was too unhealthy for their families. Originally the site of a Franciscan convent (1716), it is internationally known for the **Cementerio de la Recoleta** (Recoleta Cemetery, 1822), whose elaborate crypts and mausoleums cost more than many, if not most, *porteño* houses and apartments.

Biblioteca Nacional
AGÜERO 2502, TEL. 011/4806-4729
OPEN WEEKDAYS 10 A.M.– 9 P.M.,
WEEKENDS NOON–9 P.M.
WWW.BIBNAL.EDU.AR
On the site of the former presidential residence (which moved to the northern suburb of Olivos in 1958), Italian architect Clorindo Testa's

national library is a concrete monolith whose construction took more than three decades before its formal inauguration in 1992. Barely a decade later, it's showing plenty of wear and tear, in part because its pathways and pyramids have proved a serendipitous godsend to *porteño* skateboarders and stunt bikers.

Still, the library makes a major contribution to the capital's cultural life, hosting lectures by literary figures, exhibits by local artists, and major expositions like 2002's "Evita, una vida, una historia, un mito"—a remarkably thorough and thoroughly remarkable retrospective on Evita's life and influence, on the 50th anniversary of her death. On the other hand, its administration has been chaotic and priceless items have disappeared in recent years.

The library website has a regularly updated events calendar.

WALKING TOUR: RETIRO

At the north end of the Florida pedestrian mall, surrounded by mansions than were once single-family residences but now house government offices, **Plaza San Martín** is the starting point of almost any stroll through Retiro. The most extravagant of the mansions is the 12,000-square meter **Palacio Paz** (1909), at the west end of the Plaza.

Filling a triangular lot bounded by Maipú, Avenida Santa Fe, and Marcelo T. de Alvear, the **Palacio Haedo,** is a neo-Gothic mansion that would seem truly lavish in any other context than its proximity to the Palacio Paz. Argentina's national park service occupies the Haedo.

On the plaza's north side, the 1905 art nouveau **Palacio San Martín** (Arenales 761) was originally a complex of three houses built for the Anchorena family. Purchased by the state in 1936 for the Ministerio de Relaciones Exteriores y Culto (Foreign Ministry), it serves primarily protocol and ceremonial purposes since the ministry moved to modern headquarters across the street. The Palacio San Martín is open for public visits.

At the plaza's southeast edge, the 1935 **Edificio Kavanagh** (Florida 1035) is a 33-story high-rise that was Buenos Aires's first skyscraper. Built in 14 months and inspired by the Chicago skyscrapers of the 1920s, this Deco landmark was and is a symbol of the capital's modernization. Unfortunately, it literally overshadows the nearby **Basílica Santísimo Sacramento** (San Martín 1035), a 1916 construction based on its Parisian namesake and sponsored by Mercedes Castellano de Anchorena (who built and lived in the Palacio San Martín with her children and their families).

Plaza San Martín's most recent major addition is the **Monumento a los Caídos de Malvinas,** a marble monument that lists the names of those who died in the 1982 war over the Falkland (Malvinas) Islands. Across Avenida del Libertador to the northeast, the **Plaza Fuerza Aérea Argentina, Plaza del Carril,** and **Plaza Canadá** are extensions of Plaza San Martín. Plaza Fuerza Aérea Argentina, once known as Plaza Britania, was renamed after the Falklands War, in which Argentina's air force was the only branch of the services that performed credibly. Its centerpiece, though, is still architect Ambrose Poynter's **Torre de los Ingleses** (1916), a clock tower resembling London's Big Ben that was donated by the once-substantial, but now diminishing, Anglo-Argentine community.

Casa Museo Ricardo Rojas

CHARCAS 2837, TEL. 011/4824-4039
OPEN WEEKDAYS 10 A.M.–5 P.M., SAT. 1–5 P.M.,
SUN. 10 A.M.–2 P.M.

Ricardo Rojas (1882–1957) was a poet, essayist, and playwright who, unlike many Argentine intellectuals who saw their society as a struggle between civilization and barbarism, tried to reconcile indigenous and immigrant aspects of South American development. Perhaps because of his provincial origins in the Andean northwestern city of Tucumán, he considered highland South America's pre-Columbian civilizations equal to those of Europe—an attitude rare among Argentines.

Rojas's 1929 house, designed by architect Angel Guido to the author's specifications, incorporates elements from both traditions. Its facade is a colonial-style replica of the Tucumán house in which the country now known as Argentina declared its independence in 1815. Yet Rojas consciously incorporated Incaic ornamentation into the building design, according to his *doctrina euríndica* (Euro-Indian doctrine), which posited a harmonious fusion of indigenous, Hispanic, creole, and cosmopolitan influences.

Donated to the state by Rojas's wife Julieta Quinteros a year after the author's death, the house features an impressively decorated ves-

Immediately across Avenida Ramos Mejía is the **Estación Retiro** (1915), a recently restored relic of the British-run railroad era, where trains once ran to Argentina's northern and northwestern provinces. Today, though, it receives mostly suburban commuter trains on the Mitre and San Martín lines. To the northeast, long-distance buses from the **Estación Terminal de Omnibus** (1982) have replaced nearly all the long-distance trains; much of area immediately north of the bus terminal is a dubious *villa miseria* (shantytown).

To the northwest, foreign diplomatic missions acquired several impressive mansions that did not become state property, including the **Palacio Pereda** (Arroyo 1130), now occupied by the Brazilian Embassy. In March 2002, Israeli ambassadors from all over Latin America came to the dedication of the **Plaza Embajada de Israel** (Arroyo and Suipacha), where a 1992 car-bomb destroyed the embassy that had occupied the site since 1950. The embassy's outlines are still visible on the wall of the building next door, while 22 freshly planted trees commemorate the diplomatic personnel and passersby who lost their lives here.

South of Plaza San Martín are a handful of other landmarks, most notably the beaux arts **Centro Naval** (Naval Center, 1914) at Avenida Córdoba and Florida; the nautical-theme doors were the work of architects Jacques Dunant and Luis Gastón Mallet. Literary great Jorge Luis Borges resided in the apartment building at **Maipú 994,** immediately south of the Museo de Armas. Across Avenida 9 de Julio, opposite Plaza Lavalle at the corner of Libertad, the sumptuous plateresque **Teatro Nacional Cervantes** (1921) is one of the capital's most important theater venues; state-run, it also houses the **Museo Nacional del Teatro** (National Theater Museum).

Prosperous Retiro is a barrio where people purchase rather than make art, and its numerous contemporary galleries around Plaza San Martín are almost all worth a look. There is one major art museum, the **Museo Municipal de Arte Hispanoamericano Isaac Fernández Blanco** (Suipacha 1422). At the barrio's southwestern edge, a block north of the Teatro Nacional Cervantes, the **Museo de la Shoá** (Montevideo 919) is Argentina's Holocaust museum.

tibule, a patio embellished with bas-reliefs of Incan and Spanish colonial origins, and a Cuzco-style balcony. The colonial-style furniture is of dark polished wood.

Admission to the Casa Museo Ricardo Rojas costs US$.35 pp for guided tours conducted by motivated, congenial personnel.

Cementerio de la Recoleta
JUNÍN 1790, TEL. 011/4803-1594
OPEN DAILY 7 A.M.–6 P.M.

For the quick and the dead alike, Recoleta is Buenos Aires's most prestigious address. The roster of residents within its cemetery walls represents wealth and power as surely as the inhabitants of surrounding Francophile mansions and luxury apartment towers hoard their assets in overseas bank accounts. Arguably, the cemetery is even more exclusive than the neighborhood—enough cash can buy an impressive residence, but not a surname like Alvear, Anchorena, Mitre, Pueyrredón, or Sarmiento.

Seen from the roof of the Centro Cultural Recoleta immediately to the east, the cemetery seems exactly what it is—an orderly necropolis of narrow alleyways lined by ornate mausoleums and crypts that mimic the architectural styles of B.A.'s early-20th-century belle epoque. Crisscrossed by a few wide diagonals but with little greenery, it's a densely *de*populated area that receives hordes of Argentine and foreign tourists.

Many, if not most, go to pat the crypt of Eva Perón, who overcame her humble origins with a relentless ambition that brought her to the pinnacle of political power with her husband, general and president Juan Perón, before her sudden and painful death from cancer in 1952. Even Juan Perón, who lived until 1974 but spent most of his post-Evita years in exile, failed to qualify for Recoleta and lies across town in the more democratic Cementerio de la Chacarita.

There were other ways into Recoleta, however. One unlikely tomb is that of boxer Luis Angel Firpo (1894–1960), the "Wild Bull of the Pampas," who nearly defeated Jack Dempsey for the world heavyweight championship in New York in 1923. Firpo, though, had pull—one of his sponsors was Félix Bunge, a powerful landowner whose family owns some of the cemetery's most ornate constructions.

The economic crisis of the past several years has had an impact on one of the world's grandest graveyards. Even casual visitors will notice that more than a few mausoleums have fallen into disrepair, as once-moneyed families can no longer afford their maintenance. Municipal authorities, recognizing the cemetery's importance to tourism, have intensified overdue repairs to sidewalks and the most significant sculptures, and improvements are noticeable.

Many private travel agencies offer guided tours on demand; the municipal tourist office sponsors occasional free weekend tours.

Museo Nacional de Bellas Artes

AVENIDA DEL LIBERTADOR 1473, TEL. 011/4803-0802
OPEN TUES.–FRI. 12:30–7:30 P.M.,
WEEKENDS 9:30 A.M.–7:30 P.M.
WWW.MNBA.ORG.AR

Argentina's traditional fine arts museum mixes works by well-known European artists, such as Degas, El Greco, Goya, Kandinsky, Klee, Monet, Picasso, Renoir, Rodin, Tintoretto, Toulouse-Lautrec, and Van Gogh, with their Argentine counterparts, including Antonio Berni, Ernesto de la Cárcova, León Ferrari, Raquel Forner, Cándido López, Benito Quinquela Martín, Prilidiano Pueyrredón, and Lino Spilimbergo.

Iglesia de Nuestra Señora del Pilar, Recoleta

© WAYNE BERNHARDSON

Sights

In total, it houses about 11,000 oils, watercolors, sketches, engravings, tapestries, and sculptures. Among the most interesting are the works of López, an army officer who recreated scenes from the Paraguayan war (1864–1870) in a series of minutely detailed oils despite losing his right arm to a grenade.

Oddly enough, architect Julio Dormald designed the building, in a prime location on the Avenida del Libertador's north side, as a pumphouse and filter plant for the city waterworks in the 1870s, but the renowned architect Alejandro Bustillo adapted it to its current purpose in the early 1930s. The collections are generally stronger on classic than contemporary art.

Admission is free of charge; there are guided tours Tuesday–Friday at 4 and 6 P.M., and weekends at 5 and 6 P.M.

Immediately behind the museum, the **Asociación Amigos del Museo Nacional de Bellas Artes** (Avenida Figueroa Alcorta 2280, tel. 011/4803-4062 or 011/4804-9290, www.aamnba.com.ar) regularly sponsors well-attended interviews with well-known Argentine artists, such as Guillermo Kuitca, Juan Carlos Distéfano, Aldo Sessa, and others. Check their Spanish-English website for the most current events, which are normally free of charge.

Palermo

Buenos Aires's largest barrio, Palermo enjoys the city's widest open spaces, thanks to 19th-century dictator Juan Manuel de Rosas, whose private estate stretched almost from Recoleta all the way to Belgrano, between present-day Avenida del Libertador and the Río de la Plata. Beaten at the battle of Caseros by rival caudillo Justo José de Urquiza, a onetime confederate from Entre Ríos province, Rosas spent the rest of his life in British exile. The property passed into the public domain and, ironically enough, the sprawling **Parque Tres de Febrero** takes its name from the date of Rosas's defeat in 1852.

Once part of the capital's unsavory *arrabales* (margins), its street corners populated by stylish but capricious *malevos* (bullies) immortalized in the short stories of Jorge Luis Borges, Palermo hasn't entirely superseded that reputation—in some areas, poorly lighted streets can still make visitors uneasy. Yet it also has exclusive neighborhoods, such as **Barrio Parque**, also known as **Palermo Chico**, across Avenida del Libertador immediately north of Recoleta.

Centro Cultural Islámico Rey Fahd
AVENIDA BULLRICH 55, TEL. 011/4899-1144
OPEN MON., WED., AND FRI. NOON–1 P.M. (TOURS)
WWW.CCISLAMICOREYFAHD.ORG
Built with Saudi funds on three hectares of land donated by former President Carlos Menem's scandal-ridden administration, Buenos Aires's Islamic cultural center is a pharaonic monument to megalomania. Holding up to 2,300 worshippers, in a high-rent neighborhood, it rarely draws more than a few hundred to Friday prayers. Unless Buenos Aires becomes the

© WAYNE BERNHARDSON

Former President Carlos Menem arranged the land deal that brought the Centro Cultural Islámico Rey Fahd to Buenos Aires.

WALKING TOUR: RECOLETA AND BARRIO NORTE

The centerpiece of Recoleta, the capital's most exclusive residential barrio, is its **Cementerio de la Recoleta;** flanking the cemetery is the colonial **Iglesia de Nuestra Señora de Pilar** (1732), a Jesuit-built baroque church that's a national historical monument.

Surrounding much of the church and cemetery are sizable green spaces, including **Plaza Intendente Alvear** and **Plaza Francia**, the latter home to a growing Sunday crafts fair that's steadily working its way toward the cemetery; there are also many street performers and a legion of *paseaperros* (professional dog walkers), some with a dozen or more canines under their control. On the southeastern corner, along Robert M. Ortiz, are some of Buenos Aires's most exclusive cafés, most notably **La Biela.**

Despite the existence of these mainstays, parts of Recoleta have plunged into commercial kitsch. You can now visit a place called Dakar that's guarded by an Indiana Jones figure on an antique motorcycle, and even the inevitable sore-thumb McDonald's. Immediately across from the cemetery's southwestern wall, the weekend decibel level along the new Vicente López pedestrian mall could raise Evita from the dead.

Recoleta has other sights and activities, however. Alongside the church is the **Centro Cultural Ciudad de Buenos Aires,** one of the capital's most important cultural centers with an interactive museum, exhibition halls, and a full events calendar. Facing Plaza Francia, the **Museo Nacional de Bellas Artes** (1933) is the national fine arts museum. Several other plazas stretch northwest of the museum, along Avenida del Libertador toward Palermo.

The apartment building at **Posadas 1567,** between Ayacucho and Callao, was Eva Perón's residence. Nearby, the **Palais de Glace** (Posadas 1725) is a former skating rink that now houses the **Salas Nacionales de Cultura,** with an ample events schedule.

Recoleta's other landmarks and attractions are scattered around the barrio. A block west of the cemetery, the neo-Gothic **Facultad de Ingeniería** occupies an entire block fronting on Avenida Las Heras between Azcuénaga and Cantilo. Four blocks farther north, architect Clorindo Testa's **Biblioteca Nacional** occupies the grounds of the former presidential palace; the last head of state to actually live there was Juan Domingo Perón, along with his wife Evita.

Facing Plaza Rodríguez Peña, one of Barrio Norte's most striking buildings is the **Palacio Pizzurno,** now occupied by the Ministerio de Cultura y Educación (Culture and Education Ministry). Originally built as a girls' school, the building owes its blend of Spanish and German styles to architects Hans and Carlos Altgelt. Officially known as the Palacio Sarmiento

Mecca of a South American hajj, it will remain a questionable project, utterly out of proportion with it surroundings.

According to its Saudi director, though, the mosque, its ancillary constructions, and its grounds are intended to become South America's major Muslim cultural center. Unfortunately, its tedious guided tours only offer generalities about Islam, with little about Argentina's Muslim community and even less about this particular mosque's origins.

South America's largest Islamic center is open for guided tours only. Female visitors must put on tunics—some women have shown up in shorts and other clothing that would be considered truly offensive in the Muslim world—but need not cover their heads.

Jardín Botánico Carlos Thays
AVENIDA SANTA FE 3951
OPEN DAILY 8 A.M.–8 P.M. IN SUMMER;
9 A.M.–6 P.M. IN WINTER

One of Buenos Aires's shadiest spots, this botanical garden boasts a wide variety of trees from around Argentina and the world. Originally part of Parque Tres de Febrero, it dates

Medicina lends its name to this part of Barrio Norte. The multistory building contains two museums, the **Museo Houssay de Ciencia y Tecnología,** named for Argentina's 1947 Nobel Prize winner, and the morbidly intriguing **Museo de Anatomía José Luis Martínez** (open noon–4 P.M. weekdays when classes are in session, free), which displays every possible human organ pickled in formaldehyde. (UBA med students, by the way, are notorious for pranks and practical jokes with stray body parts.)

Barrio Norte's western sector boasts a substantial literary and artistic tradition. A plaque marks the **Casa María Luisa Bombal,** on Juncal between Azcuénaga and Uriburu, where the Buenos Aires–based Chilean novelist (1910–1980) lived many years. Jorge Luis Borges's widow María Kodama established the **Fundación Internacional Jorge Luis Borges** (Anchorena 1660, tel. 011/4822-8340), which has begun a series of Borges-focused city tours. Writer Ricardo Rojas lived at the **Casa Museo Ricardo Rojas** (Charcas 2837).

The innovative paintings of Borges's close friend Alejandro Schulz Solari are on display at the **Museo Xul Solar** (Laprida 1212, tel. 011/4824-3302). For equally spontaneous but more contemporary work, see the elaborate spray-can street art by **Buenos Aires Graff** (www.bagraff.com), covering the walls from the corner of Charcas and Sánchez de Bustamante; its own work has been vandalized, though.

Eva Perón once resided in this apartment building at Posadas 1567, Recoleta.

© WAYNE BERNHARDSON

after education-oriented 19th-century president, it takes its popular name from three career teachers, all brothers, for whom the block-long street immediately behind it was named.

Four blocks west, fronting on Paraguay, the Universidad de Buenos Aires's **Facultad de**

from 1892, when famed French landscape architect Carlos Thays requested its separation from the park to create a roughly eight-hectare space bounded by Avenida Santa Fe, República Árabe Siria (ex-Malabia), and Avenida Las Heras.

Thays was successful enough that when U.S. conservationist John Muir visited in 1911, he found the gardens "well laid out for future development. The park, by its tree life, shows the fertility of the soil in this country. The begum tree grows better in Palermo than in some parts of Australia, where it is native."

More than 30 sculptures dot the garden, including those of Thays and Patagonia explorer Francisco P. Moreno; near the Árabe Siria side stands one of the last of the hideous grottos placed around city parks by 1880s mayor Torcuato de Alvear.

The city's Dirección General de Espacios Verdes also operates a gardening school and a specialized library here. The main entrance to the fenced and gated triangular garden is at the Plaza Italia end of the property, but the mid-block entrance on Árabe Siria is usually open as well.

WALKING TOUR: PALERMO

Buenos Aires's largest barrio, Palermo divides into several more manageable areas that can make several distinct excursions. Some of the areas are patrician, some newly fashionable, but all of them are interesting.

North of Recoleta along Avenida Libertador, home to many embassies and enormous mansions still occupied by single families, **Barrio Parque** boasts some of Buenos Aires's highest property values. One of its landmarks is the **Instituto Nacional Sanmartiniano**, housing the research institute on national hero José de San Martín's life, on **Plaza Grand Bourg**. Built to mimic San Martín's home-in-exile in Boulogne sur Mer, France—but a third larger—it no longer serves as a museum, since its collections have moved to San Telmo's Museo Histórico Nacional.

Barrio Parque has several other museums, however, including the gaucho-oriented **Museo de Motivos Argentinos José Hernández** (Avenida del Libertador 2373). Dating from 1918, the beaux arts **Palacio Errázuriz** (Avenida del Libertador 1902) is a former private residence and national historical monument that contains the **Museo Nacional de Arte Decorativo**. The new kid on the block, though, is the state-of-the-art **Museo de Arte Latinoamericano de Buenos Aires** (Malba, Avenida Figueroa Alcorta 3415), which concentrates on contemporary Latin American artists.

Across Avenida del Libertador from Barrio Parque, the **Botánico** is an upper-middle-class neighborhood that takes its name from the **Jardín Botánico Carlos Thays,** though it also abuts the **Jardín Zoológico** (zoo) and **Parque Las Heras** (the former site of a federal prison). Once a neighborhood of imposing *palacetes,* (mansions, or small palaces) the Botánico is still affluent but less so than it was when, in 1948, Eva Perón enraged the neighbors by appropriating one of those mansions to create the **Hogar de Tránsito No. 2** (Lafinur 2988), a home for single mothers that now houses the **Museo Eva Perón.** For a glimpse of what the neighborhood used to look like, visit the 1911 **Edificio La Colorada** (Cabello 3791), a 24-unit apartment building of imported British brick; created for officials on the British-run railways, it features a skylighted central patio that was unusual in its time.

South of Parque Las Heras and across Avenida Santa Fe (one of Palermo's main traffic arteries) **Alto Palermo** is a densely built area that has given its name to one of the city's major shopping centers. The real center of action, though, is slightly northwest at **Palermo Viejo,** where **Plaza Serrano** (also known as **Plaza Cortázar**)

Jardín Japonés

AVENIDA CASARES AND AVENIDA ADOLFO BERRO,
TEL. 011/4804-4922
OPEN DAILY 10 A.M.–6 P.M.
WWW.JARDINJAPONES.COM.AR

An oasis of calm in the city's rush, Buenos Aires's Japanese garden opened in 1967, when Crown Prince Akihito and Princess Michiko visited Argentina. Administratively part of the Jardín Botánico, it enjoys better maintenance and, because there's chicken wire between the exterior hedges and the interior fence, it's full of chirping birds rather than feral cats.

Like Japanese gardens elsewhere, it mimics nature in its large koi pond (a bag of fish food goes for US$.20), *taki* (waterfall), and *shinzen jima*

(isle of the gods), but also culture in its *sambashi* (pier), *tourou* (lighthouse), *yatsuhashi* (bridge of fortune), *taiko bashi* (curved bridge), *tobi ishi* (path of stones), and *yusanju no to* (tower of thirteen eaves). There is also a *vivero kadan* (plant nursery) with bonsai trees at reasonable prices.

In addition, the garden contains a **Monumento al Sudor del Inmigrante Japonés** (Monument to the Effort of the Japanese Immigrant), erected during the military regime of 1976–1983 (a plaque bearing the name of dictator Jorge Rafael Videla as "president" has recently been replaced). Argentina has a small but well-established Japanese community in the capital and in the suburban community of Escobar.

Admission to the Jardín Japonés costs US$1 for

is a major nightlife nucleus; stylishly inventive restaurants and bars, plus clothing and design outlets, have made this one of the city's most fashionable neighborhoods. Jorge Luis Borges set his poem "La Fundación Mítica de Buenos Aires" (The Mythical Foundation of Buenos Aires) on the block bounded by Guatemala, Serrano, Paraguay, and Gurruchaga.

Palermo Viejo further subdivides into **Palermo Soho,** a trendy term to describe the area south of Avenida Juan B. Justo, and the more northerly **Palermo Hollywood,** where many *porteño* TV and radio producers have located their studios. Shaded by sycamores, many of Palermo Viejo's streets still contain low-slung *casas chorizos* (sausage houses) on deep, narrow lots. Picturesque *pasajes* (alleyways), such as Russel, Santa Rosa, and Soria, with their squat houses, were cozy centerpieces of architect Antonio Buschiazzo's Villa Alvear *microbarrio* that now hosts hyperactive nightlife.

Borges himself lived at **José Luis Borges (formerly Serrano) 2135,** a street recently renamed for the literary great (though still marked by a plaque, the house here is a recent replacement for Borges's residence). The nondescript modern apartment building at **Aráoz 2180** shares the onetime address of legendary revolutionary Ernesto Guevara, but is not the house in which "Che" lived. One of the most interesting private residences is the **Casa Jorge García** (Gorriti 5142), whose garage facade features Martiniano Arce's *filete* caricatures of the García family.

In addition to Borges, Palermo has a wide literary tradition. Guevara was a prolific if politically polemical writer. Additionally, the **Casa Museo Evaristo Carriego** (Honduras 3784) was the residence of a poet and Borges contemporary who died young (1883–1912); a single room holds period (though not original) furniture, while volumes of literature and poetry fill its library.

North of the Zoológico, the Sociedad Rural Argentina has rented out its historic **Predio Ferial** as the site of events ranging from traditional livestock shows to book fairs. The area's most conspicuous new landmark is the controversial **Centro Cultural Islámico Rey Fahd,** built with Saudi money on land acquired from the Menem administration, on Avenida Intendente Bullrich.

At the northern end of the barrio, overlapping Belgrano, **Las Cañitas** is a new gastronomic and nightlife area challenging Palermo Viejo among *porteño* partygoers; the nearby **Museo Nacional del Hombre** complements Monserrat's Museo Etnográfico.

adults, US$.35 for children; there are free guided tours at 11 A.M., and 3 and 4:30 P.M. Saturdays. In addition to the garden features, it includes a fine *confitería*/restaurant and an exhibition hall.

Jardín Zoológico Eduardo Ladislao Holmberg

AVENIDA LAS HERAS AND AVENIDA SARMIENTO,
TEL. 011/4011-9900
OPEN WEEKDAYS 10 A.M.–6 P.M.,
WEEKENDS 10 A.M.–6:30 P.M.
WWW.ZOOBUENOSAIRES.COM.AR

When Palermo was his private preserve, dictator Juan Manuel de Rosas kept his own collection of exotic animals. When, according to one legend, his pet jaguar ran in fright from a group of female visitors, he sarcastically suggested that it was because the animal "had never seen so much ugliness in one place." In the not-too-distant past, because of political cronyism, one could have made a similar comment about the zoo; since the 1990s, though, the once-decrepit Buenos Aires zoo passed into private hands and, rejuvenated, became a facility that is once again a favorite with *porteño* families.

What is now the zoo, an 18-hectare area bounded by Avenida Sarmiento, Avenida Las Heras, República de India, and Avenida del Libertador, was separated from Parque Tres de Febrero in 1888. Its first director was Eduardo Ladislao Holmberg, who saw it primarily as a

THE PORTEÑO PSYCHE

When grad student Mariano Ben Plotkin returned from Berkeley to Buenos Aires on vacation, his aunt asked him about the cost of living in California, which she found astonishingly cheap. Asking him for an item-by-item accounting, the *porteña* psychoanalyst listened patiently and, when he finished, she commented, "Oh, now I understand—there you don't need to budget for psychoanalysis."

New Yorkers may chatter about their therapists, but *porteños* can more than match them—in Buenos Aires, psychoanalysis and other therapies are not for the upper and upper-middle classes alone. During registration at the Universidad de Buenos Aires medical school, a proliferation of flyers offers psychoanalysis and psychotherapy with UBA professionals—the first session free—for individuals, couples, and groups. Flyers in the Subte declare that "Asking for help is the start of solving the problem" and tempts commuters with "unlimited sessions."

To some degree, the recent obsession with therapy may have been a function of economic crisis, and even the former *corralito* banking restrictions have been interpreted in this context. According to an early 2002 interview by National Public Radio's Martin Kaste, a Freudian psychiatrist made the case that "Money has a certain symbolic equivalence to the penis. People put their money in the bank, but at the moment they want to withdraw it they lose their money, so this produces a castration anxiety."

Another commented that "sexual desire has also been caught in the *corralito*—men worry about lack of desire and premature ejaculation, and women are unable to have orgasms." The 2002 Festival de Tango even included a session on *Tango de Autoayuda* (Self-Help Tango) by Mexico-based Argentine Liliana Felipe.

In a different context, angry real-estate brokers picketed the residence of caretaker President Eduardo Duhalde, himself a former realtor, but not necessarily in the hope that they would get any relief for a frozen real-estate market. Rather, proclaimed one of the protestors, "This turned into our therapy, a place to set our anguish free."

Therapy, though, is not just a function of the times; it has a long history here, beginning with the 1930s arrival of Jewish refugees from Europe. Ben Plotkin himself has chronicled this tale in *Freud on the Pampas: the Emergence and Development of a Psychoanalytic Culture in Argentina* (Stanford University Press, 2001).

Many of Buenos Aires's 30,000 or so shrinks practice in Palermo's so-called Villa Freud, an area bounded by Avenida Santa Fe, Avenida Las Heras, Avenida Scalabrini Ortiz, and Avenida Coronel Díaz. Many area businesses play on this reputation, including the Bar Sigi (Salguero and Charcas), and patients can top off their medications at the Farmacia Villa Freud (Medrano 1773, tel. 011/4825-2612). One online magazine specializes in listings for professional office rentals. Even acting classes are often exercises in therapy.

Several institutions contribute to the capital's therapeutic ambience. The Asociación Psicoanalítica Argentina (Rodríguez Peña 1674, tel. 011/4812-3518, www.apa.org.ar) organized a month-long exhibition on *Psychoanalysis, Culture and Crisis* at the Microcentro's Centro Cultural Borges. Buenos Aires's Museo de Psicología Horacio Piñeiro (Avenida Independencia 3063, 3rd fl., tel. 011/4957-4110, open 1–3 P.M. weekdays and 10 A.M.–noon Tues. and Thurs.) recounts the experimental efforts of an early-20th-century pioneer.

The locus of Villa Freud, though, is the bookstore Librería Paidós (Avenida Las Heras 3741, tel. 011/4801-2860, www.libreriapaidos.com.ar), inconspicuously located in the Galería Las Heras. It now has a Barrio Norte branch (Avenida Santa Fe 1685, tel. 011/4812-6685) as well.

While *porteños* and other Argentines continue to feel the need for therapy, their Chilean neighbors may have had the last word. In the midst of the 2002 crisis, a satirical Santiago newspaper published a short note under the headline "New Foundation, Argentines Anonymous, Created." According to the article, "A group whose members hope to rehabilitate themselves from their nationality met yesterday for the first time. At the beginning, each one must announce his name and then continue, 'I am an Argentine.'"

research facility, but by the early 20th century it was drawing more than 150,000 recreational visitors per annum. From the early 1920s, authorities built decorative fountains and lakes, a monkey island, tanks for hippopotami and crocodiles, an aviary, and other large enclosures in lieu of cages and pits.

After the 1940s, there were various projects to shift the deteriorating facility to the outskirts of town, given the potential real estate value of this large property in a prime neighborhood, but local objections in the 1980s kept the zoo in the present location. Today, it holds some 2,500 animals of some 350 different reptile, mammal, and bird species; it also includes sculptures of important figures in Argentine natural history, including Domingo F. Sarmiento, Florentino Ameghino, Clemente Onelli, and William Henry Hudson. For children, there are a *granja infanta* (petting zoo), a *calesita* (merry-go-round), a *trencito* (miniature train), and a *laberinto* (maze).

In addition to the standard enclosures, the zoo also features a reptile house, a tropical rainforest exhibit, and an aquarium that includes a sea lion pool (with deafeningly inappropriate hip-hop music). The concessionaire has repaired historic structures within the park, but it could do more; and despite warnings, the public toss unsuitable food to the animals.

The Jardín Zoológico, with entrances opposite Plaza Italia and at Avenida Sarmiento and Avenida del Libertador, charges US$2 general admission per adult but is free for children under age 13. Retirees and people with disabilities enter free Tuesday–Friday. The US$3.50 "passport" includes access to the aquarium, the reptile house, and the tropical rainforest exhibit.

M Museo de Arte Latinoamericano de Buenos Aires (MALBA)

AVENIDA FIGUEROA ALCORTA 3415,
TEL. 011/4808-6500
OPEN WED. NOON–9 P.M., THURS.–SUN. NOON–8 P.M.
WWW.MALBA.ORG.AR

Buenos Aires's newest, most deluxe art museum is a striking steel-and-glass structure dedicated exclusively to Latin American art rather than the European-oriented collections of so many Argentine art collections. Designed by Córdoba architects Gastón Atelman, Martín Fourcade, and Alfredo Tapia, the building devotes one entire floor to the private collection of Argentine businessman Eduardo F. Constantini, the motivating force behind the museum's creation; the second floor offers traveling exhibitions, often from foreign countries.

The most famous works are by the Mexican artists Frida Kahlo and Diego Rivera, but there are also works by Antonio Berni, the Chilean Robert Matta, the Uruguayan Pedro Figari, and others. Since the 2002 economic crisis, Malba curator Marcelo Pacheco has focused primarily on contemporary Argentine art, both for the museum's own exhibitions and those it sends abroad, rather than importing megabucks exhibits from overseas.

Admission to the Museo de Arte Latinoamericano de Buenos Aires costs US$2.30 except Wednesdays, when it's free. Adults over age 65 pay half.

Museo de Motivos Argentinos José Hernández

AVENIDA DEL LIBERTADOR 2373, TEL. 011/4803-2384
OPEN WED.–FRI. 1–7 P.M.,
WEEKENDS AND HOLIDAYS 3–7 P.M.
WWW.NAYA.ORG.AR/MUJOSE

It's tempting to call this the "museum of irony," as Argentina's most self-consciously gaucho-oriented institution sits smack in the middle of what may be the country's single most urbane, affluent, and cosmopolitan neighborhood, also home to many international diplomatic missions. Named for the author of the epic *gauchesco* poem *Martín Fierro,* it specializes in rural Argentiniana, regional history, and occasional special exhibitions on similar themes.

Even more ironically, the land-rich oligarch Félix Bunge built the house, a derivative French-Italianate building with marble staircases and other extravagant features. Originally

EVITA ON TOUR

Eva Perón became famous for her 1947 visit to Europe when, representing an Argentina that emerged from WWII as an economic powerhouse, she helped legitimize a shaky Franco regime in Spain and, despite missteps, impressed other war-ravaged European countries with Argentina's potential. But even her death five years later did not stop her touring.

Millions of *porteños* said "adiós" to Evita in a funeral cortege that took hours to make its way up Avenida de Mayo from the Casa Rosada to the Congreso Nacional, where her corpse lay in state before finding temporary repose in the headquarters of the Confederación General del Trabajo (CGT), the Peronist trade union. There, the enigmatic Spanish physician Pedro Ara gave the body a mummification treatment worthy of Lenin, in preparation for a monument to honor her legacy.

Evita remained at the CGT until 1955, when the vociferously anti-Peronist General Pedro Aramburu overthrew her husband, ordered her removed, and eventually (after a series of whistle stops that included a visit to an officer who apparently became infatuated with the mummy) exiled her to a pseudonymous grave near Milan, Italy. For Aramburu, even Evita's cadaver was a symbolic reminder of Peronism's durability.

Despite banning the Peronist party, Aramburu had reason to worry. For many years, Argentines dared not even speak Perón's name, while the former strongman lived in luxury

© WAYNE BERNHARDSON

Pilgrims and tourists crowd a Recoleta cemetery alleyway to pass by Eva Perón's tomb.

near Madrid. In 1970, though, as Argentine politics came undone in an era of revolutionary ferment, the left-wing Peronist Montoneros guerrillas kidnapped Aramburu and demanded to know Evita's whereabouts.

known as the Museo Familiar Gauchesco de Carlos Guillermo Daws after the family who donated its contents, it became the Museo de Motivos Populares Argentinos (Museum of Argentine Popular Motifs) José Hernández. The military dictatorship of 1976–1983 later deleted the inflammatory word "popular" (which in this context also means people's) from its official name. Thus, perhaps, it could justify depicting Argentine gentry like the Martínez de Hoz family—one of whose scions was the dictatorship's economy minister—as archetypes of a bucolic open-range lifestyle.

That said, the museum has many exhibits worth seeing, ranging from magnificent silverwork and vicuña textiles created by contemporary Argentine artisans to pre-Columbian pottery, indigenous crafts, and even a typical *pulpería* or rural store. Translations of Hernández's famous poem, some in Asian and Eastern European languages, occupy a prominent site.

Admission costs US$.35 except Sunday, when it's free of charge. The museum is normally closed in February.

When Aramburu refused to answer, they executed him and issued a public statement that they would hold the retired general's body hostage until Evita was returned to "the people." A common slogan of the time was "Si Evita viviera, sería Montonera" (If Evita were alive, she would be a Montonera" (If Evita were alive, she would be a Montonera), but Perón himself detested the leftists—even as he cynically encouraged their activism to ease his return to power.

The police found Aramburu's body before the proposed postmortem prisoner-swap could take place, but a notary in whom Aramburu had confided came forward with information as to Evita's whereabouts. In September 1971, Perón was stunned when a truck bearing Evita's casket and mutilated corpse arrived at his Madrid residence; remarried to dancer María Estela (Isabelita) Martínez, he neither expected nor wanted any such thing. His bizarre spiritualist adviser José López Rega, though, used the opportunity to try to transfer Evita's essence into Isabelita's body, as the mummy remained in the attic.

Perón returned to popular acclaim in 1973—leaving Evita in Madrid—and was soon elected president with Isabelita as his vice president. Meanwhile, the Montoneros once again kidnapped Aramburu—this time from his crypt in Recoleta cemetery—until Evita's return.

Angry but increasingly ill and senile, Perón died the following year, but now-president Isabelita flew Evita on a charter from Madrid to Buenos Aires and then sent her to the presidential residence at Olivos, north of the capital. The cadaver stayed there until March of 1976, when General Jorge Rafael Videla's brutal military junta overthrew Perón's living legacy.

Evita, for her part, finally achieved the "respectability" that she so resented throughout her rise to power. Though she was an illegitimate child who went by her mother's Basque surname Ibarguren, she landed in the family crypt of her father Juan Duarte (a provincial landowner)—only a short stroll from Aramburu's tomb.

Even that may not be the end of Evita's wanderings. In mid-2002, there were rumors of yet another move—to the Franciscan convent at Defensa and Alsina in San Telmo. (Ironically, the convent was set afire by Peronist mobs in 1955 and is also the place where her confessor Pedro Errecart is buried.)

Another possibility is Juan Perón's *quinta* (country house) in the northern suburb of San Vicente, where a new mausoleum would reunite the two (Perón presently rests at Chacarita cemetery). Astonishingly, in the midst of Argentina's ongoing economic crisis, in 2003, caretaker President Eduardo Duhalde made this a priority, but it's languished for lack of funds and family objections. The major obstacle to the move, it seems, is that Peronist politicians like the idea better than the Duarte heirs do.

Museo Eva Perón

LAFINUR 2988, TEL. 011/4807-9433
OPEN DAILY EXCEPT MON. 11 A.M.–8 P.M.
WWW.MUSEOEVITA.ORG

At her most combative, to the shock and disgust of neighbors, Eva Perón chose the prosperous Botánico for the **Hogar de Tránsito No. 2,** a shelter for single mothers from the provinces. Even more galling, her Fundación de Ayuda Social María Eva Duarte de Perón acquired architect Estanislao Pirovano's imposing three-story mansion, built for José María Carabassa in 1923, to house the transients in their transition to the capital.

Since Evita's death in 1952, the neighborhood has undergone steady if undramatic change, as middle-class multistory apartment blocks have replaced most of the elegant single-family houses and distinctive apartment buildings that once housed the *porteño* elite (many of whom have since moved to Zona Norte suburbs, such as Olivos and San Isidro). Fifty years later, on the July 26th anniversary of her death—supporting Tomás Eloy Martínez's contention that Argentines are "cadaver cultists," celebrating their heroes on the day of their death, rather than on the day of their birth—Evita's great niece

© WAYNE BERNHARDSON

In the 1940s, Eva Perón outraged neighbors of Palermo's wealthy Botánico neighborhood by opening the Hogar de Tránsito No. 2, a home for unwed mothers that's now a museum honoring her memory.

María Carolina Rodríguez officially opened the Museo Eva Perón "to spread the life, work and ideology of María Eva Duarte de Perón."

Five years in the making, this is the first Argentine museum to focus specifically on a woman. The 2002 economic crisis and *corralito* banking restrictions placed much of the work on volunteer shoulders, but since then it has expanded coverage to include video footage from both her film and political careers.

What it largely lacks, as yet, is a critical perspective that would make it possible, again in Rodríguez's words, "to understand who this woman was in the 1940s and 1950s, who made such a difference in the lives of Argentines"—a goal not necessarily consistent with her other stated aims, which do more to promote Evita's iconic image. Rather than a balanced account of her life, the museum's initial stage is more an homage that divides Evita's life into phases: Eva Duarte (her childhood and adolescence, acting career, and first encounters with Juan Perón), Eva Perón (marriage to Perón, becoming Argentina's first lady, and the Spanish journey that brought her international attention), Evita (as her political influence grew through the Fundación Eva Perón), and her death and legacy.

All this material is professionally presented but, with a couple of minor exceptions, it sidesteps the issue of personality cults that typified both Evita and her husband. One minor exception is the display of the Anglo-Argentine author Mary Main's *The Woman with the Whip*, published in Argentina as *La Mujer del Látigo* under the pseudonym María Flores.

Whereas this hatchet-job biography at least suggests Evita's polarizing effect on Argentine society, the museum would do well to display excerpts and other similar materials to suggest how her opponents viewed her. While the curators refrain from presenting the opponents' case, the exhibits here tell barely half the Evita story.

Admission costs US$1.70 pp. The museum also contains a library, a graphic archive, and a film and video library, open 2–8 P.M. weekdays. The museum shop has a selection of Evita souvenirs, and there's a café/restaurant as well.

ⓜ Parque Tres de Febrero

Argentine elites got their revenge on José Manuel de Rosas with the creation of Parque Tres de Febrero. Not only does the equestrian **Monumento a Urquiza** (Avenida Sarmiento and Avenida Figueroa Alcorta) commemorate Rosas's conqueror at the battle of Caseros, but Unitarist President Domingo F. Sarmiento's name graces one of the park's main avenues. Sarmiento, Rosas's implacable enemy, oversaw the estate's transformation during his presidency (1868–1874).

In the early 20th century, British diplomat James Bryce described what the area had become:

> *On fine afternoons, there is a wonderful turnout of carriages drawn by handsome horses, and still more of costly motor cars, in the principal avenues of the Park; they press so thick that vehicles are often jammed together for fifteen or*

© WAYNE BERNHARDSON

Palermo's Jardín Japonés offers a soothing retreat from the bustling city.

twenty minutes, unable to move on. Nowhere in the world does one get a stronger impression of exuberant wealth and extravagance. The Park itself, called Palermo, lies on the edge of the city towards the river, and is approached by a well-designed and well-planted avenue.

Today, by contrast, the park is a more democratic destination. There are no more carriages and the few automobiles go slower than elsewhere in the city. On weekends, in particular, it gets plenty of picnickers, walkers, joggers, in-line skaters, and bicyclists who enjoy its verdant serenity and other recreational and cultural attractions.

Among those attractions are the **Jardín Japonés** (Japanese Gardens, Avenida Casares and Avenida Adolfo Berro) opposite Plaza Alemania; the **Planetario Galileo Galilei** (Avenida Sarmiento and Belisario Roldán); the **Rosedal** (Rose Garden, Avenida Iraola and Avenida Presidente Pedro Montt); the nearby **Museo de Artes Plásticas Eduardo Sívori** (Avenida Infanta Isabel 555), a painting and sculpture museum; the **Hipódromo Argentino** (racetrack, Avenida

del Libertador and Avenida Dorrego); and the **Campo Argentino de Polo** (polo grounds, directly across Avenida del Libertador).

At the park's northeast corner, the **Nuevo Circuito KDT** is a velodrome where cyclists can work out without worry about the pace of motor-vehicle traffic. To its north, beyond park boundaries, the landmark **Club de Pescadores** sits at the end of a long pier extending into the river. The park's greatest drawback is the proximity of **Aeroparque Jorge Newbery,** the city's domestic airport; its relocation, proposed but apparently stalled, would open up an even larger area to public use.

Rosedal

Reached by a gracefully arching bridge over a narrow neck of the **Lago del Rosedal,** an artificial lake, Parque Tres de Febrero's rose garden contains a diversity of both bush roses and climbers on pergolas. Its southeast corner contains the **Jardín de los Poetas,** a sculpture garden of famous literary figures, mostly Spanish speakers, such as Argentina's Jorge Luis Borges and Alfonsina Storni and Guatemala's Miguel Angel Asturias, but also global greats, such as Shakespeare.

Belgrano

Readily linked to central Buenos Aires by Subte, bus, and train, Belgrano remains a barrio apart. In fact, before becoming a barrio of the capital, it was a separate city and then, briefly in the 1880s, served as the country's capital. After the Buenos Aires provincial capital moved to the new city of La Plata, Buenos Aires became the federal capital and, in 1887, it absorbed Belgrano into the city.

Its main thoroughfare Avenida Cabildo is a disorientingly noisy commercial boulevard, with a cluster of cinemas and theaters as well, but the tree-lined streets immediately to the east contain most points of interest.

Museo De Arte Español Enrique Larreta

AVENIDA JURAMENTO 2291, TEL. 011/4783-2640
OPEN WED.–SUN. 3–8 P.M.

When many Argentine writers were forging a national literature, Enrique Larreta's novels evoked nostalgia for the Spanish motherland, and his Belgrano house and art collection reflect that orientation. Most of the items either come from Spain or reflect Spanish traditions: polychrome religious carvings and *retablos* (altarpieces), *bargueños* (gilt boxes), tapestries, carpets, braziers, ceramics, paintings, and furniture from the 13th to the 20th centuries. The 19th-century fans, with elaborately painted landscapes, are exceptional.

The museum's rooms are large enough to present an enormous number of artifacts without seeming cluttered. Look for special exhibitions, such as the display of regional costumes given to Evita Perón during her 1947 Spanish tour—which took place at a time when Francisco Franco's dictatorship was desperately seeking legitimacy after the defeat of Nazi Germany and Fascist Italy in World War II.

The grounds are no less impressive, with formal Andalusian gardens and an open-air theater that offers dramatic and musical performances, including tango, in the summer months. The theater entrance is on the Vuelta de Obligado side of the building.

Admission to the Museo Larreta costs US$1, but is free Thursday. There are guided tours Sunday at 4 and 6 P.M. Like many other museums, it usually closes the entire month of January.

Belgrano's Iglesia La Redonda plays a key role in Ernesto Sabato's psychological novel *On Heroes and Tombs.*

© WAYNE BERNHARDSON

Sights

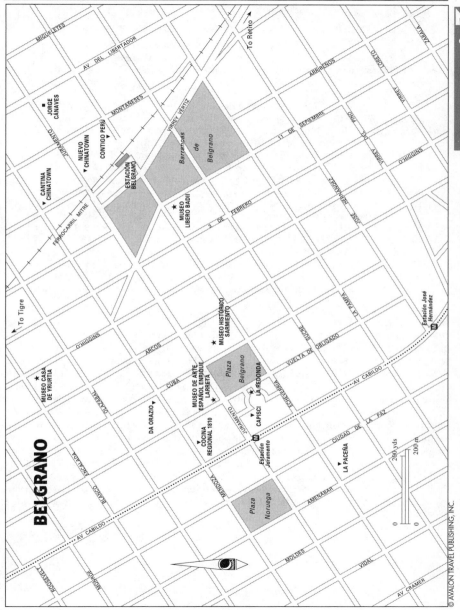

BELGRANO

To Tigre

MIGUELETES

AV. DEL LIBERTADOR

JORGE
CANAVES

NUEVO
CHINATOWN

CONTIGO PERÚ

CANTINA
CHINATOWN

MONTAÑESES

ESTACIÓN
BELGRANO

FERROCARRIL MITRE

VIRREY VERTIZ

Barrancas de Belgrano

MUSEO
LIBERO BADII

3 DE FEBRERO

To Retiro

ARRIBEÑOS

11 DE SEPTIEMBRE

JOSÉ HERNÁNDEZ

VIRREY DEL PINO

O'HIGGINS

ZABALA

LORETO

VIRREY

MUSEO CASA
DE YRURTIA

O'HIGGINS

ARCOS

CUBA

DA ORAZIO

ECHAURÍA

BLANCO ENCALADA

AV. CABILDO

MUSEO HISTÓRICO
SARMIENTO

MUSEO DE ARTE
ESPAÑOL ENRIQUE
LARRETA

COCINA
REGIONAL 1810

JURAMENTO

CAPISCI

Estación
Juramento

Plaza
Belgrano

LA REDONDA

ECHEVERRÍA

SUCRE

VUELTA DE OBLIGADO

LA PAMPA

AV. CABILDO

CIUDAD DE LA PAZ

LA PACEÑA

Estación José
Hernández

Plaza
Noruega

MENDOZA

AMENÁBAR

MOLDES

VIDAL

AV. CRAMER

ROOSEVELT

MONROE

200 yds

200 m

0

0

© AVALON TRAVEL PUBLISHING, INC.

WALKING TOUR: BELGRANO

Only a block off Cabildo, the **Plaza General Manuel Belgrano** hosts a fine Sunday crafts market; immediately to its east, the 1865 landmark **Iglesia de la Inmaculada Concepción** (Vuelta de Obligado 2042), colloquially known as **La Redonda** for its circular floor plan, figures prominently in Ernesto Sabato's psychological novel *On Heroes and Tombs.*

North of the plaza, the **Museo de Arte Español Enrique Larreta** (Juramento 2291) belonged to the Hispanophile novelist and still contains his private art collection; the museum offers outstanding special programs. When Belgrano was briefly Argentina's capital, both the executive and legislative branches met at what is now the **Museo Histórico Sarmiento** (Cuba 2079), honoring President Domingo F. Sarmiento. A few blocks northwest of the plaza, the **Museo Casa de Yrurtia** (O'Higgins 2390) was the residence of sculptor Rogelio Yrurtia, creator of San Telmo's *Canto al Trabajo.*

The famous landscape architect Carlos Thays turned **Barrancas de Belgrano** proper, on the river terrace three blocks east of Plaza Belgrano, into a shady public park; it now includes a fenced dog park, where *paseaperros* can take their charges for off-leash romps. Just across from the park, the **Museo Libero Badii** (11 de Septiembre 1990) exhibits works by one of the country's most innovative sculptors.

Across the tracks from the Barrancas, along Arribeños north of Juramento, Belgrano's **Chinatown** grew rapidly in the 1990s but has languished in the current hard times. The number of Chinese restaurants and other businesses, however, remains higher than it was a decade ago—Belgrano residents who need *feng shui* consultants can find them here.

Museo Histórico Sarmiento

CUBA 2079, TEL. 011/4783-7555
OPEN TUES.–FRI. 2–7 P.M., SUN. 3–7 P.M.
WWW.MUSEOSARMIENTO.GOV.AR

When President Nicolás Avellaneda felt insecure in Buenos Aires in mid-1880, he briefly shifted both the government's executive and the legislative branches to Juan A. Buschiazzo's Italian Renaissance building (1874), originally designed for the Municipalidad de Belgrano. After the congress declared Buenos Aires the federal capital and conflict subsided, the building returned to municipal authorities until 1938, when it became a museum honoring Argentine educator and president (1868–1874) Domingo Faustino Sarmiento—on the 50th anniversary of his death.

Though Sarmiento never lived here, the exhibits contain many of his personal possessions and a model of his birthplace, in San Juan province. He detested provincial warlords like Rosas and Facundo Quiroga, after whom he titled his polemic *Facundo: Or, Civilization and Barbarism,* still used as a text in many Latin American studies courses in English-speaking countries.

In addition to Sarmiento's life, the museum includes displays on Avellaneda and the near–civil war of the 1880s that resulted in Buenos Aires's federalization. There is also an 11,000-volume library.

Admission to the Museo Histórico Sarmiento costs US$.35, but is free Thursday; guided tours take place at 4 P.M. Sunday, though it may close on weekends in summer.

Outer Barrios

Beyond its most touristed barrios, Buenos Aires has a variety of worthwhile sights that range from the relatively mundane to the morbid. Most of them are less easily accessible by Subte, but have regular *colectivo* (city bus) service.

Ⓜ Cementerio de la Chacarita

GUZMÁN 680, TEL. 011/4553-9338
OPEN DAILY 7 A.M.–6 P.M.

Buenos Aires's second cemetery may be a more affordable final destination than Recoleta, but eternity at the Chacarita can still mean notoriety. Many high-profile Argentines in fields ranging from entertainment to religion and politics (sometimes the lines between the categories are blurred) rest at Chacarita.

The most universally beloved is tango singer Carlos Gardel, who died in a 1935 plane crash in Medellín, Colombia. Hundreds of admirers from around the globe have left plaques on his tomb, many thanking him for miracles, and every June 26 they jam the Chacarita's streets—gridded like a small city—to pay homage. As often as not, the right hand of his bronze statue holds a lighted cigarette and a red carnation adorns his lapel.

In terms of devotion, probably only Spanish-born faith-healer-to-the-aristocracy Madre María Salomé can match Gardel; on the 2nd of every month—she died October 2, 1928—her tomb is covered in white carnations. She gained fame as the disciple of Pancho Sierra, the *curandero gaucho* (gaucho healer) of Salto, in Buenos Aires province.

Other famous figures entombed at Chacarita include pioneer aviator Jorge Newbery, for whom the city airport is named (he died in a 1914 plane crash); tango musicians Aníbal "Pichuco" Troilo (seated playing his *bandoneón*) and Osvaldo Pugliese; poet Alfonsina Storni; La Boca painter Benito Quinquela Martín; and theater and film comedian Luis Sandrini, whose bronze statue often holds a red carnation in its hand.

Certainly the most famous, though, is Juan Domingo Perón, whose remains lie in a vault across town from his equally famous wife Evita. His remains are incomplete, though—in June 1987, stealthy vandals entered the crypt, amputating and stealing the caudillo's hands in a crime that has never been resolved. People speculated, though there's no evidence, that the thieves sought Perón's fingerprints for access to supposed Swiss bank accounts.

Chacarita's role as the capital's most democratic cemetery dates from its origins, when it buried yellow-fever victims of the 1870s epidemic in then-mosquito-ridden San Telmo and La Boca. The barrio, also known as Chacarita, takes its name from a Quechua term meaning a small farm; during the 17th century, it was a Jesuit agricultural property known as La Chacarita de los Colegiales, on the city's outskirts.

The Cementerio de la Chacarita covers 95 blocks with a total of 12,000 burial vaults, 100,000 gravesites, and 350,000 niches. It's only a short walk from Estación Federico Lacroze, on the Subte's Línea B.

In addition to Chacarita, there are two contiguous but formally separate cemeteries nearby: the **Cementerio Alemán** (German Cemetery, Avenida Elcano 4530, tel. 011/4553-3206) and the **Cementerio Británico** (British Cemetery, Avenida Elcano 4568, tel. 011/4554-0092). Both keep identical hours to Chacarita's.

The Británico is more diverse, with tombs belonging to Armenian, Greek, Irish, Jewish, and many other immigrant nationalities. The Anglo-Argentine Lucas Bridges, son of pioneer Anglican missionaries in Tierra del Fuego and author of the classic Fuegian memoir *The Uttermost Part of the Earth,* was buried here after dying at sea en route from Ushuaia. The Alemán features a large but politically neutral monument to Germany's World War II dead—no German or German-Argentine wants to be associated with the Third Reich.

THE OTHER SOUTH

According to Jorge Luis Borges, the south of Buenos Aires is the key to understanding the city, but fairly few foreigners get to know its unassuming working-class neighborhoods. Such Barrios as Barracas, Nueva Pompeya, Parque Patricios, and Boedo may lack San Telmo's colonial romance, La Boca's garish colors, and Recoleta's haughty chic, but they tell much more about the way most *porteños* work and live—even if reaching their spread-out sights is more challenging than elsewhere in the city.

In **Barracas,** immediately south of San Telmo, the emblematic British biscuit factory **Bagley** (Avenida Montes de Oca 169) was once a household word that, after its acquisition by a French multinational, now stands empty despite demonstrations against its closure at the end of 2004. Not so far away, the former chocolate-maker **Aguila** (Herrera 803) suffered the same fate before housing a failed Home Depot and then, more successfully, its Argentine counterpart Easy. Fortunately, despite the change in function, the recyclers preserved Aguila's classic facade.

With its working-class history, it's not surprising that left-of-center political movements would take root here. In 1904, Alfredo Palacios became the first Socialist deputy elected to the Argentine congress; the architecturally idiosyncratic party headquarters **Casa del Pueblo de Barracas** (Alvarado 1963) was his legacy to the barrio. Socialists have been linked with Freemasonry, as in the headquarters of the **Hijos del Trabajo** (San Antonio 814), also known as the Casa Egipcia (Egypt House); dating from 1890, the *casa chorizo* (sausage house) was recently restored to its original form, intricate design, and wild colors. Twin sphinxes guard the doorway lintel of its outlandish facade.

British capital built the railways that connected Buenos Aires with its suburbs and the rest of the country, influencing life immeasurably. In some instances, this influence came in the form of landmark architecture: In a style

known as Catalonian Modernist, **Estación Barracas** (Pasaje Darquier and Villarino), now known as Estación Hipólito Yrigoyen, differs greatly from most other stations on the Roca line south from Constitución.

In an effort to recast this area as a tourist zone, city government has promoted film production facilities on this picturesque cobbled passageway, and the **Casa del Polaco Goyeneche,** a *tanguería* named for the great singer, occupies a nearby corner. Its revival still has far to go, though.

Many laborers crowded into *conventillos* like those of La Boca or San Telmo, but there were also progressive efforts to accommodate working families. Near the Estación Solá cargo facilities, the 300 cottage-style units of the **Barrio Ferroviario**

© WAYNE BERNHARDSON

Recently restored, its facade repainted in bright colors, Barracas's Hijos del Trabajo (sausage house) has long been the headquarters of the capital's Freemasons.

(Australia 2700) are now 120 years old and crumbling, but in their time they were exemplary.

Between 1917 and 1925, the Acción Católica Popular (People's Catholic Action) created the **Barrio Monseñor Espinoza** (Alvarado and Perdriel), a classic *barrio obrero* (workers' barrio) that's resisted industrial decline. Originally financed by government credits, this park-like 60-house greenbelt has remained a model of its kind.

Barracas is not all work, though. Along the railroad embankment, **Pasaje Lanín** is a cobbled three-block-long diagonal where painter Marino Santamaría and his neighbors have covered some 40 houses with colorfully abstract schemes, turning the whole street into an *objet d'art*. Santamaría's own works are for sale in his home studio (Pasaje Lanín 33, 15/5728-3364).

Immediately west of Barracas, the barrio of **Parque Patricios** has undergone a steady metamorphosis from when, at various times, it was the site of slaughterhouses, a cemetery for yellow fever victims, and a garbage dump known as the Barrio de las Quemas (Barrio of the Incinerators) or Barrio de las Latas (Barrio of the Tin Cans). By the early 1900s, though, the intention was to create a "Palermo de los Pobres" (Palermo of the Poor) with broad open spaces—if only to brake the weekend invasion of working-class families into areas frequented by *"gente decente"* (decent people).

Authorities designated the renowned landscape Charles Thays to do so in the barrio's namesake **Parque Patricios,** bounded by Uspallata, Monteagudo, Caseros, and Almafuerte. Thays's efforts, though, never achieved the enduring success here that they did elsewhere in the city and the country.

One challenge was to house the workers, and the prestigious Jockey Club went so far as to build a *barrio obrero* here to try to mitigate militant labor discontent. In January 1919, though, during a strike against the Fábrica Pedro Vasena steel factory, police strikebreakers incited street battles that culminated in the notorious *Semana Trágica:* Over several days, more than a thousand workers died. In an ominous precedent, spurred by paranoia over Russian Bolshevism, the police armed paramilitary forces who attacked Jewish immigrants in Once and Villa Crespo.

Southwest of Parque Patricios, in **Nueva Pompeya,** Avenida Sáenz leads to the Riachuelo and the ornately neocolonial **Puente Alsina,** a 1930s landmark that's easily the city's most picturesque bridge; it also gave its name to a tango and a movie. The barrio is also the site of a balconied water tower, in a *barrio obrero* bounded by Einstein, Traful, Gramajo Gutierrez and Cachi, that figures prominently in Ernesto Sabato's remarkable novel *On Heroes and Tombs.*

North of Pompeya and west of Parque Patricios, **Boedo** was a transitional barrio whose leftist intellectualism had its roots in an upwardly mobile working class that moved here from Patricios. Among the Grupo de Boedo" literary figures, many of whom lived elsewhere but met here, were Antonio Zamora, who translated Maxim Gorki into Spanish, and noirish novelist Roberto Arlt.

The barrio is probably best known, though, for tango lyricist Homero Manzi, who described it wistfully in the tango *Sur;* in fact, the intersection of Avenida Boedo and Avenida San Juan is known as the **Esquina Homero Manzi** and is home to a commercial *tanguería* of that name. These days, though, the barrio's free thinking survives at locales like **Café Margot** (Avenida Boedo 857).

While Borges and others may have respected The South, that didn't mean they ventured too deeply into it; Borges, who spent much of his working life at San Telmo's Biblioteca Nacional, lived in comfortable Retiro, and few residents of the wealthy northern barrios go here. Travel agencies, though, do organize guided visits. (For suggestions, see the *Organized Tours* entry in the *Know Buenos Aires* chapter.)

Escuela de Mecánica de la Armada (ESMA)

Escuela de Mecánica de la Armada (ESMA)

AVENIDA LIBERTADOR 8200

Buildings often cause controversy, but none quite so much as the Escuela de Mecánica de la Armada (ESMA, Naval Mechanics' School) in Núñez, beyond Belgrano near the Buenos Aires province border. It was not the architecture of this handsome neoclassical building that raised havoc, though—rather, it was the fact that during the 1976–1983 military dictatorship, more than 5,000 *desaparecidos* (disappeared persons) passed through the country's most notorious clandestine torture center.

Before his term expired in 1999, President Carlos Menem—himself a victim of the repression, though he later pardoned his jailers—relocated the institution to Puerto Belgrano, near the naval town of Bahía Blanca in southern Buenos Aires province. At the same time, he ordered the ESMA's demolition and its replacement by a dubious "monument to national unity." In the end, the public outcry prevented the building's destruction.

Menem's decrees infuriated human rights groups and city officials, who saw the former ESMA as the most gruesomely suitable location for a Museo de la Memoria (Museum of Memory) that would preserve and present documentary records, oral histories, sound, film, and photographs of the military's brutal *Guerra Sucia* (Dirty War) against its own citizens. Authorized in 1996, the museum long lacked a physical facility, but in early 2005 President Néstor Kirchner and Buenos Aires mayor Aníbal Ibarra announced agreement to move remaining naval educational facilities elsewhere and open the ESMA grounds to visits. It will be years, though, before the proposed museum takes shape.

M Museo Argentino de Ciencias Naturales Bernardino Rivadavia

ANGEL GALLARDO 490, TEL. 011/4982-1154
OPEN DAILY 2–7 P.M.
WWW.MACN.SECYT.GOV.AR

Housing one of the country's largest and best-kept natural history collections, the Museo Argentino de Ciencias Naturales Bernardino

Sights

LA FERIA DE MATADEROS

Gauchesco traditions thrive in the weekend Feria de Mataderos, where city-bound *paisanos* (countrymen) and would-be *paisanos* immerse themselves in the nostalgia of the *campo,* or countryside. In addition to a diverse crafts selection, this spirited street fair features open-air *parrilladas* (mixed grills) and regional delicacies like tamales, plus live music and dancing in rural styles, such as *chamamé,* gaucho horseback races, and even—during Carnaval—a neighborhood *murga* (troupe) to kick off the season in the style of northwestern Jujuy province.

Despite some exaggeratedly nationalistic overtones, the Feria generates genuine enthu-siasm. It dates from the mid-1980s under the sponsorship of a Jewish *porteña,* Sara Vinocur, who still directs it as the link between city authorities and neighborhood residents.

In the southwesterly barrio of Mataderos, in the streets surrounding the arcades of the former Mercado de Hacienda at Lisandro de la Torre and Avenida de los Corrales, the Feria (www .feriademataderos.com.ar) is about an hour from the Microcentro by *colectivo* No. 180 and *ramal* (branch) 155 from Tucumán, Talcahuano, or Lavalle. In summer, it takes place 6 P.M.–midnight on Saturdays; the rest of the year, it starts at 11 A.M. Sundays.

Rivadavia veers between the traditional stuff-in-glass-cases approach and more sophisticated exhibits that provide ecological, historical, and cultural context. Its imposing quarters, dating from 1937, are only one-third the size of the original grandiose project, but they have some exquisite details: bas-relief spider webs around the main entrance and sculpted owls flanking the upper windows, for instance.

The main floor contains geological and paleontological exhibits, including a reconstruction of the massive Patagonian specimens *Giganotosaurus carolini* (the world largest carnivorous dinosaur) and the herbivore *Argentinosaurus huinculensis* (whose neck alone measures about 12 meters). Other prized items are meteorites from the Campo de Cielo field in Santiago del Estero province. There is also an aquarium, plus material on marine flora, mollusks, and deep-sea creatures, a diorama of seagoing megafauna, such as sharks, rays, giant squid, and sailfish, and Antarctic fauna, plus a sperm whale cranium.

The second floor stresses mostly South American mammals (including marine mammals), comparative anatomy, amphibians and reptiles, birds, arthropods, and botany, with an ecology exhibit still in preparation.

Admission costs US$.70 for patrons seven years and older. There is also a library, open 11 A.M.–4 P.M. weekdays.

Restaurants

In creative gastronomy, Buenos Aires may well be the continent's top city and many of its restaurants would be first-rate anywhere in the world. Over the past decade-plus, the scene has become more cosmopolitan, adventurous, and nuanced. Brazilian, Japanese, Thai, Vietnamese, and other once-exotic cuisines—not to mention high-quality variations on Argentine regional dishes—have stepped out of the kitchen and onto the stage.

Many areas have fine restaurants, but the best barrios for dining out include the Microcentro, Palermo, Retiro, and Recoleta. Palermo, though, is ground zero—the Palermo Viejo, Palermo Hollywood, and Las Cañitas neighborhoods seem to have sprouted stylish, sophisticated, and creative new eateries on every corner and in between.

For most of the 1990s, restaurant dining was financially challenging except for cheap cafeteria lunches and *tenedor libre* (literally, free fork) buffets. The peso collapse, though, has made it possible to eat diverse and imaginative food for a fraction of its former cost—at least for visitors with dollar or euro salaries.

Places to eat range from hole-in-the-wall *comedores* (eateries) or fast-food *bares* (unavoidably but misleadingly translated as bars) with no formal menu in bus and train stations, to cafés, *confiterías* (tea houses), and elegant *restaurantes* or even the *restó* (a trendy affectation for places that aspire to creative cook-

Buenos Aires's Best

In the last few years, dining out in Buenos Aires has become a highlight in itself, and there are many superb choices that can't make this extremely idiosyncratic list.

ℕ **Best Pizza:** The deceptively simple *fugazzeta,* with mozzarella and sweet onions, is a favorite at **Pizzería Güerrín**'s standup counter, but the cheeseless *fugazza* may be even better (page 93).

ℕ **Best Business Lunch:** Where else but **Sabot** do business leaders and politicians finish off their midday power lunch with tea from the forbidden coca leaf? The Italo-Argentine food and the good-humored service are the real stars, though (page 93).

ℕ **Best Beef:** It's no contest—**Cabaña Las Lilas** raises its own beef and serves it succulent, with views of the Puerto Madero yacht harbor. Prices are higher than elsewhere, but it's worth every peso (page 96).

ℕ **Best Buffet:** In high-rent Retiro, **Juana M.** produces standard Argentine dishes at a high quality-to-price ratio, with the best salad bar in town (page 100).

ℕ **Best Empanadas:** You can eat cheaper, and you can eat better, but you can't eat cheaper *and*

better than the tangy *salteñas* at Palermo Viejo's **La Cupertina** (page 103).

ℕ **Best Dessert:** Brazil's diverse cuisine has made fairly few inroads here, but if more *porteños* sample the *maracuyá* (passion fruit) mousse from Palermo Soho's **Maria Fulô**, their friends will come running to try it—and everything else on the menu (page 106).

ℕ **Best Outdoor Dining:** Planting a sub-Arctic forest in muggy Buenos Aires goes against all global warming cautions, but Palermo Hollywood's **Olsen** is as audacious in its landscaping as it is in its Scandinavian/Patagonian cuisine (page 108).

ℕ **Best Pasta:** It's hard to go wrong with *porteño* pasta, but Palermo's **Bella Italia Café Bar** gets the edge over its identically named restaurant because of its higher quality-to-price ratio (page 109).

ℕ **Best Seafood:** The seafood tapas and fish dishes at Palermo's **Nemo** usually include at least one Paraná delta freshwater catch, which can be hard to find in the capital (page 112).

ℕ **Best Genuinely Spicy Food:** Only a handful of *porteños* can handle the hottest, most flavorful dishes that Las Cañitas's **Lotus Neo Thai** has to offer (page 112).

ery). A bar, of course, can also be a drinking establishment; this is usually obvious in context. And a café is both more and less than its English-language equivalent would suggest, though it does serve food. (See the sidebar *Dining Vocabulary and Etiquette* in this chapter for a more complete explanation.)

One good source on the latest developments in the fast-evolving restaurant scene is Alicia Delgado's and María Esther Pérez's annual, sort-of-bilingual (Spanish plus fractured English summaries) *Los Recomendados,* published by Editorial El Ateneo. This lightweight paperback

provides information on 100 of the best restaurants in the capital and Gran Buenos Aires.

The Friday edition of the daily tabloid *Clarín* offers a variety of restaurant reviews. For English readers, Dereck Foster's Sunday *Buenos Aires Herald* column offers some of the latest suggestions; a separate column covers Argentine wines.

MEALS AND MEALTIMES

By North American and European standards, Argentines are late eaters except for *desayuno* (breakfast). *Almuerzo* (lunch) usually starts around 1 or 2 P.M., *cena* (dinner) around 9 P.M. or later—often much later. *Porteños* often bide their time between lunch and dinner with a late afternoon *té* (tea) usually consisting of a sandwich or some sort of pastry or dessert; it can be very substantial.

Since *porteños* often eat *after* the theater or a movie, around 11 P.M. or even later on weekends, anyone entering a restaurant before 9 P.M. may well dine alone. One advantage of an early lunch or dinner is that fewer customers mean fewer smokers; this is not foolproof, but statistically things are on your side.

Breakfast and Brunch

Most Argentines eat only a light breakfast of coffee or tea with *pan tostado* (toast, occasionally with ham and/or cheese), *medialunas* (croissants), or *facturas* (pastries, also eaten for afternoon tea); *medialunas* may be either *de manteca* (buttery and sweet) or *salada* (saltier, baked with oil). *Mermelada* (jam) usually accompanies plain *tostados*.

An occasional side dish, eggs may be *fritos* (fried), *revueltos* (scrambled), or sometimes *duros* (hardboiled). In some fashionable restaurant zones, such as Palermo Viejo and Las Cañitas, a more elaborate Sunday brunch has become an option.

Lunch

Lunch is often the day's main meal, usually including an *entrada* (appetizer), followed by a *plato principal* (entrée) accompanied by a *guarnición* (side dish) and a *bebida* (soft drink) or *agua mineral* (mineral water) and followed by *postre* (dessert).

Upscale Buenos Aires restaurants customarily offer a fixed-priced weekday lunch (*menu ejecutivo*) that makes it possible to eat well and stylishly without busting the budget, but this is less common in the provinces. It's also possible to find local fast-food items like *hamburguesas* (hamburgers), sandwiches, pizza, and pasta without resorting to international franchises.

Té

Té, the third of four meals in the typical Argentine day, can range from a late-afternoon sandwich to the equivalent of afternoon tea, with elaborate cakes and cookies, and is often a social occasion as well. Presumably intended to tide people over until their relatively late dinnertime, it often becomes larger and more elaborate than its name would imply.

Dinner

Dinner resembles lunch, but in formal restaurants it may be substantially more elaborate

DINING VOCABULARY AND ETIQUETTE

Restaurant vocabulary is mostly straightforward. The usual term for menu is *la carta; el menú* is almost equally common, but can also mean a fixed-price lunch or dinner. The bill is *la cuenta. Cubiertos* are silverware, a *plato* is a plate, and *vaso* is a glass. A *plato principal* is a main dish or entrée.

Note that one might ask for a *vaso de agua* (glass of water), but never for a *vaso de vino* (literally, but incorrectly, a glass of wine); rather, ask for a *copa de vino*. When speaking English, native Spanish speakers frequently make a similar error in requesting "a cup of wine."

Many but not all Argentine restaurants assess a small *cubierto* (cover charge, not silverware

in this case) for dishes, silverware, and bread. This is not a *propina* (tip); a 10 percent tip is the norm, but Argentines themselves often ignore this norm, especially in times of economic crisis. A good rule of thumb is that anyone able to afford a restaurant meal can afford a tip.

A professional waiter, usually in uniform, is a *mozo;* this term, by the way, is totally innocuous in the River Plate region but an insult in neighboring Chile, where it implies rural servitude. A waitress, regardless of age or marital status, is a *señorita.* When trying to attract a server's attention, it's also possible to use such terms as *señor* or even *jóven* (young man or woman, so long as the individual is not obviously elderly).

(and more expensive), and it can be a major social occasion. Argentines dine late—9 P.M. is early, and anything before that may earn incredulous "What are you doing here?" stares from waiters. The exception to this rule is at tourist-oriented areas, like the Puerto Madero complex, where restaurateurs have become accustomed to North Americans and northern Europeans lodged at nearby luxury hotels, who often won't wait any later than 7 P.M.

"Fast Food" Snacks

Argentina has some of the continent's best snack food. The best of the best is the empanada, a flaky phyllo-dough turnover most frequently filled with ground beef, hard-boiled egg, and olive, but it may also come with ham and cheese, chicken, onion, and (rarely) with tuna or fish. Also available in B.A., the spicier ground beef *salteña* comes from northwestern Argentina; the tangy empanada *árabe* (lamb with a touch of lemon juice) is harder to find. Empanadas *al horno* (oven-baked) are lighter than empanadas *fritas* (fried, sometimes in heavy oil).

Argentine pizza is also exceptional, though usually less diverse in terms of toppings than North American pizza. For slices, try the cheeseless *fugazza* with Vidalia sweet onions or its cousin *fugazzeta,* enhanced with ham and mozzarella. Many *porteños* embellish their slices with *fainá,* a baked garbanzo dough that fits neatly atop.

WHAT TO EAT

Argentina is famous for beef—in abundance—and grains, but fresh fruit, vegetables, and an underrated wealth of seafood add diversity to the country's cuisine. The stereotypical beef diet has serious shortcomings, and visitors will have no difficulty finding alternatives, especially in Buenos Aires.

According to historian John C. Super, whatever the Spanish invasion's negative consequences, it improved a pre-Columbian diet that was, by some accounts, nutritionally deficient (often protein-poor). In Super's opinion:

The combination of European and American foods created diversified, nutritionally rich diets. Crop yields were higher than those in Europe, and longer or staggered growing seasons made fresh food available during much of the year. The potential for one of the best diets in the history of the world was evident soon after discovery of the New World. For Europeans, the introduction of livestock and wheat was an essential step in creating that diet.

When Europeans first set foot in South America, in the densely populated Andean region the staple foods were beans, squash, and a variety of potatoes and other tubers. The diet was low in animal protein—only the llama, alpaca, guinea pig, and wild game were readily available, and these not in all areas.

The Spanish introductions blended with the indigenous base to create many of the edibles found on Argentine tables today. European grains, like wheat and barley, which yielded only a four-to-one harvest ratio in Europe, reached at least two to three times that in the Americas. Furthermore, the abundance of seafood, combined with the increase of European livestock and the high productivity of European fruits, like apples, apricots, grapes, pears, and many others, resulted in a diverse food production and consumption system which, however, is changing today.

The stereotype that the Argentine diet consists of beef and more beef is not entirely mistaken, but local cuisine has always had a Spanish touch and, for more than a century, a marked Italian influence. Though red meat consumption may be diminishing among more affluent Argentines, it remains the entrée of choice among lower classes. Thanks to the Italian immigration, though, a diversity of pastas is available almost everywhere.

Buying Groceries

Abundant across the city, North American–style supermarkets, such as Coto, Disco, and Norte, carry an abundance of processed foods but usually a lesser variety (and quality) of fresh

CATTLE CULTURE ON THE PAMPAS

From his hotel room on the Avenida de Mayo, U.S. poet Robert Lowell once wrote that he could hear "the bulky, beefy breathing of the herds." Ever since feral livestock transformed the Pampas in the 16th century, displacing the native guanaco and rhea, cattle have been a symbol of wealth and the foundation of the Argentine diet. Riding across the pampas, Charles Darwin found the reliance on beef remarkable:

> I had now been several days without tasting any thing besides meat: I did not at all dislike this new regimen; but I felt as if it would only have agreed with me with hard exercise. I have heard that patients in England, when desired to confine themselves exclusively to an animal diet, even with the hope of life before their eyes, have scarce been able to endure it. Yet the Gaucho in the Pampas, for months together, touches nothing but beef…. It is, perhaps, from their meat regimen that the Gauchos, like other

carnivorous animals, can abstain long from food. I was told that at Tandeel, some troops voluntarily pursued a party of Indians for three days, without eating or drinking.

Recent research has suggested that this diet has not been quite so universal as once imagined—urban archaeologist Daniel Schávelzon has unearthed evidence that, for instance, fish consumption was greater in colonial Buenos Aires than people thought—but there's no doubt that the *porteño parrilla* is a culinary institution. Beef may not be healthy in the quantities that some Argentines enjoy, and many of them will even admit it. But few *porteños* can bypass the capital's traditional restaurants—or even the tourist-oriented grills where flamboyantly clad urban gauchos stir the glowing coals beneath a vertical spit—without craving that savory beef.

For most Argentines, *bien cocido* (well done) is the standard for steak, but *jugoso* (rare) and *a punto* (medium) are not uncommon.

produce than may be available in corner markets. Many of them, though, have cheap *cafeterías* with surprisingly good food.

In areas where supermarkets are fewer, almost all neighborhoods have corner shops where basic groceries and fresh produce are available, usually within just a few minutes' walk from wherever you're staying. Butchers are numerous, fishmongers somewhat less so.

Vegetarianism

While vegetarian restaurants are relatively few except in Buenos Aires proper, the ingredients for quality vegetarian meals are easy to obtain, and many eateries prepare dishes, such as pasta and salads, which are easily adapted into a vegetarian format. Before ordering pasta, verify whether it comes with a meat sauce; in the Southern Cone countries (Argentina, Chile, Paraguay, and Uruguay), *carne* means "beef," and waiters or waitresses

may consider chicken, pork, and similar products as part of another category—sometimes called *carne blanca* (literally, white meat). Faced with a reticent cook, you can always claim *alergia* (allergy).

Grains

Trigo (wheat), a Spanish introduction, is most commonly used for *pan* (bread), but it's also common in the form of pasta. *Arroz* (rice) is a common *guarnición* (side order).

Maíz (maize or corn) is a main ingredient in many dishes, including the traditional Italian polenta. Maize leaves often serve as a wrapping for traditional dishes like *humitas,* the northwestern Argentine equivalent of Mexican tamales.

Legumes, Vegetables, and Tubers

Salads are almost invariably safe, and all but the most sensitive stomachs probably need not be concerned with catching bugs from greens washed in tap water. (Note that restaurant salads are usually too large for a single person and often sufficient for two.)

Porotos (beans of all sorts except green beans) are traditional in families of Spanish descent. Other common legumes include *chauchas* (green beans), *arvejas* (peas), *lentejas* (lentils), and *habas* (fava beans).

In many varieties, *zapallo* or *calabaza* (squash) remains part of the traditional diet, as does the *tomate* (tomato). Many Old World vegetables are also widely consumed, including *acelga* (chard), *berenjena* (eggplant), *coliflor* (cauliflower), *lechuga* (lettuce), and *repollo* (cabbage). *Chiles* (peppers) are relatively uncommon; Argentine cuisine is rarely *picante* (spicy), except for dishes from the Andean northwest, and even those rarely challenge palates accustomed to Mexican or Thai cuisine.

Native to the central Andes, *papas* (potatoes) grow in well-drained soils at higher elevations in northwestern Argentina; *papas fritas* (French fries) are universal, but spuds also appear as *purée* (mashed potatoes) and in Italian dishes as *ñoquis* (gnocchi). Other common tubers include *zanahorias* (carrots) and *rábanos* (radishes).

Fruits

Temperate Argentina produces many of the same fruits as northern-hemisphere farms do, often available as delicious fresh juices. Items like *manzana* (apple), *pera* (pear), *naranja* (orange), *ciruela* (plum), *sandía* (watermelon), *membrillo* (quince), *durazno* (peach), *frambuesa* (raspberry), and *frutilla* (strawberry) will be familiar to almost everyone. When requesting *jugo de naranja* (orange juice), be sure it comes *exprimido* (fresh-squeezed) rather than out of a can or box.

Also widely available, mostly through import, are tropical and subtropical fruits like banana and *ananá* (pineapple). Mango, *maracuyá* (passion fruit), and similar tropical fruits are uncommon but not unknown.

The *palta* (avocado), a Central American domesticate known as *aguacate* in its area of origin, often appears in Argentine salads.

Meats and Poultry

Prior to the Spanish invasion, South America's only domesticated animals were the *cuy* (guinea pig, rare in what is now Argentina), the llama, the alpaca, and the dog (sometimes used for food). The Spaniards enriched the American diet with their domestic animals, including cattle, sheep, pigs, and poultry, including chicken and ducks.

Carne, often modified as *carne de vacuno,* or *bife* (beef) is the most common menu item in a variety of cuts. Among them are *bife de*

Bife de chorizo often fills the grill in Buenos Aires.

© WAYNE BERNHARDSON

chorizo (sirloin or rump steak), *bife de lomo* (tenderloin), *asado de tira* (rib roast), and *matambre* (rolled flank steak). *Milanesa* is a breaded cutlet or chicken-fried steak that, at cheaper restaurants, can be intolerably greasy.

The widest selection is usually available in the *parrillada* or *asado,* a mixed grill that includes prime cuts but also *achuras,* a broad term that encompasses offal, such as *chinchulines* (small intestines), *mollejas* (sweetbreads), *criadillas* (testicles), *morcilla* (blood sausage), and *riñones* (kidneys). *Asado* can also mean a simple roast. *Chimichurri* is a garlic-based marinade that often accompanies the *parrillada.*

Sausages, such as the slightly spicy *chorizo,* may also form part of the *asado;* in a hot-dog bun, it becomes *choripán.* *Panchos* are basic hot dogs, while *fiambres* are processed meats.

Cordero (lamb), often roasted on a spit over an open fire, is a fairly common item from Argentine Patagonia, while farmed *ciervo* (venison) and *ñandú* (rhea) are becoming more common. *Cerdo* (pork) appears in many forms, ranging from simple *jamón* (ham) to *chuletas* (chops) to *lomito* (loin) and *matambre de cerdo* (pork flank). *Chivo* (goat) or *chivito* (the diminutive) is a western Argentine specialty that sometimes appears on menus in the capital; note that the Uruguayan *chivito* means something very different—a steak sandwich or plate slathered with eggs, fries, and other high-calorie extras.

Stews and casseroles include *carbonada,* which consists of beef, rice, potatoes, sweet potatoes, corn, squash, and fruit like apples and peaches, and *puchero,* of beef, chicken, bacon, sausage, *morcilla,* cabbage, corn, garbanzos (chickpeas), peppers, tomatoes, onions, squash, and sweet potatoes. Broth-cooked rice serves as a garnish.

Ave (poultry) most often means *pollo* (chicken), which sometimes appears as *gallina* (literally, hen) in a casserole or stew; eggs are *huevos.* *Pavo* (turkey) is becoming more common.

Fish and Seafood

Argentina's fish and seafood may not have the international reputation of its beef, but the country's elongated coastline, extensive territorial seas, and huge freshwater rivers and lakes provide abundant options. Buenos Aires has some fine seafood restaurants, but these are less common in provincial cities and towns.

Seafood, among the most abundant sources of pre-Columbian animal protein, includes both *pescado* (fish) and *mariscos* (shellfish and crustaceans). The most common fish are *congrio* (conger eel, covering a variety of species, sometimes called *abadejo*), *lenguado* (sole or flounder), *merluza* (hake), and *trucha* (trout). *Salmón* (salmon) normally comes from Patagonian and Chilean fish farms.

Note that the cheapest restaurants often spoil perfectly fine fish by preparing it *frito* (overpoweringly deep fried), but on request almost all will prepare it *a la plancha* (grilled, usually with a bit of butter) or *al vapor* (steamed). Higher-priced restaurants will add elaborate sauces, often including shellfish.

Among the shellfish, visitors will recognize the relatively commonplace *almejas* (clams), *calamares* (squid), *camarones* (shrimp), *cangrejo* (crab), *centolla* (king crab), *mejillones* (mussels), and *ostiones* or *callos* (scallops, but beware—in Spanish restaurants, the latter word can also mean tripe), *ostras* (oysters), and *pulpo* (octopus). Spanish restaurants normally serve the greatest variety of fish and shellfish.

Desserts

Many Argentines have a sweet tooth. At home, the usual *postre* is fresh fruit, ranging from grapes (many single-family homes have their own arbors) to apples, pears, and oranges. In restaurants, this becomes *ensalada de frutas* (fruit salad) or, somewhat more elaborately, *macedonia.* *Postre vigilante,* consisting of cheese and *membrillo* (quince) or *batata* (sweet potato) preserves, is another fruit-based dessert; it also goes by the name *queso y dulce.*

Arroz con leche (rice pudding) and *flan* (egg custard, often topped with whipped cream) are also good choices, as is the Spanish custard

COOLING DOWN WITH HELADOS

Though it stems from the Italian tradition, Argentine ice cream lacks the high international profile of gelato—when a pair of *porteños* opened an ice creamery in the author's hometown of Oakland, California, they chose the compromise name of Tango Gelato, stressing its Italian origins while acknowledging its Buenos Aires way station. Buenos Aires has a remarkable number of high-quality ice creameries, and a remarkable diversity of flavors, ranging from the standard vanilla and chocolate (with multiple variations, including white chocolate and bittersweet chocolate) to lemon mousse, *sambayón* (resembling eggnog), the Argentine staple *dulce de leche* (caramelized milk, its own major food group), and countless others.

At Congreso's Heladería Cadore, owner Gabriel Famá offers up a cone of bittersweet chocolate and lemon mousse.

© WAYNE BERNHARDSON

Buenos Aires has two types of *heladerías*. The first is the chain that produces large industrial batches; some chain products are nevertheless very fine, others are truly awful, and most fall in between. The other is the small neighborhood ice creamery that creates *helados artesanales* in smaller quantities.

Gradually overshadowing the fading Freddo, **Chungo** (tel. 0800/888-248646, www.chungo.com.ar) is probably the best industrial ice cream, and is good enough by any standard; the most convenient branch is in Recoleta (Avenida Las Heras and Rodríguez Peña). **Bianca** (Avenida Scalabrini Ortiz 2295, tel. 011/4832-3357) is the Palermo franchise of a medium-sized chain that offers a wide selection of flavors. Founded by the former owners of Freddo, always-crowded **Persicco** (Salguero 2591, tel. 011/4801-5549) is putting up a challenge to the other chains.

Over the past couple decades, Congreso's **Cadore** (Avenida Corrientes 1695, tel. 011/4374-3688) has been consistently one of the city's best ice creameries, but its small storefront (often obscured by construction) gives it a much lower profile than chain stalwarts like Freddo and Chungo. As Corrientes sidewalks widen, though, it may be more conspicuous; their *chocolate amargo* (bittersweet chocolate), *mousse de limon* (lemon mousse), and *pistacho* (pistachio) deserve special mention.

Only a few blocks south, **Sorrento** (Avenida Rivadavia 2051) is both good and inexpensive; it has a second branch in La Boca (Olavarría 658).

The Microcentro is shorter on quality ice creameries than might be expected, but **Vía Flaminia** (Florida 121) is a more-than-respectable choice, as is **Patagonia Mapuche** (Avenida Córdoba and Florida), in the basement food court of Galerías Pacífico.

Monserrat's **Fridda** (Santiago del Estero 502, tel. 011/4381-1069) is an outstanding hole-in-the-wall ice creamery with giveaway prices. Across from Parque Lezama, **Florencia** (Brasil and Defensa, tel. 011/4307-6407) is San Telmo's best. Palermo Viejo's **Tempo** (J.L. Borges 2392, tel. 011/4775-2392) features unusual fruit flavors like mango and *maracuyá*. **Mento e Cannella** (Salguero and Seguí, tel. 011/4801-2346) is also worth a stop.

Belgrano's hole-in-the-wall **Gruta** (Sucre 2356, tel. 011/4784-8417) is the barrio's finest.

Restaurants

THE RITE OF MATE

It's rarely on the menu, but the single most social drink in Argentina and most of the Río de la Plata region—including Uruguay, Paraguay, and southern Brazil—is *yerba mate,* the dried, shredded leaf of *Ilex paraguayensis.*

Espresso, in its many forms, may dominate café society, but the *mate* infusion transcends commercialism. Its production is a major industry, but its consumption belongs to home and hearth. Native to the forests of the upper Río Paraná, a relative of the everyday holly, *yerba mate* became a commercial crop on colonial Jesuit mission plantations.

Transplanted Europeans took to it—the Austrian Jesuit Martin Dobrizhoffer asserted that mate "speedily counteracts the languor arising from the burning climate, and assuages both hunger and thirst." Unlike coffee and tea, though, it never really established markets across the Atlantic or even elsewhere in the Americas, except in parts of Chile.

Production diminished with the Jesuits' 1767 expulsion from the Americas, but "Paraguayan tea" kept its place in humble households and privileged palaces alike. According to the English sailor Emeric Essex Vidal, who visited Buenos Aires in the 1820s:

Mate *is in every house all day long, and the compliment of the country is to hand the* mate *cup to every visitor, the same cup and tube serving for all, and an attendant being kept in waiting to replenish for each person. Throughout the provinces, the weary traveler, let him stop at what hovel soever he may, is sure to be presented with the hospitable* mate-*cup, which, unless his prejudices are very strong indeed, will be found a great refreshment.*

In fact, the purpose of *mate* is hospitality; preparing and serving it is a ritual. It is also an equalizer, as everyone sips in turn from the same *bombilla* (metallic tube or straw) placed in the same *yerba*-stuffed *mate* (a term which also means gourd), filled by the *cebador* (brewer) with slightly-below-boiling-temperature water. It is customary to sip the gourd dry, and then return it to the *cebador,* who will pass it clockwise around the group. Note that, in this context, saying *gracias* (thank you) means that you want no more.

Not all rituals are equal, though, and *mate*'s material culture differs dramatically according to social class. Although having a servant whose sole job was to prepare and serve it is a thing of the past, upper-class households own far more elaborate paraphernalia than working-class families do—just as British nobility have more ornate tea sets than the untitled. Simple *mates*

known as *natillas.* An acquired taste is *dulce de leche,* which one international travel magazine referred to as "its own major food group." Argentines devour prodigious quantities of this sickly sweet caramelized milk, spread on just about anything; in private homes, they will often spoon it out of the jar and directly into their mouths.

Thanks to their Italian tradition, Argentine *helados* (ice cream) are popular everywhere, and the quality can be extraordinary where *elaboración artesanal* (small-scale production) is the rule. *Almendrado,* vanilla ice cream rolled with crushed almonds, is a special treat.

WHAT TO DRINK
Coffee, Tea, and Chocolate

Caffeine addicts will feel at home in Argentina, where espresso is the norm even in small provincial towns. *Café chico* is a dark viscous brew in a miniature cup, supplemented with enough sugar packets to make it overflow onto the saucer. A *cortado* comes diluted with milk—for a larger portion request a *cortado doble*—and follows lunch or dinner. *Café con leche,* equivalent to a latte, is by contrast a breakfast drink; ordering it after lunch or dinner is a serious faux pas.

© WAYNE BERNHARDSON

might be made from plain calabashes or from plastic, but others might be made of elaborately carved wood set in silver or even gold; the *bombilla,* likewise, can range from utilitarian aluminum to ceremonial silver.

Most Argentines prefer *mate amargo* (bitter, i.e. without sugar), but northerners often take it *dulce,* with sugar and fragrant herbs known as *yuyos* (literally, weeds). While it's a mostly homebound custom in Argentina, Uruguayans (who consume even more *yerba mate* than Argentines) make it a public affair as they walk the streets with leather-encased gourds and enormous thermoses. In the open-air sauna that is the Paraguayan summer, street vendors sell icecold *yerba* in the form of *tereré.*

Supermarkets sell *yerba* in bulk packages with engaging designs that look half a century old. It is also available in tea bags as *mate cocido,* which is weaker, and may be more palatable to neophytes than the first bitter sips from the freshly prepared gourd. Do not confuse it, however, with *mate de coca,* another innocuous infusion made from the leaf of the notorious coca plant.

Mate gear can be works of art even for those who don't sip Argentina's traditional bitter herbal tea.

Fortunately for its Argentine aficionados, *mate* is inexpensive. No one really has to worry, as Dobrizhoffer did, that:

If many topers in Europe waste their substance by an immoderate use of wine and other intoxicating liquors, there are no fewer in America who drink away their fortunes in potations of the herb of Paraguay.

Té negro (black tea) usually comes in bags and is insipid by most standards. Those wanting tea with milk in the British manner should ask for tea first and milk later; otherwise, they may get a tea bag immersed in lukewarm milk. Herbal teas range from the nearly universal *té de manzanilla* (chamomile) and *rosa mosqueta* (rose hips) to *mate de coca* (coca leaf), but sipping *yerba mate,* the so-called "Paraguayan tea," is one of the country's most deeply embedded customs.

Chocolate lovers will enjoy the *submarino,* a bar of semi-sweet chocolate that dissolves smoothly in steamed milk from the espresso

machine. Powdered chocolate is also available, but less flavorful.

Water, Juices, and Soft Drinks

Argentine tap water is potable almost everywhere except in some of the northerly tropical deserts; ask for *agua de la canilla.* For ice, request your drink *con hielo.* Visitors with truly sensitive stomachs might consider bottled water, which is widely available. Ask for *agua pura* or *agua mineral.* For carbonated water, add *con gas* or ask for the even cheaper *soda,* which comes in large siphon bottles.

Gaseosas (in the plural) are sweetened, bottled

soft drinks (including most of the major transnational brands but also local versions, such as the refreshing tonic water Paso de los Toros).

Fresh-squeezed *jugos* (fruit juices) are exceptionally good though limited in diversity. *Naranja* (orange) is the standard; to be sure it's fresh, ask for *jugo de naranja exprimido.*

Alcoholic Drinks

Argentina is less famous for its wines than Chile because, historically, most production has been for domestic consumption rather than export, but this is changing and superb wines are now available. Argentina is the world's fifth-largest wine producer; most vineyards are in the western and northwestern provinces of Mendoza, San Juan, and Salta, but the northern Patagonian province of Río Negro is also making progress.

Tinto is red wine, and *blanco* is white. Good wine is almost always reasonably priced, even during times of an overvalued peso and high inflation. The best restaurants have a wide selection of full bottles, and sometimes it's possible to get a *media botella* (half bottle) or wine by the glass. Argentines often mix their table wines—even reds—with carbonated water and/or ice.

An increasing number of wine bars also offer Spanish tapas, sushi, and other light meals. Keep an eye out for the red Malbec, an Argentine specialty, and the white *torrontés,* a unique varietal that's best from the vineyards around Cafayate, in Salta province.

Since the main wine regions are in western and northwestern Argentina, nowhere close to Buenos Aires, wine tourism is not an easy option from the capital. With production booming across the Río de la Plata in Uruguay, though, there is a new Ruta del Vino in the vicinity of Montevideo.

Although Argentine wines are more than worthwhile, Argentines themselves lean more toward beer, which tastes best as *cerveza tirada* (direct from the tap) rather than from bottles or cans. The most widely available beer is Quilmes, produced in its namesake suburb across the Riachuelo from La Boca. In addition to beer, *sidra* (hard cider) from apple-rich Río Negro province is widely available, sometimes on tap.

Hard liquor is not quite so popular, but whiskey, gin, and the like are available. *Ginebra bols* (different from gin) and *caña* (cane alcohol) are local specialties. Argentina's legal drinking age is 18.

PRICE KEY

$=Entrees mostly less than US$10
$$=Entrees mostly between US$10 and US$20
$$$=Entrees mostly more than US$20

Monserrat

In general, restaurants in the area from Avenida de Mayo south toward San Telmo are less inventive than rejuvenated neighborhoods in the northern barrios, but there are some exceptions and several good lunchtime options, especially west of Avenida 9 de Julio.

ITALIAN

Prosciutto $
VENEZUELA 1212, TEL. 011/4383-8058
OPEN DAILY FOR LUNCH AND DINNER
Prosciutto's classic cantina style, with intri-

cately carved century-old woodwork, hanging hams, and museum-quality restaurant gear for decoration, is a prelude to its extensive, elaborate bilingual menu—Italian first, Spanish second—and truly professional service. The most expensive item, shrimp in garlic sauce, costs around US$8, but most entrées are barely half that. The *insalatta fruti di mare* (US$4 for one, US$7 for two), a seafood salad with clams, mussels, shrimp, and calamari, is both an aesthetic and a culinary success. There's a reasonably large and well-segregated no-smoking area on the upper floor.

RESTAURANT TERMINOLOGY

The term *restaurante* (occasionally *restorán*) usually refers to places with sit-down service, but within this definition there can be great diversity. Most often, the term refers to a place with a printed menu, but this can range from any place with a basic beef and pasta menu to truly formal places with complex cuisine, elaborate wine lists, and professional waiters. It's worth emphasizing that the occupation of waiter is traditionally professional and male in Argentina, rather than a short-term expedient for university students or aspiring actors. This is changing in the capital, though—in the new, stylish restaurants of Palermo Viejo and Las Cañitas, servers are just as likely to be young and female.

The usual international fast-food villains have Buenos Aires franchises, but the best cheap food comes from *rotiserías* (delicatessens), which serve excellent takeaway food and sometimes have basic seating. Likewise, supermarkets like Coto and Disco have *cafeterías* that are excellent options for shoestring visitors.

Bares and *comedores* are generally no-frills eateries with indifferent service, offering *minutas* (short orders); the term *comedor* can also mean a hotel breakfast nook or dining room. A café, by contrast, is a place where *porteños* may dawdle over coffee and croissants, but its de facto purpose is promoting social interaction in personal affairs, business deals, and other transactions; in addition to coffee and pastries, cafés serve snacks, *minutas,* and alcoholic drinks (beer, wine, and hard liquor).

Confiterías often serve breakfast, light meals (like sandwiches), snacks (like cakes and other desserts), and a variety of coffee drinks. Generally, they are more formal than cafés, are popular destinations for afternoon tea, and some are prestigious. A number have full-scale restaurant menus, often in a separate sector of the establishment.

PERUVIAN

Status $

VIRREY CEVALLOS 178, TEL. 011/4382-8531
OPEN DAILY FOR LUNCH AND DINNER

Though uncommon in Buenos Aires, Peruvian food is worth seeking out, and plain-Jane Status may be the best of its kind in town. South of the Plaza del Congreso, it offers inexpensive home-style Peruvian dishes, such as *aji de gallina* (chicken in a walnut cream sauce over rice, with potatoes), *lomo saltado* (stir-fried beef with vegetables), and *papa a la huancaína* (a spicy potato dish) in the US$3–5 range. Some of the garnishes are far spicier than most *porteños* can handle; tangy pisco sours, foamy with cinnamon, are on the drinks menu.

REGIONAL

Trotamundos San Telmo $

DEFENSA 683, TEL. 011/4343-8342
OPEN MON.–TUES. NOON–8 P.M.,
WED.–SAT. NOON–MIDNIGHT OR LATER

In the winter of 2002, the owners of Trotamundos had the temerity to open a new restaurant in the midst of Argentina's worst economic crisis ever. Having survived the crisis, their distinctive "Patagonian bistro" features uncommon items like scallops (around US$4) and Patagonian lamb (US$3), offers a 6–9 P.M. happy hour at the bar, and even includes a basement art space. While close to the San Telmo line, it's actually in Monserrat.

SPANISH/BASQUE

Centro Vasco Francés $

MORENO 1370 , TEL. 011/4384-6210
OPEN DAILY FOR LUNCH AND DAILY EXCEPT SUN.
FOR DINNER

Distinguished by its capacious dining room, high ceilings, and waist-coated waiters, this very French Basque restaurant specializes in traditional fish dishes like *abadejo al arriero* (conger eel in a casserole form), but the kitchen can also produce more innovative items like the *tapeo patagónico* appetizer (US$10), a finger-food potpourri of smoked salami, venison, red peppers, olives, and tangy cheese, which easily feeds three. The Provençal-style fries are lighter and tastier than the average Argentine *papas fritas,* and the portions are large.

Miramar $
AVENIDA SAN JUAN 1999, TEL. 011/4304-4261
OPEN DAILY EXCEPT TUES. FOR LUNCH AND DINNER
In the barrio of San Cristóbal, near Monserrat's western edge, Miramar is a reliable *rotisería* (deli); it's also an unfashionable restaurant unsuitable for a formal meal or romantic night out, but great for inexpensive, unpretentious lunches or dinners with poised professional service. Unlike many recently gentrified—or plasticized—*porteño* cafés, this classic corner bar sports fading posters from classic Argentine movies thumb-tacked to the walls as a backdrop for surprisingly flavorful entrées like oxtail soup and *gambas al ajillo* (garlic prawns). Prices range from US$2–5 for most items.

IN BRIEF

Relocated from Recoleta, in what was once a ceramic tile factory, the cavernous **Café Molière** (Chile 299, tel. 011/4343-2623, www.molierecafe.com) offers an international menu with fixed-price meals in the US$5 range; late on weekends, it becomes a DJ-dominated disco, while the basement theater has more intimate tango floor shows.

Housed in a recycled warehouse that also serves as a venue for live theater and music, **La Trastienda** (Balcarce 460, 011/4342-7650, www.latrastienda.com) serves mostly standard Italo-Argentine dishes but, surprisingly, lacks stuffed pastas, such as ravioli. Lunchtime specials cost around US$3, individual entrées US$2.50–3.50.

Part of a complex that includes the nearby *parrilla* **Diablada** and the Italian **Campo dei Fiori, Plaza Mayor** (Venezuela 1399, tel. 011/4383-0788, www.grupoplazamayor.com) is a Spanish seafood restaurant with San Telmo style, including filete-painted lamps hanging from high ceilings, and mid-range prices.

According to *Buenos Aires Herald* restaurant critic Dereck Foster, though, B.A.'s best Spanish food comes from the basement restaurant at the **NH City Hotel** (Bolívar 160, tel. 011/4121-6464). A longstanding author's favorite is the Basque classic **Laurak Bat** (Avenida Belgrano 1144, tel. 011/4381-0682).

Microcentro

Many of the city's traditional favorites are right downtown and in nearby neighborhoods.

ARGENTINE/REGIONAL
La Candela $
MITRE 1682, TEL. 011/4383-3225
OPEN FOR LUNCH WEEKDAYS AND DINNER NIGHTLY
A step above most of Congreso's neighborhood eateries, La Candela offers a fairly conventional Argentine menu but the preparation and presentation are more painstaking. Three-course lunch specials, comprising pastas like *sorrentinos* (stuffed pastas) and meat items like grilled chicken, cost around US$3–4 with a starter and dessert included. The service is notably attentive and the décor, while not elaborate, is more than just utilitarian.

Club del Progreso $
SARMIENTO 1334, TEL. 011/4371-5053
OPEN DAILY EXCEPT SUN. FOR LUNCH AND DINNER
WWW.CLUBDELPROGRESO.COM
For a 19th-century experience with contemporary flourishes, try the Club del Progreso, in the same site since 1852—with its lofty ceilings, classic library, and other period features, this elaborate mansion served as a film location for British director Christopher Hampton's *Imagining Argentina,* starring Antonio Banderas and Emma Thompson. For about US$5–6 pp, the fixed-price meals are a little bland, but the singing waiters, with

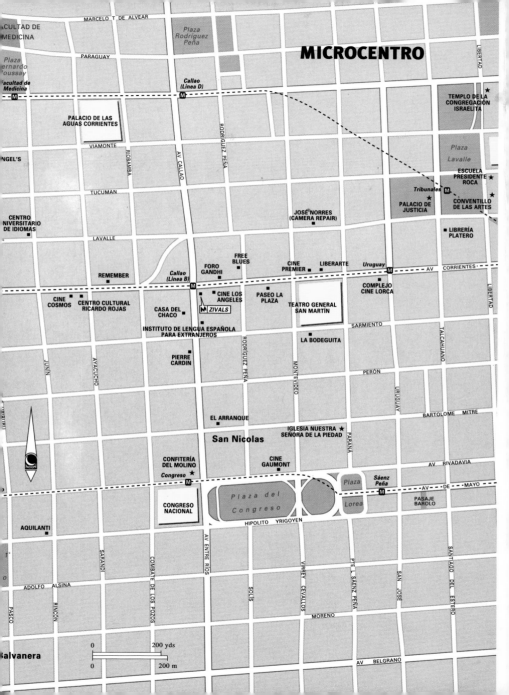

MICROCENTRO

MARCELO T DE ALVEAR

ACULTAD DE MEDICINA

Plaza Rodríguez Peña

PARAGUAY

Plaza ernardo oussay

Facultad de Medicina

Callao (Línea D)

★ TEMPLO DE LA CONGREGACIÓN ISRAELITA

PALACIO DE LAS AGUAS CORRIENTES

VIAMONTE

RIOBAMBA

AV CALLAO

RODRIGUEZ PEÑA

LIBERTAD

Plaza Lavalle

ESCUELA PRESIDENTE ★ ROCA

NGEL'S

TUCUMAN

Tribunales M

★

CONVENTILLO DE LAS ARTES ★

PALACIO DE JUSTICIA

CENTRO NIVERSITARIO DE IDIOMAS

JOSÉ NORRES (CAMERA REPAIR)

■ LIBRERÍA PLATERO

LAVALLE

FREE BLUES

FORO GANDHI

CINE PREMIER

LIBERARTE

Uruguay

AV CORRIENTES

REMEMBER

Callao (Línea B)

M

CINE LOS ANGELES

PASEO LA PLAZA

COMPLEJO CINE LORCA

LIBERTAD

CINE COSMOS

CENTRO CULTURAL RICARDO ROJAS

CASA DEL CHACO

M ZIVALS

TEATRO GENERAL SAN MARTÍN

INSTITUTO DE LENGUA ESPAÑOLA PARA EXTRANJEROS

RODRIGUEZ PEÑA

LA BODEGUITA

SARMIENTO

PIERRE CARDIN

AYACUCHO

JUNIN

MONTEVIDEO

PERÓN

URUGUAY

TALCAHUANO

EL ARRANQUE

BARTOLOME MITRE

IGLESIA NUESTRA ★ SEÑORA DE LA PIEDAD

PARANÁ

San Nicolas

CONFITERÍA DEL MOLINO

Congreso ★

CINE GAUMONT

AV RIVADAVIA

Plaza

Sáenz Peña

M

CONGRESO NACIONAL

M

Plaza del Congreso

Plaza Lorea

AV DE MAYO

PASAJE BAROLO

AQUILANTI

HIPOLITO YRIGOYEN

AV ENTRE RIOS

SARANDI

COMBATE DE LOS POZOS

SOLIS

VIRREY CEVALLOS

PTE L SAENZ PEÑA

SAN JOSÉ

SANTIAGO DEL ESTERO

ADOLFO ALSINA

RINCON

PASCO

MORENO

alvanera

| 0 | 200 yds |
| 0 | 200 m |

AV BELGRANO

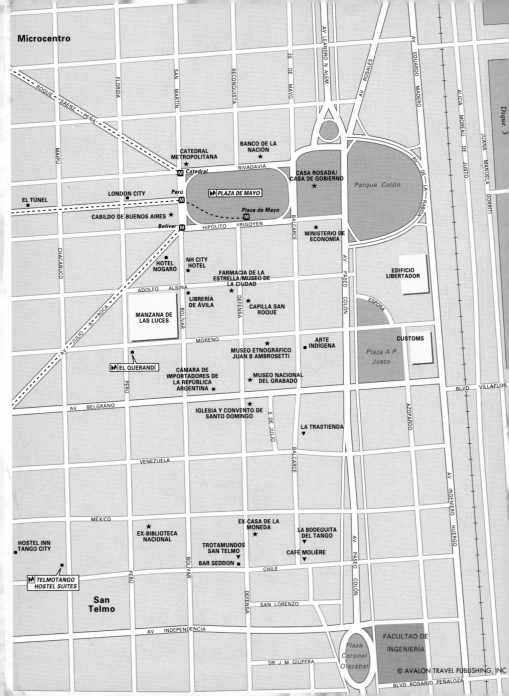

their tangos and boleros, make dining here a unique affair.

La Estancia $

LAVALLE 941, TEL. 011/4326-0330
OPEN DAILY FOR LUNCH AND DINNER

The Microcentro and nearby neighborhoods have several picture-window *parrillas* that make a fetish out of staking their steaks over glowing coals in circular barbecue pits tended by bogus gauchos in full regalia; while they play for the cliché and serve far too many tourists to be able to give patrons individual attention, the quality is good and their prices reasonable. Popular with individuals and tour groups, La Estancia is typical of its class.

Palacio de la Papa Frita $

CORRIENTES 1612, TEL. 011/4374-8063
OPEN LUNCH AND DINNER

Misleadingly named, this *porteño* classic offers an enormous Argentine and international menu—though you can certainly get its namesake French fries here, it would be a mistake to focus on them. For less than US$5, for instance, their saffron-flavored *arroz a la valenciana*, with chicken and a mixture of vegetables, can feed at least two hungry mouths. A good choice for families because it can please everyone from fussy children to discriminating adults, it has another branch (Lavalle 954, tel. 011/4322-1559) on the pedestrian mall near Avenida 9 de Julio.

ITALIAN

Broccolino $

ESMERALDA 776, TEL. 011/4322-9848
OPEN LUNCH AND DINNER
WWW.BROCCOLINO.COM.AR

Broccolino is an unfailingly reliable Italian choice, with impeccable service (all the waiters speak at least two languages) and a diverse menu ranging from pizza and pasta to seafood and beef dishes. It would be fair to say that it hasn't kept pace with some of the more innovative trends in *porteño* cuisine, but that's not necessarily bad; entrées range US$3–7, but

most are in the US$4–5 range. Because it appeals to foreign tourists, it's open as early as 7 P.M. for dinner.

El Gato Negro $

CORRIENTES 1669, TEL. 011/4374-1730
OPEN WEEKDAYS LUNCH, FRI. DINNER

Hard to characterize, El Gato Negro is a hybrid downtown institution. Its unadorned upstairs bistro serves seafood-based Italian specialties in the US$6 range, such as saffron risotto with fish, scallops, and shrimp, while most of its ground floor is a traditional *confitería* with coffee, tea, and a diversity of appetizing desserts. Few places in town, though, can match the ceiling-high cases stocked with bulk spices, teas, and dried fruits, as well as homemade jams, to take home.

🔲 Pizzería Güerrín $

AVENIDA CORRIENTES 1372, TEL. 011/4371-8141
OPEN LUNCH AND DINNER

Güerrín remains a Corrientes classic, a one-of-a-kind survivor that sells pizza by the slice at the street-side standup counter—at giveaway prices, the onion-based *fugazza* and *fugazzeta* are simply exquisite (or exquisitely simple), and the baked chicken empanadas (avoid the fried ones) are exceptional.

There are many more options for toppings, though, if you choose table seating in its vast interior. The place can be mobbed at dinnertime, but service is always quick and attentive, and the price is invariably right.

🔲 Sabot $$

25 DE MAYO 756, TEL. 011/4313-6587
OPEN WEEKDAYS 12:30–3 P.M.

Possibly downtown's best restaurant of any sort, the bankers' and powerbrokers' favorite Sabot serves Italo-Argentine dishes of the highest quality in a notably masculine environment (women are few but not unwelcome), with good-humored but extraordinarily professional service. Less formal than its clientele might imply, it's moderately expensive by current standards; choice entrées include *matambre de cerdo* (rolled pork),

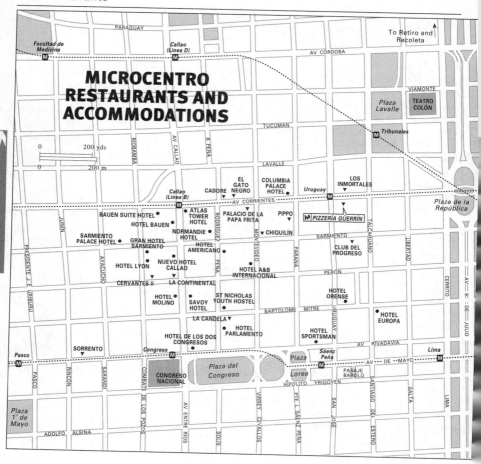

MICROCENTRO RESTAURANTS AND ACCOMMODATIONS

chivito (roast goat), and fish dishes. For an unexpected post-meal infusion, try the *mate de coca* brewed from fresh coca leaves (for digestive purposes only!).

IN BRIEF

For the financially challenged, one of B.A.'s best values is the supermarket **Coto** (Viamonte 1571), which has very cheap but remarkably good cafeteria food.

Another Microcentro classic is **Los Inmortales** (Avenida Corrientes 1369, tel. 011/4373-

5303), a pizzeria seemingly unchanged since the days of Carlos Gardel, whose photographs line the walls.

For a more typical *porteño* experience than the more *gauchesco* grills, try one of the no-frills *parrillas* like Congreso's **Pippo** (Paraná 356, tel. 011/4374-0762) or **Chiquilín** (Montevideo 321, tel. 011/4373-5163).

In the same location since 1929, near the junction of the two pedestrian malls, **ABC** (Lavalle 545, tel. 011/4393-3992) seems a relic of the Austro-Hungarian empire, with its continental atmosphere and menu of sau-

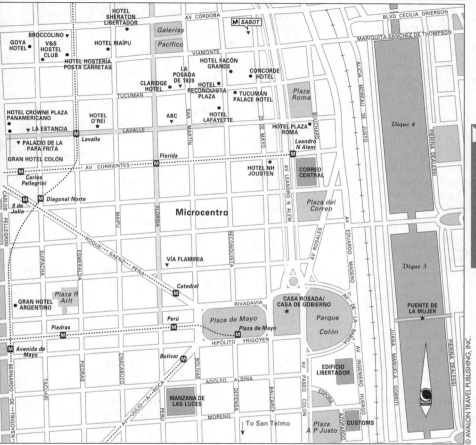

Restaurants

sage, schnitzel, and goulash. It's a popular lunch spot for businessmen and bankers from La City.

On the edge of the financial district, lunchtime favorite **La Posada de 1820** (Tucumán 501, tel. 011/4314-4557) serves a standard but above-average Argentine menu of beef and pasta at reasonable prices (US$3–6 per entrée) in bright, cheerful surroundings accented with burnished wood.

Puerto Madero

Over the past few years, redeveloped Puerto Madero has made a big impact on the restaurant scene, but more because of the area's overall appeal than because of its quality—there's only one really outstanding restaurant. Most places, though, have outdoor as well as indoor seating, and when the weather's fine it's a great option for people-watching along the yacht harbor. Because the area is popular with foreigners who stay at nearby luxury hotels, restaurants here are accustomed to dealing with dinnertimes as early as 7 P.M.

ARGENTINE/REGIONAL

ⓜ Cabaña Las Lilas $$
ALICIA MOREAU DE JUSTO 516,
TEL. 011/4313-1336
OPEN DAILY FOR LUNCH AND DINNER
WWW.LASLILAS.COM
Opposite the northerly Dique No. 4, arguably B.A.'s best *parrilla*, Cabaña Las Lilas serves only beef from its own *estancias* in Buenos Aires, Santa Fe, San Luis, and Chaco provinces; its *bife de chorizo* (US$10) may be the most succulent in town. As it's often packed despite its size, reservations are advisable; if you have to wait, they provide complimentary champagne and snacks.

With its high quality and impeccable service, this is the one can't-miss for beefeaters, well worth its relatively high prices (US$15 and

up for entrées). In fact, it's Puerto Madero's only truly memorable restaurant, though many others are suitable for lunch.

IN BRIEF

At the north end of Dique No. 4, **La Madeleine** (Avenida Alicia Moreau de Justo 102, tel. 011/4315-6200) serves a respectable beef, chicken, and pasta menu, with lunchtime specials in the US$5 range.

Puerto Sorrento (Alicia Moreau de Justo 410, tel. 011/4319-8730) is the barrio's best seafood choice, but **La Parolaccia del Mare** (Alicia Moreau de Justo 1160, tel. 011/4343-0038, www.laparolaccia.com) deserves consideration for its US$5 lunch specials.

On the west side of Dique No. 3, **Rodizio**, (Alicia Moreau de Justo 840, tel. 011/4334-3638) is a Brazilian-style *parrilla*.

Across the basin, **Il Gran Caruso** (Olga Cossentini 791, tel. 011/4515-0707) is a cavernous Italian restaurant with moderately priced lunch specials; pasta and seafood entrées range from around US$7–9.

Nearby **Asia de Cuba** (Pierica Dealessi 750, tel. 011/4894-1328, www.asiadecuba.com.ar) has a promising menu of sushi, sashimi, tempuras, and curries that help give it its name (the Cuba part is a mystery, though). In practice, though, its prices exceed its quality except for weekday lunch specials.

San Telmo

Despite San Telmo's tourist allure, it lags behind other barrios in gastronomic appeal. That's not to say there is nothing worth trying, but for the most part they're better lunchtime bargains than dinnertime indulgences.

ARGENTINE/REGIONAL

Bar El Federal $

PERÚ AND CARLOS CALVO, TEL. 011/4300-4313
OPEN DAILY FOR LUNCH AND DINNER

Dating from 1864, El Federal looks its age—in a positive way, with its worn tiled floor and its indescribably intricate carved wooden bar, symmetrically embellished with stained glass and a central clock (which no longer ticks off the minutes but reinforces the feeling of timelessness). The menu is large but the house specialty is turkey ravioli (US$3), with any of a variety of sauces; there's re-

San Telmo's classic Bar El Federal makes some of B.A.'s best ravioli.

freshing hard cider on tap. So out of style that it's stylish again, this classic also contains a bookstore; in hot weather, note, the bathrooms become virtual ovens.

La Casa de Esteban de Luca $

DEFENSA 1000, TEL. 011/4361-4338
OPEN DAILY EXCEPT MON. 9:30 A.M.–1 A.M.

In a late-colonial house designated a national historical monument, just north of Plaza Dorrego, La Casa de Esteban de Luca serves a diversity of international dishes along with the conventional *parrillada*. Prices are midrange—US$5–8 for entrées.

DesNivel $

DEFENSA 855, TEL. 011/4300-9081
OPEN DAILY FOR LUNCH (EXCEPT MON.)
AND DINNER

Sunday visitors to the Plaza Dorrego flea market queue up outside DesNivel, and many locals swear by it as well, for *parrillada* and pasta at bargain prices. In reality, though, it's almost indistinguishable from dozens of other *parrillas porteñas*—perfectly acceptable, but nothing out of the ordinary except for the crowds that often make it claustrophobic.

Dios los Cria $

CHILE 502, TEL. 011/4300-7340
OPEN DAILY FOR LUNCH AND
TUES.–SAT. FOR DINNER

With rustic décor and casual but competent service, this corner restaurant serves regionally based Argentine food, such as empanadas Norte (slightly spicy beef), Pampa (chicken), and Patagonia (lamb) for appetizers, plus entrées, such as lamb and trout in the US$7–9 range. Lunchtime specials (US$3) can include abundant dishes, including *costillas de cerdo a la riojana,* northwestern Argentine pork chops garnished with a fried egg, bacon, peas, and potatoes. On weekends, it sometimes offers live music.

Restaurants

© WAYNE BERNHARDSON

1880 $

DEFENSA 1665, TEL. 011/4307-2746
OPEN DAILY EXCEPT MON. FOR LUNCH AND DINNER
If you're looking for a traditional parrilla that oozes barrio atmosphere without DesNivel's crowds, visit 1880, immediately opposite Parque Lezama. Festooned with filete by San Telmo artist Martiniano Arce, it draws almost exclusively local residents, with entrées (including pasta dishes like ñoquis as well) in the US$3–4 range.

Territorio $

ESTADOS UNIDOS 500, TEL. 011/4307-0896
OPEN DAILY FOR LUNCH AND
TUES.–SAT. FOR DINNER
Territorio prepares uncommon items, such as Patagonian sandwiches of smoked venison, and other regionally based dishes, but also Peruvian-style stir-fried lamb with vegetables (US$4) and *tables* of smoked meats and cheeses (US$3). Fine homemade bread and free olives complement the main plates. Portions are substantial, but the desserts sound better than they really are.

Though it's small, Territorio has a good selection of brews on tap and in bottles. There's a separate non-smoking section, but the sidewalk seating can be too sunny at lunchtime; the music and noise level is moderate.

FRENCH

Abril $

BALCARCE 722, TEL. 011/4342-8000
OPEN WEEKDAYS NOON–4 P.M. AND DAILY
EXCEPT SUN. 8 P.M.–MIDNIGHT
Outside the San Telmo mold, Abril is a small French-style bistro whose fixed-price lunches and dinners are more diverse and lighter than the usual Argentine *minutas*. The service is good and friendly, even when the restaurant is understaffed; painted in soothing pastels, its interior patio (partly enclosed and air-conditioned) makes a serene retreat in an otherwise bustling city.

INTERNATIONAL

Pappa Deus $

BETHLEM 423, TEL. 011/4361-2110
OPEN DAILY FOR LUNCH AND DAILY
EXCEPT MON. FOR DINNER
WWW.PAPPADEUS.RESTAURANT.COM.AR
In a late-18th-century house with both indoor and sidewalk seating, Plaza Dorrego's Pappa Deus is more creative than most San Telmo eateries, incorporating touches like arugula and sun-dried tomatoes into the menu; the homemade pastas include a tremendous pumpkin-stuffed ravioli. On Sunday market days, though, it can be a little too hectic to enjoy a lunch here. Entrées cost a moderate US$4–5, but there are even cheaper fixed-price lunches; desserts are relatively pricey.

SPANISH/CATALAN

Hostal del Canigó $

CHACABUCO 863, TEL. 011/4304-5250
OPEN DAILY FOR LUNCH AND DINNER
Occupying the classic dining room of the Casal de Catalunya cultural center, with its dark mahogany woodwork and Spanish tiles, Hostal del Canigó specializes in Catalonian seafood, other Spanish dishes, and the occasional standard Argentine item.

URUGUAYAN

Medio y Medio $

CHILE 316, TEL. 011/4300-7007
OPEN WEEKDAYS LUNCH AND DINNER,
SAT. LUNCH ONLY
Taking its name from the blend of sparkling and white wines popular with Uruguayans, Medio y Medio (literally, half and half) bursts with lunch-goers in search of Uruguay's caloric/cholesterol overdose known as the *chivito,* a steak sandwich garnished with lettuce, cheese, tomato, and bacon (note that, in the Argentine context, *chivito* normally means kid goat). A fried egg crowns the *chivito al plato,* a dinner plate that includes a larger cut of beef plus potato salad, green salad, and French fries.

IN BRIEF

The northwestern Argentine provinces of Salta and Jujuy produce spicier-than-normal empanadas and stews like *locro,* available cheaply at **La Carretería** (Brasil 656, tel. 011/4300-5564).

The no-frills **La Vieja Rotisería** (Defensa 963, tel. 011/4362-5660) is an economical (entrées US$3–5) *parrilla.*

Several places in the vicinity of Plaza Dorrego offer pretty good tango shows along with Sunday lunch, including **El Balcón** (Humberto Primo 461), which has a US$3 *parrillada,* and **Mitos Argentinos** (Humberto Primo 489, tel. 011/4362-7810). The latter hosts live music, including rock bands, late at night on weekends.

La Boca

La Boca is no gourmet ghetto, but there's enough good food for lunch—most people visit the barrio during the daytime—and even an occasional dinnertime foray.

ARGENTINE/REGIONAL

La Barbería $

PEDRO DE MENDOZA 1959, TEL. 011/4303-8526
OPEN DAILY 11 A.M.–8 P.M.
WWW.LABARBERIA.COM.AR

With umbrella-shaded sidewalk seating on the Vuelta de Rocha, its facade and interior adorned with dazzlingly colorful *filete,* La Barbería serves empanadas, tapas, pasta, pizza, sandwiches, and seafood, plus beer and cold hard cider straight from the tap. The food's not bad but it's fairly expensive for simple food, as you're paying as much or more for the daytime tango dancers on the sidewalk.

El Obrero $

AGUSTÍN CAFFARENA 64, TEL. 011/4362-9912
OPEN LUNCH AND DINNER
EXCEPT SUN. AND HOLIDAYS

In an area where taxis are obligatory at night and maybe even advisable in the daytime (though some cabbies have trouble finding it), El Obrero is where Argentine and foreign celebrities go slumming for steaks. Its walls are plastered with posters of soccer icon Diego Maradona and little else except photos

of high-profile clientele on the order of Bono and Robert Duvall—it hasn't even taken down the image of disgraced ex-President Fernando De la Rúa. There is no printed menu—check the chalkboards scattered around the dining room. No entrée exceeds about US$3–5, and most are cheaper.

IN BRIEF

Next door to La Barbería, the almost indistinguishable El Corsario (Pedro de Mendoza 1981, tel. 011/4301-6579) has been up for sale, but likely will continue with its empanadas-style menu.

The **Caminito Tango Club** (Del Valle Iberlucea 1151, tel. 011/4301-1520) offers a lunchtime tango show in addition to its menu of beef, seafood, and pasta, with most entrées in the US$3–6 range.

Across the block from La Bombonera stadium, **La Cancha** (Brandsen 697, tel. 011/4362-2975) draws *Xeneize* soccer fans for standard Argentine fare and some Spanish dishes.

Only a block off Avenida Almirante Brown, several garishly painted pizza-and-pasta cantinas draw the Argentine tourist crowd for lunch and dinner: **Tres Amigos** (Necochea and Suárez, tel. 011/4301-2441); **Il Piccolo Vapore** (Necochea and Suárez, tel. 011/4301-4455), immediately across the street; and **Gennarino** (Necochea 1210, tel. 011/4301-6617).

Balvanera

Gastronomic points of interest are scattered around Balvanera and its bordering barrios.

JAPANESE

Ichisou $$

VENEZUELA 2145, TEL. 011/4942-5853
OPEN WEEKDAYS NOON–2:30 P.M. AND DAILY
EXCEPT SUN. 7–11:30 P.M.

Notably Japanese in its minimalist décor and cuisine, Ichisou occupies an improbable Once location with no other restaurants and few other businesses of any kind. Relatively expensive by current standards, with lunch for US$10 and up, it may be a lesser value than some more recent additions to the Asian scene, but discriminating diners and longtime consumers vouch for its authenticity and quality.

IN BRIEF

Congreso's **La Continental** (Avenida Callao 202) has fine chicken empanadas and pizza slices, including a particularly choice *fugazzeta;* there are several other branches around town.

Known for its Pantagruelian portions, **Cervantes II** (Perón 1883, tel. 011/4372-8869) is the place to load up on carbs like ravioli, gnocchi, and the like. Most entrées are large enough for two people at this utilitarian but agreeable place, whose service is professional.

Since the 1940s, **La Viña del Abasto** (Jean Jaurés 3007, tel. 011/4963-4890) has served Gardel's old neighborhood with standard Argentine dishes. Opposite the renovated Mercado del Abasto, offering a similar menu, **La Recova del Abasto** (Anchorena 557, tel. 011/4866-4244) is a pioneer on a pedestrian mall that hasn't yet matched redevelopers' plans.

Favored by the late tango legend Astor Piazzola, **Pierino** (Billinghurst 809, tel. 011/4864-5715) is an Italian-style cantina with outstanding pastas in the US$3–5 range. Olive-lovers should check the open barrels at **La Casa de las Aceitunas** (Guardia Vieja 3602, tel. 011/4862-0280).

Retiro

While Retiro isn't a gastronomic focus in the same way that Palermo is, it has a smattering of quality eateries.

ARGENTINE/REGIONAL

Juana M. $

CARLOS PELLEGRINI 1535, TEL. 011/4326-0462
OPEN LUNCH AND DINNER EXCEPT SAT. LUNCH

In an inconspicuous location, close to Retiro and Recoleta luxury hotels, this cavernous basement restaurant serves *parrillada* and pasta dishes in the US$3–5 range, including unlimited access to a spectacularly diverse salad bar (reason enough to eat here). Steel girders support the high ceilings and local artists' paintings decorate the walls, while the plain white wooden tables make a certain no-frills style statement.

Good for groups on a budget, with a quick kitchen and friendly service, it has a small tobacco-free section; its main drawback is a high noise level, even when it's not all that full. It closes for vacation the first two weeks of January.

ITALIAN

Filo $

SAN MARTÍN 975, TEL. 011/4311-0312
OPEN DAILY NOON–2 A.M.
WWW.FILO-RISTORANTE.COM

In the sector newly known as the Nuevo Bajo, Filo is B.A.'s hippest and most adventurous pizzeria (along with *parrillada,* even when pizza is good, it stands obstinately among the capital's most conservative cuisines). In both food and décor, the basics are Mediterranean, but the details are avant garde (such as its basement art space, which showcases contemporary *porteño* painters and sculptors).

Filo occupies a long, deep lot where a stylish bar—tightly stretched cattle hides protect it from footmarks—leads to a split-level dining area. The pizzas, starting around US$5 and large enough for two adults with reasonable appetites, feature a light thin crust and uncommon toppings, such as artichoke hearts. Other Italian specialties, likewise embellished with contemporary touches, are also available, and there's a large list of Argentine and foreign wines.

At lunchtime, Filo is popular with bankers and business people, but at night it becomes a fashion-conscious scene, and it can get distractingly noisy—and not just from bad techno. The food, though, remains the centerpiece, and the service is enthusiastic.

SPANISH

Tancat $

PARAGUAY 645, TEL. 011/4312-5442
OPEN DAILY EXCEPT SUN. FOR LUNCH AND DINNER

Even in the midst of economic crisis, the *tasca*-style Tancat remains wildly popular for lunches (around US$3–5 pp); don't miss the *jamón serrano* (ham) appetizer. Reservations are almost essential for tables, which are few, but individual lunch-goers can slide into a seat along the long wooden bar, which is backed by shelves of wines covered with business cards, posters, and photos. Its Spanish owner delivers a personal greeting to everyone who comes through the door.

THAI

Empire Bar $

TRES SARGENTOS 427, TEL. 011/4312-5706
OPEN LUNCH AND DINNER WEEKDAYS,
DINNER ONLY SAT.

Though it has split from Las Cañitas's culinary landmark Lotus Neo Thai, the Empire Bar still offers a fine Thai menu with some spicy dishes (by *porteño* standards, at least). Midday specials go for around US$3, most other entrées for US$4–6, and there's a 6–9 P.M. happy hour at the bar. While the food remains the same, the décor is contemporary.

VEGETARIAN

La Esquina de las Flores $

AVENIDA CÓRDOBA 1587, TEL. 011/4813-3630
OPEN WEEKDAYS 11:30 A.M.–4 P.M.
WWW.ESQUINADELASFLORES.COM.AR

A pioneer in the organic sector, La Esquina de las Flores has become a *porteño* institution not just for its health-food market and upstairs restaurant, but also for its efforts at diversifying the Argentine diet through public workshops and radio and TV programs, and its judicious discrimination in terms of where it purchases what it sells. Both sit-down service and take-away meals are available, and it's possible to buy many items, such as spices, that are difficult to find elsewhere in the city. When the restaurant proper is closed, the downstairs counter still has most of the same menu for several hours more.

IN BRIEF

Supermercado Disco (Montevideo 1037) has an upstairs cafeteria that offers a surprisingly good, cheap, and diverse selection of fast food. **Alimentari** (San Martín 899, tel. 011/4313-9382) is a popular breakfast and lunch cafetería.

Costumbres Criollas, (Esmeralda 1392, tel. 011/4393-3202) prepares spicy Tucumán-style empanadas and other northwestern Argentine dishes. **Lo de Alvarado** (Marcelo T. del Alvear 1521, tel. 011/4812-3462) serves similar fare from adjacent Salta province.

Tourist-oriented *parrillas* are numerous but almost invariably good—two of the best are **Las Nazarenas** (Reconquista 1132, tel. 011/4312-5559) and **La Chacra** (Avenida Córdoba 941, tel. 011/4322-1409).

Chile, better known for its diverse seafood and

produce than its beef, has a longstanding Retiro presence in **Los Chilenos** (Suipacha 1042, tel. 011/4328-3123). It doesn't, however, suggest gastronomic advances in the Chilean capital of Santiago, one of South America's welcome surprises.

La Esquina de las Flores has a next-door vegetarian competitor in **Lotos** (Avenida Córdoba 1577, tel. 011/4814-4552), which is more cafeteria-style and also has market produce and takeaway dishes.

Recoleta and Barrio Norte

Recoleta has some of Buenos Aires's swankiest restaurants, but also some of its best bargains.

SPANISH

José Luis $$
AVENIDA QUINTANA 456, TEL. 011/4807-0606
OPEN DAILY FOR LUNCH AND DINNER
A Recoleta stalwart, José Luis is an Asturian seafood restaurant that stresses fresher and lighter dishes than most of its counterparts, though the food falls short of truly elite. The menu is enormous, with some very expensive imported Spanish items that reflect neighborhood standards; more affordable are starters like the refreshing gazpacho (US$4) and main dishes like the *lomo de merluza* (hake filet, garnished with *jamón serrano* and clams, US$10).

Less formal than it looks from outside, José Luis's latticed walls and ceilings face a subtropical patio with a rushing waterfall, but when big groups dine here, the noise level inhibits quiet conversation, and it lacks a tobacco-free area. It has a big wine list and, while there's no wine by the glass, there are half-bottles of decent Argentine wines. The mostly female wait staff is professional and *simpática*.

Oviedo $$
BERUTI 2602, TEL. 011/4822-5415
OPEN DAILY FOR LUNCH AND DINNER
WWW.OVIEDORESTO.COM.AR
Internationally recognized Oviedo specializes in Spanish seafood but also serves Patagonian lamb and standards like steak, with most entrées in the US$7–20 range. Unfortunately, its owners seem to think its air-purification system justifies its being a cigar bar as well.

Los Pinos $
AZCUÉNAGA 1500, TEL. 011/4822-8704
OPEN DAILY FOR LUNCH AND DINNER
Occupying an old-style apothecary, its stained wooden cases still stocked with antique bottles and rising nearly to the ceiling, this Barrio Norte favorite offers fixed-price lunch and dinner specials in the US$3–5 range, with substantial choice; the à la carte menu of beef, seafood, and pasta is not much more expensive, as the comparably priced entrées include a side order. The service is well-intentioned but inconsistent.

IN BRIEF

For spicier northwestern Argentine dishes like *locro*, one of the best values is **El Sanjuanino** (Posadas 1515, tel. 011/4804-2909); the empanadas are particularly choice. **La Querencia** (Junín 1308, tel. 011/4821-1888) belongs to a small chain offering similar fare but also some more elaborate dishes.

Bar Rodi (Vicente López 1900, tel. 011/4801-5230) bursts with Recoleta diners in search of beef and pasta, though it's far less stylish than other nearby eateries. Across from the cemetery, **Tenorio** (Junín 1793, tel. 011/4802-6214) is a mid-range *parrilla* with outdoor seating and a self-conscious, even aggressive hipness.

Pizza Cero (Schiaffino 2009, tel. 011/4807-1919) is an above-average pizza chain in both price and quality.

Charging US$8–10 pp, the Middle Eastern buffet at the **Restaurant del Club Sirio** (Pacheco de Melo 1902, tel. 011/4806-5764) is open nightly except Sunday.

There are several mostly interchangeable

mid-range to upscale restaurants in the Village Recoleta complex at Vicente López and Junín, including **La Strada** (Vicente López 2008, tel. 011/4802-0905), which has good pasta and excellent desserts, sidewalk seating, and somewhat erratic service. **Monaco** (Vicente López 2052, tel. 011/4807-5330) features pizza and sandwiches, but also prepares decent fish dishes, such as *merluza* (hake) with an almond sauce; it has good house wines and good service. **Kugenhaus** (Azcuénaga 1570, tel. 011/4805-8512) sells Middle European–style pastries and take-out dishes.

Palermo

Palermo is, without question, Argentine cuisine's center of innovation. The main geographical areas of interest are Palermo Viejo (which is subdivided into Palermo Soho near Plaza Serrano—also known as Plazoleta Cortázar—and Palermo Hollywood north of Avenida Juan B. Justo); the Botánico (between Avenida Las Heras and Avenida del Libertador); and Las Cañitas (the area between Avenida Luis María Campos and the Campo Argentino de Polo). That said, there are other options scattered around the city's largest barrio.

ARGENTINE/REGIONAL

Cabernet $$
BORGES 1757, TEL. 011/4831-3071
OPEN DAILY NOON–2 A.M.
While its Palermo Soho location places it in Argentine cuisine's new wave, this elegant restaurant and wine bar owes much to the handsomely traditional features of the defunct downtown Clark's. Dishes, such as glazed lamb, accompanied by a spinach-based risotto, tweak conventional tastes without alienating them; the portions are sufficient but not gluttonously large. The wine list *is* large.

Where Cabernet differs from most other Palermo restaurants is the preservation and restoration, rather than recycling, of the corner building it occupies. While the pastel yellow exterior and large picture windows may not be quite traditional, the surviving *vitraux*, along with its burnished interior woodwork and chandeliers, link the past with the present. It also has a large, attractive patio for outdoor dining and a well-segregated tobacco-free area.

Club del Vino $–$$
CABRERA 4737, TEL. 011/4833-0048
OPEN MON.–SAT. FROM 8:30 P.M.
Known for a diversity of live music in its intimate theater, the Club del Vino is also a fine and stylish restaurant with, as its name would suggest, an exceptional wine list. The diverse menu includes the usual beef dishes (US$3–4), but also more creative entrées, such as rabbit stew (US$4), conger eel with tomato and basil (US$3), chicken breast in orange sauce (US$3), and stuffed trout with almonds (US$5). While both the food and décor lack the flamboyance of other Palermo Soho restaurants, that's not necessarily a bad thing. It also maintains a sufficiently segregated tobacco-free area.

La Cupertina $
CABRERA 5300, TEL. 011/4777-3711
OPEN TUES.–SAT. 11:30 A.M.–3:30 P.M.
AND DAILY EXCEPT MON. 7:30–11 P.M.
For quality-to-price ratio, the hands-down best choice for empanadas and regional dishes is Palermo Soho's La Cupertina, which also wins points for its invitingly rustic style with sturdily handsome wooden chairs and tables. The chicken empanadas, *pizzetas, locro* (a spicy stew), and *humitas en chala* (similar to tamales, wrapped in corn stalks) are exquisite and so cheap that price is irrelevant, even with wine; try also the desserts, especially the Spanish custard *natillas* and *arroz con leche*. Its only drawback is inconsistent (if well-intentioned) service.

Restaurants

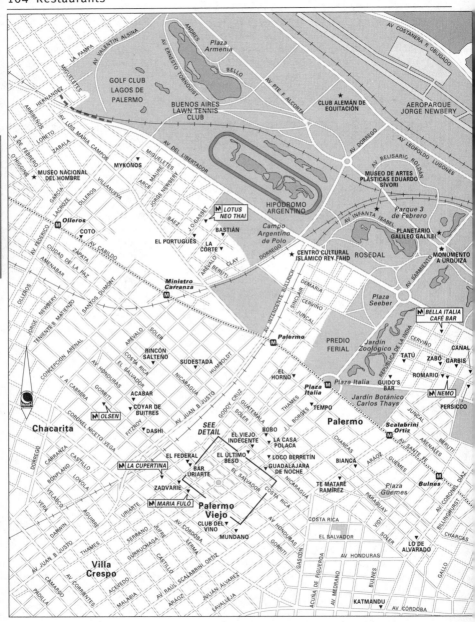

PALERMO RESTAURANTS

Río de la Plata

CLUB DE PESCADORES

Punta Carrasco

0   500 yds
0   500 m

COSTA SALGUERO GOLF CENTER

AV CASARES

Dársena F

AV PRESIDENTE RAMON S CASTILLO

JARDÍN JAPONÉS

JERONIMO SALGUERO

CASTEX CALVIA

AUTOPISTA PRESIDENTE A U ILLIA

Plaza Alemania

JUEZ TEDIN

SAN MARTIN DE TOURS

MENTA E CANNELLA

RIGGIERI

BULNES

Plaza Grand Bourg

Plaza Naciones Unidas

CABELLO

Plaza República de Chile

AV PTE FIGUEROA ALCORTA

Recoleta

AV GENERAL LAS HERAS

AUTOMOVIL CLUB ARGENTINA

AV DEL LIBERTADOR

Parque Las Heras

PEÑA

FRENCH

HOSPITAL RIVADAVIA

JUNCAL

AGÜERO

AV PUEYRREDON

HAEDO

Ⓜ Agüero

LELÉ DE TROYA ▼

LA PAILA

COSTA RICA

CABERNET ▼

RUSSEL

UN GALLO PARA ESCULAPIO ▼

FREUD & FAHLER ▼

URIARTE

EL SALVADOR

SANTA

CANTINA LA PLAZITA

ROSA

XALAPA ▼

BAR 6 ▼

PAMPA ▼

KAYOKO ▼

HONDURAS

Plaza Serrano

LA ESQUINA DE LAS FLORES

SOCIAL PARAISO ▼

SPIRIT ▼

SORIA

ARMENIA

THAMES

J L BORGES

GURRUCHAGA

GORRITI

PARAGUAY

ECUADOR

© AVALON TRAVEL PUBLISHING, INC.

El Federal $

HONDURAS 5254, TEL. 011/4832-6500

OPEN MON.–SAT. LUNCH AND DINNER

Not to be confused with its near namesake in San Telmo, Palermo Soho's El Federal attracts an upmarket clientele for high-priced versions of regional specialties from throughout the country: potatoes and quinoa from Jujuy, *cabrito* (goat) from the western Cuyo provinces, *jabalí* (wild boar) from Bariloche, and Patagonia lamb. Entrées start in the US$6–7 range.

Lelé de Troya $

COSTA RICA 4901, TEL. 011/4832-2726

OPEN LUNCH AND DINNER

Showcasing Palermo Soho's informality, Lelé de Troya does the traditional but adds nouvelle touches that set it well apart from run-of-the-mill Argentine food. The braised mixed vegetables that accompany the Patagonian lamb (US$8), for instance, come enclosed in a light, flaky phyllo dough. There's also a good dessert list.

Physically, Lelé is invitingly casual from its corner entrance, where an arbor of verdant climbing vines shades the sidewalk tables, to its rooftop terrace, where a canopy of sycamores overhangs the weekend *asados.* In between, there's a wine bar and at least a dozen different dining rooms, painted in bright primary colors, on three levels. In the daytime, a central skylight illuminates the open kitchen and one of the dining areas.

Loco Berretín $

GURRUCHAGA 1946, TEL. 011/4833-0768

OPEN DAILY EXCEPT MON. 12:30 P.M.–2 A.M.

WWW.LOCOBERRETIN.COM

A recent arrival on the scene, Loco Berretín makes *porteño* food with a Palermo Soho touch: grilled freshwater fish *pacú* with a tangy lemon sauce accompanied by a red pepper mousse (US$7). In addition to fine food for lunch and dinner, Berretín becomes a nighttime tango bar (note the mannequin *malevo,* or thug, lurking outside the entrance) with wine, live music, and skilled dancers,

Restaurants

though it's not an over-the-top floor show. In fact, after the performance, the dancers invite the public to join in an impromptu *milonga*.

La Paila $

COSTA RICA 4848, TEL. 011/4833-3599
OPEN TUES.–SAT. LUNCH AND DINNER
Even more specifically regional than most places of its sort, La Paila prepares a Catamarca-based cuisine of empanadas, *guiso* and *locro* (both stews), llama steaks, quinoa-based dishes, and tamales, plus sweets (*mate* with homemade bread and regional jams). The US$3.50 lunch special is an exceptional value.

The regional emphasis extends to the wine list, with bottles from Catamarca, Salta, and La Rioja provinces. In addition, there's live folk-loric music on Friday and Saturday nights, but occasionally Sunday afternoons as well; in part a cultural center, La Paila sells indigenous crafts and also has a library.

Pampa $

HONDURAS 5143, TEL. 011/4832-6487
OPEN DAILY FROM 10 A.M.
Pampa waves the flag for traditional Argentine dishes, including *bife de chorizo* and *pastel de papas*. It does so, though, with creative touches, such as a chopped garnish of onions with green and red peppers to flavor the beef, as well as *papas ruedas* (fries, but in the form of perfectly cooked mini-doughnuts). The *ensalada patria* of fresh spinach, goat cheese, strips of wild-boar bacon, and sun-dried tomatoes is also a winner; garnished with raspberries, strawberries, and currants, the dark-chocolate mousse makes an almost perfect dessert. Portions are large enough to satisfy, but not so large as to encourage overeating.

Pampa occupies an especially narrow "sausage house" patio with great natural light and sturdy, traditional furnishings. At the same time, they've also built some sidewalk seating around a street tree.

Rincón Salteño $

CARRANZA 1996, TEL. 011/4775-9777
OPEN DAILY FOR LUNCH AND DINNER
In Palermo Hollywood, this northwestern Ar-gentine specialist offers unique *empanadas de charqui*, of freeze-dried llama meat (US$.50 each), along with other typical dishes like *humitas, locro,* and especially *chivito al horno* (roast goat, garnished with sweet-potato rounds, US$5). Decorated with appropriately regional style, it also has sidewalk seating and a small interior patio.

ASIAN

Sudestada $

GUATEMALA 5602, TEL. 011/4776-3777
OPEN DAILY FOR LUNCH AND DINNER
One of the city's first and finest Southeast Asian restaurants, Sudestada's punning name comes from its region of origin but also from the term for the South Atlantic storms that often drown Buenos Aires. Just over the Palermo Hollywood line, this Vietnamese kitchen can be slow, but it does allow single diners to order a half-portion of starters.

BRAZILIAN

Maria Fulô $

CABRERA 5065, TEL. 011/4831-0103
OPEN MON.–SAT. FROM 8 P.M.
WWW.MARIAFULORESTO.COM.AR
After a brief closure, Palermo Soho's brilliant Brazilian restaurant has reopened as good as ever, in bright new quarters with a small interior patio for open-air dining. For US$5, the *ximxim de galinha* of chicken breast, shrimp, and cashews in coconut milk is exquisite enough, but the *maracuyá* (passion fruit) mousse may be the city's best dessert. Entrées fall into the US$4–9 range.

FUSION

Acabar $

HONDURAS 5733, TEL. 011/4772-0845
OPEN NIGHTLY 8 P.M.–2 A.M.
Young and hip, its very name a double en-tendre with sexual connotations, Acabar is a Palermo Hollywood bar/restaurant with a lab-yrinth of rooms and eclectic décor even down

to the physical menu itself—which consists of piles of cue cards. Strong on pastas, such as ravioli and gnocchi, Acabar also is notable for its *entrada oriental* of hummus, tabouleh, pita bread, and the like (US$3.50), plus good mixed drinks, but its wine list is limited. The service is attentive, and there's a small but reasonably well-segregated tobacco-free area.

Bar 6 $
ARMENIA 1676, TEL. 011/4833-6807
OPEN MON.–SAT. FROM 8 A.M.
With its high ceilings and mezzanine loft, popular Bar 6 embodies the modishly recycled Palermo Soho aesthetic. Quality entrées like *ojo de bife* (ribeye steak), stir-fried vegetables, and polenta with goat cheese fall into the US$7 range, but the menu is less diverse than some others in the neighborhood. Even on weeknights, reservations are advisable for a table; otherwise, eat at the bar. Air quality is mediocre despite the open floor plan.

Bar Uriarte $
URIARTE 1572, TEL. 011/4834-6004
OPEN DAILY FOR LUNCH AND DINNER
WWW.BARURIARTE.COM.AR
Exuding post-industrial chic, Bar Uriarte's kitchen is visible from the street and from the entryway aisle that leads to a long wooden bar. At the back, a spacious, sparsely decorated dining area draws natural light from a large picture window. Atop concrete floors, simple but handsome wooden furniture looks onto a patio where potted citrus trees and gardenias stand before a brick-wall background covered by ficus vines and ornamental conifers.

Uriarte's food is a tasty Mediterranean blend of starters, including provoletta, thin-crusted pizzas with unusual toppings (at least for Argentina), like asparagus, and heartier main dishes, such as *matambre de cerdo* (pork flank) with pumpkin puree. The US$8 brunch, on weekends and holidays, is an excellent way to sample Uriarte's best, but weekday lunch specials cost only half that. The service is attentive and there's a weeknight happy hour from 7–10:30 P.M.

On the downside, some tables are too close together, it lacks a non-smoking area, and the music is dreary elevator electronica (with an occasional tango touch). Staircases at each end of the building lead to a mezzanine with a few additional tables and an art space (www.espaciouriarte.com.ar).

Bobo $
GUATEMALA 4882, TEL. 011/4774-0505
OPEN FOR LUNCH AND DINNER
WWW.BOBOGOURMET.COM.AR
On the ground floor of its namesake hotel, this comfortably stylish Palermo Soho restaurant prepares very fine three-course lunches (US$6), plus entrées like spider-crab *sorrentinos* (US$6), whole trout with a buttered almond and fennel sauce (US$8), and an intriguing dessert menu. Its creators have preserved the traditional woodwork of the recycled building, integrating it with clean interior lines and a contemporary color scheme. There's plenty of space between the metal-frame tables, topped with handsome dark wood, and comfortable armless easy chairs for seating. In addition, Bobo has an effectively segregated non-smoking area.

La Corte $
ARÉVALO 2977, TEL. 011/4775-0999
OPEN WEEKDAYS FOR DINNER ONLY,
WEEKENDS FOR BREAKFAST AND LUNCH
At the fashionable end of Las Cañitas's offerings, La Corte is a hybrid restaurant, bar, and chic household-goods outlet. It serves Sunday buffet brunch (US$6), but also entrées like stir-fry vegetables and fresh fish; à la carte portions, though, are small for an Argentine restaurant. It's spacious, with high ceilings and some sidewalk seating, but the service can be absent-minded and the drum-machine music can be truly irritating.

Malevo $
MARIO BRAVO 908, TEL. 011/4861-1008
OPEN WEEKDAYS FOR LUNCH AND DINNER,
SAT. FOR DINNER
WWW.MALEVO-RESTAURANT.COM.AR
In Almagro, on the fringe of Palermo Viejo, Malevo's menu is an eclectic mix of wok-fried

vegetables, meats, fish, tempura, and the like, with most entrées in the US$3–4 range. Painted in bright Mexican hues—the walls around its 15 or so tables adorned with paintings for sale—it continues to be a solid neighborhood bistro. Excellent lunch specials (around US$3.50) include items like stuffed calamari, while entrées like *lomo a la pimienta* (pepper steak) go for about US$3. Desserts include *mousse de maracuyá* (passion fruit, but not the equal of Palermo's Maria Fulo's).

Olsen $–$$

GORRITI 5870, TEL. 011/4776-7677
OPEN TUES.–SAT. FROM NOON, SUN. FROM 10 A.M.

One of B.A.'s most creative restaurants, this Palermo Hollywood locale serves what might be called Scandinavian *criollo* cuisine, with dishes like ravioli with goat cheese (US$5) and pork roast with raspberry sauce (US$7). The bar serves the standard aperitifs but also a literally dizzying variety of vodka-based cocktails. The mashed potatoes that accompany some dishes finish with a hot radish flourish, while bread consists of bagels and pretzels, with light dips to accompany them. The flatware is distinguished for its irregularity, as if each piece were custom-made for this restaurant.

Olsen is as notable for its ambience as its food, having devoted at least part of what was once a *PH* (horizontal house) lot into a sculpture garden that replicates a Scandinavian boreal forest of birches, cypresses, and pines. A canvas-covered deck permits al fresco dining even when it's drizzling, while sliding-glass doors, open in fine weather, separate the deck and the interior, which has a soaring high ceiling and mezzanine seating. A central woodstove rises to the roof.

Olsen's noise level is only moderate but, on the downside, it lacks a non-smoking section. The service is attentive, but a little short of the standards set by the food.

Social Paraíso $

HONDURAS 5182, TEL. 011/4831-4556
OPEN TUES.–SAT. FOR LUNCH AND DINNER

At this intimate nouvelle-cuisine place in Palermo Soho, the US$3.50 lunch specials feature items like bruschetta and risotto; other entrées fall into the US$4–6 range. It also has innovative desserts.

Te Mataré Ramírez $

PARAGUAY 4062, TEL. 011/4831-9156
OPEN NIGHTLY EXCEPT MON. FOR DINNER
WWW.TEMATARERAMIREZ.COM

In a category of its own, definitely not a place to bring the kids or even sup alone, this self-styled "aphrodisiac restaurant" is notorious for suggestive food and décor. Diners are slow to order as they ogle the salacious menu while contemplating entrées (around US$10) like *la vertiente inagotable de tu deseo* (the inexhaustible spring of your desire, beef in a merlot sauce with vegetable tempura) and *cierro los ojos y me abismo en el mar del placer* (I close my eyes and sink into a sea of pleasure, swordfish with a salad of fava beans, bacon, and carrots in tomato vinaigrette).

Desserts include *estímulo lurioso* (lustful stimulation, ice cream with a sauce of forest fruits), and *amantes que se comparten* (shared lovers, a chocolate fondue with fruit, brownie, coconut, and fig truffles).

Ramírez's major drawback is poor air quality—go on weeknights or early on weekends, before the smokers monopolize the relatively small dining room. In addition to the food, it hosts occasional live theater (humorously sexual but far from pornographic) and jazz.

El Viejo Indecente $

THAMES 1907, TEL. 011/4775-2666
OPEN LUNCH AND DINNER
WWW.VIEJOINDECENTE.COM.AR

Taking its name from a collection of stories by Charles Bukowski—something of a deity among *porteño* Bohemians—El Viejo Indecente mocks itself as an outpost for lowlifes (the name means dirty old man). In fact, it's a casual bar/restaurant that's not so trendy as some other Palermo Soho locales, though it has its artsy side—the colorful tile fragments artistically embedded in the sidewalk add to its ramshackle charm.

The food is good enough, especially at weekday lunchtime when main menu entrées go for half price; the *fajitas de pollo* aren't exactly what you might expect from a Tex-Mex restaurant in the northern hemisphere, but they're not bad, and the cheap carpaccio starter deserves a taste. Several nights a week it has live music.

Zabó $-$$
UGARTECHE 3154, TEL. 011/4804-6816
OPEN LUNCH AND DINNER
WWW.ZABORESTAURANT.COM

Difficult to categorize, this promising new Botánico restaurant's "creative kitchen" features the usual meat dishes and pastas, but also Jewish matzo, Indonesian satay, and seafood (including swordfish). The lunch specials, comprising 1–3 courses, cost no more than US$5 but can still include imaginative items, such as a ceviche/sashimi starter.

The spacious dining room gets fine natural light and has glistening hardwood floors, while Japanese maples and bamboo decorate a secluded back patio. There is a non-smoking section and, admirably, they make the effort to ask which you prefer. The bar, meanwhile, makes a killer *caipirinha* and other mixed drinks.

ITALIAN

Bella Italia $$
REPÚBLICA ÁRABE SIRIA 3285, TEL. 011/4802-4253
OPEN DINNER ONLY

Under the same ownership as the nearby café, Bella Italia is a more formal restaurant, in one of a handful of horizontal houses that have survived the high-rise boom in the densely populated, upper-middle-class sector of the Botánico between Avenida Las Heras and Avenida Libertador. The carpaccio (US$3) and shrimp risotto (US$7) merit special mention, there's wine by the glass, and it has a small but reasonably well-segregated tobacco-free section. Its décor is more elaborate and the service more professional than the café, but its food is not demonstrably superior.

◪ Bella Italia Café Bar $
REPÚBLICA ÁRABE SIRIA 3330, TEL. 011/4807-5120
OPEN DAILY 7 A.M.–1 A.M.

One of B.A.'s best Italian venues, worth a Bo-

tánico detour from elsewhere in town, this is the informal, moderately priced café version of a nearby restaurant whose other unlikely location is Fort Worth, Texas. For around US$4, it has outstanding squash gnocchi with a subtle cream sauce, along with fine cannelloni, panini, and salads. It blends distinctively Argentine touches with Mediterranean villa–style décor of Doric columns. Sofa-style benches and small tables line one wall, and bright but diffuse light illuminates the space thanks to a central skylight; other chairs are freestanding. It has friendly management, good service, a handful of shady sidewalk tables, and is cash-only.

Un Gallo para Esculapio $
URIARTE 1795, TEL. 011/4831-7977
OPEN DAILY 8 A.M.–DINNER
WWW.GALLOPARAESCULAPIO.COM.AR

Inordinately popular on weekends because of its diverse live-entertainment schedule, El Gallo is a sprawling venue whose main-level bar/restaurant has very good Italian food—try the *ravioles de calabaza* (squash ravioli)—though it doesn't fit easily into any category. The kitchen will also prepare half-portions of starters, such as *rabas* (breaded squid rings), for single diners.

Wine by the glass is also available in this lively, friendly atmosphere. A variety of seating is available, including sidewalk, patio, and interior, the last of which features booths and easy chairs as well as freestanding tables and chairs. On the downstairs sound system, a diverse music ranges from indigenous South American to North American blues but is never loud enough to disrupt conversation. Live music shows take place Thursday–Sunday, anywhere from 9 to 11 P.M.

Guido's Bar $
Ú DE LA INDIA 2843, TEL. 011/4802-2391
OPEN WEEKDAYS 7 A.M.–1:30 A.M.,
SAT. 7 A.M.–5 P.M.

Facing the zoo, an elaborately *fileteado* facade distinguishes this tiny but personable neighborhood cantina. Standard Italian entrées are in the US$4–6 range, but the US$8 lunch (including dessert and drink, plus a digestive *limoncello*) is an excellent value. Its character also comes from the movie stills (Frank, Dino, and Sammy) and posters that clutter its walls, along with such *piropos* (aphorisms) as "I don't mind if you point out my failures, but I can't stand constructive criticism."

El Último Beso $

NICARAGUA 4880, TEL. 011/4832-7711
OPEN MON.–TUES. NOON–8 P.M.,
WED.–SUN. TO 2 A.M.

In fashion-conscious Palermo Soho, "The Last Kiss" has transformed a traditional Palermo house into a low-key restaurant. The lunch menu (around US$5) features starters, such as the mushroom omelette, and entrées, such as stir-fried chicken and vegetables. Pasta and risotto entrées fall into the US$5 range, while beef and fish dishes are slightly more expensive.

To the sounds of standards like "Don't Get Around Much Anymore" (all the music is in English), lunch-goers and diners sit on elongated sofas beneath soft interior pastels, or at French-style chairs and tables. There's also garden seating beneath a rose arbor with fountains and ficus shrubs.

Último Beso is also an afternoon teahouse with panini and cakes.

JAPANESE

Dashi $$

FITZ ROY 1613, TEL. 011/4776-3500
OPEN MON.–SAT. FOR LUNCH AND DINNER
WWW.DASHI.COM.AR

Appropriately enough for its Palermo Hollywood location, Dashi hosted Antonio Banderas, Melanie Griffith, and Emma Thompson for Banderas's birthday celebration, but the food is the enduring star here. Dashi's sushi and sashimi are visually stunning and gastronomically more than satisfying, and the desserts are surprisingly good—though their names (e.g. Monte Fuji) are more Japanese than the sweets themselves. The building itself has large picture windows, high ceilings, and contemporary furnishings, but the service can be a little absent-minded for a restaurant with its aspirations.

Jardín Japonés $

AVENIDA CASARES 2966, TEL. 011/4800-1322
OPEN WED.–MON. 10 A.M.–6 P.M.
AND 7:30 P.M.–MIDNIGHT
WWW.JARDINJAPONES.COM

No other city restaurant can match the soothing view from the dining room at the Jardín Japonés, with its curving paths, koi ponds, picturesque bridges and temples, and meticulously maintained gardens. Even better, after years of mediocrity, the food finally matches the view, with combined boards of succulent sushi and sashimi in the US$6–7 pp range, as well as dishes like pot stickers and *teppanyaki*. Daytime visitors must pay the US$1 admission fee to the park itself, but at night, when the rest of the park is closed, there is no extra charge.

Kayoko $

GURRUCHAGA 1650, TEL. 011/4832-6158
OPEN DAILY EXCEPT SUN. FROM 6:30 P.M.
WWW.KAYOKO-PALERMO.COM.AR

In Palermo Soho, barely a block off Plaza Serrano, Kayoko serves a diversity of authentic and economical Japanese food ranging from *donburi* to tempura and *teppanyaki,* as well as an exceptional sushi/sashimi mix (US$13) for two; on the downside, the ginger is a little sour. The interior style is equally authentic, but in fine weather, dining on the shady street-side deck is a real pleasure; the service is attentive.

MEXICAN

Mexican food is often none too authentic in Buenos Aires, as most *porteño* palates can't handle truly spicy food, but there are some reasonable choices.

Guadalajara de Noche $

GURRUCHAGA 1881, TEL. 011/4832-8971
OPEN TUES.–SUN. FROM 8:30 P.M.
WWW.GUADALAJARADENOCHE.COM.AR

Recently relocated from Recoleta to Palermo Soho, this is a respectable representative for ceviche (US$3) and mixed fajitas (US$5), but some staple Mexican *antojitos,* such as guacamole and enchiladas, are not always available. Guadalajara goes so far as to say that their food is spicy only by request, but visitors accustomed to authentic Mexican food will probably have to ask for extra.

Xalapa $
EL SALVADOR 4800, TEL. 011/4833-6102
OPEN TUES.–FRI. FOR DINNER,
SAT. FOR LUNCH AND DINNER
The kitchen at Xalapa makes a pretty good guacamole, decent margaritas, and pretty good entrées starting around US$3, though the *carnitas* (shredded pork) are not up to snuff. Sidewalk seating snakes around the Palermo Soho corner lot in good weather, but there's also appropriately attractive interior décor for when it's raining.

PARRILLADA
El Portugués $
BÁEZ 499, TEL. 011/4771-8699
OPEN DAILY 11 A.M.–2 A.M.
One of Las Cañitas's signature restaurants, with interior and sidewalk seating, this *parrilla* serves a half-portion of *bife de chorizo* that some diners might consider a double—consider sharing and then order more if you're still hungry. Though it dominates the intersection of Báez and Ortega y Gasset with its restaurant, a separate pizzeria, and a small grocery, El Portugués, unfortunately, does not see fit to serve wine by the glass.

PERUVIAN
Zadvarie $
URIARTE 1423, TEL. 011/4831-2719
OPEN TUES.–SAT. FOR LUNCH AND DINNER,
MON. FOR DINNER ONLY
An oddball option for Palermo Soho, Zadvarie has a large menu of fusion-style dishes, but is more notable for its Peruvian specialties. For US$7, for instance, it prepares a great *crocante de cerdo,* a well-cooked pork dish with a side of grilled sweet potatoes and a tangy onion and red-pepper salad. Peruvian-style pisco sours, flavored with Angostura bitters, and desserts like the tropical fruit *lucuma* parfait are on the menu. There are also the standard ceviche and wine by the glass.

Zadvarie falls short in its décor, which is

starkly post-industrial except for the appealing rooftop terrace; though a bamboo roof provides some shade, it's best on a warm night.

POLISH
La Casa Polaca $
JORGE LUIS BORGES 2076, TEL. 011/4899-0514
OPEN TUES.–SAT. 8 P.M.–12:30 A.M.
Though they don't have the high profile of Spaniards and Italians, Polish immigrants have been a noteworthy presence in Argentina. Distinctly unhip compared to its neighbors—unless you consider Polish coats-of-arms the latest in cool—the Casa Polaca (Polish House) has a huge and remarkably diverse menu based on quality versions of ethnic specialties like pierogi. Meals are inexpensive, the service is friendly, and its daytime classes also make it the place to brush up on your Polish.

SPANISH/SEAFOOD
Coyar de Buitres $
HONDURAS 5702, TEL. 011/4774-5154
OPEN MON.–SAT. FROM 6 P.M.
New on the seafood scene, Palermo Hollywood's Coyar de Buitres bills itself an oyster bar, but other appetizers, such as ceviche (US$3.50), and more elaborate seafood dishes, such as calamari over braised greens (US$7) and the catch-of-the-day special (US$8), fill out most of the rest of the menu. There are also meat dishes, and comfortable sidewalk seating supplements the limited seating at this corner bar. If there's a downside, it's the irritating electronic music, even when the volume is low.

Mundano $
MALABIA AND CABRERA, TEL. 011/4831-5667
OPEN TUES.–SUN. NOON–4 P.M. AND 8 P.M.–1 A.M.
WWW.MUNDANO.RESTAURANT.COM.AR
On a shady corner lot, Mundano's entrance is really a portal to an inviting Mediterranean garden where, in fine weather, there's no need to walk a step farther to enjoy a menu of tapas and fish dishes, with the occasional beef and pasta diversion. The lunch or dinner special, about US$7 with dessert and wine included, is an

outstanding value, and service is good as well. Those who venture a little farther can enjoy the airy interior or the sunny first-floor terrace.

Ⓜ Nemo $

CABELLO 3672, TEL. 011/4803-5878
OPEN NIGHTLY FOR DINNER

Originally a branch of Palermo Soho's Spirit, Nemo is a Botánico favorite that's establishing its own identity for light entrées, including seafood-based pastas (around US$5), and a diverse but steadily evolving fish menu (US$5–8), including at least one freshwater catch. Its *cuarto tapeo mare* (US$5), suitable for two diners, makes an outstanding appetizer. What *Buenos Aires Herald* food writer Dereck Foster calls the capital's "consistently best seafood restaurant" has spare décor, limited sidewalk seating, and a small but effectively segregated tobacco-free area.

Spirit $

SERRANO 1550, TEL. 011/4833-4360
OPEN DAILY 9 A.M.–MIDNIGHT OR 1 A.M.

While the quality of Palermo Soho restaurants surrounding Plazoleta Cortázar is generally lower than those just a short walk away, the tapas and oyster bar Spirit is a major exception. More often packed than not, it draws crowds for the quality of its seafood tapas (US$12), sufficient for two people, and other fairly priced Spanish dishes. The early opening hour makes it suitable for brunch.

THAI
Ⓜ Lotus Neo Thai $$

ORTEGA Y GASSET 1782, TEL. 011/4771-4449
OPEN DAILY EXCEPT MON. FOR DINNER ONLY

Reached by a narrow staircase that eventually reveals an expansive first-floor dining room with floor-hugging tables and cushions, Lotus was Argentina's Thai-food pioneer. A quiet locale with soothing music and striking lotus-themed décor, it's still one of few places in the country where it's possible to taste truly spicy Southeast Asian dishes, flavorful plates that challenge the palate even of those accustomed to it. Despite 2002's steep devaluation, Lotus

remained, and still is, relatively expensive, but it's worth the splurge.

IN BRIEF

One of the cheapest choices, but by no means bad, is the citywide supermarket **Coto** (Avenida Cabildo 545), which has an inexpensive cafeteria.

Lo de Alvarado (Mansilla 3428, tel. 011/4825-1133) sells takeaway *salteñas*, as does **Tatú** (Cabello 3918, tel. 011/4802-2816). The hole-in-the-wall **El Horno** (Güemes 4689, tel. 011/4773-8364) offers even spicier Bolivian *salteñas*.

Plaza Serrano is Palermo Viejo's heartbeat and, though it's not the best spot for dining, there are acceptable choices, like **Cantina La Plazita** (Serrano 1636), with standard Argentine dishes for US$2–3.

Only a short distance from Plaza Serrano, try **Freud & Fahler** (Gurruchaga 1750, tel. 011/4833-2153), which has a US$3.50 lunch menu with choices like fish, risotto, and ravioli, plus starters and wine.

For vegetarians, the capital's vegetarian landmark **La Esquina de las Flores** (Gurruchaga 1632, tel. 011/4832-8528) has a Palermo Soho market, café, and takeaway outlet.

On the barrio's western border, **Katmandu** (Avenida Córdoba 3547, tel. 011/4963-1122) gets high marks from the capital's small Indian community of about 150 people. Most entrées cost about US$3–4; it's open nightly except Sunday for dinner.

Romario (Cabello 3700, tel. 011/4511-4444) is the Botánico branch of an enormously popular pizza chain that also sells good empanadas. Nearby **Garbis** (Scalabrini Ortiz 3190, tel. 011/4511-6600) has outstanding hummus and a variety of kebabs but stick with the lamb rather than chicken, as the latter tends to dry out. Some more elaborate kebabs (around US$10) are large enough for two, so ask before ordering.

Canal (Salguero and Cerviño, tel. 011/4802-6511) is a spacious, contemporary *parrilla* that serves a gigantic half-portion of *bife de chorizo* and a Caesar salad more than large enough for two. Prices are midrange.

In Las Cañitas, near the entrance to the Palermo polo grounds, **Bastián** (Arévalo 3056, tel. 011/4771-5755) is primarily a *parrilla* that uses dense *quebracho* firewood from the Chaco, but also serves Argentine standards like gnocchi and empanadas. **Mykonos** (Olleros 1752, tel. 011/4779-9000) is a Greek/Mediterranean venue that's a longstanding barrio presence.

In the heart of Palermo Soho, **Mark's Deli and Coffee House** (El Salvador 4701, 011/4832-6244, 8:30 A.M.–9:30 P.M. Mon.–Sat., 10 A.M.–7 P.M. Sun.) is a U.S.-style deli, bright and cheerful with indoor and patio seating, outstanding sandwiches in the US$4 range, and choice sweets, including cookies and brownies; there's a small selection of wines by the glass and large and refreshing glasses of lemonade for those hot afternoons.

Belgrano

Perceived as remote—though it's only 20 minutes from downtown by Subte—Belgrano gets few foreign visitors and even fewer casual diners. Its Chinatown, though, offers B.A.'s best mainstream Asian food, and a handful of other places deserve a visit.

CHINESE
Cantina Chinatown $
MENDOZA 1700, TEL. 011/4783-4173
OPEN WEEKDAYS NOON–3:30 P.M. AND
7 P.M.–MIDNIGHT, WEEKENDS NOON–MIDNIGHT
Belgrano's compact Chinatown is home to a gaggle of moderately priced, mostly Cantonese, restaurants. Drawing Chinese diners from other parts of town, Cantina Chinatown serves abundant portions and some spicy dishes, such as kung pao beef, which may not seem quite so spicy to an experienced palate, but extra hot sauce is available.

ITALIAN
Capisci $
VUELTA DE OBLIGADO 2072, TEL. 011/4788-4400
OPEN DAILY 7 A.M.–2 A.M.
(24 HOURS ON WEEKENDS)
Directly opposite Plaza Belgrano and alongside La Redonda, Capisci occupies a weathered brick building whose still detailed facade is the backdrop for ample outdoor seating in fine weather. Risottos and good pasta dishes, with a variety of sauces, fall in the US$5 range, and there's also good lemonade and other refreshing drinks ideal for a break from the Sunday *feria*. On the downside, the barrio pigeons are increasingly aggressive thieves.

PERUVIAN
Contigo Perú $
ECHEVERRÍA 1627, TEL. 011/4780-3960
OPEN DAILY EXCEPT MON. 10 A.M.–MIDNIGHT
In a cul-de-sac near the railroad tracks, Contigo is a Peruvian spot, which, from humble beginnings, has become a neighborhood success—its ambience now matches the quality of its tangy pisco sours and traditional specialties, like *ají de gallina*. Prices are moderate, even cheap. The upside is the attentive service, the downside is dueling TVs—though one could argue that this is authentically Peruvian.

IN BRIEF
For Chinese food, another worthwhile choice is **Nuevo Chinatown** (Juramento 1656, tel. 011/4786-3456).

Economical **Cocina Regional 1810** (Mendoza 2320, tel. 011/4784-3063) serves Tucumán-style empanadas, as well as *humita en chala* and tamales (corn-based plates resembling their Mexican namesake), and stews like *locro*. **La Paceña** (Echeverría 2570, tel. 011/4788-2282) serves similarly spicy empanadas and the like from northwestern Argentina and Bolivia.

Da Orazio (Cuba 2220, tel. 011/4786-0088) is an elegant, highly regarded Italian choice, open for dinner only, with most entrées in the US$5–6 range.

M Restaurants

Arts and Leisure

Since independence, Argentina's impact on the arts has been remarkable for a geographically remote country with a relatively small population. Many Argentines have been eloquent writers and a much greater number are voracious readers. In the visual arts, particularly modern art, they have been innovative, and their architecture has often been grand even if derivative of Europe.

Classical music has always held a place in *porteño* society, but the city also exported the tango to Europe (where it became respectable) and around the world. It presently has one of the most vigorous rock-music scenes since 1960s London or San Francisco, creatively adapting polysyllabic Spanish to a frequently monosyllabic music. Likewise, Argentine cinema, theater, and dance have all been influential beyond the country's borders.

Even in the midst of Argentina's 2001–2002 financial crisis and loan default, one sector of Argentine society that showed resilience was arts and entertainment. After Tomás Eloy Martínez, a Tucumán native and professor of Spanish at Rutgers, the State University of New Jersey, won the Spanish Alfaguara literary prize (US$175,000) in 2002 for *El Vuelo de la Reina* (a novel about crime and corruption), he remarked, "One of Argentina's riches is forgotten but it is

Buenos Aires's Best

Best Café: Unlike *tanguerías* that reinvent themselves "for export," Monserrat's venerable **Café Tortoni** became a tourist attraction, and has remained one, by being itself (page 117).

Best Wine Bar: Like the tango, the Argentine wine industry is booming. For those who can't visit the bodegas of Mendoza, Palermo's **Club del Vino** is the place to sample up-and-coming wines, followed by a walk through its museum, dinner at its restaurant, and live music at its intimate theater (page 121).

Best Recycled Mansion: The bartenders and waitresses may not be your servants, but unwinding at Retiro's **Milión** will give you at least an inkling of how the *porteño* elite retreated from the capital's unruly streets (page 122).

Best Rock Club: Even if post-Cromañon remodeling costs it some of its edge, the roar of the audience and the rhythm of commuter trains that roll overhead will still shake the roof of **The Roxy**, in Palermo's Parque 3 de Febrero, when legends like Charly García take the stage (page 122).

Best Tango Floor Show: It falls short of a participatory *milonga,* but the producers, musicians, singers, and dancers at Monserrat's **El Querandí** manage to convey something of the tango's history and emotion, in a smaller supper-club setting than the Vegas-style spectacles elsewhere in town (page 128).

Best *Milonga:* Because *milongas* vary so greatly, ranging from no-frills social clubs to genuine landmarks designed for the purpose, with crowds that range from cordial to cliquish, it's particularly hard to choose the "best." The Confitería Ideal's **A Toda Milonga,** though, is an institution whose well-worn walls and floors best evoke tango's bittersweet nostalgia (page 129).

Best Gallery: Since it opened in the 1950s, **Galería Rubbers** has been on the cutting-edge of Argentine and Latin American modern art (its new Recoleta showroom is a recent development, though) (page 138).

Best Community Theater: Even native speakers from other countries may not understand everything that goes on in La Boca's **Teatro Catalinas Sur,** but this committed cast of nonprofessional actors, musicians, and singers communicate the epic of Argentine history even to spectators who lack even a single word of Spanish (page 140).

Best Cultural Center: Alongside the world-famous Cementerio de la Recoleta, the **Centro Cultural Ciudad de Buenos Aires** hosts some of Argentine art's most cutting-edge exhibitions—its 2005 León Ferrari retrospective was a scandal to some and a revelation to others—and its music, theater, and cinema programs also stand out in a neighborhood often derided for smug elitism (page 146).

Arts and Leisure

© WAYNE BERNHARDSON

Actors at Teatro Catalinas Sur take a bow after performing *We Came from Far Away.*

the quality, the leadership of our culture. [In that field] we can speak as equals to the U.S. or France."

Entertainment in Buenos Aires does not mean events alone, though cinema, live theater, live music, and discos feature prominently. Still, for many *porteños,* even sitting for hours in a café or *confitería* conversing and people-watching qualifies as entertainment. Sometimes, all these categories may overlap—the world-famous Café Tortoni, for instance, is a traditional meeting place, but it's also a restaurant, a bar, and a venue for live music and dance, including tango floor shows and participatory *milongas.*

Nightlife

In terms of entertainment, Buenos Aires is a 24-hour city that has as much to offer as New York or London. Argentines in general and *porteños* in particular are night people—discos and dance clubs, for instance, may not even *open* until 1 A.M. or so, and they stay open until dawn. That said, not everything of interest takes place at those hours.

All the Buenos Aires dailies have thorough event listings, especially in their end-of-the-week supplements. These include *La Nación* (Thursday); *Ambito Financiero,* the *Buenos Aires Herald*'s "getOut!" section and *Clarín* (all on Friday). *Clarín*'s Friday edition includes "Sí!," a youth-oriented pullout section. There are also listings in the German-language *Argentinisches Tageblatt* (Saturday) and *Página 12* (Sunday). In addition, there are listings in the monthly *Viva Bue,* a freebie distributed by the national and municipal tourist offices; in *Wipe* (www.wipe.com.ar), a privately distributed monthly brochure; and in the weekly *Llegás a Buenos Aires* (www.llegasabuenosaires.com).

For tickets to events at major entertainment venues (Teatro Gran Rex, Paseo La Plaza, La Trastienda, Teatro Nacional Cervantes, Teatro Astral, Teatro Astros, Teatro Margarita Xirgú, Niceto Club, The Roxy, and Centro Cultural

In Palermo, *porteños* enjoy a sidewalk café along Avenida del Libertador.

Recoleta's La Biela is one of the barrio's institutions for breakfast, brunch, and all-day people-watching.

Borges) and to sporting events (for soccer teams, such as Boca Juniors, River Plate, and San Lorenzo), contact **Ticketek** (tel. 011/5237-7200, www.ticketek.com.ar). Ticketek, which adds a US$1.50 service charge to most tickets, has outlets in the a Microcentro at the Teatro Gran Rex (Avenida Corrientes 857); in Barrio Norte at Lee-Chi (Avenida Santa Fe 1670, Local 42) and at Musimundo (Avenida Santa Fe 1844); in Palermo at Shopping Alto Palermo (Avenida Santa Fe 3253); and in Belgrano at Play (Avenida Cabildo 2082).

For discount tickets to certain events, including tango shows, cinemas, and live theater, try *carteleras,* agencies that offer last-minute specials. Among them are **Cartelera Espectáculos,** (Lavalle 742, tel. 011/4322-1559), on the downtown pedestrian mall; **Cartelera Baires** (Avenida Corrientes 1382, Local 24, tel. 011/4372-5058, open 10 A.M.– 10 P.M. Mon.–Thurs., 10 A.M.– 11 P.M. Fri., 10 A.M.–midnight Sat., and 2–10 P.M. Sun.); and **Cartelera Vea Más** (Avenida Corrientes 1660, Local 2, tel. 011/6320-5319, open 10 A.M.–10 P.M. daily), in the Paseo La Plaza complex.

CAFÉS

La Biela   RECOLETA
AVENIDA QUINTANA 596/600, TEL. 011/4804-0449
OPEN SUN.–FRI. 7 A.M.–3 A.M., SAT. 8 A.M.–4 A.M.
WWW.LABIELA.COM

Recoleta's La Biela is *the* classic breakfast and people-watching spot, though even after devaluation it remains a relatively pricey place to eat. In good weather, try the patio, beneath the shade of the palms, bulbous *palo borracho* trees, and the giant *gomero* or *ombú* (which needs wooden beams to support its sprawling thick branches). It's slightly more expensive to eat outside, though, and the outdoor service can be inconsistent.

Café Tortoni   MONSERRAT
AVENIDA DE MAYO 825, TEL. 011/4342-4328
OPEN DAILY 7 A.M.–2 A.M.
WWW.CAFETORTONI.COM.AR

No single institution embodies *porteño* tradition better than Monserrat's Tortoni, founded in 1858. Originally facing Avenida Rivadavia, it acquired a new frontage on Avenida de Mayo as city mayor Torcuato de Alvear redeveloped the area in the 1880s. Though most tourists come for coffee and croissants, the bar serves good mixed drinks (US$6) that come accompanied by a sizable *tabla* (that easily feeds two people) of sliced salami, paté, cheese, olives, and other snacks; separately, drinks cost only about US$2.50–3 each.

(For more details on the Tortoni, see the separate entry in the *Sights* chapter.)

Confitería Ideal   MICROCENTRO
SUIPACHA 384, TEL. 011/5265-8069
OPEN DAILY FROM 9 A.M.
WWW.CONFITERIAIDEAL.UNLUGAR.COM

Superannuated but hanging on, the worn-around-the-edges Ideal is one of the Microcentro's most traditional settings for coffee and croissants, and for *milongas*. Huge pillars support oval ceilings with multiple chandeliers, but one gets the notion that when a light bulb burns out it never gets replaced; the mahogany walls are in good shape, but the upholstered chairs are coming apart at the seams, and the floor tiles are cracked, stained, and worn from a century of shuffling shoes.

Then again, maybe this sort of slow corrosion is the essence of tango's bittersweet nostalgia. Ideal served as backdrop for director Alan Parker's cinematic Madonna-fest *Evita* and Sally Potter's even more appalling *The Tango Lesson*. Rumor says the Ideal is to undergo a renovation, but so far it's just rumor.

(For information on the Ideal's afternoon *milongas,* see the *Milonga* section in this chapter.)

Confitería Richmond   MICROCENTRO
FLORIDA 468, TEL. 011/4322-1341
OPEN MON.–SAT. 7 A.M.–10 P.M.
WWW.RESTAURANT.COM.AR/RICHMOND

In contrast with the Ideal, the elegant Richmond looks as good as the day it opened more than eight decades ago; one of Jorge Luis Borges's favorites, it draws the *porteño* elite for both breakfast and afternoon tea, and also serves as a bar and restaurant. Its woodwork, chandeliers, tables, and upholstery are all in primo condition and, thanks to the ample nonsmoking section at the front, non-puffers don't have to hike through clouds of toxic gases. Prices are higher

© WAYNE BERNHARDSON

Café Tortoni and the Academia Nacional del Tango, Monserrat

here than elsewhere, though, and the service can be a little lacking.

In Brief

Monserrat's **London City** (Avenida de Mayo 599) is a traditional choice for afternoon tea.

The distinguishing feature at Retiro's **Florida Garden** (Florida 889, tel. 011/4312-7902) is the paintings that adorn its supporting columns. Tables are uneven, and the food—the *medialunas* (croissants) in particular—is mediocre, but it has a devoted clientele.

In Palermo, patrons from the Las Cañitas sector and nearby Belgrano jam the sidewalk tables at **Café de la Imprenta** (Migueletes 868, tel. 011/4777-8205) for what may be the city's most succulent *medialunas.*

BARS AND CLUBS

The distinction between cafés and bars is not always obvious—in fact, it's often more a continuum than a dichotomy. Some of the more stylish (or pretentious) bars often go by the English word pub, pronounced as in English,

THE UNGRATEFUL DEAD AND THE CROMAÑON LEGACY

In December 2004, Argentine *rock nacional* got a wake-up call when a fan of the suburban Buenos Aires group Los Callejeros set off a flare that started a fire in the Once nightspot República Cromañon; with escape routes either bolted or wired shut to prevent sneak entries, nearly 200 of the group's fans died, mostly of smoke inhalation. It was the worst non-natural disaster in Argentine history.

In what was clearly an unnecessary tragedy, the aftermath was in many ways worse. Instead of deferring to the courts to identify and prosecute the culprit who set off the flare—the primary responsible party—opportunistic sectors of the public seemed most interested in scapegoating city mayor Aníbal Ibarra. While there were indications of shoddy inspections and even corruption in the city fire department, even Cromañon owner Omar Chabán, jailed for his responsibility in the matter, did not come in for the vituperative criticism that Ibarra did.

Soon, it became obvious, there were problems with many entertainment venues, especially those used for rock shows. According to one estimate, 95 percent of performance spaces were not up to snuff. The official response was an immediate shutdown of many live-entertainment options, including some very innocuous *milongas* (tango aficionados are unlikely to set off fireworks), in a two-week orgy of inspections, but this was more symbolic than genuine. In such a short time, effective compliance was impossible, and many clubs remained closed more than two months later because of a shortage of inspectors.

Though a judge ordered the detention of band manager Diego Argañaraz (whose wife died in the fire) in addition to Chabán, there seemed to be little, if any, public interest in the band's responsibility (the crowd was, by some estimates, four times Cromañon's capacity of about 1,000 spectators). Nobody, for that matter, raised the issue of high-powered and dangerous fireworks, whose availability makes New Year's Eve so nerve-wracking in the capital.

In the short run, the Cromañon disaster brought B.A.'s nightlife nearly to a standstill. In all likelihood, tighter municipal supervision will eliminate some, if not many, of the most precarious locales. On the plus side, those that remain should be safer, and *porteños* will still find a way to party all night. For all its ferocity, even Argentina's onerous 1976–1983 dictatorship felt unable to restrain B.A.'s night owls, even as Chile and other similar regimes enforced rigid curfews.

and many call themselves Irish. A number of these line Reconquista and other nearby streets in Retiro's so-called Nuevo Bajo area, where usually circumspect *porteño* drinkers become boozers on St. Patrick's Day.

Since the República Cromañon disaster of December 2004, when nearly 200 rock fans died of fire and smoke inhalation in the Once district, many live music venues were shut down at least temporarily for safety inspections, and it's unclear how many will reopen. It's worth mentioning that nearly all entertainment venues were subject to this increased scrutiny, including some prestigious theaters and even modest *milongas*. In the absence of definitive information, some locales get only brief mentions below.

Bárbaro   RETIRO
TRES SARGENTOS 415, TEL. 011/4311-6856
OPEN WEEKDAYS 7 A.M.–4 A.M., SAT. 10 A.M.–4 A.M.
More casual than any other bar in its barrio, this pioneer pub takes its punning name from a *lunfardo* term roughly translatable as cool. And it is, but unpretentiously so, with slightly rickety wooden chairs and peanut shells scattered on both the main floor and the mezzanine.

Bar Plaza Dorrego   SAN TELMO
DEFENSA 1098, TEL. 011/4361-0141
OPEN DAILY 8 A.M.–3 A.M.
At the corner of its namesake plaza, with large streetside windows that blend it with the scene outside during the *Feria,* this well-worn bar makes an ideal place to take a break from Sunday

© WAYNE BERNHARDSON

In Palermo's Las Cañitas district, Van Koning is a gathering place for Dutch expats.

flea marketing. In good weather, on non-market days, their plaza tables make it possible to enjoy a beer or snack in the open air.

Bar Seddon   MONSERRAT
DEFENSA 695, TEL. 011/4342-3700
OPEN DAILY EXCEPT MON. FROM 7 P.M.

Relocated to the edge of San Telmo, after the demolition of its classic 25 de Mayo locale in the Microcentro, Bar Seddon has made a successful transition to the capital's oldest neighborhood. It's never easy to recapture an earlier era but the current corner building, with its dark stained central bar, simple wooden tables, and casual ambience, has at least come close. There's live blues Friday and Saturday nights, tango Thursday and Sunday nights; at other times, the recorded music tends toward blues and Bob Marley. The food menu is simple but palatable pub grub.

Blues Special Club   LA BOCA
ALMIRANTE BROWN 102, TEL. 011/4854-2338
OPEN FRI. AND SAT. NIGHTS
WWW.BLUESSPECIALRECORDS.COM.AR

In an appropriate down-at-the-mouth location opposite San Telmo's Parque Lezama,

the Blues Special has traditionally flown in performers from Chicago and other blues hotbeds in the States, but the economic crisis has limited that practice. It does have its own house band, though, and other figures from the local blues scene play here on weekends only (late).

La Bodeguita   MICROCENTRO
SARMIENTO 1594, TEL. 011/4375-3388
OPEN WEEKDAYS NOON–MIDNIGHT OR LATER,
SAT. 8 P.M.–2 A.M.

In the Congreso district, La Bodeguita is a wine bar with live music and an international restaurant menu.

Buller Brewing Company   RECOLETA
PRESIDENTE RAMÓN ORTIZ 1827,
TEL. 011/4808-9061
OPEN DAILY FROM NOON
WWW.BULLERPUB.COM

Opposite Recoleta's landmark cemetery, Buller's is a brew pub that produces up to seven varieties of beer: light lager, cream ale, honey beer, Oktoberfest, India pale ale, stout, and an occasional surprise. The kitchen, meanwhile, provides a credible menu of tapas, seafood, pizza, and other pub grub, with particularly good panini and the sandwich version of the Uruguayan *chivito*. There's shady garden seating, but increasingly aggressive pigeons can be a problem.

Café Bar Banderín BALVANERA
GUARDIA VIEJA 3601, TEL. 011/4862-7757
OPEN WEEKDAYS 8 A.M.–9 P.M., SAT. 8 A.M.–4 P.M.

With their multiple giant TV screens, Recoleta's slick sports bars have glitz, but for traditionalists the Banderín is B.A.'s ultimate sports bar. Decorated with soccer pennants dating decades back, it recalls the era when *porteños* argued about, rather than gawked at, soccer. There's TV now, but the mid-'50s atmosphere survives.

Cervecería Dalinger PALERMO
(Hollywood)
GORRITI 5801, TEL. 011/4777-2827
OPEN TUES.–SUN. FROM 6 P.M.

A recent appearance on the scene, the promising Dalinger is a spacious brew pub with several custom beers on tap—stout, honey, etc.—as well as the usual suspects. The service is good, and the pub grub more than passable, with individual pizzas for less than US$3 and other items, such as ceviche. As it grows more popular, though, there'll probably be the temptation to put more tables closer together, and it may get noisier and smokier.

▶️ Club del Vino PALERMO
CABRERA 4737, TEL. 011/4833-0048
OPEN MON.–SAT. 8 P.M.–1 A.M.

One of Palermo's most genteel entertainment venues, the Club del Vino is an almost seamless combination restaurant and wine bar, with a separate theater seating a maximum of about 150 people for live music, which frequently includes tango. Just as often, though, it's folk music, such as Chango Spasiuk's accordion-based *chamamé,* from the northeastern province of Misiones. Prices for shows vary but are generally reasonable, starting around US$4, and the air quality's not bad by *porteño* standards.

La Dama de Bollini RECOLETA
PASAJE BOLLINI 2281, TEL. 011/4805-6399
OPEN NIGHTLY
WWW.LADAMA-DEBOLLINI.COM.AR

Larger than it looks from outside, this casual but engagingly decorated bar enjoys a picturesque site on a secluded, cobbled alleyway behind Hospital Rivadavia. Jorge Luis Borges, who evoked images of 19th-century knifefighters on the street in his poem *El Pasaje de los Cuchilleros* (The Cutthroats' Alleyway), participated in the 1984 founding of its weekly *café literario.*

Embellished with canvases by local artists, and boasting a small interior patio, the Bollini's brick walls and arches make it an outpost of San Telmo style in a Recoleta location. Its frequent live shows feature jazz, tango, and even Celtic music, but they are fewer in summer than during the rest of the year. Drinks are reasonably priced and there's a pub-grub menu, but food isn't why people come here—avoid the *picada* of bite-sized meats, cheeses, olives, and the like, which is far inferior to those elsewhere in the city.

Downtown Matías MICROCENTRO
RECONQUISTA 701, TEL. 011/4311-0327
OPEN MON.–SAT. FROM 9 A.M.
WWW.MATIASPUB.COM.AR

At the Microcentro branch of Buenos Aires's oldest Irish-style pub, with a dark-stained wooden bar, booths, and free-standing tables, patrons consume a variety of beers on tap, including Guinness, Harp, and Kilkenny, along with a huge selection of whiskies and other hard liquor. At lunchtime, downtown workers pack the place for pub lunches in the US$4 range, while most drinks cost US$2–3. There's a 7–11 P.M. happy hour.

In addition to the usual bar offerings, depending on the night, Matías showcases live music (including Celtic). It also has branches in nearby Retiro (San Martín 979, tel. 011/4312-9844) and more distant Belgrano (Echeverría 3195, tel. 011/4545-1050).

Arts and Leisure

Druid In   RETIRO
RECONQUISTA 1040, TEL. 011/4312-3688
OPEN WEEKDAYS NOON–1 A.M., SAT. FROM 8 P.M.
At the Irish end of the spectrum, the Druid In is popular with the downtown crowd for its pub-grub lunches in the US$5 range, including staples like steak and kidney pie, but also Argentine *minutas,* such as *milanesas.* At night, drinkers crowd into the cozy booths for beer, wine, and whiskey, sometimes to the accompaniment of live Celtic music. The front section of the building is tobacco-free.

Foro Gandhi   MICROCENTRO
AVENIDA CORRIENTES 1743, TEL. 011/4374-7501
OPEN SUN.–THURS. 10 A.M.–10 P.M.,
FRI.–SAT. 10 A.M.–MIDNIGHT
WWW.GALERNALIBROS.COM
In new quarters on theater row, the artsy Gandhi is a hybrid blend of bookstore, coffeehouse, and cultural center whose offerings include films, poetry readings, tango shows, and theater.

Gran Bar Danzón   RETIRO
LIBERTAD 1161, TEL. 011/4811-1108
OPEN MON.–FRI. FROM 7:30 P.M., SAT. FROM 8:30 P.M., SUN. FROM 8 P.M.
WWW.GRANBARDANZON.COM.AR
On the edge of Recoleta, showcasing more than 200 Argentine labels, the Danzón is a sophisticated wine bar that doubles as a restaurant. Drinkers can lounge on the comfy chairs and sofas or sit at the long bar; the dining area is separate. The music could be better—it tends toward *marcha,* as Argentines call techno—and softer. Conversation can be tough when the place fills, but the staff is cordial and the wine-by-the-glass selection is impressive.

There's a fine sushi special at happy hour (7–9 P.M., though the sushi chef takes Mondays off). For US$20, a diverse sushi plate can satisfy three hungry diners.

Milión   RETIRO
PARANÁ 1048, TEL. 011/4815-9925
OPEN WEEKDAYS FROM 5:30 P.M.,
WEEKENDS FROM 7:30 P.M.
WWW.MILION.COM.AR
Bordering Barrio Norte, Milión is a tapas bar occupying three stories of an extraordinary 1913 French Academicist mansion; only minimally altered for its current use, it offers garden, patio, and interior seating, but get there early to be seated outside. The second floor holds a gallery with rotating exhibits by local artists and photographers. Restaurant entrées cost in the US$3.50–6 range.

Niceto Club   PALERMO
NICETO VEGA 5510, TEL. 011/4779-6396
OPEN THURS.–SAT. FROM 9 P.M.
WWW.NICETOCLUB.COM
Having become one of the area's top live-music venues over the last several years, the Niceto Club is really a multi-space nightspot with three bars. The live music comprises a diversity of styles, from rock and jazz to reggae, salsa, and just about anything else. After the live music ends some time around 1 A.M. or so, it hosts all-night DJ dance parties.

Los Porteños   RECOLETA
AVENIDA LAS HERAS 2100, TEL. 011/4809-3548
OPEN DAILY 8 A.M.–MIDNIGHT
In a corner building, Los Porteños has reasonably priced drinks, a decent bar-food menu, friendly staff, and an unpretentious crowd with a good age mix, as well as better air quality than most *porteño* bars. Unfortunately, its Friday and Saturday live-music programs, which held only about 70 people for blues and Latin music, have been suspended, at least for the moment. On live-music nights, there's a modest cover charge.

The Roxy   PALERMO
AVENIDA SARMIENTO AND AVENIDA CASARES, TEL. 011/4899-0314
WWW.THEROXYBSAS.COM.AR
In the misleadingly named Arcos del Sol (literally, Arches of the Sun), squatting beneath a railroad bridge in Parque Tres de Febrero,

the Roxy shakes when trains pass overhead and leaks in heavy rainstorms. It also rocks, thanks to performers of the caliber of Charly García, who make it just what rock 'n' roll is supposed to be—rowdy and sweaty but not violent. Programs usually take place weekends, after 10 P.M., but days and times are inconsistent. It's also had some post-Cromañon problems that have slowed its reopening.

Shamrock   BARRIO NORTE
RODRÍGUEZ PEÑA 1220, TEL. 011/4812-3584
OPEN WEEKDAYS FROM 6 P.M.,
WEEKENDS FROM 8 P.M.
WWW.THESHAMROCKBAR.COM

Sometimes derided as a pick-up bar, this Barrio Norte version of an Irish pub holds happy hour, for beer and a limited number of house drinks, until midnight. In the basement, there's DJ techno for dancing Thursday–Sunday, with no cover for women but US$3–4 for men (though, by some accounts, they waive the cover for foreign boozers as opposed to *porteños,* who nurse their drinks for hours on end).

Van Koning   PALERMO
BÁEZ 325, TEL. 011/4772-9909
OPEN DAILY FROM 7 P.M.

With its solid wooden beams and furniture, and appropriately dark interior, Van Koning is a Netherlands-style pub that capitalizes on the Argentine fixation with all things Dutch (the fascination may have begun with Holstein cattle, but became an obsession when the country acquired its own royalty with the 2002 marriage of Máxima Zorreguieta to Crown Prince William). Dutch expats hold a special gathering here the first Wednesday of every month.

In Brief

Monserrat's **@lternativa** (Hipólito Yrigoyen 851) is a dance club that plays electronic music but also hosts punk and metal bands. **Eldorado** (Hipólito Yrigoyen 947, tel. 011/4334-2115) features live music acts.

The capital's Goths gather Saturday nights at Monserrat's **Requiem** (Avenida de Mayo 948, tel. 011/4331-5870, www.requiemgothic.com).

On the Microcentro/Retiro border, **La Cigale** (25 de Mayo 722, tel. 011/4312-8275) has electronica and, on occasion, live music. Bar lunches cost about US$4.

San Telmo's **Africa 1** (Balcarce 958, tel. 011/4300-6454) is a reggae and salsa venue, while nearby **Tabaco Rock** (Estados Unidos 265) is a tiny locale featuring live rock bands. Both are open weekends only.

Constitución's **Cemento** (Estados Unidos 1234, tel. 011/4304-6228) is a cavernous warehouse that hosts *rock nacional* groups on the way up. Often threatened with closure, even before the Cromañon disaster, it somehow keeps hanging on.

A restaurant by day, La Boca's **El Samovar de Rasputín** (Del Valle Iberlucea 1251, tel. 011/4302-3190) is a lively blues-and-rock venue on weekends, with regular jam sessions.

Balvanera's **Remember** (Corrientes 1983, tel. 011/4953-0638) is a small (120-capacity) multipurpose venue that offers live theater—mostly one-person acts—but it's primarily a pub that also offers music (jazz and blues, but even metal on occasion).

Typical of British/Irish–style pubs in Retiro's Nuevo Bajo are **John John** (Reconquista 924, tel. 011/4313-1428), which has good, reasonably priced drinks, an "erotic happy hour" Wednesdays, and live music on weekends, and **The Kilkenny** (Marcelo T. de Alvear 399, tel. 011/4312-7291), which has Irish beers on tap, plenty of whiskey, and live bands around midnight. Outside the immediate neighborhood is **The Temple Bar** (Marcelo T. de Alvear 945, tel. 011/4322-0474, www.thetemplebar.com.ar).

In the Village Recoleta complex southwest of the cemetery walls, **Locos por el Fútbol** (Vicente López 2000, tel. 011/4807-3777) has larger-than-life-size TV screens for soccer matches. Around the corner, the **World Sports Café** (Junín 1745, tel. 011/4807-5444) is similar but not quite so overwhelming.

The **Hard Rock Café** (Avenida Pueyrredón 2501, tel. 011/4807-7625, www.hardrock.com) is the Recoleta branch of the worldwide hamburger/rock 'n' roll memorabilia chain.

Fronting on Plaza Serrano, Palermo Soho's **República de Acá** (Serrano 1549, tel. 011/4581-0278, www.republicadeaca.com.ar) is a combination comedy club, karaoke bar, and relatively expensive Internet café.

Between Plaza Serrano and Plaza Italia, darkly lit and suggestively decorated, Palermo Soho's **Mundo Bizarro** (Guatemala 4802, tel. 011/4773-1967) is a self-consciously hip bar that attracts a youthful crowd and polarized responses from its patrons: Within a few minutes, you'll either love it or hate it.

In Palermo's Las Cañitas neighborhood, a pair of dependable, side-by-side bars mix strong drinks: **Voodoo** (Báez 340, tel. 011/4772-2453) and **Jackie O.** (Báez 344, tel. 011/4774-4844), which serves a particularly fine *caipirinha*.

JAZZ VENUES

Clásica y Moderna
BARRIO NORTE
AVENIDA CALLAO 892, TEL. 011/4812-8707
OPEN SUN.–THURS. 8 A.M.–2 A.M.,
FRI.–SAT. 8 A.M.–4 A.M.

With a quirky clutter of antique barrels and bicycles, this brick-walled hybrid of bookstore-café and live jazz venue has occupied the same Barrio Norte location since 1938. Once frequented by writers and intellectuals like Alfonsina Storni and Leopoldo Lugones, it has since seen performances by the likes of Susana Rinaldi, Mercedes Sosa, and Liza Minelli. Pop, rock, and tango singer Roberto Sánchez (popularly known as Sandro or to his true devotees as El Maestro) donated the piano from his personal collection.

While it's a top live-music venue, Clásica y Moderna is also a fine choice for breakfast or lunch, while reading the house's selection of daily newspapers and magazines.

Espacio Ecléctico
SAN TELMO
HUMBERTO PRIMO 730, TEL. 011/4307-1966
OPEN TUES.–FRI. NOON–9 P.M., WEEKENDS 3–9 P.M.
WWW.ESPACIOECLECTICO.COM.AR

In a luminous locale that serves also as an art space, Espacio Ecléctico has regular jazz events. Meanwhile, it also presents live theater, dance,

film, and even an annual event for photographers to present their coffee-table books.

Notorious
BARRIO NORTE
AVENIDA CALLAO 966, TEL. 011/4813-6888
OPEN MON.–SAT. 8 A.M.–MIDNIGHT,
SUN. 11 A.M.–MIDNIGHT
WWW.NOTORIOUSBAR.COM.AR

It's hard to classify Notorious, which is a hybrid of jazz café, sophisticated but unpretentious restaurant, and CD store where patrons can don headphones to preview music while munching on a variety of self-styled gourmet sandwiches. In addition to its dining room, the site for live-music performances at night, it has a large and woodsy rear garden.

It's probably most notable, though, for live music, primarily jazz, that takes place nearly every night at 9 or 10 P.M.

TANGO AND TANGUERÍAS

Tango can be music alone, music and song, music, song, and dance, or a theatrical combination of all three. Many visitors mistake floorshow spectacles for the essence of tango, but these tourist-oriented events can be a deceptive introduction to tango as a widespread, even democratic cultural phenomenon. For spectators conscious of their limitations, they can be entertaining and, in their own way, satisfying.

Tanguerías with floor shows range from relatively modest and simple programs at low prices to extravagant productions at high (sometimes excessive) cost. Even the latter, though, can be a bargain when the peso sinks or discount tickets are available through *carteleras*.

Many, but by no means all, tango venues are in the southerly barrios of Monserrat, San Telmo, and Barracas, with a few elsewhere and in outlying barrios.

Bar Sur
SAN TELMO
ESTADOS UNIDOS 299, TEL. 011/4362-6086
OPEN DAILY 8 P.M.–3 A.M.
WWW.BAR-SUR.COM.AR

Despite celebrity clientele, such as Antonio Banderas, Lucio Benetton, Robert Plant, and

THE TANGO, THE TANGUERÍA, AND THE MILONGA

For foreigners visiting Buenos Aires, one of the city's legendary attractions is the tango, the dance that conquered European salons despite its dubious origins in the Argentine capital's *arrabales* (outskirts) and brothels. What they usually see, in high-priced dinner-show *tanguerías,* are pairs of lithe and sexy dancers executing acrobatically intricate steps to the sounds of a professional orchestra in an elaborate setting, often a recycled historical building. It's impressive and professional, but what locals often deride as "for export" (in English) is not the experience of most *porteños.*

For *porteños,* dance is a participatory pastime at *milongas,* informal gatherings that take place at modest neighborhood locales often lacking even a stage, normally with recorded music, and charging only a modest admission charge. *Milongueros,* those who frequent *milongas,* may dance tango, but that's not the only option—the term itself describes a common style of music and dance, in two-four time, traditional to the Río de la Plata region. A *milonga* can also mean a spontaneous outbreak of dancing at a party.

Tanguerías, whatever their appeal, are for tourists. *Milongas* belong to the barrio, but tourists are welcome if they want to see—and perhaps dance—the tango as a popular art form in which couples from their teens to their *tercera edad* (retirement age) take part. The *milonga* is more than just the tango; it's a part of the *porteño* experience that transcends the stereotype of youth and beauty.

Arts and Leisure

Mario Vargas Llosa, Bar Sur remains a relatively spontaneous and informal tango-show venue open late every night except Sunday. Prices for the dinner spectacular have risen into the US$28 range, including pizza and empanadas to snack on, but this is one of the more highly rated locales.

La Bodeguita del Tango   MONSERRAT
BALCARCE 682, TEL. 011/4343-0777
OPEN THURS.–SAT. FROM 9 P.M.

In the basement of Café Molière, weekend shows at La Bodeguita tend toward the theatrical end of the spectrum, but the actor/singers and musicians are highly professional and the venue itself intimate enough that it's a more than satisfactory experience. On some nights, it has non-tango but usually dance-oriented programs, such as tap.

Café Tortoni   MONSERRAT
AVENIDA DE MAYO 825, TEL. 011/4342-4328
OPEN NIGHTLY FROM 9 P.M.
WWW.CAFETORTONI.COM.AR

There's no need to repeat details on the leg-

endary Tortoni here (see the entry in the *Sights* chapter instead), but it does host live tango song-and-dance shows most nights at its Sala Alfonsina Storni, separate from the main part of the café, for around US$7 pp plus drinks and food. Show times can vary slightly, as some nights there's a late program around 11 or 11:30 P.M.

Centro Cultural   SAN TELMO
Torquato Tasso
DEFENSA 1575, TEL. 011/4307-6506
OPEN WED.–SAT. FROM 10 P.M.

Opposite Parque Lezama, frayed around the edges but brimming with intensity, the Torquato Tasso provides more genuine barrio ambience than any other live-tango venue. Drawing performers of the caliber of Susana Rinaldi and La Chicana, it has notably authentic details—the tabletops, for instance, are all decorated with *filete* numbers, and wistful tangophile artwork lines the walls from the streetside stage to the bar at the back.

While its live-music offerings have increased, the Tasso still offers its Sunday night *milonga,*

THE GAUCHO BALLET

In the Palermo fairgrounds of the Sociedad Rural Argentina, dancers from the prestigious Ballet Brandsen and acrobatic riders, chosen from thousands of male applicants from around the country, have given Buenos Aires its folkloric equivalent to the tango spectaculars that have long been a staple of the *porteño* tourist circuit. Staged several times weekly, the Opera Pampa is a stylized account of Argentine history from the Andean past and arrival of the Spaniards to the settlement of the pampas, through song, dance, and spectacular horsemanship.

Like elaborate tango floorshows, Opera Pampa is vulnerable to criticism for stereotyping historic episodes, such as the campaign against the Ranquel people and the civil wars of the 19th century. At the same time, the choreographers have done an extraordinary job of integrating more than 50 dancers and some 20 riders into a fluid spectacle on what must be one of the world's biggest stages. The ballet showcases traditional rural dances, such as the male *malambo* (rather like gaucho tap dancing with

riding boots) and the couples' *chacarera* (more typical of farm settlements).

Opera Pampa (Avenida Sarmiento 2704, Palermo, tel. 011/4777-5557, www.operapampa.com.ar) takes place Thursday through Sunday, rain or shine; the doors open at 8 P.M. Even when it rains, its covered stands keep spectators dry. The show alone costs US$40 pp, while the combination show and *asado* (after the show) costs US$60 pp.

Spectators opting for the *asado* sit on the west side of the stands, reached by a red carpet across the sandy surface where *estancieros* traditionally show their finest livestock; show-only clients sit on the east side. Opera Pampa has transformed the adjacent western pavilion into a cavernous *parrilla* where dinner guests can enjoy empanadas and a glass of wine before the show, and browse the goods at a variety of gaucho-themed shops; after the show, they file into the *parrilla* for an all-you-can-eat buffet of roasted meats, plus salads, wine, and a sampling of traditional desserts.

with recorded music, around 11 P.M. Admission costs around US$1.50; in addition, it holds tango classes throughout the week.

El Chino   NUEVA POMPEYA
BEAZLEY 3566, TEL. 011/4911-0215
OPEN FRI.–SAT. FROM 10 P.M.
WWW.BARELCHINOFILM.COM.AR

In an untouristed southern barrio, El Chino became a tourist hangout thanks to the rugged authenticity of its late owner Jorge Eduardo Garcés, whose nickname (the Chinaman) was the source of the bar's name. Arrive well before midnight to get a table, though the live music—definitely not of the floor-show genre—may not start until later. The food is, for lack of a better description, working-class Argentine.

Cinema director Daniel Burak, who has made both a TV documentary and a feature film about the bar, is responsible for the website above, which is not official but does tell a great deal about El Chino.

Esquina Carlos Gardel   BALVANERA
CARLOS GARDEL 3200, TEL. 011/4867-6363
OPEN NIGHTLY
WWW.ESQUINACARLOSGARDEL.COM.AR

It's tempting to dismiss the Esquina Carlos Gardel, which veers dangerously close to a Vegas-style floor show, as time-warp tango that plays to the cliché. With a few exceptions, dancers clad in stereotypical early-20th-century dress stress the most acrobatic moves possible at the expense of the more subtle movements that *milongueros* prefer. Nor is there any attempt to tell the story of tango, but for a brief introductory film (subtitled in English, with outstanding footage) to Gardel himself, the Abasto neighborhood, and the Mercado del Abasto's recent redevelopment.

Yet the quality of the musicians—two violinists, two *bandoneonistas,* a pianist, and a string bassist who play on an elevated stage above the dancers—is first-rate, lead dancer Carlos Copello is a near-legend, and vocalist

Roberto Minondi is exceptional. While this show in its entirety may dismay purists, there is still much to appreciate.

On the site of the now-defunct restaurant Chanta Cuatro, literally in the shadow of the redeveloped Mercado del Abasto, the Esquina Carlos Gardel is part of a municipal project to sustain the legacy of the "Morocho del Abasto" in his old neighborhood. One of the city's most ornate tango locales, seating up to 500 spectators, the Esquina offers nightly tango shows starting at US$40 pp (show only, starting at 10:30 P.M.) and US$60 pp (with dinner, starting at 8:30 P.M.). For more expensive VIP boxes, which offer the best views (especially from each side of the stage), the rates are US$80 pp and US$120 pp, respectively.

Esquina Homero Manzi   BOEDO
AVENIDA SAN JUAN 3601, TEL. 011/4957-8488
WWW.ESQUINAHOMEROMANZI.COM.AR
Named for the great tango lyricist, a collaborator with composers such as Aníbal Troilo, this former corner bar was once part of the *arrabales* (outskirts) in the barrio of Boedo. Recycled to seat nearly 500 guests, and not quite so remote as it once was, it still holds a place as part of tango history.

Dinner starts at 9 P.M. nightly; the show commences at 10 P.M. For three hours prior to dinner, there are tango lessons.

Loco Berretín   PALERMO
GURRUCHAGA 1946, TEL. 011/4833-0768
OPEN DAILY EXCEPT MON. NOON–2 A.M.
WWW.LOCOBERRETIN.COM
Loco Berretín is a fine restaurant, adding creative touches to standard Argentine cuisine, but it's also a wine bar and tango space that offers something beyond floor-show clichés (except, of course, for the mannequin *malevo* who guards the door). From a stage overlooking the bar, outstanding musicians (and occasional recorded music) accompany a small group of actor/dancers who rely on subtlety rather than flamboyance. Following the show, guests are welcome to join the dancers in bridging the gap between floor show and *milonga.*

Palermo's only dedicated tango venue, Berretín offers dinner shows that range from US$20–26 pp, depending on the menu chosen; all dinners include a half-bottle of wine or other beverage of choice. In its upstairs salon, it also offers group and private tango classes in the afternoon and evening; instructors include the dinnertime dancers.

Mitos Argentinos   SAN TELMO
HUMBERTO PRIMO 489, TEL. 011/4362-7810
OPEN SUN. 12:30–5:30 P.M. (SHOW)
It's a rock venue Friday and Saturdays nights, but Mitos's Sunday-afternoon tango show coincides with the Feria de San Pedro Telmo, almost next door on Plaza Dorrego. Both male and female tango singers are accompanied by live guitar and/or recorded music, while dancers perform to recorded music. There is no cover charge, and the food and drink are reasonably priced.

The tango orchestra at Abasto's Esquina Carlos Gardel plays on an elevated stage above the dancers.

El Querandí   MONSERRAT

PERÚ 302, TEL. 011/5199-1770
OPEN NIGHTLY FROM 8:30 P.M.
WWW.QUERANDI.COM.AR

Dating from 1920, the Querandí is another *porteño* classic; for US$51 pp, the nightly dinner (starting at 9 P.M.) and show (starting at 10:15 P.M.) tend toward the upper end of the price scale, but it's a truly elegant place. The show itself is highly theatrical—some would say excessively so—but the musicians and actor/dancers are all outstanding. For the show alone, without dinner, admission costs US$38 pp.

Señor Tango   BARRACAS

VIEYTES 1655, TEL. 011/4303-0231
OPEN NIGHTLY FROM 8 P.M.
WWW.SENORTANGO.COM.AR

Seating more than 1,500 spectators, Señor Tango is an over-the-top spectacle, with up to 40 dancers and musicians—nothing of the intimate *milonga* here. Visitors pay US$67 pp for dinner and show, which starts at 8:30 P.M.; without dinner, the show, which starts at 10 P.M., costs US$40 pp (including two drinks). All prices include transportation to and from its theater in Barracas, some parts of which are considered dodgy, especially at night.

El Viejo Almacén   SAN TELMO

BALCARCE AND AVENIDA INDEPENDENCIA,
TEL. 011/4307-6689
OPEN NIGHTLY
WWW.VIEJO-ALMACEN.COM.AR

One of the barrio's classic tango venues, occupying a late-18th-century building that's been turned into a truly charming small theater seating 240 spectators, El Viejo Almacén also does one of the city's most elaborate floor shows (sometimes exaggeratedly so). It costs US$50 pp with an 8 P.M. dinner at its restaurant, just paces away on the opposite corner of Balcarce; the show alone, which starts at 10 P.M., costs US$35 pp. The best vantage points are from the hanging balconies.

© WAYNE BERNHARDSON

Palermo Viejo's Loco Berretín is a restaurant and wine bar presenting a vision of tango that's closer to the *milonga* than a glitzy floor show.

MILONGAS

For those who want to dance or learn tango instead of watch, the best options are neighborhood *milongas,* many of which take place at cultural centers. Organized events charge in the US$2–3 range with live orchestra, less with recorded music.

According to recent estimates, more than 60 *milongas* operate in the city, some of them several nights per week. Of those, about 60 percent are less than five years old. For the most current information on dates and times, check Buenos Aires Milongas (www.buenosairesmilonga.com).

For classes, a good clearinghouse is Monserrat's **Academia Nacional del Tango** (Avenida de Mayo 833, tel. 011/4345-6968, www.anacdeltango.org.ar), directly above Café Tortoni. For truly dedicated students, it even offers a three-year degree in tango as a cultural, social, and political phenomenon.

El Arranque
SAN NICOLÁS

MITRE 1759, TEL. 011/4371-6767
OPEN TUES.–THURS. 3–10 P.M., SAT. 3–9 P.M.

One of few venues built with tango in mind, with its ample stage and mosaic floor, this urbane salon features live music at least once a month. At the same time, it has many regulars who know each other and may be skeptical of strangers; tango's unwritten codes are in full force, and for that reason, it's not so easy to fit in. Still, it's popular for its easy accessibility from all parts of the city, modest cover charge (US$1–2), and inexpensive drinks.

 A Toda Milonga
MICROCENTRO

SUIPACHA 384, TEL. 011/4729-6390
OPEN THURS. 3–9 P.M.
WWW.DOMART.COM.AR/MARRAPODITANGO

Upstairs at the well-worn Confitería Ideal, this is one of B.A.'s least formal *milongas,* where amateurs can feel comfortable and

strangers are readily accepted (though without any particular solicitousness), and there's occasional live music. Also frequented by teachers, it's a good place to make arrangements for lessons; admission costs US$1.75 pp, as do group tango lessons. Instructor Osvaldo Marrapodi also offers Tuesday lessons here, 3–11 P.M., and individual lessons by appointment, as do recommended Diego Alvaro and Zaraida Fontclara.

Club Español
MONSERRAT

BERNARDO DE IRIGOYEN 172, TEL. 011/4201-7199
OPEN THURS. 4–11 P.M.

Possibly B.A.'s most elegant tango salon, the Club Español is an architectural classic with its burnished wood, gilt elevators, marble staircases, and red carpets—a place to see as much as dance. The afternoon schedule makes it suitable for visitors who don't care to pull an all-nighter, but serious *milongueros* can close up shop here, have dinner at its restaurant, and continue the night at nearby Niño Bien.

Club Gricel
SAN CRISTÓBAL

LA RIOJA 1180, TEL. 011/4957-7157
OPEN FRI.–SAT. FROM 11 P.M., SUN. FROM 9 P.M.

Frequented most by couples, so that it's not the best place to find a partner, Gricel offers live orchestra *milongas* Friday (admission US$2) and Saturday (admission US$1.50). Sunday, at 9:30 P.M., there's a cheaper event (US$1) with recorded music. With a fine parquet floor, it can hold up to 300 dancers.

Niño Bien
CONSTITUCIÓN

HUMBERTO PRIMO 1462, TEL. 15/4147-8687
OPEN THURS. 10:30 P.M.–4 A.M.

While it's in a rather dodgy neighborhood, Niño Bien occupies the spacious ballroom of the Centro Legión Leonesa, a fairly formal venue with parquet floors, cloth-covered tables and dark wooden chairs, and an older set of dancers who dress more elegantly than at some other venues. After 11 P.M., it can be tough to get a table, at least until it thins out at around 2 A.M. or so.

Dancers of all ages show their steps at a street *milonga* in Monserrat.

Arts and Leisure

Parakultural
PALERMO

SCALABRINI ORTIZ 1331, TEL. 011/4832-6753
OPEN MON., TUES., FRI. FROM 11 P.M.–4 A.M.
WWW.PARAKULTURAL.COM.AR

In the Salón Canning, a classic no-frills *milonga* venue with perhaps the best floor in the city, Parakultural draws a younger, less traditional clientele who find mixing tango with electronica unremarkable; but that young crowd can be cliquish. On other days, particularly Saturday, the Canning may host more conventional events with less adventurous but more agreeable participants.

La Shusheta
SAN TELMO

PIEDRAS 936, TEL. 011/4361-3537
OPEN WED. 10 P.M.–3 A.M.
WWW.MANSIONDANDIROYAL.COM

It's costly to stay at the tango-themed hotel next door, but anyone with the US$2 cover charge can test his or her steps at this weekly *milonga,* in a long, narrow ballroom on a century-old hardwood floor that can accommodate up to 100 dancers (50 couples). Tables line the north wall, while there's a bar at the east end, and a food menu as well.

Novices will appreciate that the staff make a special effort for everyone to feel welcome, but its relatively small size limits the room for errors. There's even less room when, once a month or so, a live trio takes the central stage, which, like a Murphy bed, pulls out of the south wall to eat up some of the dancing area.

FLAMENCO VENUES

As tango partisans, Argentines may feel ambivalence toward Spanish music and dance, but several *porteño* venues offer flamenco shows and even lessons, almost always on weekends (as opposed to tango shows, which take place every night of the week).

Tiempo de Gitanos
PALERMO

EL SALVADOR 5575, TEL. 011/4776-6143
OPEN WED.–SUN. FOR DINNER
WWW.TIEMPODEGITANOS.COM.AR

Run by a pair of documentary filmmakers—appropriately enough for its Palermo Hollywood location—Tiempo de Gitanos (Time of Gyp-

sies) is a restaurant that specializes in flamenco dinner shows in an intimate locale adorned with souvenirs of the owners' own extensive travels. The menu tends toward tapas and paella, with beef and pasta dishes to keep the more conservative *porteño* diners contented.

Shows take place at 9 P.M. most nights but 10 P.M. on weekends, for US$13–17 pp.

In Brief

Monserrat's classic **Ávila Bar** (Avenida de Mayo 1384, tel. 011/4383-6974) and San Telmo's tapas bar **Alarico** (Chile 518, tel. 011/4300-8810) also offer flamenco shows.

GAY SOCIAL VENUES

Buenos Aires has a vigorous gay scene, traditionally centered around Barrio Norte, where lots of gay men hang out on Avenida Santa Fe between Callao and Pueyrredón, especially on Friday and Saturday nights before going to clubs. Palermo Viejo is also popular; San Telmo is developing a higher profile; and there are other scattered gathering places and gay-oriented businesses throughout the city.

With only a few exceptions, gay hangouts lack signage and, during daylight hours, they're virtually invisible. A series of widely available freebie publications keeps up with the local scene, including the monthly *La Otra Guía,* the quarterly *Gay Map Buenos Aires,* and the quarterly *Circuitos Cortos Bs As Gay.*

Dance clubs and other venues are mostly tolerant and inclusive of heterosexuals; when non-Argentine heterosexual women tire of Argentine machismo, they sometimes prefer gay bars for dancing, but some *machista* males are catching on to this.

Amerika
ALMAGRO

GASCÓN 1040, TEL. 011/4865-4416
OPEN THURS.–SAT. 1–8 A.M.
WWW.AMERI-K.COM.AR

It may claim to be in Palermo, but Amerika lies just over the Almagro line—not that it makes much difference to the mixed crowd (mostly gay, but with more than a handful of hetero-sexuals) who flock here. There are three large but separate dance floors, one with electronica, another with Latin music, and yet another with 1980s pop. Saturdays and nights immediately before holidays, a US$5 cover includes all the beer you can drink.

Angel's
BALVANERA

VIAMONTE 2168
OPEN THURS.–SAT. 1–7 A.M.
WWW.DISCOANGELS.COM.AR

One of B.A.'s most durable gay locales, Angel's is also one of few to flaunt its orientation with a conspicuous sign. Some of B.A.'s gay community consider it "unrefined," with large numbers of transvestites, but it has its public. The music, as usual, is pulsing electronica.

Bach Bar
PALERMO

CABRERA 4390
OPEN TUES.–SUN. FROM 11 P.M.
WWW.BACH-BAR.COM.AR

Bach's is a gay male and lesbian hangout that doesn't advertise the fact—there's no sign, the windows are blacked out, and there's a heavy security door—but there's usually a crowd as well. Some nights, there's live entertainment, which is often participatory, including karaoke and drag.

Boicot
PALERMO VIEJO

BULNES 1250, TEL. 011/4861-7942
OPEN FRI.–SAT. FROM 10 P.M.

Having changed its name and its clientele, Boicot is now a women-only club in a comfortable, spacious locale with contemporary style and lighting. In fact, it's the reincarnation of an earlier bar, of the same name, that occupied a site in an obscure Barrio Norte passageway.

Palacio Buenos Aires
MONSERRAT

ALSINA 940
OPEN FRI. FROM 1 A.M., SUN. 7 P.M.–1:30 A.M.

In a cavernous ballroom, a former Orthodox church that became a warehouse and has been recycled, the Palacio draws a mostly young crowd for twice-weekly electronica (the early Sunday program almost seems like a *milonga* schedule, but most people don't arrive until after 10 P.M.); other nights, it's more for general audiences. Halloween night can be a real experience here.

Pride Café
SAN TELMO

BALCARCE 869, TEL. 011/4300-6435
OPEN DAILY 10 A.M.–10 P.M.

At the corner of Pasaje Giuffra, Pride Café is a bright, cheerful corner café that serves specialty drinks, including Irish coffee, plus sandwiches and loads of sweets, including brownies, chocolate cake, cookies, muffins, and strudel. There are also mixed drinks, and happy hours 7–9 P.M. nightly. While it gets a mixed audience of gays and straights, it stays open later on Thursday nights for gay-oriented live entertainment.

Search
BARRIO NORTE

AZCUÉNAGA 1007, TEL. 011/4824-0932
OPEN NIGHTLY FROM 11:30 P.M.

Not far from the weekend hot spot of Santa Fe and Pueyrredón, Search is a small but long-lived Barrio Norte gay bar with drag shows and strippers. Having undergone several name and ownership changes, it remains a durable, reliable venue even if its inconspicuous basement facilities lack the glitz of other places.

Sitges
PALERMO VIEJO

AVENIDA CÓRDOBA 4119, TEL. 011/4861-3763
OPEN WED.–SUN. FROM 10:30 P.M.
WWW.SITGESONLINE.COM.AR

On the edge of Palermo and one of B.A.'s most popular gay and lesbian bars, Sitges packs them into three large but distinct spaces, including an ample patio, almost until daybreak. It's known for drag shows, but also gets some mainstream entertainment (such as the Joplinesque rock singer Patricia Sosa) and celebrity clientele (such as burlesque diva Moria Casán). The US$2–3 cover charge varies according to the night and includes one drink.

Arts and Leisure

The Arts

Buenos Aires has a huge inventory of museums, which range from obscure to world-class. Several of them appear in the Sights chapter, as they are highlights that many visitors will want to see, but the ones that appear here have strong appeal among niche audiences.

MUSEUMS

Buque Museo   PUERTO MADERO
A.R.A. *Uruguay* Corbeta
DIQUE NO. 4, TEL. 011/4314-1090
OPEN DAILY 9 A.M.– 9 P.M.
WWW.IRIZAR.ORG/HISTOTEC.HTML

Built in Birkenhead (one of England's biggest shipbuilding ports) in 1874, this motorized corvette served mostly as a coastal patrol vessel and a training ship until 1902, when it was up for decomissioning. The apparent loss the next year of Otto Nordenskjöld's Swedish Antarctic expedition, however, on which the Argentine ensign José María Sobral was an officer, intervened. Under the command of Lt. (later Admiral) Julián Irízar, the reinforced and refitted *Uruguay* successfully rescued the expedition, marking the beginning of Argentina's Antarctic presence. (Note: Julián Irízar's namesake icebreaker helped rescue the crew of the stranded German supply vessel *Magdalena Oldendorff* in the austral winter of 2002.)

The oldest Argentine vessel still afloat, the *Uruguay* experienced years of abandonment until its two-year restoration began in 1953, on the 50th anniversary of its Antarctic mission. Declared a national monument in 1967, it was anchored in La Boca until the mid-1990s, when it moved to Puerto Madero.

Admission to the Buque Museo A.R.A. *Uruguay* Corbeta costs US$.35.

Buque Museo   PUERTO MADERO
Fragata A.R.A. *Presidente Sarmiento*
DIQUE NO. 3, TEL. 011/4334-9386
OPEN DAILY 9 A.M.–10 P.M.

Built in Birkenhead in 1887, the frigate *Sarmiento* takes its name from Domingo F. Sarmiento, the Argentine president who founded the country's Escuela Naval (Naval School) in 1872. Its bowsprit, an effigy of the patriotic symbol La Libertad Argentina (analogous to the U.S. Statue of Liberty), crowns an iron-framed 85-meter vessel with wooden siding and copper veneer. The frigate undertook 37 international training voyages from 1899 to 1938 and served in Argentine waters in 1960. It also served a diplomatic function, having represented the country at the coronations of Edward VII in England and of Alfonso XIII in Spain, the centenary of Mexican independence, and the opening of the Panama Canal, among other occasions.

So famous as to be the subject of an Argentine feature film, the *Sarmiento* is now a museum that honors the ship's commanders and crew—including the stuffed cadaver of its canine mascot, Lampazo. (Embalming of human bodies is rare in Argentina; the most notorious human case is Eva Perón's cadaver.)

Admission costs US$.35, but children under age five climb aboard for free.

Fundación Proa   LA BOCA
AVENIDA PEDRO DE MENDOZA 1929,
TEL. 011/4303-0909
OPEN DAILY EXCEPT MON. 11 A.M.–7 P.M.
WWW.PROA.ORG

For the most part, La Boca trades on nostalgia, but the Vuelta de Rocha's cavernous Fundación Proa has become an ultra-modern display space. In a recycled three-story Italianate house, it hosts rotating exhibitions by both Argentine and international artists. In addition to painting and sculpture, there are also displays of artisans' crafts and of photography. Occasional concerts and films also take place here.

On weekends, there are guided tours for individuals, in Spanish only; tours in English cost an additional US$25 for groups up to 25 persons and must be arranged in advance. Admission to the Fundación Proa costs US$1 for adults, US$.35 for children and seniors; children under age 12 accompanied by an adult do not pay.

Museo Casa de Yrurtia   BELGRANO

O'HIGGINS 2390, TEL. 011/4781-0385
OPEN TUES.–FRI. AND SUN. 3–7 P.M.

Influenced by Auguste Rodin, sculptor Rogelio Yrurtia (1879–1950) spent much of his career in Italy and France before returning to Buenos Aires in 1921. His signature work, *Canto al Trabajo* (Ode to Labor, 1923) on San Telmo's Plazoleta Olazábal, is a worthy antidote to the pompous equestrian statues that dominated decades of *porteño* public art.

Yrurtia designed, lived, and worked in this Mudéjar residence, which he intended as a museum for his sculptures and the paintings of his wife, Lía Correa Morales; on his death, he donated the house and his works to the state.

In addition to family creations, there are some works from other artists, most notably Picasso's painting *Rue Cortot, Paris.* The garden features Yrurtia's oversized *The Boxers,* which appeared at the 1904 St. Louis World's Fair.

Admission to the Museo Casa de Yrurtia costs US$.35. Guided tours, at no additional expense, take place Sunday at 5 P.M.

Museo de Armas de la Nación   RETIRO

AVENIDA SANTA FE 702,
TEL. 011/4311-1072, EXT. 179
OPEN WEEKDAYS 1–6:30 P.M.
WWW.CIRCULOMILITAR.ORG/WEB2/MUSEO.HTM

A field day for gun fetishists and other weapons zealots, the army's museum showcases arms and armor from medieval and colonial Europe, firearms from the 15th century on, antique artillery, and a few more events-oriented items: a diorama of the 1807 British landing at Ensenada de Barragán prior to the occupation of Buenos Aires, photographs of General Julio Argentino Roca's genocidal *Campaña del Desierto* (Desert Campaign) against the northern Patagonia Mapuche in the late 19th century, and a nod to the Falklands War, in which the Argentines seem to have produced an inordinate number of heroes for forces that lost so badly. There is also a roomful of antique Asian—mostly Japanese—weapons and armor.

The controversial General Roca himself founded the museum in 1904. All the exhibits are well presented and labeled, though like many Argentine museums this one is short on interpretation. Admission costs US$.70.

Museo de Arte Moderno   SAN TELMO

AVENIDA SAN JUAN 350, TEL. 011/4361-1121
OPEN TUES.–FRI. 10 A.M.–8 P.M.,
WEEKENDS AND HOLIDAYS 11 A.M.–8 P.M.
WWW.AAMAMBA.ORG.AR

San Telmo's modern art museum showcases contemporary Argentine artists in a spacious converted warehouse with high ceilings; exhibits tend toward the abstract, with works from figures like Antonio Berni, León Ferrari, and Kenneth Kemble.

Admission costs about US$.35 but is free Wednesdays; guided tours take place daily except Monday at 5 P.M. It's closed in January.

In Belgrano's Museo Casa de Yrurtia, *The Boxers* is an example of the work of one of Argentina's most innovative 20th-century sculptors.

© WAYNE BERNHARDSON

Arts and Leisure

Museo de Artes Plásticas Eduardo Sívori

PALERMO

AVENIDA INFANTA ISABEL 555,
TEL. 011/4772-5628
OPEN TUES.–FRI. NOON–8 P.M.,
SAT.–SUN. 10 A.M.–8 P.M.
WWW.MUSEOSIVORI.ORG.AR

Shifted from downtown's Centro Cultural San Martín in 1995, the Museo Sívori occupies a Bavarian-style house (1912) with a newer cement-block annex designed specifically for painting and sculpture, along with a separate sculpture garden. Argentine artists whose works are on display include Ernesto de la Cárcova, Lino Spilimbergo, and Luis Seoanes; there are also special exhibitions in other fields, such as photography.

Admission costs US$1, but is free Wednesdays.

Museo de Esculturas Luis Perlotti

CABALLITO

PUJOL 644, TEL. 011/4433-3396
OPEN TUES.–FRI. 11 A.M.–7 P.M., WEEKENDS AND
HOLIDAYS 10 A.M.–1 P.M. AND 2 P.M.–8 P.M.

Luis Perlotti (1890–1969), an Italo-Argentine who traveled widely in the Andean highland countries of Peru and Bolivia, adapted the themes from those early American civilizations into exceptional *indigenista* sculptures, with strong social content but realist and naturalistic style. A friend and contemporary of La Boca painter Benito Quinquela Martín, Perlotti and his wife donated their Caballito house, along with about 1,000 pieces of his and others' works, to the city.

Despite its out-of-the-way location, this municipally run museum is a worthwhile detour. Admission costs US$.35, but is free Wednesdays.

Museo de la Policía Federal

MICROCENTRO

SAN MARTÍN 353, 7TH FL., TEL. 011/4394-6857
OPEN TUES.–FRI. 2–6 P.M.

It's faint but fair praise to say that Argentina's federal police are the country's most scrupulous police, if only because provincial forces are seemingly corrupt beyond salvation. This museum tells only part of the story: It focuses on material items like uniforms, badges, and weapons over the centuries, as well as the force's role in monitoring and controlling gambling, robbery, drugs, counterfeiting, con artists, and faith healers. There is also a truly gruesome room dedicated to forensic medicine, which includes dismembered bodies and other unpleasant sights.

Still, the museum is as notable for what it excludes as for what it includes. There is only the briefest mention of its repressive role in events like the 1920s anarchist uprisings and the 1970s Dirty War. The museum gives no attention to the issue of police corruption—even if the feds are virtual angels compared to the Buenos Aires provincial police, they still have plenty to answer for.

Admission is free. Children under age 16, as well as the very squeamish of any age, are not permitted in the goriest exhibits.

Museo del Cabildo

MONSERRAT

BOLÍVAR 65, TEL. 011/4343-4387
OPEN WED.–FRI. 11:30 A.M.–6 P.M., SAT. 2–6 P.M.,
SUN. 3–7 P.M.

The Plaza de Mayo's only remaining colonial structure, the Cabildo was a combination town council and prison, and the site where *criollo* patriots deposed Spanish viceroy Baltasar Hidalgo de Cisneros in 1810. The present structure preserves part of the *recova* (arcade) that once extended across the plaza.

Unfortunately, the museum itself is thin on content—a few maps, paintings, and photographs of the plaza and its surroundings, along with a portrait gallery of figures in the British invasions of 1806–1807, and the Revolution of May 1810. The real star is the building; thankfully, part of it, at least, survived 19th-century mayor Torcuato de Alvear's wrecking ball, which created the Avenida de Mayo to connect the Casa Rosada with the Congreso Nacional.

Admission costs US$.35. The interior has a small *confitería* and occasionally hosts live music events.

Museo del Cine Pablo A. Ducrós Hicken
SAN TELMO

DEFENSA 1220, TEL. 011/4361-2462
OPEN WEEKDAYS 10 A.M.–6 P.M.,
WEEKENDS NOON–6 P.M.
WWW.MUSEOS.BUENOSAIRES.GOV.AR/
MUSEODELCINE/INTRO.HTML

In recent years, the Argentine movie museum has devoted space to special exhibits, such as 1974, a key year in cinema with the death of Perón and the chaos that led to military dictatorship; comedians and comedy in the country's movies over the last century; and movie posters. Permanent displays stress topics like film technology, including a collection of antique cameras, and there's a small cinema that shows Argentine classics for free (no subtitles, though, and on the oldest films, the soundtrack can be difficult even for those with a command of *porteño* Spanish).

Around the corner from the modern art museum, the Museo del Cine also contains a library on Argentine cinema. Admission is US$.35 except Wednesdays, when it's free.

Museo del Traje
SAN TELMO

CHILE 832, TEL. 011/4343-8427
OPEN TUES.–SAT. 4–8 P.M.

Buenos Aires's Museo del Traje (Museum of Dress) might more accurately be called the Museo de Moda (Museum of Fashion), as it concentrates largely (though not exclusively) on women's clothing from colonial times to the present. In a middle-class *casa chorizo* (sausage house, so called because of its deep, narrow lot), the museum features three large patios typical of the mid-19th century; part of the building still awaits restoration.

Admission to the Museo del Traje is free, but donations are welcome.

Museo Etnográfico Juan B. Ambrosetti
MONSERRAT

MORENO 350, TEL. 011/4331-7788
OPEN WED.–SUN. 3–7 P.M.
WWW.MUSEOETNOGRAFICO.FILO.UBA.AR

Affiliated with the Universidad de Buenos Aires, the city's ethnographic museum has first-rate archaeological, ethnographic, and ethnohistorical material on Argentina's Andean northwest (on the periphery of the great civilizations of highland Peru), northern Patagonia's Mapuche, and the Tierra del Fuego archipelago. Well organized, with good narration in Spanish only, it does a lot with what it has—and what it has is pretty good.

Admission to the Museo Etnográfico costs US$.35, but retirees get in free. There are guided tours Saturday and Sunday at 4 P.M.; for English or French, it's necessary to make an advance request.

Museo Forense de la Morgue Judicial Dr. Juan Bautista Bafico
BALVANERA

JUNÍN 760, TEL. 011/4344-2035
OPEN WEEKDAYS 9 A.M.–2 P.M.

Definitely not for the squeamish, the Forensic Museum of the Morgue is primarily a resource for students from the nearby medical school. It consists of a single large hall filled with glass cases displaying mutilated body parts from famous criminal cases or suicides (some of the remains are from tattooed prisoners).

Though it's not quite so grisly as that description might sound, the Museo de la Morgue has a serious purpose and is thus not open to casual drop-ins. It's for groups of 10 or more, but by phoning at least a day ahead between 10 A.M. and 3 P.M., it's possible to join an existing group.

Admission is free; photography is prohibited. It's closed in January, February, and March.

Museo Histórico Brigadier General Cornelio de Saavedra
SAAVEDRA

CRISÓLOGO LARRALDE 6309, TEL. 011/4572-0746
OPEN TUES.–FRI. 9 A.M.–6 P.M.,
WEEKENDS AND HOLIDAYS 2–6 P.M.

Focusing on 19th-century Argentina, this historical museum occupies the grounds of the onetime rural estate of Luis María Saavedra, nephew of independence hero Cornelio de Saavedra. Expropriated after 1929, the property came under municipal control as the Parque General Paz; the building, "modified for authenticity," became a museum in 1941.

Arts and Leisure

Permanent museum exhibits include silverwork from the private collection of Ricardo Zemborain (1872–1912), who willed his possessions to the city; gems, coins, clothing, and furniture from the 18th and 19th centuries; and fashion accessories, such as *peinetones* (ornamental combs). Thematically, it covers events of the independence era and the early Argentine confederation.

The Museo Saavedra also functions as a cultural center, hosting concerts, films, and dance and theater events. Guided tours take place weekends and holidays at 4 P.M. Admission costs US$.35, but is free on Wednesday.

Museo Houssay de Ciencia y Tecnología
BARRIO NORTE

PARAGUAY 2155, 1ST FLOOR,
TEL. 011/5950-9500, EXT. 2102
OPEN WEEKDAYS NOON–4 P.M.
WWW.FMED.UBA.AR/DEPTO/HISTOMED/
HOUSSAY.HTM

This small but engaging museum at the UBA's Facultad de Medicina contains primarily educational and experimental equipment, instruments, and documents relating to Argentine medicine. Presently undergoing a long-overdue reorganization, it takes its name from physiologist Bernardo Houssay, the son of French immigrants and winner of the 1947 Nobel Prize in medicine. The museum also features some remarkable scientific curiosities, including an extraordinary German-built mechanical model of the eye dating from the late 19th century.

The Museo Houssay is only open when the university is in session. Houssay's residence, also a museum, is nearby in Once.

Museo Libero Badii
PALERMO

11 DE SEPTIEMBRE 1990, TEL. 011/4783-3819
OPEN WEEKDAYS 10 A.M.–6 P.M.

After the fall of Rosas, jurist Valentín Alsina acquired the property overlooking Barrancas de Belgrano for his *quinta* or country house, but it soon passed into the hands of the Atucha family, which built the 1870s Italian Renaissance house that survives, amid high-rises, to house this unique museum. The wildly imaginative Italian-born Badii, a naturalized Argentine, specialized in sculpture, engraving, design, collage, and illustration.

Operated under the auspices of the Fundación Banco Francés, the Museo Badii also offers special exhibits. Admission is free; ring the bell for entry.

Museo Nacional de Arte Decorativo
PALERMO

AVENIDA DEL LIBERTADOR 1902, TEL. 011/4802-6606
OPEN TUES.–SAT. 2–7 P.M.
WWW.MNAD.ORG.AR

Works ranging from Roman sculptures to contemporary silverwork, but mostly Asian and European pieces from the 17th to 19th centuries, fill the ornate four-story beaux arts residence (1918) that now houses the national museum of decorative art. Many of its 4,000-plus items are anonymous; the best-known artists are Europeans like Manet and Rodin.

Both the building and the collections once belonged to Chilean diplomat Matías Errázuriz Ortúzar and his Argentine wife Josefina de Alvear de Errázuriz, who lived less than 20 years in the house. After her death, the Errázuriz family sold both the building and the collections to the state.

Admission to the Museo de Arte Decorativo costs US$.70 except Tuesdays, when it's free. It normally closes the first two weeks of January.

Museo Nacional del Grabado
MONSERRAT

DEFENSA 372, TEL. 011/4345-5300
OPEN DAILY EXCEPT SAT. 2–6 P.M.

Occupying the Casa de la Defensa, from which *porteños* routed British invaders in 1806–1807 by pouring boiling oil and water from the roof, Buenos Aires's museum of engraving owns 15,000 works by Argentine and foreign artists including Dalí, Picasso, and Siqueiros. Its mission, though, is to present rotating exhibits, often of very high quality, from Argentine artists in the medium.

Admission to the Museo Nacional del Grabado costs US$.35, but is free on Sunday.

Museo Nacional del Hombre
PALERMO

3 DE FEBRERO 1370, TEL. 011/4784-9971
OPEN WEEKDAYS 10 A.M.–8 P.M.
WWW.INAPL.GOV.AR/MUSEO.HTM

Small but well-maintained and -organized, the Museo Nacional del Hombre (National Museum of Man) is a modest but worthy complement to Monserrat's larger and more elaborate Museo Etnográfico. Providing information on the prehistory and contemporary status of Argentina's indigenous peoples, it could use more detailed maps of individual group territories, but its 5,000 pieces are a fine representative sample of indigenous material culture.

Part of the Instituto Nacional de Antropología y Pensamiento Latinoamericano, a research and training institute, the Museo Nacional del Hombre charges US$.35 admission. The museum shop has a small but excellent crafts selection.

Museo Penitenciario Argentino Antonio Ballvé
SAN TELMO

HUMBERTO PRIMO 378, TEL. 011/4362-0099
OPEN WED. AND FRI. 2–6 P.M., SUN. 2–7 P.M.
WWW.SPF.JUS.GOV.AR/MUSEO.HTM

Once poorly organized, Buenos Aires's penal museum has undergone recent improvements, and now includes thematic exhibits including cell doors from various prisons throughout time and typically outfitted cells, including one from the women's prison this once was. From a historical perspective, the most intriguing items are photographs, including Anarchist Simón Radowitzky's release from the world's most southerly prison at Ushuaia, in Tierra del Fuego, and an elaborate wooden desk that Ushuaia inmates carved for Roberto M. Ortiz (no doubt to show their affection) during his 1938–1942 presidency. Note the large wooden apothecary cabinet in the same room as Ortiz's desk.

Half a block east of Plaza Dorrego, the museum occupies the former convent wing of the **Iglesia Nuestra Señora de Belén** (1750), a colonial structure that has experienced several remodelings; taken over by Bethlemites after the Jesuit expulsion of 1767, it became a men's prison under secular President Bernardino Rivadavia and then a women's house of detention until 1978.

Still lacking interpretive materials, the Museo Penitenciario is not worth a special trip, but can justify a stop if you're nearby during its limited hours. Admission costs US$.35.

Museo Xul Solar
BARRIO NORTE

LAPRIDA 1212, TEL. 011/4824-3302
OPEN TUES.–FRI. NOON–7 P.M., SAT. NOON–6 P.M.
WWW.XULSOLAR.ORG.AR

Obsessed with architecture and the occult, Alejandro Schulz Solari (1897–1963) was an abstract painter who produced vivid oils and watercolors. During his lifetime, his work showed in Buenos Aires, Brazil, France, and Italy; after his death, it also appeared in Miami, New York, London, Madrid, Stockholm, and other European cities. Despite his own blindness, Jorge Luis Borges left vivid descriptions of the works of his friend and contemporary, better known as Xul Solar.

The Xul Solar museum displays a large assortment of his work, mostly smallish watercolors, in utilitarian surroundings with sheetrocked walls and relatively dim light that contrast dramatically with the painter's intense colors. It also shows personal effects, such as postcards directed to famous writers like Nietzsche.

Admission to the Museo Xul Solar costs US$1 except for children under age 12 and retired persons, who pay only US$.35. It closes in the summer months of January and February.

Planetario Galileo Galilei
PALERMO

AVENIDA SARMIENTO AND BELISARIO ROLDÁN,
TEL. 011/4771-6629
OPEN WEEKDAYS 9 A.M.–5 P.M.,
WEEKENDS 1–7:30 P.M.
WWW.PLANETARIO.GOV.AR

Since it opened in 1967, Buenos Aires's planetarium has introduced more than 10 million visitors, mostly school children, to the night skies projected on its interior dome in a 360-seat auditorium. It also has a telescope for

Arts and Leisure

viewing the stars directly. There is a small artificial lake outside, the **Lago del Planetario.**

Admission to the Planetario is free except for guided tours (US$1.35 pp), which take place at 3, 4:30, and 6 P.M. weekends and holidays. Children under age five and retired persons get in free.

In Brief

Occupying part of the former Hotel Majestic, the **Museo y Archivo Histórico de la Dirección General Impositiva** (Avenida de Mayo 1317, 5th fl., tel. 011/4384-0282) focuses on the theme of taxation in a country renowned for money laundering and similar subterfuges. Alternatively known as the Museo de la Administración Federal de Ingresos Públicos, it's open 11 A.M.–5 P.M. weekdays only. Admission is free.

Bernardo Houssay, Argentina's 1947 Nobel Prize winner in physiology, resided at what is now Balvanera's **Casa Museo Bernardo A. Houssay** (Viamonte 2790, tel. 011/4961-8748, open 2–6 P.M. weekdays only), near the Facultad de Medicina Subte station.

Palermo's **Casa Museo Evaristo Carriego** (Honduras 3784, tel. 011/4963-2194, open 10 A.M.–6 P.M. weekdays only) was the residence of a *porteño* poet and Borges contemporary who died young (1883–1912).

GALLERIES

Buenos Aires has a thriving modern art scene, with the most innovative galleries in Retiro and Recoleta. Some dealers still focus on European-style works, but these will probably be of little interest to visitors, as they fail to indicate the vitality of contemporary Argentine art. The best dealers have outstanding websites that make it possible to preview their work.

Galería Federico Klemm   RETIRO

MARCELO T. DE ALVEAR 636, TEL. 011/4312-4443
OPEN WEEKDAYS 11 A.M.–8 P.M.
WWW.FUNDACIONFJKLEMM.ORG

The legacy of the Czech-born Federico Klemm, a flamboyant figure who died in 2002, this gallery at the north end of the Florida pedestrian mall is particularly good at giving young artists a jump start

through annual competitions. It's possible to get an idea of Klemm's tastes through his former TV program (www.klemmtv.com), which is now online. The gallery closes for two weeks in January.

⋈ Galería Rubbers   RECOLETA

AVENIDA ALVEAR 1595, TEL. 011/4816-1864
OPEN WEEKDAYS 10:30 A.M.–9 P.M.,
SAT. 10 A.M.–1 P.M.
WWW.RUBBERS.COM.AR

Recently moved to Recoleta, Rubbers is a contemporary gallery that's worked with modern Argentine painters, such as Antonio Berni and Xul Solar, but also with photographers, such as Aldo Sessa. They've also led the way with other Latin American artists, having been the first to exhibit Uruguay's Pedro Figari in Buenos Aires (shortly after opening in 1957), and gave the now-famous Colombian painter Fernando Botero his first contract (in 1964).

Galería Ruth Benzacar   RETIRO

FLORIDA 1000, TEL. 011/4313-8480
OPEN WEEKDAYS 11:30 A.M.–8 P.M.,
SAT. 10:30 A.M.–1:30 P.M.
WWW.RUTHBENZACAR.COM

Accessed by an inconspicuous staircase at the Florida pedestrian mall's north end, the Benzacar gallery is a bright, uncluttered subterranean space that showcases some of the capital's and the country's most avant-garde artists. Founded in 1965, it made an early-1990s list of the world's 200 best galleries, and has earned an international reputation in promoting the works of figures like Antonio Berni and León Ferrari. It also makes a point of selecting young, talented artists for their commercial debut.

Galería Vermeer   RETIRO

SUIPACHA 1168, TEL. 011/4393-5102
OPEN WEEKDAYS 11 A.M.–7 P.M., SAT. 11 A.M.–2 P.M.
WWW.GALERIAVERMEER.COM.AR

In business since 1973, perhaps not quite so avant garde as Galerí Rubbers, Vermeer is still a quality gallery that has hosted exhibitions by contemporary artists, such as Berni, Raquel Forner, Lino Spilimbergo, Xul Solar, and the Uruguayan Joaquín Torres García.

THE REBIRTH OF FILETE

The flamboyant folk art called *filete* began with Sicilian immigrants whose horse carts were art on wheels. Their symmetrical ornamental lines, enriched by elaborate calligraphy, simulated the moldings and wrought-iron ornamentation on late-19th and early-20th-century buildings—the word *filete* derives from the Italian *filetto,* meaning a strip that separates moldings.

Gradually, the Argentine capital's *fileteadores* made their craft the standard for commercial sign painting, as it drew attention to fixed businesses like restaurants, cafés, and a variety of other services. It suffered, though, during the dark days of the Proceso dictatorship (1976–1983), when the generals banned it from public transportation for its alleged unreadability. Since the return to representative government, though, *filete* has made a comeback, and skilled *fileteadores* can make a handsome living.

To see ready-made decorative plaques, visit Plaza Dorrego's Sunday Feria de San Pedro Telmo, where typical themes and subjects are tango (and tango legend Carlos Gardel), plus skillfully drawn dragons, flowers, and fruits. Many of these plaques display *piropos* (aphorisms or proverbs).

Perhaps typical of contemporary *fileteadores* is Martiniano Arce, whose San Telmo studio is literally a memorial to his craft—he has already chosen and painted his and his wife's coffins and keeps them on display in his house. He does not shy away from commercial work, saying that his art is incomplete until

Filete painter Martiniano Arce of San Telmo has decorated his own casket—and his wife's.

© WAYNE BERNHARDSON

Arts and Leisure

someone owns it—in addition to the cover for rock band Fabulosos Cadillacs' *Fabulosos Calavera* CD, he has commemorated the 10th anniversary of McDonald's in Argentina with a custom design and even painted a symbolic bottle for Coca-Cola.

For information on purchasing *filete* from markets and directly from artisans such as Arce, see the *Shopping* chapter.

Galería Zurbarán　　　　RETIRO
CERRITO 1522, TEL. 011/4815-1556
OPEN WEEKDAYS 10:30 A.M.–9 P.M.,
SAT. 10 A.M.–1 P.M.
WWW.ZURBARANGALERIA.COM.AR

While Zurbarán may not be one of B.A.'s most adventurous galleries, it's had an impressive roster of exhibitions and its website has abundant information on contemporary Argentine artists, including the *gauch-* esco caricaturist Florencio Molina Campos. It also has a separate showroom called Colección Alvear de Zurbarán (Avenida Alvear 1658, Recoleta, tel. 011/4811-3004).

THEATER

Though the last few years of economic hardship have taken the luster off some of its venues, Buenos Aires remains the theater capital of the continent. Avenida Corrientes is the traditional locus of live theater, and city administration hopes that widening the sidewalks between Avenida 9 de Julio and Avenida Callao will draw pedestrians back to the area and help restore this tradition. Meanwhile, it's still worth seeking out less conventional alternatives.

Avenida de Mayo and myriad Microcentro side streets are also home to important theaters, several of them historic. At the same time, many smaller and less conventional "off-Corrientes" venues, some of which might be called micro-theaters, add diversity. For the latest information on those, check the website Alternativa Teatral (www.alternativateatral.com).

Ranging from vulgar burlesque with elaborate stage shows to Shakespearean and avant garde drama, the theater scene is busiest June–August. The difference between traditional theaters and shoestring venues is not so much the quality of acting as the production budget; larger budgets allow much more elaborate sets at larger venues. The biggest productions can even move intact to the Atlantic beach resort of Mar del Plata for the summer.

Winter is the principal theater season, but events can take place at any time of year. For discount tickets, check carteleras or online ticket-purchasing services. All major porteño newspapers, including Ámbito Financiero, the Buenos Aires Herald, Clarín, La Nación, and Página 12, provide extensive listings and schedules.

Centro Latinoamericano de Creación e Investigación Teatral   SAN TELMO

BOLÍVAR 825, TEL. 011/4361-8358
WWW.CELCIT.ORG.AR

Known more conveniently by its acronym Celcit, this innovative theater and educational institution produces plays by modern and contemporary Latin American dramatists, such as Argentina's late Roberto Arlt and Chile's Marco Antonio de la Parra. As a company, they often take their show on the road to other Latin American locales, as far away as Mexico and Puerto Rico; the theater itself also hosts a variety of musical events.

© WAYNE BERNHARDSON

Omar Gasparini created the public mural *Escenográfico* for La Boca's Catalinas Sur theater group.

LiberArte   MICROCENTRO

AVENIDA CORRIENTES 1555, TEL. 011/4375-2341
WWW.LIBERARTETEATRO.COM.AR

Liberarte is a politically and socially conscious bookstore that also offers theater programs, mostly on weekends but occasionally on weeknights. In addition to stage plays, improv, and standup comedy, it also hosts dance (including tango) and even children's programs (at relatively early hours, around 5–6 P.M.).

Teatro Catalinas Sur   LA BOCA

BENITO PÉREZ GALDÓS 93, TEL. 011/4300-5707
WWW.CATALINASUR.COM.AR

To appreciate Catalinas Sur, a community theater group that illuminates the experience of working-class European immigrants, it's unnecessary to understand a single word of Spanish. So visual is their approach (Omar Gasparini's sets are almost psychedelically imaginative), and so expressive are the non-professional actors, singers, and musicians, the language is only secondary. Understanding *porteño* Spanish may enrich the experience of repertory works like *Venimos de Muy Lejos* (We Came from Far Away) and *El Fulgor Argentino* (a century of Argentine history through the experience of a neighborhood sports and social club), but it's not essential.

Catalinas Sur normally has Friday and Saturday night shows, but also appears in parks around the barrio and vicinity. Take a cab to the theater, a recycled warehouse in a dark and deserted part of La Boca (though plenty of people are around at show time).

Teatro de la Ribera   LA BOCA
PEDRO DE MENDOZA 1821, TEL. 011/4302-8866
WWW.TEATROSANMARTIN.COM.AR

Before his death in 1977, La Boca artist and promoter Benito Quinquela Martín donated the building that serves as headquarters for the La Boca theater group Teatro de la Ribera. Since then, it's become part of the municipal Teatro San Martin complex. Its programs tend toward works by playwrights like the politically committed Italian Nobel Prize winner Dario Fo. It also has a gallery for art exhibits, including photography.

Teatro General   MICROCENTRO
San Martín
AVENIDA CORRIENTES 1530, TEL. 011/4371-0111
WWW.TEATROSANMARTIN.COM.AR

B.A.'s single most notable theater facility, the San Martín is a multipurpose complex whose diversity of offerings helps compensate for its lack of architectural merit. Covering more than 30,000 square meters, this utilitarian building (1961) has three main auditoria, a cinema, exhibition halls, and other facilities that draw up to one million visitors per year. Students with international ID cards get 50 percent discounts for most shows, and there are many free events, as well.

Teatro Nacional Cervantes   RETIRO
LIBERTAD 815, TEL. 011/4815-8883
WWW.TEATROCERVANTES.GOV.AR

Dating from 1921, the plateresque Cervantes was originally a private initiative but, when its Spanish owners fell into financial problems, the Argentine government took it over to create a national theater. After suffering an early-1960s fire, it underwent a major renovation/expansion and now holds three separate theaters, most notably the 860-seat Sala María Guerrero. The others hold 150 and 120 seats, respectively.

While the theater still pays homage to its famous Spanish namesake by presenting his classics, most offerings now lean toward 20th-century Argentine playwrights. The building is also home to the Museo Nacional del Teatro (National Theater Museum), open 10 A.M.–6 P.M. weekdays.

In Brief

Administratively part of the Teatro San Martín complex, but a block north on the opposite side of the street, the **Teatro Presidente Alvear** (Avenida Corrientes 1659, tel. 011/4374-6076, www.teatrosanmartin.org.ar) is more attuned to popular musical revues. The **Multiteatro** (Avenida Corrientes 1283, tel. 011/4382-9140) has far smaller, character-driven productions, while the **Teatro del Pueblo** (Diagonal Norte 943, tel. 011/4326-3606, www.teatrodelpueblo.org.ar) is a company with a social conscience.

There are several smaller and less conventional "off-Corrientes" venues, some of which might be called micro-theaters—the three stages at **Teatro El Vitral** (Rodríguez Peña 344, tel. 011/4371-0948) seat 36–180 patrons.

Some companies lack regular venues in the strictest sense—they may appear spontaneously or rent theaters to put on their productions. Less conventional groups to watch for include **Teatreros Ambulantes Los Calandracas** (California 1732, Barracas, tel. 011/4302-6285) and **Teatro Callejero La Runfla** (Pasaje La Selva 4022, Vélez Sarsfield, tel. 011/4672-5708).

These groups often literally take it to the streets, performing in parks and other public venues, but the **Grupo Teatral Escena Subterránea** (tel. 011/4777-8599) takes it beneath the streets, performing in Subte cars and stations.

Arts and Leisure

CONCERT VENUES

The classical music and opera season lasts March–November but peaks in winter, June–August.

La Scala de San Telmo · SAN TELMO

PASAJE GIUFFRA 371, TEL. 011/4362-1187 OR 011/4813-5741
WWW.LASCALA.COM.AR

High culture and popular culture, of a sort, meet at this intimate performing-arts locale, in an artfully restored colonial house. While its name suggests a classical orientation, La Scala actively seeks and encourages up-and-coming talent in folk, jazz, and tango music. Part of an institution that also trains aspiring performers, it even records and distributes their efforts through its website.

While it's not a casual venue—jeans, sandals, and T-shirts are not appropriate here—La Scala is not stiffly formal either. After each show, spectators and performers mix in its cozy bar, which serves empanadas, pizza, wine, soft drinks, and coffee. Program days and times vary, but most are around 8 or 9 P.M. from Thursday to Sunday.

Teatro Avenida · MONSERRAT

AVENIDA DE MAYO 1222, TEL. 011/4381-3193

Second only to the Colón as an opera venue, the Teatro Avenida will celebrate its centennial in 2008, though this stunning Hispanophile theater sat empty for 15 years after a 1979 fire gutted its interior. When the famed Spanish dramatist Federico García Lorca came to Buenos Aires in 1933, his classic *Bodas de Sangre* (Blood Wedding) played here.

While it owes its origins to a taste for the Spanish light opera form *zarzuela,* it also hosts flamenco programs and even the occasional hybrid: Accompanied by a 40-strong orchestra, former Soda Stereo rock guitarist Gustavo Cerati debuted symphonic versions of 11 of the group's hits here in 2003.

Teatro Colón · MICROCENTRO

LIBERTAD 621, TEL. 011/4378-7344
WWW.TEATROCOLON.ORG.AR

Unquestionably, the capital's prime classical music locale remains the Colón, though the recent economic crisis meant increasing reliance on Argentines rather than high-profile foreigners (performers such as Luciano Pavarotti and Plácido Domingo have often graced the Colón's stage). At the same time, internationally known figures with local links, such as the Buenos Aires–born Israeli conductor Daniel Barenboim, have made special efforts here.

Among other performers that play the Colón are the Orquesta Filarmónica de Buenos Aires (www.eldorado.org.ar/ofba)—often with guest conductors from elsewhere in Latin America—and the Mozarteum Argentina (www.mozarteumargentino.org). Occasionally, there is a surprise, such as the rhythm-and-blues unit Memphis La Blusera, the first of its sort to take

After the Teatro Colón, Monserrat's Teatro Avenida is the capital's most prestigious performing arts venue.

© WAYNE BERNHARDSON

facade of the Teatro Colón, home to the Buenos Aires opera

the hallowed stage, in conjunction with the Orquesta Sinfónica Nacional.

The Colón is due to close for much of 2006 for needed repairs. (For more information on the theater, see the *Sights* chapter.)

Teatro Margarita Xirgú   SAN TELMO
CHACABUCO 863/875, TEL. 011/4300-2448
WWW.MXIRGU.COM.AR

In a magnificent neo-Gothic building that was once the Spanish consulate, the Margarita Xirgú is the performing-arts arm of the Casal de Catalunya cultural center, with offerings ranging from ballet to big bands, flamenco, and even opera. The wildly comedic (but musically serious) band Les Luthiers made their debut here, and the famous Catalan singer Joan Manuel Serrat has also performed on its stage.

In addition to its cultural and entertainment programs, the Xirgú complex has an outstanding restaurant.

CINEMA

Buenos Aires's traditional commercial cinema district is in the Microcentro along the Lavalle pedestrian mall west of Florida and along Avenida Corrientes and Avenida Santa Fe. In addition, there are multiplexes in the shopping malls of Puerto Madero, Retiro, and Palermo, and clusters of cinemas in the outer barrios, such as Belgrano.

Imported films generally appear in the original language with Spanish subtitles, except for animated and children's movies, which are dubbed into the local language (Cine Los Angeles specializes in these). Translations of foreign-language titles are often misleading, but the *Buenos Aires Herald* prints the original English title and translations of other foreign-language titles.

Because of devaluation, ticket prices have fallen to US$3–4 for first-run movies. Most cinemas offer half-price discounts Monday–Wednesday, and sometimes for the afternoon shows on other days. On Friday and Saturday nights, there is usually a *trasnoche* (midnight or later) showing, but even on weeknights there may be shows beginning as late as 11 P.M.

The following listings generally include cinemas that show Argentine and other foreign films, rather than multiplexes showing first-run

Hollywood features; the latter are easy to locate in the *Buenos Aires Herald* and other daily newspapers. Independent films or reprises of commercial films generally show at cultural centers or smaller venues scattered around town.

Balvanera

The two-screen **Cine Cosmos** (Avenida Corrientes 2046, tel. 011/4953-5405, www.cinecosmos.com) shows up to four different films, mostly European (Bergman is a favorite) and Latin American, on any given day.

Microcentro

The Instituto Nacional de Cine y Artes Visuales (www.incaa.org.ar) operates two central cinemas that promote mostly Argentine films: the four-screen **Complejo Tita Merello** (Suipacha 442, tel. 011/4322-1195) and the three-screen **Cine Gaumont** (Rivadavia 1635, tel. 011/4371-3050).

At the Teatro San Martín's **Sala Leopoldo Lugones** (Avenida Corrientes 1530, 10th floor, tel. 011/4371-0111, www.teatrosanmartin.org.ar), Werner Herzog is about as mainstream as it gets—most of its offerings and retrospectives tend toward obscure French, Italian, and even Korean films, but there are some real gems among these.

The two-screen **Complejo Cine Lorca** (Avenida Corrientes 1428, tel. 011/4371-5017) shows mostly European films and the occasional off-center Hollywood flick (in the *Bad Santa* vein). The three-screen **Cine Metro** (Cerrito 570, tel. 011/4382-4219) has similar offerings, but occasionally shows some of the better commercial Hollywood fare.

The three-screen **Cine Premier** (Avenida Corrientes 1565, tel. 011/4374-2113) is more strictly commercial, but usually has at least one indie-type film on the docket.

The three-screen **Cine Los Angeles** (Avenida Corrientes 1770, tel. 011/4372-2405) specializes in children's films, normally dubbed rather than subtitled.

Palermo

The **Cine Club Tea** (Aráoz 1460, tel. 011/4832-

Argentine filmmakers shoot on a San Telmo balcony.

2646, cineclubtea@uol.com.ar) is an aficionados' club that operates out of a small Palermo Viejo locale.

The **Museo de Arte Latinomamericano de Buenos Aires** (MALBA, Avenida Figueroa Alcorta 3415, tel. 4808-6500, www.malba.org.ar/web/cine.php) shows up to half a dozen classics, documentaries, and obscurities daily in its cinema, which is part of a much larger art facility that's one of the city's cultural highlights.

Recoleta

INCAA, the national film institute, operates the **Cine Palais de Glace** (Avenida Libertador 1248, tel. 011/4806-8222, www.incaa.org.ar), as part of a larger museum complex.

CULTURAL CENTERS

Buenos Aires has a multitude of municipal, national, and international cultural centers, all of which offer live entertainment and events, dance and language classes, films, and many other activities.

BUENOS AIRES ON THE SCREEN

Foreign filmmakers have found Buenos Aires both visually appealing and thematically intriguing. Argentine-born but British-based, Martin Donovan made the cult thriller *Apartment Zero* (1989), which brilliantly and even humorously portrays *porteño* life—its depiction of busybody neighbors in a Buenos Aires apartment building is priceless—even as it deals with the Dirty War savagery. British actor Colin Firth plays the protagonist, an Anglo-Argentine cinema manager.

The worst of the worst is Alan Parker's kitschy version of the already kitschy musical *Evita* (1996). Filmed partly in B.A. but also in Budapest, it's most notable for the controversy it caused with Peronist politicians obsessed with Evita's legacy and for the highly publicized meeting between Madonna and a flagrantly lecherous President Carlos Menem.

Nearly as bad, though, is British director Sally Potter's narcissistic *The Tango Lesson* (1997). For a better cinematic presentation of the tango, despite a weak story line, see Puerto Rican director Marcos Zurinaga's *Tango Bar* (1988); Zurinaga worked with his compatriot, the late Raúl Juliá, and an Argentine cast and crew, including *bandoneon* player Rubén Juárez and singer Valeria Lynch.

It's only incidental, but the hero of Dutch director Paul Verhoeven's *Starship Troopers* (1997), a hilarious adaptation of Robert Heinlein's sci-fi novel, is a *porteño*. Buenos Aires, in the process, gets vaporized by alien bugs.

U.S. actor/director Robert Duvall, a frequent Buenos Aires visitor and fervent tango aficionado, filmed the so-so thriller *Assassination Tango* (2003) on location in Buenos Aires. British director Christopher Hampton filmed the adaptation of Lawrence Thornton's novel *Imagining Argentina,* starring Emma Thompson and Antonio Banderas, in the capital and the provinces.

Most recently, Ernesto "Che" Guevara puttered off from Palermo's cobbled streets in Brazilian director Walter Salles's international hit *The Motorcycle Diaries* (2004). In a fitting footnote, Uruguayan singer-songwriter Jorge Drexler's *Al Otro Lado del Río* (To the Other Side of the River), from that movie's soundtrack, won a best original song Oscar—only days before Drexler flew home to participate in the inauguration of Tabaré Vásquez, Uruguay's first leftist president in history.

Arts and Leisure

Asociación Argentina de Cultura Inglesa
RETIRO

SUIPACHA 1333, TEL. 011/4393-6941
OPEN WEEKDAYS 3–9 P.M.,
WEEKENDS 11 A.M.–1:30 P.M.
WWW.AACI.ORG.AR

Also known as the British Arts Centre (BAC), one of the city's most active foreign cultural missions supplements its language instruction with a calendar of theater (including Shakespeare staged for kids), film cycles of British actors, directors, and even themes (such as adaptations of Agatha Christie), TV/video (would you believe Benny Hill?), and music (including Celtic). It also hosts exhibits by Argentine artists, and regular lectures and workshops.

The BAC shuts down in January, keeps limited hours in February, and resumes a full schedule in March.

Centro Cultural Borges
MICROCENTRO

VIAMONTE AND SAN MARTÍN, TEL. 011/5555-5359
OPEN MON.–SAT. 10 A.M.–9 P.M., SUN. NOON–9 P.M.
WWW.CCBORGES.ORG.AR

Adjacent to the Galerías Pacífico and named for Argentina's most famous literary figure, this 10,000-square-meter cultural center has become one of the city's top cultural attractions. In addition to a diverse schedule of performing-arts events in its Auditorio Astor Piazzola, it holds film retrospectives in its *microcine* (small cinema), as well as rotating fine-arts exhibitions, and a variety of classes and seminars on topics ranging from Borges himself to Russian literature and the works of Woody Allen.

Modern art patrons queue for a León Ferrari retrospective at the Centro Cultural in Recoleta.

Admission costs US$1, though the ground and first-floor exhibit halls are open to the public without charge.

M Centro Cultural Ciudad de Buenos Aires
RECOLETA

JUNÍN 1930, TEL. 011/4803-1040
OPEN TUES.–FRI. 2–9 P.M.,
WEEKENDS AND HOLIDAYS 10 A.M.–9 P.M.
WWW.CENTROCULTURALRECOLETA.ORG

In the 1980s, architects Clorindo Testa, Jacques Bedel, and Luis Benedit turned the 18th-century Franciscan convent alongside the Iglesia Nuestra Señora del Pilar into one of Buenos Aires's major cultural centers; it now boasts exhibition halls, a cinema, and an auditorium that is one of the most important sites for March's Festival de Tango. In addition, outside the center proper, the architects added the **Plaza del Pilar,** a stylish arcade housing the upscale Buenos Aires Design shopping mall and a gaggle of sidewalk restaurants and cafés.

Immediately after Argentine independence, General Manuel Belgrano established an art school on the site. Thereafter, though, it served as a beggars' prison until reformist mayor Tor-cuato de Alvear cleaned up the site in the 1880s; Italian architect Juan Buschiazzo turned the chapel into an auditorium and gave adjacent walls and terraces an Italianate style. Until its 1980s remodel, it served as the Hogar de Ancianos General Viamonte, a retirement home.

The Centro's other facilities include the **Museo Participativo de Ciencias** (tel. 011/4807-3260, www.mpc.org.ar), a hands-on science museum for children, whose hours vary depending on whether school is in session; and a **microcine** with repertory film cycles. Admission is free (but donations are encouraged) except for the Museo Participativo, which costs US$2 pp for those aged five and older. There are also charges for some film programs. For guided visits, make reservations (tel. 011/4803-4057).

Centro Cultural del Sur
BARRACAS

AVENIDA CASEROS 1750, TEL. 011/4306-0301
OPEN TUES.–FRI. 2–8 P.M., SAT.–SUN. 2–11 P.M.
WWW.CENTRODELSUR.ORG

In a a colonial-style house, this underappreciated cultural center hosts some of the Festival de Tango's biggest events on its open-air stage, alongside what was once the city's southern botanical garden. The building's enclosed patio is the site of an off-and-on crafts fair, and there are frequent children's and theater events on weekends. Admission is usually free, even for special events, such as the tango festival, but it's necessary to pick up tickets at least a couple hours in advance.

Centro Cultural Rector Ricardo Rojas   BALVANERA
AVENIDA CORRIENTES 2038, TEL. 011/4954-5521
OPEN WEEKDAYS 10 A.M.–7 P.M.
WWW.ROJAS.UBA.AR
One of Buenos Aires's most dynamic cultural centers, the increasingly important Rojas sponsors events and exhibitions in the visual arts (specifically photography), cinema, dance (including tango), music, and theater. In addition, it hosts lectures on science and technology, and it has special interest in *porteño* circus and the participatory *murgas* (community performance groups) that are the grassroots of the city's *carnaval*. It also co-sponsors off-site events.

The schedule above is for normal business hours; concert, exhibition, and lecture hours depend on the individual event.

Instituto Goethe   MICROCENTRO
AVENIDA CORRIENTES 319, TEL. 011/4315-3327
OPEN WEEKDAYS 9 A.M.–8 P.M.
WWW.GOETHE.DE/HS/BUE/SPINDEX.HTM
In addition to its library and German-language classes, the Goethe Institute has an ambitious schedule of films, lectures, theater, dance and music (including some very avant-garde electronica), and art and photography exhibits. Many events take place on site, but others are co-sponsored in venues like the Teatro Colón.

Salas Nacionales de Cultura   RECOLETA
POSADAS 1725, TEL. 011/4804-1163
OPEN TUES.–SUN. 2–8 P.M.
WWW.PALAISDEGLACE.ORG
A former skating rink—according to legend, Carlos Gardel was once shot in the vicinity—the Palais de Glace hosts a steady calendar of artistic and historical exhibitions, plus cultural and commercial events (see the current schedule on the website at www.artesur.com/links/palais.htm). The price of admission depends on the program; INCAA, the national cinema institute, also hosts art films here.

Arts and Leisure

Holidays, Festivals, and Events

One Uruguayan called his country *"un país de feriados"* (a country of holidays), but Argentina might be called the same; it observes all the typical national holidays and quite a few special events on top of that. The summer months of January and February, when most *porteños* leave on vacation, are generally quiet; things pick up after school starts in early March.

January
January 1 is **Año Nuevo** (New Year's Day), an official holiday.

February and March
Dates for the pre-Lenten **Carnaval** (Carnival) vary from year to year but, in Buenos Aires, most celebrations take place on weekends rather than during the week. While unlikely

ever to match the spectacle of Brazilian festivities, Carnaval is enjoying a revival, particularly with the performances of barrio *murgas* (street musicians and dancers) rather than elaborate downtown events.

Semana Santa (Holy Week) is widely observed in Catholic Argentina, though only the days from **Viernes Santo** (Good Friday) through **Pascua** (Easter) are official holidays. Many Argentines, however, use the long weekend for a mini-vacation.

Saint Patrick's Day (March 17) has acquired a certain fashionability in Buenos Aires, but some *porteños* seem to see it as an excuse to get roaring drunk at any of several nominally Irish pubs (Buenos Aires did see substantial Irish immigration in the 20th century).

In late March, the **Exposición de Otoño de**

THE RESUSCITATION OF CARNAVAL

Carnaval is traditionally a far lesser celebration in Buenos Aires than in Brazil or even Uruguay, where Montevideo's Afro-Uruguayan communities uphold the tradition of syncopated *candombe* music. *Candombe* may still be more conspicuous on the San Telmo murals of its musicians than in the Argentine capital's pre-Lenten celebrations, but it is making a comeback.

Candombe nearly disappeared after the 1870s, as overwhelming European immigration overshadowed what remained of the Afro-Argentine heritage. Elements of it survived, though, thanks to *murgas,* bands of brightly costumed dancers accompanied by drums, who adopted the music of a nearly bygone way of life. Contemporary neighborhood *murgas,* with their subtext of political protest by an underclass betrayed by its owners, display a revived urgency.

In 2005, more than a hundred *murgas* of colorfully clad leaping dancers and pounding drummers participated in neighborhood *corsos* (parades). Bearing names like Los Amantes de La Boca (The Lovers of La Boca), Los Amos de Devoto (The Lords of Devoto), La Locura de Boedo (The Madness of Boedo), Los Mocosos de Liniers (The Snots of Liniers), Los Reyes del Movimiento (The Kings of Rhythm), and Los Quitapenas (The Sorrow Busters), they continued the revival of a tradition that nearly died with the 1976–1983 dictatorship.

Nevertheless, this protest music and dance has offered a colorful outlet in hard times. Popular commercial musicians, such as *rock nacional* icons Los Piojos, have also gravitated to this dynamic expression of disenfranchised voices.

la **Asociación Criadores de Caballos Criollos** is the best-of-breed showcase for the hardy horses of the sort that Aimé Tschiffely rode from Buenos Aires to Washington, D.C. in the 1920s. Sponsored by Balvanera's Asociación Criadores de Caballos Criollos (Creole Horse Breeders' Association, Larrea 670, 2nd fl., tel. 011/4961-3387, www.caballoscriollos.com), the event normally takes place at Palermo's Predio Ferial de la Sociedad Rural Argentina, on Avenida Sarmiento (Subte: Plaza Italia).

Though it began in 1998 on Gardel's December 11 birthday, the increasingly popular **Festival de Tango** now follows Brazilian Carnaval in March. Lasting several weeks, it includes dance competitions and numerous free music and dance events at venues like the Centro Cultural San Martín, the Centro Cultural Recoleta, and the Centro Cultural del Sur, where calendars are available; for details, contact the Festival de Tango (tel. 011/4374-2829, tel. 0800/333-7848 toll-free in Argentina, www.festivaldetango.com.ar).

April

Buenos Aires's annual book fair, the **Feria del Libro,** has been a fixture on the *porteño* literary scene for nearly three decades. Dates vary, but it lasts three weeks and sometimes extends into May. Most but not all exhibitors are from Latin America; European and Asian countries also participate, and there are regular author appearances. It has recently moved from Recoleta to Palermo's Predio Rural (Cerviño 4474, Avenida Sarmiento 2704, tel.011/4777-5500). It's sponsored by the Fundación El Libro (Hipólito Yrigoyen 1628, 5th fl., Monserrat, tel. 011/4374-3288, www.el-libro.com.ar). Admission costs about US$1.

Toward the end of the month, the **Festival Internacional de Cine Independiente** (International Independent Film Festival) proved a success even during the economic crisis of 2002 (which marked the festival's fourth year). Featuring independent movies from every continent, it takes place at various cinemas around town.

FESTIVAL BUENOS AIRES TANGO

Despite its newness—the first event took place only in 1997—the Festival Buenos Aires Tango (tel. 0800/3378-4825, www.festivaldetango.com.ar) has become one of the city's signature special events. Lasting three weeks from mid-February to early March, this festival of music, song, and dance ranges from the very traditional and conservative to the imaginative and even the daring.

Shortly after its creation, the festival moved from December to February and March to follow Brazilian Carnaval, but it is not strictly a tourist-oriented affair; it is also widely accepted and anticipated by a demanding *porteño* public. Unlike Brazilian Carnaval, it is not a mass spectacle, but rather a decentralized series of performances at relatively small, often intimate, venues around the capital. As such, it offers opportunities to see and hear not just established artists, but also developing performers.

Most of the funding for the city-sponsored festival goes to pay the artists, and admission is either free or inexpensive; however, tickets are usually available on a first-come, first-serve basis on the day of the performance. Among the locales hosting events are the Academia Nacional del Tango (Avenida de Mayo 833, Monserrat); the Centro Cultural Plaza Defensa (Defensa 535, Monserrat); the Centro Cultural General San Martín (Avenida Corrientes 1551, Congreso); the Teatro Presidente Alvear (Avenida Corrientes 1659, Congreso); the Centro Cultural del Sur (Avenida Caseros 1750, Barracas); the Centro Cultural Recoleta (Junín 1930, Recoleta); and the Anfiteatro Juan Bautista Alberdi (Juan Bautista Alberdi and Lisandro de la Torre, Mataderos).

May

May 1 is **Día del Trabajador** (International Labor Day), an official holiday. On May 25, Argentines observe the **Revolución de Mayo** (May Revolution of 1810), when *porteños* made their first move toward independence by declaring the Viceroy illegitimate. This is not, however, the major indepedendence celebration, which takes place July 9 (see the *July* section).

For more than a decade now, mid-May's **Feria de Galerías Arte BA** has shown work from dozens of Buenos Aires art galleries. Like the Feria del Libro, it takes place at the Predio La Rural in Palermo.

June

June 10 is **Día de las Malvinas** (Malvinas Day), an official holiday celebrating Argentina's claim to the British-governed Falkland (Malvinas) Islands. June 20, also an official holiday, is **Día de la Bandera** (Flag Day).

Though not an official holiday, June 24 commemorates the **Día de la Muerte de Carlos Gardel,** the anniversary of the singer's death in a 1935 aviation accident in Medellín, Colombia. Pilgrims crowd the streets of the Cementerio de la Chacarita to pay tribute, and there are also tango events.

July

July 9, **Día de la Independencia,** celebrates Argentina's formal declaration of indepedence in 1816 at the northwestern city of Tucumá. Later in the month, when school lets out, many Argentines take **Vacaciones de Invierno** (Winter Holidays), and flights and even buses out of the capital fill up fast.

During the winter holidays, the Sociedad Rural Argentina sponsors the **Exposición Internacional de Ganadería, Agricultura, y Industria Internacional,** the annual agricultural exhibition at Palermo's Predio Ferial. For more than a century, this has been one of the capital's biggest events; for details, contact the Sociedad Rural Argentina (Florida 460, tel. 011/4324-4700, www.ruralarg.org.ar).

August

August 17 is **Día de San Martín,** the official

observance of the death (not the birth) of Argentina's independence hero.

September

In early September, municipal authorities block off traffic from several blocks of Avenida Corrientes, on either side of Avenida Callao, for the **Semana del Libro** (Book Week), where booksellers from around the city and the country maintain open-air stalls.

October

October 12 is **Día de la Raza** (equivalent to U.S. Columbus Day, marking Columbus's arrival in the New World), an official holiday.

November

November 2's **Día de los Muertos** (All Souls' Day) is the occasion for Argentines to visit their loved ones' graves, though this is not the colorful event it is in Mexico and Central America.

Also in early November, the gaucho sport of *pato* holds its **Campeonato Argentino Abierto de Pato** (Argentine Open Pato Championship)

at the suburban Campo de Mayo; for more information, contact the Federación Argentino de Pato (Avenida Belgrano 530, 5th fl., Monserrat, tel. 011/4331-0222).

From mid-November to mid-December, the **Campeonato Abierto Argentino de Polo** (Argentine Open Polo Championship) takes place at Palermo's Campo Argentino de Polo (Avenida del Libertador and Dorrego, tel. 011/4774-4517). For details, contact the Asociación Argentina de Polo (Arévalo 3065, Palermo, tel. 011/4777-6444, www.aapolo.com).

December

Though the Festival de Tango has moved to March, the city still blocks off the street near the Centro Cultural San Martín for the **Milonga de Calle Corrientes,** in which partiers dance to live and recorded music on Gardel's December 11 birthday, when his grave at Chacarita also draws pilgrims.

December 25 is **Navidad** (Christmas Day), an official holiday.

Sports and Recreation

Not just a city for sightseeing, Buenos Aires also offers options for activities, ranging from the relatively calm concentration of a chess match to the energy of a pickup soccer game.

In the densely built Microcentro and other close-in barrios, there's not much open space, but hotel health clubs and private gyms are good alternatives for those who can't get out to Puerto Madero's ecological reserve, Palermo's parks, and other open spaces for a bit of exercise. Parts of these areas are closed to automobiles all week or at least on weekends.

The main spectator sport is *fútbol* (soccer), an Argentine passion. Rugby, though, is also popular; the national team, Los Pumas, has a global reputation. *Basquetbol* or *básquet* (basket) is rapidly gaining popularity and boxing may be making a comeback.

Befitting a country that grew up on horse-

back, racing and polo also draw crowds, while the indigenous *pato* is a specialist interest.

PARKS AND PROTECTED AREAS

The only unit of Argentina's national park system close to Buenos Aires is the **Reserva Natural Estricta Otamendi,** a 2,600-hectare riverside reserve on the right bank of the Río Paraná between Tigre and Zárate. Just east of Puerto Madero, however, the spontaneous colonization of a former landfill by native and introduced flora and fauna created the city's **Reserva Ecológica Costanera Sur;** ironically enough, this former rubbish tip has become a favorite destination for jogging, cycling, and weekend outings by *porteños.* (For details, see the separate entry in the *Sights* chapter.)

Many other open spaces, such as **Palermo's Parque Tres de Febrero,** appear in detail in the *Sights* chapter.

Parque Centenario

Caballito's largest open space, Parque Centenario, is a heavily used park in a mostly residential neighborhood. Also well-maintained, with a small artificial lake, the park attracts joggers, cyclists, sunbathers and dogs. It includes the city's most important natural history museum (see the *Sights* chapter for details) and a separate **Observatorio Astronómico** (Avenida Patricias Argentinas 550, tel. 011/4863-3366). The observatory's telescopes are open to the public from 9–10 P.M. Friday and Saturday nights in clear weather. Admission costs US$1 for adults, slightly less for children.

Parque Rivadavia

Extending several blocks along Avenida Rivadavia, between Doblas and Beauchef, today's Parque Rivadavia formed part of the Ambrosio Lezica estate but became municipal property in 1920; one reminder of its country origins is the remains of a *noria* or well, from which a water wheel irrigated the grounds (according to legend, one of Lezica's washerwomen was murdered here, and her ghost can still be seen carrying her own head).

Parque Rivadavia has a handful of monuments, such as José César Avanti's **Monumento a Bolívar,** which won the competition for the 1934 centenary of Venezuelan independence; finished in 1942, it is unfortunately covered with graffiti. Sculptor Luis Perlotti, whose museum is a few blocks northwest of here, carved the **Escultura a la Madre.** There is a small shrine to the Virgin of Luján, the symbol of Argentine Catholicism.

Parque Rivadavia also has a large Sunday book fair, which began spontaneously but has since been formalized. In the 2002 economic crisis, unfortunately, it also became the site of the so-called *Feria de los Desocupados,* (Jobless Fair) in which unemployed middle-class families from the barrio sold their personal belongings to pay their rents and mortgages.

BIRD-WATCHING

Within the city limits, the best bird-watching site is the Reserva Ecológica Costanera Sur, a former landfill where the spontaneous colonization of grasses, shrubs, and trees has mimicked the Paraná delta wetlands to create habitat for abundant bird life, not to mention aquatic mammals and reptiles. That said, it can't match the delta's more remote channels or the *estancias* of Buenos Aires province.

Palermo has the next largest open green spaces, but most of its parks are poor areas for bird-watching because uncontrolled numbers of feral cats have decimated avian populations; the exception is the small but beautifully maintained Jardín Japonés, where chicken wire between the hedges helps keep the felines out.

Argentina has about 3,000 dedicated bird-watchers, mostly affiliated with the Microcentro's Asociación Ornitológica del Plata (25 de Mayo 749, 2nd fl., tel. 011/4312-8958, www.avesargentinas.org.ar). The Asociación also offers bird-watching classes and organized excursions in the vicinity of the capital.

© WAYNE BERNHARDSON

The Luna Park covered stadium, a popular site for sports events and concerts, is also the place where Eva Duarte maneuvered to meet her future husband Juan Domingo Perón.

RUNNING

Many porteños have taken up running, but the congested downtown area often deters short-term visitors because the only open spaces are relatively small plazas, and the traffic (and its consequent vehicle emissions) make street-running unpleasant and even dangerous.

Easily the biggest open space, with the least traffic (pedestrians and bicycles only), is the Reserva Ecológica Costanera Sur, the former rubbish tip reinvented as parkland near Puerto Madero. The next best are the parks of Palermo and Belgrano, which also have ample open space and little traffic.

CYCLING

Buenos Aires's densely built city center, ferocious traffic, and lack of challenging terrain all make cycling at least superficially unappealing. Nevertheless, a surprising number of porteños—even including some policemen—get around on bicycles.

Though there's no really rugged terrain anywhere, mountain bikers commonly use the Reserva Ecológica Costanera Sur (where there's a 10-km per hour speed limit because bicycles have to share the trails with hikers). In addition, there are a small but growing network of paved bicycle trails and the car-free open spaces of Palermo's parks. The roads of suburban Buenos Aires province encourage some riders, though the vehicle traffic can be dangerously fast.

Rental bikes are available along Avenida de Infanta Isabel in Palermo's Parque Tres de Febrero, on both sides of the Museo Sívori. Speed riders, meanwhile, can test themselves on the track at the park's Nuevo Circuito KDT (Jerónimo Salguero 3450, tel. 011/4802-2619, open 8 A.M.–9 P.M. daily, US$.50 pp); there's another entrance on Avenida Sarmiento. Monthly membership costs only US$3 pp.

HORSEBACK RIDING

In the capital's northern barrios, it's possible to take riding lessons (in the English rather than

gaucho style) and even polo instruction. Tourist-oriented *estancias* in Buenos Aires province also provide riding opportunities.

City venues include the Club Hípico Mediterráneo (Avenida Figueroa Alcorta 4800, Palermo, tel. 011/4772-3828); the Club Alemán de Equitación (Avenida Dorrego 4045, Palermo, tel. 011/4778-7060, www.cae-hipico.com.ar); and the Club Hípico Argentino (Avenida Figueroa Alcorta 7285, Belgrano, tel. 011/4786-6240, www.clubhipicoargentino.org.ar).

TENNIS

Argentine professional tennis has long enjoyed an international reputation, thanks to star players like Guillermo Vilas and Gabriela Sabatini. In 2002, David Nalbandian of Unquillo, in Córdoba province, became the first Argentine to reach the men's finals at Wimbledon before losing to Lleyton Hewitt of Australia.

As of early 2005, the most top rated Argentine men included Juan Ignacio Chela, José Acasuso, Rodolfo Coria, David Nalbandian, and Agustín Calleri. Paola Suárez (17th) was the top-ranked Argentine woman, followed by Gisela Dulko (32nd).

While it has a high professional profile, tennis is also a popular participant sport. Though most courts are private and some require substantial membership fees, when things are slow during the week they may open to nonmembers. Possibilities include the **Buenos Aires Lawn Tennis Club** (Olleros 1510, Palermo, tel. 011/4772-0983), which also hosts high-profile professional events; and **Salguero Tennis/Paddle/Squash** (Avenida Salguero 3350, Palermo, tel. 011/4805-5144).

GOLF

Porteño golfers have one public 18-hole course and another private one, along with short courses, driving ranges, and putting greens, to test their skills. For information on facilities outside the capital, contact the Microcentro's **Asociación Argentina de Golf** (AAG, Avenida Corrientes 538, 11th fl., tel. 011/4325-1113, www.aag.com.ar).

© WAYNE BERNHARDSON

Arts and Leisure

Young skateboarders and skaters fly down a ramp at Puerto Madero.

The 18-hole **Golf Club Lagos de Palermo** (Avenida Tornquist 1426, tel. 011/4772-7261) is open 7 A.M.–5 P.M. daily except Monday. Greens fees are US$7 weekdays, US$9 weekends (when reservations are advisable). The only full-sized course, in the northwestern barrio of Villa Lugano, is the private **Golf Club José Jurado** (Avenida Coronel Roca 5025, tel. 011/4605-4706).

Palermo's **Costa Salguero Golf Center** (Avenida Costanera Rafael Obligado and Salguero, tel. 011/4805-4732, www.costasalguerogolf.com.ar) has a nine-hole pitch 'n' putt course, along with a driving range and putting green. In Núñez, the private **Club Ciudad de Buenos Aires** (Avenida del Libertador 7501, tel. 011/4703-0222) also has a par-three course.

For driving and putting, there's the **AAG**'s Palermo facility (Avenida Costanera Rafael Obligado 1835, tel. 011/4802-1116), which also has a museum, a golf school, and a restaurant.

CHESS

Like most megacities, Buenos Aires has a critical mass of serious chess players. For a chess match, tournament, or instruction, contact the **Club Argentino de Ajedrez** (Paraguay 1858, Barrio Norte, tel. 011/4811-9412, http://club-argentino.tripod.com). Nonmembers are welcome to participate, but pay slightly more than members.

CLIMBING

A city whose highest natural elevation reaches barely 25 meters might seem an improbable place to pursue an activity like climbing, but a pair of gyms have climbing walls for town-bound *porteños* to practice before heading into the countryside. Serious rock climbing is possible in the Sierras de Tandil and the Sierra de la Ventana, both in southern Buenos Aires province, as well as in more remote areas in the Andean northwest and the Patagonian provinces.

City climbing gyms include Palermo's **Boulder** (Arce 730, tel. 011/4802-4113, www.elboulder.com.ar, Subte: Olleros, Línea D); and Almagro's **Fugate** (Gascón 238, tel. 011/4982-0203, www.fugate.com.ar, Subte: Castro Barros, Línea A). Both offer climbing lessons in town and also organize field trips.

WATER SPORTS

Porteños take readily to water, but the beaches along the capital's silt-laden Río de la Plata are nothing to speak of, and pollution makes them even more questionable. There are better options in suburban Tigre, on the Paraná delta, and across the river in Uruguay. Boating, fishing, and even surfing are possible in some of those areas. Note that huge numbers of *porteños* spend their summers in and around Mar del Plata, on the southern coast of Buenos Aires province, but "Mardel" is five or six hours away except by plane.

Boating and Fishing

Boating and fishing are best in and around the intricate channels of the Río Paraná, north and east of the suburb of Tigre. City-bound folks, though, choose the Reserva Ecológica Costanera Sur and the area around the Club de Pescadores, near the Aeroparque, for casting their lines. The denizens of La Boca even take their chances in the toxic sludge of the Riachuelo.

Surfing

There's no surf to speak of anywhere in northern Buenos Aires province, but the beaches east of Punta del Este, Uruguay, get some legitimate south Atlantic Ocean waves—though not so good as those in Chile (Chile's Pacific Ocean currents, though, mean much colder water).

Swimming

For those who can't get to the beaches or afford five-star hotels, Buenos Aires has several *polideportivos* (sports clubs) with inexpensive *piletas* (public pools), but they get crowded. The most central is **Polideportivo Martín Fierro** (Oruro 1310, San Cristóbal, tel. 011/4941-2054, Subte: Urquiza, Línea E). Try also **Polideportivo Parque Chacabuco** (Avenida Eva Perón 1410, Parque Chacabuco, tel. 011/4921-5576, Subte: Emilio Mitre, Línea E).

Many private pools are open to members only, with a membership fee and monthly dues, but others are open to the public at what, before devaluation, were high prices—as much

as US$20 for day use. The weak peso, though, has made it worth looking at options like the indoor pool at Congreso's **Ateneo Cecchina** (Mitre 1625, tel. 011/4374-4958); Palermo's **Club de Amigos** (Avenida Figueroa Alcorta 3885, tel. 011/4801-1213); the outdoor pool at Palermo's **Punta Carrasco** (Avenida Costanera Norte and Avenida Sarmiento, tel. 011/4807-1010, www.puntacarrasco.com.ar); and the outdoor pool at Belgrano's **Balneario Parque Norte** (Avenida Cantilo and Güiraldes, tel. 011/4787-1432).

SOCCER

Argentina is a perpetual soccer power—having won the World Cup in 1978 and 1986—and the birthplace of Diego Armando Maradona, one of the sport's legends. What its English fans like to call "the beautiful game," though, often falls short of its billing; the *Buenos Aires*

SOCCER TICKETS

For schedules and tickets, contact the first-division clubs below. *Entradas populares* (standing-room tickets) are the cheapest, but *plateas* (fixed seats) have better security. Again, wear neutral colors to avoid clashes with partisans of either side.

Boca Juniors, Brandsen 805, La Boca, tel. 011/4309-4700, www.bocasistemas.com.ar

Huracán, Avenida Amancio Alcorta 2570, Parque Patricios, tel. 011/4911-0757, www.cahuracan.com

Nueva Chicago, Avenida Justo A. Suárez 6900. Mataderos, tel. 011/4687-2538, www.nuevachicago.com.ar

River Plate, Avenida Presidente Figueroa Alcorta 7597, Núñez, tel. 011/4788-1200

San Lorenzo de Almagro, Avenida Fernández de la Cruz 2403, Nueva Pompeya, tel. 011/4914-2470, www.sanlorenzo.com.ar

Vélez Sarsfield, Avenida Juan B. Justo 9200, Liniers, tel. 011/4641-5663, fax 011/4641-5763, www.velezsarsfield.com.ar

© WAYNE BERNHARDSON

Pickup soccer games, such as this one at Puerto Madero, take place all over the city.

Herald may have said it best with the headline "Another Boring 0–0 Tie."

Though the *selección nacional* (national team) suffered an ignominious first-round exit from the 2002 World Cup, it won the 2004 Olympic gold medal at Athens. By early 2005, it ranked third in the world behind Brazil and France, but professional soccer still has many other problems.

One is the so-called *barras bravas,* the counterpart to British "football hooligans," who make the cheap seats and the area outside the stadiums unsafe. Often provided tickets and transportation by the clubs themselves, soccer goons have caused injuries and even deaths; anyone attending a match should take care to dress in neutral colors, such as brown or gray, to avoid showing an affiliation with either team.

Another problem is financial, as clubs often must sell their best players to wealthy European teams to stay solvent. Popularly known as the Millonarios, River Plate is one of the world's best-known teams, but being an Argentine millionaire isn't what is used to be—the club has had trouble meeting its payroll.

Still, Buenos Aires is a soccer-mad city,

with six first-division teams in the city proper and another six in its Gran Buenos Aires suburbs. The season runs March–December; for the most current information, check the website of the Asociación de Fútbol Argentina (www.afa.org.ar), which appears in English as well as Spanish. (For club contacts, see the sidebar *Soccer Tickets.*)

RUGBY

Argentine rugby is largely an amateur sport rather than a professional one, but the touring club Pumas has enjoyed great international success. In early 2005, the national team ranked seventh in the world, behind New Zealand, France, Australia, England, South Africa, and Ireland.

For up-to-date info on local competition, contact the Unión de Rugby de Buenos Aires (Pacheco de Melo 2120, Barrio Norte, tel. 011/4805-5858, www.urba.org.ar).

BOXING

Argentina has had international visibility in boxing since 1923, when Luis Angel Firpo

(1894–1960), the "Wild Bull of the Pampas," nearly defeated Jack Dempsey for the world heavyweight championship in New York. More than 2,500 *porteños* paid 50 centavos each to hear the Firpo-Dempsey fight broadcast live from New York at Luna Park Stadium, which became the city's prime boxing venue.

Other notable boxers have come to untimely ends: heavyweight contender Oscar "Ringo" Bonavena (1942–1976) died from a gunshot in a Reno, Nevada, brothel, and former world middleweight titlist Carlos Monzón (1942–1995) died in an automobile accident while on furlough from prison (once shot by his first wife, he was convicted of murdering his second wife in 1988).

For most of the past decade-plus, **Luna Park** (Bouchard 465, tel. 011/4311-5100) has hosted rock concerts rather than fights, but boxing has returned there in recent years. The organization that oversees Argentine boxing is the **Federación Argentina de Box** (Castro Barros 75, Almagro, tel. 011/4981-2965, www.fabox.com.ar), which maintains a smaller stadium at that address.

BASKETBALL

Argentine basketball's international profile has risen dramatically with victories over the so-called U.S. "Dream Team" in the 2002 World Basketball Championships and the 2004 Olympics. Many observers admired the Argentines' selfless team play and at least one National Basketball Association (NBA) coach cited them as an example his own team should follow.

Several Argentines have played in the NBA. One of the league's best players, 6-foot-6 (1.98-meter) guard Emanuel Ginóbili helped the San Antonio Spurs win championships (2002–2003 and 2004–2005) and made his first All-Star appearance in 2005. Rookies in 2004–2005, Chicago Bulls forward Andrés Nocioni and Detroit Pistons guard Carlos Delfino have both gotten substantial playing time.

Buenos Aires has three teams in the first division of the Liga Nacional de Basquetbol: **Boca Juniors** (Arzobispo Casanova 600, La Boca, tel. 011/4309-4748); **Obras Sanitar-**

ias (Avenida del Libertador 7395, Núñez, tel. 011/4702-4655); and **Club Atlético River Plate** (Avenida Figueroa Alcorta 7597, Núñez, tel. 011/4788-1200).

With arenas seating no more than about 3,000 spectators, basketball crowds are much smaller than those for soccer. The regular season runs early November to late March, with playoffs into mid-May.

EQUESTRIAN SPORTS

For a country raised on horseback, equestrian sports have great resonance even in the metropolis, though only the rarely played *pato* overtly reflects the gaucho tradition.

Horse Racing

The country's landmark racetrack is Palermo's **Hipódromo Argentino** (Avenida del Libertador 4101, tel. 011/4788-2800, www.palermo.com.ar). Races may take place any day of the week, but mostly Friday–Monday. General admission costs US$1, with minimum bets about the same.

Pato

For gauchos rather than gentlemen, *pato* is the anti-polo, a rural sport in which, originally, a live duck in a leather bag was flung into a goal from horseback. No longer so brutal, it uses a leather bag with handles, but the sport is clearly in decline even in the provinces.

Nevertheless, *pato* has not disappeared. For information on competitions, contact the **Federación Argentina de Pato** (Avenida Belgrano 550, 5th fl., Monserrat, tel. 011/4331-0222, www.fedpato.com.ar). Most matches take place at the **Campo Argentino de Pato** (Ruta Nacional 11 and Calle Avellaneda, Km 30, Campo de Mayo, tel. 011/4664-9211. The national championships, though, take place at Palermo's Campo Argentino de Polo.

Polo

Argentine society has always been intricately involved with horseback riding; the British in-

© WAYNE BERNHARDSON

Palermo's Campo Argentino de Polo is the site of November's Campeonato Abierto Argentino de la República, the national polo championships.

fluence made them mount polo ponies. The gaucho tradition has left its mark, though, as the Argentine style is more rugged than its British antecedent.

First held at the suburban Hurlingham Club in 1893, the **Campeonato Abierto Argentino de la República** (Argentine Open Polo Championship) moved to Palermo's Campo Argentino de Polo, near the intersection of Avenida del Libertador and Avenida

Dorrego, in 1928. This is also the headquarters of the **Asociación Argentina de Polo** (Arévalo 3065, tel. 011/4576-5600, www .aapolo.com); the Campeonato takes place beginning in mid-November, with several others throughout the year. The admission charge is about US$3 pp.

Several estancias near the capital, such as La Martina (tel. 0222/643-0777, www .lamartinapolo.com), offer lessons.

Shopping

Buenos Aires's main shopping areas are the Microcentro, along the Florida pedestrian mall toward Retiro; Retiro (especially around Plaza San Martín and along Avenida Santa Fe); Recoleta, in the vicinity of the cemetery; and the tree-lined streets of Palermo Viejo, where stylish shops sit between the newest restaurants and bars. The main street markets take place in San Telmo, Recoleta, and Belgrano.

Since the 2001–2002 financial meltdown, fewer merchants accept credit cards (though many still take debit cards). While the practice of *recargos* (surcharges) for credit-card purchases has declined in recent years, some of those still accepting credit cards have reinstituted the practice. Before handing over the plastic, shoppers should verify whether the business in question intends to collect a *recargo*.

Readers should note that the categories in this chapter are not always mutually exclusive. Both antique and souvenir shops, for instance, might sell *mate* gourds, and clothiers and souvenir sellers might offer leather jackets.

Buenos Aires's Best

N Best Shopping Center: For one-stop shopping, nothing beats **Galerías Pacífico.** Anticonsumers in the company of compulsive shoppers can pause to study its landmark murals or else seek refuge in the adjacent Centro Cultural Borges (page 160).

N Best Street Market: Like the Café Tortoni, Sunday's **Feria de San Pedro Telmo** is at least as popular with *porteños* as with foreign visitors. More than just a market, it's an event with street performers (page 161).

N Best Antiques: On San Telmo's antiques row, **Churrinche Antigüedades** has plenty for traditionalists whose standard is the "Paris of the South." At the same time, it's not so orthodox that it won't stock industrial artifacts that fit better in Palermo Soho's hippest bars (page 163).

N Best Bookstore: Everyone mourned the closure of Barrio Norte's classic Grand Splendid cinema—in a worst-case scenario, it might have become yet another evangelical storefront—but when the **El Ateneo Grand Splendid** opened its doors, with bookshelves lining the curving balconies and a café on the elevated stage, both preservationists and B.A. book buyers responded with enthusiasm (page 164).

N Best Outlet Store: For leather jackets, shoes, and other casual clothing with mostly insignificant defects, Palermo Soho's **Cardón** is the place. Its only downside is the limited availability of sizes and styles (page 166).

N Best Leather: For more than half a century, **Guido Mocasines** has created fine handcrafted shoes and accessories more affordable than its Barrio Norte and Recoleta locations might imply (page 167).

© WAYNE BERNHARDSON

Feria de San Pedro Telmo, Plaza Dorrego

N Best Vernacular Art: For readymade *filete,* the traditional sign-painting art whose revival parallels the tango boom, check out the Feria de San Pedro Telmo. For custom work, consider a craftsman, such as **Martiniano Arce** (page 171).

N Best Music Store: At the strategic corner of Corrientes and Callao, Congreso's **Zivals** is an independent store that specializes in tango but has a far wider selection of Argentine, Latin American, and world music. Its bargain bin may be the best in town (page 173).

N Best Wine Shop: Other wine retailers may be inclusive, but Palermo Viejo's **Club del Vino** is selective at what it purchases and sells. Before buying, though, you can sample the goods at its adjacent wine bar and, if you want to know how they'll go with food, at its namesake restaurant (page 175).

Shopping

Shopping Centers

Over the past decade-plus, several older landmarks have been recycled into upscale shopping centers—known in Argentina as *shoppings* (in the plural). Several of them are ideal for one-stop mall-trawling.

Buenos Aires Design   RECOLETA

AVENIDA PUEYRREDÓN 2501, TEL. 011/5777-6000
OPEN WEEKDAYS 11 A.M.–9 P.M.,
SAT. 10 A.M.–9 P.M., SUN. NOON–9 P.M.
WWW.ALTOPALERMO.COM.AR/S_BADESIGN.HTM
Under the same management as Patio Bullrich, Buenos Aires Design is a 3,000-square-meter complex of shops and restaurants on two levels alongside the cultural center and the cemetery at Recoleta. As its name suggests, it focuses on design and interior decoration, including Oriental carpets, kitchen goods, and bedroom ware. Despite the street address, it's most easily accessible from its southeast corner, near Plaza Francia.

Galerías Pacífico   MICROCENTRO

FLORIDA AND CÓRDOBA, TEL. 011/5555-5100
OPEN MON.–SAT. 10 A.M.–9 P.M., SUN. NOON–9 P.M.
WWW.GALERIASPACIFICO.COM.AR
Even compulsive anti-consumerists will appreciate this architectural landmark, which has preserved magnificent murals in its central cupola (for more details, see the separate entry in the *Sights* chapter). For a diagram of its three levels of more than 50 shops, many of which have separate but less conveniently concentrated locales elsewhere in town, check the street-level information booth at the Florida entrance. Shoppers who make purchases of more than about US$50 will receive a free lunch voucher for the basement-level Patio de Comidas.

Patio Bullrich   RETIRO

AVENIDA DEL LIBERTADOR 750, TEL. 011/4814-7400
OPEN DAILY 10 A.M.–9 P.M.
WWW.ALTOPALERMO.COM.AR/S_BULLRICH.HTM
Once a livestock auction house, Patio Bullrich has become a palatial 24,000-square-meter commercial space with more than 50 shops, plus restaurants and cinemas, on four levels. While it's not the attraction that Galerías Pacífico is, it's packed with shoppers from nearby Recoleta and also has a food court.

In Brief

Three other large centers are under the same Alto Palermo management as Patio Bullrich and Buenos Aires Design, including the sizeable but modern and undistinguished **Alto Palermo Shopping Center** (Avenida Coronel Díaz 2098, Palermo, tel. 011/5777-8000) and **Paseo Alcorta** (Jerónimo Salguero 3172, Palermo, tel. 011/5777-6500). The third

TAXES AND REFUNDS

Argentina imposes a 21 percent *Impuesto de Valor Agregado* (IVA or Value Added Tax) on all goods and services. Tourists, however, may request IVA refunds for purchases of Argentine products valued at more than 70 pesos from shops that display a "Global Refund" decal on their windows. Always double-check, though, that the decal is not out of date.

When making any such purchase, request an invoice and other appropriate forms. Then, upon leaving the country, present the forms to Argentine customs; customs will authorize payment to be cashed at Banco de la Nación branches at the main international airport at Ezeiza, at Aeroparque Jorge Newbery (for flights to some neighboring countries), or at Dársena Norte (for ferry trips to Uruguay). Refunds can also be assigned to your credit card.

At smaller border crossings, do not expect officials to be prepared to deal with tax refunds. Some crossings do not even have separate customs officials, but rather are staffed by the Gendarmería (Border Guards), a branch of the armed forces. For more information, in English, check the Global Refund website (www.globalrefund.com).

Galerías Pacífico is a recycled railroad office building transformed into an upscale shopping center.

is the recycled **Abasto de Buenos Aires** (Avenida Corrientes and Anchorena, tel. 011/4959-3400), originally a project of U.S.- Hungarian George Soros; unfortunately, the disorientingly noisy interior detracts from the magnificence of the building itself.

Street Fairs

Shopping

For sightseers and spontaneous shoppers alike, Buenos Aires's diverse *ferias* (street fairs) are one of the city's greatest pleasures.

Feria Artesanal Plaza General Manuel Belgrano   BELGRANO
JURAMENTO AND CUBA
OPEN WEEKENDS AND HOLIDAYS 9 A.M.–7 P.M.
Crafts stalls cover most of Belgrano's main square at the easy-going Feria Artesanal Plaza General Manuel Belgrano, which gets better as the day goes on and sometimes stays open well beyond its ostensible closing hour. When it rains, the stalls are well-sheltered with tarps.

Feria de la Baulera   MONSERRAT
DEFENSA 628 AT MÉXICO, TEL. 011/4325-4020
OPEN WEEKENDS 10 A.M.–7 P.M.
It doesn't fit easily into any category, but the Feria de la Baulera (Fair of the Old Trunk), alternatively known as the Primera Feria del Usado Elegante (First Fair for Elegant Discards), sells the dregs discarded by the *porteño* elite. Recently moved to the former Casa de la Moneda, it's strongest in women's clothing and accessories, but also has some good souvenirs, trinkets, and, for serious collectors, perhaps some real gems. Admission costs US$.35.

Feria de San Pedro Telmo   SAN TELMO
DEFENSA AND HUMBERTO PRIMO
OPEN SUN. 10 A.M.–5 P.M.
Easily the most prominent of all B.A.'s street fairs is Feria de San Pedro Telmo, which fills Plaza Dorrego and the surrounding streets with booths of antiques, *filete* artwork, and other crafts; authorities close Defensa to vehicle

Filete, the traditional *porteño* sign-painting art, makes for ideal souvenirs at Sunday's Feria de San Pedro Telmo, on Plaza Dorrego.

traffic. There are professional tango musicians and dancers, and the dozens of other street performers range from the embarrassingly mundane to the amazingly innovative. The neighborhood is also home to many sidewalk cafés and upscale antique shops. (For more details, see the entry in the *Sights* chapter.)

Feria Parque Lezama   SAN TELMO
DEFENSA AND BRASIL
OPEN SUN. 10 A.M.–5 P.M.
So successful is the Feria de San Pedro Telmo that it has aided the increasingly thriving Feria Parque Lezama, a Sunday crafts fair that's gradually spread north from its namesake park up Calle Defensa and under the freeway, beyond which only the broad Avenida San Juan has been able to stop it. Parque Lezama itself now gets Sunday street performers, though not so many as Plaza Dorrego.

Feria Plaza   RECOLETA
Intendente Alvear
JUNÍN AND PRESIDENTE QUINTANA
OPEN WEEKENDS AND HOLIDAYS 9 A.M.–7 P.M.
After San Telmo, the most frequented tourist

feria is probably the Feria Plaza Intendente Alvear, a crafts-oriented event that's also strong on street performers. Immediately northeast of the Centro Cultural Recoleta, it's filled the space to Avenida Libertador and begun to stretch south along Junín.

In Brief
In La Boca, permanently docked on the waterfront promenade at the Vuelta de Rocha, the former ferry *Nicolás Mihainovich* holds a number of crafts stalls. Immediately across from it, at the corner of Avenida Pedro de Mendoza and Puerto de Palos, the **Feria Artesanal Plazoleta Vuelta de Rocha** takes place weekends and holidays 10 A.M.–6 P.M.; along the length of the nearby Caminito, painters, illustrators, and sculptors sell their works in the **Feria del Caminito,** open 10 A.M.–6 P.M. daily.

It's mostly *porteños* who really appreciate southern barrios like Barracas, where the **Feria de Artesanos Criollos y Aborígenes** (Creole and Indigenous Artisans' Fair) takes place at the Centro Cultural del Sur (Avenida Caseros 1750). It's open on summer weekends only, however.

At the **Feria de Mataderos,** in the southwestern barrio of Mataderos, *gauchesco* souvenirs like knives, spurs, and silver-studded belts are the key items, but for most visitors this *feria* constitutes entertainment rather than shopping.

Antiques

For much of the 20th century, Argentina alternated between periods of prodigious prosperity and palpable penury. During the good times, Argentines both imported and produced items of great value, but during hard times they often had to dispose of them. Over time, of course, once-precious items have made their way through many owners and have ended up in the hands of antique dealers.

In San Telmo in particular, antique shops form an almost unbroken line along Calle Defensa, from Avenida San Juan in the south past Plaza Dorrego to Pasaje Giuffra on the north. The variety and quality of their goods are remarkable, but dealers know what they've got—so they're resolute bargainers. Whether you're seeking that French chess set or a YPF gasoline pump globe, expect prices to be quoted in U.S. dollars rather than pesos, and don't expect much give.

Arte Antica Antigüedades   SAN TELMO
DEFENSA 1133, TEL. 011/4362-0861
OPEN DAILY 10:30 A.M.–7 P.M.
WWW.ARTEANTICA.COM.AR
At the Europhile end of the San Telmo spectrum, Arte Antica specializes in decorations and furnishings for traditional Recoleta sensibilities, with its inventory of intricate chandeliers, Louis XV furniture, and *objet d'arts* of bronze, marble, porcelain, and terracotta. Within that tradition, at least, it's diverse: Their origins are Austrian, British, Czech, French, German, Venetian, and others.

Cándido Silva   SAN TELMO
DEFENSA 1066, LOCAL 15, TEL. 011/4361-5053
OPEN TUES.–SUN. 10 A.M.–7 P.M.
WWW.CANDIDOSILVA.COM.AR
At the back of the Galería Solar de French, Silva sells some dazzling colonial *platería* (silver work), ranging from candelabras and *mates* to statuary and even Mapuche jewelry. In addition, it stocks traditional religious art and imagery, including canvases, crucifixes, triptychs, and wooden statuary, as well as elaborately carved wooden stirrups (seen more frequently in Chile than Argentina). Its adjacent crafts shop offers credible replicas of some of the originals on sale here.

Ⓜ Churrinche   SAN TELMO
Antigüedades
DEFENSA 1031, TEL. 011/4362-7612
OPEN SUN.–FRI. 11 A.M.–6 P.M.
WWW.CHURRINCHE.COM.AR
One of San Telmo's classic antique dealers, Churrinche carries a wild array of items, ranging from formal chandeliers and lamps to the glass globes that once topped the gas pumps of the former state-run YPF petroleum company. In addition, it carries life-size classical statues for formal gardens and Francophile furniture that would still fit in Recoleta's *fin de siecle* mansions. In at least one sense, it's very literally exclusive—for security reasons, Churrinche allows no more than four shoppers at a time.

Galería Cecil   SAN TELMO
DEFENSA 845
OPEN DAILY EXCEPT MON. 10 A.M.–6:30 P.M.
Beneath a luminous skylight, in what was once an enormous cinema—a statue of Jesus now fronts the original screen—the Galería Cecil holds dozen of small to medium-sized stalls stocking just about every trinket that made its way to Buenos Aires between the late 19th century and the mid-20th. A handful of items are older or younger than the rest, and there are some larger pieces, such as furniture. A café, situated where moviegoers once strode through the doors, makes a good spot for a breather.

Shopping

Galería de la Defensa SAN TELMO

DEFENSA 1179
OPEN DAILY 8 A.M.–8 P.M.

Far less gentrified than the nearby Galería Solar de French, this worn but still distinctive gallery falls closer to the flea-market end of the continuum; a few places look as if the squatters just moved out and left everything *they* didn't want. Those with patience to sort through the dreck, though, may find the occasional gem in its cluttered locales, many of which are closed early in the week. It's busiest, and best, on the Sunday market day.

Galería Solar de French SAN TELMO

DEFENSA 1066
OPEN DAILY 11 A.M.–7:30 P.M.

Not exclusively an antiques gallery, the gentrified French is a two-story structure whose ground level resembles a picturesque urban alleyway, paved with handsome stones and shaded by an Araucaria tree and a bright red-blossoming bougainvillea. While it does have more than just a handful of antiques dealers, it also has some high-quality arts and crafts dealers, and design shops.

Books

Once the center of South America's publishing industry, Buenos Aires has lost ground to other countries, but can still boast an impressive array of bookstores, from the antiquarian to the contemporary, along with specialist dealers. They are as many—or more—cultural as commercial institutions, and they take that role seriously.

In addition to bookstores proper, there are several *ferias* (outdoor stalls) scattered throughout the city. The most central of these takes place at the south end of **Plaza Lavalle**, between Talcahuano and Libertad, 10 A.M.–6 P.M. weekdays only. There's also a big selection at **Plazoleta Santa Fe**, on the Avenida Santa Fe median strip (Subte: Palermo, Línea D). Caballito's **Parque Rivadavia** (Subte: Acoyte, Línea A) has a permanent weekend market with 85 stalls, and there are also stalls at the Línea A terminus at **Primera Junta.**

Antique Book Shop RETIRO

LIBERTAD 1236, TEL. 011/4815-0658
OPEN WEEKDAYS 10 A.M.–8 P.M.,
SAT. 10:30 A.M.–1:30 P.M.
WWW.ABEBOOKS.COM/HOME/BREITBOOKS

Antique carries a good but expensive collector's selection, in many languages, on Buenos Aires, Patagonia, and travel, as well as on guachos and Argentine art and literature. It charges premium prices: A first edition of U.S. engineer Bailey Willis's survey of Pata-

gonia, undertaken for the Argentine public works ministry, costs nearly US$700 in mint condition, with all maps.

El Ateneo MICROCENTRO

FLORIDA 340, TEL. 011/4325-6801
OPEN WEEKDAYS 9 A.M.–8 P.M., SAT. 9 A.M.–1 P.M.
WWW.TEMATIKA.COM.AR

In a striking building in the heart of the pedestrian shopping district, Buenos Aires's signature bookstore is El Ateneo's Microcentro branch, which celebrated its 90th anniversary in 2002. It has a huge selection on Argentine history, literature, and coffee-table souvenir books, plus a good selection of domestic travel titles (it is also a publishing house), some of them bilingual; unfortunately, the selection of foreign-language books has dwindled as the economic crisis has made imports expensive. The basement travel section is strong on maps.

El Ateneo Grand Splendid BARRIO NORTE

AVENIDA SANTA FE 1880, TEL. 011/4813-6052
OPEN MON.–THURS. 9 A.M.–10 P.M.,
FRI.–SAT. 9 A.M.–MIDNIGHT, SUN. NOON–10 P.M.
WWW.TEMATIKA.COM.AR

Buenos Aires's most elegant bookstore is El Ateneo's Barrio Norte branch, occupying a recycled and renovated cinema that deserves a visit simply to see its remarkable and apparently seamless transformation: The stage is a café, the opera-style boxes contain chairs for readers, and the curving walls of the upper stories are lined with bookshelves floor to ceiling. In addition to books, it has a broad selection of quality music.

Librería ABC
RETIRO

AVENIDA CÓRDOBA 685, TEL. 011/4314-8106
OPEN WEEKDAYS 9 A.M.–8 P.M.,
SAT. 9:30 A.M.–1:30 P.M.
WWW.LIBRERIASABC.COM.AR

A fixture for decades, ABC stocks books about Argentina, in both English and Spanish, including coffee-table books that make popular souvenirs. At the same time, it also carries a broad selection of paperback literature in English and German, as well as dictionaries and maps.

Librería de Ávila
MONSERRAT

ADOLFO ALSINA 500, TEL. 011/4331-8989
OPEN WEEKDAYS 8:30 A.M.–8 P.M.,
SAT. 9 A.M.–6 P.M.
WWW.LIBRERIADEAVILA.SERVISUR.COM

Occupying a notable Art Deco building, Ávila claims descent from the late-colonial Librería del Colegio—making it possibly the capital's most historic bookstore. Its classic inventory consists of titles on history, philosophy, ethnology, folklore, tango, travel literature, and the like. In addition to its well-stocked stacks, it also hosts author readings and even musical events, and has a café.

Librería L'Amateur
RETIRO

ESMERALDA 882, TEL. 011/4312-7365
OPEN WEEKDAYS 10 A.M.–6:30 P.M.

An antiquarian and rare-book dealer—its stacks look like a library from a Merchant Ivory movie—L'Amateur also holds a prodigious basement stock of maps, illustrations, and engravings from Argentina, South America, and around the world. Appealing to regional specialists and collectors, these are also works of art that are suitable for framing. While prices are high, the staff are knowledgeable, well-organized, and patient.

Librería Paidós
PALERMO

AVENIDA LAS HERAS 3741, LOCAL 31, TEL.
011/4801-2860
OPEN WEEKDAYS 9:30 A.M.–8 P.M.,
SAT. 10 A.M.–1:30 P.M.
WWW.LIBRERIAPAIDOS.COM

More than just a bookstore, the shrink's specialist Paidós has been a community institution since 1957 for countless numbers of inward-looking *porteños* preoccupied with psychology, psychoanalysis, philosophy, social theory, and (to a lesser degree) humanities. In an inconspicuous gallery location just off Plaza Alférez Sobral, it also publishes a monthly bulletin and keeps a bulletin board full of listings for various therapies and related topics, such as office rentals "suitable for professionals."

Paidós also has a Barrio Norte branch (Avenida Santa Fe 1685, tel. 011/4812-6685).

Librería Platero
MICROCENTRO

TALCAHUANO 485, TEL. 011/4382-2215
OPEN WEEKDAYS 8:30 A.M.–7 P.M.,
SAT. 8:30 A.M.–12:30 P.M.
WWW.LIBRERIAPLATERO.COM.AR

Near the Tribunales (law courts), Platero's modest storefront is a deceptive facade for what may be B.A.'s best specialist bookstore, with an enormous stock of new and out-of-print books (the latter ensconced in the basement stacks). Experienced in filling overseas requests, it does a good trade with visiting academics, who can pass hours browsing its stacks and foreign libraries.

Librerías Turísticas
RECOLETA AND BARRIO NORTE

PARAGUAY 2457,
TEL. 011/4963-2866 OR 011/4962-5547
OPEN WEEKDAYS 9 A.M.–7 P.M., SAT. 10 A.M.–1 P.M.
WWW.LIBRERIATURISTICA.COM.AR

The first Buenos Aires bookstore to specialize in travel and tourism, Librerías Turísticas carries an outstanding selection of Argentine maps and guidebooks, including its own titles (some in English) on subjects that include the capital's cafés (three volumes!), neighborhoods, archaeology, and travelogues. In addition, it has a large stock of books for professionals in the travel and tourism sector.

Shopping

In Brief

Even chain bookstores, such as **Cúspide Libros,** (Florida 628, Microcentro and Vicinity, tel. 011/4328-0973, www.cuspide.com) often carry a fine selection. Excellent independents include **Zivals** (Avenida Callao 395, Congreso, tel. 011/4371-7500, www.zivals.com); **Liber-Arte** (Avenida Corrientes 1555, Microcentro and Vicinity, tel. 011/4375-2341, www.liber-arte.com.ar), a left-of-center institution that also offers theater programs on weekends; **Li-**

brería Huemul (Avenida Santa Fe 2237, Recoleta and Barrio Norte, tel. 011/4825-2290), a history specialist; and **El Túnel** (Avenida de Mayo 767, Monserrat/Catedral al Sur tel. 011/4331-2106), named for Ernesto Sabato's *porteño* novel.

For antiquarian interests, try **Alberto Casares** (Suipacha 521, Microcentro and Vicinity, tel. 011/4322-6198, http://servisur.com/casares) or **Aquilanti** (Rincón 79, Congreso, tel. 011/4952-4546).

Clothing

Porteños, both male and female, are notorious fashion plates. The most elite clothiers line the Florida pedestrian mall and the avenues of Retiro, Recoleta, and Barrio Norte, while the edgiest inhabit Palermo Viejo. Many upmarket outlets have branches in the large *shoppings,* such as Galerías Pacífico and Patio Bullrich.

Leather goods, Argentina's traditional specialty, range from tightly woven *tiento* belts to shoes, jackets, coats, trousers, handbags, and many other items. In fact, there are two sorts of leather shops: a *marroquinería* is a place that makes leather wearables and accessories (such as belts, jackets, and shoes) while a *talabartería* produces riding boots, horse gear, and the like. This difference between the two is less obvious than it once was; a good shorthand distinction is that you can buy wearables in a *talabartería,* but not saddles in a *marroquinería.*

Alberto Vannucci
RECOLETA

AVENIDA CALLAO 1773, TEL. 011/4811-3112
OPEN MON.–SAT. 10 A.M.–1 P.M. AND 3–7 P.M.
WWW.AVANNUCCISA.COM.AR

In a prime Recoleta location, Vannucci is a clutter of the usual blankets, saddles, and other leather goods, but its specialty is polo gear for royalty, such as Prince Charles of Wales and the Prince of Dubai. The selection of mallets and saddles is particularly impressive.

Cardón
PALERMO

HONDURAS 4755, TEL. 011/4832-5925
OPEN DAILY 10 A.M.–8 P.M.

For males and females alike, the widespread Cardón chain offers casual clothing, including leather jackets, shoes, and bags, as well as jeans and jean jackets, along with an ample range of accessories. This store, though, stands out because it's an outlet for seconds and discontinued lines where it's possible to get top-quality items at a fraction of the usual prices. The selection, however, is smaller than at their regular stores.

Casa López
RETIRO

MARCELO T. DE ALVEAR 640/658,
TEL. 011/4311-3044
OPEN WEEKDAYS 9 A.M.–8 P.M., SAT. 9:30 A.M.–7 P.M., SUN. 10 A.M.–6 P.M.

López is one of the city's traditional clothiers and, as befits its location and clientele, charges premium prices. It has an additional installation at Galerías Pacífico for women's handbags and accessories in particular.

Dalla Fontana
MICROCENTRO

RECONQUISTA 735, TEL. 011/4313-4354
OPEN WEEKDAYS 9 A.M.–8 P.M., SAT. 9 A.M.–7 P.M.

Dalla Fontana is a longtime leather professional that specializes in women's wear and accessories, primarily an over-the-top selection of handbags. For men, it does carry some jackets and shoes.

Palermo Soho is the most innovative neighborhood for fashion in Buenos Aires.

Flabella
MICROCENTRO

SUIPACHA 263, TEL. 011/4322-6036
OPEN WEEKDAYS 10 A.M.–9 P.M., SAT. 10 A.M.–8 P.M.
WWW.FLABELLA.COM

Flabella works in the very specialized field of shoes for tango dancers, both male and female. A small business, it produces only about 20 pairs per day in pure leather, patent leather, chamois, red lamé, and even some combinations thereof.

Frenkel's Leather World
RETIRO

FLORIDA 1055/1075, TEL. 011/4311-2300
OPEN WEEKDAYS 9 A.M.–7:30 P.M.,
WEEKENDS 9 A.M.–6 P.M.

Leather experts since 1943, occupying two nearly side-by-side locales in the Edificio Kavanagh, Frenkel's specializes in suede and leather jackets, but there are also shoes, handbags, belts, and similar items at prices that target foreign visitors and especially the Japanese (several Japanese-Argentines work the floor). Some items are made of spotted *carpincho* (capybara) hides.

Frenkel's also sells gaucho daggers, horse gear, and *mate* paraphernalia, as well as jewelry of rodo-crosite (most easily described as a pinkish lapis lazuli). The ostensibly indigenous crafts, trite to the point of kitsch, barely deserve a glance.

Guido Mocasines
BARRIO NORTE

RODRÍGUEZ PEÑA 1290, TEL. 011/4813-4095
OPEN WEEKDAYS 9:30 A.M.–8 P.M.,
SAT. 9:30 A.M.–1 P.M.
WWW.GUIDOMOCASINES.COM.AR

Handcrafting shoes since 1952, Italian immigrant Luciano Bagnasco created one of the capital's most enduring leather stores in Guido, a Barrio Norte business that has since expanded to accessories like bags, belts, and billfolds. Some of its shoes, as inexpensive as US$40, are very economical for what is top quality footwear.

Guido's has a second Recoleta branch at Avenida Quintana 333.

Jorge Cánaves
BELGRANO

AVENIDA LIBERTADOR 6000, TEL. 011/4785-3982
OPEN MON.–SAT. 9:30 A.M.–1 P.M. AND MON.–FRI. 4–8 P.M.
WWW.JORGECANAVES.COM.AR

Founded by a two-time Olympic rider and well-equipped with polo gear, Cánaves is

Shopping

particularly strong in saddles but also carries the usual boots, blankets, mallets, and the like.

López Taibo   RECOLETA
AVENIDA ALVEAR 1902, TEL. 011/4804-8585
OPEN WEEKDAYS 10 A.M.–8 P.M., SAT. 10 A.M.–6 P.M.
WWW.LOPEZTAIBO.COM
In business since 1897, leather specialist López Taibo focuses on men's shoes but also produces briefcases and handbags and a diversity of accessories. The really interesting items are goat-suede and sheepskin jackets, but their price tags will dismay the budget-conscious. In addition to its Recoleta flagship, it also has a Galerías Pacífico branch that's open Sundays.

La Martina   RETIRO
PARAGUAY 661, TEL. 011/4576-7999
OPEN WEEKDAYS 10 A.M.–8 P.M., SAT. 10 A.M.–2 P.M.
WWW.LAMARTINA.COM
On its face, La Martina is a polo snobs' supply boutique, and there are plenty of bags, blankets, boots, mallets, saddles, spurs, and stirrups for those who don't need to work for a living. It also, however, offers a selection of its own brand-name clothing, such as 100-percent cotton trousers, which are comfortably suitable for non-riders; prices are high by local standards, but still reasonable for overseas visitors.

La Martina also has a larger Belgrano branch, La Casona de la Martina (Arribeños 2632, tel. 011/4576-0010).

Mercer   PALERMO
GURRUCHAGA 1686, TEL. 011/4833-4587
OPEN DAILY 11 A.M.–8:30 P.M.
No man older than about 25 will feel very comfortable with Mercer's sleeveless T-shirts, brightly colored high-top sneakers and calf-length jeans, but for anyone younger it's the place to shop. The bright colors and design extend to the building itself, whose facade is a diverse mosaic of brightly colored tiles surrounding a giant picture window.

Perugia   RECOLETA
AVENIDA ALVEAR 1862, TEL. 011/4804-6340
OPEN WEEKDAYS 10 A.M.–1:30 P.M. AND 2:30–8 P.M., SAT. 10 A.M.–2 P.M.
Perpetually threatening liquidation of its stock (not an unusual business tactic in Buenos Aires), Perugia is a women's footwear specialist. Strategically located across from the Alvear Palace Hotel, its oozes patrician Recoleta style (with prices to match); shoe fetishists like Imelda Marcos would feel right at home here.

Rapsodia   PALERMO
EL SALVADOR 4757, TEL. 011/4832-5363
OPEN DAILY 10 A.M.–9 P.M.
WWW.RAPSODIA.COM.AR
This women's "vintage" clothing specialist pushes gaudy, shimmering retro designs that, in their eyes, blend traditions from the Indian subcontinent with a 1970s rock 'n' roll aesthetic. In reality, it's closer to the 1960s fads that proliferated when the Beatles took up transcendental meditation with the Maharishi—though the designers do use post-Beatles imagery. In Rapsodia's case, though, the fad's enjoyed at least a little more staying power.

Rossi y Caruso   RECOLETA AND BARRIO NORTE
AVENIDA SANTA FE 1377, TEL. 011/4811-1965
OPEN MON.–SAT. 10 A.M.–8 P.M.
WWW.ROSSICARUSO.COM
Though it occupies new quarters, Rossi y Caruso's leather business dates from the 1940s and, over that time, it has catered to such celebrity clientele as Spain's King Juan Carlos, Britain's Prince Phillip, and Frank Sinatra—not to mention Argentina's own royalty, Princess Máxima Zorreguieta of The Netherlands. Its specialties include men's and women's clothing, billfolds, handbags, portfolios, purses, saddles, and silver work.

Rossi y Caruso also has a Galerías Pacífico branch.

Uma   PALERMO
HONDURAS 5225, TEL. 011/4832-2122
OPEN MON.–SAT. 11 A.M.–7:30 P.M.
WWW.UMACUERO.COM
Tanned cowhide looks different when it's

stitched to lycra in jackets, tops and trousers at this Palermo Soho *fashionista* favorite. It also has outlets in Galerías Pacífico and Patio Bullrich.

Welcome Marroquinería RETIRO

MARCELO T. DE ALVEAR 500, TEL. 011/4313-7847
OPEN WEEKDAYS 10 A.M.–2 P.M. AND 3–7:30 P.M.,
SAT. 10 A.M.–2 P.M.
WWW.WELCOME-LEATHER.COM.AR
One of Buenos Aires's best-established leather goods outlets, dating from 1930, Welcome specializes in briefcases, women's handbags, and travel bags and accessories. Within these broad categories, it has dozens of distinctive products ranging from simple purses to multi-pocketed attaches. Welcome takes two weeks' vacation in late January.

In Brief

In a jarring juxtaposition, Parisian clothier **Pierre Cardin** (Avenida Callao 220, tel. 011/4372-0560) shares space with Balvanera's Buenos Aires chapter of the Communist party.

Crafts and Souvenirs

Argentina's artisanal heritage is not so immediately evident as, say, the indigenous textile traditions of the Peruvian or Guatemalan highlands, but both the city and the countryside have characteristic crafts.

The most solidly urban expression of folk art is *filete,* the elaborate rainbow signage that, in the hands of its most skilled practitioners, approaches the finest calligraphy. Embellishing the signs of so many businesses, it even used to cover city buses. While some of this is ready-made and can be trite, many *fileteadores* will produce custom pieces at a price.

For off-the-shelf *filete,* check Sunday's **Feria de San Pedro Telmo** on Plaza Dorrego; better yet, consider hiring a *fileteador* for custom work, which starts around US$100 for a piece measuring about 20 by 30 centimeters (8 by 12 inches). If doing so, though, you'll have to give the artist at least a few days or more, depending on the size of the work.

Gaucho gear, such as the sharp, silver *facón* (knife), wide, coin-studded *rastra* (belt), silver *espuelas* (spurs), and *bombachas* (baggy trousers) all make worthwhile souvenirs. Before purchasing *bombachas,* though, be sure of what you're buying—the word also means women's underwear.

In the 19th century, when wealthy households kept servants for the sole purpose of preparing *mate,* the paraphernalia, such as the *mate* (gourd) itself and the *bombilla* (straw), were works of art; many of them are now museum pieces. Small and lightweight but distinctive, they are popular with visitors.

The *mate* is often a simple calabash but can be an elaborate carving of exotic wood; while the modern *bombilla* is often aluminum, it is traditionally silver with intricate markings and design. The *pie* (base or holder) for a formal *mate* may be made of leather.

Old *conventillos* (tenements) are being recycled as craft and souvenir centers in La Boca.

Shopping

storefront in Palermo Soho

To accompany the *mate* paraphernalia, check any supermarket for *yerba mate,* the dried leaf of *Ilex paraguayensis,* an infusion that Argentines sip in prodigious amounts. Some North American markets now carry *yerba,* especially in areas with large immigrant populations, though its consumption is most common among Argentines, Uruguayans, Paraguayans, and, to a lesser degree, Brazilians and Chileans.

There are also outlets for regional Argentine crafts, such as textiles from indigenous communities in the northwestern Andean provinces or in Patagonia. In some cases, *casas de provincia* (provincial government offices, all of which supply tourist information) display and sell products typical of the area.

Arte Étnico Argentino　　　PALERMO
EL SALVADOR 4600
OPEN WEEKDAYS 10 A.M.–7 P.M., SAT. 10 A.M.–2 P.M.
WWW.ARTEETNICOARGENTINO.COM
Its specialty is textiles—specifically woolen rugs, with abstract designs, from the Mapuche of northern Patagonia—but this ethnic art outlet also features rustically styled furniture, primarily chairs and the odd table. A few drift-

wood-style curios, carved into animal motifs, round out the offerings.

Arte Indígena　　　MONSERRAT
BALCARCE 234, TEL. 011/4343-1455
OPEN WEEKDAYS 9 A.M.–6 P.M.
Non-profit Arte Indígena contains a small but representative assortment of indigenous crafts from around the country. Items on display include Quechua tapestries from the northern highlands, carved Chané masks from Salta, Toba and Guaraní basketry from the humid northeastern lowlands, and Mapuche silver work and weavings from the southerly Patagonian provinces.

Artesanías Argentinas　　　RECOLETA AND
BARRIO NORTE
MONTEVIDEO 1386, TEL. 011/4812-2650
OPEN WEEKDAYS 9:30 A.M.–7:30 P.M.,
SAT. 10 A.M.–1:30 P.M.
WWW.ARTESANIASARGENTINAS.ORG
Artesanías Argentinas is a well-established non-profit outlet for indigenous artisans, mostly from the northeastern Mesopotamian provinces and the northwestern Andean provinces. While the selection is small, the quality of its

© WAYNE BERNHARDSON

Shopping

ceramics, knives, tapestries, and hardwood boxes and carvings (with wildlife motifs) is high. Its website, in both Spanish and very good English, does a fine job of displaying the merchandise.

Artesanías Salteñas   RECOLETA
RODRÍGUEZ PEÑA 1775, TEL. 011/4814-7562
OPEN WEEKDAYS 10 A.M.–1 P.M. AND 4–7:30 P.M.,
SAT. 10 A.M.–1 P.M.

This small Recoleta shop deals exclusively with crafts from the northwestern province of Salta, where the indigenous Andean and colonial Spanish influences are among the country's strongest. Distinctive items include artwork with colonial-style religious motifs, blankets and other textiles, decorative boxes of *cardón* cactus, furniture crafted from native woods, and traditional silver work.

El Boyero   RETIRO
FLORIDA 953, TEL. 011/4312-3564
OPEN MON.–SAT. 9 A.M.–8:30 P.M.,
SUN. NOON–8 P.M.
WWW.ELBOYERO.COM

One of the city's most diverse souvenir shops, El Boyero showcases clothing and crafts from around the country. Items on the docket range from standard dress items, such as belts, boots, hats, and shoes—all with an artisanal touch—to silver work, including gaucho knives and Mapuche jewelry, as well as *mates, bombillas,* and ceramics. In addition to the main shop, it has a Galerías Pacífico branch.

Casa del Chaco   MICROCENTRO
AVENIDA CALLAO 322, TEL. 011/4372-5209
OPEN WEEKDAYS 10 A.M.–4:30 P.M.

Though the selection may be small, Chaco province's representative in the capital provides some of the most inexpensive indigenous Wichí crafts to be found and, arguably, they're more authentic than polished items at much higher prices in Retiro and Recoleta. Pieces include carvings from the aromatic *palo santo,* ceramics, jewelry, weavings, and even the odd string instrument fashioned from a metal cooking-oil container.

ℳ Martiniano Arce   SAN TELMO
PERÚ 1089, 1ST FL., TEL. 011/4362-2739
WWW.MARTINIANOARCE.COM

One of San Telmo's best known and most flamboyant *fileteadores*—his bright yellow house draws attention to itself, and he's already painted his own casket and his wife's—Arce is happy to undertake custom work. He has no fixed hours, though, and is not available for drop-ins—phone ahead for an appointment.

Rigoletto Curioso   PALERMO
SOLER 4501, TEL. 001/6320-5310
OPEN WEEKDAYS 10:30 A.M.–8 P.M.,
SAT. 11:30 A.M.–8 P.M.
WWW.RIGOLETTOCURIOSO.COM.AR

Hard to categorize, Rigoletto is a collectors' shops with books and magazines but most notably posters and still photos from vintage films, especially but not exclusively Argentine. The real classics, with cast members like Hugo del Carril, Mirtha Legrande, Niní Marshall, and Tita Merello, cost in the US$100–170 range, though few are truly immaculate (most are in pretty good condition, though).

POSTAGE STAMPS

Correo Argentino operates a **philatelic service** for stamp collectors in the **Correo Central** (Sarmiento 189, Oficina 51). The **Federación Argentina de Entidades Filatélicas** (Argentine Federation of Philatelic Entities, Perón 1479, 4th fl., Congreso, tel. 011/4373-0122) is open 6–8 P.M. Tuesday only.

JEWELRY

Buenos Aires has many jewelers. The most typical materials, though, are not diamonds or gold but rather silver, transformed by skilled artisans into unique pieces often held together with *tiento* (finely braided leather). There is a concentration of prestigious silversmiths in the Buenos Aires province town of San Antonio de Areco, about 80 kilometers west of the capital. (For details, see the *Excursions from Buenos Aires* chapter.)

Household Goods and Furniture

Argentina's 1990s economic boom, while it may have had a shaky foundation, brought sophistication and style to design and furniture in particular. While many of these items, such as beds and tables, are large, the 2002 devaluation made them cheap enough to justify shipping them overseas. With a strengthening peso, that's increasingly a judgment call, but their quality is undeniable.

Shopping centers like Recoleta's Buenos Aires Design may have set the tone, but smaller individual designers and shops in Palermo have been the most adventurous. Their cutting-edge influence is evident even in the standard furniture shops that line Balvanera's Avenida Belgrano, west of Avenida Entre Ríos, which do not produce such unique pieces.

Calma Chicha
PALERMO
HONDURAS 4925, TEL. 011/4831-1818
OPEN MON.–SAT. 10 A.M.–8 P.M., SUN. 2–8 P.M.
WWW.CALMACHICHA.COM

Defying easy categorization, Calma Chicha stocks a smartly designed, moderately priced diversity of household goods ranging from simple but well-made cups, pitchers, and place mats to children's games, lambskin and tanned-leather rugs, and a sample of clothing. Bright, cheerful, and spacious, it's a place where even anti-shoppers can amuse themselves while their mates or friends shop till they drop.

Carpintería Pampa
PALERMO
HONDURAS 5301, TEL. 011/4831-8559
OPEN MON.–SAT. 10 A.M.–1 P.M., MON.–FRI. 4–8 P.M.

For sturdy furniture of darkly rich subtropical hardwoods, such as *lapacho* and quebracho (axe-breaker), Pampa's rustically styled tables, chairs, benches, and the like are hard to surpass. Many of its woods and other materials are recycled, such as the leaf springs, salvaged pine, and forged iron used to create a garden bench resembling the passenger seat of a sulky (the single-horse cart that was once common on the pampas).

Concepto Gea
PALERMO
NICARAGUA 4758, TEL. 011/4833-5820
OPEN MON.–SAT. 11 A.M.–7 P.M.
WWW.CONCEPTOGEA.COM.AR

Starting from a rustic base of recycled wood from northwestern Argentina, Concepto Gea

Palermo Soho's Calma Chicha stocks a wide variety of creatively designed household items.

incorporates such elements as Asian tapestries to create a hybrid, stylish furniture with bright colors and a self-conscious exoticism. Examples include sofas, dressers, and coffee tables; some items are more harmonious than others.

In addition to its furniture, Concepto Gea turns out smaller functional items, such as tabletop lamps, as well as decorative ceramics. The ample showroom offers a wide spectrum of choices.

D. Mario   PALERMO
SOLER 5108, TEL. 011/4774-7646
OPEN MON.–SAT. 9 A.M.–7 P.M., SUN. 3–7 P.M.
In materials, at least, no one can accuse D. Mario of a faux rusticism—almost everything in its showroom consists of weathered wood recycled into handsome furniture in its adjacent workshop or a larger factory in the provincial

town of Pilar. Good examples include garden benches assembled from fence battens that once helped divide paddocks on provincial *estancias* and dining room tables of solid wooden planks rescued from rubbish tips.

Urano   PALERMO
HONDURAS 4702, TEL. 011/4833-0977
OPEN MON.–SAT. 10:30 A.M.–7:30 P.M.
WWW.URANODESIGN.COM
Beds, benches, bookshelves, chairs, and tables at Urano all partake of a sleek, contemporary design that, on occasion, lapses into something dangerously close to retro 1950s fashion. Having outfitted several bars, restaurants, and other business around town, Urano also produces a large variety of accessories for bathrooms, dining rooms, and kitchens. Prices are at the high end.

Music and Video

Compact discs and cassettes of locally produced music are readily available at bargain prices since the 2001–2002 devaluation—at US$5–7 per item, it's not so risky to try something unfamiliar. Even vinyl is available in used record stores.

Many classic Argentine films are available, but rarely with subtitles. Before buying any video, verify whether it's VHS (as used in the United States) or PAL (as used in Argentina and Europe).

Disquería Oid Mortales   MICROCENTRO
AVENIDA CORRIENTES 1145, LOCAL 17,
TEL. 011/4382-8839
OPEN WEEKDAYS NOON–8 P.M.
WWW.OIDMORTALESDISCOS.COM.AR
A small shop in a large gallery, specializing in CDs, this ironically alternative music shop draws its name (Listen, Mortals!) from the first line of Argentina's pompous national anthem. Strongest in rock 'n' roll, it has some truly offbeat selections, including the obscure but legendary Thirteenth Floor Elevators, a 1960s Texas band whose lead singer Roky Erikson

was once found innocent of marijuana possession—by reason of insanity.

Free Blues   MICROCENTRO
RODRÍGUEZ PEÑA 438, TEL. 15/4057-4749
OPEN WEEKDAYS 11 A.M.–9 P.M.
Just off Avenida Corrientes, Free Blues is a collectors' shop that stuffs a lot of used CDs and vinyl in a small space. It's strong on blues and *rock nacional,* but also has a surprising amount of country music and even rockabilly. Prices are high for scarce items.

Zivals   MICROCENTRO
AVENIDA CALLAO 395, TEL. 011/5128-7500
OPEN MON.–SAT. 9:30 A.M.–10 P.M.
WWW.ZIVALS.COM
One of B.A.'s best music shops, the independent Zivals showcases a diversity of styles and artists at reasonable prices, including a larger and far better sale bin than its competitors; it is also a very fine bookstore. Its specialized website, though, focuses exclusively on tango CDs, DVDs, VHS tapes, books, and sheet music.

Shopping

In Brief

In addition to their books, the Microcentro's **El Ateneo** (Florida 340, tel. 011/4325-6801) and its Barrio Norte branch **El Ateneo Grand Splendid** (Avenida Santa Fe 1880, tel. 011/4813-6052) stock an ample selection of quality CDs.

Musimundo (Florida 259, tel. 011/4394-7203, www.musimundo.com) is a chain with numerous outlets about town, but its lowest-common-denominator stock is costing it business.

Wine

Argentine wine is underrated and was underpriced even before devaluation—in fact, it's one of few commodities that always seems reasonably priced, even in times of runaway inflation. Except for the cheapest vintages, they're rarely disappointing.

Two uniquely Argentine varietals are the red Malbec, usually from Mendoza province, and the fruity but dry white *torrontés* from Cafayate, in Salta province (*torrontés* produced elsewhere may not be bad, but it usually can't match that from Cafayate).

Avola Enoteca   PALERMO
CERVIÑO 3804, TEL. 011/4801-0299
OPEN DAILY EXCEPT SUN. 9 A.M.–9 P.M.
WWW.AVOLAENOTECA.COM.AR
A recent creation, sort of a mini–Club del

Vino, the Avola's small Botánico storefront carries a selection of lesser-known wines, mostly from Mendoza province. In the basement, though, it has also opened a stylish wine bar that seats only about 50 patrons but hosts live music, usually blues or jazz, on Saturday nights (except in the summer months of January and February).

Buenos Aires Wines   RETIRO
SANTA FE 901, TEL. 011/4312-8069
OPEN DAILY 10 A.M.–10 P.M.
WWW.BUENOSAIRESWINES.COM
A recent addition to the scene, fancying itself a wine boutique, this strategically located outlet stocks bottles from Achával Ferrer to Zuccardi, and from Salta's northern subtropical highlands to Patagonia's Río Negro valley. It

Competitively priced, quality Argentine wines are gaining ground in the international market.

© WAYNE BERNHARDSON

also allows selective tasting prior to purchase and boasts a modernistic mezzanine wine bar offering a daily tapas special, with a sample of three different wines.

◪ Club del Vino   PALERMO
CABRERA 4737, TEL. 011/4833-0048
OPEN WEEKDAYS 10 A.M.–3:30 P.M. (RETAIL HOURS)
The king of the capital's wine outlets, the Club del Vino is also (nightly except Sunday) one of Palermo Soho's top restaurants, bars, and entertainment venues. Featuring a small but beautifully presented basement wine museum, it also publishes a monthly newsletter that covers the latest on Argentine wines, and hosts special events for its members (though membership is unnecessary in order to eat, drink, or see a show).

Tonel Privado   MICROCENTRO
SUIPACHA 299, TEL. 011/4328-0953
OPEN WEEKDAYS 9 A.M.–8 P.M.
WWW.TONELPRIVADO.COM
Tonel Privado is an outstanding wine shop

with well-trained personnel, and convenient branches at several other locations, including Galerías Pacífico, with even longer hours. Its website, though, is badly out of date, with no new newsletter in the past couple years and no indication of recent wine classes.

Winery   RETIRO
AVENIDA LIBERTADOR 500, TEL. 011/4325-3400
OPEN MON.–SAT. 10 A.M.–9 P.M.
WWW.WINERY.COM.AR
Tucked beneath the highway where Avenida 9 de Julio becomes the northbound Autopista Illia, Winery is a small chain that sells Argentine wines by the glass in its ground-level restaurant/wine bar (which serves excellent lunches at moderate prices, with sushi Wednesdays and Thursdays). On its upper level, it carries a representative stock of Argentine wines ranging from the economical to the truly premium.

Winery has several other outlets around town, but most of the rest do not serve food.

◪ Shopping

Accommodations

Buenos Aires has an abundance of accommodations in all categories, from hostel dorms to extravagant luxury suites and everything in between. There's no camping in the city proper, but many excursion destinations in Buenos Aires province and Uruguay do offer that option.

Prices in Buenos Aires proper often fall in the summer months of January and February, as business travel slows to a crawl, but then rise in March. For excursion destinations, though, they rise as *porteños* flee the capital for sand, sun, and fun on the beach. Other peak seasons, when prices may rise, are Semana Santa (Holy Week) and July's winter school vacations, which coincide with patriotic holidays.

Note also that Argentine hotels levy 21 percent in Impuesto al Valor Agregado or IVA (Value Added Tax or VAT); there is also IVA in Uruguay—remember this if you take excursions there. Unless otherwise indicated, rates in this book include IVA, but if there's any question at the front desk, ask for clarification to avoid unpleasant surprises when paying the bill.

CHOOSING A HOTEL

When choosing a hotel, much also depends on personal needs and taste—by most standards, the Alvear Palace is one of the continent's and even the world's great hotels, but five-star French furnishings and a personal butler may seem excessive to someone looking for cheaper but charming boutique accommodations, such as Barrio Norte's Art Hotel. Likewise, Retiro's high-rise Sheraton might suit a business person for its location and meeting rooms, while a backpacker might prefer a hostel near the nightlife of San Telmo or Palermo.

Buenos Aires's Best

N Funkiest Decor: At the self-described **Pop Hotel Boquitas Pintadas,** not far from San Telmo in the distinctly untouristed barrio of Constitución, every room reflects the work of the flamboyant novelist Manuel Puig. Even its restaurant desserts, such as "Kiss of the Spider Woman," have Puigian names (page 181).

N Most Offbeat Decoration: What would Paris do? Puerto Madero's **Hilton Buenos Aires** has a Barbie-themed room (usually reserved for young daughters as part of a suite adjoining their parents' room, but management might not refuse discreet fetishists) (page 186).

N Best Recycled Building: French architect Philippe Starck has taken Puerto Madero's resurrection one step beyond in turning the crumbling El Porteño granary into the audaciously visionary **Faena Hotel & Universe** (page 186).

N Best Hostel: Competition's tough in this category, given how quality hostels have proliferated the last few years, but San Telmo's **Telmotango Hostel Suites** stands apart for preserving magnificent period style while maintaining a casual manner (page 187).

N Best Thematic Hotel: Guests at San Telmo's **Hotel Mansión Dandi Royal** don't just dance tango, they live it: The best instructors get them started or improve their technique, individualized service gets them to any *milonga* in town, and an à la carte breakfast is available at any hour (page 188).

N Best Views: From its north side, Retiro's **Sheraton Buenos Aires Hotel** provides panoramas from the Kavanagh building and Plaza San Martín past the monumental train stations that linked Buenos Aires to Argentina's northern and western provinces, and the current port that still connects the city to the world. To the south, there's the Hotel de Inmigrantes, where

reception area of tango-themed Hotel Mansión Dandi Royal

European arrivals first set foot on Argentine territory, and the recycled Puerto Madero waterfront (page 193).

N Best Boutique Hotel: Combining style with affordability, Barrio Norte's **Art Hotel** has transformed a former rooming house into a stylish hotel with a luminous art gallery, open to the public, that changes its exhibitions frequently (page 195).

N Best Service: At Recoleta's elegant **Alvear Palace Hotel,** a butler comes with every room (page 197).

N Best Value for the Money: On a block-long street in Palermo Soho, **Che Lulu Guest House** has stylishly designed private rooms at hostel-plus prices, within easy walking distance of the city's best restaurants, bars, and nightlife (page 198).

Visitors also should not take government-generated hotel ratings too literally as they often represent an ideal rather than a reality, and some one- or two-star places may be better values than others that rank higher on paper. National and municipal tourist officials offer accommodations lists and brochures, but these often exclude budget options and may even omit some mid-range and high-end places. Prices, especially since the 2001–2002 devaluation, may be negotiable; do not assume the *tarifa mostrador* (rack rate) is etched in stone.

Camping

While there's no camping in Buenos Aires proper, it's a traditional budget option for families and other groups, with or without their own vehicles, throughout Argentina and Uruguay. Visitors taking excursions into the countryside and even to provincial cities—some facilities are surprisingly central—may find them worth consideration. Prices rarely exceed a couple dollars per person.

Argentine and Uruguayan campgrounds are generally spacious affairs, with shade, clean toilets, and bathrooms with hot showers, and even groceries and restaurants. In summer and on weekends, though, the best sites can be crowded and noisy; remember that Argentines stay up late—very late—for their barbecues. It's often possible to find a quieter—but otherwise less desirable—site on the periphery.

Hostels

Since devaluation, shoestring travelers have streamed into Buenos Aires and the local market has responded by adapting a variety of buildings in key barrios into hostels. While the bulk of their accommodations are inexpensive dorms, almost all of them have single or double rooms as well, and some of these are so comfortable and even stylish that non-backpackers can find some exceptional values.

Hostels, of course, offer an opportunity to socialize with a spectrum of like-minded travelers and some have restaurants, bars, and other entertainment facilities. While they may not be *youth* hostels per se, some do have rambunc-

tious clientele who enjoy the city's nightlife, and potential hostellers should carefully consider whether a given hostel meets their peace-and-quiet standards.

Buenos Aires proper has several Hostelling International (HI) affiliates, where oversight ensures more than minimum standards; there are several more in the province and in Uruguay. That said, many independent hostels are at least as good and deserve consideration.

For up-to-the-minute information on official Argentine hostels, contact Hostelling International Argentina (Florida 835, 3rd fl., Oficina 319-B, tel. 011/4511-8712, www.hostels.org.ar). The competing but rather torpid Asociación Argentina de Albergues de la Juventud (AAAJ, Talcahuano 214, tel. 011/4372-7094, www.hostelling-aaaj.org.ar) has a smaller affiliate network, though there is some overlap.

Uruguay's HI representative is Montevideo's Hostelling International Uruguay (Canelones 935, tel. 598/2-9005749, www.hosteluruguay.org).

Other Budget Accommodations

Budget accommodations in Buenos Aires, the surrounding provinces, and Uruguay can cost

HIGHER PRICES FOR FOREIGNERS

In the aftermath of the 2002 peso devaluation, price levels fell for nearly everything in Argentina, including accommodations. As the year progressed, though, and the 2003 summer tourist season began, some hotels began to institute differential pricing for Argentine residents and foreign visitors, and this practice has continued to the present.

The increase has been particularly noticeable at the top of the accommodations scale, where foreigners may pay 40 percent or so more than Argentines, but much may depend on the individual traveler's language and negotiating skills. The trend in hotel prices is likely a steady move upward, but prices are nevertheless cheaper than they were in the years when the peso and the dollar were at par.

THERE'S NO PLACE LIKE HOME

Rather than just renting a hotel room, visitors spending at least a week in Buenos Aires should consider renting an apartment and living in a neighborhood. Shopping in the same place everyday, buying a newspaper from the corner kiosk, learning the bus lines and Subte system, and establishing a rapport with the *portero* (doorman) give a traveler the chance to feel like part of local society. It's especially good if you wish to stay in a neighborhood like Palermo, which still has relatively limited accommodations.

Daily newspapers, like *Clarín, La Nación,* and the *Buenos Aires Herald,* all have rental listings. For short-term rentals, though, the best option may be an agency, such as **B y T Argentina Travel & Housing** (tel. 011/4821-6057, 011/4821-1783, or 011/4825-6202, www.bytargentina.com); its online inventory of apartments and other housing is a good way to familiarize yourself with the options. Other possibilities include **BA House** (tel. 011/4851-0798, www.bahouse.com.ar), which has a smaller selection of housing in a more geographically restricted area, and **Alojargentina** (tel. 011/5219-0606, www.alojargentina.com.ar).

and toilet (*baño general* or *baño compartido*) or offer a choice between shared and private bath (*baño privado*); bathtubs are unusual. In some cases, they have ceiling fans and even cable TV, but there is often an extra charge for cable and almost always a surcharge for air-conditioning (referred to as a/c throughout this book).

Travelers intending to stay at budget accommodations should bring their own towels. Likewise, as many budget hotels have thin walls and squeaky floors, earplugs are a good idea. Many but by no means all establishments include breakfast in their rates; ask to be certain.

Mid-Range Accommodations

Mid-range hotels generally offer larger, more comfortable, and better-furnished rooms (almost always with private bath) than even the best budget places. Ceiling fans, cable TV, and even a/c are common, but they may not have on-site parking. Some have restaurants. Rates can range anywhere from US$30 to US$100 d; some are better values than their high-end counterparts.

While star ratings can be misleading as to quality, it's worth mentioning the main distinction between two- and three-star accommodations. Generally, the former have showers, while the latter have bathtubs as well.

High-End Accommodations

Upscale hotels with top-flight service, which can range well upwards of US$100 per night, are few outside the capital and major resort areas. In the capital, amenities often include restaurants and bars, swimming pools and gym facilities, business centers and conference rooms, and in-room broadband or WiFi Internet connections.

Some are traditionally elegant places in privileged neighborhoods like Recoleta; others are business-oriented downtown accommodations, while still others are cutting-edge options in pioneer neighborhoods like Puerto Madero. Invariably, they offer secure onsite parking.

Outside the capital, these are mostly resort hotels that lack the business facilities.

as little as US$5 pp. Ranging from dingy fleabags with mattresses that sag like hammocks to simple but cheerful and tidy places with firm, new beds, they go by a variety of names that may be misleading as to their quality.

Hospedajes are generally family-run lodgings with a few spare rooms; *pensiones* and *casas de huéspedes* are comparable, nearly interchangeable terms. Some may have long-term residents as well as overnight guests. *Residenciales* (singular *residencial*) are generally buildings constructed with short-stay accommodations in mind, but may also have semi-permanent inhabitants. All of these places may even go by the term *hotel,* though usually that belongs to a more formal category.

There are some exceptionally good values in all these categories. Many have shared bath

Some of the best options in this category are country inn resorts on *estancias,* offering traditional hospitality and ambience with style unmatchable at other high-end places. Again, prices may be upwards of US$100—often substantially upwards.

Monserrat

Most budget accommodations in the vicinity of the Plaza de Mayo are only so-so and fairly interchangeable, but there are some exceptions. There are abundant mid-range options and a handful of very fine upmarket options.

UNDER US$25
Che Lagarto Youth Hostel
VENEZUELA 857, TEL. 011/4343-4845
WWW.CHELAGARTO.COM

Recently relocated to Monserrat, this casual, spacious hostel charges US$8 pp for dorm accommodations with breakfast, but also has private rooms for US$15/24 s/d with breakfast, free 24-hour Internet and the like; presently, rooms have cooling fans but a/c is in the planning stages. The entire ground floor is devoted to the Madhouse Pub, open until 1 A.M., which extends into a large wooded patio rare in this part of town.

Hotel Chile
AVENIDA DE MAYO 1297, TEL. 011/4383-7877

Once a prestige hotel, now a reliable budget-mid-range option, French architect Louis Dubois's art nouveau monument now features modernized rooms for US$14/20 s/d with private bath and breakfast. On the upper floors, airy corner balcony rooms enjoy panoramas of the Plaza del Congreso and, by craning the neck a bit eastward, the Plaza de Mayo and Casa Rosada; the location, though, also means a high decibel level.

Milhouse Youth Hostel
HIPÓLITO YRIGOYEN 959, TEL. 011/4345-9604
WWW.MILHOUSEHOSTEL.COM

Affiliated with Hostelling International, this refurbished period house is an immaculate, well-managed, well-located, and secure facility with spacious common areas that include a

kitchen and a coffee shop. Close to popular San Telmo and to public transportation to all parts of the city, its rates range from US$9 pp with breakfast in multi-bedded dorms to US$25 d for rooms with private bath. Many rooms have small balconies.

Portal del Sur Youth Hostel
HIPÓLITO YRIGOYEN 855, TEL. 011/4342-8788
WWW.PORTALDELSURBA.COM.AR

Just south of Avenida de Mayo, Po tal del Sur occupies a former *pension* (boarding house) with several floors of dorms (US$8pp) and private rooms (US$22/28 s/d) surrounding a sunny atrium, plus a rooftop terrace (with *parrilla*) and bar for relaxing and partying away from the sleeping areas. Rates include breakfast, kitchen privileges, a/c, and similar amenities; there's also a travel desk for arranging excursions and other transportation.

US$25–50
Concept Hotel
SANTIAGO DEL ESTERO 186, TEL. 011/4383-3473

In a rundown but rebounding area, the Concept Hotel is an anomaly in many ways: a high-tech budget hotel where every amenity or utility, from room lights to cable TV, is computer-controlled. Recycled almost beyond recognition, the building itself retains a few original features, such as its verdant interior patio and exposed segments of the original brick walls, but the rest seems almost futuristic. Rates start at US$22/26 s/d, with larger rooms only slightly more expensive.

Hotel Ibis
HIPÓLITO YRIGOYEN 1592, TEL. 011/5300-5555
WWW.IBISHOTEL.COM

Reservations are almost essential for the enormously popular Ibis, part of the French Accor chain. The sleek 147-room high-rise has added more than a smidgen of minimalist style and comfort to an area that had been truly run-down and, in the aftermath of the 2002 melt-down, is still recovering. Rates of US$28 s or d, plus US$2 for the optional breakfast, make it one of B.A.'s best bargains.

Hotel Napoleón
RIVADAVIA 1364, TEL. 011/4383-2031
WWW.HOTEL-NAPOLEON.COM.AR
With their superannuated '60s style, suffering from drab but somehow garish décor, the well-kept rooms here are well past their peak. Still, the friendly Napoleón will do in a pinch and the rates (US$39 s or d with breakfast, a/c, cable TV, and telephone) are competitive even if it can't come close to the Ibis.

US$50–100
Castelar Hotel & Spa
AVENIDA DE MAYO 1152, TEL. 011/4383-5000
WWW.CASTELARHOTEL.COM.AR
One of the capital's most historic lodgings, dat-ing from 1929, the four-star Castelar (US$48–57 s or d) oozes character out onto the Avenida de Mayo. In its time, it has hosted the likes of Spanish playwright Federico García Lorca (who lived in room 704 for six months), Chile's Nobel Prize–winning poet Pablo Neruda, Nobel Prize–winning scientist Linus Pauling, and many Argentine politicians. Embellished with marble, it offers comfortable, well-equipped rooms (with entire non-smoking floors), but a middling breakfast. Figure in access to its own basement spa, and it's an outstanding value even by post-devaluation standards.

ⓜ Pop Hotel Boquitas Pintadas
ESTADOS UNIDOS 1393, TEL. 011/4381-6064
WWW.BOQUITAS-PINTADAS.COM.AR
Just outside Monserrat's boundaries, Consti-tución's Boquitas Pintadas is a flamboyant five-room hostelry that takes its inspiration

from the even more flamboyant Argen-tine novelist, the late Manuel Puig. Every room features an idiosyncratic décor based on a theme from Puig's writings; all have private baths, but some are outside the rooms themselves.

Decorated in a pop art mode, Boquitas also boasts a Puig-inspired restaurant menu and a popular bar that pumps thumping techno at night and especially on weekends. Room rates range from US$41/55–US$86/115 s/d; the neighborhood itself remains marginal, but the German owners have given the place a remarkable makeover.

US$100–150
Hotel Intercontinental
MORENO 809, TEL. 011/4340-7100
WWW.BUENOS-AIRES.INTERCONTINENTAL.COM
According to magazines like *Travel & Leisure,* the swank Intercontinental consistently makes the list of Buenos Aires's best hotels. Rates start around US$160 s or d for *lujo* (luxury) rooms, which are in fact their most basic units but are still spacious and comfortable, with Internet access via the room's TV.

In addition to extensive personal and busi-ness services, two-thirds of the Intercontinen-tal's 315 rooms are nonsmoking. It also has two restaurants, a gym and pool, and considerable open space in an adjacent public plaza main-tained by hotel personnel.

Hotel Nogaró
DIAGONAL JULIO A. ROCA 562, TEL. 011/4331-0091
WWW.NOGAROBUE.COM.AR
Dating from 1930 but renovated just a few years ago, this legitimately four-star, French-style, 145-room hotel no longer offers give-away post-devaluation rates, but prices barely a third of what they are now (US$107–133 s or d with breakfast) were never des-tined to last. Amenities include telephone, cable TV, a/c, Internet connections, and in-room strongboxes.

NH City Hotel

BOLÍVAR 160, TEL. 011/4121-6464
WWW.NH-HOTELES.COM

Part of a highly regarded Spanish luxury business chain and located just south of the Plaza de Mayo, the City Hotel is a spectacularly modernized 303-room facility (dating from 1931) that had the misfortune to reopen at the nadir of Argentina's 2001–2002 economic meltdown. The bad timing, though, has meant good rates: US$106–144 s or d, for beautifully appointed rooms with all the contemporary conveniences, plus luxuries like a rooftop pool, gym, and sauna, and a highly rated Spanish restaurant.

Microcentro

Recent economic conditions have made some pretty good Microcentro hotels more affordable, but bargains are fewer as the economy stabilizes.

UNDER US$25

Hotel A&B Internacional

MONTEVIDEO 248, TEL. 011/4384-9616

A real surprise in this part of town, the A&B has injected elements of style without going big budget, having created lofts with spiral staircases and balconies (US$17/23 s/d with private bath and breakfast) by combining small street-side rooms that were once on separate floors. At the same time, they've exposed sections of the original red brick walls to give the hallways and other common areas a touch of distinction. The so-called "four-star suite" (US$27/32 s/d), though it has a small patio and a large bathroom, falls a little short of its aspirations; still, on the whole, this place offers superb value for money.

Hotel Americano

RODRÍGUEZ PEÑA 265, TEL. 011/4382-4223
WWW.HOTELAMERICANO.COM.AR

Though well-located, the undistinguished Americano is friendly enough, but its *común* rooms (US$17/20 s/d with breakfast) are claustrophobically small; if you need to stay here, the larger and comfier *especial* rooms (US$20/23 s/d) are well worth the price difference.

Hotel Europa

BARTOLOMÉ MITRE 1294, TEL. 011/4381-9629
WWW.EUROHOTEL.COM.AR

Only the exterior retains its original Art Deco style, but the Europa is a spotless, rejuvenated budget hotel for US$15/18 s/d with breakfast; a/c costs extra. A few interior rooms are relatively dark; the better rooms have exterior balconies.

Hotel Maipú

HOTEL MAIPÚ 735, TEL. 011/4322-5142

Catering to overseas visitors and close to more prestigious Retiro, the Maipú occupies an attractive but aging building whose utilitarian rooms cost US$9/11 s/d with shared bath, US$11/14 s/d with private bath. Breakfast is not included.

Hotel O'Rei

LAVALLE 733, TEL. 011/4394-7112
WWW.HOTELOREI.COM.AR

Despite a record of notoriously cranky management, the O'Rei is a longstanding backpackers' choice because of its central pedestrian mall location and low prices—US$7/10 s/d for smallish rooms with shared bath, US$12/14 s/d with private bath. It has upgraded the rooms with cable TV and ceiling fans, as well as the furniture (not extravagantly, though), and the kitchen is open to guests.

Hotel Orense

BARTOLOMÉ MITRE 1359, TEL. 011/4372-4441
WWW.HOTELORENSE.COM.AR

While it has no luxuries, the Orense is a meticulously spic-and-span budget hotel where most of the rooms front onto a luminous atrium; isolated from the street by the lobby, the rooms themselves are remarkably quiet for this part of town. Rates are US$16/20 s/d with breakfast and private bath (showers only, no tubs), telephone, and ceiling fans; there's a surcharge for a/c.

Hotel Sportsman
RIVADAVIA 1425, TEL. 011/4381-8021
WWW.HOTELSPORTSMAN.COM.AR
In Congreso, the Sportsman is a musty backpackers' special whose main appeal is low prices, but it has its adherents. Rates are US$7/11 s/d with shared bath, US$11/15 s/d with private bath; breakfast is extra. There are discounts for longer stays.

St. Nicholas Youth Hostel
BARTOLOMÉ MITRE 1691, TEL. 011/4373-5920
WWW.SNHOSTEL.COM
In the bustling Congreso area, this HI affiliate has dorm accommodations for US$7 pp (with breakfast and shared bath) and private rooms for around US$11 pp; non-Hostelling members pay slightly more. Like most other B.A. hostels, it's a handsome rehabbed period house with ample shared spaces (including a sunny rooftop terrace and even its own pub), but noise carries a little too well through the multistory atrium; consequently, it's not the best choice for the early-to-bed set.

V&S Hostel Club
VIAMONTE 887, TEL. 011/4322-0944 OR 011/4327-5131
WWW.HOSTELCLUB.COM
In a recycled early-20th-century house, this well-located, independently operated hostel offers dorm beds for as little as US$8 pp with a buffet breakfast included; rooms with private bath cost US$22/25 s/d. The building itself has central heating, a/c, and spacious and appealing common areas, including a kitchen, dining room, small gym, and a *parrilla* for barbecues.

US$25–50

Columbia Palace Hotel
AVENIDA CORRIENTES 1533, TEL. 011/4373-1906
WWW.COLUMBIAPALACEHOTEL.COM.AR
Facing the Teatro General San Martín and close to other prestigious theater venues, the Columbia Palace is worn and well past its peak, but at least it's holding its own and is suitable for a night. Rates are US$25/32 s/d with breakfast.

Goya Hotel
SUIPACHA 748, TEL. 011/4322-9269
WWW.GOYAHOTEL.COM.AR
This is one of the Microcentro's best small hotels, with 40 cozy rooms and family-style service. Rates start at US$27/33 s/d for very decent quarters with private bath (shower only), while rooms with tubs go for US$37/43 s/d; there's a handful of *presidente* rooms (US$47/53 s/d) whose bathrooms have Jacuzzis. All rates include a continental breakfast, cable TV, and a/c.

Hotel de los Dos Congresos
RIVADAVIA 1777, TEL. 011/4372-0466
WWW.HOTELDOSCONGRESOS.COM
Possibly Congreso's finest value, this rejuvenated gem boasts a stately exterior that belies the relatively low prices found in its refurbished interior: US$35/40 s/d for spacious and comfortable rooms with cable TV, a/c, telephone, and other standard amenities, as well as a buffet breakfast. Reservations are advisable for one of the stylish lofts (US$50 s or d), which have spiral staircases and Jacuzzi-equipped bathrooms.

Hotel Facón Grande
RECONQUISTA 645, TEL. 011/4312-6360
WWW.HOTELFACONGRANDE.COM
The former Hotel Italia Romanelli, a very respectable hotel in its time, has undergone a *criollo* transformation into the gaucho-themed Facón Grande, suggesting a piece of Patagonian revolutionary history in the heart of Buenos Aires. Totally rehabbed, it offers bright, cheerful midsize rooms, plus appealing common areas, on a reasonably quiet block. Rates of US$47 d are an excellent value.

Hotel Lafayette
RECONQUISTA 546, TEL. 011/4393-9081
WWW.LAFAYETTEHOTEL.COM.AR
With large and modernized rooms for US$40/50 s/d with a diverse buffet breakfast, the steadily improving Lafayette is one of the best values in its category—better than several pricier hotels in the vicinity. Along with obliging personnel, it features such amenities as cable TV, telephone, a/c, WiFi service, and the like.

Accommodations

Hotel Plaza Roma

LAVALLE 110, TEL. 011/4314-0666
WWW.HOTELPLAZAROMA.COM.AR
Opposite the historic Luna Park stadium, convenient to Puerto Madero's restaurants, cinemas, and open spaces, the Plaza Roma offers rooms with private bath, breakfast, a/c, cable TV, and telephone. Some rooms enjoy views of the Puerto Madero complex and, while prices have risen since the depths of 2002, it's still a good value for US$30/40 s/d.

Normandie Hotel

RODRÍGUEZ PEÑA 320, TEL. 011/4371-7001
WWW.HOTELNORMANDIE.COM.AR
In the Congreso district, just off Avenida Corrientes, the Normandie is a respectable mid-range choice that charges US$24/27 s/d for carpeted rooms with private bath and breakfast. There are discounts for cash payments, though, and for stays longer than five consecutive nights; as post-devaluation hotel prices rise, this is one the best values in town.

In Brief

Only a block from the Plaza del Congreso, **Hotel Parlamento** (Rodríguez Peña 61, tel. 011/4374-1410, hotelparlamento@speedy.com.ar, US$23/28 s/d) is a friendly but otherwise unremarkable option.

Though its smallish rooms are well-kept, the **Concorde Hotel** (25 de Mayo 630, tel. 011/4313-2018, www.concordehotel.com.ar, US$34/40 s/d) has not kept pace with comparably priced hotels, other than its bathrooms (which, however, lack tubs). There's a 10 percent discount for cash.

US$50–100

Atlas Tower Hotel

AVENIDA CORRIENTES 1778, TEL. 011/5217-9371
WWW.ATLASTOWER.COM.AR
One of barely a handful of attractive new hotels in Congreso, the three-star Atlas Tower has midsized rooms with all the modern conveniences, including telephone, modem and broadband Internet access, strongboxes, cable TV, and the like; the common areas are also inviting. Rates of US$47/53 s/d with breakfast are more than fair for what it offers, and there are discounts for Internet reservations.

Gran Hotel Argentino

CARLOS PELLEGRINI 37, TEL. 011/4334-4001
WWW.HOTEL-ARGENTINO.COM.AR
Housed in a striking art nouveau building a few blocks south of the Obelisco, at US$52 s or d the otherwise unremarkable Argentino is not quite the value it was immediately post-devaluation, but there are discounts for cash and for extended stays. Some will find the location on Buenos Aires's broadest avenue enthralling, but others may think it a little too fast-paced.

Gran Hotel Colón

CARLOS PELLEGRINI 507, TEL. 011/4320-3500
WWW.COLON-HOTEL.COM.AR
Only a block from the Obelisco, the business-oriented, four-star Colón isn't quite the value it was in the early post-devaluation days of 2002, but at US$80/90 s/d it's still good value by international standards and convenient to almost everything in town. Rooms with better views go for US$100 s or d, and there are also more elaborate suites; stays of three days or more get significant discounts.

Hotel Reconquista Plaza

RECONQUISTA 602, TEL. 011/4311-4600
WWW.RECONQUISTAPLAZA.COM.AR
Interesting in its design, the Reconquista Plaza has turned a corner lot into a hotel with a series of large trapezoidal rooms (even the elevators share this unusual form). Unfortunately, though it's been open only a few years, there are early signs of inconsistent maintenance (even if the staff are gracious and attentive). The rates of US$91 d, while not excessive, are higher than those at some places that are arguably better values.

Savoy Hotel

AVENIDA CALLAO 181, TEL. 011/4370-8000
WWW.GOLDENTULIPSAVOY.COM
Congreso's prime upscale option is the Savoy, now part of the Dutch Golden Tulip chain, though it has a certain institutional impersonality. Rates start at US$80 d, with larger suites at higher

prices; for stays longer than two weeks, there's a 10 percent discount. All windows are double-paned for silence, and rooms include phones (with voicemail), Internet connections and other business amenities, and a buffet breakfast.

US$100–150

Hotel Hostería Posta Carretas
ESMERALDA 726, TEL. 011/4322-8567
WWW.POSTACARRETAS.COM.AR
The Posta Carretas has an older sector with smallish and dark but quiet rooms, and a newer addition with larger, comfier rooms but a noisier street exposure. Amenities include cable TV, a/c, pool, sauna and gym, bar, restaurant, and buffet breakfast. The staff is agreeable, but at US$100 d for two-room suites and US$125 d for a more spacious junior suite, it's not B.A.'s best value.

Hotel NH Jousten
AVENIDA CORRIENTES 240, TEL. 011/4321-6750
WWW.NH-HOTELES.COM
Another affiliate of the Spanish chain, the Jousten has 85 rooms in an elegant, tastefully recycled French-style castle. Quiet despite the busy avenue thanks to double-paned windows, each room has cable TV, stereo, telephone, a/c, and Internet connections; rates are US$107/133 with buffet breakfast. The highly regarded basement restaurant serves Spanish cuisine.

US$150–200

Hotel Crowne Plaza Panamericano
CARLOS PELLEGRINI 525, TEL. 011/4348-5000
WWW.CROWNEPLAZA.COM.AR
Near the Obelisco, the Panamericano consists

of an older south tower, where rates start at US$138 s or d, and a newer north tower, beginning at US$152 s or d. Both are comfortable, but the north-tower rooms are technologically superior. All of its 400 rooms have access to amenities, including gym and rooftop pool; its restaurant, *Tomo I,* is widely considered one of the capital's best.

Hotel Sheraton Libertador
AVENIDA CÓRDOBA 680, TEL. 011/4322-2095
WWW.STARWOOD.COM
Sheraton's Microcentro hotel boasts a business center, restaurant, pool, gym, and other luxuries. The rooms themselves are showing signs of wear, with worn carpets and scuffed woodwork, even though they're still comfortable enough and the service is diligent. Rates start at US$164 s or d for a standard midsize room, with buffet breakfast included.

MORE THAN US$200

Claridge Hotel
TUCUMÁN 535, TEL. 011/4314-7700
WWW.CLARIDGE-HOTEL.COM.AR
One of the capital's classics, dating from 1946 but tastefully modernized, the Claridge charges US$229 s or d for rooms with the standard amenities in its range, including cable TV, telephone, and a work desk with Internet connection. Several floors are tobacco-free. While it's impeccable and efficient, some of its more contemporary competitors arguably offer better value for money.

Puerto Madero

B.A.'s youngest barrio has only limited accommodations—all in the highest price ranges.

US$150–200

 Hilton Buenos Aires
AVENIDA MACACHA GÜEMES 351, TEL. 011/4891-0000
WWW.BUENOS.HILTON.COM

From the outside, it's a boxy, undistinguished, modern glass palace, but the B.A. Hilton's lobby is an expansive seven-story atrium that warms the entire interior with spectacular natural light. Not reached by the narrow dark hallways of traditional hotels, its room entrances all face the atrium, while the rooms themselves are large, comfortable, well-designed and immaculately maintained. On the upper floors, west-facing rooms have great views of the Puerto Madero yacht harbor and downtown.

While the Hilton is far from dark, it's had its noir side. In Fabián Bielinsky's recent con-man film *Nueve Reinas (Nine Queens)*, its luminous lobby was one of few identifiable landmarks in a city otherwise depicted through its lowlifes and anonymously seedy bars.

Rates at the Hilton start around US$169 s or d and reach nearly US$300, but the lower rates compare favorably to some Recoleta hotels that aren't nearly so good. For a truly specialized market, room No. 538 is Barbie-themed (presumably for young daughters of parents in the adjoining room).

MORE THAN US$200

Faena Hotel & Universe
MARTA SALOTTI 445, TEL. 011/4010-9000
WWW.FAENAHOTELANDUNIVERSE.COM

There's no false modesty in the name of French architect Philippe Starck's latest project, which turned the landmark Edificio El Porteño, an early-20th-century granary, into a five-star-plus hotel. From outside, in fact, it's not evident that this red brick structure on the edge of the Reserva Ecológica is a hotel, but its interior is an unexpected revelation of continental style.

Puerto Madero's Hilton Buenos Aires was one of the locations for the con-man film *Nine Queens*.

© WAYNE BERNHARDSON

In fact, the Faena is an 83-room hotel but it's also home to permanent apartment residents and such amenities as a restaurant, a cabaret, a pool with a swim-up bar, and a library seemingly airlifted in from a 19th-century Parisian mansion. The rooms themselves—and their furnishings—look so Parisian as to be incongruous with the building, but there's no denying their quality and sophistication. In its "universe," the Faena also sells "experiences," such as polo with pros and workshops with famous photographer Aldo Sessa.

Rates at the Faena start around US$300 s or d, and rise into the US$1,200 range.

San Telmo

San Telmo's accommodations are limited and, historically, they've been mediocre at best. In recent years, though, the barrio's popularity with backpackers and other budget travelers has spawned a proliferation of quality hostel-style accommodations—some of *very* high quality.

UNDER US$25

Albergue Ester de Nadenhein
BRASIL 675, TEL. 011/4300-9321
WWW.HOSTELLING-AAAJ.ORG.AR
Near the Constitución railroad and Subte stations, the city's oldest continuously operating hostel is cheap (US$4 pp), but during school holidays, it's overrun with groups from the provinces and the kids can get rowdy. Rates include breakfast but not kitchen privileges, and the building itself is suffering from deferred maintenance.

Carlos Gardel Hostel
CARLOS CALVO 579, TEL. 011/4307-2606
WWW.HOSTELCARLOSGARDEL.COM.AR
The great *tanguero* toting a backpack is the trademark of this inviting hostel barely two blocks from Plaza Dorrego. Rooms range from dorms (US$5–6 pp) to private singles and doubles (US$8–9 pp) in a quirky building with kitchen access, comfy common areas, and free tango classes and Internet access. Rates also include breakfast.

El Hostal de San Telmo
CARLOS CALVO 614, TEL. 011/4300-6899
HTTP://WEBS.SATLINK.COM/USUARIOS/E/ELHOSTAL
A pioneer of contemporary hostel-style accommodations in Buenos Aires, this is a cozy—perhaps cramped would be closer to the truth—hostel in a prime location, but it's hard pressed to match the amenities of its more recent competitors. Dorm rates are US$10 pp; shared amenities include kitchen facilities, a large terrace with a *parrilla*, cable TV, and Internet access.

Hostel Inn Tango City
PIEDRAS 680, TEL. 011/4300-5776
WWW.HOSTEL-INN.COM
This engaging hostel has dorms (US$8 pp) and doubles (US$15 pp) with breakfast, kitchen facilities, free 24-hour Internet, tango and Spanish lessons, and plenty of other amenities. It's even dog-friendly, though owners have to take responsibility for their pets.

Hostel Nómade
CARLOS CALVO 430, TEL. 011/4300-7641
WWW.HOSTELNOMADE.COM
Barely a block from Plaza Dorrego, this cozy, friendly hostel in a traditional PH ("horizontal property," as opposed to multistory) has mostly dormitory accommodations (US$6 pp) but also a handful of private rooms (US$15 d); rates include breakfast. There's 24-hour Internet access, and common areas include a game room with a pool table.

Telmotango Hostel Suites
CHACABUCO 679, TEL. 011/4361-5808
WWW.HOSTELMOTANGO.COM
This is the pick of San Telmo's hostel accommodations, in a magnificently preserved 19th-century house with stunning common areas, including a spectacular atrium and a sunny

Accommodations

San Telmo's Lugar Gay is an intimate bed-and-breakfast in an attractively recycled century-old house.

rooftop terrace. Some of its 33 rooms are a little small, but others are sizeable and the rates (US$17–25 d with breakfast) make it arguably the barrio's best value; the cheaper rooms have shared bath. Though it's only just opened, it's likely to become a favorite not just with backpackers, but also a broader spectrum of travelers seeking both style and value.

In Brief

While San Telmo's non-hostel budget accommodations are few, **Hotel Varela** (Estados Unidos 342, tel. 011/4362-1231, hotel varela@yahoo.com.ar, US$7–9 s or d) is a no-frills but spotless and reputable backpackers' choice. Rates depend on whether the room has shared or private bath.

US$25–50

Lugar Gay de Buenos Aires

DEFENSA 1120, TEL. 011/4300-4747
WWW.LUGARGAY.ORG

With impeccable taste, its owners have recycled a century-old house into B.A.'s only bed-

and-breakfast catering exclusively to gay men, without compromising the classic style of its steep marble staircases and other traditional features. Bordering Plaza Dorrego (one balcony looks diagonally onto the plaza), it has comfortable rooms with cable TV, strongboxes, and comfortable furnishings, though some lack view windows (but not natural light). There are two sunny but secluded rooftop terraces, one of which offers river views in the distance.

Lugar Gay has only eight rooms, so reservations are imperative; rates vary from US$25/35 s/d (with shared bath) to US$35/50 s/d (with private bath). Rates include breakfast, Internet access, a shared Jacuzzi, a weight room, and a kitchenette; the entire staff can handle English.

MORE THAN US$100

Hotel Mansión Dandi Royal

PIEDRAS 922, TEL. 011/4361-3537
WWW.HOTELMANSIONDANDIROYAL.COM

Only slightly less distinctive than Boquitas Pintadas, but with a different style, the Dandi

Royal is a boutique hotel whose primary clientele are foreigners who come not just to dance but to live tango 24/7. At the same time, it welcomes non-dancers who enjoy its peace, quiet, and individualized service, in a magnificently recycled mansion that, according to its managers, was originally a single-family residence and once a brothel.

All the original woodwork, once covered with paint, has been stripped and restored, the walls covered with tango-themed murals and the common areas furnished with tables, chairs, and sofas from the Gardelian epoch. In three categories, the 15 rooms all have king-size beds and other modern amenities but also period touches, such as claw-foot tubs. Prices vary according to size: The "Dandi" costs US$84 s or d, the "Royal" US$127 s or d, and the "Suite Piazzola" US$169 s or d. An à la carte breakfast, included in the rates, is available at any hour (*milongueros* keep irregular schedules!); it also has a gym, a sunny terrace, a small rooftop pool, and a secluded patio.

For information on Dandi Royal's tango packages, see the *Special Interests* entry in the *Know Buenos Aires* chapter.

Balvanera

Most Balvanera budget hotels are on the borders of Monserrat and the Microcentro, within a few blocks of the Congreso Nacional.

UNDER US$25

Gran Hotel Sarmiento
SARMIENTO 1892, TEL. 011/4374-8069
WWW.HOTELGRANSARMIENTO.COM
Some exterior rooms in this 30-unit, French-style "petit hotel" have wrought-iron balconies; its original carved and stained banisters, as well as marble staircases, contribute to a genuine but faded gentility. At US$13/17 s/d without breakfast, the amiable Sarmiento remains a better value than some places that cost twice as much; its simple amenities include a/c and ceiling fans.

US$25–50

Hotel Bauen
AVENIDA CALLAO 360, TEL. 011/4372-1932
Following the 2002 peso collapse, the old Hotel Bauen closed, but in mid-2004 it reopened as a unique, employee-run hotel cooperative—the first of its kind in the country, though some smokestack factories have seen similar experiments. With more labor than capital available, its unadorned rooms (US$30/33 s/d with breakfast) provide basic comforts.

The new Bauen is perhaps most notable for the sense of community among its staff, who are quickly rehabbing common areas like the bar, restaurant, and the basement club, which features live jazz, rock, and techno on weekends.

Hotel Lyon
RIOBAMBA 251, TEL. 011/4372-0100
WWW.HOTEL-LYON.COM.AR
For families or groups of friends, one of the capital's best options is the Lyon, which has spacious apartment-style rooms—ranging from 40 to 65 square meters—starting at US$38 s or d with breakfast. For stays longer than three days and paid in cash, there's a 15 percent discount.

Molino Hotel
AVENIDA CALLAO 164, TEL. 011/4374-9112
WWW.MOLINOHOTEL.COM.AR
Slightly worn but still tidy, the 60-room Molino is a perfectly decent choice in its price range (US$23/27–US$27/30 s/d with private bath, breakfast, telephone, and a/c). Rates for the midsized rooms vary depending on whether the baths have showers or tubs.

Nuevo Hotel Callao
AVENIDA CALLAO 292, TEL. 011/4372-3861
WWW.HOTELCALLAO.COM.AR
In a stylish building crowned by a corner cupola, near the theater district, the upgraded 45-room

Accommodations

Callao has kept both its architectural and practical integrity while maintaining moderate prices. Rates are US$25/35 s/d with breakfast; make reservations for the more distinctive cupola rooms, which, however, are cooled by ceiling fans rather than a/c.

Sarmiento Palace Hotel
SARMIENTO 1953, TEL. 011/4953-3404
WWW.HOTELSARMIENTO.COM.AR

On a shady, leafy block unusually close to the densely built Microcentro, the 120-room Sarmiento enjoys a reputation for personalized attention. For US$30/38 s/d with breakfast, the midsized rooms have dated décor and older a/c units but upgraded baths; a handful of larger, more expensive suites (US$64 s or d) include whirlpool tubs. Common areas include a bar, a small gym, and a sunny third-floor deck.

US$50-100

Bauen Suite Hotel
AVENIDA CORRIENTES 1856, TEL. 011/4370-0400
WWW.BAUENSUITE.COM

More business-oriented than its former affiliate around the Callao corner, Congreso's other Bauen is a high-rise hotel with spacious, well-maintained suites (40 square meters with kitchenettes), incongruously decorated in a sort of Southeast Asian mode. Rates start at US$53 s or d, with breakfast and taxes included.

US$100-150

Abasto Plaza Hotel
AVENIDA CORRIENTES 3190, TEL. 011/6311-4466
WWW.ABASTOPLAZA.COM

Opposite the Mercado del Abasto, the former Holiday Inn has tried to reinvent itself as a five-star tango-theme hotel, and in truth it does have nearby tango landmarks: the market itself, the Esquina Carlos Gardel *tanguería,* and the Gardel museum. It also offers tango lessons, but they can't afford to ignore business clients (there's an ample business center); other amenities include a gym, a pool, and a solarium. There are several different kinds of rooms, ranging from standard to luxury suites, and dedicated tobacco-free floors. Rates fall into the US$121–145 s or d range.

Retiro

True budget accommodations are scarce in the northern barrios, but there are a few options. Many upscale Retiro hotels are close to extravagant Recoleta and often claim to be part of that barrio.

UNDER US$25

Recoleta Youth Hostel
LIBERTAD 1216, TEL. 011/4812-4419
WWW.TRHOSTEL.COM.AR

Boasting the most prestigious location in its category, this HI-affiliated hostel occupies an erstwhile mansion typical of Francophile Recoleta (though it lies geographically within Retiro, it is *close* to the Recoleta line). Bunks in multi-bedded rooms with shared bath and separate lockers cost US$8 pp, but it also has private rooms for US$18 d; all rates include breakfast. There are ample shared spaces, including kitchen facilities.

US$25-50

Gran Hotel Orly
PARAGUAY 474, TEL. 011/4312-5344
WWW.ORLY.COM.AR

While prices have risen since the depths of the 2002 devaluation, the 180-room Orly is often full at rates of US$30/35 s/d, breakfast and taxes included, because it offers good value for money. Close to Plaza San Martín, Puerto Madero, and the Microcentro, its rooms are utilitarian but utterly reliable.

US$50-100

Argenta Tower Hotel & Suites
JUNCAL 868, TEL. 011/4325-0607
WWW.ARGENTA-TOWER.COM.AR

For expansive rooms with all the modern conveniences at moderate prices, it's hard to top the 100 suites at the Argenta Tower. On a quiet block almost equidistant between the Microcentro and Recoleta, it's popular with business clients for its full-service facilities, including high-speed Internet connections in every room, but is also a fine tourist choice. Rates start at US$77 s or d for substantial studio suites, but even larger rooms are not that much more expensive.

Bisonte Palace Hotel
MARCELO T. DE ALVEAR 910, TEL. 011/4328-4751
WWW.HOTELESBISONTE.COM
For a hotel in this neighborhood, only a block off Santa Fe, the four-star Bisonte offers good value for both business and pleasure. Rates are US$67/79 s or d for soundproofed rooms with a/c, buffet breakfast, and distinctive touches, such as a newspaper of your choice in the morning.

Carlton Hotel
LIBERTAD 1180, TEL. 011/4812-0081
WWW.SOLANS.COM
The Carlton is a decent business hotel, with well-furnished midsize rooms and buffet breakfast but without luxuries. Its rising rates of US$57/63 s/d with breakfast have more to do with its location than with its presumptive four-star status.

Dazzler Hotel
LIBERTAD 902, TEL. 011/4816-5005
WWW.DAZZLERHOTEL.COM
Overlooking Plaza Libertad, the Dazzler prides itself on "park view" rooms that overlook the plaza's dense wooded canopy. Rates are US$85 s or d, reasonable enough in this part of town, but the hotel (which opened in the dark days of 2002) is showing early signs of corner-cutting or substandard workmanship. While the facilities and amenities are still good enough, and the service is assiduous, by the next edition of this book the Dazzler could be running as fast as it can just to stay in the same place.

Hotel Lancaster
AVENIDA CÓRDOBA 405, TEL. 011/4312-4061
WWW.LANCASTERHOTEL-PAGE.COM
Graham Greene, appropriately enough, once stayed at the British-styled Lancaster, which figures briefly in his novels *The Honorary Consul* and *Travels with My Aunt*. Really a hotel of another era, exceptionally well-preserved from Greene's time, it still boasts marble staircases, burnished woodwork, and aging but fully functional fixtures. Rates are US$58/62 s/d with breakfast; there's an English-style pub on the ground floor.

Impala Hotel
LIBERTAD 1215, TEL. 011/4816-0430
WWW.HOTELIMPALA.COM.AR
Superbly located for a hotel in its category, the three-star Impala has smallish but modern, comfortable, and immaculate rooms for US$50/60 s/d with an ample buffet breakfast. Amenities include a business center.

US$100–150

Américas Towers Hotel
LIBERTAD 1070, TEL. 011/4815-7900
WWW.GRUPOAMERICAS.COM.AR
Almost next door to its sister Hotel de las Américas, this is a 100-room business-oriented facility that has virtually identical services (plus a fitness center) and slightly higher rates (US$110/125 s/d).

Hotel Conquistador
SUIPACHA 948, TEL. 011/4328-3012
WWW.ELCONQUISTADOR.COM.AR
Just off Avenida Santa Fe, the Conquistador is a modern multistory hotel appealing primarily to commercial travelers, with its business center, meeting rooms, workout facilities, and the like. Rates starting at US$116 s or d include a buffet breakfast.

Hotel Crillón
AVENIDA SANTA FE 796, TEL. 011/4310-2000
WWW.HOTELCRILLON.COM.AR
The Crillón's Parisian style is not quite classic—it dates only from 1968, long after B.A.'s early-20th-century Francophile building boom—but its details and especially its staff project the feeling of a more venerable and far

more exclusive place. Near Plaza San Martín, its rooms offer all the contemporary comforts, including a/c, cable TV, telephone, WiFi Internet access, voicemail, and even a cell phone; the corner rooms, though, are larger and have better views toward the Plaza. Rates start at US$109 s or d, with buffet breakfast.

Hotel de las Américas
LIBERTAD 1020, TEL. 011/4816-3432
WWW.GRUPOAMERICAS.COM.AR
Renovated not so long ago, this 150-room hotel has king-size beds, telephones, dataports, voicemail, double-paned windows, bar and restaurant, and parking. The service is almost uniformly professional except for the front desk, which can show apparent indifference toward some requests; on the other hand, they'll open the breakfast salon at 5 A.M. for guests who have an early flight. Rates are US$85/105 s/d with an elaborate breakfast buffet.

Hotel Presidente
CERRITO 850, TEL. 011/4816-2222
WWW.HOTELPRESIDENTE.COM.AR
Oriented toward business travelers, the well-located Presidente is a modern high-rise with 181 rooms, 28 suites, and 35 apartments. Rates start at US$106 d with breakfast, cable TV, Internet, gym and sauna, parking, room service, and other amenities. Its 24-hour business center appeals to the international crowd, as do its non-smoking rooms.

US$150–200

Feir's Park Hotel
ESMERALDA 1366, TEL. 011/4131-1900
WWW.FEIRSPARK.COM.AR
Barely two blocks from Plaza San Martín and only half a block from Avenida del Libertador, the 115 spacious suites at Feir's Park offer slightly lower prices than other nearby luxury facilities. Some of them, though, have awkward floor plans: The executive suites (US$160 s or d) are bright and cheerful where the sunlight penetrates from their outdoor terraces, but the light can't easily penetrate to the recesses of their long, narrow interiors. The ambassador suites (US$189 s or d) have better floor plans but smaller terraces.

Hotel Park Plaza Kempinski
PARERA 183, TEL. 011/6777-0200
WWW.PARKPLAZAHOTELS.COM
In a quiet location on the edge of fashionable Recoleta, the 54-room Park Plaza Kempinski

Popular with package tours, Retiro's high-rise Sheraton Buenos Aires Hotel is close to Puerto Madero.

© WAYNE BERNHARDSON

has that Francophile style, but it's less appealing and slightly less well-maintained than its nearby competitors. So-called "luxury" rooms (US$152 s or d) are really overpriced; the executive suites (US$229 s or d), with their sleeping lofts, are more interesting but there are better values in the vicinity.

 Sheraton Buenos Aires Hotel
SAN MARTÍN 1225, TEL. 011/4318-9000
WWW.STARWOODHOTELS.COM
Near Puerto Madero, across from Plaza Fuerza Aérea Argentina, the massive 742-room highrise Sheraton gets lots of international business trade but also plenty of tourists, especially in summer. Executive suites occupy most of the upper floors.

In addition to its accommodations, the Sheraton has tennis courts, an ample fitness center, a complex of indoor and outdoor swimming pools, two restaurants, and a gallery of high-class shopping options. The views from its 24th floor may be the best in the city, with panoramas ranging from Plaza San Martín to the Retiro railroad stations and bus terminal, the current freight port, and the Buquebus passenger terminal, plus glimpses of Puerto Madero. Most of this floor, unfortunately, is closed to the public.

Rates start at US$181 s or d, but executive suites go for around US$242 s or d.

MORE THAN US$200

Caesar Park Hotel
POSADAS 1232, TEL. 011/4819-1100
WWW.CAESAR-PARK.COM
Operated by a Mexican chain, the extravagant Caesar Park seems to aspire to the Alvear Palace's traditional greatness, but it's closer to a nouveau riche pretender. An imposingly large lobby is the gateway to large and comfortable rooms—the smallest is 36 square meters—that enjoy access to a state-of-the-art business center, pool and spa, and lush gardens. Upper rooms have unobstructed river views.

Rates start at US$271 s or d, with buffet breakfast included. There are entirely tobacco-free floors, and the service is impeccable.

Retiro's Four Seasons Hotel Buenos Aires consists of a classic art nouveau mansion and this newer high-rise tower.

Four Seasons Hotel Buenos Aires
POSADAS 1086, TEL. 011/4321-1200
WWW.FOURSEASONS.COM
Operated by an international chain, this luxury hotel consists of a 1990s tower with a contemporary sensibility, but also includes seven suites in an adjacent Belle Epoque mansion large and opulent enough to satisfy any Francophile visitor—the presidential suite covers 180 square meters. In aspirations and style, if not quite precisely in location, this hotel embodies the Recoleta sensibility. Rates start at US$350 s or d per night with a lavish breakfast. In 2004, it made the *Travel & Leisure* list of top-ten Latin American hotels, while *Conde Nast Traveler* called it South America's best.

Marriott Plaza Hotel
FLORIDA 1005, TEL. 011/4318-3000
WWW.MARRIOTT.COM
Now under international-chain control, the landmark (1909) Plaza Hotel overlooks Plaza San Martín at the north end of the Florida pedestrian mall. Though it's undergone a significant

modernization, its German baroque charm survives and, with the Alvear Palace, this is one of the capital's truly elegant classics. Rates start at US$200–300 s or d and climb from there, but there are occasional discounts.

Park Tower Hotel
AVENIDA LEANDRO N. ALEM 1193, TEL. 011/4318-9100
WWW.STARWOODHOTELS.COM
Dating from 1996, the Park Tower is the adjacent Sheraton's nouveau riche stepbrother—the two share a parent corporation, as well as gym and pool facilities, and even some doorways. The Park Tower, though, distinguishes itself from its elder, slightly aging sibling; in fact, it's distinguished itself enough to make the 2004 *Travel & Leisure* top-ten list of Latin American hotels, on the heels of the Alvear Palace and a few steps ahead of the Four Seasons.

Famous figures who have enjoyed the 23rd floor presidential suite include Brad Pitt, Bill and Hillary Clinton, and Luciano Pavarotti. In February 2005, populist President Hugo Chávez of Venezuela caused a commotion when Argentine *piquetero* (picketer) sympathizers—not usually seen on properties like these—gathered in hopes of meeting him. The Park Tower's rates start at US$339 s or d.

Sofitel Buenos Aires
ARROYO 841, TEL. 011/4131-0000
WWW.SOFITEL.COM
If the Caesar Park is a failed effort to surpass the Alvear Palace's Parisian elegance, the Sofitel Buenos Aires comes closer to the mark: This modernization of the neoclassical Torre Mihanovich (1929) is a more credible effort at blending the Francophile tradition in *porteño* hotels with current design trends and modern functions. Rates for its 144 luminous rooms start at US$260 s or d, but ostensible "luxury" rooms (US$297 s or d) have larger bathrooms and slightly better views on one of the city's quietest blocks, known for its upscale art galleries. The lobby is an architectural masterpiece.

Recoleta and Barrio Norte

Like Retiro, the Recoleta/Barrio Norte area has few budget accommodations, but among the ones it has, some are excellent. Some of the city's top upmarket hotels are here.

UNDER US$25
Alfa Hotel
RIOBAMBA 1064, TEL. 011/4812-3719
WWW.ALFAHOTEL.COM.AR
This is a small but well-kept and well-priced Barrio Norte choice with rates starting at US$22/25 s/d, but some slightly more expensive rooms have undergone substantial upgrades. All rooms have private bath, cable TV, telephone, and a/c, and breakfast is included; there's a 10 percent discount for cash payments.

Hotel del Prado
PARAGUAY 2385, TEL. 011/4961-1192
WWW.HOTELDELPRADO-BA.COM.AR
Near the Facultad de Medicina, the Prado is a simply but tastefully remodeled older building with a quiet interior, good beds, and friendly owner-operators. Rates are US$13/17 s/d for rooms with private bath, a modest buffet breakfast, cable TV, telephone, and ceiling fans but no a/c. Discounts are possible for stays of three days or more.

Juncal Palace Hotel
JUNCAL 2282, TEL. 011/4821-2770
WWW.JUNCALPALACEHOTEL.COM.AR
Though Buenos Aires hotel prices have generally been rising, the 26-room Juncal Palace seemingly sits in a time warp, with rates (US$15/19 s/d) closer to the 2002 peso crash than the recent recovery. Once a single-family home, this 1930s Art Deco building, em-

bellished with glistening oak woodwork and Carrara marble staircases, is situated in a solid Barrio Norte location.

Southern House BA
ANCHORENA 1117, TEL. 011/4961-6933
WWW.SOUTHERNHOUSEBA.COM

At US$5–7 pp, there's no cheaper Barrio Norte option than this new hostel, which has huge dorm rooms with perhaps a few too many beds, but there are also large common areas and a kitchen; its finest feature is the large and lushly landscaped interior patio. It needs to build at least one more common bathroom, though; one private room does have its own bath.

US$25–50

Ayacucho Palace Hotel
AYACUCHO 1408, TEL. 011/4806-1815
WWW.AYACUCHOHOTEL.COM.AR

It's less palatial than either its name or the elegant exterior suggests, but this is a solid, quiet mid-range hotel with friendly staff and 70 smallish but immaculate and well-furnished rooms. Rates of US$30/40 s/d include breakfast, and all the bathrooms have tubs. It's also on or near several key bus lines.

Guido Palace Hotel
GUIDO 1780, TEL. 011/4812-0674
WWW.GUIDOPALACE.COM.AR

Extraordinarily friendly, this modest hotel has personality—the tiny antique elevator is a classic—but no frills other than its prime Recoleta location. The rooms are small but well-kept with decent natural light, but most bathrooms have showers rather than tubs. Rates (US$37/44 s/d) do *not* include breakfast, but its adjacent café will provide room service at no extra charge.

Hotel Príncipe
LAPRIDA 1454, TEL. 011/4821-9818
WWW.HOTEL-PRINCIPE.COM.AR

Rooms at the modest Príncipe are really mini-apartments with a refrigerator and sink (but no other kitchen facilities) for US$25/33 s/d with breakfast. While it's sound enough, its strongest point is its Barrio Norte location.

Prince Hotel
ARENALES 1627, TEL. 011/4811-8004
WWW.PRINCEHOTEL.COM.AR

In an almost ideal location on a shady but central street, the modest Prince Hotel offers cozy, quiet, and well-kept rooms, with attractive color schemes, in a building dating from 1917. Amenities include a/c and cable TV; rates of US$27/32 s/d with breakfast are more than fair for a place with truly attentive, friendly personnel.

US$50–100
⚄ Art Hotel
AZCUÉNAGA 1268, TEL. 011/4821-4744
WWW.ARTHOTEL.COM.AR

Behind the reception desk, shelves of bulky law books make a misleadingly formal entryway to this creatively rehabbed, 36-room boutique hotel and art space that was once a rooming house. Having stripped decades of paint to reveal its natural wood features, it has three kinds of rooms: "small and cozy" (US$65 s or d), queen (US$80 s or d), and king (US$90 s or d), all with breakfast. All rooms have high-speed Internet connections, and stylish but unpretentious furnishings disguise the cable TV and mini-bar.

Exhibits at the street-level art space, which change monthly, show well thanks to natural illumination from the fifth-floor skylight. All works are for sale, and this part of the hotel is open to the public during normal business hours.

Hotel Bel Air
ARENALES 1462, TEL. 011/4021-4000
WWW.HOTELBELAIR.COM.AR

In an ideal Barrio Norte location, only the elegant 1920s facade remains unchanged in this classy, modernized 77-room hotel, which has separate smoking and non-smoking floors. One room has facilities for guests with disabilities.

011 54114804 - 9837

On the ground level, the Bel Air has an inviting restaurant and wine bar, as well as a Business Corner with free Internet access (also available in the rooms). Rates run from US$85/95–US$90/100 s/d with breakfast.

Hotel Plaza Francia

5411

EDUARDO SCHIAFFINO 2189, TEL. 011/4804-9631
WWW.HOTELPLAZAFRANCIA.COM

Close to Recoleta restaurants, entertainment, and open spaces, as well as the cemetery, the Plaza Francia is a cozy multi-story hotel with rooms ranging from standard interior (US$68 s or d) to deluxe exterior (US$77 s or d) and junior suites (US$98 s or d), with buffet breakfast and amenities like a business center. Some rooms face busy Avenida Libertador and the highest have river views, but effective sound insulation keeps things quiet.

Mayflower Suites

POSADAS 1557, TEL. 011/4878-7500
WWW.MAYFLOWERSUITES.COM.AR

Recently rehabbed and located just down the block from Evita's old Recoleta haunts, the Mayflower is a modern boutique-style hotel with ample-sized rooms (about 30 square meters) and affordable prices (US$97 s or d) for the area. In a neighborhood where Francophilia runs rampant, its clean simplicity adds a welcome note of variety.

Wilton Hotel

AVENIDA CALLAO 1162, TEL. 011/4811-1818
WWW.HOTELWILTON.COM.AR

For US$75 s or d with breakfast, the Wilton is a solid mid-range hotel, though its formal four-star category seems an exaggeration. Its 120 rooms are simply decorated but spacious enough, though those facing the avenue might not be suitable for light sleepers. Rates include a buffet breakfast and access to its gym and business center.

US$100–150

Design Suites

MARCELO T. DE ALVEAR 1683, TEL. 011/4814-8700
WWW.DESIGNSUITES.COM

Though not quite new, the Design Suites is a still-sparkling boutique-style hotel with a striking ground-floor solarium and twin towers of 20 spacious suites each; amenities include cable TV, telephone, Internet and fax connections, kitchenette, minibar, a/c, strongbox, and Jacuzzi. Rates start at US$121 s/d for standard rooms but rise to USD$169 s/d for two-room suites.

Recoleta's Alvear Palace Hotel consistently makes the lists of Latin America's top hotels.

US$150–200

Etoile Hotel
ROBERTO M. ORTIZ 1835, TEL. 011/4805-2626
WWW.ETOILE.COM.AR

Facing Recoleta's famous cemetery, the high-rise Etoile is a modern place that lacks the character of older upscale *porteño* hotels but partly compensates with its location and services. Accommodations range from large bedrooms with interior light to very large suites with cemetery and plaza views; all have balconies, and many have been so recently updated that the scent of new construction lingers. Rates, from US$120 to US$200 s or d, include breakfast and access to the 14th-floor spa.

MORE THAN US$200

Ⓜ Alvear Palace Hotel
AVENIDA ALVEAR 1891, TEL. 011/4805-2100
WWW.ALVEARPALACE.COM

Since 1928, the Alvear Palace Hotel has symbolized *porteño* elegance and luxury—not to mention wealth and privilege. Even during and after the 2002 crisis, it has maintained both its standards and its prices—rack rates start around US$410 s or d and range up to US$3,000 for the royal suite; room amenities include Egyptian cotton sheets and Hermés toiletries. Francophobes may find the *ancien régime* décor cloying, but both *Travel & Leisure* and *Condé Nast Traveler* have consistently ranked it at or near the top of Latin America's hotel list and as one of the world's finest.

Loi Suites Recoleta
VICENTE LÓPEZ 1955, TEL. 011/5777-8950
WWW.LOISUITES.COM.AR

Its neoclassical columns make a misleading approach to one of the city's most contemporary hotels, only a few years old and a design pioneer for its open floor plan and use of natural light—with its retractable roof, the spectacular central pool house doubles as a breakfast solarium. Its 112 identically decorated rooms, for which rates range from US$150 to US$230 s or d, vary in size only.

Palermo

Palermo's traditional budget accommodations, in the immediate vicinity of Plaza Italia, are generally not bad, but with a couple notable exceptions they're unremarkable. In recent years, though, Palermo Viejo has witnessed an influx of quality hostels, bed-and-breakfasts, and a handful of boutique hotels that are easy walking distance to restaurants and nightlife, but not so close that it's impossible to sleep at a reasonable hour. The neighborhood itself is well served by public transportation, both Subte and buses.

UNDER US$25

Casa Jardín
CHARCAS 4422, TEL. 011/4774-8783
WWW.CASAJARDINBA.COM.AR

Billing itself a "creative hostel," the intimate Casa Jardín can accommodate only about 13 guests in an art-infused ambience with ample common spaces and gregarious management who act more like friends than business owners (though it's efficiently run). Dorm accommodations cost US$10 pp, while private rooms cost US$15/27 s/d; all baths are shared, however. Like nearby El Firulete, Casa Jardín is tobacco-free except for the balconies and the enormous rooftop terrace.

El Firulete Hostel
GUEMES 4499, TEL. 011/4770-9259
WWW.EL-FIRULETE.COM.AR

Once a single-family house, this luminous Palermo Viejo hostel has comfortable, freshly painted dorms (US$6 pp) and private rooms (US$22/24 s/d) with breakfast and shared bath only; reached by a narrow, wooden spiral staircase, the upstairs bar

Ⓜ Accommodations

and terrace are great for socializing but far enough from the accommodations that getting a good night's sleep is feasible. El Firulete claims to be Buenos Aires's first WiFi hostel, and is also a non-smoking facility except for the rooftop terrace.

Tango Backpacker's Hostel
THAMES 2212, TEL. 011/4776-6871
WWW.TANGOBP.COM
In the sleep-all-day, party-all-night sector of Palermo Soho, this HI affiliate occupies a grand old house that boasts a rooftop terrace with a *parrilla* for barbecues, a large kitchen, and free Internet access, plus dining and partying recommendations from the staff, who also lead inexpensive guided tours around town. Rates range from US$8 pp in dorms to US$20 s in small private rooms.

In Brief
Hotel Pacífico (Santa María de Oro 2554, tel. 011/4771-4071. www.hotelpacifico.com.ar, US$17/24 s/d) has decent rooms with a/c and cable TV, breakfast included. The upstairs rooms are airier at the 56-room **Hotel Panamé** (Godoy Cruz 2774, tel. 011/4771-4041, www.paname-hotel.com.ar, US$17/25 s/d), a respectable choice with private bath, breakfast, and cable TV.

US$25–50

B&B Bayres
AVENIDA CÓRDOBA 5842, TEL. 011/4772-3877
WWW.BAYRESBNB.COM
Strictly speaking, it's in Villa Crespo, but this spacious, sunny, and well-furnished bed-and-breakfast is literally just across the avenue from Palermo Hollywood, with its abundant restaurants and bars. With only six guest rooms, its owners cater to gay men and lesbians; three rooms use shared baths while the other three have private baths, but all have access to the ample common spaces, including an enormous living room and a large, sunny terrace. Rates range from US$25/35–US$40/50 s/d with buffet breakfast, depending on the facilities; the more expensive rooms have their own private terraces.

Che Lulu Guest House
EMILIO ZOLÁ 5185, TEL. 011/4772-0289
WWW.LULUGUESTHOUSE.COM
On a block-long street where the original cobbles still show through slabs of pavement, Che Lulu is an artist-inspired bed-and-breakfast where seven small but colorful rooms with rustically styled furniture go for bargain prices, ranging from US$15 q to US$33 d with breakfast. Their main shortcoming is a lack of closet space, which can mean living out of a suitcase or backpack.

The large common areas, well-isolated from the bedrooms in this three-story house, make staying at the Lulu a sociable experience. While close to a busy avenue and a suburban railroad line, it's quiet and also easy walking distance to the restaurants and nightlife of both Palermo Soho and Palermo Hollywood.

Hotel Palermo
GODOY CRUZ 2725, TEL. 011/4774-7342
WWW.HOTEL-PALERMO.COM.AR
The barrio's oldest hotel, the Palermo began life as accommodations for *estancieros* who came to the capital for livestock shows at the nearby Sociedad Rural, but the cattle barons have since found more sumptuous alternatives. Rates are US$20/27 s/d for smallish but impeccable rooms that, post-renovation, lack the character they once had.

Torre Cristóforo Colombo
SANTA MARÍA DE ORO 2747, TEL. 011/4777-9622
WWW.TORRECC.COM.AR
Rising well above everything else in this quiet, leafy neighborhood, the Colombo tower contains 160 fully equipped suites with kitchenettes and patios, accommodating 2–4 persons. Rates start around US$50 s or d with breakfast included, but the larger units cost substantially more. Until the opening of Palermo Hollywood's Home Buenos Aires, this was the only barrio hotel with a pool.

US$50–100

Como en Casa

GURRUCHAGA 2155, TEL. 011/4831-0517
WWW.BANDB.COM.AR

Como en Casa is a charming house on a narrow but deep lot dating from 1926. Its 11 cozy rooms feature high ceilings and share inviting common areas and several shady patios. Rates, ranging from US$25/35–US$60/70 s/d with continental breakfast, depend on whether or not the room has a private bath. Como en Casa offers Internet access and English-speaking personnel, but lacks a/c.

In Brief

The **Alpino Hotel** (Cabello 3318, tel. 011/4802-5151, www.hotel-alpino.com.ar, US$47/52 s/d) is a solid three-star hotel in a desirable area that has few accommodations of any sort.

US$100–150

Bobo Hotel

GUATEMALA 4882, TEL. 011/4774-0505
WWW.BOBOHOTEL.COM

This self-deprecatingly style-conscious Palermo Soho boutique hotel takes its name from U.S. author David Brooks, who coined the ironic term "bourgeois bohemians" to describe middle-class individuals with counter-cultural pretensions (in Spanish, for what it's worth, *bobo* is synonymous with stupid). Still, with its seven individually distinctive rooms and gourmet bar/restaurant, this has quickly become the classiest option in a barrio that still has relatively few accommodations, and an ideal location for anyone who wants dozens of other gourmet dining options within easy walking distance. Rates range from US$97–US$145 s or d, depending on the room.

Hotel Home Buenos Aires

HONDURAS 5860, TEL. 011/4779-1008
WWW.HOMEBUENOSAIRES.COM

While it hadn't yet opened during the research period, this promising boutique hotel deserves a look for its imaginative design, spacious rooms and suites, and ample common spaces, including a large garden with pool that's uncommon in this part of town. With neighboring properties, it forms a mini-greenbelt that's remarkably quiet for such a lively neighborhood.

Built to E.U. standards, including access for guests with disabilities, by an Argentine-British-Irish partnership, it's just far enough from Palermo Hollywood's densest bunching of bars and restaurants to ensure a quiet night's rest. Rates range from US$90–110 s or d for the 14 beautifully designed rooms, and up to US$250 s or d for suites, one of which is a secluded poolside apartment.

Malabia House

MALABIA 1555, TEL. 011/4832-3345 OR 011/4833-2410
WWW.MALABIAHOUSE.COM.AR

Occupying a painstakingly remodeled 19th-century *casa chorizo,* Malabia House has become a stylish bed-and-breakfast with magnificent natural light, glistening wooden floors, handsome furnishings, and small but attractive patio gardens. Standard ground-floor rooms (US$79/109 s/d with breakfast) have external private baths; more expensive upstairs rooms (US$97/139 s/d) have a/c and interior baths. There's a 10 percent discount for cash payment.

Accommodations

Excursions from Buenos Aires

When *porteños* tire of the city, there are plenty of nearby escapes both within Buenos Aires province and beyond it. Truly unique are the intricate channels of the Río Paraná delta, easily reached by launch from the increasingly fashionable northern suburb of Tigre, itself easily reached by train. One of the highlights is the island of Martín García, a colonial fortress and onetime prison camp that offers nature trails and historic architecture.

Built on a grid resembling that of Washington, D.C., the streets of the provincial capital of La Plata, only an hour southeast, feature imposing architecture and cultural resources (including theaters and museums) that many national capitals cannot match. An hour west of Buenos Aires, the city of Luján, with its towering basilica, is a major pilgrimage destination and also boasts an impressive complex of historical museums. Another half-hour west, San Antonio de Areco is Argentina's symbolic gaucho capital.

For those wishing to go farther afield, daily ferries cross the Río de la Plata to the Uruguayan destinations of Carmelo (a quiet riverside resort), the town of Colonia (a UNESCO World Heritage Site for its 18th-century core), the capital city of Montevideo (a repository of colonial and art deco architecture), and the Atlantic beach resort of Punta del Este (traditionally overrun by Argentines in January and February).

Best Excursions

⋈ **Best Ex-Prison:** Just off the Uruguayan coast, its bedrock rising out of the River Plate's muddy waters, **Isla Martín García** has been a colonial fortress and even a political penal colony, but today it's an absorbing historical and natural getaway from Buenos Aires's bustle (page 208).

⋈ **Best Pilgrimages:** The truly devout can walk 62 kilometers from Buenos Aires to the chamber of the Virgencita, Argentina's patron saint, in Luján's **Basílica Nacional Nuestra Señora de Luján.** The rest can go by bus, train, or car to appreciate the city's **Complejo Museográfico Enrique Udaondo,** a remarkable complex of historical museums (pages 211 and 212).

⋈ **Best Time Trip:** In the placid pampas west of Luján, Argentina's gaucho capital of San Antonio de Areco embodies a romantic vision of the countryside's past. Revel in that romantic idealization at **Parque Criollo y Museo Gauchesco Ricardo Güiraldes,** San Antonio's gaucho museum and 97-hectare park celebrating the *gauchesco* literature of Ricardo Güiraldes (page 218).

⋈ **Most Ambitious Museum:** With all the aspirations of an international city, Buenos Aires province's capital, La Plata, boasts an assemblage of century-old buildings and prestigious educational institutions, including its landmark natural sciences museum **Museo de La Plata.** It makes an ideal day trip from Buenos Aires (page 231).

⋈ **Best Spontaneous Revival:** An endangered neighborhood not so long ago, Montevideo's colonial **Ciudad Vieja** has revived with an energy and style that resembles Buenos Aires's Palermo Viejo, with restaurants, bars, live music, theater, museums, and cultural centers (page 241).

⋈ **Best Winery Excursion:** At the moment, historic **Establecimiento Juanicó** is best-prepared to receive visitors for tours, tasting, and

wine barrels at Establecimiento Juanicó

meals, but other Montevideo-area wineries are catching up fast (page 254).

⋈ **Best Colonial Complex:** It's not just another stamp in your passport—barely an hour from Buenos Aires, in the Uruguayan city of Colonia, the **Barrio Histórico** has the best preserved colonial core in all the Southern Cone countries. It's a UNESCO World Heritage Site, and rightly so (page 257).

⋈ **Best Country Inn:** It's benefited from traffic from the nearby Four Seasons Resort at Carmelo, but the restaurant, winery, and cheeses at the stylishly modernized **Finca y Granja Narbona** are making it an essential stopover in an otherwise out-of-the-way corner of the Uruguayan littoral. For those not at the Four Seasons, Narbona has its own upscale accommodations (page 269).

⋈ **Culture in a Vacuum:** Punta del Este proper may be a monument to brainless hedonism, at least in summer, but painter Carlos Páez Vilaró's nearby hotel, restaurant, and museum **Casapueblo** is literally and figuratively a work of art (page 279).

© WAYNE BERNHARDSON

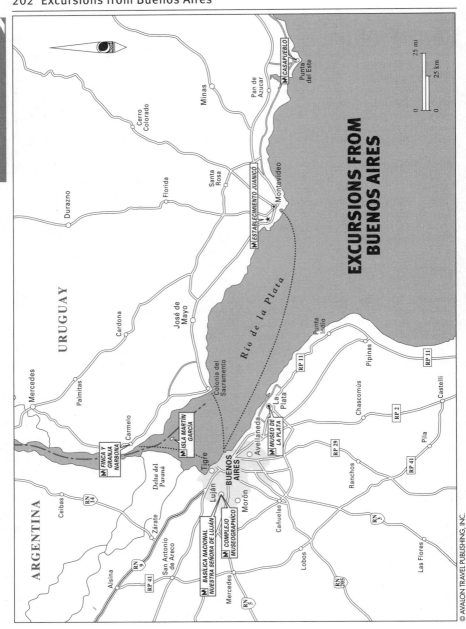

EXCURSIONS FROM BUENOS AIRES

© AVALON TRAVEL PUBLISHING, INC.

In general, this chapter's excursions cover afternoon getaways, day trips, or weekend destinations that do not require air travel (that's an option for Uruguay, but not a particularly good one because ferries are faster); for this reason, popular but more distant sites, such as the southern Buenos Aires province beach resort of Mar del Plata and the thunderous Iguazú Falls, on the Brazilian border, do not appear here; they do appear in detail, though, in the author's *Moon Handbooks Argentina*.

PLANNING YOUR TIME

For the bulk of the excursions here, Buenos Aires is a hub for departures in all directions. For the most part, it's simplest to return to the capital before taking any other excursion.

The exception to this rule is Uruguay: Visitors can travel to Carmelo, Colonia, or Montevideo and return directly to Buenos Aires, but it's also possible to arrange convenient loops, of varying lengths, by public transportation. The simplest would be to take the ferry or catamaran to Colonia for at least an overnight stay or preferably longer, continuing overland to Montevideo and perhaps to Punta del Este for several days more. Instead of returning to Colonia, it's quicker (though more expensive) to take the high-speed catamaran from Montevideo back to Buenos Aires.

Likewise, it's possible to vary the trip by taking a catamaran from the riverside Buenos Aires suburb of Tigre to the placid Uruguayan port of Carmelo, then continue to Colonia and to Montevideo or vice versa, before recrossing the river to Buenos Aires. Punta del Este would be an easy extension from Montevideo.

Tigre

After decades of decay, the flood-prone riverside city of Tigre is experiencing a renaissance. The train stations are completely renovated, the streets clean, the houses brightly painted (and many restored), and it remains the point of departure for delta retreats and historic Isla Martín García. In a decade, the population has zoomed from a little more than 250,000 to nearly 300,000.

The number-one attraction near Buenos Aires, Tigre and its Paraná Delta are barely half an hour by train from the capital. When the capital swelters in summer heat, the delta's maze of forested channels offers shady relief, just close enough for an afternoon off, but there's plenty to do for a day trip, a weekend, or even longer. The fewer than 4,000 people who inhabit the 950 square kilometers of "the islands" traditionally bring their produce to Tigre's Mercado de Frutos.

HISTORY

Tigre began as a humble colonial port for Buenos Aires–destined charcoal from the delta,

languishing until the railroad connected to the capital in 1865. From the late 19th century, it became a summer sanctuary for the *porteño* elite, who built imposing mansions, many of which survive. Prestigious rowing clubs constructed extravagant headquarters and ran regattas on the river, but after the 1920s, Tigre settled into a subtropical torpor until its recent revival.

ORIENTATION

Tigre is 27 kilometers north of Buenos Aires at the confluence of the north-flowing Río Tigre and the Río Luján, which drains southeast into the Río de la Plata. The delta's main channel, parallel to the Río Luján, is the Río Paraná de las Palmas.

East of the Río Tigre, the town is primarily but not exclusively commercial. West of the river, it is largely residential.

SIGHTS

On the Río Tigre's right bank, along Avenida General Mitre, stand symbols of the town's early

Club de la Marina (Naval Club) in Tigre

elegance, the 1873 **Buenos Aires Rowing Club** (Mitre 226) and the 1910 **Club Canottierri Italiani** (Mitre 74). Though both still function, they're not the prominent institutions they once were.

Unfortunately, Tigre's rebirth has also brought fast-food franchises and the dreadful **Parque de la Costa** (Vivanco 1509, tel. 011/4002-6000, www.parquedelacosta.com.ar, open 11 A.M.–midnight Wed.–Sun.), a cheesy theme park. Admission, valid for all rides and games, costs US$7 pp for adults, US$5 for children under age 10.

East of the Parque de la Costa is the **Puerto de Frutos** (Sarmiento 160, tel. 011/4512-4493); though the docks of this port no longer buzz with products of launches from the deepest delta islands, it's home to a revitalized crafts fair that's open 11 A.M.–7 P.M. daily, but is liveliest on weekends. Handcrafted wicker furniture and basketry, as well as flower arrangements, are unique to the area.

West of the river, in the residential zone, the present-day **Museo de la Reconquista** (Liniers 818, tel. 011/4512-4496, open 10 A.M.–6 P.M. daily except Mon. and Tues., free) was the Spanish Viceroy's command post while

the British occupied Buenos Aires during the 1806–1807 invasions. Not merely a military memorial, it also chronicles the delta, ecclesiastical history, and Tigre's golden age from the 1880s to the 1920s.

Several blocks north, fronting on the Río Luján, the **Museo Naval de la Nación** (Paseo Victorica 602, tel. 011/4749-0608, 8 A.M.–12:30 P.M. Mon.–Thurs., 8 A.M.–5.30 P.M. Fri., and 10 A.M.–6:30 P.M. weekends and holidays, US$.65) occupies the former **Talleres Nacionales de Marina** (1879), a naval repair station that closed as naval ships got too large for its facilities; it now chronicles Argentine naval history from its beginnings under the Irishman Guillermo Brown to the present.

At the confluence of the Río del la Reconquista and the Río Luján and dating from 1910, the belle epoque **Tigre Club** (Paseo Victorica 972, tel. 011/4749-3411) now serves as the municipal cultural center. It's all that remains of a complex that included the earlier Tigre Hotel, built in the town's heyday but demolished after upper-class *porteños* abandoned the area for Mar del Plata in the 1930s.

ACCOMMODATIONS AND FOOD

In a classic Tudor-style mansion on the Río Tigre's west bank, the family-run **Casona La Ruchi** (Lavalle 557, tel. 011/4749-2499, www.casonalaruchi.com.ar, US$30 d) has six spacious rooms that stay cool even on hot days, thanks to the building's stone-block exterior and high ceilings; there are three shared baths. With its sprawling and lushly landscaped gardens, and a sizeable pool, it's an exceptional value and just across the street from the port for launches to Carmelo, Uruguay.

Standard Argentine eateries are a dime a dozen at the Puerto de Frutos. One fine choice is **Lo de Negri** (Sarmiento 3, tel. 011/4749-6235, lunch only), a *parrilla* that does roaring weekend business but still manages to combine above-average food with quick and friendly service. Entrées, such as *lomo a la pimienta* (pepper steak) with creamed potatoes, run about US$6.

For a more elaborate menu on a shady riverside terrace with good service, west of the Río Tigre, try **María Luján** (Paseo Victorica 611, tel. 011/4731-9613, www.marialujan.com.ar). Homemade pastas cost around US$3, more elaborate dishes around US$5, and the weekday *menú ejecutivo* (lunch special) around US$6. A full dinner with wine will cost around US$10; it's open from 8 A.M. until the last diner staggers out the door.

INFORMATION

In the Nueva Estación Fluvial is Tigre's **Ente Municipal de Turismo** (Mitre 305, tel. 011/4512-4497 or 0800/888-8447 toll-free, www.tigre.gov.ar, open 9 A.M.–5 P.M. daily). It distributes a particularly good map of the city and delta.

The private website **Tigre Tiene Todo** (www.tigretienetodo.com) is also useful for services.

TRANSPORTATION

Tigre is well-connected to Buenos Aires by bus and train, but the heavy traffic on the Panamericana Norte makes the bus slow. Through the delta, there are numerous local launches and even international service to the Uruguayan ports of Carmelo and Nueva Palmira.

Boat

From Tigre's Nueva Estación Fluvial (Mitre 319), several companies offer *lanchas*

Wicker baskets and furniture are popular purchases at Tigre's Puerto de Frutos.

© WAYNE BERNHARDSON

For a century, rowing has been a popular pastime at Tigre and throughout the Delta del Paraná.

colectivas, river-bound buses that drop off and pick up passengers at docks throughout the delta. Among them are **Interisleña** (tel. 011/4749-0900), **Líneas Delta Argentino** (tel. 011/4749-0537, www.lineasdelta.com. ar), and **Jilguero** (tel. 011/4749-0987). **Marsili** (tel. 15/4413-4123) and **Giacomotti** (tel. 011/4749-1896) use smaller *lanchas taxi.*

Cacciola (Lavalle 520, tel./fax 011/4749-0329, www.cacciolaviajes.com) has daily launches to Carmelo, Uruguay, at 8:30 A.M. and 4:30 P.M. (US$11, 2.5 hours), with bus connections to Montevideo (US$7 more). Fast, new catamarans make the trip quicker and more comfortable than it was just a few years ago, but it also means they use broader, less scenic channels to get there.

Líneas Delta Argentino also operates launches to the Uruguayan town of Colonia (US$13, 3.5 hours) daily at 1 P.M.; it also goes to Nueva Palmira, Uruguay (three hours; US$11), west of Carmelo, at 7:45 A.M. daily, with an additional Friday sailing at 5 P.M. While launches leave from Cacciola's international terminal, sales take place at Delta Argentino's on the opposite bank of the river.

Bus

The No. 60 *colectivo* from downtown Buenos Aires runs 24 hours a day, but when traffic is heavy, reaching Tigre can take two hours.

Train

Tigre has two train stations. From Retiro, Trenes de Buenos Aires (TBA) operates frequent commuter trains on the Ferrocarril Mitre from the capital to **Estación Tigre;** it's also possible to board these trains in Belgrano or suburban stations. The best-maintained and best-run of any rail line into Buenos Aires province, it charges only US$.35 each way.

Also from Retiro, a separate branch of the Mitre line runs to Estación Bartolomé Mitre, where passengers transfer at Estación Maipú to the **Tren de la Costa** (tel. 011/4002-6000, www.trendelacosta.com.ar), a tourist train that rumbles through several riverside communities and shopping centers to its terminus at Tigre's **Estación Delta,** at the entrance to the Parque de la Costa. This costs about US$.50 weekdays and US$1 weekends (when it's a day pass valid for all stations on the route).

© WAYNE BERNHARDSON

Catamarans to Carmelo, Uruguay, leave from Tigre's Puerto Fluvial Internacional.

Vicinity of Tigre

Tigre itself may have been revitalized, but many rusting hulks still line the shore of the Paraná's inner channels. Farther from Tigre, where colonial smugglers often hid from Spanish officials, summer houses stand on *palafitos* (pilings) to prevent—not always successfully—being flooded.

Many operators at Tigre's Nueva Estación Fluvial and the Puerto de Frutos offer 40- to 90-minute excursions that are, not quite literally, enough to get your feet wet in the delta. It's also possible to use the *lanchas colectivos* to get where you want to go, including hotels and restaurants. One word of warning: *Porteño* powerboaters, especially those on so-called personal watercraft, can be as reckless as motorists on the capital's roadways—don't jump in the water without looking around first.

One of the closest excursions is the **Museo Histórico Sarmiento**, (Río Sarmiento and Arroyo Los Reyes, tel. 011/4728-0570, open 10 A.M.–6 P.M. Wed.–Sun., free). In a house

dating from 1855, built from fruit boxes and now protected by glass, President Domingo F. Sarmiento had his summer residence here; the museum preserves some of his personal effects. There is also a one-kilometer footpath through a gallery forest typical of the delta.

For a quick sightseeing orientation, **Catamaranes Interisleñas** (Lavalle 499, tel. 011/4731-0261) has several spacious ships offering one- to two-hour excursions in the immediate vicinity of town. These leave from Escalera 12, a riverside staircase at Mitre and Vivanco on the Río Tigre's right bank, and from the Muelle Municipal, in the 500 block of Lavalle on the left bank.

Accommodations and Food

Both accommodations and dining options are increasing in the delta and are accessible by launches from Tigre.

About 50 minutes from Tigre by Interisleña, **Hostería l'Marangatú** (Río San Antonio 181, tel. 011/4728-0752, www.i-marangatu.com.ar, US$23 pp weekdays, US$27 pp weekends and holidays) has 10 rooms; rates include breakfast and dinner.

About 90 minutes from Tigre by Delta Argentino launch, **Hotel Laura** (Río Paraná de las Palmas, tel. 011/4728-1019, www.riohotel-laura.com.ar, US$63 d) has both accommodations and a large restaurant that sometimes offers river fish like surubí. There are discounts for stays of two nights or more.

Nearby the island of Martín García and the Uruguayan coast, the delta's most exclusive option is the new **La Pascuala Delta Lodge** (Arroyo Las Cañas, tel. 011/4728-1253, www.lapascuala.com, US$150/250 s/d with full board), which has 15 bungalow-suites and no neighbors within sight, for a truly placid getaway. Rates include kayaks, pedal boats, and other sporting gear, but not instruction or guides for them. Transportation out and back costs US$25 pp more on their own boat.

About 25 minutes from Tigre by Inter-isleña launch, **La Riviera** (Río Tres Bocas, tel. 011/4728-0177) offers outdoor dining in good weather, with a wide selection of beef, fish, and pasta dishes.

ISLA MARTÍN GARCÍA

Rising out of the Río de la Plata, almost within swimming distance of the Uruguayan town of Carmelo, the island of Martín García boasts a lush forest habitat, a fascinating history, and an almost unmatchable serenity compared to the frenzy of the federal capital and even provincial suburbs.

History

Spanish navigator Juan Díaz de Solís was the first European to see the island, naming it for a crewman who died there in 1516. In colonial times, it changed hands often before finally settling under Spanish control in 1777; in 1814, Guillermo Brown, the Argentine navy's Irish founder, captured it for the Provincias Unidas del Río de la Plata

Reached by boat from Tigre, Isla Martín García's theater is the most distinctive of the island's many historic buildings.

© WAYNE BERNHARDSON

(United Provinces of the River Plate). For a time, mainlanders quarried its granite bedrock for building materials.

For a century, 1870–1970, the navy controlled the island and often used it as a political prison and a regular penal colony, though it was also a quarantine base for European immigrants. The famous Nicaraguan poet Rubén Darío (1867–1916) lived briefly on the island in the early 1900s, while serving as Colombian consul in Buenos Aires.

Political detainees have included Presidents Marcelo T. de Alvear (in 1932, after his presidency), Hipólito Yrigoyen (twice in the 1930s), Juan Domingo Perón (1945, before being elected president), and Arturo Frondizi (1962–1963). In World War II's early months, Argentine authorities briefly incarcerated crewmen from the German battleship *Graf Spee,* scuttled off Montevideo in December 1939.

Although the island passed to the United Provinces at independence, it was not explicitly part of Argentina until a 1973 agreement with Uruguay (which was one of the United Provinces). After the navy departed, the Buenos Aires provincial Servicio Penitenciario (Penitentiary Service) used it as a halfway house for run-of-the-mill convicts, but it was also a detention and torture site during the military dictatorship of 1976–1983.

Orientation
Only 3.5 kilometers off the Uruguayan coast but 33.5 kilometers from Tigre, 168-hectare Martín García is not part of the sedimentary delta, but rather a pre-Cambrian bedrock island rising 27 meters above sea level. Its native vegetation is a dense gallery forest, and part of it is a *zona intangible,* a provincial forest reserve.

Sights
Uphill from the island's *muelle pasajero* (passenger pier), opposite the meticulously landscaped **Plaza Guillermo Brown,** the island's **Oficina de Informes** was, until recently, the Servicio Penitenciario's headquarters; it now houses provincial park rangers. Along the south shore are several *baterías* (gun emplacements).

At the plaza's upper end stand the ruins of the onetime **cuartel** (military barracks that later became jail cells). Clustered together nearby are the **Cine-Teatro,** the former theater, with its gold-tinted rococo details; the **Museo de la Isla** (Island Museum) and the former Casa Médicos de Lazareto, the quarantine center now occupied by the **Centro de Interpretación Ecológica** (Environmental Interpretation Center). A bit farther inland, the island's **faro** (lighthouse, 1881) rises above the trees, but is no longer in use. To the north, the graves of conscripts who died in an early-20th-century epidemic dot the isolated **Cementerio** (cemetery).

At the northwest end of the island, trees and vines grow among the crumbling structures of the so-called **Barrio Chino** (Chinatown), marking the approach to the **Puerto Viejo,** the sediment-clogged former port. Across the island, beyond the airstrip, much of the same vegetation grows in the **zona intangible,** which is closed to the public.

Activities
Though the island offers fine walking and outstanding bird-watching, the river is unsuitable for swimming. The restaurant **Comedor El Solís,** however, has a swimming pool open to the public.

Accommodations and Food
Crowded in summer and on weekends, **Camping Martín García** (tel. 011/4728-1808) charges US$2 pp for tent campers, with discounts for two or more nights; reservations are advisable for hostel bunks with shared bath (US$2.50 pp) or with private bath (US$3.50 pp). Cacciola's *Hostería Martín García* charges US$43 pp for overnight packages with full board that include transportation from Tigre. Each additional night costs US$14 pp.

Cacciola's own restaurant **Fragata Hércules** is decent enough, but **Comedor El Solís** is at least as good and a bit cheaper; in winter, however, the Solís may be closed. **Panadería Rocío** is known for its fruitcakes.

Transportation
On the Río Tigre's west bank, **Cacciola** (Lavalle 520, tel. 011/4749-0329, www.cacciolaviajes.com) offers day trips Tuesday, Thursday, Saturday, and Sunday at 9 A.M., but get there half an hour earlier. Arriving at the island around noon, the tour includes an aperitif on arrival, a guided visit, and lunch at Cacciola's *Fragata Hércules.* The tour returns to Tigre around 5 P.M., but again get to the dock early. There is ample time for just roaming around.

Cacciola also has a Microcentro office (Florida 520, 1st fl., Oficina 113, tel. 011/4393-6100). Fares for a full-day excursion are US$21 for adults, US$19 for children ages 3–9, including port charges. An overnight stay at the *hostería,* including transportation and full board, costs US$43 pp.

CARICATURING THE GAUCHO

Few non-Argentines know Florencio Molina Campos by name, but many more have seen his paintings. These benign caricatures exaggerated the gaucho's physical features and showed his horses, with oversized heads and expressive eyes, as a physical extension—even an equal partner—of the pampas' legendary horseman.

Buenos Aires–born of a landowning family, Molina Campos (1891–1959) spent his summers on family *estancias* in Buenos Aires and Entre Ríos provinces. That experience introduced him to the gauchos' traditional virtues of courage, honor, hospitality, and sacrifice, and his art communicated those traits without patronizing his subjects. Following a 1926 exhibition of *motivos gauchos* (gaucho motifs) in Palermo's Sociedad Rural, he taught drawing at the Colegio Nacional Nicolás Avellaneda for 18 years but continued to travel extensively around the country.

He became famous, though, after the Fábrica Argentina de Alpargatas, which made the linen slippers still common in today's Argentina, hired him to illustrate calendars that sold 18 million copies over 12 years. After traveling to the United States to study animation, he did similar work for the Minneapolis-Moline mills. He also worked on the Walt Disney cartoons *Goofy se Hace Gaucho* (Goofy Becomes a Gaucho), *El Volador Gaucho* (The Flying Gaucho), *El Gaucho Reidor* (The Laughing Gaucho), and *Saludos, Amigos* (Greetings, Friends), though he resigned when Disney's producers rejected his suggestions to make them more "authentic."

In addition to showing them in the United States, Molina Campos exhibited his paintings, as well as photographs and silver work, in the United Kingdom, France, and Germany. Some of his gaucho-themed works even appear as tiled murals in the Buenos Aires subway (Estación Constitución, Línea C) and on the walls surrounding the provincial Casa de Gobierno in the city of La Plata.

Now a residential suburb of Gran Buenos Aires, the city of Moreno (with a population

COURTESY OF F. MOLINA CAMPOS EDICIONES · WWW.MOLINACAMPOS.NET

El Payador

of almost 380,000) is only 36 kilometers west of the capital, but in Molina Campos's time, it was still *tierra de gauchos* (gaucho land). Built in the style of a mid-19th-century *estancia* house, the **Museo Florencio Molina Campos** (Florencio Molina Campos 348) has kept no regular hours for nearly four years, but groups can make arrangements for special guided visits through the Fundación Molina Campos (Ruggieri 2758, Buenos Aires, tel. 011/4804-9312, www.molinacampos.net).

Plans are in the works to move the museum collections to new facilities in Buenos Aires, but this is unlikely to happen very soon. Meanwhile, the simplest way to reach Moreno is by TBA's Línea Sarmiento, an electrified commuter line, from Estación Once in Buenos Aires. From the Moreno station, it's about a 15-minute walk along Avenida Libertador and Calle Molina Campos (ex-Güemes) to the museum; take a left at the end of the hospital grounds and walk three blocks more.

Luján

History and legend blend in the pampas city of Luján, Argentina's single most important devotional center. Modern Luján, though, is an incongruous potpourri of piety and the profane, where pilgrims purchase shoddy souvenirs and, after making their obligatory visit to the landmark basilica, party until dawn.

Luján may merit a visit for the truly devout and for those with an intellectual interest in orthodox Catholicism, but what really shines is its complex of historical museums in handsome colonial buildings—recent improvements have turned Luján from a mildly interesting side trip into a nearly obligatory one.

As a sacred symbol, Luján gets four million visitors per year, mostly on weekends and for religious holidays like Easter and May 8 (the Virgin's day). Also important are events like October's Peregrinación de la Juventud (Youth Pilgrimage), a 62-kilometer walk from Once that acquired a semi-political character during the Dirty War, but has since returned to its devotional origins. For most foreigners, it makes a better day trip than an overnight, unless *estancia* accommodations are an option.

HISTORY

Legend says that, in 1630, an oxcart loaded with a terra-cotta image of the Virgin Mary stuck in the mud, unable to move until gauchos removed the statue. Its devout owner, from the northwestern province of Santiago del Estero, took this as a sign that the Virgin should remain at the spot and built a chapel for her. Apparently, though, Argentina's patron saint was not totally immovable—she has since shifted to more opulent accommodations in the French Gothic basilica, five kilometers from her original abode.

ORIENTATION

On the right bank of its eponymous river, Luján (population 78,005) is about 65 kilometers west of Buenos Aires via RN7. Most points of interest are on and around Avenida Nuestra Señora de Luján, the broad avenue that enters town from the north, while most services are eastward toward the central Plaza Colón.

SIGHTS

The basilica may be Luján's most imposing site, but its museums have undergone a professional transformation that transcends the standard stuff-in-glass-cases approach of so many provincial institutions.

Basílica Nacional Nuestra Señora de Luján

Glazed in silver to protect her from deterioration, clothed in white and blue robes, the ceramic Virgin is a diminutive 38-centimeter

Cabildo Rose Garden and Basílica Nacional Nuestra Señora de Luján, Buenos Aires Province

image that was baked in Brazil. In the 1880s, on a trip to Europe, the French Lazarist missionary Jorge Salvaire created her elaborate crown; apparently deciding that was not enough, he worked tirelessly to build the Gothic basilica whose pointed spires now soar 106 meters above the pampas. Not completed until 1937, its facade has been undergoing a slow but thorough restoration. Pope John Paul II said Mass here in 1982, only a few days before Argentina's surrender in the Falklands war.

Twice removed from the world outside, the Virgencita (little virgin) inhabits a separate *camarín* (chamber) behind the main altar; begging her help, pilgrims proceed at a snail's pace past plaques left by their grateful predecessors.

The Basílica Nacional Nuestral Señora de Luján (San Martín 50, tel. 02323/412070, www.basilicadelujan.org.ar, open 7 A.M.–8 P.M. daily) overlooks the barren Plaza Belgrano. Immediately west of the basilica, the **Museo Devocional** (San Martín 51, tel. 02323/420058, open 1–6 P.M. weekdays except Mon., 10 A.M.– 6 P.M. weekends) holds larger *ex-votos* (gifts left in thanks for her help).

Construction of the Basílica Nacional Nuestra Señora de Luján began in the 1880s.

© WAYNE BERNHARDSON

Complejo Museográfico Enrique Udaondo

On the west side of Avenida Nuestra Señora de Luján, immediately north of the basilica, the former *cabildo* (colonial town council, 1797) and the **Casa del Virrey** (House of the Viceroy, 1803) hold one of the country's finest museum assemblages. No viceroy every lived in Luján, by the way, but the Marqués de Sobremonte once spent a few hours in the house.

Porteño architect Martín S. Noel's 1918 restoration of the *cabildo* took some liberties with the building's original unadorned facade and a few other features. Still, the three hectares of buildings and well-kept grounds, bounded by Lezica y Torrezuri, Lavalle, San Martín, and Parque Ameghino, are distinguished for their contents as well.

Within the *cabildo* and the Casa del Virrey, the **Museo Histórico** has a thorough display on Argentine history, with a dazzling assortment of maps, portraits, and artifacts (such as caudillo Facundo Quiroga's blood-stained *vicuña* poncho) that bring history to life. The museum box office, at the corner of Avenida Nuestra Señora de Luján and Lavalle, has a salon for special exhibits.

Immediately north, the **Museo de Transporte** houses an extraordinary collection of horse carriages in mint condition, including hearses, a carriage that belonged to General Mitre, and the stuffed carcasses of Gato and Mancha, the hardy Argentine *criollo* horses that 1930s adventurer A. F. Tschiffely rode from Buenos Aires to Washington, D.C. There is also a Dornier seaplane co-built by Spaniards and Argentines, and the country's first-ever locomotive, from the Ferrocarril Oeste. The main showroom's upper level is devoted to an elaborate exhibit on *mate* and its ritual, from colonial times to the present.

The **Complejo Museográfico** (tel. 02323/420245, open noon–6 P.M. Wed.–

Fri., 10:15 A.M.–6:30 P.M. weekends and holidays, US$.35) has a box office at the corner of Avenida Nuestra Señora de Luján and Lavalle; admission is valid for all museum facilities.

RESTAURANTS

For breakfast and dessert, the best choice is **Berlín** (San Martín 135, tel. 02323/440780), half a block east of the basilica. Calle 9 de Julio, just north of the basilica, consists of undistinguishably cheap *parrillas,* lined up wall-to-wall, frequented primarily by pilgrims.

The exposed bricks in its 18th-century adobe exterior sag like a syncline and weeds may be sprouting on the roof, but that gives the **1800 Restaurant** (Rivadavia and Almirante Brown, tel. 02323/433080) part of its charm. That wouldn't mean much, though, if their menu of meat, pasta, and fish and seafood (around US$4 for entrées) were not so good, the service so agreeable, and the *pulpería* interior equally charming. Add fresh summer raspberries from El Bolsón for dessert and good wine by the glass, and there's nothing to complain about.

Befitting Luján's ecclesiastical importance, the traditional choice for a more formal family lunch or dinner is the cross-town, Carmelite-run **L'eau Vive** (Constitución 2112, tel. 02323/421774, open noon–2:15 P.M. daily except Mon. and 8:30–10 P.M. except Sun. and Mon.). Fixed-price lunches or dinners, in the US$4–6 range, lean toward French specialties; they sometimes stop to observe a recorded version of *Ave Maria.* The main dining room is tobacco-free.

ENTERTAINMENT AND EVENTS

For most visitors to Luján, entertainment consists of spontaneous barbecues in Parque Ameghino or, when campgrounds are really crowded, on the median strip of Avenida Nuestra Señora de Luján. In February, though, there's the annual **Encuentro de la Fe y la Historia** (Encounter of Faith and History), a four-day festival that blocks off Avenida Nuestra Señora de Luján for folkloric music by the

likes of Antonio Tarragó Ros and Soledad Pastorutti (who prefers to use her first name only).

Alternatively, the rest of the year, there are movies at the **Cine Nuevo Numancia 1** (San Martín 398, tel. 02323/430860) and drinking and dancing at the **Old Swan Pub** (San Martín 546, tel. 02323/433346).

ACCOMMODATIONS

Many if not most pilgrims choose cheap camping; in fact, on major religious holidays, pilgrims camp just about anywhere there's open space, including Avenida Nuestra Señora de Luján's median strip. More formally, across the Río Luján about 10 blocks north of the basilica, shady **Camping El Triángulo** (Avenida Carlos Pellegrini, RN7, Km 69.5, tel. 02323/430116, US$4 d) also rents tents for about US$1.50 per day.

Across from the bus terminal, **Hotel Royal** (9 de Julio 696, tel. 02323/421295, US$10/13 s/d) has smallish but otherwise adequate rooms; it has a restaurant, but a buffet breakfast costs US$1.25 more. On the east side of the basilica, the well-managed **Hotel de la Paz** (9 de Julio 1054, tel. 02323/428742, US$14/21 s/d) is a dignified inn that's been around for nearly a century. Rates include breakfast, cable TV, and private bath; weekday rates are about 10 percent less.

Rates at **Hotel del Virrey** (San Martín 129, tel. 02323/420797, US$13/23 s/d) include private bath and breakfast. The 45-room **Hotel Hoxón** (9 de Julio 769, tel. 02323/429970, www.hotelhoxon.com.ar, US$14/23–US$17/26 s/d) is a major step up, and the only place in town with its own pool.

INFORMATION AND SERVICES

At the west end of Lavalle, Luján's municipal **Dirección de Turismo** (Parque Ameghino s/n, tel. 02323/433500, open 9 A.M.–1 P.M. weekdays only) is located in the Edificio La Cúpula. The helpful, non-governmental **Coprotur** (9 de Julio 938, tel. 02323/428680, open 8 A.M.–8 P.M. daily) a block north of the basilica, actually operates out of a kiosk on Plaza Belgrano, opposite its storefront.

TRANSPORTATION

Luján has road and rail connections with Buenos Aires. The bus station is within walking distance to everything, while the train station is across town. Cheap *remises* can carry up to four passengers for a minimal fare.

Bus

The **Estación Terminal de Ómnibus** (Avenida Nuestra Señora del Rosario between Almirante Brown and Dr. Reat, tel. 02323/420044) is three blocks north of the basilica. **Transportes Atlántida** (Línea 57, tel. 02323/420032, Interno 24) connects Luján with Palermo's Plaza Italia (US$1.50, 1.5 hours).

Train

TBA's **Línea Sarmiento** (Avenida España and Belgrano, tel. 02323/421312, www.tbanet.com.ar) goes to and from the capital's Estación Once

© WAYNE BERNHARDSON

The religious center of Luján, in Buenos Aires province, is also a magnet for Argentine bikers.

(Subte: Plaza Miserere, Línea A), but it's necessary to change trains in Moreno. The fare is only about US$.60, but it takes at least two hours.

VICINITY OF LUJÁN

Luján proper may draw the faithful, but some points of interest in the vicinity have little or nothing to do with faith. Even as folk musicians are charming listeners in the Basílica's shadows, heavy metal bands in nearby **Jáuregui** are energizing February's annual **Motoencuentro As de Espadas,** an annual bikers' gathering. During the 2005 event, Argentine rock/blues guitarist Norberto Napolitano (better known as Pappo, he once shared the Madison Square Garden stage with B.B. King) literally made an impact here when he skidded his Harley under the wheels of an oncoming car; in all likelihood the accident scene (RN 5, Km 71) will become a pilgrimage site for his followers.

About 15 kilometers north of Luján, bypassed by time, the dying railroad, and relocated RN 7, the village of **Carlos Keen** has undergone a tourism revival thanks to its well-preserved 19th-century architecture, restaurants, and teahouses. In mid-February 2005, though, it also drew 18,000 music fans to the alcohol-free (and thus orderly) **Festival CampoKonex** (www.campokonex.com.ar), to hear *rock nacional* icons, including Charly García and Luis Alberto Spinetta, but also folk-oriented figures, such as *chamamé* accordionist Chango Spasiuk.

Estancias still play an important role in the local economy and society: **Estancia Las Lilas** produces beef for its Buenos Aires restaurant nearby, and politician-crooner Ramón (Palito) Ortega (who once sought a government subsidy to bring Frank Sinatra to Buenos Aires!) owns **Estancia La Negrita.** The most interesting of them, though, is the historic **Estancia Los Talas,** which is open to day-trippers and overnight guests.

Estancia los Talas

In the same family for nearly two centuries—

except for a time in the 1840s when tyrant José Manuel de Rosas confiscated it—the 890-hectare Estancia los Talas raises dairy cattle and produces honey for the Argentine market. As an *estancia* open to guests, it's arguably the most authentic of the bunch: it's oldest adobe dates from 1824 and the main house, where most visitors stay in high-ceilinged, slightly musty rooms furnished with antiques, from 1840.

Approached through a long avenue of mature eucalyptus, Los Talas is also the unlikely home to the **Fundación Archivo y Biblioteca Jorge M. Furt,** guarding a 40,000-volume library of rare books and documents that belonged to the renowned philologist who resided here. In partnership with the Universidad Nacional San Martín, it includes valuable material, such as the archive of early Argentine intellectual, educator, and politician Juan Bautista Alberdi, whose ideas on immigration—"to populate is to govern"—became part of Argentine orthodoxy.

The library itself draws scholars from around Argentina and overseas; for what it's worth, the building itself is a 1950s addition to the main house, but it so closely mimics the original style that it's nearly impossible to distinguish it. Los Talas' literary connections are even older, though: poet Esteban Echeverría (1805–1851) lived and wrote here before Rosas's persecution drove him to exile in Uruguay.

The Furt family still operates Estancia los Talas (RP 47 Km 19, tel. 02323/494995, biblioteca_furt@yahoo.com.ar), which charges US$21 pp for its Día de Campo, which includes as *asado,* afternoon tea, and unlimited use of their horses and the swimming pool. Full-board accommodations cost around US$48 pp; three or four days' notice is advisable before a visit. A *remise* from downtown Luján costs around US$6 for up to four persons.

San Antonio de Areco

Bidding for UNESCO World Heritage Site status, the 18th-century town of San Antonio de Areco is Argentina's unofficial gaucho capital, host to its biggest gaucho festivities, and home to a concentration of traditional craftsmen and artists difficult to match in any other town its size. It's an irony, though, that many of those most closely associated with the gaucho traditions have Italian-immigrant surnames.

San Antonio was the home of *gauchesco* novelist Ricardo Güiraldes, who wrote *Don Segundo Sombra* (1927) here. It was also the location for director Manuel Antín's 1969 movie, which featured the author's recently deceased (September 2002) nephew Adolfo Güiraldes in the title role of a dignified rustic whose practical wisdom leaves a lasting imprint on a landowner's son.

While some small pampas towns have been struggling since 2002, San Antonio (population 17,820) emits an air of tidy prosperity, with many of its Italianate colonial-style houses and other buildings restored or recycled. The local real-estate market is booming with an influx of *porteño* refugees from the big-city bustle.

San Antonio's biggest event is November's **Día de la Tradición,** celebrating the gaucho heritage, but weekends are busy all year round. The pace is always relaxed, though, with greater deference to pedestrians and cyclists than anywhere else in the country. Many Arequeños, in fact, use bicycles to get around, and hotels often provide free *bicis* to their guests.

ORIENTATION

San Antonio de Areco is 113 kilometers west of Buenos Aires via RN8, which continues west toward San Luis, Mendoza, and the Chilean border. On the right bank of the Río Areco, it forms a mostly regular grid west of the highway; the commercial street of Alsina, leading south from the main Plaza Ruiz de Arellano, is the liveliest part of town.

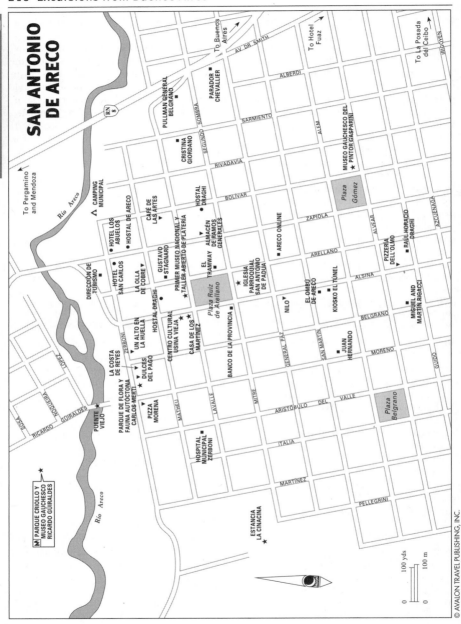

SAN ANTONIO DE ARECO

© AVALON TRAVEL PUBLISHING, INC.

SIGHTS

San Antonio is so pedestrian-friendly that, in a country where motorists rarely even slow down for crosswalks, townsfolk often stroll in the middle of the street. That's not really recommended, but San Antonio's leisurely pace and compact core do make it attractive for walkers and cyclists.

Unlike most central plazas, San Antonio's **Plaza Ruiz de Arellano** is not the lively hub of local life, but it's an appealingly shady park surrounded by historic buildings and monuments: the **Casa de los Martínez,** site of the original *estancia* house, is at the northwest corner; the **Iglesia Parroquial San Antonio de Padua** (Parish Church, 1869) is on the south side; and the **Palacio Municipal** (1885), part of which has become the Draghi family's **Taller y Museo de Platería Criolla y Civil y Salón de Arte,** a combination museum, silversmith's workshop, and art gallery, is on the plaza's north side. In the plaza's center, the **Monumento a Vieytes** memorializes San Antonio native Juan Hipólito Vieytes (1762–1815), a participant in the 1810 revolution that eventually brought Argentine independence.

THE PAMPA GAUCHA

The pampas west of Buenos Aires were transformed by the herds of cattle that proliferated on them after the Spanish invasion and by the horsemen who lived off those herds, making the pampas gaucho country. Eventually, and ironically, though, the free-ranging gauchos became the peons of the sprawling *estancias* (cattle ranches) that occupied almost every square centimeter of this prime agricultural land.

Unofficially, San Antonio de Areco is Argentina's gaucho capital, and the *estancias* that surround it are some of the country's most historic. The city of Luján, however, is equally if not more historic, with outstanding museums, and is also one of South America's major devotional centers.

Half a block north of the Plaza, dating from 1901, the **Centro Cultural Usina Vieja** is an antique power plant recycled into a fine museum and cultural center. Three blocks northwest, facing the river, the **Parque de Flora y Fauna Autóctona Carlos Merti** (Zerboni and Moreno, tel. 02326/453783, open 9 A.M.–noon and 2–7 P.M. daily, US$.35) is a small zoo. Across the street, the restored **Puente Viejo** (1857) over the Río Areco may have been the country's first toll bridge; originally designed for cart traffic, it lent its atmosphere to the movie version of *Don Segundo Sombra*. It's now a bike, horse, and pedestrian shortcut to the **Parque Criollo y Museo Gauchesco Ricardo Güiraldes,** a museum memorializing the author's *gauchesco* romanticism.

It's not the only *gauchesco* institution in town, though: Luis Gasparini, son of the late painter Osvaldo Gasparini, continues to paint and operate the **Museo Gauchesco del Pintor Gasparini.** At the intersection of RN8 and Soldado Argentino, at the south end of San Antonio, the remains of both Ricardo Güiraldes and Segundo Ramírez (the author's model for the fictional Don Segundo Sombra) repose in the **Cementerio Municipal.**

For a day in the country without really leaving town, visit **Estancia la Cinacina** (Mitre 9, tel. 02326/452045, www.lacinacina.com.ar), only six blocks west of Plaza Ruiz de Arellano, on Tuesday, Friday, and Sunday. For about US$13 pp, the visit includes snacks, a city tour, lunch, and folkloric music and dance; from Buenos Aires, with transportation, it costs about US$30 pp.

Centro Cultural Usina Vieja

Handsomely recycled as a museum and events center, San Antonio's century-old power plant holds permanent collections of odds and ends, such as an experimental biplane built here, and a good sample of work by San Antonio's artisans. It's also managed impressive exhibits that recreate overlooked everyday institutions, like the simple barbershop and *botica* (apothecary), while the garden holds an array of antique farm machinery.

While it has plenty of good artifacts, the

Centro Cultural Usina Vieja (Alsina 66, tel. 02326/452021, open 11 A.M.–5 P.M. daily except non-holiday Mondays, free) presents little historical and cultural interpretation.

Museo Gauchesco del Pintor Gasparini

Since the death of his father, Luis Gasparini continues to live in and operate this *gauchesco* art museum, which has half a dozen rooms devoted to the gaucho sculpture, silverwork, and painting (including works by Benito Quinquela Martín and Lino Spilimbergo, among others). There is also a chapel, an atelier with the family's own *gauchesco* works, and a library; appropriately enough, there's a hitching post outside for those who arrive on horseback.

The Museo Gauchesco (Alvear 521, tel. 02326/453930, gaspa@arecoonline.com.ar, open 9 A.M.–8 P.M., 365 days a year, free) is located just off Plaza Gómez.

The Iglesia Parroquial San Antonio de Padua overlooks San Antonio de Areco's Plaza Ruiz Arellano.

Parque Criollo y Museo Gauchesco Ricardo Güiraldes

Set on 97 hectares of parkland, San Antonio's gaucho museum is a romantic idealization of the already romantic *gauchesco* literature of Ricardo Güiraldes, whose family lived on the nearby Estancia La Porteña. Created by the provincial government in the 1930s, the museum lacks the authenticity of the *estancia* itself (which is open to visits). It does, though, offer genuinely ironic insights into the way Argentines—even *porteños*—have internalized the gaucho heritage.

The irony, of course, was that the landowning novelist Güiraldes, however sincere, presumed to speak for the illiterate gaucho—a defiantly independent figure who became a humble, dependent laborer on the oligarchy's *estancias*. Nowhere is this clearer than in the principal **Casa del Museo,** a 20th-century replica of an 18th century *casco* (big house): It devotes two rooms to Güiraldes himself; another to his wife Adelina del Carril; another to his painter cousin Alberto; a **Sala de los Escritores** to *gauchesco* literature, including Walter Owen's English-language translation of José Hernández's epic poem *Martín Fierro;*

a **Sala Pieza de Estanciero** that includes the bed of tyrant landowner Juan Manuel de Rosas (who exploited gauchos ruthlessly but counted them among his most enthusiastic allies); and, finally, a **Sala del Gaucho** that stresses horse gear and *gauchesco* art, but not the gaucho's marginal status.

The Casa del Museo gives only a partial account of the gaucho; the surrounding park contains the **Pulpería La Blanqueada,** a real 19th-century roadhouse with a life-size gaucho diorama. Nearby are three other aging structures, **La Ermita de San Antonio,** an adobe chapel with an image of its patron saint; the **La Tahona** flour mill (1848); and the **Galpón y Cuarto de Sogas,** a carriage house.

Reached by the Puente Viejo shortcut, the Museo Gauchesco (Camino Ricardo Güiraldes s/n, tel. 02326/455839, open 11 A.M.–5 P.M. daily except Tues.) costs US$1 pp except for retired persons, who pay US$.35, and children under age 12, who get in free.

Primer Museo Nacional y Taller Abierto de Platería

Recycling a century-old residence that was

in near ruin, silversmith Juan José Draghi has enriched the moribund Plaza Ruiz de Arellano with his new museum/shop and adjacent bed-and-breakfast. In addition to the opportunity to see a master craftsman and his employees at work, there are displays of museum-quality gaucho gear that reflect their regions of origin. *Facones* (gaucho knives) and spurs from the featureless pampas are unadorned, for instance, while their highly ornamented counterparts from Mesopotamian provinces, such as Entre Ríos and Corrientes, reflect the exuberant natural environment of riverside gallery forests.

Some items displayed in the shop—such as ceremonial silver bridles that take a year to produce and cost up to US$20,000—are custom jobs awaiting shipment. Others, such as cutlery with intricately threaded leather handles and ritual silver *mates* may be available for over-the-counter purchase.

The Museo (Lavalle 387, tel. 02326/454219, open 9 A.M.–1 P.M. and 4–8 P.M. weekdays, 9 A.M.–8 P.M. Sat., US$1.75) offers guided visits from 10:30 A.M., on the half-hour, in very good English as well as Spanish.

FIESTA DE LA TRADICIÓN

Since 1934, November's Fiesta de la Tradición has feted San Antonio's gaucho heritage with guided visits to historic sites, lectures by top folklorists, crafts fairs, and folk music and dance—plus, of course, flamboyant displays of horsemanship on Plaza Ruiz de Arellano. While the principal **Día de la Tradición** is theoretically November 10, the festivities normally stretch over two weekends, climaxing on the final Sunday. Reservations are critical for anyone who wants to stay in San Antonio proper rather than in the surrounding countryside or neighboring towns.

SHOPPING

San Antonio's silversmiths are the country's finest, so don't expect to find any bargains—a silver mate can cost up to US$1,500, though there are, of course, cheaper versions. Other typical silver dress items include the long-bladed *facón* (gaucho knife), *rastra* (coin-studded belt), and *espuelas* (spurs).

Silversmith Juan José Draghi's magnificent new museum/shop and bed-and-breakfast

Silversmith Juan José Draghi has transformed a rundown house into a museum and shop.

THE ESTANCIAS OF ARECO

In the vicinity of San Antonio, several historic *estancias* grow soybeans and raise livestock, but tourism pays the bills. All of them are quality establishments that take overnight guests and even offer "day in the country" excursions, including an *asado* and rural activities like horseback riding. Camping is not out of the question, at least at La Porteña.

Estancia La Porteña

San Antonio's most emblematic *estancia*, La Porteña has belonged to the Güiraldes family since the early 19th century. Of all the area's farms, it has the finest grounds; French landscape architect Carlos Thays, who created major public parks, like Palermo's Jardín Botánico and Mendoza's Parque General San Martín, designed the plan, including the stately avenue of elm-like hackberries that leads to the main house.

La Porteña has only a few guest rooms, so reservations are essential. Beef is the standard menu, but the kitchen will happily accommodate vegetarians with pasta and other meatless dishes, served in a dining room filled with French and British antiques. La Porteña eschews television, but there's a large swimming pool and a library. English is spoken.

Estancia La Porteña (tel. 02326/453770, cell 02325/15-684179, www.estancialaportenia.com.ar) is about six kilometers northeast of San Antonio via RP 8 and RN 41. Accommodations cost US$131 d with full board, pool access, and use of horses; it also has a nearby campground (tel. 02326/453402, US$4 pp), but this is effectively segregated from the main grounds.

Estancia El Ombú de Areco

Named for Argentina's wide-crowned national tree, El Ombú de Areco belonged to General Pablo Ricchieri, who first forced military conscription onto Argentina's youth. Set among four hectares of formal gardens, with a pool, on a 300-hectare property, it's the area's most lavish *estancia* in terms of furnishings, facilities, and activities: satellite TV and video, telephone, horseback and bicycle riding, and games. There are six impeccable double rooms and three triples, with full board; vegetarians should verify the menu, which leans heavily toward beef.

Estancia El Ombú de Areco (tel. 02326/492080, cellular 02325/15-682598, www.estanciaelombu.com, US$120/180 s/d) is about 11 kilometers northeast of San Antonio via RN 8, paved RP 41, and graveled RP 31. It also offers "day in the country" visits for US$35 pp and arranges transportation from the capital and its airports for guests. It also has a Gran Buenos Aires contact (Cura Allievi 1280, Boulogne, Buenos Aires Province, tel. 011/4710-2795).

are major contributions to San Antonio's appeal. Other silversmiths include Raúl Horacio Draghi (Guido 391, tel. 02326/454207), who also works in leather; Gustavo Stagnaro (Arellano 59, tel. 02326/454801, www.stagnaro.com.ar); and Miguel and Martín Rigacci (Belgrano 381, tel. 02326/456049).

Camilo Fiore (Avenida Vieytes 632, tel. 02326/452804) is a custom boot-maker, while Cristina Giordano (Sarmiento 112, tel. 02326/452829) is a weaver.

El Ombú de Areco (Alsina and San Martín) is a commercial dealer in leather, silver, ropes, and crafts, and is a good place for an overview of what's available.

Juan Hernando (Moreno 279, tel. 02326/456425) is a spectacular antiques dealer that looks more like a museum, in a recycled brick building with high ceilings and plenty of space to admire the merchandise. El Tramway (Segundo Sombra 411, 02326/455561) is an equally spacious, but less stylish and more cluttered, antiquarian.

RESTAURANTS

San Antonio has a pair of passable pizzerias, downtown's **Pizzería Dell'Olmo** (Alsina 365, tel. 02326/452506) and **Pizza Morena** (Zerboni and Moreno, tel. 02326/456391), near the river.

Estancia La Bamba

Less elegant than La Porteña and less luxurious than El Ombú, Estancia La Bamba is a little rougher around the edges, but its unique personality—it began as a *posta* (way station) on the colonial Camino Real rather than as an *estancia* per se—gives it a unique ambience. The least formal of the big three, it is perhaps the most relaxed of them all.

In addition to its accommodations, La Bamba has recently rebuilt its former carriage house into a country *pulpería* with Saturday-evening (7 P.M.) celebrations of gaucho *guitarreadas* and folkloric dances, along with traditional country food and wine. There's a US$2.50 cover charge, and reservations are advisable.

La Bamba, which served as a set for director María Luisa Bemberg's 19th-century drama *Camila,* can accommodate 11 persons in five rooms in the main house, another four in a cottage suitable for a family, and four more in an annex. Amenities include a swimming pool, game and video rooms, and activities, including horseback riding, bird-watching, fishing, and the like. High-season rates range from about US$90 to US$165 pp with full board, depending on the room.

Estancia La Bamba (tel. 02326/456293, tel. 011/4732-1269 in Buenos Aires, www.la-bamba.com.ar) is about 13 kilometers north-east of San Antonio via RN 8, RP 41, and RN 31. It also offers "day in the country" visits for about US$45 pp.

Estancia El Rosario de Areco

Only six kilometers southwest of San Antonio, El Rosario raises polo ponies and offers a polo school, with two full playing fields on about 80 hectares of land. Non-players and even non-riders, though, will appreciate the design ingenuity that has turned its former stables into 16 remarkably comfortable, spacious, and tasteful suites.

In addition to the accommodations, part of a *casco* that includes a main house dating from the 1890s, owner Francisco Guevara has built a conical open-sided *quincho* (a covered shelter for barbeques) for *asados*. There are also living and dining areas just far enough from the sleeping quarters to ensure peace and quiet, and a pool for guests.

Rates at El Rosario de Areco (tel. 02326/451000, www.rosariodeareco.com.ar) are US$140 pp with full board (including drinks) and activities included. "Day in the Country" visits cost US$60 pp. Guevara tries not to mix overnight guests and day-trippers, nor unrelated groups, so reservations are essential—preferably as far in advance as possible. It also hosts business groups on retreat and has WiFi Internet access and a dedicated conference room.

La Costa de Reyes (Belgrano and Zerboni, tel. 02326/452481) serves primarily *parrillada* but also pasta, with friendly service and good prices; most entrées are in the US$3–4 range. Immediately across the street, **Un Alto en la Huella** (Zerboni and Belgrano, tel. 02326/455595) has similar offerings and prices.

Recently relocated to an 1890s house, still recreating the atmosphere of a traditional *pulpería,* **Puesto La Lechuza** (Segundo Sombra 188, tel. 2326/454542) serves home-cooked Argentine food—your basic *bife de chorizo* and a salad, but also appetizers of homemade salami, cheese, bread, and *empanadas.* There's usually live music on weekends; if not, ask owner Marcelo Salazar to play "Whiter Shade of Pale" on the antique Parisian organ.

Also relocated, to a charmingly recycled house whose original brickwork shows through the plaster, the **Almacén de Ramos Generales** (Zapiola 143, tel. 02326/456376, www.ramos-generalesareco.com.ar) is primarily a *parrilla* but also has fine pastas and the occasional oddity, such as the Basque seafood casserole *txan gurro,* which includes king crab, tuna, red peppers, and tomatoes. Its cozy walls festooned with bottles, ladles, padlocks, paintings, posters, and photographs, it also makes particularly good desserts and sells homemade salami and cheeses.

ESTANCIA OPERATORS

Over the past decade-plus, weekending in the countryside of Buenos Aires province has become an increasingly popular option for those wishing to escape the capital. As *estancia* owners have struggled to diversify economically, some even make more income from hosting tourists than they do growing grain or raising livestock. Some *estancias* aim at day-trippers, but most of them prefer overnight guests. Some are reasonably priced places with limited services, but others are magnificent estates with castle-like *cascos* (big houses), elaborate services, including gourmet meals, and recreational activities, such as horseback riding, tennis, swimming, and the like.

Affiliated with the Sociedad Rural Argentina, the **Red Argentina de Turismo Rural** (Florida 460, 4th fl., tel. 011/4328-0499, www.raturestancias.com.ar) represents *estancias* in northern and southern Buenos Aires province, as well as in the northwestern Argentine provinces, Córdoba, and even some in Patagonia.

Another exceptional choice is **Café de las Artes** (Bolívar 70, tel. 02362/15-511684), very strong on pastas, including homemade gnocchi with a beet sauce. Likewise loaded with antiques and art works, it discourages smoking, but hasn't quite been able to pull the trigger on tobacco abusers.

Nilo (Alsina 234, tel. 02326/452341) is the best of several fine ice creameries. **La Olla de Cobre** (Matheu 433, tel. 02326/453105, www.laolladecobre.com.ar) produces fine artisanal chocolates and other sweets, while **Dulces del Pago** (Zerboni 136, tel. 02326/454751, www.delpagodeareco.com.ar) specializes in fruit preserves.

ACCOMMODATIONS

Despite its tourist tradition, San Antonio proper has good but limited accommodations; in recent years, some hotels have

expanded and the level of services has improved, as even some moderately priced accommodations have added such features as swimming pools and air-conditioning.

During November's Fiesta de la Tradición, when reservations are imperative, visitors may lodge in communities for miles around. Prices often rise on weekends, when reservations are advisable, but informal bed-and-breakfast accommodations may also be available—ask at the tourist office.

At the north end of town, the **Camping Municipal** (Zapiola s/n) is cheap (US$2 per site for up to four campers) and shady, but heavy rains can flood the lowest-lying sites.

Hotel San Carlos (Zapiola and Zerboni, tel. 02326/453106, www.hotel-sancarlos.com.ar, US$10/14 s/d weekdays, US$18 d weekends) remains an exceptional value, with cable TV, a pair of smallish pools (one with Jacuzzi), and other amenities, including free bicycles. It's expanded, though, and can get a little noisy when kids play around the pool. A few cozy rooms have what might be called micro-closets.

Immediately across the street, the smallish rooms at modern **Hotel Los Abuelos** (Zapiola and Zerboni, tel. 02326/456390, www.sanantoniodeareco.com/losabuelos, US$13–17 s or d) are comfortable enough, but what might have been a secluded central garden has instead become a dreary driveway and parking lot. Rates include private bath, high ceilings with fans, telephone, cable TV, and swimming pool; skip the mediocre breakfast (US$1).

Next door, recently reopened **Hostal de Areco** (Zapiola 25, tel. 02326/456118, www.hostaldeareco.com.ar, US$10/15 s/d weekdays, US$20 d weekends) is not quite pristine, but it has large to huge rooms, ample and inviting common spaces in classic San Antonio style, and a spacious, woodsy, and pool-less garden that ensures quiet during the siesta hours.

Until recently, Areco proper lacked really stylish accommodations, but **Hostal Draghi** (Lavalle 387, tel. 02326/454219, draghi@lq.com.ar, US$23–33 d) is filling that niche nicely. Entered from Matheu, immediately behind the Draghi family's museum on Plaza Ruiz de Arellano, this converted garage (combined with new construction) recreates traditional San Antonio style on fountain-studded grounds. Furnished with antiques, the spacious rooms have high ceilings, kitchenettes, and distinctive design flourishes that reflect a silversmith's attention to detail; some but not all have Jacuzzi-equipped tubs. Free bicycles are also available, and museum admission and tours are free for guests.

Other options, in less appealing locations near the highway, are **La Posada del Ceibo** (Irigoyen between RN8 and Avenida Dr. Smith, tel. 02326/454614, www.laposadadelceibo.com.ar, US$20 d), with breakfast, private bath, cable TV, and pool; and **Hotel Fuaz** (Avenida Dr. Smith 488, tel. 02326/452487, US$13 d), with air-conditioned rooms with breakfast. More spacious rooms cost just a little more.

INFORMATION

San Antonio's **Dirección de Turismo** (Zerboni and Ruiz de Arellano, tel. 02326/453165, ww.arecotur.com.ar, open 8 A.M.–8 P.M. daily) publishes the monthly *Don Segundo,* a useful commercial miniguide with a town map; other handouts include a glossy list of tourist-oriented services and a map of local artisans.

SERVICES

Correo Argentino (Alvear and Aristóbulo del Valle) is the post office. **Kiosko El Túnel** (Alsina 264) provides long-distance service, while **Areco Online** (Arellano 285-A) has reliable Internet access. Money is available through ATMs at several banks, including **Banco de la Provincia** (Mitre and Alsina).

For medical emergencies, there's the **Hospital Municipal Zerboni** (Moreno and Lavalle, tel. 02326/452759).

TRANSPORTATION

Just off the highway, on the east side of town, San Antonio's **Parador Chevallier** (Avenida Dr. Smith and General Paz, tel. 02326/453904, tel. 011/4000-5255 in Retiro) has up to 12 buses daily to San Antonio (US$4, 1.5–2 hours). Just to the north, **Pullman General Belgrano** (Avenida Dr. Smith and Segundo Sombra, tel. 02326/454059) has four buses daily to and from Retiro.

© WAYNE BERNHARDSON

Sulkies, single-horse carriages, are not unusual to see on the streets of San Antonio de Areco.

Lobos and Vicinity

South of Buenos Aires, RN 3 and its spur RN 205 might be called the "Ruta de Polo" for the scattered *estancias* that keep gigantic, closely cropped lawns in primo condition for a sport that's the dominion of the elite. At the same time, ironically enough, one of the area's largest towns is the birthplace of the *caudillo* and working-class hero Juan Domingo Perón.

ORIENTATION

Lobos (population 26,801) is about 100 kilometers southwest of Buenos Aires via RN 3 and RN 205. Plaza 1810 is the center of its regular grid.

MUSEO JUAN DOMINGO PERÓN

For all his transformative impact on Argentine public life, and the persistence of a personality cult that allows hero-worshippers from extreme left to extreme right to claim his legacy, Juan Domingo Perón's hometown and birthplace museum is strangely understated. It's almost as if its curators decided that the story of the obscure army officer who became Latin America's stereotypical strongman is so well known that no commentary is necessary—a handful of his personal documents, family and political photos, and smiling portraits are sufficient.

The museum's own history is at least as interesting, dating from 1953 (when Perón was still president). Following his 1955 overthrow, it had to close until his 1973 return from exile; it stayed open only a few years until another coup closed it in 1976. Even after the 1983 return to constitutional government, it took six years more to reopen definitively.

Though it's undergone substantial remodeling since its construction in 1894, a year before the caudillo's birth, the building itself is a national historical monument. Perón's former office desk, as well as furniture and other personal belongings from his Spanish home in exile, fill several rooms.

The museum's most offbeat exhibit—having no connection whatsoever to Perón—is the skull of the famous gaucho *bandido* Juan Moreira, shot dead by police only a few blocks away in 1874. Moreira's life has been the subject of movies in 1936, 1948, and 1973, so he's probably overdue for a cinematic update.

The Museo Juan Domingo Perón (Presidente Perón 482, tel. 02227/424404, open 10 A.M.–noon and 3–6 P.M. Wed.–Sun.) is located five blocks south of Plaza 1810.

LA MARTINA POLO RANCH

While the genteel sport of polo might seem antithetical to Argentina's gaucho tradition, the two come together at La Martina. Like many *estancias,* it's open to the general public, but its specialist public is polo riders from as far afield as the United States, the United King-

Juan Domingo Perón's boyhood home is a modest museum in Lobos, Buenos Aires province.

© WAYNE BERNHARDSON

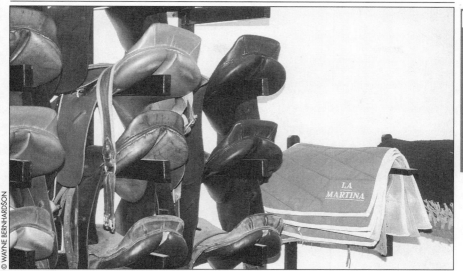

© WAYNE BERNHARDSON

Polo saddles cover the walls at La Martina Polo Ranch, between Buenos Aires and Lobos.

dom, and even Malaysia. It owes a good part of its reputation to its status as the home of international legend Adolfo Cambiaso, the Willie Mays of the sport, and its 88 hectares include two full-size fields.

At the same time, La Martina gets plenty of weekend visitors from the capital, as they enjoy its two finely furnished guesthouses, oak-shaded brick patio, broad lawns, tennis courts, and riding trails. If it gets crowded, the century-old *casco* (big house) is also available for accommodations. There are few visitors during the week, except for Buenos Aires companies who hold corporate retreats here.

"Day in the Country" excursions from Buenos Aires cost US$72 pp, including an arrival snack, a full lunch (including empanada appetizers, the traditional *asado,* a salad buffet, dessert, wine or soft drinks, and coffee or tea), and a late-afternoon tea with homemade cakes. In addition, day-trippers can use the pool, tennis courts, and the ranch's horses for riding (polo-playing day-trippers, though, pay US$194 pp).

Overnight accommodations at La Martina

cost US$194/339 s/d with full board and all activities; for polo players, rates are US$387 pp. Polo players tend to stay four or five days, and there are special packages for them.

La Martina Polo Ranch (tel. 0226/430772, www.lamartinapolo.com) is about 50 kilometers southwest of Buenos Aires via the Ezeiza-Cañuelas freeway, and 50 kilometers northeast of Lobos; most of the staff speak good English. For visitors who don't care to drive, Lobos Bus drops passengers at the Puente Vicente Casares, an overpass barely a 10-minute walk from La Martina's gates.

ESTANCIA & POLO CLUB LA CANDELARIA

For many Argentines, especially landowners, France was the ideal of elegance, but few have taken it so far as Manuel Fraga, who built an outlandish Norman-style *castillo* on the pampas in the early 1900s. Now, though, anyone who wants to feel like the guest of nobility can spend the night on this 400-hectare *estancia,* which doubles as a polo ranch.

With its painstakingly carved, stained,

© WAYNE BERNHARDSON

Near Lobos, Estancia La Candelaria's Norman-style castle reflected the Francophile aspirations—or pretensions—of Argentina's landed elite.

and burnished woodwork, meticulously detailed *vitraux*, and furniture that may indeed have come from French castles, "El Castillo" has an unquestionable air of upper-class privilege. Almost indescribably ornate, its interior includes an elaborate dining room (used only for special occasions, as visitors dine in a separate facility), a game room with a large pool table, and several high-ceilinged guestrooms that range from relatively modest doubles to sprawling suites.

Famed French landscape architect lined La Candelaria's roads with casuarinas and eucalyptus, studded its broad lawns with more than 240 species of trees, and punctuated them with classical statuary. Given its painstaking design, La Candelaria has the ambience of an exclusive planned village, rather than a ranch.

No longer in the Fraga family, Estancia Candelaria (RN 205 Km 114.5, tel. 02227/424404, www.lacandelaria.com.ar) is about 15 kilometers south of Lobos. Rates, with full board, range from US$47/60 s/d

in the Spanish colonial-style bungalows to US$113/200 s/d in the castle's finest suite. Included is unlimited access to recreational facilities: bicycles, swimming pool, tennis courts, and horses (but not polo ponies—polo packages are separate).

ACCOMMODATIONS AND FOOD

Other than the surrounding *estancias,* the best option is the **Aquae Sulis Spa & Resort** (Independencia s/n, tel. 02227/424330 in Lobos, tel. 011/4658-1226 in Buenos Aires, www.aquaesulis.com.ar, US$180–214 d), a full-service spa that has 28 luxury rooms and a restaurant. Multi-day packages permit use of all facilities until late afternoon on the day of departure.

For day visitors, there's downtown's **La Marina** (Buenos Aires and Suipacha, tel. 02227/431097), which has good pastas and pizzas in the US$4 range. **Helados Florencia** (9 de Julio 365, tel. 02227/431105) has fine and very inexpensive ice cream.

INFORMATION

Lobos's **Consejo Asesor de Turismo** (Salgado 40, tel. 02227/431450, open 10 A.M.–7 P.M. weekdays, 10 A.M.–6 P.M. weekends) is located opposite Plaza 1810. Even when it's closed, there's a large, detailed map that's helpful in finding the sights.

TRANSPORTATION

La Martina (US$2.25, 45 minutes) and Lobos (US$4, 1.5 hours) are both easily reached by **Lobos Bus** (Mitre 1762, Congreso; Buenos Aires 579, Lobos, tel. 02227/431346). Reservations are essential for this very efficient service.

La Plata

In 1882, after barely avoiding civil war following the federalization of the city of Buenos Aires, indignant provincial authorities expropriated six square leagues in the former Municipio de la Ensenada to create their new capital of La Plata. Provincial Governor Dardo Rocha chose Pedro Benoit's standard grid, superimposed with diagonals like those of Washington, D.C., to be embellished with pretentious neoclassical and Francophile buildings that have, nevertheless, achieved a remarkable harmony over time.

While government is its reason for existence, La Plata (population 553,002) has become one of the country's major cultural centers, with first-rate universities, theaters, concert halls, libraries, and museums. In January and February, though, when politicians go on vacation and university students return to their families, the cultural calendar thins out and many museums close.

ORIENTATION

La Plata is 56 kilometers southeast of Buenos Aires via the Autopista Buenos Aires–La Plata, the recently completed freeway between the two cities. The city itself consists of a rectangular grid, with regularly distributed plazas, but the connecting diagonals (which run north-south and east-west) can make the layout disorienting to pedestrians—a slight wrong turn can send you far out of your way.

Most public buildings are on or around Plaza Moreno, La Plata's precise geographical center, but its commercial center is near Plaza San Martín, six blocks northeast. Unlike most Argentine cities, its streets and avenues are numbered rather than named; locations are most commonly described by their intersections and cross streets rather than building numeration.

SIGHTS

In 1882, Governor Dardo Rocha laid La Plata's **Piedra Fundacional** (Foundation Stone) in the center of sprawling **Plaza Moreno,** which fills four full blocks bounded by Calle 12, Calle 14, Calle 50, and Calle 54. Along with architects

© WAYNE BERNHARDSON

The Museo de La Plata is one of Argentina's top natural history facilities.

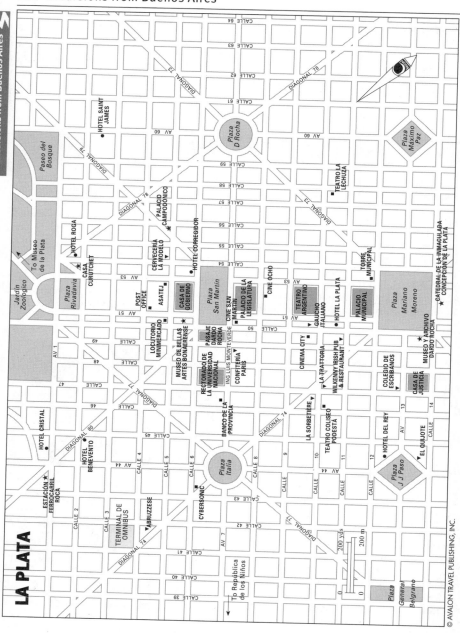

LA PLATA

© AVALON TRAVEL PUBLISHING, INC.

PARQUE ECOLÓGICO CULTURAL GUILLERMO E. HUDSON

B eyond La Boca, across the Riachuelo, the Zona Sur of Gran Buenos Aires is a low-profile, no-go zone for most tourists, but it's home to some offbeat sights. About midway to La Plata, at the Berazategui exit off the new freeway, the site where the late *cumbia* star Rodrigo Bueno rolled his car in 2000 has become a pilgrimage site for working-class fans convinced he was a saint. Near the slum suburb of Florencio Varela is Los 25 Ombúes, a onetime farm that was home to naturalist/novelist William Henry Hudson.

Known to Argentines as Guillermo Enrique, Hudson was the Argentine-born son of New Englanders Daniel Hudson and Carolina Kimble, who moved to Argentina in 1836. Born in 1841, Hudson passed his youth on the farm, which took its name from the *ombú* trees that once surrounded the humble house in what was then a wild and remote area. Today, the 18th-century adobe is a museum and the centerpiece of a 54-hectare forest and wetland preserve.

Hudson, who left Argentina for England in 1869, reminisced about his pampas days in *Long Ago and Far Away* (1918), but also left other memorable South American stories in *Idle Days in Patagonia* (1893) and *The Purple Land* (1885, republished in 1904). His main interest, though, was natural history, particularly birds.

Alongside Hudson's birthplace, which holds his books and family documents, some of the original 25 trees still stand. The best time to see the park is after the spring rains, when the wetlands still teem with bird life—but also with mosquitoes.

The Parque Ecológico Cultural Guillermo E. Hudson (tel. 011/4901-9651) is about midway between Buenos Aires and La Plata. The easiest way here is to take the train from Constitución (Buenos Aires) to Estación Florencio Varela and bus No. 324, Ramal (Branch) 2. This will get you to within a few hundred meters of the entrance, which is up a dirt road.

Ernesto Meyer and Emilio Coutaret, Benoit designed the French neo-Gothic **Catedral de la Inmaculada Concepción de la Plata** at the plaza's southwest corner.

Rocha himself resided in what is now the **Museo y Archivo Dardo Rocha,** fronting on Calle 50 on the plaza's northwest side. Two blocks west, the French-style **Casa de Justicia** fills an entire block bounded by Avenida 13, Calle 47, Calle 48, and Calle 14.

On the northeast side of Plaza Moreno, fronting on Calle 12, Hannover architect Hubert Stiers built the elegant German Renaissance **Palacio Municipal** (1886), whose main **Salón Dorado** is adorned with marble staircases, imported oak floors, German stained-glass windows, and bronze chandeliers. Two blocks away, bounded by Calle 9, Calle 10, Avenida 51, and Avenida 53, the **Teatro Argentino** is a performing-arts center that has finally replaced a far more dignified building that burned to the ground in 1977.

Two blocks northeast, facing Plaza San Martín on Avenida 7, Hannoverian architects Gustav Heine and Georg Hagemann designed the provincial **Palacio de la Legislatura** in the German Renaissance style of the Palacio Municipal. Across the plaza, fronting on Calle 6, Belgian architect Julio Doral designed the Flemish Renaissance **Casa de Gobierno,** home to the provincial executive branch and, seemingly, a challenge to the federal capital's nondescript Casa Rosada. The surrounding walls feature a remarkable set of murals by Rodolfo Campodónico (see the sidebar *The Campodónico Murals* for details).

Across Avenida 51, the **Museo de Bellas Artes Bonaerense** (Avenida 51 No. 525, tel. 0221/421-8629, www.lpsat.net/museo, open 10 A.M.–7 P.M. weekdays, 10 A.M.–1 P.M. and 3–7 P.M. weekends) is a contemporary art museum.

At the northwest corner of Plaza San Martín, La Plata's first railroad station is now the

THE CAMPODÓNICO MURALS

Stretching around the grounds of the Casa de Gobierno, Rodolfo Campodónico's 28 vivid historical and thematic murals are a welcome addition to La Plata's cultural scene. The former mostly include scenes from major events in Argentine history, and the latter deal with ways of life and figures from folk culture, music, and literature.

Dating from 1999, the murals that cover the walls from Avenida 51 along Calle 5 and Avenida 53 deal with the country's history. Their titles and their subjects are as follows: *Primeros Habitantes*, (First Inhabitants); *Solís and el Río de la Plata*, the Spanish discovery of the Río de la Plata; *Las Fundaciones*, the early settlements of Pedro de Mendoza and Juan de Garay; *Ataque al Fuerte Sancti Spiritus, 1536*, the Querandí assault on Mendoza's settlement; *El Mestizaje*, the blending of the indigenous and European-immigrant populations; *La Virgen de Luján*, Argentina's patron saint; *Exodo de los Indios Quilmes*, the forced deportation of the Quilmes people from northwestern Argentina to Buenos Aires; *Invasiones Inglesas*, the British invasions of the early 19th century; *Los Colorados del Monte*, the Federalist soldiers of the backcountry; *El Fusilamiento de Dorrego* (The Execution of Colonel Dorrego); *Combate de Vuelta de Obligado*, a battle in the war with Paraguay; *Telégrafo, Alumbrado y Ferrocarril*, the arrival of the telegraph, barbed wire, and the railroad; *Campañas al Desierto*, the war against the Patagonian indigenous people; and *Los Inmigrantes*, the European immigration.

At the corner of Calle 5 and Avenida 51, the more thematic murals are as follows: *Los Isleños*, (residents of the delta); *La Construcción*, the building of urban Argentina; *Campesinos* (peasants); *Las Canteras*, (stone quarries); *Pescadores del Mar*, (maritime fishermen); *Industria Pesada* (heavy industry); *Pescadores del Río* (river fishermen); *Homenaje al don Atahualpa Yupanqui*, an homage to the late folksinger; *Homenaje a José Hernández*, an homage to the author of the epic poem *Martín Fierro*; *La Doma*, on breaking wild horses; *Pulpería y Posta*, the rural stores and way stations; *Saladeros*, the 19th-century plants that salted beef and cattle hides; *Asado, Mate, Yerba*, the cultural bellwethers of the barbecue and the ritual herbal tea; and *Homenaje a Molina Campos*, an homage to *gauchesco* caricaturist Florencio Molina Campos.

Unfortunately, though, some of the murals are showing signs of weathering. Without remedial attention, they will soon deteriorate.

Pasaje Dardo Rocha (1887), home to several museums and other cultural institutions. Two blocks farther on, the **Rectorado de la Universidad Nacional** (1905), on Avenida 7 between Calle 47 and 48, now houses university offices. About three blocks east of the plaza, topped by a view tower, the **Palacio Campodónico** (1892) fills a small triangular lot bounded by Diagonal 70, Calle 5, and Calle 56. Expropriated by the provincial government in 1976, it's now a cultural center with rotating exhibitions.

Several blocks northeast, facing Plaza Rivadavia, the **Casa Curutchet** (Calle 53 No. 320, tel. 0221/482-2631, www.capba.com.ar, open 10 A.M.–2:30 P.M. weekdays only, US$1.70) was designed by the famed Swiss architect Le Corbusier as a private residence and office for Dr. Pedro Curutchet. One of only two Le Corbusier works in the western hemisphere (the other is Harvard University's Carpenter Center for the Visual Arts), the Casa Curutchet was built in 1948.

Across Avenida 1, the 60-hectare **Paseo del Bosque** is a forested park that contains recreational and educational facilities, including the **Anfiteatro Martín Fierro,** an outdoor theater; the exceptional natural sciences museum, **Museo de La Plata;** the **Observatorio Astronómico** (Astronomical Observatory); the **Jardín de la Paz** (Peace Garden), with small pavilions for each country with diplomatic representation in Argentina; and the **Jardín Zoológico** (Zoo).

WAYNE BERNHARDSON

Completion of La Plata's Catedral de la Inmaculada Concepción took more than a century after the planting of its foundation stone in 1889.

Catedral de la Inmaculada Concepción de la Plata

Construction of La Plata's cathedral is a story in itself, even by the standards of Argentine public-works projects. Begun in 1885, it did not open officially until 1932, and its three crowning towers went unfinished until 1999. So long, in fact, did the project take that the building underwent its first restoration (1997) even before its completion!

Overlooking Plaza Moreno, its **Museo de la Catedral** (Calle 14 between 51 and 53, open 8 A.M.–noon and 2–7 P.M. daily) offers special exhibitions on such subjects as colonial religious art. A recently opened elevator goes to *miradores* (overlooks) at the 42-meter and 63-meter levels, from 9 A.M.–7:30 P.M. daily; for more info, contact the Fundación Catedral (tel. 0221/427-3504).

Jardín Zoológico

At the west end of the Paseo del Bosque, La Plata's 14-hectare, Victorian-style zoo billets more than 180 native and exotic species, including giraffes, elephants, lions, monkeys, and rhinoceri. Admission to the Jardín Zoológico (Paseo del Bosque s/n, tel. 0221/427-3925) costs US$.70 pp; children under 12 get in free. Hours are 9 A.M.–7 P.M. daily, but the gates close to incoming visitors at 6:15 P.M.

Museo de La Plata

Patagonian explorer Francisco Pascasio Moreno donated his personal collections of anthropological, archaeological, and paleontological artifacts to Argentina's premier natural history museum, which opened in 1888 under his own lifetime directorship. Today, more than 400,000 visitors per annum view at least some of the 2.5 million items in its 21 exhibition halls, which also deal with botany, geology, zoology, and other fields.

The four-story building is a monument to its era, its exterior a hybrid of Greek regional styles with indigenous American—Aztec and Incaic—flourishes. Home to the Universidad Nacional de La Plata's natural sciences department, its interior also contains classrooms, libraries, offices, workshops, and storage space. The museum's public displays, though, have still not evolved far beyond taxonomy and its founder's 19th-century Darwinism.

The Museo de La Plata (Paseo del Bosque 1900, tel. 0221/425-7744, www.fcnym.unlp.edu.ar/museo) is open 10 A.M.–6 P.M. daily except for Mondays and New Year's Day, May Day, and Christmas Day; when other holidays fall on Monday, it is open. Admission costs US$1 pp for those over 12 years of age; there are guided tours at 2 and 4 P.M. weekdays except Monday, and hourly on weekends from 10:30 A.M.–4:30 P.M.

Museo y Archivo Dardo Rocha

Benoit also designed the residence of La Plata's founder (1838–1921), whose varied career included stints as a journalist, soldier, diplomat, provincial legislator, national

Excursions from Buenos Aires

Excursions from Buenos Aires

Now a cultural center, La Plata's Pasaje Dardo Rocha began its life as a train station.

© WAYNE BERNHARDSON

senator, and provincial governor. The museum, though, focuses on Rocha's personal effects, including furniture, art works, clothing, housewares, documents, and photographs, to the virtual exclusion of his role in the controversial shift of the provincial capital from Buenos Aires.

The Museo y Archivo Dardo Rocha (Calle 50 No. 933, tel. 0221/427-5591, open 9 A.M.– 6 P.M. weekdays, 10 A.M.–1 P.M. and 3–6 P.M. weekends) is more an homage than an analytical or interpretive institution.

Observatorio Astronómico de La Plata

Part of the Universidad Nacional de La Plata, the local observatory has both modern telescopes and historical instruments from the 19th century. Guided tours take place every Friday at 8:30 P.M. in March, 7 and 8 P.M. April–September, 7:30 P.M. in October and November, and 8:30 P.M. October–December.

The Observatorio Astronómico de La Plata (Paseo del Bosque s/n, tel. 0221/423-6953, www.fcaglp.unlp.edu.ar, US$1 pp) requires reservations for guided tours.

Pasaje Dardo Rocha

Formerly the Estación 19 de Noviembre, La Plata's first major railroad station, the French classic–style Pasaje Dardo Rocha has undergone an adaptive reuse that has turned it into a major cultural center with several museums, plus cinemas, auditoriums, conference rooms, cafés, and other features. The municipal tourist office is also here.

Opened in 1999, the **Museo de Arte Contemporáneo Latinoamericano** (Calle 50 between Calles 6 and 7, tel. 0221/427-1843, www.macla. laplata.gov.ar, open 10 A.M.–8 P.M. Tues.–Fri., 2–10 P.M. weekends) features works by modern Latin American artists. There are guided tours at 9 A.M. and 2 P.M. weekdays only.

The **Museo Municipal de Arte** (tel. 0221/ 427-1198, open 10 A.M.–7 P.M. weekdays except Mon., and 4–9 P.M. weekends) is a painting and sculpture museum focusing primarily on local artists. Dedicated exclusively to photography, the **Museo y Galería Fotográfica** (MUGAFO) keeps the same hours.

Teatro Argentino

Finally rebuilt after its destruction by fire in

1977, the hideous **Teatro Argentino** reopened in October 2000 with a presentation of *Tosca*. With all the elegance of a multistory parking lot, this 60,000-square-meter concrete structure looks like the product of the military dictatorship that approved it—a fortified bunker that (had it been complete) might have bought the general and admirals a little more time in power after their 1982 Falklands debacle.

Still, the new Teatro Argentino looks and sounds better within than without and remains one of the country's major performing-arts venues, with its own orchestra, chorus, ballet, and children's chorus. Its principal theater is the Sala Alberto Ginastera, seating more than 2,000 spectators; smaller halls seat 300–700. Past performers include Arthur Rubenstein, Ana Pavlova, Andrés Segovia, and Richard Strauss.

The Teatro Argentino (Avenida 51 between Calle 9 and Calle 10, tel. 221/429-1700, tarelacionespublicas@ed.gba.gov.ar) offers guided tours at 10:30 A.M. and 2 P.M. daily except Monday, by reservation only. These cost US$1 pp except for bilingual English-Spanish tours, which cost US$1.50 pp. There are discounts for seniors and students.

ARTS AND ENTERTAINMENT

For event tickets, try **Ticketek** (Calle 48 No. 700, corner of Calle 9, tel. 021/447-7200, www.ticketek.com.ar).

Cinema

La Plata has three downtown movie theaters: the six-screen **Cine Ocho** (Calle 8 No. 981, between Avenidas 51 and 53, tel. 0221/482-5554); the four-screen **Cine San Martín** (Calle 7 No. 923, between Avenidas 50 and 51, tel. 0221/483-9947); and the three-screen **Cinema City** (Calle 50 No. 723, between 9 and 10, tel. 0221/4223-5456). All share a common website (www.cinemalaplata.com).

Performing Arts

La Plata is a major theater and live-music center, whose major venue is the **Centro de las Artes Teatro Argentino** (Avenida 51 between

Calle 9 and Calle 10, tel. 0800/666-5151 toll-free). Its box office (tel. 0221/429-1733) is open 10 A.M.–8 P.M. daily except Monday. The Teatro Argentino provides free transportation from Buenos Aires for ticket holders.

Another major performing-arts locale is the **Teatro Coliseo Podestá** (Calle 10, between Calle 46 and Calle 47, tel. 0221/424-8457). More intimate productions take place at spots like the **Teatro La Lechuza** (Calle 58 No. 757, tel. 0221/424-6350).

RESTAURANTS

For breakfast, coffee, or pastries, the best option is the tobacco-free **Confitería París** (Avenida 7 and Calle 49, tel. 0221/482-8840).

The **Colegio de Escribanos** (Avenida 13, between Calles 47 and 48) is a lunchtime favorite for lawyers and judges from the nearby Tribunales. Plaza Paso's **El Quijote** (Avenida 13 and Avenida 44, tel. 0221/483-3653) specializes in seafood.

La Trattoría (Calle 47 and Diagonal 74, tel. 0221/422-6135) is a casual Italian restaurant with sidewalk seating, while **Abruzzese** (Calle 42 No. 457, tel. 0221/421-9869) is more formal. Open for dinner only, **Gaucho Italiano** (Calle 50 No. 724, between 9 and 10, tel. 0221/483-2817) serves 50 varieties of pizzas, *tablas* of meats and cheeses, and pastas with a hybrid pampas touch. There's a tobacco-free area, but the background music is a dreadful and inappropriate techno.

The line between places to eat and places to drink is not always obvious in La Plata. The best blend of the two is the classic **Cervecería El Modelo** (Calle 5 and Calle 54, tel. 0221/421-1321), which prepares terrific sandwiches, plus draft beer and hard cider with free unshelled and unsalted peanuts. There's a fairly large tobacco-free area, and sidewalk seating in fine weather.

Another option is the **Wilkenny Irish Pub & Restaurant** (Calle 50 No. 797, tel. 0221/483-1772, www.wilkenny.com.ar), a legitimately Irish-style pub in the heart of La Plata. The food includes pub grub like lamb stew (though the bulk of the menu is

Argentine and there are even a couple Chinese dishes), plus Irish beers (Guinness, Harp, and Kilkenny) on tap by the pint and half-pint. Lunch or dinner entrées cost around US$3–5; there's a larger selection of bottle brews, plus Irish and specialty coffees.

For ice cream, try **La Sorbetière** (Calle 47 and Calle 10).

ACCOMMODATIONS

Frayed but friendly, no-frills **Hotel Saint James** (Avenida 60 No. 377, tel. 221/421-8089, www.hotelsj.com.ar, US$9/13 s/d) is the best choice for the truly budget-conscious, but it's often full. Rates include breakfast, private bath, and telephone.

On a quiet block near the Paseo del Bosque, **Hotel Roga** (Calle 54 No. 334, tel. 0221/421-9553, www.hotelroga.com.ar, US$14/19 s/d) is modern, friendly, and comfortable; rates include private bath, breakfast, and parking. There's a 5 percent surcharge for credit-card payments.

Near the train station, **Hotel Cristal** (Avenida 1 No. 620, tel. 0221/424-5640, www.hotelcristallp.com.ar, US$16/22 s/d) is a decent choice.

Rates at centrally located, 70-room **Hotel La Plata** (Avenida 51 No. 783, tel./fax 0221/422-9090, www.weblaplatahotel.com.ar, US$18/24 s/d) include breakfast *and* dinner, a phenomenal value for what is a very good hotel with a/c, cable TV, and similar conveniences.

At the intersection of Avenidas 13 and 44, **Hotel del Rey** (Plaza Paso 180, tel. 0221/427-0177, www.hoteldelrey.com.ar, US$19/24 s/d–US$40 d) is a 10-story tower with 40 well-kept midsize rooms and suites with all the modern conveniences. The higher rates correspond to suites.

The utilitarian exterior at **Hotel San Marco** (Calle 54 No. 523, tel. 0221/422-7202, www.sanmarcohotel.com.ar, US$23/28 s/d) disguises what is also a pretty good hotel.

The star of La Plata's accommodations scene, though, is the restored **Hotel Benevento** (Calle 2 No. 645, at the corner of Diagonal 80, tel. 0221/423-7721, www.hotelbenevento.com.ar, US$22 s–US$26/30 s/d). In a century-old building that once housed the provincial labor ministry, its rooms have high ceilings, traditional balconies, and modernized baths (showers only). It's worth mentioning that the singles are truly small (though still comfortable).

Now part of the Howard Johnson chain, the

REPÚBLICA DE LOS NIÑOS

Conceived by Evita Perón, executed by 1,600 laborers under Perón provincial governor Domingo Mercante, and officially opened by Juan Perón himself, the children's amusement park of República de los Niños was once a 53-hectare golf course built for the English meat packer Swift.

In the northern La Plata suburb of Manuel Gonnet, República de los Niños displays a melange of architectural miniatures from around the world, ranging from the medieval Europe of Grimm's fairy tales to Islamic mosques and the Taj Mahal. According to some accounts, it inspired Walt Disney to create Disneyland and Walt Disney World, but the Argentine park did not open until 1951—a decade after Disney visited the country.

In the context of mid-century Peronism, what with its origins as an expropriated foreign property and a destination for working-class children, República de los Niños sent a political message that may not be obvious to non-Argentines. It also includes replicas of the Argentine presidential palace, legislature, and courts—with the obvious implication that its youthful public could aspire to office (and apparently to graft—there's also a jail).

Admission to República de los Niños (Camino General Belgrano and 501, Manuel Gonnet, tel. 0221/484-1409, www.republica.laplata.gov.ar, open 10 A.M.–10 P.M. daily except Mon.) costs US$.70 except for children under age seven; a miniature steam train makes the rounds of the park. Parking costs US$1.

From Avenida 7 in downtown La Plata, bus Nos. 518 and 273 go to República de los Niños, but not all No. 273s go all the way.

four-star, 110-room high-rise **Hotel Corregidor** (Calle 6 No. 1026, tel. 0221/425-6800, www.hojoar.com, US$37 s or d) is a good upscale value, though the Benevento has more style.

INFORMATION

In the Pasaje Dardo Rocha, the improved **Información Turística La Plata** (Calles 6 and 50, tel. 0221/427-1535, www.laplata.gov.ar, open 9 A.M.– 6 P.M. daily) is the municipal tourist office. It distributes far-better city maps, informational brochures, and bus schedules than in the recent past, and the staff is more accommodating. It works under the **Dirección de Turismo** (Diagonal 79 at Calle 8, tel. 0221/422-9764), open 9 A.M.–6 P.M. weekdays in the historic Palacio Campodónico.

In the high-rise Torre Municipal, the **Dirección Provincial de Turismo** (Calle 12 and Avenida 53, 13th fl., tel. 0221/429-5553, www.vivalaspampas.com.ar, open 9 A.M.–3 P.M. weekdays only), though sometimes bureaucratic, can be surprisingly helpful for out-of-town sights.

SERVICES

As a provincial capital, La Plata has a full complement of services.

Banco de la Provincia has an ATM on Avenida 7 between Calle 46 and Calle 47, while **Banco Nación** has one at the corner of Avenida 7 and Calle 49. There are many others, however.

For postal services, **Correo Argentino** is at the corner of Avenida 51 and Calle 4.

Locutorio Minimercado (Avenida 51 and Calle 5) provides long-distance phone and Intenet services. Near Plaza Italia, **Cybersonic** (Diagonal 74 and Calle 6, tel. 0221/489-5511) is open 24 hours for Internet access.

Asatej (Avenida 5 No. 990, at the corner of Avenida 53, tel. 0221/483-8673, laplata@asatej.com.ar) is a branch of Argentina's student- and youth-oriented travel agency.

TRANSPORTATION

Air

La Plata has no airport, but Manuel Tienda León (tel. 0221/425-1140) provides door-to-door transportation to Buenos Aires's Ezeiza and Aeroparque.

Bus

La Plata's **Terminal de Omnibus** is at Calle 42 and Calle 4, tel. 0221/421-2182; **Costera Metropolitana** (tel. 0800/222-6798) has frequent buses to and from Retiro (US$1.50, one hour), but also picks up and drops off passengers along the capital's Avenida 9 de Julio.

Train

The century-old **Estación Ferrocarril General Roca** is at Avenida 1 and Avenida 44, tel. 0221/423-2575. **Transportes Metropolitana SA General Roca** (TMR, tel. 011/4304-0021) operates around 50 weekday trains from Constitución (Buenos Aires) to La Plata (1.5 hours, US$.50); the number drops to around 35 or 40 trains on weekends and holidays. The last train returns to Constitución around 10:30 P.M., but they start up again around 3 A.M.

Excursions from Buenos Aires

Montevideo, Uruguay

Montevideo is a metropolis of 1.6 million people—almost half the country's inhabitants—but Uruguay's capital has somehow managed to maintain a small-town feel. Its revived colonial quarter, the Ciudad Vieja, is a pedestrian-friendly grid of narrow streets with distinctive plazas, dotted with restaurants, bars, antique shops, cultural centers, and galleries—though there are still *conventillos,* one-time mansions taken over by squatters.

Montevideo's port, superior to Buenos Aires in every aspect except access to the pampas, has given it an international flavor. Having begun to appreciate the Ciudad Vieja's potential, authorities plan to link the nightlife and restaurant zones along the streets of Bartolomé Mitre and Sarandí with the similarly picturesque port zone.

East of the Ciudad Vieja, dense sycamores line most streets on either side of Avenida 18 de Julio, and the avenue itself is home to a smattering of classical mansions and early-20th-century Deco-style buildings. The southeastern suburban barrios toward Palermo and Pocitos enjoy access to sandy riverside beaches—something Buenos Aires's muddy shoreline cannot match.

Montevideo is also a bureaucratic city, home to Uruguay's major political institutions and the administrative headquarters for Mercosur, the shaky common market in which Argentina, Brazil, and Paraguay also participate. In between the two South American giants, Uruguay still plays the role of political buffer.

HISTORY

The determined resistance of Uruguay's aboriginal Charrúa peoples discouraged permanent European settlement until the early 18th century; since then, the country's history has been that of a buffer—first between colonial Spain and Portugal, and then between republican Argentina and Brazil. Bruno Mauricio de Zabala's 1726 founding of fortified Montevideo was a direct response to Portuguese activity along the river, but also to Northern European smugglers and privateers. The first settlers arrived from Buenos Aires and the Canary Islands (rural Uruguayans are still known as *Canarios*).

At that time, though, it was a pretty primitive place. On the initial houses, according to one historian, "Leather made the protective roofs.... Nails being scarce, wire unheard of, rope and cord undreamed of. . . leather was used as cables, as chisels, in all manner of joining and riveting." By the late 18th century, though, Montevideo had acquired an air of permanence.

After several years under Brazilian rule in the 1820s, Montevideo spent most of the 1840s under siege from Buenos Aires strongman Juan Manuel de Rosas before finally achieving political and economic stability in the 1850s. Most surviving colonial buildings date from the early 19th century, after which today's Centro, east of the entrance to the Ciudadela (walled city)

Montevideo's Banco de la República reflects an epic view of Uruguay's history.

TRAVEL IN URUGUAY

Because so many travelers to the Argentine capital cross the Río de la Plata to Uruguay, Montevideo, Colonia, Carmelo, Punta del Este, and some other destinations are covered in this handbook. For the most part, conditions are similar to those in Argentina.

Visas and Officialdom

Very few nationalities need advance visas for Uruguay, but requirements can change—if in doubt, contact Uruguay's Buenos Aires consulate. Ordinarily, border officials give foreign tourists an automatic 90-day entry permit.

Health

Uruguay requires no vaccinations for visitors entering from any country, and public health standards are among the continent's highest.

Money and Prices

The Argentine political and economic meltdown of 2001–2002 had severe repercussions on the Uruguayan economy. With Argentines unable to travel because of their own weak peso, Uruguayan hotel occupancy fell, but the Uruguayan peso slipped more slowly than the Argentine peso; because of the weak dollar, Uruguayan price levels have remained somewhat higher than in Argentina.

Traditionally, Uruguay has the continent's most liberal banking laws; exchange houses are numerous, and bureaucracy is minimal for U.S. cash and travelers' checks. The U.S. dollar operates as a parallel currency, at least in the tourist sector, where hotel and restaurant prices are often quoted in both; Argentine currency may be accepted, but often at a poor rate. In areas away from the heavily touristed coast, acceptance of foreign currency is less common.

Banks keep limited hours—normally 1–5 P.M. weekdays only. ATMs are common in Montevideo, Colonia, and Punta del Este, but in smaller towns they may not work with foreign plastic. Keep a close eye on exchange rates, and avoid buying too many pesos if the rate is unstable.

Interestingly, Uruguay has phased the faces of generals and politicians out of its banknotes, which now feature artists and writers like Joaquín Torres García (Ur$5), Eduardo Acevedo Vásquez (Ur$10), Juan Zorrilla de San Martín (Ur$20), José Pedro Varela (Ur$50), Eduardo Fabini (Ur$100), Pedro Figari (Ur$200), Alfredo Vásquez Acevedo (Ur$500), Juana de Ibarbourou (Ur$1,000), and Dámaso Antonio Larrañaga (Ur$2,000). The one-peso coin, though, remains the stronghold of independence hero General José Gervasio Artigas.

Communications

Despite privatization pressures, Uruguayan communications remain under the state monopoly Antel. Long-distance phone and Internet offices are fewer than in Argentina, but still numerous enough. Uruguay's country code is 598; each city or town has a separate area code, ranging from one to three or even four digits. Note that while most Montevideo telephone numbers have seven digits, a handful of informational and public-service numbers have only four digits, and a very few have eight. Rural and suburban numbers can have between four and six digits.

Getting Around

Distances in Uruguay are short and roads are good. Rental cars are readily available, but the cost of gasoline is high—in excess of US$1 per liter.

Uruguayan buses resemble Argentine ones—modern, spacious, and fast—and service is frequent on most routes. Most, though not all, towns have a main bus terminal, usually on the outskirts of town; some bus lines have separate ticket offices in more central locations.

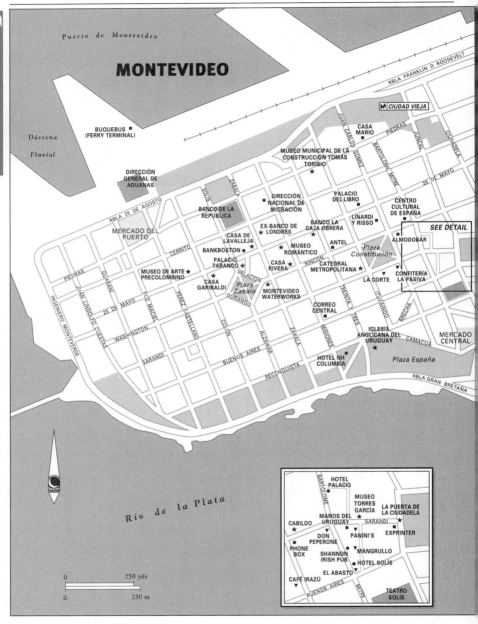

Puerto de Montevideo

MONTEVIDEO

Dársena
Fluvial

RBLA FRANKLIN D ROOSEVELT

CIUDAD VIEJA

BUQUEBUS
(FERRY TERMINAL)

CASA
MARIO

PIEDRAS

JUNCAL

CIUDADELA

JUAN CARLOS GOMEZ

BARTOLOME MITRE

MUSEO MUNICIPAL DE LA
CONSTRUCCIÓN TOMÁS
TORIBIO

DIRECCIÓN
GENERAL DE
ADUANAS

25 DE MAYO

RBLA 25 DE AGOSTO

ZABALA

SOLIS

DIRECCIÓN
NACIONAL DE
MIGRACIÓN

PALACIO
DEL LIBRO

CENTRO
CULTURAL
DE ESPAÑA

BANCO DE LA
REPÚBLICA

LINARDI
Y RISSO

MERCADO DEL
PUERTO

CERRITO

EX-BANCO DE
LONDRES

BANCO LA
CAJA OBRERA

SEE DETAIL

CASA DE
LAVALLEJA

ALMODOBAR

PIEDRAS

GUARANI

JUAN LINDOLFO CUESTAS

INGENIERO MONTEVERDE

BANKBOSTON

MUSEO
ROMÁNTICO

ANTEL

Plaza
Constitución

MUSEO DE ARTE
PRECOLOMBINO

PALACIO
TARANCO

CASA
RIVERA

RINCON

CATEDRAL
METROPOLITANA

CONFITERÍA
LA PASIVA

CASA
GARIBALDI

VALACION

Plaza
Zabala

MONTEVIDEO
WATERWORKS

LA CORTE

25 DE MAYO

ECU MACIEL

PEREZ CASTELLANO

DURANGO

COLON

ALZAIBAR

TREINTA Y
TRES

ITUZANGO

BRECHA

WASHINGTON

CORREO
CENTRAL

MISIONES

ZABALA

BUENOS AIRES

IGLESIA
ANGLICANA DEL
URUGUAY

CAMACUA

MERCADO
CENTRAL

SARANDI

RECONQUISTA

HOTEL NH
COLUMBIA

Plaza España

RBLA GRAN BRETAÑA

Río de la Plata

HOTEL
PALACIO

BARTOLOME

MUSEO
TORRES
GARCÍA

LA PUERTA DE
LA CIUDADELA

MANOS DEL
URUGUAY

SARANDI

CABILDO

EXPRINTER

PANINI'S

DON
PEPERONE

PHONE
BOX

MANGRULLO

SHANNON
IRISH PUB

HOTEL SOLIS

EL ABASTO

MITRE

CAFÉ IRAZÚ

BUENOS AIRES

TEATRO
SOLIS

0   250 yds

0   250 m

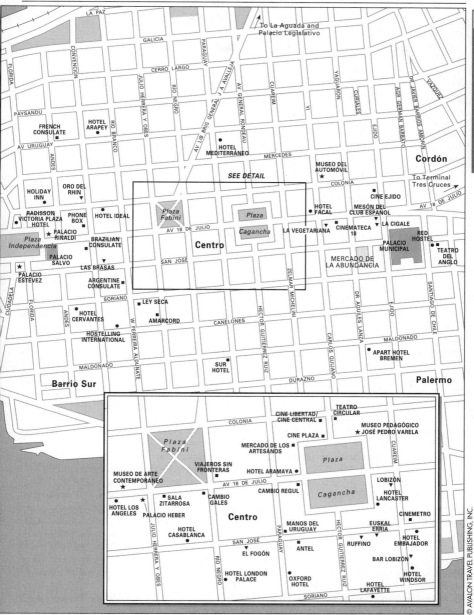

gradually superseded the Ciudad Vieja.

From the 1850s, Montevideo followed Buenos Aires's economic example, as British investment, particularly in the railroads, fostered European immigration and the export of produce from countryside to capital and then overseas. For a time, this made Uruguay one of South America's most prosperous countries, with generous social welfare policies, but the economically active sector of the population was eventually unable to support a large pensioner class. Beginning in the 1960s, economic stagnation led to revolutionary political upheaval and, in reaction, a military dictatorship (1973–1985) from which the country and the capital slowly but steadily recovered until recent economic setbacks.

For all this, Montevideo continues to dominate the countryside politically, economically, and culturally, even more than Buenos Aires does Argentina. Still, there has been a political tension between the countryside and the city, which has consistently voted the left-of-center Frente Amplio (Broad Front) into municipal power, but was unable to elect its candidates nationwide until former city mayor Tabaré Vásquez won the presidency in 2004.

ORIENTATION

East of Buenos Aires, Montevideo occupies a hilly site on the left bank of the Río de la Plata. Passengers from Buenos Aires normally arrive at the Buquebus hydrofoil port on the Rambla 25 de Agosto, on the north side of the Ciudad Vieja, a gentrifying colonial grid of narrow streets west of Plaza Independencia. East of Plaza Independencia lies the commercial Centro, split in half by the east-west thoroughfare Avenida 18 de Julio; businesses cluster around Plaza del Entrevero and Plaza Cagancha. South of the Centro, Barrio Sur is home to much of Montevideo's Afro-Uruguayan community; to the north, La Aguada is an improving area that's home to the national legislature and a new suburban train station. The riverside *rambla* (street or boulevard) leads southeast to suburban barrios with large wooded parks and sandy beaches.

SIGHTS

Most of Montevideo's sights are concentrated in the compact Ciudad Vieja, but quite a few are also scattered around the Centro and neighboring barrios. The Ciudad Vieja's more northwesterly parts, around the port, have a history of petty crime problems after dark, but Montevideo's increased popularity with South Atlantic cruise ships has spurred municipal authorities to improve security here.

Municipal authorities have also produced an informative walking-tour map of the city, with details on many historic structures. It's widely available at tourist offices and hotels throughout the city.

The Centro and Vicinity

About three blocks east of Plaza Independencia, construction of **Plaza Fabini** (1964), also known as **Plaza del Entrevero** for the monument by sculptor José Belloni, opened a view down the diagonal Avenida Libertador General Lavalleja toward the barrio of La Aguada, site of the Uruguayan congress. At the southeast corner of the plaza, dating from 1894, the ornate French-style **Palacio Heber** (Avenida 18 de Julio 998) was built as a private residence but now holds the **Museo de la Moneda y del Gaucho,** on Uruguay's financial and rural history. The **Museo de Arte Contemporáneo** (Avenida 18 de Julio 965, 2nd fl., tel. 02/900-6662, open 2–8 P.M. daily) is across the street.

Two blocks farther east, Avenida 18 de Julio splits **Plaza Cagancha** (dating from 1836, but handsomely remodeled in 1995) in two. At its northeast corner, the **Museo Pedagógico José Pedro Varela** (Plaza Cagancha 1175, tel. 02/902-0915, www.crnti.edu.uy/museo) deals with the evolution of Uruguayan public education. Hours are 9 A.M.–7 P.M. weekdays only from mid-March to mid-December; the rest of the year, hours are 8 A.M.–noon weekdays. Admission is free.

A short distance northeast, the Automóvil Club del Uruguay's **Museo del Automóvil** (Colonia 1251, 6th fl., 2–7 P.M. daily except

SOUTH AMERICA'S SWITZERLAND

Uruguay shares many features with its larger neighbor, so much so that even some Uruguayans will reluctantly suggest that the country might as well be an Argentine province—and when Argentines pack the beaches of Punta del Este in summer, it often seems like one. Uruguayans themselves, while their appearance and accent differ little from that of their neighbors, do not have the reputation for arrogance that other Latin Americans often attribute to Argentines.

Nor do they bear the stigma of corruption—Uruguay ranks in the top 25 of Transparency International's clean government rankings according to perceived corruption levels. For that reason, and its traditional social welfare policies, Uruguay long held a reputation as the "Switzerland of South America," though its own 1971–1984 dictatorship subverted that assessment.

Uruguay has many attractions not easily found in the immediate vicinity of Buenos Aires—long, sandy beaches beneath rising headlands, extensive oceanside dunes, and verdant rolling hill country. It also has a lively capital city in Montevideo, one of the Southern Cone's cultural treasures in the UNESCO World Heritage Site town of Colonia, and the high-powered summer resort of Punta del Este.

Still, when Argentina sneezes, Uruguay catches cold, and the Argentine political and economic collapse of 2001–2002 hit the country hard. With their currency devalued and bank accounts frozen, Argentines could not even afford to travel across the river—except to fetch money from their Uruguayan accounts, which were also briefly frozen despite Uruguay's tradition of free-market banking. The Uruguayan peso also fell, though not so far as the Argentine currency, giving the Uruguayan tourist industry some breathing room by making it more competitive and attractive to Brazilians.

With an improving economy, some Argentines have begun to return to Uruguay for their summer holidays, though they're spending less freely than they once did. Prices are, in general, about 15–20 percent higher than in Argentina, though much depends on individual indulgences and tastes.

Montevideo and Colonia are both easily accessible by ferry and catamaran from downtown Buenos Aires. Montevideo is the country's transport hub, with bus services west toward Colonia and east toward Punta del Este. There are also catamarans from the Argentine river port of Tigre through the Paraná delta to the Uruguayan riverside town of Carmelo.

Mon., free) sports a collection of classic cars seen less frequently on Uruguay's streets and highways than they once were.

To the southeast, dating from 1904–1909, the art nouveau **Mercado de la Abundancia** (San José 1312) is a national historical monument that's been recycled as a crafts outlet and cultural center. Immediately east, but fronting on Avenida 18 de Julio, the ponderous **Palacio Municipal** (1929–1930) sits atop the site of the former British cemetery—appropriately enough for a monument to bureaucracy.

From Plaza Fabini, Avenida Libertador provides an unobstructed northeast view toward the neoclassical **Palacio Legislativo** (1908), the home of Uruguay's legislature and the work of Vittorio Meano. Meano, who also contrib-

uted to Buenos Aires's Teatro Colón and the Argentine Congreso Nacional, died in a mysterious gunshot incident before the Montevideo building's completion. Brightly illuminated after dark, at the north end of Avenida Libertador, the **Palacio Legislativo** (tel. 02/200-1334) offers weekday guided tours in both Spanish and English, hourly from 8:30 A.M.–6:30 P.M.

Ⓜ Ciudad Vieja

Plaza Independencia, dating from 1836 but remodeled completely in 1936, is a civic center marking the boundary between the colonial Ciudad Vieja to the west and the republican Centro to the east. The best starting point for an introduction to downtown Montevideo, its

© WAYNE BERNHARDSON

entrance to the Mercado del Puerto, Ciudad Vieja, Montevideo

literal centerpiece is the massive equestrian statue atop the **Mausoleo de Artigas,** the subterranean crypt of independence hero José Gervasio Artigas. On the south side of the Plaza, the **Palacio Estévez** (1873) served as the presidential palace for a century-plus; it is still home to the **Museo de la Casa de Gobierno** (Plaza Independencia 776, tel. 02/1515, ext. 902, open 10 A.M.–5 P.M. weekdays), with guided tours available.

From the plaza, the late-afternoon sun illuminates architect Mario Palanti's photogenic **Palacio Salvo** (1922), a 26-story baroque hotel since converted into apartments, at the foot of Avenida 18 de Julio. Palanti designed the building to be visible from its Buenos Aires doppelganger Pasaje Barolo, which he also built. From the Salvo's upper floors, in December 1939, British spies observed the German battleship *Graf Spee* taking refuge in neutral Uruguay for a few days as permitted by international law, before its captain scuttled it in the river.

Montevideo has perhaps the finest assemblage of Art Deco architecture in the Southern Cone countries. Immediately across the avenue from the Palacio Salvo, dating from

1929, the apartment building **Palacio Rinaldi** (Plaza Independencia 1356) is one of the best specimens; note the decorative relief panels on the facade.

Upon its creation in 1836, Plaza Independencia symbolized a break with the colonial past; at its west end, the **La Puerta de la Ciudadela** (1746) is one of the last remaining fragments of the fortifications that surrounded what is now the Ciudad Vieja. Passing through the gate, the pedestrian mall Sarandí is a portion of the partly rejuvenated colonial quarter; the first major point of interest is the **Museo Torres García,** dedicated to one of Uruguay's most notable 20th-century artists.

Opposite the museum, wall-to-wall with restaurants and bars, the narrow pedestrian mall Bacacay branches south to the 1837 **Teatro Solís,** a historic performing-arts venue.

Sarandí continues to **Plaza Constitución,** the colonial *plaza mayor* (1726) and predecessor to Plaza Independencia. Surrounded by colonial buildings, including the landmark **Catedral Metropolitana** (1790) and the neoclassical **Cabildo** (colonial council, 1804), the sycamore-shaded plaza also features

Juan Ferrari's post-colonial central fountain. The **Cabildo** contains the **Museo y Archivo Histórico Municipal** (Juan Carlos Gómez 1362, tel. 02/915-9685, open 2:30–7 P.M. weekdays except Mon.), the municipal historical museum.

Two blocks south of Plaza Constitución, Montevideo merchant Samuel Fischer Lafone (founder of the Falkland Islands Company) commissioned the 1845 **Iglesia Anglicana del Uruguay** (Anglican Church of Uruguay), which was dismantled in the 1930s to allow construction of the Rambla Francia and then rebuilt. Four blocks north of the church, dating from 1941, the facade of the **Banco La Caja Obrera** (25 de Mayo 500) displays extraordinary bas-reliefs by Edmundo Prati.

Recently rehabbed, the architectural **Museo Municipal de la Construcción Tomás Toribio** (Piedras 528, open 2–6 P.M. weekdays except Mon.) is located two blocks farther north. Three blocks west, dating from 1926–1938, the monumental **Banco de la República** (Cerrito 351) fills an entire block bounded by Piedras, Solís, Zabala, and Cerrito.

Four blocks west of Plaza Constitución, French landscape architect Edouard André created **Plaza Zabala** (1880), named for the city's founder, on the site of the former Casa de Gobierno and an even earlier fortress. Occupying an irregular lot immediately to the north, the **Palacio Taranco** (25 de Mayo 376) houses the **Museo de Arte Decorativo.**

In the immediate vicinity of Plaza Zabala, several historic buildings are units of the **Museo Histórico Nacional** (National History Museum): the **Casa Rivera** (Rincón 437); the 1831 **Museo Romántico** (25 de Mayo 428); the **Casa de Lavalleja** (Zabala 1469); and the 1830 **Casa Garibaldi** (25 de Mayo 314).

The museums are not the only points of interest. At Rincón and Zabala, the former **Montevideo Waterworks** dates from the late 19th century. A little more than a block to the north, the neoclassical 1890 **Banco de Londres** (Zabala 1480) is slowly undergoing rehab as the **Biblioteca Americanista** (Americanist Library).

Northwest of Plaza Zabala, the **Mercado del Puerto** (1868), on the Pérez Castellano pedestrian mall, is one of the capital's top tourist destinations for its seafood restaurants and casual atmosphere. The imposing building to its north, across the Rambla 25 de Agosto, is the Deco-style **Dirección General de Aduanas** (1923), the customs headquarters.

Museo Torres García

Pictured on Uruguay's five-peso banknote, Joaquín Torres García (1874–1949) was a Picasso contemporary who became widely known for both abstract and figurative work. Spending much of his career in Barcelona, Paris, and New York, he also produced historical portraits of *Hombres Célebres (Famous Men)*, which in one instance he retitled *Hombres, Héroes y Monstruos (Men, Heroes and Monsters)*, according to his interpretation of individuals such as Bach, Beethoven, Columbus, and Rabelais. The museum includes samples of the Torres García's legacy, but also works by contemporary artists.

The Museo Torres García (Sarandí 683, tel. 02/916-2663, www.torresgarcia.org.uy) is open 9 A.M.–6 P.M. daily except for January 1, May 1, July 18, and December 25. Admission costs US$4 pp for foreigners; guided visits in Spanish and English are available. There is a museum bookshop and gift shop.

Teatro Solís

Montevideo's performing-arts counterpart to Buenos Aires's Teatro Colón, the neoclassical Teatro Solís (1856) has showcased performers of the caliber of Enrico Caruso, Arturo Toscanini, Vaslav Nijinsky, and Mstislav Rostropovich. Half a century older than the Colón—though Rosas's blockade delayed its completion—its facade features eight Ionic columns; the symmetrical lateral wings were a later addition. The horseshoe-shaped auditorium seats 1,600 spectators, considerably fewer than the Colón, but with outstanding acoustics.

Having completed a major renovation, the Teatro Solís (Buenos Aires 678, tel. 02/1950-3323 or 02/1950-3324, www.teatrosolis.org.uy)

presents a full schedule of classical music, ballet, opera, and drama.

Palacio Taranco

Occupying an irregular lot opposite Plaza Zabala, the opulent Palacio Taranco (1907–1908) is the equal of Buenos Aires's French Renaissance palaces, with antique furniture, sparkling parquet floors, and marble fireplaces in almost every room. In 1979, it saw the signing of a papal mediation that avoided war between Argentina and Chile over a territorial dispute in the southern Beagle Channel.

The Palacio Taranco is also home to the **Museo de Arte Decorativo** (25 de Mayo 376, tel. 02/915-1101, open 12:15–6 P.M. Tues.–Sat., 2–6 P.M. Sun., free) with a collection of European artwork on its upper floors and a basement gallery with brightly decorated classical Greek and Roman ceramics and bronzes, plus early Islamic ceramics from what is now Iranian territory.

Opposite Plaza Zabala, but entered around the corner, the museum occupies an irregular lot. There are guided tours at 4:30 P.M. every day the museum is open.

Museo Histórico Nacional

Montevideo's national historical museum consists of several Ciudad Vieja houses with distinct histories, contents, and perspectives. Admission to all of them is free of charge, but their hours differ.

The most broadly historical of them is the **Casa Rivera** (Rincón 437, tel. 02/915-6863, www.mec.gub.uy/museo/rivera, open 11 A.M.–5 P.M. weekdays, 11 A.M.–4 P.M. Sat.), a handsome late-colonial residence that was once the residence of General Fructuoso Rivera, the country's first president; the upper floor, with wrought-iron balconies at every window and an octagonal watchtower, are late-19th-century additions. The museum's display on pre-Hispanic Uruguay is more than just a token tribute to the country's aboriginal inhabitants (note the Charrúa sculpture by Juan Luis Blanes). It's most notable, though, for the massive canvases of Uruguayan political and military figures, and of independence-era battles.

Dating from 1782 but dramatically remodeled in the early 1830s, the **Casa Montero** houses the **Museo Romántico** (25 de Mayo 428, tel. 02/915-5361, www.mec.gub .uy/museum/romantico, open 10 A.M.–5 P.M. weekdays except Monday). Also known as the *Palacio de Mármol* (Marble Palace) for its elaborate materials, its museum traces the tastes of upper-class Montevideo inhabitants from independence to the early 20th century through their household artifacts.

Dating from 1873, the **Casa de Lavalleja** (Zabala 1469, tel. 02/915-1028, www.mec .gub.uy/museo/lavalleja, open 10 A.M.–5 P.M. weekdays only) was the residence of Juan de Lavalleja, who led the "33 Orientales" whose landing in 1825 began the liberation from Brazil. The two-story building (uncommon in colonial times) served as Montevideo's first theater; it's still an impressive building, but its contents are fairly ordinary and scantier than other historical museums.

Italian adventurer Giuseppe Garibaldi, who aided Uruguay's anti-Rosas resistance in the 1840s, lived in the 1830 Spanish neoclassical **Casa Garibaldi** (25 de Mayo 314, tel. 02/915-4257, www.mec.gub.uy/museum/garibaldi, open by appointment only).

Mercado del Puerto

Originally intended as a Chilean train station, the British prefab port market—whose wrought-iron superstructure bears a strong resemblance to Santiago's historic Mercado Central—never made it out of Montevideo harbor. Erected just south of the port complex in 1868, its stalls and grills served stevedores and other laborers for nearly a century, but several decades ago the restaurants gradually grew more sophisticated, adding sidewalk seating and turning it into a tourist attraction.

Always packed for lunch into the late afternoon (when it closes for the day), the Mercado is an informal venue whose surrounding streets teem with artisans, artists, and musicians. It's possible to eat well on stools at the grills, where you can pick your cut off the coals, but there is also table service. The interior, which features a wooden "Big Ben" clocktower, would look more appealing if owners removed all the illuminated plastic signs promoting an international soft drink company that needs no more publicity.

Museo de la Moneda y del Gaucho

French architect Alfred Massüe designed the ornate French-style Palacio Heber (1896–1897) as a private residence for wealthy widow Margarita Uriarte de Heber, whose second marriage to politician Luis Alberto de Herrera took place here. Later sold to the Peirano family, then acquired by the Banco de la República, it was restored in 1985 to house two outstanding museums on Uruguayan economic history and the country's gaucho heritage: the Museo de la Moneda y del Gaucho (Avenida 18 de Julio 998, tel. 02/900-8764, www.brounet.com.uy/Novedades/Museo/museo.htm, open 10 A.M.–5 P.M. weekdays only, free).

Of the two museums, the second-floor Museo del Gaucho is the better—in fact, even if the presentation romanticizes the past, its assortment of gaucho artifacts equals anything in Argentina. The items range from the usual saddles, spurs, stirrups, and belts to lances, *facones* (knives), and elaborate silver *mates* (gourds) and *chifles* (carved horns for drinking), plus paintings and sculptures by contemporary Uruguayan artists. All in all, it's the one Montevideo museum not be missed.

The Museo de la Moneda, on the first floor, is more pedestrian but does house an impressive collection of colonial coins and medals, not to mention Uruguayan public and private banknotes that offer insights into the country's economic history. Banknotes of 500,000 pesos, for instance, recall the disastrous hyperinflation of the 1980s.

Museo de Arte Precolombino

It's a work-in-progress, but Montevideo's new pre-Columbian art museum, Museo de Arte Precolombino (MAPI, 25 de Mayo 279, open noon–4 P.M. weekdays except Mon., 11 A.M.–4 P.M. Sat., free), is impressive both for its collections and for a magnificent restoration of a historic building. Only the ground floor, with lithic artifacts from Uruguay and ceramics from the central Andes, really functions as a museum, but as renovation proceeds the upper-floor display space will expand beneath the broad skylights that let natural light flood into the building.

Originally intended as a spa in the late 19th century, the building became Uruguay's defense ministry before the military abandoned it in the 1990s. The facade and some downstairs exhibit halls are complete, along with a stage now used for small live-music events (the tiled floor where spectators sit was originally a swimming pool).

ENTERTAINMENT

Montevideo is not quite Buenos Aires for nightlife, but the Ciudad Vieja is gearing up along once moribund Bartolomé Mitre, nearly wall-to-wall with bars and restaurants. Most of these places are within staggering distance of each other but, as buses run less frequently than in Buenos Aires, it may be necessary to take a cab home.

Bars and Pubs

Part of its namesake apart-hotel, the intimate bar at **Bremen** (Maldonado 1308, tel. 02/902-2094) occasionally hosts local tango singers (not dancers), backed by guitar, with spontaneous audience participation.

Ley Seca (Soriano 952, tel. 02/908-2481) has live music Thursday through Sunday. **Amarcord** (Julio Herrera y Obes 1231, tel. 02/901-9381) has live rock and pop music.

In the Ciudad Vieja, the **Shannon Irish Pub,** (Bartolomé Mitre 1381, tel. 02/916-9585) is a clone of its Buenos Aires counterparts. Punning the name of the award-winning Spanish cinema director, **Almodobar** (Rincón 626, tel. 02/916-6665) is a cavernous but friendly pub/bar with red brick walls, a fine sound system, and live music some nights.

© WAYNE BERNHARDSON

The recently restored Teatro Solís is Montevideo's top performing arts facility.

Cinema

Downtown Montevideo has several movie theaters, including the **Cine Plaza** (Plaza Cagancha 1129, tel. 02/901-5385); the **Cine Libertad** and **Cine Central** (both at Avenida Rondeau 1383, tel. 02/901-5384); the **Cinemateca 18** (Avenida 18 de Julio 1286, tel. 02/900-9056); the **Cine Ejido** (Ejido 1377, tel. 02/901-4242); and the **Cinemetro** (San José 1211, tel. 02/901-0772).

The **Centro Cultural de España** (Rincón 629, tel. 02/915-2250) hosts art exhibits and free films.

Tango

Tango is almost as popular in Montevideo as in Buenos Aires. Within the Mercado Central, **Fun Fun** (Ciudadela 1229, tel. 02/915-8005) is the city's classic tango venue.

Though less youthful than its name implies, the Mercado de la Abundancia's **Joventango** (San José 1312, tel. 02/901-5561, http://canelones.chasque.net/joventango) does host regular tango events, including classes and *milongas*.

Theater

In addition to its cinemas, Montevideo has several live-theater venues, including the landmark **Teatro Solís.** Among them are several downtown theaters: the **Teatro del Centro** (Plaza Cagancha 1164, tel. 02/902-8915); the **Teatro Circular** (Avenida Rondeau 1388, tel. 02/901-5952); and the **Teatro del Anglo** (San José 1426, tel. 02/902-3773).

Other Performing Arts

The **Sala Zitarrosa** (Avenida 18 de Julio 1008, tel. 02/901-7303, www.salazitarrosa.com.uy) hosts events almost every night, ranging from evangelical and rock 'n' roll concerts to movies and live theater.

Upstairs at the Mercado Central, the **Complejo Cultural Mundo Afro** (Ciudadela 1229, tel. 02/915-0247, webs.demasiado.com/mafro) stresses Afro-Uruguayan theater and dance.

SHOPPING

The **Mercado de los Artesanos** (Plaza Cagancha 1365, tel. 02/901-0158) has a diversity of crafts. The recycled **Mercado de la Abundancia** (San José 1312, tel. 02/901-3438) has downstairs crafts stalls and upstairs *parrillas*.

For a broader crafts selection from around the country, try **Manos del Uruguay** (Sarandí 686, tel. 02/915-5345, www.manos.com.uy) in the Ciudad Vieja and downtown (San José 1111, 022/900-4910).

The Ciudad Vieja is the place to look for antiques and artwork, at places like **Galería Latina** (Sarandí 671, tel. 02/916-3737). For leather, try the Ciudad Vieja's **Casa Mario** (Piedras 641, tel. 02/916-2356, www.casamario leather.com), which sets the standard.

Also in the Ciudad Vieja, **Librería Linardi y Risso** (Juan Carlos Gómez 1435, tel. 02/9157129, www.linardiyrisso.com) is a specialist bookstore dealing with Uruguayan literature and history, and Latin America in general. Once the studio of artist Joaquín Torres García, it has been frequented by literary figures ranging from Pablo Neruda to Mario Benedetti and Juan Carlos Onetti.

Palacio del Libro (25 de Mayo 577, tel. 02/915-7543) is another large antiquarian bookseller.

RESTAURANTS

It's hard to go wrong at the historic **Mercado del Puerto** (Pérez Castellano 1569). Some of its gaggle of *parrillas* (beef grills) and other restaurants are, according to *Buenos Aires Herald* restaurant critic Dereck Foster, "scruffy looking but they have wonderful food."

At **La Pradera,** for instance, grilled chicken costs about US$3–4, top beef cuts around US$6–7, and fish dishes like *abadejo gitana* (conger eel spiced with paprika) around US$4–7. **La Posada de Don Tiburón** (tel. 02/915-4278) has indoor/outdoor seating (enjoy the pepper swordfish steak, abundant portions, and good service).

Best by consensus, the *tasca*-style **El Palenque** (tel. 02/915-4704) is a place where Galician owner Emilio Portela specializes in seafood (US$5–10 for most entrées), hams hang from the ceiling, and there's both indoor and patio seating. Particularly choice items include the *rabas* (squid rings) appetizer (US$6), swordfish steak (US$8), and the mixed seafood

grill (US$26), generous enough to feed three hungry adults.

The innovation center for Uruguayan dining is the Ciudad Vieja, where imaginative new options seem to open on an almost daily basis. **Café Irazú** (Juan Carlos Gómez 1315, tel. 02/916-6419) has the area's best, most reasonably priced breakfasts, with Brazilian coffee in a bright, cheerful locale. Relatively expensive by neighborhood standards, **Café Bacacay** (Bacacay 1306, tel. 02/916-6074) gets the pre- and post-theater crowd, thanks to its proximity to the Teatro Solís. There's also the classic **Confitería La Pasiva** (Juan Carlos Gómez and Sarandí, tel. 02/915-8261), on Plaza Constitución.

Panini's (Bacacay 1339, tel. 02/916-8760) is an upmarket sidewalk café with an excellent, diverse Italian menu that features entrées like *ravioli neri* (black ravioli) in the US$6–10 range, plus fine desserts, Uruguayan wines, and ambience.

The name may sound like a chain cliché, but **Don Peperone** (Sarandí and Bartolomé Mitre, tel. 02/915-7493) deserves consideration for fine lasagna and *pizzetas,* as well as good desserts and good service. There's both inside and sidewalk seating.

More subdued than some Ciudad Vieja restaurants, with simple décor in a neighborhood obsessed with fashion, **Mangrullo** (Bacacay 1327, tel. 02/916-3112) serves pasta stuffed with wild game, such as jabalí (boar), ciervo (deer), and nutria (beaver), but also beef dishes and has a good local wine list.

El Abasto (Mitre 1308, Bacacay 1309, tel. 02/916-9026, www.paninis.com.uy) is the fashionable face of *parrillada,* with outstanding meats in the US$5–8 range, a fine selection of Uruguayan wines, and equally fine service in agreeable surroundings.

Upscale **La Corte** (Sarandí 586, tel. 02/915-7592) has a sophisticated international menu.

Downtown's **Bar Lobizón** (Zelmar Michelini 1264, tel. 02/901-1334) serves a fairly extensive pub-style menu of meat, pasta, chicken, and sandwiches with an accompaniment of rock music; it gets most of its business at night. Its namesake **Lobizón** (Zelmar Michelini 1329, tel. 02/902-5999), one block north on the opposite side of the street, is more of a lunchtime cafeteria.

For short orders, snacks, and coffee, there's the *confitería* **Oro del Rhin** (Convención 1403, tel. 02/902-2833).

Since Uruguayans are even more notorious carnivores than Argentines, traditional downtown *parrillas* like **Las Brasas** (San José 909, tel. 02/900-2285) and **El Fogón** (San José 1080, tel. 02/900-0900) always draw crowds. For variety, **La Vegetariana** (Carlos Quijano 1334, tel. 02/900-7661) is one of several branches of the capital's main meatless chain.

Other ethnic food is primarily European, at venues like the **Mesón del Club Español** (Avenida 18 de Julio 1332, tel. 02/901-5145) and the Basque **Euskal Erria** (San José 1168, tel. 02/902-3519).

For seafood by the river, try **Che Montevideo** (Rambla Gandhi 630, tel. 02/710-6941), with ample outside seating. *Parrilla* costs in the US$8–10 pp range.

La Cigale (Ejido 1337) serves outstanding ice cream.

ACCOMMODATIONS

Montevideo has abundant accommodations, with several excellent values in the budget and midrange categories—especially since the recent devaluation. Choices are relatively few, however, in the Ciudad Vieja, the city's most interesting barrio.

Under US$25

Hotel Casablanca (San José 1039, tel. 2/901-0918, US$9/12 s/d) has modernized rooms in an older building, and an owner whose moods range from brusque to charmingly *simpática* (friendly).

Hotel Cervantes (Soriano 868, tel. 02/900-7991, US$9/13 s/d), a crumbling classic that's now a historical monument, dates from 1928. Designed with direct telephone connections to Buenos Aires—a novelty in those days—it was the favorite accommodations of figures

like tango singer Carlos Gardel, folksinger Atahualpa Yupanqui, and writers Jorge Luis Borges, Adolfo Bioy Casares, and Julio Cortázar; Cortázar conceived his short story "La Puerta Condenada" in room No. 205.

The shoestring **Hotel Arapey** (Avenida Uruguay 925, tel. 02/900-7032, www.arapey.com, US$12/15 s/d) has rooms with tacky but serviceable contemporary furnishings. It's certainly not a desperation choice. **Hotel Los Angeles** (Avenida 18 de Julio 974, tel. 02/902-1072, US$15/20 s/d) is a large (100 rooms) older (1928) hotel that retains some of its original features, such as high ceilings and common areas, but it's showing wear and tear.

Many youthful international travelers enjoy the **Hostelling International** (Canelones 935, tel. 02/908-1234, www.hosteluruguay.org, US$6–7 pp) affiliate, in an early 20th-century house on a tree-lined block. Rates depend on whether you're a Hostelling member or not, Uruguayan or not, and your age; dorm-style accommodations come with kitchen facilities, expansive common areas, information, and Internet access.

It has competition, though, from the newly created, lively **Red Hostel** (San José 1406, tel. 02/908-8514, www.redhostel.com, US$10 pp in dorms, US$26 d), a beautiful three-story home with a rooftop terrace surrounded by a canopy of sycamores. There are only a handful of private rooms; in addition to accommodations, it has kitchen and Internet facilities, and a small bar.

Classic in style, the no-frills **Hotel Palacio** (Bartolomé Mitre 1364, tel. 02/916-3612, US$12/19 s/d) now lags behind better budget choices in the Ciudad Vieja, but it's worth consideration if you can get one of the two sixth-floor rooms with enormous balconies and expansive views of the old city.

For style and character on a budget, try the nooks and crannies of the Ciudad Vieja's **Hotel Solís** (Bartolomé Mitre 1314, tel. 02/915-0279 or 02/916-4900, www.hotelsolis.20m.com, US$10/16–US$16/21 s/d). Rates for simple but attractive rooms with high ceilings and eclectic furnishings, in a two-story flatiron that Uruguayan president Baltasar Brum erected for his mistress in 1901, depend on whether the room has a shared or private bath, but all have balconies. There are also many good restaurants and bars in the vicinity and, while it's quieter than their density might suggest, the Solís is probably best for those who prefer to stay up late.

US$25–50

Accommodations at the well-managed **Hotel Mediterráneo** (Paraguay 1486, tel. 02/900-5090, www.hotelmediterraneo.com.uy, US$14/18 s/d–US$22/26) range from utilitarian standard rooms to more spacious "superior" rooms with a/c and free Internet connections; rates include a Brazilian-style buffet breakfast of croissants and fresh fruit. Street-side rooms get a steady drone from passing vehicles on nearby Avenida Lavalleja.

The highly recommended **Sur Hotel** (Maldonado 1098, tel. 02/908-2025, www.surhotel.com, US$21–27 d) is an attractively rehabbed hotel, on a quiet block, with gracious management; the more expensive rooms have Jacuzzis. Breakfast costs US$2 extra.

The central **Hotel Lancaster** (Plaza Cagancha 1334, tel. 02/902-1054, www.lancasterhotel.com, US$22/32 s/d) has very decent if unadorned rooms.

The best option in this category, though, is the German-run **Apart Hotel Bremen** (Maldonado 1308, tel./fax 02/903-2094, www.bremenmontevideo.com, US$30/35–US$75/85 s/d). This magnificently remodeled century-old building, with stained-glass skylights and windows, has been transformed into stylish one- and two-bedroom apartments with cable TV, fax, T-1 Internet connections, and kitchenettes. Rates depend on size; the offices are half a block north, on Aquiles Lanza between Maldonado and Canelones.

Hotel Lafayette (Soriano 1170, tel. 02/902-4646, fax 02/902-1301, www.lafayette.com.uy, US$28/36 s/d) is a contemporary hotel with spacious rooms and breakfast. Tobacco-free rooms are available, and there are business facilities (including WiFi), a gym, and other amenities.

Immaculate and cheerful rooms more than compensate for a bland exterior at the **Hotel London Palace** (Río Negro 1278, tel. 02/902-0024, www.lphotel.com, US$35/45 s/d). Amenities at this excellent midrange hotel include a Brazilian-style buffet breakfast (plenty of fresh fruit), a/c, and parking.

The high-rise **Hotel Embajador** (San José 1212, tel. 02/902-0012, www.hotelembajador.com, US$35/45 s/d) has 120 rooms with a/c, cable TV, a Brazilian buffet breakfast, parking, swimming pool, and the like; the rooms are spacious but not quite so good as at the London Palace.

The 137-room **Holiday Inn** (Colonia 823, tel. 02/902-0001, www.holidayinn.com.uy, US$40/45 s/d) is the local rep of the international chain, but it's in a slightly dodgy neighborhood.

US$50–100

The **Oxford Hotel** (Paraguay 1286, tel. 02/902-0046, www.oxford.com.uy, US$40/52 s/d) is a well-kept 1960s structure that's perfectly acceptable; rates include breakfast, a late afternoon snack, and parking. Some rooms, though, are a little small.

Overlooking the river, on the south side of the Ciudad Vieja, the Spanish NH chain has rehabbed the **Hotel NH Columbia** (Rambla Gran Bretaña 473, tel. 02/916-0001, www.nh-hotels.com, US$55 d), which offers 138 rooms including a dozen suites, with buffet breakfast and conveniences including Internet access and a fitness center.

Under international-chain ownership after years as a Sun Myung Moonie outpost, the **Radisson Victoria Plaza Hotel** (Plaza Independencia 759, tel. 02/902-0111, fax 02/902-1628, toll-free in the United States 800/333-3333, www.radisson.com, US$95 s or d) has expanded to include a state-of-the-art casino. It has a 24-hour business center, a full-service spa, and many other luxuries.

INFORMATION

The **Ministerio de Turismo** (Rambla 25 de Agosto and Yacaré, tel. 02/1885, www.turismo.gub.uy, open 9 A.M.–6:30 P.M.

weekdays only) occupies spacious new port headquarters, opposite the Mercado del Puerto. Its Aeropuerto Carrasco branch (tel. 02/601-1757) is open 8 A.M.–8 P.M. daily.

The municipal **Módulo de Información al Turismo** (Avenida 18 de Julio and Ejido, tel. 02/1950, ext. 1830, www.montevideo-invita.com.uy, open 10 A.M.–6 P.M. daily) is a helpful kiosk in front of the Intendencia de Montevideo.

At Terminal Tres Cruces, the main bus station, the **Asociación de Hoteles y Restaurantes** (AHRU, Bulevar Artigas 1825, tel. 02/409-7399, open 8 A.M.–9 P.M. weekdays, 9 A.M.–9 P.M. weekends) maintains a particularly helpful information office.

SERVICES

As the capital and only real metropolis in a small country, Montevideo has a full range of services.

Consulates

Several Latin American, North American, and European countries have diplomatic representation in Montevideo, including Argentina (W.F. Aldunate 1281, tel. 02/902-8623); Brazil (Convención 1343, 6th fl., tel. 02/901-2024); Canada (Plaza Independencia 749, Oficina 102, tel. 02/902-2030); France (Avenida Uruguay 853, tel. 02/902-0077); Germany (La Cumparsita 1435, tel. 02/902-5222); the United Kingdom (Marco Bruto 1073, tel. 02/622-3630); and the United States (Lauro Muller 1776, tel. 02/418-7777).

Immigration

For visa or tourist-card extensions, the Ciudad Vieja's **Dirección Nacional de Migración** (Misiones 1513, tel. 02/916-0471) is open 8:15 A.M.–1:30 P.M. in summer; the rest of the year, hours are 12:30–7 P.M.

Money

There's a growing number of ATMs, such as the Ciudad Vieja's **BankBoston** (25 de Mayo 391). On the west side of Plaza Independen-

cia, **Exprinter** (Sarandí 700) changes travelers checks, as do exchange houses like **Cambio Gales** (Avenida 18 de Julio 1048) and **Cambio Regul** (Avenida 18 de Julio 1126).

Postal Services

The *Correo Central* (main post office) is at Buenos Aires 451, in the Ciudad Vieja.

Telephone, Fax, and Internet

Antel, the national telephone company, has long-distance Telecentros at Rincón 501 in the Ciudad Vieja (San José 1102) and at the Tres Cruces bus terminal. All three have Internet access for fixed amounts of time—minimum 15 minutes.

For Internet access, try the **Phone Box** (Sarandi 606 in the Ciudad Vieja and Andes 1363 in the Centro); the latter is open 24 hours.

Travel Agencies

Partnering with Hostelling International, **Viajeros sin Fronteras** (Río Negro 1354, 2nd fl., Oficina 8, tel. 02/902-8848, www.sinfronteras.com.uy) arranges excursions around Montevideo and the country.

TRANSPORTATION

Air

Montevideo's **Aeropuerto Internacional de Carrasco** (tel. 02/604-0330) is about 15 kilometers northeast of downtown, on the highway toward Punta del Este.

From December to April, **American Airlines** (Sarandí 699 bis, tel. 02/916-3979) offers three nonstops per week from Miami. Otherwise, it's only a short hop across the Río de la Plata from Buenos Aires with American and with **United Airlines** (Plaza Independencia 831, Oficina 501, tel. 02/902-4630). Both fly from New York and Miami to B.A.; United also flies from Chicago.

Aerolíneas Argentinas (Convención 1343, 4th fl., tel. 02/902-3694), which flies from Miami to B.A., has the most frequent connections across the river from Buenos Aires. Other options from North America are via São Paulo or Rio de Janeiro, Brazil, with **Pluna/Varig** (Plaza Independencia 804, tel. 02/604-4080, www.pluna.aero) or **TAM** (Colonia 820, tel. 02/901-8451); or via Santiago de Chile with Pluna or **LAN** (Colonia 993, 4th fl., tel. 02/902-3881).

From Europe, the only direct connections are twice-weekly services from Madrid via Rio de Janeiro, with Pluna/Varig.

Uair (Plaza Independencia 759, 7th fl., tel. 02/908-7417, www.uair.com) flies to the Argentine cities of Rosario, Córdoba, and Mendoza, and the Brazilian city of Curitiba, with connections elsewhere in Brazil.

Boat

Comfortable high-speed ferries from Buenos Aires take less than three hours to cross the Río de la Plata. The rehabbed Puerto Fluvial, on the Rambla 25 de Agosto, is convenient to the Ciudad Vieja, Montevideo's colonial core.

Buquebus has its office in the Edificio Santos (Rambla 25 de Agosto de 1825 and Yacaré, tel. 02/916-8801 or 011/4316-6500, www.buquebus.com). Buquebus's *Juan Patricio* and *Atlantic III* have smallish, close-together tourist-class seats that recline only slightly; the on-board cafeteria serves pretty dire sandwiches, empanadas, and a few other items. There are two or three sailings per day, depending on the season and the day of the week; fares range from US$58–70 pp depending on the class.

Buquebus also operates a bus-ferry combination via Colonia up to five times daily (US$35–44 pp).

THE COUNTRY OF HOLIDAYS

Uruguay's devastating 1973–1985 dictatorship, followed by economic changes in which a relatively small working population could no longer support a large pensioner class, undercut the country's traditionally generous social welfare state. One feature still survives, though: Uruguay remains the País de los Feriados—the country of holidays.

Uruguay celebrates all the typical holidays that Argentines and most other South Americans do—**New Year's Day** (January 1), **Labor Day** (May 1), **Día de la Raza** (Columbus Day, October 12), and **Día de la Familia** (Christmas, December 25); Uruguayan workers get those days off. They also enjoy an official holiday on **Epifanía** (Epiphany, January 6).

April 19 marks the **Desembarco de los 33,** the 1825 date on which 33 returning exiles, with Argentine assistance, landed on the Banda Oriental to begin the campaign for independence from Brazil. May 18's **Batalla de Las Piedras** (Battle of Las Piedras) commemorates a key independence battle.

June 19 is the **Natalicio de Artigas;** unlike the Argentines' celebration of José de San Martín, Uruguayans honor their great national hero on the date of his birth rather than his death. July 18 is **Jura de la Constitución** (Constitution Day), while August 25 is **Día de la Independencia** (Independence Day).

Oddly enough for a self-proclaimed secular country, Uruguay officially acknowledges November 2 as the **Día de los Muertos** (All Souls' Day). This is particularly peculiar as it does *not* acknowledge **Semana Santa** (Holy Week) in March or April as such—rather, this time is **Semana Criolla** (Creole Week) or even **Semana de Turismo** (Tourism Week). Though this may occur only shortly after the end of the January and February summer vacations, many Uruguayans take the entire week off, rather than just Good Friday.

Uruguay's **Carnaval,** on the Monday and Tuesday before Ash Wednesday, is what Buenos Aires's must have been before the decimation of the Afro-Argentines; Montevideo's Barrio Sur still has a visible Afro-Uruguayan population that practices *candombe* (Afro-Uruguayan music and dance) ceremonies. Although these are not official holidays, they are popular ones.

As if all that were not enough, each Uruguayan is officially entitled to take the day off on his or her birthday.

At Terminal Tres Cruces, **Cacciola** (tel. 02/401-9350, www.cacciolaviajes.com) has bus-launch service to Tigre (US$18, eight hours) via Carmelo. Departures are at 12:30 and 10:45 A.M. weekdays, 12:30 A.M. and 1:30 P.M. Saturday, and 1 P.M. Sunday.

Bus

About three kilometers northeast of Plaza Independencia, Montevideo's modern and orderly **Terminal Tres Cruces** (Bulevar Artigas and Avenida Italia, tel. 02/401-8998, www .trescruces.com.uy) is a full-service bus terminal and shopping center with a helpful tourist information office, money exchange and ATM, baggage storage, toilets, restaurants, public telephones, and Internet access.

Although the ferry from Buenos Aires is far faster and more convenient, there is direct bus service from Montevideo to Retiro (US$25, nine hours) four times nightly with **Bus de la Carrera** (tel. 02/402-1313), once nightly with **Cauvi** (tel. 02/401-9196); and once nightly with **General Belgrano** (tel. 02/401-4764).

Domestically, Montevideo is the hub for Uruguayan bus services, eastbound toward Maldonado and Punta del Este, and west-bound toward Colonia and Carmelo. **Bus del Atlántico** (tel. 02/408-6668) serves Maldonado and Punta del Este (US$5, two hours); companies serving Colonia (US$5, two hours) include **COT** (tel. 02/408-6668), **Chadre** (tel. 02/1717), and **Turil** (tel. 02/1990). For Carmelo, there's Chadre as well as **Sabelín** (tel. 02/1717) and **Intertur** (tel. 02/401-7729).

Car Rental

Rental agencies include **Alquilato** (Piedras 306, tel. 02/916-5195); **Dollar** (J. Barrios Amorín 1186, tel. 02/402-6427); **Europcar** (Bulevar Artigas 1875, tel. 02/401-0575); **Localiza** (Paysandú 1570, tel. 02/409-2737); and **Multicar** (Colonia 1227, tel. 02/902-2555).

Train

This is not a very practical way of getting around much of Uruguay, but dedicated trainspotters can catch the local to the suburbs of Canelones and 25 de Agosto (US$1.50, two hours) from the new **Estación Central** (Río Negro s/n, tel. 02/929-0125), just north of the handsome but rundown old station.

The Montevideo Wine Country

In San Francisco's 2002 World Wine Market, the most impressive Latin American exhibitor turnout came not from traditional powerhouses Argentina and Chile, but rather from little-known Uruguay. Over the past decade or so, about 10 percent of the country's 300 wineries have begun to switch from traditional jug wines, for exclusively domestic consumption, to fine wines for more sophisticated Uruguayan palates and for export.

Uruguay produces many of the same varietals as Argentina, including the reds cabernet sauvignon, malbec, and merlot, and the whites chardonnay and sauvignon blanc, but its signature grape is the red tannat, of French Basque origin. Accounting for about a third of Uru-guayan production, this smooth, deep red varietal is uncommon elsewhere.

According to Daniel Pisano, who owns a small vineyard on Montevideo's outskirts, Uruguay's annual yield of 100 million bottles is roughly equivalent to Chile's giant Concha y Toro winery. Unlike Argentina and Chile, Uruguay does not need to irrigate its vineyards, and its lowland soils and rolling topography are very different from the mostly alluvial soils in those countries.

If the Uruguayans cannot match their continental rivals in quantity, they're hoping to establish a niche market through quality. To this end, Pisano and other exporters have formed an alliance, the Asociación de Bode-

© WAYNE BERNHARDSON

Of French Basque origins, the tannat is Uruguay's quintessential grape variety.

gas Exportadoras de Vinos Finos de Uruguay (www.winesofuruguay.com) to promote their wines overseas. More importantly for readers of this book, they've organized a fledgling Ruta del Vino (wine route) barely half an hour from the capital city.

Most of the families here have Italian or Galician backgrounds, but the dominant winemaking tendency is French. Specifically, they adhere to the idea of *terroir,* a regional approach in which the product of each vineyard represents its own soils, climate, grapes, and wine-making skills. The Montevideo area resembles Bordeaux in its mild, humid climate and clayey soils but gets more sun than its French counterpart.

While Uruguay's wine route may be in its infancy, it's not hard to arrange a visit, though some smaller family-run vineyards need at least a day's advance notice and may not always be able to provide an English-speaker. All of them, though, treat visitors as if they were family—there are no wine snobs here.

Though the wineries are close to Montevideo, some can be hard to find; it's easier to hire

a *remise* (car and driver) than to navigate the maze of rural roads or struggle with the multitude of public bus lines.

BODEGA BOUZA

The closest winery to Montevideo, Bouza is perhaps the most ambitious of them all, a high-tech facility—all stainless steel tanks and state-of-the-art equipment—that's transformed a crumbling 1940s winery. At the same time, it's rapidly renovating aging brick buildings, while preserving their facades, to accommodate overnight guests and create a restaurant.

Bouza's vineyards include 10 hectares of well-established tannat, merlot, and chardonnay, but they've planted another 13 of tannat, merlot, tempranillo, and the unusual dry white albariño. Like all the other wineries described here, this is a family enterprise, where even fairly young children participate in the harvest, manual grape selection, and other tasks.

In addition to its wines, Bouza intends to become a wine museum; it's also home to owner Juan Luis Bouza's growing collection of historic *cachilas* (antique automobiles, most of which await restoration) and even rail cars. When complete, the restaurant will hold special events rather than keep regular hours. Accommodations, though, will keep a more regular schedule.

Actually part of Montevideo Rural (Greater Montevideo), Bodega Bouza (Camino de la Redención 7658 bis, tel. 02/323-3872, www .bodegabouza.com) figures to become one of the top destinations for wine-oriented visitors to Uruguay.

BODEGA DELUCCA

Educated as a plant pathologist in Pennsylvania and France, Reinaldo de Lucca views wine as a "living being" and he takes a craftsman's approach, with constant visual monitoring of the vineyards and the wine-making process. About half his production consists of fine wines, with about 20 percent exported; the main reds are tannat, merlot, syrah, and

Laborers and family members at Montevideo's Bodega Bouza select the best chardonnay grapes from the recent harvest.

cabernet sauvignon, with tannat/merlot and tannat/syrah blends. The whites are sauvignon blanc and the uncommon marsanne.

De Lucca (Ruta 48, Km 13.1, El Colorado, Canelones, tel. 02/367-8076, www.deluccawines.com) has a small tasting room but a larger facility is in the works. The website, by the way, is in impeccable English; if possible, try to give them 48 hours' advance notice of a visit.

VIÑEDOS Y BODEGA FILGUEIRA

While it's been in the Filgueira family for more than 80 years, only in the past five or six has their bodega begun to produce fine wines, primarily tannat but also cabernet sauvignon, merlot, and sauvignon blanc, from freshly planted vines on only 12 hectares. All of them come in standard, oak, and premium lines, where the quality generally depends on yield (6,000–

9,000 kg per hectare, with the lower yields corresponding to higher quality). The odd duck is the white sauvignon gris (sauvignon grigio, if you prefer).

Bodega Filgueira (Ruta 81, Km 7, Cuchilla Verde, Canelones, tel. 033/46438, www.bodegafilgueira.com) has an intimate tasting room in its modernized bodega, but plans to build a larger visitor facility. It needs 24 hours to arrange a visit; the staff handle English well, and the website also features excellent English text.

ESTABLECIMIENTO JUANICÓ

Probably the country's closest thing to an industrial winery, Juanicó produces about a quarter of all Uruguayan wines, and half of that is still jug wines for domestic consumption. At the same time, it's one of the leaders in fine wines and its facilities, dating from the 1840s but modernized within, are the most historic and picturesque of any Montevideo winery (though Bouza, when finished, will be at least a close second).

On 600 hectares of rolling terrain, some 240 of them in vineyards and most of the rest in forest, Juanicó dates from colonial times. It takes its name from Francisco Juanicó, who built the current *cava* (wine cellar) around 1840, but the property passed through several hands, including the state oil company ANCAP, before being sold to the Deicas family in 1979. It employs 100 permanent laborers, plus another 100 during the March harvest, to produce a diversity of reds (tannat, merlot, cabernet sauvignon, cabernet franc, pinot noir, petit verdot, shiraz) and whites (chardonnay, gewürztraminer, sauvignon blanc, viognier). Some vintages from its Preludio line have become collectors' items.

Juanicó is well-prepared to receive visitors, having converted the ground level of its historic *cava* into a restaurant and events center that can accommodate large groups for *asados* and tastings, but it also has a more intimate subterranean dining room suitable for small groups. The latter is a de facto museum, filled with antique winemaking gear and a gallery of tannat-oriented artwork.

Excursions from Buenos Aires

© WAYNE BERNHARDSON

Establecimiento Juanicó is one of Uruguay's most historic wineries.

Juanicó (Estación Juanicó s/n, Juanicó, Canelones, tel. 033/59725, www.juanico .com) is actually the easiest of all the wineries to find—the property fronts directly on Ruta 5, about 37.5 kilometers northwest of Montevideo. While Uruguay has no "wine train" on the order of California's Napa Valley, it's conceivable to arrive on the slow suburban commuter train from downtown Montevideo—Juanicó station is easy walking distance from the property's entrance—but service is erratic.

BODEGA CÉSAR PISANO

On 30 hectares, dating from the 1920s, the Pisano vineyards produce at least half a dozen premium varietals, including tannat, cabernet sauvignon, chardonnay, and sauvignon blanc, with others on the way. One interesting varietal is the dry white torrontés, normally grown on alluvial soils in high desert climates, such as Argentina's Salta province, rather than on low-altitude clay in humid Uruguay.

Bodega Pisano (Camino de los Ingleses, Ruta 68, Km 29, tel. 02/368-9007, www

.pisanowines.com) is a family business, with at least three generations directly involved in the process at all levels. For visits, it prefers specialized groups, with some advance notice. The bodega's cook prepares an excellent *asado* that includes, unusually for this part of the world, lightly grilled vegetables (rather than the overdone style so common in lowest-common-denominator Southern Cone cookery).

BODEGA CARLOS PIZZORNO

A fourth-generation family enterprise, Pizzorno started switching from jug wines to fine wines in the late 1980s to become a boutique winery on 15 hectares planted to tannat, cabernet sauvignon, merlot, sauvignon blanc, and chardonnay. Unusual for this area, it also produces sparkling wine from its chardonnay and sauvignon blanc.

Bodega Carlos Pizzorno (Ruta 32, Km 23, Canelón Chico, tel. 02/368-9601, www.pizzornowines.com) welcomes visits, but normally needs 48 hours advance notice. There's a small tasting and sales room, and a truly warm welcome for visitors.

tannat grapevines at Bodega Carlos Pizzorno, near Montevideo, Uruguay

© WAYNE BERNHARDSON

Colonia del Sacramento

Only a short sail across the river from Buenos Aires, Colonia del Sacramento's picturesque 18th-century architecture has made it a UNESCO World Heritage Site and tourist town, but it's still a neighborly place whose residents sip *mate* on the sidewalk and chat across cobbled sycamore-shaded streets. Its unhurried pace—local motorists even stop for pedestrians—could not contrast more with the Argentine capital's frenetic tempo.

Traditionally, Argentines descend upon Colonia in overwhelming numbers in summer and on weekends, though traditional price differentials have diminished. The town suffered dramatically from the Argentine meltdown—a large majority of its annual visitors are *porteños*—but business has recovered quickly as the neighboring economy has risen from the depths of 2001–2002.

One positive consequence of the crisis has been the postponement of a megaproject—a 42-kilometer series of five bridges from Punta Lara, near the Buenos Aires provincial capital of La Plata, across the river to a point seven kilometers east of Colonia. The Argentine-Uruguayan Comisión Binacional Puente Buenos Aires Colonia (Buenos Aires Colonia Binational Bridge Commission) has long promoted this environmentally suspect project for purposes of improving communications within the Mercosur common market, but it remains on hold. Still, its potential impact on tiny Colonia is enormous.

Many foreign visitors cross the river on day trips from Buenos Aires. That's a good option for anyone short on time, but Colonia's worth at least an overnight stay and preferably more.

HISTORY

Colonia do Sacramento (its original Portuguese name) dates to 1680, at a time when Buenos Aires was a backwater of Spain's mercantile empire and nearly all trade had to pass through the viceregal capital of Lima and then across the Andes and over the pampas. The Portuguese Manoel de Lobo established the settlement directly opposite Buenos Aires on the Río de la Plata's *Banda Oriental* (Eastern Shore), in order to exploit the Paraná delta's labyrinthine channels for contraband.

Colonia, then, became the focus of a continual tug-of-war between Spain and Portugal. A 1750 agreement to hand it over to the Spaniards failed when Jesuit missions, which operated with near-total autonomy until the Jesuits' 1767 expulsion from the Americas, refused to cede any of their upper Paraná territory. By the time the Spaniards finally established themselves in Colonia in 1777, the newly created Virreinato del Río de la Plata had made the contraband economy nearly superfluous, as foreign imports could use the port of Buenos Aires.

Beginning in the mid-19th century, Swiss, Italian, and German immigration gave the surrounding area a dairy- and farm-based prosperity, but Montevideo's rapid growth deflected infrastructural and industrial development toward the capital. Spared by the capital, Colonia's **Barrio Histórico,** its 18th-century core, remained largely intact for the evolution of the local tourist industry.

ORIENTATION

Colonia is less than an hour by high-speed catamaran or two-plus hours by ferry from Buenos Aires. It is 180 kilometers west of Montevideo via Ruta 1, a smoothly paved two-lane highway that enters town from the east and turns southwest toward the ferry port.

The town itself consists of two distinct areas: a conventional grid west of Ruta 1, centered on Plaza 25 de Agosto, and the narrow irregular streets of the Barrio Histórico west of Ituzaingó, marking the limits of the peninsular *ciudadela,* the walled colonial city. The main commercial street is east-west Avenida General Flores, which runs the length of the town on the south side of Plaza 25 de Agosto.

 BARRIO HISTÓRICO

Nearly all of Colonia's sights are in the Barrio Histórico, including its numerous museums, open 11:30 A.M.–5:45 P.M. daily in summer; they usually close Mondays the rest of the year. Entrance tickets, which cost about US$.50, may be purchased at the Museo Municipal and the Museo Portugués only, but are also valid for the Archivo Regional, the Museo Indígena, the Museo Español, and the Museo de los Azulejos. Individual tickets cost US$.20.

Early Colonia was a *ciudadela,* a walled

© WAYNE BERNHARDSON

a brick and cobble house on Colonia's Calle del Comercio

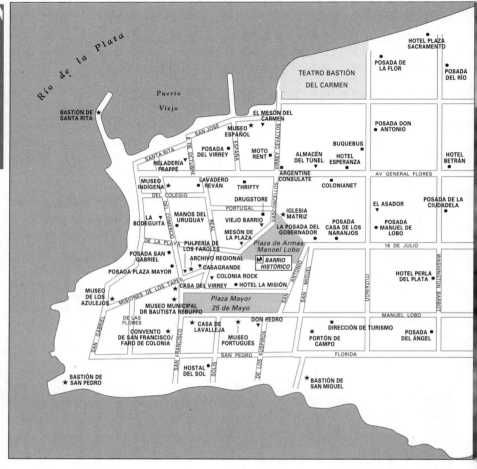

fortress protected from sea and land by *bastiones* (bulwarks) like the southerly **Bastión de San Miguel,** the westerly **Bastión San Pedro** and **Bastión Santa Rita,** and the northerly **Bastión del Carmen.**

The entrance to the Barrio Histórico is the reconstructed **Portón de Campo** (1745), a gate approached by a drawbridge. To the west, several major landmarks surround the irregular quadrangle of **Plaza Mayor 25 de Mayo:** the **Museo Portugués** (Portuguese Museum,

1730), the **Casa de Lavalleja** (once the home of independence figure Juan Antonio Lavalleja), the **Museo Municipal Dr. Bautista Rebuffo** (Municipal Museum, also known as the **Casa del Almirante Brown,** though the founder of the Argentine navy never lived there), and the 17th-century ruins of the **Casa del Virrey** (also misleadingly named as no viceroy ever lived in Colonia).

At the plaza's southeast corner, low-slung colonial houses line both sides of the sloping,

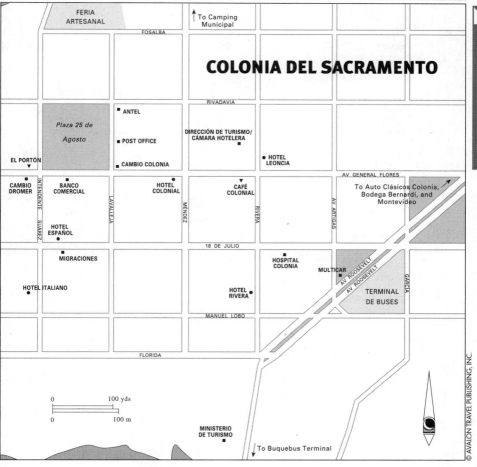

COLONIA DEL SACRAMENTO

FERIA ARTESANAL

To Camping Municipal

FOSALBA

RIVADAVIA

ANTEL

Plaza 25 de Agosto

POST OFFICE

DIRECCIÓN DE TURISMO/ CÁMARA HOTELERA

HOTEL LEONCIA

EL PORTÓN

CAMBIO COLONIA

AV GENERAL FLORES

CAMBIO DROMER

BANCO COMERCIAL

HOTEL COLONIAL

CAFÉ COLONIAL

To Auto Clásicos Colonia, Bodega Bernardi, and Montevideo

HOTEL ESPAÑOL

INTENDENTE

LAVALLEJA

MENDEZ

RIVERA

AV ARTIGAS

SUAREZ

18 DE JULIO

MIGRACIONES

HOSPITAL COLONIA

MULTICAR

AV ROOSEVELT

AV ROOSEVELT

GARCIA

HOTEL ITALIANO

HOTEL RIVERA

TERMINAL DE BUSES

MANUEL LOBO

FLORIDA

0   100 yds
0   100 m

MINISTERIO DE TURISMO

To Buquebus Terminal

© AVALON TRAVEL PUBLISHING, INC.

roughly cobbled **Calle de los Suspiros** (Street of Sighs); one of the city's most emblematic structures (though a private residence) is the pink stucco with red tiles at the corner of Calle San Pedro.

At the Plaza Mayor's southwest corner, ruins of the 18th-century **Convento de San Francisco** nearly surround the 19th-century **Faro de Colonia** (lighthouse; open 11 A.M.–7 P.M. daily, US$.60), an almost pristine restoration. Climbing its 118 steps is the best workout in town (and an enjoyable one when it's not humid); from the top, Buenos Aires, Quilmes, and even La Plata are visible in good weather. At some times of the year, the late closing hour makes it a fine place to see the sunset.

North of the plaza, dating from 1770, the **Archivo Regional** (Misiones de los Tapes 115) belongs to the simple architectural style known as *rancho portugués,* its adobe walls topped by a tile roof. The archive's contents are scanty, but the building is a relic of the

© WAYNE BERNHARDSON

The *rancho portugués* architectural style is typical of Colonia's Calle de los Suspiros.

era when, according to Jesuit priest Martin Dobrizhoffer, Colonia boomed with contraband wealth:

> *The houses are few and low, forming a village, rather than city, yet it is far from despicable; opulent merchants, wares of every kind, gold, silver, and diamonds are concealed beneath its miserable roofs.*

To the west, on the riverfront, the **Museo de los Azulejos** traces local architectural history through its elaborate tilework. To the north, on Calle del Comercio, is the modest **Museo Indígena,** which displays indigenous tools, such as scrapers and *boleadoras,* plus some clippings on the pre-Columbian Charrúa and the romantic *indigenismo* of Uruguayan writer Juan Zorrilla de San Martín (1855–1931).

Northeast of the Plaza Mayor, the landmark **Iglesia Matriz** (1699) extends along the north side of the **Plaza de Armas Manoel Lobo,** but its twin-towered facade fronts on Calle Vasconcellos. Despite its early appearance, it has undergone major modifica-

tions due to combat damage, fire, and even an explosion of an arsenal during the Brazilian occupation of 1823.

On the north side of the peninsula, the two-story **Museo Español** (1725) was originally a private residence. Immediately north is the **Puerto Viejo,** the former port. The **Teatro Bastión del Carmen** (Virrey Ceballos and Rivadavia) integrates part of the colonial bulwarks and the Fábrica Caracciolo, a former soap factory, into the city's principal performing-arts center.

Museo de los Azulejos

This collection (Misiones de los Tapes 104) of decorative tilework dates mostly from the mid-19th century—before then, beautification was a low priority in a city that was in an almost constant state of war. The stenciled artisanal tiles, many of them imported from France, vary slightly in size, shape, and design.

Sections of the floor and ceiling of the mid-18th-century building are original, others of subsequent brick. Some ceramic roof tiles are *tejas musleras,* so called because they were formed on the thighs of mulatto women.

THE VANISHING CACHILAS

Not so long ago, the finest assortment of antique automobiles south of Havana filled the streets of Colonia and Montevideo. In what was an open-air museum for vintage wheels, it wasn't unusual to see Model A Fords, Daimlers, Studebakers, and Willys parked at the curbs and rolling down Uruguay's roadways. Uruguay owed this abundance of classic cars (which they call *cachilas*) to its history of alternating good fortune and misfortune.

A prosperous country in the first half of the 20th century, Uruguay imported a wide variety of vehicles from Europe and the United States, but economic and political decline forced Uruguayans to maintain and operate what, in most other countries, would have been museum pieces. At times, it seemed, there were so many classic cars that the streets looked like sets for Mafia movies.

This began to change when, in the 1970s, foreign collectors began to discover the abundance of *cachilas*. As the country's fleet of motor vehicles modernized with the renewal of automobile imports from Argentina and Brazil during the 1990s boom, these stylish relics slowly but inexorably began disappearing.

Although not so numerous as they once were, the *cachilas* have spawned their own niche within the automotive sector. Scouts still scour the garages of provincial towns and the backroads of the interior for hidden treasures worthy of restoration and sale to collectors. This, in turn, has created a job market for artisans (sometimes elderly) who can restore and reproduce irreplaceable items, such as wooden dashboards and leather upholstery. There's a market for parts as well as for entire vehicles.

Uruguayans are aware of their automotive legacy, and the law defines historic vehicles as part of the national patrimony. Except in a few high-profile cases, though, this has not restricted their sale and export, for which there is a strong incentive—cars that cost a few thousand dollars when they were built can, in restored condition, fetch nearly US$100,000.

While the clock may be ticking for the *cachilas* that for so many decades lent their personalities to Uruguayan streets, roads, and highways, they haven't quite disappeared. Even now, along the highway from Montevideo to Punta del Este, there are roadside lots where the vehicles range from rusting wrecks to fairly well-conserved specimens awaiting a savior.

Even as its presence diminishes, the *cachila* keeps a high profile in the public consciousness. On being sworn into office in March 2005, newly elected Uruguayan president Tabaré Vásquez chose a family treasure, a Model T Ford that had belonged to his wife's father, for the traditional parade down Avenida del Libertador.

cachilas on the street in Colonia, Uruguay

© WAYNE BERNHARDSON

Museo Español

The Spanish museum (San José 152) actually consists of two buildings, a mid-18th-century, two-story Portuguese residence and a mid-19th-century addition to the east. Its contents are mostly ordinary, though the narrative of events (in Spanish only) is thorough. What raises it above the routine are the historical portraits by contemporary Uruguayan artist and Colonia resident José Páez Vilaró, which complement the otherwise archaic materials.

Museo Municipal
Dr. Bautista Rebuffo

Unlike its Portuguese counterpart, Colonia's municipal museum displays more potential than accomplishment. Occupying the so-called **Casa de Almirante Brown** (1795, but rebuilt in the 1830s), it's a bit musty, both physically and in concept (or lack of it). While it's a little more informative than in past years, it's still pretty much a stuff-in-glass-cases affair that could benefit from a professional curator to organize and interpret its documents and artifacts on aboriginal Uruguay, the struggle between Spain and Portugal, and Uruguay's early residents—plus fossils and a mass of deteriorating taxidermy specimens. One recent addition is material on the bullfights—long since outlawed—that brought Argentine tourists to nearby Real de San Carlos.

It would also be informative to add material on Colonia's transformation over the past 20 years, and its almost total dependency on the Argentine tourist trade. Still alive in his nineties, the elderly gentleman from whom the museum takes its name has resisted tampering with the exhibits, though some Montevideo professionals have indicated a willingness to volunteer their efforts.

Museo Portugués

Built under Portuguese dominion beginning in 1730, the former **Casa de Ríos** underwent a late-18th-century reconstruction under the Spaniards. With help from the Portuguese government, its collections have improved dramatically—it has an excellent sample of maps on the Portuguese voyages of discovery (high-quality copies of the Lisbon originals), an extraordinary assortment of professionally displayed porcelain ceramics, and period clothing.

OTHER SIGHTS
Auto Clásicos Colonia

Still, on occasion, *cachila* owners park their antique cars at the curbs of the Barrio Histórico, but it's not such a common sight as it was in the past because collectors have bought up and exported so many of them. About three kilometers east of the port, though, on the west side of Ruta 1 toward Montevideo, there's usually an assortment of Chevrolets, Fords, and other aging wrecks in the process of restoration or customization at this specialist auto repair shop. While it's not exactly tourist-oriented, they're happy to let visitors walk around and snap photos of the process during normal work hours. For more information, contact owner Marco Torres (tel. 09/431-4235, marco29_524@hotmail.com).

Bodega Bernardi

Colonia can't match Montevideo's increasingly sophisticated wineries, but this unpretentious, low-tech bodega, dating from 1892, has begun to supplement its jug wine production with an increasing variety of fine reds, mostly merlot and tannat, as well as their Isabella rosé, produced from the so-called "strawberry grape." They also make about 300 bottles per year of the deeply colored dry white moscato giallo, but the house specialty is several varieties of distilled grappa, once a state monopoly in Uruguay.

Founded by Italian-Swiss immigrants, Bernardi is open for drop-in visits but needs advance notice to be sure of accommodating English speakers. With 24 hours notice, they can prepare a *tabla* of *fiambres* (cold cuts), cheeses, and empanadas to accompany a tasting of wine and grappa.

Bodega Bernardi (Ruta 1, Km 171.5, tel. 052/24762, vigneto@adinet.com.uy, open 9 A.M.–

noon and 2–5:30 P.M. Mon.–Sat., 10 A.M.–2 P.M. Sun.) resides on undulating terrain about seven kilometers east of Colonia; it's ideal for a bike ride.

FOOD

Until recently, Colonia's restaurants have displayed more colonial style than culinary imagination. The standard has been the *parrilla,* though this is changing as local cuisine diversifies.

For *parrillada,* El Asador (Ituzaingó 168, tel. 052/24204) is a no-frills choice that's maintained its popularity over the years, so it must be doing something right. El Portón (General Flores 333, tel. 052/25318) is a more upmarket alternative.

Café Colonial (General Flores 432, tel. 052/21542) is essentially a sandwich spot, but it's good at what it does. Almacén del Túnel (General Flores 227, tel. 052/24666) is a traditionally good restaurant with fixed-price lunches.

Facing the Plaza Mayor, Don Pedro (Suspiros 99, tel. 052/22867) is a shady sidewalk café with excellent homemade pasta (around US$3), chivitos, and unfortunately aggressive pigeons—watch your bread.

The Barrio Histórico's Casagrande (Misiones de los Tapes 143, tel. 052/20654) prepares somewhat more elaborate short orders than most Uruguayan restaurants do. Pulpería de los Faroles (Misiones de los Tapes 101, tel. 052/25399) has one of the Barrio Histórico's more diverse menus, but prices are moderate.

Viejo Barrio (Vasconcellos 169, tel. 052/25399) may not have Colonia's best food, but it's decent enough, the portions are large, and the service easily the most attentive, entertaining, and extroverted in town. Pastas and seafood in the US$3–6 range are the best options.

El Mesón del Carmen (San José 170, tel. 052/23090) serves a US$5 lunch or dinner menu, but also serves à la carte dishes ranging from fish and shellfish to pastas, in garden surroundings. Most entrées are in the US$6–10 range but some specialties are costlier.

La Bodeguita (Del Comercio 167, tel. 052/25329, www.labodeguita.net) has excellent beef dishes (around US$6) with varied sauces and a fine wine list, but it is most popular for its pizza. Its split-level wooden deck is a great place to watch the sunset and, after the sun goes down, the lights of Buenos Aires in the distance.

Mesón de la Plaza (Vasconcellos 153, tel. 052/24807) may be Colonia's most ambitious restaurant, with an adventurous menu that sometimes includes sturgeon, which is now being farmed in northwestern Uruguay (caviar production is also beginning). The garden has a covered patio where it's possible to dine al fresco even when it rains.

Heladería Frappé (General Flores and 8 de Octubre) has Colonia's best ice cream.

ENTERTAINMENT

In a creatively readapted colonial building, Colonia Rock (Misiones de los Tapes 157, tel. 052/28189) serves mixed drinks and bar food. There is sidewalk seating and an interior patio, and there's live music Saturday nights.

The immensely popular, idiosyncratic El Drugstore (Vasconcellos 179, tel. 052/25241) has expanded its space, diversified its food menu, and also has live music some nights. One of its prime attractions is a parked *cachila* with the front seat removed to allow for a comfy cushion seat and a table for candlelight dining.

SHOPPING

The artisans' cooperative Manos del Uruguay (Del Comercio 158, tel. 052/28286) has a Barrio Histórico outlet in the Paseo del Sol complex. Colonia's permanent Feria Artesanal (Crafts Fair, Suárez and Fosalba, two blocks north of Plaza 25 de Agosto) is open 9:30 A.M.–7:30 P.M. daily.

ACCOMMODATIONS

Colonia's accommodations, always pretty good, have improved—even modest places have a/c and cable TV. Nothing that appears in the listings below is even close to marginal, but some are better than others.

Colonia's El Drugstore is popular day and night for its food and entertainment.

Less than US$10

In a eucalyptus grove at the Real de San Carlos, five kilometers north of town, the **Camping Municipal de Colonia** (tel. 052/24444, US$2.50 pp) can get crowded and noisy in summer. Easily reached by public transportation, it also rents *cabañas* with private bath (US$6 pp).

US$10–25

Hotel Colonial (General Flores 440, tel. 052/30347, hostelling_colonial@hotmail.com, US$6 pp with breakfast) is the local Hostelling International affiliate.

Hotel Español (Manoel Lobo 377, tel. 052/30759, elespaniol@adinet.com.uy, US$6–8 pp) has also reincarnated itself as a hostel; the higher prices correspond to rooms with private bath. Breakfast costs US$1.50 extra.

Some rooms at **Hotel Rivera** (Rivera 131, tel. 052/20807, www.hotelescolonia.com/rivera, US$15/23 s/d with breakfast) are small and slightly dark, but they're also perfectly maintained and it's exceptionally quiet. Rooms with a/c, rather than fans, are slightly more expensive.

Rates at **Posada del Río** (Washington Barbot 258, tel. 052/23002, www.colonianet.com/delrio, US$15/23 s/d) include start-of-the-art a/c, attractive patios, and an ample breakfast served on the terrace, but it's fallen behind some more recent options. Service remains good and friendly, however.

US$25–50

Fittingly enough, all the cheerful, spacious rooms take their names from flowers at **Posada de la Flor** (Ituzaingó 268, tel. 052/30794, posada_delaflor@yahoo.com.ar, US$20/30 s/d). Some but not all rooms have a/c.

In the heart of the historic district, **Posada San Gabriel** (Del Comercio 127, tel. 052/23283, psangabriel@adinet.com.uy, US$22–27 s or d) has cheaper rooms at ground level, while the more expensive upstairs rooms have river views. Both, though, have a colonial style remarkable for a place in this price range in this location.

Posada de la Ciudadela (Washington Barbot 164, tel. 052/22683, US$15 pp) is a small, family-run hotel long popular with budget-conscious visitors.

Hotel Perla del Plata (Washington Barbot 121, tel. 052/25848, www.colonianet.com/perladelplata, US$25/35 s/d) has immaculate but styleless midsize rooms and a patio that's blindingly sunny at midday. It's no desperation choice, though.

Likewise, compared with other Colonia hotels, **Hotel Leoncia** (Rivera 214, tel. 052/22369, www.hotelleoncia.com, US$28/38 s/d) may lack personality, but the rates are fair enough. It does have an indoor pool with, uniquely, a retractable roof.

It has plenty of competition, but the beautifully furnished rooms at **Posada del Ángel** (Washington Barbot 59, tel. 052/24602, www.posadadelangel.net, US$40–50 s or d) offer some of the finest style for money in town, with (almost literally) heavenly murals in a luminous building. Though it lies outside the historic district, it's still quiet enough and has a gym and also a pool, alongside an ancient fig tree. The costlier rooms, some with river views, are upstairs, more spacious, and even brighter.

In a mid-19th-century building, **Posada del Virrey** (España 217, tel. 052/22223, www.posadadelvirrey.com.uy, US$50 d) is one of many good, stylish Barrio Histórico hotels; note the elaborately carved Czechoslovakian doors. The staff can handle English and German; some more expensive rooms come with Jacuzzis.

Substantially upgraded **Hotel Esperanza** (Avenida General Flores 237, tel. 052/22922, www.hotelesperanzaspa.com, US$50 d) now includes a pool, spa, and gym, but it's not quite so stylish as most hotels in the historic district.

US$50–100

Just down the block from the more conspicuous Posada del Gobernador, **Posada Casa de los Naranjos** (18 de Julio 219, tel. 052/24630, www.colonianet.com/naranjos, US$25/45 s/d–US$60 d) is a handsome colonial house with friendly ownership, a large lush garden and a pool, but has some minor drawbacks: Two street-side rooms

Hostal del Sol is typical of accommodations in Colonia's Barrio Histórico.

lack a/c because building codes prohibit altering its historic facade, and a couple others are slightly dark because their windows face an interior passageway.

One of Colonia's old reliables, **Hotel Beltrán** (General Flores 311, tel. 52/22955, www.colonianet.com/hbeltran, US$60 d) has pleasing rooms around a central courtyard.

Posada Manuel de Lobo (Ituzaingó 160, tel. 052/22463, www.colonianet.com/posadamdelobo, US$35/45 s/d–US$65 d) has eight contemporary rooms and beautifully landscaped patios in an ideal location. The largest suite has an in-room whirlpool tub.

Cozy is no euphemism at the two-story **Hotel La Misión** (Misión de los Tapes 171, tel. 052/26767, tel. 011/4372-0892 in Buenos Aires, www.lamisionhotel.com, US$55 d), whose 12 rooms surround a lushly landscaped central patio. Embodying the best in Colonia style, the common areas are no less engaging.

The classic facade at **Posada Don Antonio** (Ituzaingó 232, tel. 052/25344, www.colonianet.com/donantonio, US$50–60 d) conceals a mostly modern but still appealing hotel with a large pool and landscaping that's helping to soften its once-rough edges. The cheaper rooms have fans but lack a/c.

Reopened under new ownership, the Barrio Histórico's traditional luxury choice **La Posada del Gobernador** (18 de Julio 205, tel. 052/22918, posadadelgobernador@adinet.com.uy, US$55/60 s/d) still fills rapidly, but its style is less colonial than its grounds. For an extra US$10–15, guests can postpone checkout until 6 P.M., when catching the boat back to Buenos Aires.

Near the Bastión de San Miguel, **Hostal del Sol** (Solís 31, tel. 052/23179, cell 15/4415-2605 in Buenos Aires, US$60 d) is a lovingly restored and lavishly furnished 19th-century house with high ceilings, in the quietest part of the Barrio Histórico.

Posada Plaza Mayor (Del Comercio 111, tel. 52/23193, www.hotelplazamayor.com, US$65 d) is a spectacularly restored mansion with shady patios, lush gardens, and 15 rooms with modern conveniences, including a/c and private baths with Jacuzzis. Still, the rooms retain colonial style—some beds nestle in arched alcoves—and furnishings. The upper dining room has excellent river views.

On a sycamore-shaded block, **Hotel Italiano** (Intendente Suárez 103, tel. 052/27878, hitaliano@adinet.com.uy, US$40–70 d) has undergone a dramatic expansion and modernization with every detail virtually perfect, including luminous and attractive common areas, a large outdoor pool, and a smaller indoor one; the facade, though, still fits into Colonia's historical style. The lower prices correspond to smaller but very decent rooms, but only a little more money brings more space and better amenities; the most expensive suites have whirlpools.

More than US$100

Currently expanding to include a casino and a cinema, the **Hotel Plaza Sacramento** (Washington Barbot 283, tel. 52/30460, www.plazasacramento.com, US$95–125 s or d) may be stretching the limits for construction in the Barrio Histórico. What's there now is tasteful, but its expansion bears critical examination.

INFORMATION

The municipal **Dirección de Turismo** (General Flores 499, tel. 052/23700, www.colonia.gub.uy, open 8 A.M.–7 P.M. or a little later daily) is well-stocked with brochures and usually has an English speaker in summer at least; there's a branch on the Plazoleta 1811, near the Puerta de Campo, tel. 052/28506.

Adjacent to the main tourist office, Colonia's private **Cámara Hotelera** (tel. 052/27302, open 9 A.M.–5 P.M. daily, and sometimes a bit later) provides information on accommodations.

There is a ferry port branch of the national **Ministerio de Turismo** (tel. 052/24897, open 9 A.M.–3 P.M. daily).

SERVICES

Consulate

Argentina's consulate (General Flores 209,

tel. 052/22093) is open noon–5 P.M. weekdays only.

Immigration

For visa matters, visit Migraciones (18 de Julio 365, tel. 052/22126).

Laundry

Lavadero Reván (General Flores 90) can do the washing.

Medical

Hospital Colonia is at 18 de Julio 462, tel. 052/22579.

Money

Visitors coming for the day needn't bother to change money, as Argentine pesos and U.S. dollars are both widely accepted (euros are a novelty, so don't count on their being accepted). Avoid changing money at the ferry port proper, where rates are significantly lower than at downtown's **Cambio Colonia** (General Flores 401) or **Cambio Dromer** (General Flores 350). **Banco Comercial** (General Flores 356) has an ATM.

Postal Services

El Correo is at Lavalleja 226.

Telephone and Internet

Antel (Rivadavia 420) has long-distance telephone service and Internet access. **Colonianet** (General Flores 240) has Internet access as well.

TRANSPORTATION

Boat

Buquebus (Ituzaingó 205, tel. 052/22975 or 011/4316-6500, www.buquebus.com) can sell tickets for its own fast catamarans (US$37, one hour to Buenos Aires) and slower, cheaper ferries (US$17–23, about 2.5 hours), as well as services by Ferrylíneas.

Catamarans and ferries leave from the Puerto de Colonia, the ferry port at the foot of Avenida Roosevelt, where Buquebus has a separate ticket office (tel. 052/23030).

Bus

Colonia's **Terminal de Buses** (fronting on Avenida Roosevelt, also bounded by Vicente García and Manoel de Lobo, tel. 52/30288) occupies a triangular site. **Turil** (tel. 052/25246) and **COT** (tel. 052/23121) go frequently to Montevideo (US$6, two hours), while Berrutti goes to Carmelo (US$2.25, 1.5 hours) six times each weekdays, five times Saturday and thrice Sunday.

Rental Cars, Motorbikes, and Bicycles

Thrifty (General Flores 172, tel. 052/22939) rents bicycles, motor scooters, golf carts, and automobiles at reasonable prices. **Multicar** (Manoel Lobo 505, tel. 052/24893) also rents cars, while **Moto Rent** (Virrey Cevallos near Avenida General Flores) has scooters and golf carts.

Carmelo

Rediscovered by Argentine tourists in the years before the 2001–2002 crash, the town of Carmelo (population 24,000) is a secluded river port where the Río Uruguay and the Río Paraná Guazú unite to form the Río de la Plata. It's not fair to compare it with historic Colonia, but Carmelo does exude a certain century-old calm and charm, and visitor services are improving.

Yachting and water sports are the main activities; getting there used to be half the fun, but Cacciola's fast, new catamarans from Tigre now use broader river channels rather than the smaller (but less comfortable) launches that used to weave through the lush gallery forests of the Paraná delta islands en route to the Uruguayan side.

Founded in 1758 on a swampy site near the ominously named Arroyo de las Víboras (Arroyo of Vipers), Carmelo moved to the more promising Arroyo de las Vacas (Arroyo of Cattle) in 1816, after petitioning independence hero José Gervasio Artigas.

ORIENTATION

In the department of Colonia, Carmelo is 75 kilometers northwest of Colonia del Sacramento via paved Ruta 21, and 235 kilometers from Montevideo via Ruta 1, Ruta 22 (which bypasses Colonia), and Ruta 21. Its recreational focus is the area around the arroyo, but most services line both sides of Calle 19 de Abril, to the north.

SIGHTS

Running along the north bank of the arroyo, the **Rambla de los Constituyentes** is the starting point for riverside excursions. The human-powered **Puente Giratorio** (Revolving Bridge, 1912), the first of its kind in the country, crosses the arroyo to the **Yacht Club Carmelo.**

In the town proper, dating from 1860, the **Casa de Ignacio Barrios** (19 de Abril 246) was the residence of a major Uruguayan independence figure and is now the **Casa de la Cultura,** also housing the city's tourist office.

the riverfront esplanade at Carmelo, Uruguay

© WAYNE BERNHARDSON

© WAYNE BERNHARDSON

The restaurant at Carmelo's Finca y Granja Narbona is also a wine tasting room.

Four blocks west, facing the placid Plaza Artigas, the **Templo Histórico del Carmen** (Barrios and J.P. Varela) dates from 1830; it's the focus of July 16's Festival de la Virgen del Carmen, honoring Carmelo's patron saint. The adjacent **Archivo y Museo Parroquial** (open 10 A.M.–noon and 6–8 P.M. weekdays, free), originally built in 1848 as a school, focuses on local and ecclesiastical history, with artifacts from the original settlement on the Arroyo de las Víboras, and an antique selection of carved religious statuary. It also has a gallery of paintings by local talent Gregorio Gil Martín and a small crafts shop that's mostly but not exclusively kitsch.

La Estancia de Narbona

Near Carmelo's original site on the Arroyo de las Víboras (Km 263 of Ruta 21 toward Nueva Palmira, open to the public 9 A.M.–5 P.M. Tues.–Fri.), this crumbling 18th-century *estancia* sits atop a prominent hillock just north of the highway. Uruguay still has many *estancias,* but few can match the antiquity of Narbona's *casco* (main house), chapel, and *campana* (bell tower), but it needs urgent attention to arrest the decay.

 Finca y Granja Narbona

Carmelo has its own little Ruta del Vino, and Finca y Granja Narbona, about 13 kilometers north of town, may be the gem of the bunch. Eduardo Cantón, its Argentine owner, has preserved all the venerable vineyard buildings and recycled them into a stylish restaurant that also serves as a tasting room, as well as an upmarket bed-and-breakfast above the bodegas themselves. As if that weren't enough, there's a remarkable collection of antique wine-making equipment and an equally remarkable assortment of *cachilas,* the antique automobiles that are slowly disappearing from Uruguayan highways.

Finca y Granja Narbona (Ruta 21 Km 267, tel. 0542/9041, www.fincaygranjanarbona.com, US$150 d) is about 13 kilometers north of Carmelo. Restaurant meals cost about US$20 pp; it also sells its own wine, primarily the red Tannat and white Viognier, as well as eight-kilogram rounds of its homemade Parmesan cheese.

Four Seasons Resort Carmelo

Eight kilometers north of town, attracting an international clientele for whom it's a destination in its own right rather than just a place to sleep, the luxury **Four Seasons Resort Carmelo** (Ruta 21, Km 262, tel. 0542/9000 in Carmelo, tel. 011/4321-1710 in Buenos Aires, www .fourseasons.com/carmelo, US$360–390 s or d) has made *Travel & Leisure*'s list of the world's 50 most romantic hotels, thanks to its dispersed rooms and elegant use of Asian décor.

On a former pine and eucaluptus plantation that includes a huge outdoor pool and its own riverside beach, its 44 rooms are equally divided between split-level apartments and sprawling bungalows. All feature handsomely crafted teakwood furniture, fireplaces, and considerable privacy and quiet. It has a spectacular spa, a somewhat smaller indoor pool, and arranges excursions, including horseback rides and winery visits for guests. Across the highway, golfers may play at the 18-hole course, and there are also bicycles and tennis courts.

The Four Seasons also flies in its own guests from Buenos Aires's Aeroparque, often as part of a package with its sister hotel in Retiro; few visitors come for fewer than two or three days. Its main drawback is that, because it's so self-contained, guests here have little contact with ordinary Uruguayans other than the English-speaking hotel staff, who are not necessarily typical.

FOOD

In town proper, there's nothing much more than the standard *chivito*, but try **Perrini** (19 de Abril 440, tel. 0542/2519) or **El Refugio** (Playa Seré, tel. 0542/2325), south of the bridge. The best around is probably the Four Seasons Resort Carmelo's all-day restaurant **Pura** (Ruta 21, Km 262, tel. 0542/9000), which does a fine job with the seared freshwater *boga,* accompanied by grilled vegetables and pumpkin puree, or its night-time-only Italian restaurant **Mandara.** On the grounds of its namesake winery, **Finca Narbona** (Ruta 21 Km 267, tel. 0542/9041) comes close in quality and is far more authentically Uruguayan in style (though its owner is an Argentine). Both are substantially better, and more expensive, than anything in town.

ENTERTAINMENT

For most Carmelitanos, entertainment is billiards or video games, but the town's **Cine Teatro Uamá** (Uruguay 220, tel. 0542/4830) is a 500-seat Deco landmark that shows recent movies and occasionally hosts live theater.

ACCOMMODATIONS

In recent years, new hotels have opened and others have modernized; rates have risen in pesos, but devaluation has kept them competitive in dollar terms.

Two campgrounds charge around US$2.50 pp: **Camping Don Mauro** (Ignacio Barros and Arroyo de las Vacas, tel. 0542/2390) and **Camping Náutico Carmelo** (Embarcadero s/n, tel. 0542/2058).

Hotel Bertoletti (Uruguay 171, tel. 0542/2030, US$7/13 s/d) lacks personality but is otherwise acceptable. Near the docks, **Hotel Rambla** (Uruguay 55, tel. 0542/2390, bomba@adinet.com.uy, US$7–12 pp) lacks a/c but is otherwise a good value with breakfast included; the cheaper rooms correspond to upper floors, as there's no elevator.

Hotel Centro (Uruguay 370, tel. 0542/4488, US$12 pp) is tidy enough, but several of the rooms are dark, their small windows facing an already shady corridor. Directly above it, though, **Hospedaje Renée y Alcides** (Uruguay 368, tel. 0542/2028, US$12) is a family-run bed-and-breakfast-style place that's an outstanding value.

Behind the well-preserved Italianate facade of **Hotel Timabe** (19 de Abril and Solís, tel. 0542/4525, timabe@adinet.com.uy, US$20/32 s/d), there stands a modern, comfortable hotel with luminous midsized rooms that's probably the best choice in town proper. On the downside, the shower-only bathrooms are tiny. Across the Arroyo de las Vacas, **Hotel Casino Carmelo** (Rodó s/n, US$30/45 s/d) has bed-and-breakfast accommodations but also packages with half board (US$70 d) or full board (US$100 d).

INFORMATION

The municipal **Oficina de Turismo** (19 de Abril 246, tel. 0542/2001, turiscar@adinet.com.uy), in the Casa de la Cultura, the town cultural center, keeps erratic hours but is presumably open at least 8 A.M.–2 P.M. daily. Across the street and down the block, there's a more reliable private office (19 de Abril 213, tel. 0542/5389).

SERVICES

Directly on the central Plaza Independencia, **Banco Comercial** (Uruguay 401) has an ATM.

For long distance, **Antel** is on Ingeniero Barrios just west of Uruguay. **Ciber Computer** (Uruguay 372) offers Internet access.

Hospital Artigas (Uruguay and Artigas, tel. 0542/2107) can handle medical problems.

TRANSPORTATION

The Four Seasons Resort flies its guests to and from Buenos Aires via the airstrip at nearby Balneario Zagargazú. For others, though, bus and boat are the primary options.

Berrutti (Uruguay 337, tel. 0542/2504) has six buses each weekday to Colonia (US$2.25, 1.5 hours), beginning in Nueva Palmira, and is the only company on this route; there are only five Saturday and three Sunday buses. Several Montevideo (US$7, three hours) carriers share offices on 18 de Julio between Uruguay and 19 Abril (tel. 0542/2987): Sabelín/Klüver, Chadre, and Intertur.

On the waterfront, **Cacciola** (tel. 0542/3042) crosses to Tigre (US$11, 2.5 hours) at 4 A.M. and 2:30 P.M. daily except Saturday, when the afternoon departure is at 5 P.M., and Sunday, when the only departure is at 5:30 P.M.

Budget (19 de Abril 241, tel. 0542/7073) provides rental cars.

Punta del Este and Maldonado

High-rise hotels soar behind sandy Atlantic beaches and elegant vessels crowd the sprawling yacht harbor at Uruguay's Punta del Este, one of South America's flashiest summer getaways—ironically enough, a place where a colonial Jesuit priest remarked that "you see nothing here but a few cabins, the abodes of misery." In January and February, the southern summer, Punta irrupts with flamboyant Argentine celebrities who make the covers and gossip columns of glossy Buenos Aires magazines. In 1832, though, Charles Darwin spent 10 solitary weeks searching for natural-history specimens at a "quiet, forlorn town" that is now the jewel of the "Uruguayan Riviera."

It was in the late 1970s, as money from the corrupt Argentine military dictatorship flowed in, that Punta del Este began to grow up—literally so, as high-rise hotels and flats replaced single-family homes. On the peninsula, only the southernmost sector of El Faro, whose landmark lighthouse limits other buildings to three stories, has been spared.

Truth be told, there's not that much to see in Punta del Este itself, but the compact peninsula that juts into the ocean is the place where wealthy Argentines come to play and be seen in a frenetic summer season—except when the Argentine currency collapses. Avenida Gorlero is the axis of Punta's hyperactive nightlife, but the beaches along Rambla Artigas, which rings the peninsula, are the focus of sunny summer days. Under different names, the *rambla* connects the peninsula to the riverside beaches to the west and to the ocean beaches to the east.

Maldonado, by contrast, is a business

In otherwise hyperactive Punta del Este, the El Faro (lighthouse) neighborhood is a beacon of calm.

© WAYNE BERNHARDSON

and administrative center that's been largely eclipsed by Punta's rapid growth and glitter, but still retains vestiges of its colonial origins. Founded in 1755, the fortified city fell briefly under British control during the invasion of Buenos Aires in 1806.

Darwin may have disparaged Maldonado as a place whose few residents were mostly land-owners and merchants "who do all the business for nearly 50 miles around," but modern Maldonado is far better than that. In recent years, however, quite a few businesses have closed, and the city's economy is moribund compared with Punta's.

ORIENTATION

Punta del Este and Maldonado are about 130 kilometers east of Montevideo via Ruta I—a four-lane toll road—and Ruta 93.

Punta del Este proper occupies a compact peninsula that juts south into the Atlantic, separating the rugged surf of the Playa Brava (Wild Beach) to the east from the calmer Playa Mansa to the west. This is the point that divides the Atlantic Ocean from the Río de la Plata; in practice, Punta del Este is a much larger area that includes the departmental capital of Maldonado and a multitude of residential suburbs.

The peninsula itself divides into two separate grids: To the north, on both sides of Avenida Juan Gorlero and side streets, is the high-rise hotel area with its restaurants and shopping; to the south, named for its lighthouse, the El Faro neighborhood is quieter, more residential, less pretentious, and more economical.

Punta del Este streets are commonly known by their numbers, though they also have names. Addresses below include both except in the case of Avenida Juan Gorlero, known consistently as Gorlero.

Punta del Este and Maldonado have gradually grown together, but Maldonado's center is a regular colonial rectangular grid centered on Plaza San Fernando. Outside the city center, thoroughfares like Avenida Roosevelt and Bulevar Artigas connect the streets of irregular

suburban neighborhoods. The Rambla Claudio Williman follows the riverside beaches to the west, while the Rambla Lorenzo Batlle Pacheco tracks along the ocean beaches. Buses along each *rambla* pick up and drop off passengers at numbered stops, known as *paradas*.

SIGHTS

Punta del Este is the place to go and to people-watch, but Maldonado has more historic sites. The *rambla* around the peninsula is a wide, pedestrian-friendly circuit that encourages walkers (Uruguayan drivers, by the way, respect pedestrians more than their Argentine counterparts, but there are plenty of Argentines here, so caution still applies).

Maldonado

Remodeled in 1975 and planted with dawn redwoods, Maldonado's **Plaza San Fernando** features a statue of independence hero José Gervasio Artigas, a fountain, and an amphitheater for musical events.

On the west side of the plaza, the neoclassical **Catedral San Fernando de Maldonado** (1895) took nearly a century to complete; Antonio Veiga sculpted its altar, while the image of the Virgen de Santander came from the steamer *Ciudad del Santander,* which sank near Isla de Lobos in 1829.

At the plaza's southwest corner, the Spaniard Bartolomé Howel designed the **Cuartel de Dragones y de Blandengues,** masonry military barracks with impressive iron gates, whose grounds fill an entire block bounded by 25 de Mayo, 18 de Julio, Pérez del Puerto, and Dodera. Built between 1771 and 1797, it includes the **Museo Didáctico Artiguista** (tel. 042/225378, open 1–7 P.M. daily), dedicated to Uruguay's independence hero. In addition, it holds the fine arts **Museo Nicolás García Uriburu** (open 7 A.M.–11 P.M. daily except Mon., free).

Two blocks east, the **Museo San Fernando de Maldonado** (Sarandí and Pérez del Puerto, tel. 042/231786, open 1–7 P.M. daily except Mon., free) served as the colonial customs

© WAYNE BERNHARDSON

Chilean sculptor Mario Irarrázabal, who created Punta del Este's *Mano en la Playa (Hand on the Beach),* has similar works in Antofagasta and Puerto Natales, Chile.

house and prison; it now houses a fine arts facility with rotating exhibitions, and a permanent collection of puppets from Uruguay and around the world.

Two blocks west of the Cuartel de Dragones y de Blandengues, the **Plaza Torre del Vigía** (1800) surrounds a colonial tower built high enough to allow sentries to sight passing boats on the river.

A block north of Plaza San Fernando, better organized than in the past, the eclectic **Museo Regional R. Francisco Mazzoni** (Ituzaingó 789, tel. 042/221107, open 1–6 P.M. daily except Mon., free) occupies an 18th-century house filled with colonial-style furnishings and natural-history items. It has also added a modern art gallery in a rehabbed outbuilding.

Punta del Este

Avenida Juan Gorlero is Punta del Este's throbbing heart, open for business all night in summer and on weekends, but at other times it can seem positively sedate. Lively **Plaza Artigas,** fronting on Gorlero between Arrecifes (25) and El Corral (23) is the site of a perennial crafts fair, the **Feria de los Artesanos** (open 6 P.M.–1 A.M. daily in sum-

mer, 11 A.M.–5 P.M. weekends only the rest of the year).

It's almost always sedate near the **Faro de Punta del Este** (1860), a 43-meter lighthouse built by Tomás Libarena with a crystal prism brought from France. A spiral staircase of 150 steps, not open to the public, leads to the top.

On the Playa Mansa side of the peninsula, the sheltered **Puerto Nuestra Señora de la Candelaria** has 400 slips for visiting yachts, but it's also a good place for wildlife watching. Southern sea lions often haul up in the vicinity, and the shorebirds include grebes, gulls, sandpipers, terns, and other species.

On the Atlantic side, **Playa El Emir** is Punta's most popular surfing beach; to the north, note the *Mano en la Playa (Hand on the Beach)* by Chilean sculptor Mario Irarrázabal, who built a similar but much larger piece in the Atacama Desert.

Calmer riverside beaches stretch west along the Rambla Williman toward and beyond Punta Ballena. To the east, the Rambla Lorenzo Batlle Pacheco passes a series of beaches facing the open Atlantic. All of these have *paradores,* simple restaurants with beach service.

In the summer high season, Punta del Este is a magnet for yachts from around the the world.

© WAYNE BERNHARDSON

For those who can't make it to artist Carlos Páez Vilaró's Casapueblo, at Punta Ballena, there's a representative sample of his work at his **Galería Atelier Casapueblo** (Solís 720, tel. 042/446594, www.carlospaezvilaro .com), in the basement of Hotel Palace.

ENTERTAINMENT

Punta del Este has a good selection of cinemas, including the three-screen **Cine Casino** (Gorlero and Inzaurraga (31), tel. 042/441908); the **Cine Fragata** (Gorlero 798, tel. 042/440002); the Galería Atlántica's **Cine Gorlero,** (Gorlero and Los Muergos (27), tel. 042/444437); the the Galería Libertador's **Cine Libertador** (Gorlero and Los Arrecifes (25), tel. 042/444437); and the five-screen **Cines Lido** (El Remanso (20) and Inzaurraga (31), tel. 042/440911).

Bars

Near the yacht harbor, **Moby Dick** (on Rambla Artigas between Virazón (12) and 2 de Febrero (10)) is open in summer only.

SHOPPING

Manos del Uruguay has a leather shop on Gorlero (22) between Inzaurraga (31) and Las Focas (30) in Punta del Este. Uruguayan artists display their work at **La Ciudadela,** at the corner of Mareantes (13) and Virazón (12).

RESTAURANTS

Punta del Este has a larger and more fashionable selection of restaurants than Maldonado, but Maldonado does have some excellent values.

Maldonado

Al Paso (18 de Julio 888, tel. 042/222881) is a well-established, reliable *parrilla,* with most entrées in the US$3.50–5 range except for fish dishes, which are slightly more expensive. **Pizzería El Oasis** (Sarandí 1105, tel. 042/234794) is also popular for its *parrillada.*

Try **El Grillo** (Ituzaingó and Sarandí) for *chivitos* (steak sandwiches) and other short orders. The **Círculo Policial de Maldonado**

(Pérez del Puerto 780, tel. 042/225311) has inexpensive lunch and dinner specials.

Open weekends only, the relatively expensive **Mesón del Centro Español** (18 de Julio 708, tel. 042/224107) specializes in Spanish seafood.

Punta del Este

Sumo (Gorlero between El Corral (23) and La Galerna (21), tel. 042/446729) has Punta's finest cheap *chivitos*, as well as pizzas and other short orders. **La Pasiva** (Gorlero and Los Meros (28), tel. 042/441843) is an inexpensive pizzeria.

El Pobre Marino (Solís (11) and Virazón (12), tel. 042/443306) is a relatively inexpensive seafood restaurant. Other seafood choices include the Basque-style **Gure Etxe** (Virazón (12) and La Salina (9), tel. 042/446858) and the pricier **El Viejo Marino** (Solís (11) and El Foque (14), tel. 042/443565, www.elviejomarino.com).

It would take a long time to work your way through the extensive Italian menu at **Il Barretto** (La Salina (9) between El Trinquete (8) and 2 de Febrero (10), tel. 042/447243, www .ilbarreto.com.uy), where everything is casual except for quality dishes like swordfish steak (US$8), seafood risotto (US$13), and a lemon mousse so light that a breeze might blow it away. Packed at night, less so for lunch, it recreates the color scheme of an Italian villa, with brightly painted tables and rustically styled wooden chairs. It also has a large wine list and, for the budget-conscious, a US$9 lunch special (cash only) that includes either a starter or dessert, a main dish (either *pizzeta* or grilled catch of the day), and drink.

Blue Cheese (Rambla Artigas and El Corral (23), tel. 042/440354) is a well-established French restaurant. **Bungalow Suizo** (Rambla Batlle Pacheco at Parada 8, near Avenida Roosevelt, tel. 042/482358) is a local favorite specializing in fondue at mid-range prices.

Between the peninsula and Maldonado, **La Bourgogne** (Pedragosa Sierra and Avenida del Mar, tel. 042/482007) is a highly regarded (and expensive) French restaurant that flavors its entrées with herbs from its own gardens (the herbs themselves are also for sale here).

Lo de Tere (Rambla Artigas and La Galerna (21), tel. 042/440492, www.lodetere.com) is one of Punta's top international/Italian restaurants, famous for its *taglierini neri* (black pasta) with seafood. Entrées are expensive, in the US$8–10 and up range. So are the desserts, but don't miss the *maracuyá* (passion fruit) parfait. The budget-conscious should note that the first four parties that arrive for lunch before 1 P.M. or for dinner before 9 P.M. get a 40 percent discount; all others before those hours get a 20 percent discount. There is a good tobacco-free area and outdoor seating for sunny days and warm evenings.

Its chairs and tables painted in a riot of primary colors, with walls by Carlos Páez Vilaró, **La Tuttie** (La Salina (9) and El Trinquete (8), tel. 042/447236) serves a wide variety of seafood, such as *corvina negra* and swordfish, in the US$6–8 range for entrées, with a 5 percent discount for cash. There's wine by the glass, but the desserts are not so good as the fish dishes.

Hacienda Las Palomas (El Trinquete (8) between La Salina (9) and Díaz de Solís (11), tel. 042/449410, www.haciendalaspalomas .com) serves passable Mexican food (around US$6 for *antojitos*, US$8 for fajitas) and margaritas to the sound of recorded mariachis. Service is erratic.

The best ice creamery is **Arlecchino** (Gorlero between La Galerna (21) and Comodoro Gorlero (19).

ACCOMMODATIONS

Accommodations are far fewer but generally cheaper in Maldonado than in Punta del Este proper; unless otherwise indicated, the lodgings below are in Punta. Rates are highly seasonal; January and February are the peak months, and at that time it's hard to find singles—expect to pay for a double even if you're traveling solo. February prices often drop a bit from January; the rest of the year, and especially when times are hard, rates are negotiable.

The private **Centro de Hoteles y Restoranes** (Plaza Artigas s/n, tel. 042/440512, www.puntadelestehoteles.com, open 10 A.M.– 8 P.M. all year) is the best single information source for accommodations and very helpful to those in desperate need of a bed.

Under US$25

Maldonado's best value is the no-frills **Hotel Isla de Gorriti** (Zelmar Michelini 884, tel. 042/225223, US$10 pp with shared bath).

Hostelling International's former facility has closed, but hostellers have a new and better alternative in **1949 Hostel** (Calle 30 and Calle 18, tel. 042/440719, www.1949hostel .com, US$15 pp), which has shared dorm rooms with private baths, private lockers, breakfast, and a bar with a sort of beach view. It's only a short walk from the Punta bus terminal.

US$25–50

On the north side of Maldonado's Plaza San Fernando, **Hotel Le Petit** (Florida and Sarandí, tel. 042/223044) charges US$27 d in summer, slightly less the rest of the year.

Also on the plaza, the nearby **Hotel Colonial** (18 de Julio 841, tel. 042/223346, hotelcolonial@adinet.com.uy, US$20/32 s/d) has rooms with private bath and TV, and a separate bar with Internet service; off-season rates fall to US$12/20 s/d.

Maldonado's **Hotel Catedral** (Florida 823, tel. 042/242513, hotel_catedral@yahoo.com, US$42 d) has rooms with private bath, plain furnishings, heat, and ceiling fans, but no a/c.

US$50–100

Hotel Marbella (Inzaurraga (31) No. 615, tel. 042/441814, US$39/55 s/d) is a respectable middle-class hotel with reasonable comforts except for the breakfast room, which can be uncomfortably crowded even when the hotel isn't all that full. Rates fall to only US$15 pp off-season.

In the middle of all the action, **Hotel Península** (Avenida Gorlero 761, tel. 042/441533, hotpenin@adinet.com.uy, US$44/62 s/d) has quieter, terraced interior rooms that face the pool rather than the street.

Near the lighthouse, the **Petit Hotel** (La Salina (9) No. 717, tel. 042/441412,

hotelpetit@multi.com.uy, US$60–90 d) is a minor gem—a small, cheerful, family-run hotel with quiet, attractive gardens and other common areas; the higher rates correspond to garden rooms. It's an outstanding value with continental breakfast, cable TV, and telephone, and discounts for cash, though some may find the color scheme—pistachio and violet exterior, pink and blue interior—not to their taste.

One of the peninsula's oldest hotels, dating from 1911 but unrecognizably modernized in the 1980s, the **Gran Hotel España** (La Salina (9) No. 660, tel. 042/440228, www.granhotel espana.net, US$60/70 s/d) also enjoys a fine location near the lighthouse.

In the same vicinity, rates at the architecturally utilitarian but very friendly **Atlántico Hotel** (Capitán (7) and Dos de Febrero (10), tel. 042/440229, hatlanti@adinet.com .uy, US$70 d) has cable TV, telephone, swimming pool, and a buffet breakfast. Off-season rates fall by half.

As quiet as Punta gets, **Hotel Galicia** (Sotileza 718, tel. 042/444992, hotelgalicia@hotmail. com, US$70 s or d) has small but immaculate rooms directly opposite the lighthouse.

Hotel San Fernando (Las Focas (30) No. 691, between Baupres (18) and El Remanso (20), tel. 042/440720, hotelsanfernando@hotmail. com, US$77 d) is a modern hotel with a rooftop terrace. Each of the 60 rooms has a/c, a strongbox, and other standard conveniences.

Rooms at **Hotel Champagne** (Gorlero 828, tel. 042/445276, www.hotelchampagne.com. uy, US$80 d) are simple but attractively furnished.

At the **Palace Hotel** (Avenida Gorlero and Solís (11), tel. 042/441919, palacepunta@ hotmail.com, US$50/90 s/d), most rooms look onto the palm-studded grounds, which have a substantial pool. Far larger than it appears from its modest entrance, the hotel also has a restaurant and a quiet bar.

Over US$100

On the peninsula, the **Punta del Este Golden Beach Resort & Spa** (El Mesana (24) No.

34, tel. 042/441314, www.golden-beach.com, US$190 s or d) is a luxury spa facility that has some real off-season bargains. The 800-pound gorilla of Punta del Este accommodations is **Hotel Conrad** (Rambla Williman and Avenida Chiverta, tel. 042/491111, www.conrad.com.uy, US$300 s or d), a 302-room megahotel-casino just north of the peninsula.

INFORMATION

Punta del Este and Maldonado each have separate tourist representatives under the municipal **Secretaría de Turismo** (www.maldonado.gub.uy).

Widely available around town, the free weekly *Que Hacemos Hoy* is a guide to what's going on, at least among the self-anointed beautiful people who dominate Punta's social scene.

Maldonado

For most purposes, the municipal **Oficina de Información Turística** (25 de Mayo 761, tel. 042/250490, open 8 A.M.–8 P.M. daily), on the south side of Plaza San Fernando, is the most convenient source of information.

Punta del Este

In the Punta del Este bus terminal, the municipal **Secretaría de Turismo** (tel. 42/494042) is open 10 A.M.–6 P.M. daily, sometimes later in summer. Nearby, the private **Liga de Fomento** (Rambla Williman, Parada 1, tel. 42/446519) keeps similar hours.

At the western approach to town, there's another municipal **Oficina de Informes** (Rambla Williman, Parada 24 (Las Delicias), tel. 042/230050), normally open 8 A.M.–7 P.M. daily, though it often keeps later hours in January and February.

The national **Ministerio de Turismo** (Gorlero 942, tel. 042/441218) is open 10 A.M.–2:30 P.M. and 5:30–10 P.M. daily.

SERVICES

Punta del Este and Maldonado have similar but not identical services.

Consulate

Argentina operates a seasonal consulate on the Península, normally 4–8 P.M. weekdays, from mid-December to mid-March and July to early August. It's a moving target, changing its abode from year to year, but most recently it was at Gorlero and 19 (Comodoro Gorlero), tel. 042/440789.

Immigration

For visa matters, Maldonado's **Dirección Nacional de Migraciones** (Ventura Alegre between Sarandí and Román Guerra, tel. 042/237624) is open 12:30–7 P.M. weekdays.

Laundry

In Punta del Este, **Mr. Lav** (El Mesana (24), between Las Focas (30) and Las Gaviotas (29)) is open 10 A.M.–6 P.M. daily.

In Maldonado, try **Espumas del Virrey** (Zelmar Michelini 1081, tel. 042/220582).

Medical

The **Hospital de Maldonado** (Ventura Alegre s/n, tel. 042/225852) is about eight blocks northwest of Plaza San Fernando.

Money

In Punta del Este, **BankBoston** has an ATM on Gorlero (22) between La Galerna (21) and Comodoro Gorlero (19), but there are several others. In Maldonado, **Banco BBVA** has an ATM on Florida, on the north side of Plaza San Fernando.

Maldonado has several exchange houses in the vicinity of Plaza San Fernando, including **Cambio Porto** (Florida 764) and **Cambio Dominus** (25 de Mayo and 18 de Julio).

Postal Services

There's a Punta del Este post office on Gorlero between Izaurraga (31) and La Angostura (32). In Maldonado, the post office is on Ituzaingó between Sarandí and Román Guerra.

Telephone and Internet

In Punta del Este, **Antel** is at Arrecifes (25) and El Mesana (24). **Spot Internet,** at Gorlero and

Las Focas (30), has good Internet access, but there are many others.

In Maldonado, **Antel** is at the corner of Joaquín de Viana and Florida.

TRANSPORTATION

Punta del Este and Maldonado have air connections with Buenos Aires, land links with Montevideo, and bus-boat combinations as well.

Air

Aeropuerto Internacional Laguna del Sauce (tel. 042/559389) is about 15 kilometers west of Maldonado. There are regular airport shuttles from Punta del Este's bus terminal.

On the ground level of the Edificio Santos Dumont, **Aerolíneas Argentinas** (Gorlero between Inzaurraga (31) and Las Focas (30), tel. 042/444343) shuttles frequently to Buenos Aires's Aeroparque. So does **Pluna/Varig** (Avenida Roosevelt and Parada 9, tel. 042/490101), which serves several Brazilian cities in summer.

American Falcon (Gorlero 910, tel. 042/449381) also links Laguna del Sauce to Aeroparque.

Uair (Edificio Miguens, Inzaurraga (31) and El Remanso (20), tel. 042/449775, www.uair .com) flies to the Argentine cities of Rosario and to Córdoba and Mendoza, and the Brazilian city of Curitiba.

Boat

In the Punta del Este bus terminal, **Buquebus** (Local 9, tel. 042/484995 or 011/4316-6500) makes bus-boat connections to Argentina via, Piriápolis, Montevideo, and Colonia.

Bus

Most services into the area stop over at **Terminal Maldonado** (Avenida Roosevelt s/n, tel. 042/225701) and proceed to **Terminal Punta del Este** (Playa Brava, tel. 042/489467), near the isthmus. **Bus del Atlántico** (tel. 042/489205) has such frequent services to Montevideo that reservations are rarely necessary.

To get around town, **Maldonado Turismo,** in the Galería Mejillón (La Angostura (32) and Gorlero, tel. 042/495504, www.maldonadoturismo.com) links Punta del Este with the easterly suburbs of La Barra and Manantiales. Its buses leave from immediately behind the bus terminal.

Rental Cars

Rental agencies include **Avis** (Inzaurraga (31) between Gorlero and El Mesana (24), tel. 042/442020); **Europcar** (El Mesana (24) and Las Gaviotas (29), tel. 042/495017); **Hertz** (Inzaurraga (31) between Gorlero (22) and El Remanso (20), tel. 042/489778; **Localiza** (Gorlero and La Angostura (32), tel. 042/492685); and **Thrifty** (Gorlero and Los Muergos (27), tel. 042/447462).

Vicinity of Punta del Este and Maldonado

In addition to water sports and sunbathing in the day and partying at night, there are some worthwhile sights in the vicinity of Punta del Este and Maldonado.

ISLA GORRITI

From the yacht harbor, frequent launches (US$4 rt) cross to and from Isla Gorriti, immediately west of the peninsula. In addition to its beaches and *parador* restaurants, Gorriti holds the remains of the **Baterías de Santa Ana,** a colonial Spanish fortress.

ISLA DE LOBOS

About eight kilometers southeast of the Playa Brava, in the open Atlantic but readily visible from the mainland, the otherwise barren 41-hectare Isla de Lobos is home to a breeding colony of about 200,000 southern sea lions *(Otaria byronia).* It was once home to the southern elephant seal *(Mirounga leonina),* but uncontrolled hunting for its blubber eliminated the species here.

Topped by a lighthouse (1906), the rocky

© WAYNE BERNHARDSON

Casapueblo, Punta Ballena, Uruguay

islet has been a tourist draw since 1920, though landings are not permitted. Rising 43 meters above the ocean, the structure boasts South America's most powerful sea-level light, with a range of 22.5 nautical miles.

Isla de Lobos played a grim historic role during the British invasion of 1806, as the British marooned Spanish prisoners here without food or water. Many died attempting to swim to the mainland.

For visits to Isla de Lobos, contact **Calypso Charters y Excursiones** (Rambla Artigas and Calle 21, tel. 042/446152, marina charters@netgate.com.uy). The two-hour excursion, which normally leaves at 11 A.M. daily, costs US$28 pp, half that for kids up to 12 years old.

M CASAPUEBLO

Lacking right angles and so blindingly white that you need sunglasses to approach it, Uruguayan painter Carlos Páez Vilaró's whimsical Mediterranean-style villa, which resembles the rounded mud nest of the *rufous hornero* (ovenbird), is the area's most unusual sight. On a sloping headland at Punta Ballena, 10 kilometers west of Punta del Este, it's a showcase for unconventional art—Páez Vilaró is clearly a Picasso admirer—and Casapueblo has grown over the years to include a hotel, a restaurant, and a bar.

Parts are open to the public for a small charge, others to members only. Hours are 10 A.M.–6 P.M. daily; for those unable to make the excursion, Páez Vilaró now has a downtown gallery on the Península.

Accommodations at **Club Hotel Casapueblo** (tel. 042/579386, www.clubhotel.com.ar) start around US$85/110 s/d, but are lower in the off-season.

LA BARRA DE MALDONADO

Until the 1940s, when the construction of summer houses began apace, La Barra de Maldonado was a modest fishing village. The undulating **Puente Leonel Viera** (1965), a bridge crossing the Arroyo de Maldonado, opened up the area east of Punta del Este to beachside development.

Conspicuous because of the kitschy great white shark at its entrance, just across the bridge in Barrio El Tesoro, Barra's **Museo del Mar** (Los Bucaneros s/n, tel. 042/771817, www.vivapunta.com/museomar, open 10 A.M.–8:30 P.M. daily in summer, 10 A.M.–6 P.M. weekends and holidays only the rest of the year, US$2 for adults, US$1 for children) houses an impressive collection of shells and corals. It also covers historical material on Punta del Este, including photography and information on individuals such as Juan Gorlero, the former Maldonado mayor and tourism promoter for whom Punta's main avenue is named.

The 28-room beachfront **La Posta del Cangrejo** (Km 11.3, tel. 042/770021, www .lapostadelcangrejo.com, US$120/150 s/d–US$300 d) has hosted the rich and powerful since the 1960s, when it housed Kennedy-administration officials for a legendary meeting of the Organization of American States and the Argentine-born Cuban delegate, Ernesto "Che" Guevara tweaked their noses (figuratively speaking, at least). Former U.S. president George H. W. Bush also experienced the Mediterranean elegance of La Posta's suites in 1990. Its restaurant comes highly recommended.

JOSÉ IGNACIO

Beyond La Barra, about 30 kilometers east of Punta del Este, the former fishing village of José Ignacio has become a magnet for those—like plutocrat Argentine cement heiress Amalia de Fortabat—who'd rather not advertise their presence on the Uruguayan Riviera. Fishing boats still sell the day's catch on the beach, and the most conspicuous landmark is the 32.5-meter **Faro José Ignacio** (1877), a lighthouse with a visibility of 16.5 nautical miles and a light visible for nine nautical miles.

Since 1973, the fourth-generation, family-run **Santa Teresita** (Las Calandrinas s/n, tel. 0486/2004) has become famous for its "gourmet home-cooking." Known as the home of the seaweed omelette, it also offers specialty appetizers, such as ceviche with a dozen different dips, and entrées like *pescado a mi manera* (literally, fish my way) in the US$7–10 range, plus desserts like lemon mousse ice cream. It's open for lunch and dinner in summer, lunch only the rest of the year, and has both indoor and outdoor seating.

Repeat patrons swear that Santa Teresita is even better than celebrity restaurateur Francis Mallman's nearby, more highly publicized (and more highly priced) **Los Negros** (Los Teros and Costanera del Faro, tel. 0486/2018), which uses fresh ocean fish and whose dining rooms all have ocean views.

Know
Buenos Aires

The Land

Buenos Aires sits atop the coastal margin of the almost unrelentingly flat, pampas grasslands, whose beef and grain exports made Argentina a wealthy country throughout much of the 19th and 20th centuries. The city has little relief—its highest elevation is only about 25 meters—except along the original *barrancas* (riverbanks), which now lie well inland because of landfill along the Río de la Plata's muddy estuary. The only other significant body of water is the heavily polluted Riachuelo, a tributary that forms part of the city's southern boundary; the densely built city has covered all the smaller arroyos.

The Río de la Plata, misleadingly glossed into English as the River Plate (it literally means the River of Silver), is one of the world's great river systems—in terms of length, width, and flow, it's in a class with the Amazon, Nile, and Mississippi. Originating in the heights of the Bolivian altiplano and draining an area of more than 3.1 million square kilometers, in reality it's an estuary at the confluence of the Río Paraná (length 3,945 km) and the Río Uruguay (length 1,650 km).

Its delta, northwest of Buenos Aires proper, is a series of islands in a maze of muddy channels whose sedimentary surface is largely covered by dense gallery forest. The combined flow of the Paraná and Uruguay carries sediments far out into the south Atlantic Ocean.

GEOGRAPHY

The Ciudad Autónoma de Buenos Aires is a compact, politically autonomous federal district surrounded by contiguous suburbs of Buenos Aires province. It occupies 192 square kilometers on the right bank of the Río de la Plata.

Together with the federal capital, the conurbation of Gran Buenos Aires (Greater Buenos Aires) includes 24 contiguous and surrounding *partidos* (roughly translatable as counties): Almirante Brown, Avellaneda, Berazategui, Estéban Echeverría, Ezeiza, Florencio Varela, General San Martín, Hurlingham, Ituzaingó, José C. Paz, La Matanza, Lanús, Lomas de Zamora, Malvinas Argentinas, Merlo, Moreno, Morón, Quilmes, San Fernando, San Isidro, San Miguel, Tigre, Tres de Febrero, and Vicente López.

CLIMATE

In the southern hemisphere, Buenos Aires's seasons are reversed from those in the northern hemisphere: The summer solstice falls on December 21, the autumnal equinox on March 21, the winter solstice on June 21, and the vernal equinox on September 21. For most Argentines, the de facto summer months are January and February, when schools are out of session and families take their holidays.

Thanks to its mid-latitude setting (34° 37' S) and proximity to the Atlantic Ocean, Buenos Aires's climate is humid and temperate, with annual precipitation of about 1.2 meters distributed evenly throughout the year. It resembles southern parts of the United States's eastern seaboard except in winter, when temperatures remain mild and frosts are rare. Summer can be uncomfortably hot and humid, as temperatures frequently exceed 30°C and thunderstorms are common. *Pamperos* (southwesterly cold fronts) and *sudestadas* (southeasterly cool, high winds) are the most problematical climatic phenomena; snow is unheard of.

Flora and Fauna

As one of the world's largest cities, Buenos Aires has no truly untouched natural habitat, but many birds, fish, and other wildlife survive among the gallery forests, channels, and oxbow lakes of the Río Paraná delta. Many of these plants and animals are opportunistic species that have colonized the former landfill east of Puerto Madero.

Like many other cities, the capital is home to unfortunately large numbers of stray dogs and even larger numbers of feral cats that infest areas like Palermo's Jardín Botánico (botanical garden). Because of its presence, the pigeon sometimes seems to be the only bird species to survive in substantial numbers.

CONSERVATION ORGANIZATIONS

For information on protected areas, a few of which are in the vicinity of Buenos Aires, contact the **Administración de Parques Nacionales** (Avenida Santa Fe 690, Retiro, tel. 011/4314-9325, www.parquesnacionales.gov.ar, 10 A.M.–5 P.M. weekdays only). Although its selection of brochures on national parks and other protected areas is improving, the staff themselves are best informed on the country's most high-profile destinations, such as Parque Nacional Iguazú and Parque Nacional Los Glaciares; on lesser units, they don't know much.

The **Fundación Vida Silvestre Argentina** (Defensa 251, Monserrat, tel. 011/4331-4864, www.vidasilvestre.org.ar) is a pro-wildlife and habitat advocacy organization. Membership rates, including the newsletter *Otioso,* start around US$16 per annum; higher-priced memberships include the foundation's magazine, *Revista Vida Silvestre.*

Bird-watchers can get information from the **Asociación Ornitológica del Plata** (25 de Mayo 749, 2nd floor, Microcentro, tel. 011/4312-1015, www.avesargentinas.org.ar); its library is open to the public 3–9 P.M. Wednesdays and Fridays.

Argentina's branch of **Greenpeace** (Mansilla 3046, Barrio Norte, tel. 011/4962-0404, www.greenpeace.org.ar) is very active and outspoken on local, national, and international environmental issues; actor Ricardo Darín is one of its high-profile members.

FLORA

The main trees of the Paraná delta gallery forest are medium-size species, such as the contorted *ceibo (Erythrina crytagalli),* whose blossom is Argentina's national flower; the *sauce criollo (Salix humboldtiana),* a native willow; and *canelón (Rapanea iaetevirens).*

Seasonally flooded areas along the river feature sizeable marshes of large herbaceous plants like rushes, totora reeds, cattails, and bunch grasses. There are also "floating islands" of aquatic vegetation in calm, protected areas of the delta.

FAUNA

Marine, Coastal, and Aquatic Fauna

In the La Plata estuary's murky, sediment-filled waters, it can be difficult to spot any kind of aquatic fauna, but ocean-going fish species like the yellow corvina *(Micropogonias furnieri)* and the black corvina *(Pogonias cromis),* as well as crustaceans, such as crabs, and shellfish, such as mussels, do hide in the water. The outstanding marine mammal is the La Plata river dolphin *(Pontoporia blainvillei).* The nutria, or La Plata river otter *(Lutra platensis),* is also present here and farther up the estuary.

Terrestrial and Freshwater Fauna

In the upper reaches of the Plata estuary, as far as the confluence of the Paraná and the Uruguay, freshwater game fish like the *boga (Leporinus obtusidens), dorado (Salminus brasiliensis), sábalo (Prochilodus platensis), surubí (Pseudoplatystoma coruscans),* and *tararirá (Hoplias malabaricus)* mix with some oceanic species.

Marshes along the river provide habitat for mammals like the *carpincho* or capybara *(Hydrochoerus capybara,* a Rottweiler-sized rodent) and the marsh deer *(Blastocerus dichotomus)*. The amphibian *rana criolla* (Creole frog, *Leptodactylus ocellatus)* is large (up to 130 mm in length) and meaty enough that it's occasionally eaten.

Birds

In the gallery forests along the Plata estuary, common birds include the *boyero negro* or black cacique, an oriole-like species that breeds in hanging nests; the rufous-capped antshrike *(Thamnophilus ruficapillus);* and *pava de monte* (black guan, *Penelope obscura).* Typical aquatic species include coots, ducks, and swans.

Marshland species include the *junquero* (marsh wren, *Phleocryptes melanops),* the poly-

chromatic *sietecolores* (literally, seven colors; *Thraupis bonariensis),* and the striking *federal,* with black plumage crowned by a scarlet hood. There are also several species of rails and crakes.

Invertebrates

In such a dense urban environment, of course, the most conspicuous invertebrates are usually cockroaches, flies, and mosquitoes, but Buenos Aires remains free of contagious insect-borne diseases like malaria and dengue. Nonetheless, in well watered rural areas like the Paraná delta, mosquitoes can be a real plague, so a good repellent is imperative.

The Cultural Landscape

In immediate pre-Columbian times, bands of nomadic Querandí hunter-gatherers peopled what is now Buenos Aires and its surrounding pampas. Living in smallish bands with no permanent settlements, they relied on wild game like the guanaco (a relative of the domestic llama) and the flightless, ostrich-like *ñandú* (rhea), as well as fish for subsistence. What remains of their material culture is primarily lithic (arrowheads, spearheads, and the rounded stone balls known as *boleadoras)* and ceramics.

AGRICULTURE AND THE LANDSCAPE

The arrival of the Spaniards, of course, brought major transformations. Though their initial efforts at colonizing the pampas failed because of Querandí resistance and their own poor preparation, feral European livestock—cattle and horses—proliferated almost beyond belief on the nearly virgin grasslands. By the late 19th century, large rural estates known as *estancias* produced hides, beef, and then wool for export to Europe via Buenos Aires; in the 20th century, Argentine agriculture diversified with grain exports. The pattern of large rural landholdings persists in Buenos Aires province, but the capital has expanded onto lands that were only recently agricultural.

SETTLEMENT LANDSCAPES

Cities, of course, differ greatly from the countryside. By royal decree, Spanish colonial cities were organized according to a rectangular grid surrounding a central plaza where all the major public institutions—*cabildo* (town council), cathedral, and market—were located. Buenos Aires was no exception to the rule; though the transformation from colonial city to modern metropolis obliterated many landmarks, the essential grid pattern remains.

Traditionally, in colonial barrios such as San Telmo, houses fronted directly on the street or sidewalk, with interior patios or gardens exclusively for family use; houses set back from the street were rare. This pattern has persisted to the present, though materials have changed from adobe to reinforced concrete and multistory apartment buildings have replaced traditionally low-slung structures.

Though it's unusual to find houses with large yards or gardens of the North American suburban model in the capital city, they're common enough in the northern suburbs and a few other areas—often surrounded by high fences and state-of-the-art security.

Environmental Issues

Like other global megacities, the Capital Federal and its suburbs suffer from environmental degradation, though not all indicators are negative.

AIR POLLUTION

Buenos Aires's aging diesel buses may be the primary culprit in the capital's declining air quality, but private vehicles (some of which still run on leaded gasoline) and taxis contribute more than their share. Superannuated factories, with their subsidized smokestacks, are another source.

One advantage that Buenos Aires has over some other cities is the frequency of rain and even thunderstorms that clear pollutants from the air. Storms, though, also ensure that airborne pollutants hit the ground and drain onto city streets and eventually into the waterways.

WATER POLLUTION

Buenos Aires may have potable drinking water, but the success of the early hides and livestock industry, and then of heavy industry, has left a legacy of polluted waterways. The textbook example is the Riachuelo, in the working-class barrio of La Boca. Its water more closely resembles sludge than water; its bottom sediments, thanks to chemical runoff from factories in La Boca and in nearby Avellaneda, are an even greater toxic hazard. To give credit where it's due, there's been progress in removing rusting hulks from the Vuelta de Rocha, near the popular tourist area of Caminito, but that's the easy part.

NOISE POLLUTION

Just as motor vehicles cause most of the city's air pollution, they produce most of its noise pollution, due partly to inadequate mufflers. According to one study, vehicular noise accounts for 80 percent of levels that, at corners like Rivadavia and Callao, reach upwards of 80 decibels.

Aeroparque Jorge Newbery, the capital's domestic airport, rates highly for convenience and accessibility, but noisy jet takeoffs and landings are particularly bothersome to residents of Palermo and Belgrano. Interestingly enough, it's these middle- and upper-class barrios, and not working-class neighborhoods, that have to put up with these high decibel levels. Plans to close Aeroparque are on the table, but it's unlikely to happen before the next edition of this book.

SOLID WASTE

Like other megacities, Buenos Aires produces prodigious amounts of trash—according to the municipal waste management agency Ceamse, garbage trucks collect 14,000 tons per day from city streets. This misleading statistic, though, overlooks the issue of what's not collected because opportunistic *cartoneros* or *cirujas* (the latter, an ironic *lunfardo*, or slang, term derived from the Spanish word for surgeon, but meaning street scavengers), who appeared in force during the 2001–2002 economic crisis, recycle items left for streetside pickup.

Recycling might seem a solution to the problem, but *cartoneros* break open sealed plastic garbage bags to extract recyclables; when garbage trucks collect the broken bags, much of the remaining materials fall into the street (augmenting the trash that thoughtless *porteños* have already tossed there). Municipal authorities have attempted, so far without success, to create a formal recycling program that would require city residents to separate recyclables in the bags they place on the streets nightly.

There's also a dark side to informal recycling. Some *cartoneros*—apparently in league with criminal elements—have absconded with valuable bronze and other precious metals that cover utility boxes and similar objects accessible from the street. Sold and melted into ingots, the stolen items are virtually untraceable.

Another sort of solid waste is even more problematic. Greenpeace Argentina has protested an agreement with Australia to import that country's nuclear waste for reprocessing near the suburb of Ezeiza. Argentina's constitution prohibits storage of nuclear waste, though Argentina has its own aging 357-megawatt Atucha I reactor near the town of Lima, northwest of the capital.

URBAN FORESTRY

Buenos Aires has some 375,000 street trees of more than 500 species. The *fresno* (European ash, *Fraxinus excelsior*) comprises nearly half the total, and the sycamore is the next most common. The distribution of trees, however, is uneven—the northern barrios are woodsier—but even then, many specimens are in poor condition. Thunderstorms often knock down branches and even entire trees.

Municipal authorities estimate that at least 110,000 additional trees would be desirable, but inadequate maintenance is working against the existing urban forests, and the economic crisis works against afforestation. A new law that permits private parties to plant their own street trees from a list of approved species could help close the gap.

ENERGY

Argentina is self-sufficient in fossil fuels and has substantial hydroelectric resources in the subtropical north and along the Andean foothills, but Argentine governments have promoted nuclear power since the 1950s. Although the country has renounced any intention to build nuclear weapons, the 357-megawatt Atucha I reactor has powered the capital's electrical grid since 1974. For much of the time since then, it has operated at reduced capacity thanks partly to the availability of cheaper hydroelectricity, but also due to inadequate maintenance; the controling Comisión Nacional de Energía Atómica (CNEA, National Atomic Energy Commission) is not known for its transparency. Atucha I is due to close in 2014.

History

Buenos Aires's origins are, in some ways, as murky as the muddy Río de la Plata. Everyone agrees that bands of Querandí hunter-gatherers roamed the southern banks of the river, but their encampments of *toldos* (tents of animal skins) shifted with the availability of game, fish, and other resources. No Querandí settlement could reasonably be called a city, a town, or even a village.

THE FIRST BUENOS AIRES

Buenos Aires proper dates from January 1536, when the Spaniard Pedro de Mendoza, commanding a fleet of at least a dozen ships and perhaps as many as 2,500 men plus nearly 100 horses, landed on its shores. Mendoza came to establish a colony, but his summer arrival was too late for planting and the colonists suffered from food shortages during the cool, wet winter. Spanish demands for food and supplies provoked violent and effective Querandí opposition; within five years, the insecure colonists abandoned their settlement.

Traditionally, Argentine histories place Mendoza's settlement on the *barrancas* (natural levees) of what is now Parque Lezama, in the barrio of San Telmo, and a monument to Mendoza is one of the park's highlights. Though it's now well inland, thanks to nearly five centuries of landfill, during Mendoza's time it directly fronted on the river.

Porteño author Federico Kirbus, though, has argued that Mendoza's expedition didn't land anywhere near Parque Lezama or even within the area that now comprises the Capital Federal. Instead, relying on historical accounts of the time complemented by field observations, he concludes that the first Buenos Aires may have been some distance up what is now the Paraná delta, closer to the provincial town of Escobar, before several centuries of sedimentary deposition would have filled in the river and complicated navigation for such a large fleet as Mendoza's. Although the evidence is circumstantial rather than definitive, it's an intriguing hypothesis.

BUENOS AIRES BECOMES PERMANENT

While Mendoza's initial settlement failed, some expedition members sailed up the Paraná to found Asunción, capital of present-day Paraguay. Almost four decades later, in 1580, Juan de Garay led an expedition in the opposite direction to found Santa Fe; he also refounded Buenos Aires, settling 60 colonists near what is now the Plaza de Mayo. Garay fell victim to the Querandí within three years, but the settlement he established—peopled by *mancebos de la tierra* (offspring of Spaniards and native Guaraní)—survived.

On the river's muddy banks, the location had little to recommend it as a port, but this was largely irrelevant—the new Buenos Aires was subordinate to Asunción, which was in turn subordinate to the Viceroyalty of Lima and the Spanish capital of Madrid via a long, indirect overland-and-maritime route. It took nearly two centuries for Buenos Aires, a backwater of Spain's American empire, to match Lima's viceregal status.

COLONIAL BUENOS AIRES

Barred from direct contact with Europe by Spain's mercantile bureaucracy, early colonial Buenos Aires had to survive on the resources of the sprawling pampas. The Querandí and other indigenous groups had subsisted on guanacos, rheas, and other game, in addition to edible fruits and plants they gathered, but these resources were inadequate and culturally inconceivable for the Spaniards.

The Mendoza expedition, though, had left behind horses that thrived on the lush but thinly populated pastures of the pampas, and the proliferation of the Garay expedition's escaped cattle soon transformed the Buenos Aires backcountry into a fenceless feral cattle ranch.

The presence of horses and cattle, nearly free for the taking, spawned the gaucho culture for which Argentina became famous. Durable hides were the primary product; perishable beef had little market value.

Buenos Aires had no easily accessible markets in which to sell their hides, though, because hides were too low-value a product to ship to Spain via Lima and Panama; consequently, there developed a vigorous contraband trade with British and Portuguese vessels in the Paraná delta's secluded channels. As this trade grew, Spain acknowledged Buenos Aires's growing significance by making it capital of the newly created Virreinato del Río de la Plata (Viceroyalty of the River Plate) in 1776. Reflecting its significance and the need to curb Portuguese influence, the viceroyalty even included the bonanza silver district of Potosí in present-day Bolivia, then known as Alto Perú (Upper Peru).

The city's population, only about 500 in the early 17th century, grew slowly at first. By 1655, it was barely 4,000, and it took nearly a century to reach 10,000 in 1744. By the time of the new viceroyalty, though, the population exceeded 24,000, and nearly doubled again by the early 19th century. Open to European commerce as Madrid loosened its reins, the livestock economy expanded with the development of *saladeros* (meat-salting plants), adding value to beef that was almost worthless before.

Unlike the densely populated central Andean area, where the Spaniards established themselves atop an already hierarchical society and exploited the native population through tribute and forced labor, Buenos Aires lacked an abundant labor force. The improving economy and growing population—which consisted of peninsular Spaniards, *criollos* (creoles, American-born Spaniards), *indígenas* (indigenous people), and mestizos (the offspring of Spaniards and *indígenas*)—soon included African slaves. Increasing political autonomy and economic success accelerated the end of Spanish rule.

The Dissolution of Colonial Argentina

Appointed by the Spanish crown, all major viceregal officials governed from Buenos

Aires, and economic power was also concentrated there. Outside the capital and isolated by geographic barriers, provincial bosses created their own power bases. When Napoleon invaded Spain in the early 19th century, the glue that held together Spain's colonial possessions began to dissolve, leading to independence in several steps.

Contributing to the move toward independence was a changing sense of identity among the people of what is now Argentina. In the early generations, the Spanish settlers of course identified themselves as Spaniards, but over time *criollos* began to differentiate themselves from *peninsulares* (European-born Spaniards). It bears mention that while the mestizos and even the remaining indigenous population may have identified more closely with Argentina than with Spain, it was the *criollo* intelligentsia who found the Spanish yoke most oppressive, and to whom the notion of independence had the greatest appeal.

The South American independence movements commenced on the periphery, led by figures like Argentina's José de San Martín, Venezuela's Simón Bolívar, and Chile's Bernardo O'Higgins, but their heroism was built on a broad support base. In Buenos Aires, this base developed as opportunistic and unauthorized British forces took advantage of Spain's perceived weakness and occupied the city in 1806 and 1807.

As the shocked Viceroy Rafael de Sobremonte fled Buenos Aires for Córdoba, city residents organized a covert resistance that, under the leadership of the Frenchman Santiago de Liniers, dislodged the invaders. Based on the belief that Spain's legitimate government had fallen and as reflection of their confidence, the *porteños* chose Liniers as viceroy in an open *cabildo*. The royalist Liniers, ironically enough, died at the hands of independence fighters during the 1810 Revolution.

Returning from Spain to Buenos Aires, San Martín led independence armies against royalist forces deployed from Peru, in what is now northwestern Argentina. In 1816, in the city of Tucumán, delegates of the Provincias Unidas del Río de la Plata (United Provinces of the River Plate) issued a formal declaration of independence. But this was only a loose confederation that glossed over differences between Federalist caudillos—provincial landholders and warlords intent on preserving their fiefdoms—and the cosmopolitan Unitarists of Buenos Aires.

The struggle between Federalists and Unitarists was slow to resolve itself; according to historian James Scobie, "It took 70 years for Argentina to coalesce as a political unit." Even today, tensions between the provinces and the central government have not disappeared, but it took a Federalist to ensure the primacy of Buenos Aires.

REPUBLICAN ARGENTINA AND BUENOS AIRES

Having achieved independence, the Provincias Unidas were less successful in creating institutions. Several attempts at agreeing upon a constitution failed, resulting in a series of mini-states that quarreled among themselves. In Buenos Aires, the largest province, Federalist *caudillo* Juan Manuel de Rosas took command and ruled from 1829 until his overthrow in 1852. The shrewd, ruthless Rosas did more than anyone else to ensure the primacy of the city, which, nevertheless, did not become the country's capital until 1880.

By the time Rosas took power, Buenos Aires's population had grown to nearly 60,000; in 1855, only a few years after he left, it reached 99,000. In 1833, Charles Darwin (who admired the loyalty of Rosas's followers even as he questioned the dictator's ruthlessness) was impressed with the city's size and orderliness:

Every street is at right angles to the one it crosses, and the parallel ones being equidistant, the houses are collected into solid squares of equal dimensions, which are called quadras. On the other hand the houses themselves are hollow squares; all the rooms opening into a neat little courtyard. They are generally only one story high, with flat roofs, which are fitted with seats, and are much frequented by the inhabitants in summer. In the centre of the town is the Plaza, where the public offices, fortress, cathedral, &c., stand. Here also, the old viceroys, before the revolution had their palaces. The general assemblage of buildings possesses considerable architectural beauty, although none individually can boast of any.

In the early independence years, Unitarist visionaries like Mariano Moreno and Bernardino Rivadavia had advocated an aggressive immigration policy to Europeanize the young republic, but Rosas's dictatorial rule, obstinate isolationism, and continual military adventures deterred immigration. His defeat at the battle of Caseros (1853) opened the country to immigration and accelerated the diversification of the economy from extensive *estancias* and *saladeros* to the more intensive production of wool and grains for export.

For the city, still a provincial rather than a national capital, this meant explosive growth—its population more than doubled to 230,000, by 1875. In 1880, when the other provinces forced the federalization of Buenos Aires, irate provincial authorities shifted their own capital to the new city of La Plata, but the newly designated federal capital continued to grow. By the early 20th century, it became the first Latin American city with more than a million inhabitants.

THE PORTEÑOS GET A PORT

Unfortunately, for a fast-growing city of *porteños,* Buenos Aires was a poor natural port. Its muddy river banks and shallow waters made loading and unloading slow, laborious, expensive, and even hazardous, as freighters had to anchor in deep water and transfer their cargo to shallow-draft lighters. Before it could become a great commercial port, Buenos Aires would have to speed up a process that took months rather than weeks for the average steamship.

Everyone agreed port improvements were imperative, but there were different visions of how to accomplish them. Engineer Luis Huergo offered the simplest and most economical solution: to broaden, dredge, and straighten the Riachuelo to provide better access to existing port facilities at La Boca and Barracas, in the city's southern barrios. As so often happens in Argentina, though, political influence trumped practical expertise, as the congress approved wealthy downtown businessman Eduardo Madero's vague plan to transform the mudflats into a series of deep *diques* (basins) immediately east of the central Plaza de Mayo, even as work advanced on the Riachuelo option.

Approved in 1882, Puerto Madero took 16 years to complete, came in well over budget, caused a scandal because of shady land dealings, and finally even proved inadequate for the growing port traffic. Only improvements at La Boca and the 1926 opening of Retiro's Puerto Nuevo (New Port) finally resolved the problem, but port costs remained high.

FROM GRAN ALDEA TO COSMOPOLITAN CAPITAL

Federalization gave the city a new mayor—Torcuato de Alvear, appointed by President Julio Argentino Roca—and Alvear immediately imposed his vision on the newly designated capital. Instead of the traditionally intimate *Gran Aldea,* Buenos Aires was to become a city of monuments, a cosmopolitan showpiece symbolizing Argentina's integration with the wider world. Where single-story houses once lined narrow colonial streets, broad boulevards like the Avenida de Mayo soon linked majestic public buildings, such as the Casa Rosada presidential palace and the Congreso Nacional (the federal legislature).

Newly landscaped spaces like the Plaza de Mayo, Plaza del Congreso, and Plaza San Martín, not to mention the conversion of Rosas's former Palermo estate into parklands, reflected the aspirations—or pretensions—of an ambitious country. Some, though, castigated Alvear for favoring upper-class barrios, such as Recoleta, Palermo, and Belgrano, over struggling immigrant neighborhoods, like San Telmo and La Boca.

Peronists honor Evita on the 50th anniversary of her death, July 26, 2002, at Cementerio de la Recoleta.

As immigrants streamed into town from Spain, Italy, Britain, Russia, and other European countries, such differential treatment exacerbated growing social tensions. In 1913, Buenos Aires became the first South American city to open a subway system, beneath the Avenida de Mayo, but in poorer neighborhoods large families squeezed into *conventillos* (tenements) and struggled on subsistence wages. The gap between rich and poor frequently exploded into open conflict. In 1909, following police repression of a May Day demonstration, anarchist immigrant Simón Radowitzky killed police chief Ramón Falcón with a bomb. In 1919, President Hipólito Yrigoyen ordered the army to crush a metalworkers' strike during what is now recalled as La Semana Trágica (The Tragic Week).

Ironically, Yrigoyen pardoned Radowitzky a decade later, and his was the first administration to suffer one of repeated military coups that plagued the country for most of the 20th century. The dictatorship that followed him continued the policy of demolishing narrow co-

lonial streets to create broad thoroughfares like Corrientes, Córdoba, and Santa Fe, all parallel to the Avenida de Mayo, and the crosstown boulevard Avenida 9 de Julio. The populist Perón regimes of the 1940s and 1950s, despite public deference to working-class interests, splurged on pharaonic works projects, heavy and heavily subsidized industry, and unsustainable social spending that squandered the country's post–World War II surpluses.

THE DIRTY WAR AND ITS AFTERMATH

As Gran Buenos Aires grew, encompassing ever more distant suburbs, the capital and its vicinity became home to more than one-third of the country's population; by 1970, it had more than eight million inhabitants. Continued political instability, though, became almost open warfare until 1976, when the military ousted President Isabel Perón (widow of Juan Perón, who died shortly after returning from exile in 1973) in a bloodless coup that introduced the most systematic and bloodiest reign of terror in Argentine history.

Under its euphemistically named Proceso de Reorganización Nacional (Process of National Reorganization), the military's *Guerra Sucia* (Dirty War) may have claimed 30,000 Argentine lives, ranging from leftist urban and rural guerrillas to suspected sympathizers and large numbers of innocent bystanders whose links to armed opposition groups were tenuous at best. Many more were imprisoned and tortured, and more still were either sent or escaped into exile. Only a few courageous individuals and groups, such as Nobel Peace Prize winner Adolfo Pérez Esquivel and the even more famous Madres de la Plaza de Mayo, who marched around Buenos Aires's main plaza in quiet defiance, dared risk public opposition.

One rationale for the military coup was political corruption, but the military and their civilian collaborators were just as adept at diverting international loans to demolish vibrant but neglected neighborhoods and to create decadent monuments, such as freeways that went nowhere. Much of the money, of course, found its way into offshore bank accounts. The horror ended only after the military underestimated the response to their 1982 invasion of the British-ruled Falkland (Malvinas) Islands; after a decisive defeat, the military meekly ceded control to civilians. The main coup plotters and human-rights violators went to prison—an unprecedented occurrence in Latin America, even if they were later pardoned.

Following the 1983 return to constitutional government, Argentina underwent several years of hyperinflation in which President Raúl Alfonsín's Radical government squandered an enormous amount of good will. The succeeding Peronist government of Carlos Menem overcame hyperinflation by pegging the Argentine peso at par with the U.S. dollar through a "currency basket" that ensured the country would print no more pesos than it had hard currency reserves to back them.

Menem's strategy, Economy Minister Domingo Cavallo's brainchild, brought a decade of economic stability during which foreign investment flowed into Argentina, and Buenos Aires was one of the main beneficiaries. Privatization of inefficient state-run monopolies, which had had thousands of so-called *ñoquis* (ghost employees) on the payroll, brought major improvements in telecommunications, transportation, and other sectors. The financial and service sectors flourished, and ambitious urban renewal projects, like the transformation of Puerto Madero into a fashionable riverfront of lofts and restaurants, gave *porteños* a sense of optimism through most of the 1990s.

There was a dark side to the boom, however: "crony capitalism," in which associates of the president enriched themselves through favorable contracts for privatization. Governmental reform did not touch the provinces, which maintained large public payrolls for patronage, and even printed their own *bonos* (bonds), "funny money" that further reduced the confidence of international investors.

After the resignation of Menem's hapless successor Fernando De la Rúa in December of that same year, the country had a series of three caretaker presidents in two weeks. Following a dubiously extra-constitutional congressional vote, Peronist Eduardo Duhalde (whom De la Rúa had defeated two years earlier) stepped into office, serving until 2003, when Néstor Kirchner was elected president. In a controversial move, Duhalde ended Cavallo's convertibility policy and devalued the peso, which lost nearly 75 percent of its value within a few months. At the same time, he continued the De la Rúa administration's *corralito* policy, which restricted bank withdrawals to maintain hard currency reserves but also strangled the economy of the city and the country.

As the economy stagnated and unemployment rose, homelessness also rose and scavengers became a common sight even in prosperous barrios like Palermo and Belgrano. Strikes, strident pickets blocking bridges and highways, and frustration with politicians and institutions like the International Monetary Fund (IMF) contributed to the feeling of *bronca* (aggravation). Yet somehow, the city, with its blend of neighborhood integrity, cosmopolitan sophistication, and rich cultural life, continued to function.

Touching bottom by late 2002, the country gradually rebounded as the devalued peso made agricultural exports competitive internationally, and consequent low wages made some traditional smokestack industries viable again. Devaluation also brought a tourism boom from neighboring countries and overseas, and the *corralito*'s end unleashed domestic demand. Unemployment fell as well, though it remained alarmingly high.

Government and Politics

Argentine politics is often contentious and includes little consensus. Since the end of the military dictatorship of 1976–1983, though, it has been remarkably stable and peaceful, all things considered. The major exception, of course, was the storm of political and economic protest that led to five demonstrators' deaths in the Plaza de Mayo on December 20, 2001. The country had three provisional presidents in two weeks before Senator Eduardo Duhalde of Buenos Aires province, who had lost the 1999 presidential election to De la Rúa, assumed the office in a dubiously extra-constitutional congressional vote.

Argentines' lack of faith in institutions, however, led to barrio activism through *asambleas populares* (popular assemblies) and less-constructive extra-constitutional practices, such as *escrache,* in which groups of citizens loudly and publicly demonstrate against politicians, judges, bankers, or representatives of other institutions at their homes or workplaces. *Es-craches,* which often deteriorate into shouting matches, originated as a tactic to identify and publicize the whereabouts of alleged torturers and murderers from the military dictatorship after a series of pardons and other measures limited their prosecution.

Unlike 1970s Argentina, though, early-21st-century Argentina was imploding rather than exploding, and the villains were not always as conspicuous as they were in previous years and decades. Many placed the blame on former president Carlos Menem and his "neo-liberal" free market policies and corruption, as well as foreign banks and institutions, such as the International Monetary Fund (IMF).

Other Argentine politicians, though, could be singled out for blame. Duhalde's "pesification" policy benefited his own industrial clients by turning their dollar debts into devalued pesos and decimated individual Argentines' personal savings.

Argentina's fractious politics often leave little room for compromise, as the mere existence of the Intransigent Party might suggest.

ORGANIZATION

Buenos Aires is Argentina's capital and also its economic powerhouse and cultural cornerstone. Like Washington, D.C., it is a geographically and administratively separate federal district; the 24 *partidos* (counties) of Gran Buenos Aires belong to Buenos Aires province, the most populous and important of the country's 23 provinces.

Superficially, Argentina's constitution resembles that of the United States. The popularly elected President leads the executive branch; a bicameral legislature consists of an upper house, the Senado (Senate), and a lower Cámara de Diputados (Chamber of Deputies); the Corte Suprema (Supreme Court) is the independent judiciary.

In practice, institutions are often weak and dysfunctional. The president dominates the system, often ruling by decree when the legislature obstructs his agenda, and the Corte Suprema is notoriously vulnerable to political pressure.

Much depends on individuals, as institutions are weak. The charismatic President Carlos Menem (1989–1999), for instance, exercised unquestionable power despite (or perhaps because of) his ethical shortcomings, while successors like Fernando De la Rúa (1999–2001) and Eduardo Duhalde (appointed in 2001 to serve until 2003) have proved ineffectual even with legislators of their own parties.

Politically, the Capital Federal holds a special constitutional status as the Ciudad Autónoma de Buenos Aires (Autonomous City of Buenos Aires, which is similar to the District of Columbia in the United States), with its own elected mayor and legislature. (Until 1996 reforms, the president appointed the mayor and legislature.) Unlike the largely disenfranchised voters of Washington, D.C., though, the Buenos Aires voters enjoy voting representation in the Congreso Nacional (National Congress) as well.

POLITICAL PARTIES

Although the Peronists, or Justicialists, are the country's largest political party, the capital's most important political force has been

Alianza, an alliance of the rather misnamed Radical party (a middle-class institution that seems to function better in opposition than in power) and the slightly left-of-center Frente del País Solidario (Frepaso, National Solidarity Front). The current mayor is the Alianza's Aníbal Ibarra.

Whereas nearly 20 parties are represented in the 63-member legislature, several have only a single seat. None is close to a majority, though they often form transitory *bloques,* usually to obstruct others.

The Peronists, Radicals, and similar entities, however, are barely parties in the European or North American sense—it might be more accurate to call them movements. Voters, for instance, cannot vote directly for candidates, but only for lists chosen by party bosses to reward loyalists.

More often than not, the major Argentine parties are patronage machines that, after mobilizing their most militant members for elections, reward them with well-paid public posts that may not actually involve working for their paychecks. Such "ghost employees" are called *ñoquis* after the inexpensive potato pasta traditionally served the 29th of each month in restaurants and cash-strapped households—the insinuation is that they start making their appearance in the office just in time to collect their first-of-the month salary.

Historically, many officeholders have used their supporters for political intimidation instead of dialogue. Ever since the default of 2001, though, political affiliations mean even less than they did in the past. Many Argentines have assumed a "plague on all your houses" attitude toward politicians in general. In fact, ambitious individuals, ranging from populist Elisa Carrió (a left-wing member of the Cámara de Diputados) to conservative businessman Mauricio Macri (president of the Boca Juniors soccer team), have consciously distanced themselves from traditional parties.

ELECTIONS

On a national level, Argentina operates under an 1853 constitution, amended in 1994 to permit the president's re-election while reducing his or her term from six to four years; no president may serve more than two consecutive terms. Each of the 23 provinces, as well as the Buenos Aires federal district, chooses three senators; in the 257-member Cámara de Diputados, each province has a delegation proportionate to its population. The population and corresponding number of delegates is subject to revision with each new census. Senators serve six-year terms, deputies four-year terms.

Porteño voters choose the city's 63-member Poder Legislativo by proportional representation for four-year terms; half the legislature is renewed every two years. Term limits prohibit both the mayor and legislators from serving more than two consecutive terms without a lapse of at least four years.

BUREAUCRACY

The government institutions most travelers are likely to come into contact with are immigration, customs, and police. Immigration and customs generally treat foreigners fairly, but Argentine police are notoriously corrupt. The capital's Policía Federal are not quite so bad as the Buenos Aires provincial police, a "mafia with badges" who are particularly infamous for shaking down motorists for bribes after stopping them for minor equipment violations.

Repeated attempts at reforming the police have invariably ended in failure, but the recent creation of community police forces in some municipalities and a tourist police in Buenos Aires have brought some optimism. Still, a poll of newly recruited Buenos Aires provincial police yielded the disturbing response that nearly half of them would not arrest a relative accused of a crime.

The politicized administrative bureaucracy remains one of Argentina's most intractable problems due to the continuing presence of *ñoquis* at the federal, provincial, and municipal levels. Abuses are not so extreme as they were in the past, when individuals often drew multiple paychecks without performing any work whatsoever, but bloated government payrolls are still cause for concern.

While the privatizations of the 1990s reduced federal sector employment by nearly two-thirds, they had little impact on the provinces. Provincial payrolls still include nearly 1.4 million Argentines—many in what might be more accurately called positions rather than jobs. For the tourist, it may be gratifying to find a tiny, obscure museum open 60 hours per week and staffed by three people, but the cumulative economic impact of such practices has been catastrophic.

In practical terms, lack of a professional civil service means a lack of continuity, as officials lose their jobs with every change of administration; continuing political influence in the bureaucracy means an abundance of uninterested and often ill-qualified officials who take their time dealing with any but the most routine matters. It also means nepotism and corruption—Transparency International consistently ranks Argentina among the world's worst countries in its annual survey of perceived corruption. In 2004, of 146 countries surveyed, Argentina was 108th (tied with Albania, Libya, and the Palestinian Authority); on the South American continent, only Ecuador (112th), Venezuela (114th), Bolivia (122nd), and Paraguay (140th) rated lower.

THE MILITARY

Because of repeated 20th-century coups and the notably vicious 1976–1983 Dirty War dictatorship, the Argentine military earned a reputation as one of the worst ever on a continent infamous for armed repression. Its ignominious collapse in the 1982 Falkland Islands War, followed by public revelations of state terrorism and the conviction of the top generals and admirals responsible for kidnapping, torture, and murder, helped civilian authorities overcome the tradition of military impunity.

Since the 1983 return to constitutional government, civilian governments have eliminated conscription, the military budget has declined to barely 1 percent of the GDP (less than half that of neighboring Chile), and Argentine forces have undertaken more strictly military operations, such as peacekeeping missions in the Balkans. Although periods of political disorder, such as 2001–2002, always bring coup rumors, the military appears to have little or no interest in taking the reins of government.

The size of the military services has also been reduced, with only about 100,000 soldiers, sailors, and other personnel in uniform, though these are heavily weighted toward noncommissioned officers. Defense minister José Pampuro has said, "We conceive Argentina as a defensive country," but in recent years, he has directed investment in updated equipment for the army, navy, and air force. He has also added that involving the military in domestic security "would be a mistake," given its recent history.

Nevertheless, there remains an ugly reminder of military fanaticism in Colonel Mohamed Alí Seineldín, who earned a life term in a military prison after mounting a rebellion against the constitutional government in 1989. Inexplicably, in 2003, outgoing president Duhalde granted him a gratuitous pardon.

A fundamentalist Catholic despite his name, Seineldín has taken to making bizarre public statements regarding oral and anal sex. He has also made the bewildering assertion that the CIA and the Fuerzas Armadas Revolucionarias de Colombia (FARC, the leftist Colombian guerrilla forces) are conspiring to destabilize Argentina (as if Argentines were incapable of doing so themselves).

Despite the country's reputation for dictatorial bellicosity, two Argentines have won Nobel Peace Prizes: foreign minister Carlos Saavedra Lamas (1936) for mediating a Chaco War settlement between Paraguay and Bolivia, and Adolfo Pérez Esquivel (1984) for publicizing the 1976–1983 military dictatorship's human rights abuses.

Economy

The urban economy is mostly administrative, financial, and service-oriented. The capital remains the country's major port, but most industrial jobs are in provincial suburbs like Avellaneda. Along with northern Argentina's Iguazú Falls and Patagonia's Moreno Glacier, the city is one of the country's top tourist attractions.

To most foreign observers, Argentina's economy is an enigma. Rich in natural resources and having a well-educated populace and modern infrastructure, for most of seven decades it has lurched from crisis to crisis, with the notable exception of the stable, prosperous 1990s. In late 2001, it stunned the world and even many Argentines by defaulting on part of its US$141 billion foreign debt, triggering a political and economic meltdown comparable to the 1930s Great Depression. In the first quarter of 2002, the economy shrank 16.3 percent, marking 14 consecutive quarters of contraction; while steady growth has resumed since early 2003, it's still a long road back.

Argentina emerged from World War II in an enviable position, but the government of the charismatic General Juan Domingo Perón and its successors squandered enormous budget surpluses from agricultural exports by funding bloated state enterprises. Those enterprises, in collusion with corrupt labor leaders, became industrial dinosaurs impossible to reform. Then, during the 1970s and 1980s, large loans destined for massive public works projects filled the pockets—or Swiss bank accounts—of the nefarious generals and their civilian collaborators who ruled the country.

Corruption and deficit spending resulted in hyperinflation that reached levels of 30 percent or more *per month*. Shortly after taking power in 1989, President Carlos Menem's administration became the first Argentine government in recent memory to tackle the inflation problem through Economy Minister Domingo Cavallo's "convertibility" policy; Cavallo's "currency basket" fixed the Argentine peso at par with the U.S. dollar, and required the government to back every peso printed with a dollar or other hard currency.

Selling off unprofitable state enterprises,

such as Aerolíneas Argentinas, the state tele-communications enterprise Entel, and most of the extensive railroad network, made convertibility possible. Inflation dropped to zero and, after an initial glitch, there was steady economic growth. But the 1995 Mexican "tequila" crisis, followed by a Brazilian devaluation that reduced Argentine competitiveness, led to increasing unemployment and recession. After a brief recovery, convertibility proved to be an economic straitjacket that, by the De la Rúa administration's second year, was unsustainable.

In a desperate move, De la Rúa reappointed Cavallo to the Economy Ministry, but a run on bank deposits brought severe restrictions on withdrawals, known collectively as the *corralito* (literally, little fence). The *corralito's* unpopularity triggered Cavallo's resignation and De la Rúa's downfall. De la Rúa's successor, Eduardo Duhalde, made things even worse by eliminating convertibility, changing dollar-based savings accounts to peso-based accounts at a 1:1.4 rate, and floating the local currency (leaving it open to market forces to find its own level rather than intervening to control the market) so that those accounts soon lost most of their value. At the same time, in a classic case of Argentine "crony capitalism," the new president converted dollar debts to peso debts at a rate of 1:1, benefiting the large industrialists who were his political base.

With devaluation, according to the Economist Intelligence Unit, in less than a year Buenos Aires went from the world's 22nd most expensive city (of 131 surveyed) to the 120th. As the peso plummeted from 1:1 to 1:3.5 in only a few months, disciplined savers saw their frozen wealth evaporate, while those who had accumulated large debts saw their dollar burdens reduced. Devaluation also meant renewed inflation, though not at the nightmarish 1980s levels because banking restrictions limited the cash in circulation.

Eventually, the devalued peso made Argentine exports more competitive, though the Duhalde administration contradictorily slapped a new tax on export profits in excess of US$5 million. Banks took the brunt of criticism for not repaying their depositors (though some were solvent enough), but government restrictions prevent them from doing so.

In 2002, the Argentine economy contracted by about 11 percent, but in 2003–2004 it enjoyed eight straight quarters of growth in the 8-percent range. Part of this performance, though, stemmed from the fact that there was nowhere to go but up, and it will take strong management and reform to maintain that pace as the boost from devaluation dissipates.

Meanwhile, low levels of investment because of Argentina's unwillingness (or incapability) to repay its massive foreign debt could derail the recovery. At the same time, some economists fear that the presently overheated economy could revive inflationary pressures in a country with a history of fiscal irresponsibility.

The economist Arturo Porcezanski, for instance, believes the only way to stabilize prices is to adopt the dollar as Argentina's currency, asserting, "Any effort to convince Argentines that the peso is worth anything is in vain. They only have faith in the dollar." In a similar sentiment, Cavallo remarked that "forcing Argentines to save in pesos would be as difficult as forcing them to learn to speak Chinese instead of Spanish."

This, of course, has long been the case: For decades, Argentines have speculated on the dollar in times of crisis. In the 1970s, when Montoneros guerrillas headed by Rodolfo Galimberti kidnapped businessman Jorge Born, they demanded and got a ransom of US$60 million—at a time when that was *real* money. In an only-in-Argentina scenario, the pardoned Galimberti later became the business partner of the man he abducted.

EMPLOYMENT, UNEMPLOYMENT, AND UNDEREMPLOYMENT

Despite a recovering economy, Argentine unemployment remains high by most standards—estimates as of early 2005 are around 13 percent—and many people are underemployed as well. These figures are probably not quite so bad in Buenos Aires as in the provinces,

© WAYNE BERNHARDSON

Paseaperros (professional dog walkers) are a common sight in Buenos Aires.

but street, bus, and subway vendors are far more numerous than in the past, and the number of people rummaging through garbage for recyclables is shocking even to Argentines.

During the early-2002 economic crisis, many unemployed individuals spent the night in line to buy dollars at Banco de la Nación and private exchange houses, in hopes of selling their spots to those who did have sufficient pesos to purchase dollars. Similarly, individuals waited in lines outside the Italian consulate and other European missions to sell their places in line for passports and visas.

While unemployment figures can help gauge trends, observers and analysts should not take them too literally. Many Argentines work *en negro* (in black, i.e. off the books), avoid paying taxes, and do not show up in official statistics. This does not mean that unemployment figures are irrelevant, but interpreting them requires a critical eye.

AGRICULTURE

Since the 19th century, the Argentine pampas have developed from the meat locker and

woolshed of the world to one of its main granaries, growing corn, wheat, oats, sorghum, and soybeans, among other crops. The country's agriculture has diversified, though, to include vegetables, such as potatoes, onions, carrots, squash, beans, and tomatoes, and fruit crops like apples, pears, and grapes. Its grape harvest has helped make Argentina the world's fifth-largest wine producer.

Other commercial crops include subtropical cultigens, such as sugar cane, olives, tea, yerba mate, and tobacco, mostly in provinces to the north and west of the capital. Agriculture accounts for roughly 11 percent of GDP but, at roughly US$12 billion per year, it delivers about a third of all exports by value.

INDUSTRY

Argentina's industrial heyday was the immediate post–World War II period, when President Juan Domingo Perón invested vast sums in manufacturing products, such as steel, chemicals, and petrochemicals; the military controlled large parts of the economy, including its own weapons manufacture and support industries.

© WAYNE BERNHARDSON

Since the 2002 peso collapse, many poor Argentines earn a subsistence as *cartonero* scavengers.

Despite the privatization of the 1990s, much of Argentine industry is still inefficient and unable to compete without state assistance—or cronyism. The 2002 exchange rate collapse revived ailing factories as production costs fell in real terms, but the superannuated sector is likely to face similar problems in the near future, barring unprecedented investment in modernization.

Accounting for about 35 percent of GDP, the industrial sector also includes food processing, motor vehicles, consumer durables, textiles, printing, metallurgy, and steel. Much of this activity is concentrated in the southern suburbs of Avellaneda and Quilmes, across the Riachuelo.

three years later the poverty figure had fallen by 10 percent.

Statistics can be misleading, though. According to World Bank figures from the calendar year 2000, with the Argentine peso at par with the U.S. dollar, the country's per capita income was US$7,460, while that of neighboring Paraguay was US$1,470. As the flailing Argentine peso sank to nearly a quarter of its former value, these two figures would have been roughly comparable in dollar terms; yet it would be difficult to argue that Argentina's standard of living, no matter how dire the economy, was ever equivalent to that of impoverished Paraguay.

RICH AND POOR

Historically, the disparity between rich and poor in Argentina has been far less extreme than in other Latin American countries, but the meltdown of 2001–2002, with its devastating impact on the middle class, has resurrected the issue. In early 2002, more than half of all Argentines were considered to fall beneath the poverty line, and six million (one-sixth of the population) were considered indigent, though

EDUCATION

Literacy is formally high, nearly 97 percent, one of the highest in the Americas. Education is free through high school and compulsory to age 12, but the curriculum is rigid. Some public secondary schools, most notably the Colegio Nacional Buenos Aires, are even more prestigious than some of their private bilingual counterparts.

Public universities like the capital's Universidad de Buenos Aires and the Universidad Nacional de La Plata, in the provincial capital, are generally superior to private universities. Public university education is free of charge, but has generated a surplus of high-status degrees in fields like law, psychology, and sociology—and not enough in hands-on disciplines like engineering and computer science.

School teachers generally do not receive university degrees, but attend special teachers' colleges. Frequent teacher strikes have disrupted both primary and secondary instruction throughout the country. There is vocational and technical training as well, but these skills enjoy little respect, even when those jobs pay more than white-collar positions or office work.

Several Argentine scientists have won Nobel Prizes, including Bernardo Houssay (Medicine, 1946), Luis Federico Leloir (Chemistry, 1972), and César Milstein (Medicine, 1984). One continual concern is the "brain drain" of educated Argentines overseas; Milstein, for instance, spent his most productive years in England because Perón-era political pressures at Argentine universities made research impossible. Many talented individuals, though, have left simply because the economy has failed them.

TOURISM

For many overseas visitors, Buenos Aires is the gateway to globally famous attractions like the subtropical Iguazú Falls in the northern province of Misiones and the Perito Moreno Glacier in Patagonia's Santa Cruz province. Still, Buenos Aires is an attraction its own right—on the entire continent, Rio de Janeiro is probably the only other city with an international profile anywhere close to the Argentine capital.

Thanks partly to the tourist sector, Buenos Aires's economy remains relatively prosperous compared to that of the provinces. According to figures for the first eleven months of 2004, the city received about 2.5 million foreign visitors. If previous years are any indication, nearly 15 percent of these visitors were from North America and about 22 percent from Europe. Most of the remainder came from the neighboring countries of Uruguay, Brazil, Paraguay, Bolivia, and Chile.

These figures have risen rapidly over previous years, as the political situation has stabilized since 2002 and devaluation has made the city a bargain. According to projections, from December of 2004 to March of 2005, 1.9 million foreigners (almost 42 percent of all visitors) would spend more than US$600 million in the city.

Many other visitors to Buenos Aires, of course, come from the provinces, drawn by family and other personal links, the city's cultural attractions, and the fact that devaluation has made foreign travel too expensive for many Argentines.

The People

According to the 2001 census, Argentina's population is 36,223,947. Of these, 2,768,772 reside in Buenos Aires, the Capital Federal; this is a decline of 8 percent from the 1991 census, when its population was 2,965,403. Another 8,684,953 reside in the 24 counties of Gran Buenos Aires, for a total of 11,453,725.

POPULATION GEOGRAPHY

Nearly a third of all Argentines live in the Capital Federal and Gran Buenos Aires. Most of the rest are also city dwellers, in population centers such as Rosario, Córdoba, Mar del Plata, Mendoza, Salta, and other provincial capitals and cities. The southern Patagonian provinces of Chubut, Santa Cruz, and Tierra del Fuego are very thinly populated.

Indigenous Peoples

Argentina has the smallest indigenous population of any South American country except Uruguay, but many Kollas (Quechuas) from northwestern Argentina and Mapuches from the southern Patagonian provinces reside in

THE AFRO-ARGENTINES AND THEIR "DEMISE"

In a country of immigrants, the heritage of many Argentines is often conspicuous. According to some accounts, there are even more Argentines with Italian surnames than *Gallegos* of Spanish ancestry. Anglo-Argentines are prominent and have their own daily newspaper, and German-Argentines still support a weekly. Buenos Aires has numerous Jewish community landmarks, and so-called *Turcos* of Middle Eastern descent, such as former President Carlos Menem, have made their mark in politics.

Yet an Afro-Argentine population, that, by official statistics, once comprised nearly a third of the city's population has been nearly invisible. When the revolutionary government of 1810 tentatively banned the slave trade three years later, nearly 10,000 of more than 32,000 *porteños* were of African origin. As late as 1838, the figure was nearly 15,000 of almost 63,000. Yet in 1887, the number had dropped to only 8,000 among more than 430,000 city residents.

After the turn of the century, Afro-Argentines virtually fell off the city map. In the 1970s, newspaper and magazine articles even puzzled over the disappearance of a community that fought honorably in the 19th-century civil and regional wars, supported a variety of social and charitable organizations, sponsored a lively local press, and made substantial contributions to the arts. How and why this could have happened was, seemingly, an enigma.

Two plausible hypotheses were widely accepted. One was that Afro-Argentines were made into front-line cannon fodder, particularly in the war with Paraguay, where they suffered disproportionate casualties. Another was that the 19th-century yellow fever epidemics in San Telmo, where many Afro-Argentines lived, decimated their numbers as wealthier *criollos* moved to higher, healthier ground in the northern suburbs.

Historian George Reid Andrews, though, challenged the orthodoxy by arguing that there was slim evidence for either hypothesis and, moreover, little for the disappearance of the community itself. What he did learn, through examination of archival materials and the capital's Afro-Argentine press, was that the community itself was unconcerned with demographic decline but clearly worried about its socioeconomic status.

As the slave trade ended by the mid-19th century and massive European immigration transformed the city a couple decades later, Afro-Argentines were clearly a declining *percentage* of the population, but that does not explain their plunging absolute numbers. Andrews, though, found that Argentine authorities and opinion-makers consciously excised the Afro-Argentine presence in an attempt to promote the country as a European outpost in the Americas.

the capital. There is also a handful of Tobas, Matacos, and others from Chaco and Santa Fe provinces, and Guaraní in the Mesopotamian provinces, especially Misiones.

Simple population statistics, though, may understate contemporary Argentina's indigenous legacy. According to a DNA study by Universidad de Buenos Aires geneticist Daniel Corach, 56 percent of all Argentines have some indigenous ancestry, though only 10 percent of those qualify as "purely" indigenous.

Ethnic Minorities

Argentina is a country of immigrants, both recent and not-so-recent, and the capital reflects that history. Spaniards, of course, first colonized what is now Argentina, but a 19th-century influx of Italians, Basques, English, Irish, Welsh, Ukrainians, and other nationalities made Buenos Aires a mosaic of immigrants; Italo-Argentines even came to outnumber Argentines of Spanish origin.

Some immigrant groups retain a high vis-

Some of this, certainly, owed its origins to a racism that was present from early independence times. The political opponents of Bernardino Rivadavia, a presumed mulatto who served as president in 1826–1827 before his forced resignation, stigmatized him with the epithet "Dr. Chocolate." Modern Argentine school children are taught proudly that the country was among the first to abolish slavery, in 1813, but these measures were so half-hearted that the institution lingered nearly another half-century.

More insidiously, though, census-takers systematically undercounted Afro-Argentines by equally half-hearted efforts that sometimes even avoided the neighborhoods in which they lived. When summarizing the data, they minimized the black presence by creating vague new racial categories, such as *trigueño* (wheat-colored), and incorporating individuals with African background into them. Eventually, in Andrews's words, the Afro-Argentines of Buenos Aires were "forgotten, but not gone."

Even as more and more European immigrants streamed into Argentina, Afro-Argentines kept alive such institutions as the Shimmy Club, a social organization that held regular dances only half a block off Avenida Corrientes, into the 1970s. Here, at regular intervals, rhythmic drum-based *malambo, milonga,* and *zamba* filled the hall and, on occasion, spilled out into the street.

Andrews thought that Argentine society was absorbing blacks and, indeed, defining them as whites in accordance with an unspoken ideology, even as their societal contributions survived. In recent years, though, there has been a small but complex revival of black culture in Buenos Aires that involves Afro-Argentines (now estimated at about 3,000) but also Afro-Uruguayans, Afro-Brazilians, Cape Verde Portuguese (perhaps 8,000), and Cubans and Africans. This has not always been convivial, as the remaining Afro-Argentines clearly distinguish themselves from the latecomers even as they share some cultural features.

More and more individuals with African origins may be visible on Buenos Aires streets, but Argentine society's continued refusal to acknowledge their presence and its own African heritage may be their greatest adversary. Created in 1996, the Fundación Africa Vive (Africa Lives Foundation) claims there are more than two million Argentines of African descent; according to director María Magdalena Lamadrid, "A single drop of blood is enough" to define an Afro-Argentine.

Yet in 2002, when Lamadrid herself attempted to fly to Panama to participate in a conference on the life of Dr. Martin Luther King Jr., immigration officials detained the fifth-generation Argentine on suspicion of carrying a false passport. One said, allegedly, that "she can't be black and Argentine."

ibility, most notably a Jewish community that numbers at least 200,000 and is historically concentrated in Balvanera's Once district. Since the onset of the 2001–2002 economic crisis, though, many have needed assistance from Jewish community organizations, and significant numbers of Argentine Jews have emigrated or considered emigrating to Israel despite insecurity there. It's worth mentioning that still-unsolved terrorist incidents in Buenos Aires killed 29 people in the Israeli Embassy in Retiro in 1992 and 87

people in Once's Asociación Mutua Israelita Argentina (AMIA), a Jewish cultural center, in 1994; most Jewish community landmarks are well fortified.

Middle Eastern immigrants are less numerous, but have occupied high-profile positions—the most notable example of this is former president Carlos Menem, of Syrian descent. Argentines misleadingly refer to anyone of Middle Eastern descent as *turcos* (Turks), a legacy of the initial immigration from the region.

Asian faces have become more common in recent years. There has long been a community of about 30,000 Japanese-Argentines, concentrated in the capital and the Gran Buenos Aires suburb of Escobar. Belgrano also has a modest Chinatown near the Barrancas. Many Koreans work in Once and live in the southern barrio of Nueva Pompeya.

Other South Americans, mostly Bolivians, Paraguayans, and Peruvians, flocked to Argentina during the early 1990s boom. They generally work at menial jobs, and many have returned home since the economic meltdown of 2001–2002. They are mostly concentrated in certain neighborhoods—Peruvians in Congreso, Paraguayans in Constitución, and Bolivians in Nueva Pompeya.

LANGUAGE

Spanish is Argentina's official language, but English is widely spoken in the tourist and business sectors of the economy. Foreign language use is also vigorous among ethnic communities, such as Italo-Argentines, Anglo-Argentines, and German-Argentines. The Anglo-Argentine and business communities even support a daily tabloid, *The Buenos Aires Herald,* while the German-Argentine community has the weekly *Argentinisches Tageblatt.*

Buenos Aires also has its own distinctive street slang, known as *lunfardo,* which owes its origins to working-class immigrant communities. Many *lunfardo* words have worked their way into everyday Argentine speech even though they may be unintelligible at first to those who have learned Spanish elsewhere. Some are fairly obvious in context, such as *laburar* instead of *trabajar* for work or labor, but others are obscure.

While many of its idioms are crude by standards of formal Spanish, *lunfardo* has acquired a certain legitimacy among Argentine scholars. There is even an academy for the study of *porteño* slang, the Academia Porteña del Lunfardo (Estados Unidos 1379, Monserrat, tel. 011/4383-2393).

Culture and the Arts

VISUAL ARTS

Because of its small, dispersed settlements, Argentina mostly lacked the great tradition of colonial religious art of the populous central Andean highlands, which developed their own styles of painting and sculpture in the churches of Peru and Bolivia. As a political and demographic entity, the Viceroyalty of the Río de la Plata did not even exist until the late 18th century and, according to *porteño* art critic Jorge Glusberg, "Buenos Aires was practically devoid of any cultural life." Glusberg has gone so far as to claim that the colonial period, "characterized by subordination to the European models currently in vogue," lasted until after World War II.

Glusberg may underrate the work of some early painters and sculptors, but there is no question that innovative Argentine artists have flourished artistically, if not always financially, since then—in both figurative and abstract modes. His English-language *Art in Argentina* (Milan: Giancarlo Politi Editore, 1986) is a readable and well-illustrated introduction to currents in contemporary Argentine art, though it needs an update. The same is true of Rafael Squirru's Spanish-only *Arte Argentino Hoy* (Ediciones de Arte Gaglianone, Buenos Aires, 1983), with color displays of 48 20th-century painters and sculptors.

Buenos Aires galleries range from prosaically traditional to truly daring. While gallery-hopping, watch for street art in the form of elaborate graffiti (see the website www.bagraff.com) and *filete,* the traditional line painting that once decorated horse carts, trucks, and buses; experiencing something of a revival, it now graces many cafés and restaurants, and has even returned to some buses. (For an overview of Buenos Aires galleries, see the *Shopping* chapter.)

In 1965, controversial *porteño* sculptor León Ferrari created *La Civilización Occidental y Cristiana (Western and Christian Civilization)* to protest the bombing of Vietnam.

Painting

One of Argentina's first notable artists, European-trained Prilidiano Pueyrredón (1823–1870) painted landscapes and people of rural Buenos Aires. Other early painters of note included Eduardo Sívori (1847–1918) and Ernesto de la Cárcova (1866–1927), both of whom manifested concern with social issues, such as poverty and hunger.

One of Argentine painting's extraordinary stories, though, is Cándido López (1840–1902), a junior army officer who lost his right forearm to gangrene after being struck by a grenade in battle against Paraguay. Remarkably, López painted more than 50 oils of war scenes with his left hand; even more remarkably, his paintings were not romanticized scenes of combat

heroism, but vivid landscapes depicting routine activities—ordinary encampments and river crossings, for instance—in addition to the occasional battle.

Benito Quinquela Martín (1890–1977) chronicled the struggles of immigrant factory workers and stevedores in his vivid oils of La Boca, many of which reside in his namesake museum in the barrio. One of Argentina's modern art pioneers Argentina was Jorge Luis Borges's friend Xul Solar (1887–1963; real name Alejandro Schulz Solari), who dealt with esoteric and mystical themes in his watercolors. His works are displayed in a Barrio Norte museum in his honor.

One of Argentina's best-known modern artists is the versatile Antonio Berni (1905–1981), who worked in painting, drawing, engraving, collage, and sculpture. His socially conscious canvases, such as *Juanito Laguna Bañándose entre Latas (Juanito Laguna Bathing in the Trash)*, have fetched astronomical prices in the international art market. His *Monstruos (Monsters)* is a series of three-dimensional works (1964–1971) that depicts the nightmares of Ramona Montiel, a prostitute who dreams of war, death, and destruction.

In conjunction with other artists, including Lino Spilimbergo (1896–1964), Juan Carlos Castagnino (1908–1972), Galician-born Manuel Colmeiro (1901–1999), and Demetrio Urruchúa (1902–1978), Berni was an adherent of the politically conscious Nuevo Realismo (New Realism) movement. The movement's greatest public legacy is the ceiling murals in the recycled Galerías Pacífico shopping center, under the influence of the famed Mexican painter David Alfaro Siqueiros.

Spilimbergo, when not collaborating on such projects, specialized in geometric forms, still lifes, and lighted landscapes. Castagnino specialized in rural, even gauchesque, landscapes, and Colmeiro and Urruchúa were both socially oriented painters and muralists.

Influenced by pop art, self-taught Jorge de la Vega (1930–1971) alternated figurative and abstract geometrical work; in his series of *Monstruos* or *Bestiario,* he attached objects, such as coins, sticks, and especially mirrors, to his canvases, deforming both the subject and the viewer.

One of Argentina's rising modern painters is Guillermo Kuitca, born in 1960 to a Russian-Jewish immigrant family. Kuitca contrasts small figures with large environments and transforms everyday abstractions, such as floor plans and road maps (most effectively in his *Kristallnacht II,* an observation on the Nazi genocide against German Jews). He also creates abstract visual expressions of popular music themes like the anti-lynching classic "Strange Fruit" and the Rolling Stones's "Gimme Shelter."

Daniel Barreto (born 1966) adapts popular figures, like the folk saint Difunta Correa of San Juan province and the rural bandit Gaucho Antonio Gil of Corrientes province, into colorful paintings that transcend the kitsch often associated with those figures.

Sculpture

Buenos Aires is a city of monuments; unfortunately, many if not most of them are pretentious busts of ostensible statesmen and colossal equestrian statues of military men like national icon José de San Martín, caudillo Justo José Urquiza, and Patagonian invader Julio Argentino Roca. The Rodin-influenced Rogelio Yrurtia (1879–1950), though he did create the mausoleum of President Bernardino Rivadavia, displayed his talents better in statues like the larger-than-life-size *The Boxers,* displayed at his house and museum in the barrio of Belgrano; even better is his working-class tribute *Canto al Trabajo (Ode to Labor),* on San Telmo's Plazoleta Olazábal.

Those following Yrurtia have been far more daring. León Ferrari (born 1920) created the prescient *La Civilización Occidental y Cristiana (Western and Christian Civilization,* 1965), a sardonic Vietnam-era work that portrays Christ crucified on a diving F-105. His 2005 retrospective at the Centro Cultural Recoleta drew howls of protest and a lawsuit from the Catholic Church that briefly shut it down. Ironically enough, the controversy gave Ferrari front-page publicity that he could never

have paid for: After the courts dismissed an injunction against the exhibition, more than a thousand art lovers and curiosity seekers per day queued up to an hour or more to see it.

Like Ferrari, Juan Carlos Distéfano (born 1933) blends sculpture and painting in works like *El Rey y La Reina* (1977), a disturbingly lifelike representation of a couple shot to death in an automobile. In the context of its time, it was a thinly disguised portrayal of extrajudicial executions carried out by military and paramilitary death squads after the 1976 coup. Remarkably, the work was shown publicly, on the Florida pedestrian mall, shortly thereafter.

Albert Heredia (born 1924) mocks the pomposity of monumental public art in works such as *El Caballero de la Máscara (The Masked Horseman).* The title is misleading, as this headless parody of an equestrian statue is a collage of materials that ridicules 19th-century strongmen and their modern counterparts. Heredia originally titled it *El Montonero,* a reference to the early Federalist cavalry, but could not exhibit the piece under its original name because the leftist guerrilla movement Montoneros was a hot-button issue at the time.

In contrast to politically committed sculptors like Ferrari and Heredia, Yoël Novoa creates cleverly entertaining caricatures of *porteños* and Buenos Aires street scenes in papier mâché.

ARCHITECTURE

Because Buenos Aires languished as a backwater of the Spanish colonial empire until the creation of the Viceroyalty of the River Plate in the late 18th century, little remains of its precarious early architecture. (There are older, more impressive early colonial constructions in the northwestern provinces of Jujuy, Salta, Tucumán, and Córdoba.)

Nevertheless, the barrios of Monserrat, San Telmo, and some others boast a selection of worthwhile colonial buildings, many but not all of them churches. Vernacular architecture styles include the distinctive *casa chorizo,* a long, narrow construction—sometimes barely wider than an adult's arm span—on deep lots.

The wood-frame, metal-clad houses of La Boca derive their traditional bright primary colors from the fact that early residents scavenged their paint from ships on the Riachuelo.

For most of the 19th century, *porteño* architecture evolved from its Spanish colonial origins to an Italianate style. Beginning in the early 20th century, the reigning architectural fashion was a beaux arts academicism, both for public buildings and the ornate *palacetes* (mansions) of the landowning oligarchy. Some of these Parisian-style residences became public buildings when the Great Depression bankrupted and impoverished—relatively speaking, of course—Argentina's first families. Many French professionals, including landscape architect Carlos Thays, worked on *porteño* projects in what has been called, with some exaggeration, "the Paris of the South."

From the 1930s onward, the capital developed greater residential and commercial density with buildings such as the Edificio Kavanagh, a handsome 30-story high-rise on Plaza San Martín. Barrios like Recoleta and Palermo that were once almost exclusively single-family residences or *propiedades horizontales* (horizontal properties, or *PHs*) are now filled with soaring apartment blocks. Some of these are handsome, others much less so.

The late 20th century saw some hideous developments, such as Italian-born Clorindo Testa's brutalist Biblioteca Nacional (National Library) in Palermo (in fairness, the building's interior is more attractive and practical than its hideous exterior would suggest). One positive development is the recycling of historical structures, such as the Galerías Pacífico and the Mercado del Abasto into contemporary shopping centers, and the former brick warehouses at Puerto Madero into fashionable restaurants, hotels, and residential lofts.

The best general guide to Buenos Aires's architecture, the Spanish-language *Buenos Aires: Guía de Arquitectura* (1994), edited by Alberto Petrina, includes suggested walking tours, architectural drawings, and sharp black-and-white photographs. Readers who know even basic Spanish can benefit from it.

MUSIC AND DANCE

Argentines are musical people, their interests ranging from folk, pop, rock, and blues to classical. The country's signature sound and dance is the tango, both as instrumental and with lyrics; in its plaintiveness and melancholy, it's a cultural counterpart to the blues.

In their musical interests, Argentine performers are versatile and unselfconscious about crossing boundaries—folksinger Mercedes Sosa, for instance, has sometimes performed with the talented but erratic rock musician Charly García. Throughout most of the 1990s, major international artists in both classical and popular music toured the country, but the peso's collapse placed many of them beyond the public's means. (Some have recently begun to return.) Nevertheless, qualified local performers were able to take up much of the slack, even at locales like the Teatro Colón, which traditionally attracts big overseas names.

Classical Music and Dance

Since its completion in 1908, the **Teatro Colón** has been the preeminent high-culture venue on the continent and perhaps in the entire southern hemisphere (the Sydney Opera House cannot boast the Colón's history). Thanks to the presence of the Colón, the **Teatro Avenida,** and other classical venues, early-20th-century Argentina produced an abundance of classical composers, particularly in the fields of opera and ballet.

Among the notable figures of the time were Héctor Panizza (1875–1967); Constantino Gaito (1878–1945), who produced *gauchesco* ballet, such as *La Flor del Irupé* (The Flower of Irupé); Felipe Boero (1884–1958), and Italian-born Pascual De Rogatis (1880–1980). Possibly the most distinguished, though, was Juan José Castro (1895–1968), whose career suffered because of his outspoken opposition to the 1943 military government and the subsequent Perón regime. Castro's ballets include *Mekhano* and *Offenbachiana.*

The Spanish composer Manuel de Falla (1876–1946) spent the last seven years of his life in Alta Gracia—a provincial Córdoba town that was also the boyhood home of Ernesto "Che" Guevara—following the victory of Perón's ally Francisco Franco in the Spanish Civil War. Franco's regime had executed Falla's friend, playwright Federico García Lorca.

One of the outstanding figures in Argentine ballet is Roberto García Morillo (1911–1996), whose works include *Usher* and *Harrild*. Arnaldo D'Espósito (1897–1945), Luis Gianneo (1897–1968), and Alberto Ginastera (1916–1983) were his contemporaries. A later generation of opera composers includes Valdo Sciamarella (born 1924), Mario Perusso (born 1936), and Gerardo Gandini (born 1936).

Contemporary Argentine classical music boasts figures like Daniel Barenboim (born 1942), a pianist and conductor who has held posts at the Orchestre de Paris, the Chicago Symphony Orchestra, and the Deutsche Staatsoper Berlin among others. Barenboim (also an Israeli citizen who has played in the West Bank in defiance of Israeli government objections) is a versatile figure who has, among other achievements, recorded tango and other popular music. He performed at the Colón during the economic crisis of 2002, when the theater could not afford to pay high-profile international acts.

Pianist Martha Argerich (born 1941), though she lives in Brussels, has sponsored competitions in Buenos Aires. She has drawn rave reviews from *The New York Times* for her Carnegie Hall concerts and has won a Grammy for Best Instrumental Soloist.

U.S.-based Osvaldo Golijov (born 1960) is responsible for classical works like *The St. Mark Passion,* but is flexible enough to work on movie soundtracks (for British director Sally Potter's widely panned *The Man Who Cried*) and even with rock bands like Mexico's Café Tacuba.

Rosario-born but Europe-based tenor José Cura (born 1962) has drawn attention as a credible successor to Luciano Pavarotti on the international opera scene. Among ballet performers, by far the most significant is Julio Bocca (born 1967), a prodigy who has performed in New York, Paris, and elsewhere.

He has formed his own company, the Ballet Argentino, and continued to perform in Argentina even during the economic crisis.

Popular Music

Argentine popular music takes many forms, from the Andean northwest's folk tradition to the accordion-based immigrant *chamamé* of the northeastern lowlands and Buenos Aires's hard-nosed *rock nacional*. Its centerpiece, though, remains the tango, which overlaps categories—many classical composers and performers (see the preceding *Classical Music and Dance* section) have incorporated tango into their repertoires.

Tango: Tango overlaps the categories of music and dance, and even within those categories there are distinctions. As music, the tango can be instrumental but it gained its initial popularity and international reputation through the *tango canción* (tango song) as projected by the legendary Carlos Gardel and others (though to a lesser degree). One *porteño* songwriter has described the tango as "a sad feeling that is danced," and there is no doubt that it appeals to nostalgia for things lost—an old flame or the old neighborhood, for instance.

The charismatic Gardel, whose birth date and birthplace are both topics of controversy, attained immortality after dying young in an aviation accident in Medellín, Colombia in 1935. According to his diehard admirers, "Gardel sings better every day." Uruguayan-born Julio Sosa (1926–1964), who also died young in a car accident, was nearly as important; at a time when Peronism was outlawed, his subtle smile and on-stage gestures evoked the exiled caudillo.

Orchestral tango, as opposed to that of the *tango canción,* is the legacy of bandleaders and composers like Osvaldo Pugliese (1905–1995), Aníbal "Pichuco" Troilo (1914–1975), and especially Astor Piazzola (1921–1992), whose jazz influences are palpable. Important lyricists include Enrique Santos Discépolo (1901–1951), also a composer, and Homero Manzi (1907–1951).

Practiced by skilled and sexy dancers in San

Telmo and Monserrat night clubs, the "tango for export" floor show is popular with tourists, but tells only part of the story. The tango is not exclusive to the young and lithe—in fact, one could easily argue that its nostalgia lends it to older individuals with longer memories—and a recent revival has made it just as popular with mixed-age audiences at *milongas* (informal dance clubs).

Tango remains a daily presence in the lives of *porteños,* with both a 24-hour FM radio station (FM 92.7) and a cable TV channel, Sólo Tango. Contemporary performers of note include several women, such as Eladia Blásquez (born 1931), Susana Rinaldi (born 1935), and Adriana Varela (born 1958). Pop singers, such as Sandro and Cacho Castaña (born 1942), have also sung tango, and the much younger Omar Giammarco produces tango-flavored music using accordion instead of *bandoneón* in his *quinteto.* La Chicana is a tango song group that adds a flute to the traditional instrumental mix and even works with rock musicians.

Folk: Tango is arguably an urban folk music, but Argentina's true folk tradition stems from *payadores,* gauchos who sang verses to guitar accompaniment; in dance, it sometimes takes the form of the *malambo,* a competitive male-only affair that, despite its identification with the Pampas, contains echoes of flamenco. An older current derives from the northwestern Andean provinces and their link to the Bolivian and Peruvian highlands, featuring the *zampoña* (panpipes) and *charango,* a tiny stringed instrument that uses an armadillo shell as its sound box.

Born in Buenos Aires province, the late Atahualpa Yupanqui (1908–1992) belongs to these purist traditions, as does the Salta-based group Los Chalchaleros, an institution for more than half a century. Tucumán native Mercedes Sosa (born 1935) also comes from this tradition but is less of a purist, having even performed with the brilliant but erratic rock musician Charly García. Their contemporary León Gieco (born 1951) crosses the line into folk-rock and even rap.

Tomás Lipán, an Aymará Indian from the northwestern village of Purmamarca in Jujuy province, embodies the region's Andean folk roots but adds urban touches like the *bandoneón* to create an Argentine hybrid. Soledad Pastorutti (born 1980), who goes by her first name only as a performer, is a self-conscious folkie who sings and dresses in an exaggerated *gauchesco* style.

Immigrant communities have left their mark in *chamamé,* an accordion-based music typical of the humid lowland provinces along the Río Paraná and the Río Uruguay, north of Buenos Aires to the Brazilian and Paraguayan borders. Among the notable performers are Antonio Tarragó Ros (born 1947) and Chango Spasiuk (born 1968); the latter comes from a Ukrainian immigrant community in the province of Misiones.

Rock and Pop: It's no exaggeration to say that Buenos Aires, like London or San Francisco in the mid- to late 1960s, has one of the most vigorous rock scenes ever. Despite the handicap of trying to fit a multisyllabic language into a monosyllabic musical idiom, the practitioners of *rock nacional* have had remarkable success.

In terms of live music, there seems to be something happening every night. One downside to this is that some top bands have a small but pugnacious hard core of fans who tend to crowd the stage; most visitors unaccustomed to the scene will probably prefer to stand back a bit. The other drawback, ostensibly being remedied, is the questionable safety conditions; a catastrophic Once fire, in which nearly 200 fans of Los Callejeros died in December 2004, has prompted overdue inspections of the locales in which many groups play.

Argentine rock music's pioneer is Roberto Sánchez (born 1945), better known by his stage name, Sandro. As an early rock star who became a movie idol with a dominating manager, Sandro draws obvious comparisons with Elvis Presley, but "El Maestro" has also been a credible tango singer and the first Argentine to appear at Madison Square Garden. A surprisingly modest individual but also a heavy smoker who now needs oxygen on stage, he is the honoree of *Tributo a Sandro: Un Disco de Rock,* an exceptional tribute album by Argentine, Chilean, Colombian, and Mexican rock bands.

Charly García (born 1951), a founder of the legendary Sui Generis, transcends generations—many of his fans are in their 20s and even younger. García, who sings and plays mostly keyboards, incorporates women into his backing bands even as lead guitarists and saxophonists; he displays a sense of history in performing classics like Eddie Cochran's "Summertime Blues," the Byrds's "I'll Feel a Whole Lot Better," Neil Young's "Don't Let It Bring You Down," and even the obscure Small Faces gem "Tin Soldier." Rather than strict cover versions, these are adaptations, often with García's own Spanish-language lyrics.

Nearly as revered as Charly is the Dylanesque León Gieco; his album *Bandidos Rurales* (2002) bears thematic resemblance to Dylan's *John Wesley Harding*. He does a brilliant cover of Sandro's "Si Yo Fuera Carpintero," itself a brilliant Spanish-language adaptation of Tim Hardin's "If I Were a Carpenter."

Fito Páez (born 1963) and García protegé Andrés Calamaro (born 1961) also have solo careers, but many acts in the *rock nacional* idiom have a stronger group identity than individual identity. Among them are Attaque 77, Babasónicos, Los Divididos (a branch of the earlier Sumo and famous for their versions of the Mexican folk song "Cielito Lindo" and the Doors's "Light My Fire"), Las Pelotas (the other branch of Sumo), Los Piojos, Los Ratones Paranóicos (strongly influenced by the Rolling Stones), and Patricio Rey y Sus Redonditos de Ricota. Almafuerte and the power trio A.N.I.M.A.L are the leading heavy metal bands.

Grammy winners Los Fabulosos Cadillacs (best alternative Latin rock group in 1998) have toured North America, playing salsa- and reggae-influenced rock at venues like San Francisco's legendary Fillmore Auditorium. Others in this idiom include Los Auténticos Decadentes, Los Cafres, but the band of the moment is Bersuit Vergarabat.

In a category of their own are Les Luthiers, an eclectic bunch who make their own unique instruments (which defy description) and caricature the most bourgeois and authoritarian sectors of Argentine society. While musically sophisticated, their shows are as much theater as concert.

Jazz and Blues: Both traditional and free-form jazz play a part in Argentina's musical history. A fixture in the traditional jazz scene is the Fénix Jazz Band, whose vocalist Ernesto "Cachi" Carrizo says he can't sing blues in Spanish because "the blues in Spanish seems as absurd to me as tango in English."

Better known outside strictly Argentine circles is saxophonist Gato Barbieri (born 1932), who also wrote the soundtrack for *The Last Tango in Paris*. Hollywood regular Lalo Schifrin (born 1932), famous for TV and movie soundtracks like *Bullitt, Cool Hand Luke,* and *Mission Impossible,* originally moved north to play piano with Dizzy Gillespie. Schifrin, who also writes classical music, makes a brief onscreen appearance as an orchestra conductor in the opening sequence of the Hannibal Lecter gore-fest *Red Dragon* (2002); his father, Luis, was concertmaster of the Teatro Colón's orchestra.

Buenos Aires has a robust blues scene, thanks to individuals like the late guitarist Pappo and groups like La Mississippi and Memphis La Blusera, who have even taken their act to the stage of the Teatro Colón (almost causing nausea from classical music critics). The female vocal trio Las Blacanblus treats blues standards in a distinctive style with minimal accompaniment—only guitar and piano. International blues figures such as B.B. King, and many less-famous but still credible foreign artists, have also played in B.A.

CINEMA

Given the country's political and economic instability, it's surprising that Argentine cinema has been as productive and successful as it has. In the year 2000, for instance, Argentine directors managed to make 30 full-length features and four documentaries. In October

2002, the American Cinemateque showed a dozen new films in the three-day New Argentine Cinema 2002 in Hollywood's Egyptian Theater, with attendance by Argentine directors and actors.

Special effects are generally limited, and it's worth noting that Argentine films, like European ones, tend to be more character- than plot-driven. There are plenty of outstanding directors and actors, and quite a few films from the last 20 years, in particular, are available on video.

Not only have Argentines made good films, but foreign directors have found Buenos Aires an interesting locale for filming—all the more so now that the peso's collapse has made it inexpensive to shoot in the capital. Readers who know Spanish should look for film critic Diego Curubeto's *Babilonia Gaucha* (Buenos Aires: Editorial Planeta, 1993), on the relationship between Argentina and Hollywood; Curubeto also wrote *Cine Bizarro* (Buenos Aires: Editorial Sudamericana, 1996), on idiosyncratic films from Argentina and elsewhere.

Alquileres Lavalle (Lavalle 1199, tel. 4476-1118) rents and sells Argentine videos in the original Spanish. Argentine videos, however, use European PAL technology, which is incompatible with the North American VHS system.

Argentine Directors, Movies, and Actors

In its earliest years, Argentine cinema dealt almost exclusively with *porteño* topics, such as Carnaval; even given the capital's Afro-American traditions, it's startling to see Argentine actors in blackface. Later, tango legend Carlos Gardel worked extensively in Hollywood as well as Buenos Aires, starring in films such as *El Día Que Me Quieras* (The Day You Love Me, 1935).

Over the years, several Argentine films have made respectable showings at the Oscars. Director Sergio Renán's *La Tregua (The Truce,* 1975), based on a story by Uruguayan Mario Benedetti, was the first nominated for best foreign-language film; it lost to the tough competition of Federico Fellini's *Amarcord.*

María Luisa Bemberg (1922–1995), astonishingly enough, made her first feature at the age of 58, but made up for lost time with films like *Camila,* nominated in 1984; it was based on the true story of 19th-century heiress Camila O'Gorman, her Jesuit lover, and their persecution by the Rosas dictatorship. In 1985, director Luis Puenzo's *The Official Story* won the Oscar for his treatment of the controversial issue of military adoptions of infant children of "disappeared" parents during the 1976–1983 Dirty War; it stars Norma Aleandro, a highly respected theater actress and director. Puenzo drew scorn, though, for implying that some Argentines were unaware of extrajudicial tortures and murders.

Based partly on Adolfo Bioy Casares's novella *The Invention of Morel,* Eliseo Subiela's *Man Facing Southeast* won a nomination in 1986; the plot of the 2001 Hollywood production *K-Pax,* starring Kevin Spacey and Jeff Bridges, bears a remarkable resemblance to Subiela's work. Most recently, in 2002, Juan José Campanella's maudlin *Hijo de la Novia* (The Bride's Son) received a nomination; Ricardo Darín plays the title role, a type-A *porteño* restaurateur whose father wants to give Darín's Alzheimer's-stricken mother a belated church wedding.

The Oscars, though, showcase only a small percentage of Argentine films and are not necessarily representative. Often subtly and sometimes overtly political, they are frequently eloquent and passionate but also introspective—partly due, perhaps, to the popularity of psychoanalysis in the capital.

Subiela's *The Dark Side of the Heart* (1992), an erotic love story with both humor and pathos, takes place in Buenos Aires and Montevideo; based loosely on the life of *porteño* poet Oliverio Girondo, it features a cameo by Uruguayan poet Mario Benedetti.

Bemberg also made the English-language *Miss Mary* (1986), starring Julie Christie in the tale of an English governess on an Argentine *estancia,* and *I Don't Want to Talk About It* (1992), a truly peculiar romance starring the late Marcelo Mastroianni and set in a conservative provincial town (the filming took place in the Uruguayan city of Colonia, across the river from Buenos Aires).

Adolfo Aristarain (born 1943) directed the versatile Federico Luppi in the Spanish-language thriller *Time of Revenge* (1981), a labor drama available on video, and in *A Place in the World* (1992). The latter is a socially conscious film that was disqualified for an Oscar nomination because it was unclear whether it was an Uruguayan, Argentine, or Spanish production (most of the filming took place in Argentina's scenic San Luis province). Aristarain also directed the English-language film *The Stranger* (1986), a psychological thriller with Peter Riegert, Bonnie Bedelia, and cameos from a cast of Argentine stars, but its ingenious structure can't compensate for a plot full of holes.

Other films have gotten less international recognition but are worth seeing, such as Bruno Stagnaro's and Adrián Caetano's low-budget *Pizza, Birra, Faso* (1997), an unsentimental story of *porteño* lowlifes trying to get by. Ricardo Darín shares the lead with Gastón Pauls in Fabián Bielinsky's *Nine Queens* (2001), the twist-filled noirish tale of *porteño* con-men who strike up a partnership in crisis-racked Buenos Aires.

Politically committed director Fernando "Pino" Solanas (born 1936), a left-wing Peronist, dealt with the theme of expatriation in *The Exile of Gardel* (1985). Tango legend Astor Piazzola wrote the soundtrack and also appears in the film, which, appropriately enough for a film whose title figure may have been born in France, takes place in Paris.

The prolific Leopoldo Torre Nilsson (1924–1978), who shot nearly 30 features in his relatively short lifetime, adapted Manuel Puig's novel *Boquitas Pintadas (Painted Lips)*, a story of hypocrisy and petty jealousies in a small provincial town, to the screen in 1974. Torre Nilsson also filmed *La Guerra del Cerdo (War of the Pigs*, 1975); set in Palermo, it's a discomforting adaptation of Adolfo Bioy Casares's story of generational conflict and political polarization in the immediate pre-coup years. Argentine jazz legend Gato Barbieri wrote the soundtrack.

Director Héctor Olivera (born 1931) has turned two of Osvaldo Soriano's satirical novels into movies: *A Funny Dirty Little War* (1983), which depicts the comic consequences of a military coup in a provincial town (but has nothing to do, directly at least, with the 1976–1983 dictatorship); and *Una Sombra Ya Pronto Serás (Shadows*, 1994), a road movie that encourages disorientation by making it impossible to tell where the movie takes place. Federico Luppi (born 1936) appeared in the former.

Starting with a bungled robbery in Buenos Aires, Marcelo Piñeyro's *Wild Horses* (1995) becomes a road romance that ends with a chase in the Patagonian province of Chubut. Héctor Alterio, who plays opposite Norma Aleandro in *Hijo de la Novia,* is a hostage who goes along for the ride.

Gustavo Mosquera directed the innovative *Moebius* (1996), really a collaborative film-school project set mostly in a Borgesian Buenos Aires subway; a disappearing train, audible but not visible, serves as a metaphor for Dirty War victims. Displaying great creativity and technical proficiency on a shoestring budget, its anachronisms—antique dial telephones alongside cell phones, for instance—imply that despite modernization and the return to representative government, remnants of the old Argentina remain.

In addition to his Argentine films, Federico Luppi has appeared in two outstanding films by Mexican director Guillermo del Toro: the sci-fi thriller *Cronos* (1992) and the politically charged ghost story *The Devil's Backbone,* set during the Spanish Civil War. Luppi also played the lead role of a socially committed physician in U.S. director John Sayles's *Men with Guns* (1997), an eloquent parable on political violence in Latin America.

Norma Aleandro (born 1936), best known overseas for *The Official Story,* has won many international acting awards. She has also appeared opposite Anthony Hopkins in Sergio Toledo's *One Man's War,* a human-rights drama set in Paraguay.

Cecilia Roth (born 1958), who appeared with Luppi in *A Place in the World,* has worked

the Argentine trinity of Carlos Gardel, Evita Perón, and Diego Maradona

frequently with maverick Spanish director Pedro Almodóvar, most recently in *All About My Mother* (1999).

THEATER

Porteños, traditionally, are theatergoers. In the year 2000, for example, more than 300,000 attended programs at both the Teatro Colón and the Teatro General San Martín combined, and nearly 200,000 went to the Teatro Cervantes. Even in September 2002, at the nadir of the country's worst economic crisis ever, there were 110 plays showing at 70 theaters, and three new theaters opened their doors the first weekend of that month.

The theater tradition dates from late colonial times, when creation of the Virreinato del Río de la Plata gave the city a certain legitimacy and pretensions, at least, to high culture. Over the course of the 19th century, the area's theater culture developed through institutions like the *sainete,* a humorous performance dealing with immigrant issues.

Formal theater dates from the late 19th century, thanks to the patronage of the Montevideo-born Podestá family, who built theaters in Buenos Aires and La Plata. Influential early playwrights included Montevideo-born Florencio Sánchez (1875–1910), who wrote *sainetes* but drew much of his inspiration from Ibsen; Gregorio de Laferrere (1867–1913), who wrote comic plays; and Roberto Payró (1867–1928), also a novelist.

Twentieth-century European dramatists, such as Federico García Lorca and Jean Cocteau, found that the Buenos Aires theater scene justified the long trip across the Atlantic in the days before jets. Among Argentina's best-loved 20th-century performers are comedian Luis Sandrini (1905–1980) and Lola Membrives (1888–1969); the best-known contemporary playwright is Juan Carlos Gené. Norma Aleandro, while primarily known for her films, is active as a theater director.

Religion

Roman Catholicism remains Argentina's official and dominant religion, but evangelical Protestantism, with its street preachers and storefront churches, is growing even in sophisticated Buenos Aires, mostly but not exclusively among the working-class population. Other religions have fewer adherents, though there's still a sizeable Jewish community and a small but growing Muslim presence.

Catholicism in particular has left the city with many of its greatest landmarks, ranging from the colonial churches of San Telmo and Recoleta to the dignified neoclassical Catedral. Immigrant Protestant communities are also responsible for ecclesiastical landmarks like the Danish and Swedish churches of San Telmo and the impressive Russian Orthodox dome opposite Parque Lezama, also in San Telmo.

ROMAN CATHOLICISM

Starting with the famous Dominican Bartolomé de las Casas in Mexico, factions in the Church have wrestled with the contradictions between its official mission of recruiting and saving souls and its duty to alleviate the misery of those who have experienced secular injustice and persecution. Argentina is no exception—figures such as the late Cardinal Antonio Quarracino were outright apologists for the vicious military dictatorship of 1976–1983, but others lobbied against its excesses and for return to democracy. Some more militant clergy worked in the slums under the influence of "liberation theology," and some lost their lives in the aftermath of the 1976 coup.

Folk Catholicism, including spiritualist practices, often diverges from Church orthodoxy in the veneration of unofficial saints, like the Difunta Correa of San Juan province, and even historical figures like Juan and Evita Perón, tango legend Carlos Gardel, and healer Madre María, all of whose tombs are in Buenos Aires's landmark cemeteries at Recoleta and Chacarita. Novelist Tomás Eloy Martínez has sardonically labeled his countrymen as "cadaver cultists" for their devotion to those dead and gone.

PROTESTANTISM

Anglicans were the original bearers of Protestantism in Argentina, but Scandinavian communities were numerous enough to justify construction of Danish and Swedish churches. More recent Protestant denominations are often shrill evangelicals; nearby Uruguay's capital city of Montevideo is one of the centers for Reverend Sun Myung Moon's cultish Unification Church.

OTHER RELIGIONS

The Argentine constitution guarantees freedom of religion, and adherents of non-Christian faiths are not rare, if not exactly widespread or numerous. The largest and most conspicuous of these other religions is Judaism, as the capital's Jewish community is at least 200,000 strong (a planned community census may well reveal a larger number). The government of Saudi Arabia sponsored the construction of Palermo's Centro Islámico Rey Fahd, whose capacity is disproportionately large for the capital's relatively small community of observant Muslims.

Getting There

Most overseas visitors arrive by air, though many also arrive overland from Chile, Bolivia, Uruguay, Paraguay, and Brazil. Almost all of the latter arrive by bus or private vehicle; there is no international rail service. There are ferry connections to Uruguay.

BY AIR

Buenos Aires has regular air links with North America, Europe, and Australia/New Zealand, plus less-frequent routes from southern Africa across the Atlantic (usually via Brazil). It is, however, a relatively expensive destination during peak periods, such as Christmas/New Year's and Holy Week holidays; an Advance Purchase Excursion (APEX) fare can reduce the bite considerably, but may have minimum- and maximum-stay requirements, allow no stopovers, and impose financial penalties for any changes. Economy-class (Y) tickets, valid for 12 months, are more expensive but allow maximum flexibility. Travelers staying more than a year, though, have to cough up the difference for any interim price increase.

Discount ticket agents, known as consolidators in the United States and "bucket shops" in Britain, may offer the best deals but often have drawbacks—they may not, for instance, allow mileage credit for frequent-flyer programs. Courier flights, on which passengers give up some or all of their baggage allowance to a company sending equipment or documents to overseas affiliates or customers may be even cheaper but are less common to Latin America than to other parts of the world. These are also available for short periods only and often leave on short notice.

Other options include Round the World (RTW) and Circle Pacific routes that permit numerous stopovers over the course of much longer multi-continental trips, but putting these itineraries together requires some effort. Two useful resources for researching airfares are the third edition of Edward Hasbrouck's *The Practical Nomad* (Emeryville, CA: Avalon Travel Publishing, 2004) and the same author's *The Practical Nomad Guide to the Online Marketplace* (Emeryville, CA: Avalon Travel Publishing, 2001).

While airlines reduced their services to Buenos Aires after the economic collapse of 2001–2002, as far fewer Argentines could afford to travel overseas and business travel from overseas likewise declined, the recent recovery has meant increased air traffic. American Airlines, for instance, has reinstituted non-stops to and from Dallas.

Airports

Buenos Aires has two airports, both operated by the private concessionaire Aeropuertos Argentinos 2000 (tel. 011/5480-6111, www.aa2000.com.ar). The main international facility is Aeropuerto Internacional Ministro Pistarini, 35 kilometers southwest of downtown, popularly called Ezeiza after its Buenos Aires province suburb. The other is Aeroparque Jorge Newbery, within the capital's boundaries at Avenida Costanera Rafael Obligado s/n (*sin número,* or unnumbered), Palermo; Aeroparque is primarily domestic but has a handful of international flights from neighboring countries.

International passengers leaving from Ezeiza pay a US$30.50 departure tax, payable in local currency or U.S. dollars, but it's partially included in the ticket price. On flights of fewer than 300 kilometers to neighboring countries, such as Uruguay and Chile (from Mendoza), the tax is only US$16.50, and on domestic flights it's US$2. Again, these fees are normally included in the ticket price.

From North America

Miami, Atlanta, Washington, D.C. (Dulles), New York, Dallas, and Los Angeles are the main gateways to Buenos Aires. Aerolíneas Argentinas is the traditional flagship carrier,

INTERNATIONAL AIRLINES IN BUENOS AIRES

Unless otherwise indicated, the airline offices below are in the Microcentro.

Aerolíneas Argentinas: Perú 2, Monserrat, tel. 0810/222-86527
AeroMéxico: Reconquista 737, 3rd fl., tel. 0800/666-0133
Air Canada: Avenida Córdoba 656, tel. 011/4327-3640
Air Europa: Avenida Santa Fe 962, 1st fl., Retiro, tel. 011/4327-1700
Air France: San Martín 344, 23rd fl., tel. 0800/222-2600
Air New Zealand: Marcelo T. de Alvear 590, 10th fl., Retiro, tel. 011/4315-5494
Alitalia: Avenida Santa Fe 887, Retiro, tel. 011/4310-9999
American Airlines: Avenida Santa Fe 881, Retiro, tel. 011/4318-1111
American Falcon: Avenida Santa Fe 963, Retiro, tel. 011/4328-0543
Avianca: Carlos Pellegrini 1163, 4th fl., Retiro, tel. 011/4394-5990
British Airways: Carlos Pellegrini 1163, Retiro, tel. 0800/666-1459
Copa: Carlos Pellegrini 989, 2nd fl., Retiro, tel. 0810/222-2672
Cubana de Aviación: Sarmiento 552, 11th fl., tel. 011/4326-5291
Delta: Carlos Pellegrini 1141, 12th fl., Retiro, tel. 0800/666-0133
Iberia: Carlos Pellegrini 1163, 1st fl., Retiro, tel. 011/4131-1000
KLM: Suipacha 268, 9th fl., tel. 011/4326-8422
LAN: Cerrito 866, Retiro, tel. 011/4378-2200
Lloyd Aéreo Boliviano (LAB): Carlos Pellegrini 141, tel. 011/4323-1901
Lufthansa: Marcelo T. de Alvear 590, 6th fl., Retiro, tel. 011/4319-0600
Malaysia Airlines: Suipacha 1111, 14th fl., Retiro, tel. 011/4313-4698
Mexicana: Avenida Córdoba 755, 1st fl., Retiro, tel. 011/4000-6300
Pluna: Florida 1, Microcentro, tel. 011/4342-4420
Qantas: Avenida Córdoba 673, 13th fl., Retiro, tel. 011/4114-5800
South African Airways: Avenida Santa Fe 1141, 5th fl., Retiro, tel. 011/5556-6666
Southern Winds: Avenida Santa Fe 784, Retiro, tel. 0810/777-7979
Swiss International: Avenida Santa Fe 846, 1st fl., Retiro, tel. 011/4319-0000
Transportes Aéreos de Mercosur (TAM): Cerrito 1026, Retiro, tel. 011/4819-4800
United Airlines: Avenida Eduardo Madero 900, 9th fl., Retiro, tel. 0810/777-8648
Varig: Avenida Córdoba 972, 4th fl., Retiro, tel. 011/4329-9211

Note: At press time, Southern Winds was experiencing difficulties due to withdrawal of state subsidies, and its state-owned affiliate Lafsa was in limbo. Currently Aerolíneas Argentinas/Austral is the only reliable domestic airline, though the Chilean airline LAN is due to begin services between Argentine cities.

AIRPORT TRANSPORTATION

There's a variety of options to and from the airports, ranging from *colectivos* (city buses) to shuttles, taxis, and *remises* (meterless taxis that quote a fixed price for the trip).

Colectivos

Colectivos provide the cheapest transportation to and from the airports, but they are more practical for close-in Aeroparque than distant Ezeiza, as they take circuitous routes on surface streets. To Aeroparque (about US$.25), the alternatives are No. 33 from Plaza de Mayo, the Microcentro and Retiro; No. 37-C ("Ciudad Universitaria") from Plaza del Congreso, Avenida Callao, Avenida las Heras, and Plaza Italia; No 45 northbound from Plaza Constitución, Plaza San Martín, or Retiro; and No. 160-C or 160-D from Avenida Las Heras or Plaza Italia. Return buses leave from the Avenida Costanera Rafael Obligado, a short walk outside the terminal.

To Ezeiza (about US$.80), the backpackers' choice is the No. 86-A ("Aeropuerto"), from La Boca to Plaza de Mayo, Plaza del Congreso, Plaza Once, and onward, but the roundabout route takes up to two hours. *Servicio Diferencial* buses cost more (about US$2.50) but have more comfortable reclining seats. In Ezeiza, both leave from a stop at the Aerolíneas Argentinas terminal, a short distance from the main international terminal.

Shuttles

Manuel Tienda León (Avenida Madero and San Martín, tel. 011/4315-5115 or 800/777-0078, www.tiendaleon.com.ar) runs 35 shuttle buses daily to and from Ezeiza (US$8 pp) between 4 A.M. and 11:30 P.M. There are 25 daily to Aeroparque (US$3) between 8:30 A.M. and 10:45 P.M.; most buses from Ezeiza make connections to Aeroparque for domestic flights.

Taxis and Remises

Taxis and *remises* offer similar services, but taxis are metered and *remises* (generally newer and more spacious vehicles) are not. Offering door-to-door service, they are no more expensive than shuttles for three or more persons. Manuel Tienda León and many other companies, such as Transfer Express (tel. 0800/444-4872) and Naon Remises (tel. 011/4545-6500, remisesnaon@sinectis.com.ar) offer *remises* to Aeroparque (US$6) and Ezeiza (US$18). Both *remises* and taxis usually add the cost of the toll road to Ezeiza, which is less than US$1.

but other options include American Airlines, Copa, Delta, LAN (Chile), Mexicana, Southern Winds, and TAM Mercosur. Aerolíneas Argentinas, American, Delta, and United have the only nonstop services; others require changing planes elsewhere in Central or South America.

Canadian passengers can avoid connections in the United States by taking Air Canada from Toronto, some days nonstop and others via Santiago de Chile.

From Mexico, Central America, and the Caribbean

Mexicana flies six times weekly from Mexico City via Cancún, while LAN has regional connections via Santiago de Chile.

Copa flies daily from Panama, with connections throughout Central America.

Cubana flies twice weekly from Havana, while Avianca has connections to the Caribbean, Central America, and Mexico via Bogotá.

From Europe

From Europe, there are direct services to Buenos Aires with Aerolíneas Argentinas (from Rome and Madrid, with connections from London and Paris); Air Europa (from Madrid); Air France (from Paris); Alitalia (from Milan and Rome); British Airways (from London); Iberia (from Barcelona and Madrid); KLM (from Amsterdam via São Paulo); Lufthansa (from Frankfurt); Southern Winds (from Madrid); Swiss International (from Zurich and Geneva); and TAM (from Paris via São Paulo).

From Asia, Africa, and the Pacific

The most direct service from the Pacific is Aerolíneas Argentinas transpolar flight from Sydney and Auckland, though Qantas also flies from Sydney and Auckland to Santiago de Chile, and also links up with LAN flights via Tahiti, Easter Island, and Santiago, or with LAN via Los Angeles. From Japan, it's easiest to make connections via Los Angeles.

South African Airways flies six times weekly from Johannesburg to São Paulo, where TAM and Varig offer connections to Buenos Aires. Malaysia Airlines flies twice weekly to Cape Town, Johannesburg, and Kuala Lumpur.

Within South America

Buenos Aires has connections to the neighboring republics of Uruguay, Brazil, Paraguay, Bolivia, Chile, and elsewhere on the continent. There are no flights to the Guyanas, however.

Some international airlines fly to and from Ezeiza to Montevideo, **Uruguay,** but most flights to the Uruguayan capital leave from the closer Aeroparque. There are also flights from Aeroparque to Punta del Este, Uruguay's popular summer resort and weekend getaway. Aerolíneas Argentinas and Pluna are the main carriers, but American Falcon also has a few flights.

To **Brazil,** the main destinations are São Paulo and Rio de Janiero, but there are also flights to Florianópolis, Porto Alegre, Curitiba, and other cities. The main carriers are Aerolíneas Argentinas, TAM, and Varig.

Flights to **Paraguay** go to the capital city of

Asunción, with TAM and Varig; some TAM flights continue to São Paulo (Brazil).

Lloyd Aéreo Boliviano flies to the lowland **Bolivian** city of Santa Cruz de la Sierra and on to Cochabamba and the highland capital of La Paz, as does AeroSur. Aerolíneas also flies to Santa Cruz, and TAM has connections to Santa Cruz and Cochabamba via Asunción.

Discount fares are often available from travel agents but are less common in Latin America than elsewhere; the major exception is the highly competitive Buenos Aires–Santiago de Chile route: European carriers like Air France and Lufthansa try to fill empty seats between **Chile** and the Argentine capital, where most transatlantic passengers board or disembark. This has kept fares low on competitors like Aerolíneas Argentinas and LAN.

Flights to **Peru, Ecuador, Colombia,** and **Venezuela** are all via capital cities, though some carriers stop elsewhere en route. Aerolíneas Argentinas goes to Lima and Caracas; Aeroméxico goes to Lima en route to Mexico City; and Avianca flies to Bogotá.

From Elsewhere in Argentina

In addition to international air service, there is a network of domestic airports and airlines centered in Buenos Aires; indeed, to fly between Argentine cities, changing planes in Buenos Aires is almost unavoidable. Since none of the excursions in this book requires flying, these destinations and airlines are covered only generally here. Unless otherwise indicated, all of them use Aeroparque, the city airport.

Please note that in early 2003 some Argentine domestic airlines began to charge differential rates for Argentine residents and foreigners in dollars; while fares are moderate by international standards, Argentines can pay substantially less.

Aerolíneas Argentinas has domestic as well as international flights. Their domestic branch Austral (Perú 2, Monserrat, tel. 011/4320-2345) flies to destinations ranging from Puerto Iguazú on the Brazilian border to Ushuaia in Tierra del Fuego.

Southern Winds (Avenida Santa Fe 764,

tel. 011/4515-8600, www.sw.com.ar) serves a large number of domestic destinations from Aeroparque, but its future is shaky since withdrawal of government subsidies in the aftermath of a drug scandal tied to its international services.

American Falcon (Avenida Santa Fe 963, Retiro, tel. 0810/222-3252, www.americanfalcon.com.ar) flies from Aeroparque to Iguazú, the northwestern city of Salta, the Patagonian resorts of Bariloche, and Puerto Madryn.

Líneas Aéreas del Estado (LADE, Perú 714, San Telmo, tel. 011/4361-7071) is the Argentine air force's heavily subsidized commercial aviation branch. Miraculously surviving budget crises and privatizations, it flies to southern Buenos Aires province and Patagonia on a wing and a deficit.

BY LAND
Bus
Buenos Aires's main bus station is Retiro's Estación Terminal de Omnibus (Avenida Ramos Mejía 1860, tel. 011/4310-0700, www.tebasa.com.ar). The sprawling three-story building is home to nearly 140 bus companies that cover the entire country and international destinations as well. It's walking distance from the northern terminus of Subte Línea C, at the Retiro train station.

The ground floor is primarily for freight; buses leave from first-floor *andenes* (platforms), but ticket offices are on the second floor. On the first floor, the Centro de Informes y Reclamos (tel. 011/4310-0700) provides general bus information and also oversees taxis that serve the terminal; direct any complaints about taxi drivers to them. There is also a separate tourist office, open 7:30 A.M.–1 P.M. only.

For international buses, reservations are a good idea, especially during the summer (January and February) and winter (late July) holiday periods, but also on long weekends like *Semana Santa* (Holy Week). Prices vary according to the quality of service, ranging from ordinary reclining seats to more spacious *servicio diferencial* and nearly horizontal *coche cama*.

Domestic bus services to the provinces do not appear in detail here. (For transportation to areas beyond the federal capital, see the appropriate geographical entry in the *Excursions from Buenos Aires* chapter.)

Several companies take the roundabout 600-kilometer route to **Montevideo, Uruguay,** which takes longer (eight hours) than the ferry but costs (US$24) less than half: Bus de la Carrera (four nightly, tel. 011/4313-1700); Cauvi (one nightly, tel. 011/4314-6999); and General Belgrano (one nightly, tel. 011/4315-1226). All leave between 9:30 and 11:30 P.M.

To the Paraguayan capital of **Asunción** (US$27–37, 17 hours), the main carriers are Nuestra Señora de la Asunción (tel. 011/4313-2349) and Chevalier Paraguaya (tel. 011/4313-2325). For **Brazilian destinations,** such as Foz do Iguaçu (US$36, 18 hours), Porto Alegre (US$42, 20 hours), São Paulo (US$80, 38 hours), and Rio de Janeiro (US$90, 42 hours), try Pluma (tel. 011/4313-3893) or Crucero del Norte (tel. 011/4315-1652).

For the trans-Andean crossing to **Santiago, Chile** (US$45, 21 hours), carriers include Fénix Pullman Norte (tel. 011/4313-0134) and Transporte Automotores Cuyo (TAC, tel. 011/4313-7012). For the Peruvian capital of **Lima** (via Chile, US$110, a 68-hour marathon), the choices are El Rápido Internacional (tel. 011/4313-3757) and Ormeño Internacional (tel. 011/4313-2259).

Car, Motorcycle, and Bicycle
Overland travel from North America or elsewhere is problematical because Panama's Darien Gap route to Colombia is impassable for motor vehicles, time-consuming, very difficult, and potentially dangerous even for those on foot. The route passes through areas controlled by drug smugglers, guerrillas, and/or brutal Colombian paramilitaries.

For travelers whose primary interest is the city, a vehicle is unnecessary, as public transport is cheap and excellent (parking, meanwhile, is next to impossible). Those visiting other parts of the continent, though, might consider shipping a vehicle, which is recommended over renting a car for extended trips. While rental cars are easy to find in both Argentina and Uruguay, crossing borders with them can be complicated (though not impossible) and requires extra expense for insurance and notarial documents. To locate a shipper, check the Yellow Pages of your local phone directory under Automobile Transporters. These are normally freight consolidators rather than the companies that own the ships—the latter will charge higher container rates. Since many more people ship vehicles to Europe than to South America, it may take patience to find the right shipper; one recommended North American consolidator is McClary, Swift & Co. (360 Swift Avenue, South San Francisco, CA 94080, tel. 650/872-2121, www.glomato.com/swift), which has agents at many U.S. ports.

Argentine customs has improved in recent years, so shipping a vehicle into the country is easier than it used to be. Vehicles arrive at the Estación Marítima Buenos Aires (Dársena B, Avenida Ramon Castillo and Avenida Maipu, Retiro, tel. 011/4311-0692, 011/4317-0675, or 011/4312-8677); here it is necessary to present your passport, vehicle title, and the original *conocimiento de embarque* (bill of lading), and to fill out a customs application. You will then obtain an appointment with a customs inspector to retrieve the vehicle, which involves about US$300 for port costs and another US$200 for the shipper; if the vehicle has been in port longer than five days, there will be additional charges. The vehicle can remain legally in Argentina for eight months, with an eight-month extension possible; of course, any visit to a neighboring country restarts the clock. In the event of any difficulty, consult a private *despachante de aduana* (customs broker), such as José Angel Vidal Labra (tel. 011/4345-7887, vidla@sinectis.com.ar).

Another option is via Chile, whose ports are less bureaucratic and safer for the vehicle than those of Argentina. The recommended and most probable ports of entry are San Antonio (southwest of Santiago), and Valparaíso (northwest of the capital). It pays to be there within a couple days of the vehicle's arrival, or stor-age charges can mount up. Leave the gas tank as nearly empty as possible (for safety's sake) and leave no valuables—including tools—in the vehicle.

To arrange a shipment from San Antonio or Valparaíso, contact the Santiago consolidator Ultramar (Avenida El Bosque Norte 500, 18th fl., Las Condes, tel. 02/6301000, www.ultramar.cl). For a trustworthy customs agent to handle the paperwork, contact the office of Juan Alarcón Rojas (Fidel Oteíza 1921, 12th fl., Providencia, Santiago, tel. 02/2252780, alrcon@entelchile.net); Chile's country code is 56.

Bicycles, of course, can be partially dismantled, packaged, and easily shipped aboard airplanes, sometimes for no additional charge. There is rarely any additional paperwork for bringing a bike into the country, but many of the same overland travel concerns apply, like bad road conditions and drivers.

Vehicle Documents, Driver's License, and Equipment: Most South American countries, including Argentina, Chile, Uruguay, and Brazil, have dispensed with the cumbersome *Carnet de Passage en Douanes* that required depositing a large bond in order to import a motor vehicle. Officials at the port of arrival or border post will issue a 90-day permit on presentation of the vehicle title, registration, bill of lading (if the vehicle is being shipped), and your passport. For shipped vehicles, there are usually some small but relatively insignificant port charges (unless the vehicle has been stored more than a few days).

Before traveling to Argentina, obtain an International or Interamerican Driving Permit. (Travelers intending to visit Uruguay should note that that country officially recognizes only the latter, though in practice they appear more flexible.) These permits are available through the American Automobile Association (AAA), or its counterpart in your home country, and are normally valid one calendar year from date of issue. Strictly speaking, they are not valid without a state or national driver's license, but Argentine police usually ignore the latter. Another form of identification, such as a national ID card or passport, is also necessary.

The police pay close attention to vehicle documents—*tarjeta verde* (green card) registration for Argentine vehicles, customs permission for foreign ones, and liability insurance (though many Argentines drive without it, it is reasonably priced from many insurers, including the Automóvil Club Argentino, the national automobile club). Vehicles without registration may be impounded on the spot. Argentine vehicles should have proof of a *verificación técnica* (safety inspection).

At roadside checkpoints, the police are also rigid about obligatory equipment, such as headrests for the driver and each passenger, *valizas* (triangular emergency reflectors), and *matafuegos* (one-kg fire extinguishers). In any instance of document irregularity or minor equipment violation, provincial police in particular may threaten fines while really soliciting *coimas* (bribes). A firm but calm suggestion that you intend to call your consulate may help overcome any difficulty.

Road Hazards: Buenos Aires traffic is so fast and ruthless that it's amazing that Jorge Luis Borges, or any other blind person, could survive it—it's tough enough on sighted people in prime physical condition. According to statistics, 60–70 percent of the city's traffic fatalities are pedestrians; most culprits, unsurprisingly, are male drivers between 19 and 35 years of age. According to government statistics, the national traffic fatality rate of 25 per 100,000 residents is nearly double that of the United States, and more than triple that of Germany; one journalist has referred to its 38 deaths per day as a "weekly Cromañon," after the disastrous fire that killed nearly 200 *porteño* rock music fans in December 2004.

Porteño drivers in the city and stray cattle in the countryside might seem trouble enough, but the recent economic crisis has created an intractable movement of *piqueteros* (picketers, demonstrators protesting unemployment and other issues) who mount *piquetes* (roadblocks) to disrupt traffic. While they focus on stopping

commercial traffic, picketers slow down everything else as well; never try to run a roadblock, as doing so can raise their wrath. If necessary, feign solidarity and, in all likelihood, you'll pass without incident.

Train

There are no international rail services to or from Buenos Aires and only a few long-distance domestic services, mostly to the Atlantic beach resorts of southern Buenos Aires province. (See the *Getting Around* section for information on suburban and long-distance trains.)

BY RIVER

From Buenos Aires, there are ferry connections across the river to the Uruguayan capital of Montevideo, but also to the resort town of Piriápolis (summer only) and to the charming 18th-century town of Colonia. From the suburban river port of Tigre, there are launches to the Uruguayan river ports of Carmelo and Nueva Palmira.

Buenos Aires to and from Colonia and Montevideo

From Puerto Madero's Dársena Norte, at the foot of Avenida Córdoba, Buquebus (Avenida Antártida Argentina 821, tel. 011/4316-6500, www.buquebus.com) sails to Colonia, Montevideo, and Piriápolis; it also has a ticket outlet at Avenida Córdoba 879, Retiro. Services and fares vary, depending on the vessel—the ferry *Eladia Isabel,* for instance, has the cheapest but slowest crossing to Colonia (three hours, US$17–23), while the high-speed ferries *Juan Patricio* and *Patricia Oliva III* cover the much longer distance to Montevideo (US$52–67) in about the same time.

Tigre to and from Carmelo and Nueva Palmira

Cacciola Viajes (Florida 520, tel. 011/4393-6100, www.cacciolaviajes.com) connects the northern Buenos Aires province suburb of Tigre with the Uruguayan riverside resort of Carmelo.

Getting Around

Even as automobiles clog the streets of Buenos Aires and other cities, most Argentines still rely on public transportation to get around. Services in the capital and Gran Buenos Aires are frequent and reasonably well-integrated, but not perfectly so.

A local miracle, at least for visitors who can understand Spanish, is the free service (tel. 131 from any public or private telephone) that tells you the best Subte or bus route between any two points in the city; simply tell the operator exactly where you are, and he or she will tell you the closest stop.

COLECTIVOS (BUSES)

More than 200 separate bus routes serve the *capital federal* and Gran Buenos Aires, but most visitors and even residents need to know only a few of them to get around easily. It's useful, however, to have one of the annually updated city atlases, such as the *Guía Lumi* or the *Guía*

T, which include detailed bus routes. There are also abbreviated pocket versions of the bus lines. All are readily available at newsstand kiosks and bookstores.

Route signs at fixed stops often but not always list the bus's itinerary. If you don't have a written guide, ask someone for help—*porteños* often know the system by heart and are generous with information. Fares depend on distance traveled, but within the capital most are US$.30 or less; after you tell the driver your destination, he will enter the fare in the automatic ticket machine, which takes only coins but does give small change. Though the driver will often give warning of your stop, his politeness may cease when he hits the accelerator.

TRAIN

Buenos Aires has two types of rail systems: the Subte (subway) that serves the Capital Federal, and a series of surface commuter trains, run by

© WAYNE BERNHARDSON

The No. 60 is one of BA's most heavily used bus lines.

RIDING THE SUBTE

Operated by the private concessionaire Metrovías, the state-owned Subterráneos de Buenos Aires comprises five alphabetically designated lines, four of which (A, B, D, and E) begin in Monserrat or the Microcentro and serve outlying northern and western barrios, with numerous stations in between. Línea C is a north-south connector line between major railway stations at Retiro and Constitución.

An additional north-south connector line, Línea H, is under construction between Once and outlying southern barrios, beneath Avenida Pueyrredón and Avenida Jujuy. Three other lines have been proposed, but construction has not yet begun.

Subte hours are 5 A.M. to about 11 P.M. Monday–Saturday, but the system opens later (around 8 A.M.) and closes earlier (about 10:30 P.M.) Sundays and holidays, when services are less frequent. Fares are 70 centavos; to save time, purchase magnetic tickets in quantities of 2, 5, 10, and 30 rides. Two or more people may use the same ticket (legally) by passing it back and forth across the turnstile; you do not need a ticket to exit the system.

Before going through the turnstiles, be sure of the direction you're headed; at some stations, trains in both directions use the same platform, but at others the platforms are on opposite sides. Some stations have one-way traffic only; in those cases, the next station down the line usually serves one-way traffic in the other direction.

For complaints or problems, contact Metrovías's Centro de Atención al Pasajero (tel. 0800/555-1616 toll-free).

Subte Routes

Línea A begins at Plaza de Mayo in Monserrat and runs beneath Avenida Rivadavia to Primera Junta, in the barrio of Chacarita.

Línea B begins at Avenida Leandro Alem in the Microcentro and runs beneath Avenida Corrientes to Federico Lacroze in the barrio of Chacarita, where it connects with the suburban Ferrocarril Urquiza. A recent northwesterly extension continues to Tro-

nador and Avenida los Incas and is due to reach Villa Urquiza.

Línea C connects Retiro (which has northern suburban commuter surface rail lines) with Constitución, the transfer point for southern suburban commuter surface lines; Línea C also has transfer stations for all other Subte lines.

Línea D begins at Catedral on Plaza de Mayo and runs beneath Avenida Santa Fe and Avenida Cabildo through Palermo and Belgrano to Congreso de Tucumán, in the barrio of Núñez.

Línea E begins at Bolívar on the Avenida de Mayo and goes to Plaza de los Virreyes, in the barrio of Flores. At Plaza de los Virreyes, there's a light-rail extension known as the Premetro.

Presently under construction, **Línea H** should open by late 2006. The first stretch will begin at Caseros, in the southern barrio of Nueva Pompeya, and connect with Plaza Miserere (Once), on Línea A; it will eventually extend north to Recoleta and Retiro.

entrance to Subte Línea A, at Plaza de Mayo

© WAYNE BERNHARDSON

Suburban train commuters arrive from the suburbs at Estación Retiro.

several private companies, that connect downtown with more distant suburbs.

Subte

Popularly known as the Subte, the Buenos Aires subway opened in 1913. South America's first underground railway, the 13th in the world, it has modernized and expanded in recent years, but its antique cars, with their varnished but worn woodwork and elaborately tiled but chipped murals, recall the prosperity and optimism of early-20th-century Argentina. Privatized in 1994, the Subte is still the fastest way to get around the capital.

Metrovías (www.metrovias.com.ar), a private concessionaire, operates the five existing underground lines and is building a sixth transverse line from Retiro through Recoleta, Once, and the southern part of the city, which will shorten many trips by reducing the need to transfer in the Microcentro. At present, there are 67 stations for 39.5 kilometers of track within the capital; in 2003, the system carried more than 225 million passengers. While this figure was lower than in previous years, it probably reflected growing

unemployment rather than riders abandoning the system.

Since taking over the system, Metrovías has also improved the rolling stock, extended existing lines, modernized many stations, and built new ones. Electronic tickets have replaced the traditional Subte *fichas* (tokens) but, while this is perhaps more efficient than in the past, it means lots of litter. Another negative development is the system of SUBTV monitors that show nonstop advertising. Though some of the newest cars are air-conditioned, ventilation remains poor in many stations. Improvement plans are in progress.

Suburban Trains

With few exceptions, suburban trains are less useful to short-term visitors than they are to commuters from Buenos Aires province. They are very cheap and, while some may be improving, most lag well behind the Subte.

The most useful and best is the Ferrocarril Mitre, operated by Trenes de Buenos Aires (TBA, tel. 011/4317-4400, www .tbanet.com.ar), which connects the classic Estación Retiro (Avenida Ramos Mejía 1302) with Belgrano and Zona Norte suburbs, including Vicente López, Olivos, Martínez, San Isidro, and Tigre. Another branch of the line goes to Villa Ballester, for connections to Reserva Natural Estricta Otamendi.

TBA also operates the Ferrocarril Sarmiento from Estación Once (Avenida Pueyrredón y Bartolomé Mitre, Subte: Plaza Miserere), which goes to western destinations like Moreno, with connections to Luján. Unlike the immaculate, state-of-the-art Mitre, this is a rundown line on which vendors even sell switchblades.

Transportes Metropolitano (tel. 0800/666-358736) operates the Ferrocarril Roca from Estación Constitución, at Avenida Brasil and Lima, to the Buenos Aires provincial capital of La Plata and intermediate points, but its service and maintenance are poor.

TAXI AND REMISE

Buenos Aires has an abundant fleet of taxis, painted black with yellow roofs. Since a spate of robberies that began some years ago, nearly all of them are now so-called **radio taxis** (which means you may call in advance for a cab). Some people prefer the security of phoning for a cab, but many if not most *porteños* still flag them down in the street. If in doubt, lock the back doors so that no one can enter the cab by surprise.

All regular cabs have digital meters. It costs about US$.55 to *bajar la bandera* (drop the flag, i.e. switch on the meter) and another US$.05 per 100 meters. Verify that the meter is set at minimum fare.

Drivers do not expect tips and sometimes, to avoid having to make change, will even round the fare *down*. It's best to carry small bills rather than have to rely on the driver's making change, especially if he has just come on shift. Since there are some dishonest drivers, before handing over the bill you may want to ask if he can change a large note, stating the amount of the note you're handing over.

Remises are radio taxis that charge an agreed-upon rate based on distance; the dispatcher will let you know the fare when you call, based on the pickup and drop-off points.

Hotels, restaurants, and other businesses will gladly ring taxis and *remises* for customers and clients.

CAR RENTAL

Aggressive drivers, traffic congestion, and lack of parking make driving in Buenos Aires inadvisable, but some visitors may consider this option for excursions beyond the capital. To rent a car, you must show a valid driver's license and a valid credit card and be at least 21 years old.

Both local and international agencies maintain offices in Buenos Aires, where rental costs are typically lower than elsewhere in the country but higher than in North America. Since the 2002 devaluation, prices are more volatile, but they usually involve a fixed daily amount plus a per-kilometer charge; unlimited mileage deals are normally for rentals of a week or longer. Insurance is additional.

Prior to devaluation, Argentina had some of the most expensive gasoline in the Americas except for Uruguay, but prices have fallen in dollar terms—at least temporarily, even as they

Driving in Buenos Aires has its risks.

CAR RENTALS

The following rental agencies have representatives in Buenos Aires:

Avis: Cerrito 1527, Retiro, tel. 011/4326-5542

Dollar: Marcelo T. de Alvear 449, Retiro, tel. 011/4315-8800

Hertz: Paraguay 1138, Retiro, tel. 011/4816-8001

Localiza: Rivadavia 1126, Microcentro, tel. 011/4382-9267

Thrifty: Carlos Pellegrini 1576, Retiro, tel. 011/4326-0418

rose in peso terms. Regular gasoline now goes for about US$.59 per liter, premium for about US$.65 per liter, and super for about US$.69 per liter. *Gasoil* (diesel) is typically cheaper than gasoline, about US$.50 per liter, but the differential is shrinking. Because gasoline prices are unregulated, they may rise quickly.

Anyone driving in Buenos Aires should know that the Microcentro, bounded by Avenida Leandro Alem, Avenida Córdoba, Avenida de Mayo, and Avenida 9 de Julio is off-limits to private passenger vehicles weekdays, 7 A.M.–7 P.M.

BICYCLE

Cycling may not be the safest way of getting around Buenos Aires's chaotic traffic, but the number of cyclists has risen with the economic crisis. According to city government statistics, the number of cyclists rose by more than 50 percent from 2000 to 2001. For trips shorter than five kilometers, according to their calculations, the bicycle is both cheaper and faster than public transportation.

If riding around Buenos Aires, side streets may be safer than fast-moving avenues, but they are also narrower, with less room for maneuvering. Traffic is not so wild on weekends as on weekdays, and parts of downtown are virtually deserted on Sunday.

There are still few dedicated bike paths, ex-

cept for the *bicisenda* that runs from Palermo to Retiro parallel to Avenida Figueroa Alcorta and Avenida Libertador. Cyclists should exit west at the *fin bicisenda* sign to avoid the *villa miseria* (shantytown) behind the Retiro train and bus stations. New bike lanes have appeared on Avenida San Juan and Avenida Independencia, to be shared with automobiles, which must observe a speed limit of 40 km per hour.

The capital's main bicycle advocacy organization is the Asociación de Ciclistas Urbanos (Avenida Díaz Vélez 5563, Caballito, tel. 011/4981-0578, www.geocities.com/acubicicleta).

WALKING

Thanks partly to its gentle topography, Buenos Aires is a walker's city or, one might even say, a jaywalker's city. Jaywalking is endemic, perhaps because it's not much more dangerous than crossing at the crosswalk with the light—for an overwhelming majority of *porteño* drivers, crosswalks are no more than decorative. While making turns, drivers weave among pedestrians rather than slowing or stopping to let them pass.

That said, in congested areas, pedestrians can often move faster than automobiles. In addition, barrios like San Telmo, La Boca, Recoleta, Palermo, and Belgrano (with their shady sidewalks and expansive parks) are particularly rewarding to pedestrian explorers; the summer heat and humidity, though, make it essential to consume plenty of fluids. Thundershowers make an umbrella advisable.

ORGANIZED TOURS

Some of the city's best guided tours are available through the municipal tourist office on Saturday and Sunday, often but not always with English-speaking guides. The *Buenos Aires Herald*'s Friday "getOut!" section and *Clarín*'s event section both contain listings, but the complete schedule also appears in *Cultura BA,* a weekly giveaway tabloid from the city government; they are also posted on the city government's website (www.buenosaires.gov.ar). In case of rain, the tours are canceled.

TRAVEL AGENCIES

North of Plaza San Martín, Retiro's **American Express** office (Arenales 707, tel. 011/4310-3535, amexbueemp@aexp.com) offers the usual services and cashes its own travelers' checks without additional commission.

Swan Turismo (Cerrito 822, 9th fl., Retiro, tel./fax 011/4129-7926, www.swanturismo.com.ar) is a full-service travel agency that's earned a reputation for willingness and ability to deal with some of the Argentine travel system's eccentricities.

There are also several student-oriented agencies, such as Retiro's nonprofit **Asatej**, in the Galería Buenos Aires (Florida 835, 3rd fl., tel. 011/4311-6953, www.asatej.com.ar). Since the Argentine economic crisis has reduced overseas travel by young Argentines, Asatej has shifted its focus to incoming tourism and is good at searching out the best airfares for anyone, not just students.

The **Asociación Argentina de Albergues de la Juventud** (AAAJ, Talcahuano 214, tel./fax 011/4372-7094, www.hostelling-aaaj.org.ar) also provides student-travel services. Also university-oriented is Balvanera's **Turismo Unión Buenos Amigos** (TUBA, Sarmiento 1967, 1° "12," tel. 011/4953-3773, www.tuba.com.ar), in the Congreso neighborhood.

Recently opened, the local affliate of STA Travel, **Startravel** (Avenida Córdoba 679, 3° C, tel. 011/5199-4445, www.startravel.com.ar), has made excellent first impressions.

For conventional tours of the capital and vicinity, including the Microcentro, Recoleta and Palermo, and San Telmo and La Boca, a frequent choice is **Buenos Aires Visión** (Esmeralda 356, 8th fl., tel. 011/4394-2986, www.buenosaires-vision.com.ar).

Jorge Luis Borges's widow María Kodama leads fortnightly Borgesian tours, free of charge, sponsored by municipal tourism authorities and her own **Fundación Internacional Jorge Luis Borges** (Anchorena 1660, tel. 011/4822-8340); phone for schedules.

Highly recommended **Eternautas** (Avenida Roque Sáenz Peña 1124, 4° B, tel. 011/4384-7874, cell 15/4173-1078, www.eternautas.com) is an organization of professional historians who offer inexpensive walking tours (as little as US$2) and longer half-day excursions, such as "El Otro Sur," a fascinating three-hour bus tour (US$5 pp) through working-class southern barrios like Barracas, Nueva Pompeya, Parque Patricios, and Boedo. They also go farther afield to such places as La Plata and Luján (including the historic Estancia Los Talas) for US$27.

Run by a Rick Steves' Europe guide who spends most of the year in Buenos Aires, **In Depth Travel** (cell 15/5174-4440, www.in-depth.com.ar) offers a variety of walking tours, including a distinctive Art Nouveau circuit (US$20 pp, 3–4 hours). English, Spanish, and Portuguese are spoken.

By its very name, **Tangol** (Florida 971, 1st fl., Local 59, tel. 011/4312-7276, www.tangol.com) combines those two *porteño* passions, tango and soccer (*¡goooooooooooolll!*) in its offerings. It also does excursions farther afield, in Buenos Aires province and elsewhere. For a commercial website, it's surprisingly informative as well.

Travel Line Argentina (Esmeralda 770, 10th fl., Oficina B, tel. 011/4393-9000, www.travelline.com.ar) conducts specialty excursions, such as its "Evita Tour" (US$30, six hours), which takes in the CGT labor headquarters, Luna Park Stadium, the Perón and Duarte residences, and other locales associated with Evita's meteoric career.

One unique option is **Cicerones de Buenos Aires** (tel. 011/4330-0800, www.cicerones.org.ar), a non-profit that matches visitors with enthusiastic non-professional guides who can provide a resident's perspective on the city.

Visas and Officialdom

Citizens of neighboring countries—Bolivians, Brazilians, Chileans, Uruguayans, and Paraguayans—need only national identity cards to enter Argentina. In the western hemisphere, most other nationalities need passports; only Cubans, Belizeans, and a few others need an advance visa. Likewise, citizens of the European Union and Scandinavian countries, Switzerland, Israel, Australia, and New Zealand need only passports. Citizens of nearly all African and Asian countries, except for South Africa and Japan, need advance visas.

Regulations change, though, so check the visa page of Argentina's Ministerio de Relaciones Exteriores (Foreign Relations Ministry, www.mrecic.gov.ar/consulares.html). (See also the sidebar *Argentine Consulates in Other Countries* in this chapter for addresses and telephone numbers of key Argentine embassies and consulates.)

Argentina routinely grants 90-day entry permits to foreign visitors in the form of tourist cards that, theoretically, must be surrendered on departure from the country; in practice, it's the passport stamp that counts. For US$100, the entry is renewable for 90 days at the Dirección Nacional de Migraciones (Avenida Argentina 1355, Retiro, tel. 011/4317-0237, 8 A.M.–1 P.M. weekdays only).

In the provinces, renewal can be done at any office of the Policía Federal (Federal Police), but in smaller towns the police may not be accustomed to conducting renewals. Buenos Aires visitors may find it cheaper and simpler to take a day trip on the ferry to Colonia, Uruguay, which will reset the 90-day period.

Formally, arriving visitors must have a return or onward ticket, but enforcement is inconsistent—if you have a Latin American, North American, or Western European passport, for instance, it is unlikely you will be asked to show the return ticket. The author has entered Argentina many dozens of times over many years, at Buenos Aires's international airport and some of the most remote border posts, without ever having been asked for the return or onward ticket.

Airlines, though, may feel differently and not permit a passenger without a roundtrip ticket to board a flight to Argentina. Likewise, if the arriving passenger comes from an Eastern European, Asian, or African country, he or she may be asked for proof of return transport. Immigration officials have a great deal of discretion in these matters.

Always carry identification, since federal and provincial police can request it at any moment, though they rarely do so without reason. Passports are also necessary for routine transactions, like checking into hotels, cashing travelers' checks, and even payment by credit card.

Dependent children under age 14 traveling without both parents presumably need notarized parental consent, but the author's daughter has visited Argentina many times with only one parent, and has never been asked for such a document.

Argentine-born individuals, if their parents were not Argentines or if they have been naturalized elsewhere, sometimes experience obstacles from immigration officials. Generally, they may enter the country for no more than 60 days on a non-Argentine document. Argentine passports renewed outside the country expire on reentry, making it necessary to renew them with the Policía Federal, a bothersome and time-consuming process on a short trip.

LOST OR STOLEN PASSPORTS

Visitors who suffer a lost or stolen passport must obtain a replacement at their own embassy or consulate. After obtaining a replacement passport, it's necessary to visit the Dirección Nacional de Migraciones to replace the tourist card.

CUSTOMS

Notorious for truly egregious corruption, Argentine customs has improved from the days of

FOREIGN CONSULATES IN ARGENTINA

As a major world capital, Buenos Aires has a full complement of embassies and consulates that provide services to foreign visitors. A country's embassy and consulate often share an address, but when the addresses are separate the list below provides the address of the consulate, as they are primarily responsible for dealing with individuals traveling for either business or pleasure.

Australia: Villanueva 1400, Palermo, tel. 011/4777-6580, www.argentina.embassy.gov.au

Belgium: Defensa 113, 8th fl., Monserrat, tel. 011/4331-0066, www.diplobel.org/argentina

Bolivia: Avenida Belgrano 1670, 1st fl., Monserrat, tel. 011/4381-0539

Brazil: Carlos Pellegrini 1363, 5th fl., Retiro, tel. 011/4515-6500, www.brasil.org.ar

Canada: Tagle 2828, Palermo, tel. 011/4808-1086, www.dfait-maeci.gc.ca/argentina

Chile: San Martín 439, 9th fl., Microcentro, tel. 011/4394-6582, www.embajadadechile.com.ar

Denmark: Leandro N. Alem 1074, 9th fl., Retiro, tel. 011/4312-6901

France: Santa Fe 846, 3rd fl., Retiro, tel. 011/4312-2409, www.embafrancia-argentina.org

Germany: Villanueva 1055, Palermo, tel. 011/4778-2500, www.buenos-aires.diplo.de

Ireland: Avenida del Libertador 1064, 6th fl., Recoleta, tel. 011/5787-0801, www.irlanda.org.ar

Israel: Avenida de Mayo 701, 10th fl., Monserrat, tel. 011/4338-2500, http://buenosaires.mfa .gov.il

Italy: Marcelo T. de Alvear 1149, Retiro, tel. 011/4816-6132, www.ambitalia-bsas.org.ar

Japan: Bouchard 547, 17th fl., Microcentro, tel. 011/4318-8200, www.ar.emb-japan.go.jp

Mexico: Arcos 1650, Belgrano, tel. 011/4789-8826, www.embamex.int.ar

Netherlands: Olga Cossentini 831, 3rd fl., Edificio Porteño Plaza 2, Puerto Madero, tel. 011/4338-0050, www.embajadaholanda.int.ar

New Zealand: Carlos Pellegrini 1427, 5th fl., Microcentro, tel. 011/4328-0747, www.nz embassy.com

Norway: Esmeralda 909, 3rd fl., Retiro, tel. 011/4312-2204, www.noruega.org.ar

Paraguay: Viamonte 1851, Balvanera, tel. 011/4814-4803

Peru: Florida 165, 2nd fl., Microcentro, tel. 011/4334-0970

Spain: Guido 1760, Recoleta, tel. 011/4811-0070, www.mae.es/consulados/buenosaires

Sweden: Tacuarí 147, Monserrat, tel. 011/4342-1422, www.swedenabroad.com

Switzerland: Santa Fe 846, 10th fl., Retiro, tel. 011/4311-6491, www.eda.admin.ch/buenosaires_emb

United Kingdom: Dr. Luis Agote 2412, Recoleta, tel. 011/4808-2200, www.britain.org.ar

United States of America: Colombia 4300, Palermo, tel. 011/5777-4533, http://buenosaires.us embassy.gov

Uruguay: Avenida Las Heras 1915, 5th fl., Recoleta, tel. 011/4807-3040

ARGENTINE CONSULATES IN OTHER COUNTRIES

Argentina has wide diplomatic representation throughout the world, even though economic difficulties have reduced this presence over the past couple of decades. In capital cities, embassies and consulates often, though not always, share an address; people planning a visit to Argentina should go to consulates rather than embassies for visas and other inquiries.

Australia: Embassy—John McEwen House, 7 National Circuit, 2nd fl., Barton ACT, tel. 02/6273-9111, www.argentina.org.au
Consulate—44 Market Street, 20th fl., Sydney NSW, tel. 02/9262-2933

Bolivia: Azpiazu 497, Sopocachi, La Paz, tel. 02/241-7737

Brazil: Praia Botafogo 228, Sobreloja 201, Edificio Argentina, Rio de Janeiro, tel. 21/2533-1646
Avenida Paulista 2313, Sobreloja, São Paulo, tel. 11/3897-9522

Canada: 90 Sparks St., Ste. 620, Ottawa, Ontario K1P 514, tel. 613/236-2351, www.argentina-canada.net
1 First Canadian Place, Ste. 5840, Toronto, Ontario M5X 1K2, tel. 416/955-9075
2000 Peel St, Montréal, Québec H3A 2W5, tel. 514/842-6582, www.consargenmtl.com

Chile: Vicuña Mackenna 41, Santiago, tel. 02/582-2608
Pedro Montt 160, 7th fl., Puerto Montt, tel. 065/253966
21 de Mayo 1878, Punta Arenas, tel. 056/261532

France: 6 Rue Cimarosa, Paris, tel. 1/4434-2200

Germany: Kleiststrasse 23–26, 4th fl., Berlin, tel. 30/226-6890

New Zealand: 142 Lambton Quay, 14th fl., Wellington, tel. 04/476-8331, www.arg.org.nz

Paraguay: Banco Nación, 1st fl., Palma 319, Asunción, tel. 021/445646
Artigas 960, Encarnación, tel. 071/201066

Switzerland: Jungfraustrasse 1, Bern, tel. 31/356-4349

United Kingdom: 27 Three Kings Yard, London W1Y 1FL, tel. 20/7318-1340

United States of America: 1811 Q St. NW, Washington, D.C. 20009, tel. 202/238-6460
5550 Wilshire Blvd., Ste. 210, Los Angeles, CA 90036, tel. 323/954-9155, www.consuladoargentino-losangeles.org
800 Brickell Ave., Penthouse 1, Miami, FL 33131, tel. 305/373-1889, www.consuladoargentinoenmiami.org
245 Peachtree Center Ave., Ste. 2101, Atlanta, GA 30303, tel. 404/880-0805, www.consuladoargentinoatlanta.org
205 N. Michigan Ave., Ste. 4209, Chicago, IL 60601, tel. 312/819-2610
12 W. 56th St., New York, NY 10019, tel. 212/603-0403, www.consuladoargentinoennuevayork.com
3050 Post Oak Blvd., Ste. 1625, Houston, TX 77056, tel. 713/871-8935

Uruguay: Wilson Ferreira Aldunate 1281, Montevideo, tel. 02/902-8623
Avenida General Flores 226, Colonia, tel. 052/22093

the so-called *aduana paralela* (parallel customs) and normally presents no obstacle to tourists. Short-term visitors may import personal effects, including clothing, jewelry, medicine, sporting gear, camping equipment and accessories, photographic and video equipment, personal computers, and the like, as well as 400 cigarettes, two liters of wine or alcoholic beverages (adults over 18 only), and up to US$300 of new merchandise.

Customs inspections are routine, but at Buenos Aires's international airports, river ports, and at some land borders, incoming checked baggage may have to pass through X-ray machines; do not put photographic film in checked baggage. Fresh food will be confiscated at any port of entry.

A recent development for border-crossers is the Economy Ministry's currency declaration, intended to prevent money laundering and tax evasion. No visitor entering or leaving Argentina may carry more than US$10,000 in cash or travelers' checks, without formally declaring that amount. Anything undeclared over the limit is subject to confiscation.

At some remote border posts, the Gendarmería Nacional (Border Guard) handles all formalities, from immigration to customs to agricultural inspections. Visitors arriving from drug-producing countries like Colombia, Peru, and Bolivia may get special attention at border posts.

POLICE AND MILITARY

Argentina is notorious for police corruption. For this reason, *porteños* and other Argentines scornfully call both federal and provincial police *la cana*—an insult that should never be used to their faces.

The Policía Federal (Federal Police) are marginally more professional than provincial forces like that of Buenos Aires province; the latter is almost universally detested for harassing motorists for minor equipment violations and, even worse, for their *gatillo fácil* (hair-trigger) response to minor criminal offenses. This behavior is not completely unwarranted, however—many police officers have died at the hands of well-armed criminals (who are themselves sometimes police officers).

Police officers often solicit *coimas* (bribes) at routine traffic stops. To avoid paying a bribe, either state your wish to consult your consulate, or use broken Spanish even if you understand the language well. Either one may frustrate a corrupt official sufficiently to give up the effort.

Since the end of the 1976–1983 dictatorship, the Argentine military has lost prestige and appears to have acknowledged its inability to run the country, despite the occasional fringe group clamor in favor of a coup. Still, security is heavy around military bases and photography and video are taboo—signs that say *No Fotografiar o Filmar* are common.

Conduct and Customs

Porteños, like New Yorkers, have a stereotyped reputation for brusqueness and some of them complain that, especially in times of crisis, "nobody respects anybody here any more." In many contexts, though, they are remarkably courteous people.

Politeness goes a long way with bus drivers, officials, shopkeepers, and others with whom you may have contact. It's always good form to offer the appropriate polite greeting

buenos días (good morning), *buenas tardes* (good afternoon), or *buenas noches* (good evening or good night), depending on the time of day.

In terms of general conduct, both women and men should dress conservatively and inconspicuously when visiting churches, chapels, and sacred sites. This, again, is an issue of respect for local customs, even if *porteños* themselves don't always observe it.

VIVEZA CRIOLLA

Argentines in general, and *porteños* in particular, are infamous for *viveza criolla,* an inadmirable trait (roughly translatable as cunning, or perhaps guile) that somehow draws grudging respect in a country where playing by the rules often means being left behind. To achieve this sort of respect, though, you need to be successful at "artful deception."

Such was not the case for José María González, a former colonel and director of the army's Museo de Armas, who, just before his retirement in July of 2002, was shocked, *shocked,* to find valuable items missing. Soon afterward, federal police arrested him for sneaking at least 28 antique pieces out of the museum and into his private collection. The police also found a substantial illegal arsenal of modern firearms on the properties of González's presumed civilian accomplice.

An even more colorful example was the convicted counterfeiter who, in the early independence years, falsified his own release papers from jail but had the misfortune to be executed for it. These days, many motorcyclists flaunt the traffic code by wearing helmets on their elbows, as apparently there's no requirement to use them on their heads (putting aside the question of where their brains are).

Certainly the best cinematic exploration of *viveza criolla* is Fabián Belinsky's *Nine Queens,* in which the con-men partners Ricardo Darín and Gastón Pauls match wits in tricking their victims (and each other, perhaps). In real life, the most famous example is probably Diego Maradona, who illegally scored the winning goal against England in the 1986 World Cup, then praised "the hand of God" for helping him.

Tips for Travelers

SPECIAL INTERESTS

Work

While the Argentine economy is recovering from its 2002 implosion, unemployment is still high and remunerative work can be hard to come by even for legal residents, let alone visitors on tourist or student visas. Nevertheless, foreigners have found work teaching English or another foreign language, working in the tourist industry, or doing casual labor in bars or restaurants. The problem with such jobs is that they either require time to build up a clientele (in the case of teaching) and may be seasonal (in the case of tourism) or poorly paid (in the case of restaurants, except in a handful of places where tips are high). Language teachers may find that few *porteños* can afford the luxury of one-on-one lessons.

Ideally, obtaining a work permit from an Argentine consulate is better than attempting to obtain one in-country, as employment may not begin until the permit is actually granted. Either way, the process requires submitting documents and takes some time. Some visitors, such as freelancers who do not receive payment locally, work without papers.

Business

There are few if any legal limitations on foreign businesses operating in Argentina, but because of the lingering debt default, the climate has not been conducive to investment. In by-country risk assessments, featured like sports scores on the front page of *porteño* newspapers, Argentina ranks among the world's highest investment risks—by early 2005, this key statistic was still near 5,000 compared to around 400 for neighboring Brazil and Uruguay (it was only 59 in Chile, widely regarded as having the

USEFUL BUSINESS ORGANIZATIONS

One critically important and unavoidable contact is the **Administración Nacional de Aduanas** (Azopardo 350, Monserrat, tel. 011/4338-6400). If importing equipment for permanent use, it's essential to deal with them through a *despachante de aduanas* (private customs broker).

The **Cámara de Comercio de los Estados Unidos en Argentina** (U.S. Chamber of Commerce in Argentina, Viamonte 1133, 8th fl., Microcentro, tel. 011/4371-4500, www.amchamar.com.ar) is an organization run by and for U.S. businesses.

The **Cámara Argentina de Comercio** (Argentine Chamber of Commerce, Avenida Leandro N. Alem 36, Planta Baja (ground floor), Microcentro, tel. 011/5300-9000, www.cac.com.ar) is an alliance of Argentine businesses, while the **Cámara de Importadores de la República Argentina** (Argentine Chamber of Importers, Avenida Belgrano 427, 7th fl., Monserrat, tel. 011/4342-1101/0523, www.cira.org.ar) deals primarily with exports.

The **Bolsa de Comercio de Buenos Aires** (Sarmiento 299, 1st fl., Microcentro, tel. 011/4316-7000, www.bcba.sba.com.ar) is the city's stock exchange.

The **Sociedad Rural Argentina** (Argentine Agricultural Association, Florida 460, Microcentro, tel. 011/4324-4700, www.ruralarg.org.ar) is the traditional landowners' organization.

continent's best investment climate). Around the same time, an Economist Intelligence Unit survey was even less encouraging; by its poll, only Iraq and Zimbabwe were worse investment risks.

Corruption remains an issue. Political officeholders have an unfortunate reputation for shaking down foreign companies for bribes, and customs procedures can be trying despite increasing professionalization of the service. Intellectual property rights for computer software, CD and cassette recordings, and DVDs and video tapes are problematic.

The business dailies mentioned in the Media section of this chapter are good background sources on business, at least for those who read Spanish, as are magazines like *Apertura* (www.apertura.com). Though it often lags behind on events, the most thorough English-language source is the U.S. State Department's Country Commercial Guide service (www.export.gov, but easier to access through the U.S. Embassy in Buenos Aires: http://buenosaires.usembassy.gov). Its best bets for investment include travel and tourism services, computer equipment and software, management consulting, medical equipment, energy technology, building materials and supplies, and biotechnology.

While overseas investors have been cautious in recent years, some believe that Argentina may offer high yields on investments because devaluation has depressed prices in dollar terms. Residential real estate, for instance, has been a bargain, though prices are rising from the depths of 2002. In any event, before signing any business deal, consult a local lawyer recommended by your embassy, your consulate, or a trusted friend.

Conducting business is as much a personal and social activity as an economic one; even though initial contacts may be formal, with appointments arranged well in advance, topics such as family and sports are often part of the conversation. Formality in dress and appearance is less rigid than it once was, but in sectors like banking it's still the rule.

An ability to speak Spanish well is a plus, even though many Argentine business figures speak English (more than a few have been educated in English-speaking countries). The best months for business travel are April–November; in January and February, when school lets out and *porteños* take their summer vacations, the city can seem deserted.

Language Study

Buenos Aires's cultural resources and low cost of living have made it popular with students seeking to acquire a quick competence in Spanish or improve their language skills.

The Universidad de Buenos Aires (UBA) offers limited instruction at its Laboratorio de Idiomas (25 de Mayo 221, tel. 011/4343-1196, www.idiomas.filo.uba.ar). It also offers more intensive programs (15 hours weekly for one month, US$400) at its Centro Universitario de Idiomas (Junín 224, Balvanera, tel. 011/5238-3000, ext. 24, www.cui.com.ar).

The Centro de Estudio del Español (Reconquista 715, 11th fl., tel./fax 11/4315-1156 or 11/4312-1016, www.cedic.com.ar) offers a variety of options. Group instruction, four hours daily, costs US$120 pp per week, while individual tutoring costs US$9 hourly. In addition, it arranges housing.

In new Microcentro facilities, Coined (Suipacha 90, 2nd fl., tel. 011/4331-2418, www.coined.com.ar) has 20-hour weekly intensive group courses, with supplementary individual lessons as well. Rates start in the US$250–305 range, including accommodations.

The Instituto de Lengua Española para Extranjeros (ILEE, Avenida Callao 339, 3rd fl., tel. 011/4782-7173, www.ilee.com.ar) offers conversation-based courses at various levels for US$200 per week, plus private classes (US$16 per hour). It will also help arrange accommodations.

For individual private tutoring, contact English-speaking Dori Lieberman (tel. 011/4361-4843, dori@sinectis.com.ar).

Tango

Often (but not always) inspired by films like Sally Potter's execrable *The Tango Lesson* or the Al Pacino vehicle *Scent of a Woman*, an increasing number of visitors come to Buenos Aires specifically—sometimes exclusively—to dance tango. It's not always what they expect; it's often better. Tango is an everyday presence and, if not quite 24/7, *milongas* take place every day and lessons are easy to arrange.

For those who do want to live tango 24/7, the **Mansión Dandi Royal** (Piedras 922, San Telmo, tel. 011/4307-7623, www.mansiondandiroyal.com) offers multi-day to one-week packages that include accommodations in its own boutique hotel, lessons from top instructors in its private salon, and interaction with *porteño milongueros* during its own regular Wednesday event, in a separate salon open to the public. They're also on top of the *milonga* scene elsewhere in town.

For individual tango tours, try **Tangofocus** (Santiago del Estero 145 4° H, tel. 011/4381-9153, cel. 15/4095-3023, www.tangofocus.com). It also has a U.K. contact address: 8 Mayhill Rd., Ross on Wye, Herefordshire HR9 7EU, tel. 44/7837/609388.

Travel With Children

In most ways, Argentina is a child-friendly country and Buenos Aires is a child-friendly city. In fact, since many Argentines have large extended families, some may feel little in common with people in their late 20s and older who do *not* have children. Traveling with kids can open doors.

Many of the capital's parks and plazas have playground equipment, and it's easy to mix with Argentine families there. What foreign parents may find unusual is that even toddlers may be out on the swings and slides with their families at 11 P.M. or even later. Additionally, *porteño* kids are playing across the street, around the neighborhood, and even traveling on the buses and Subte at ages when nervous North American parents are driving their kids three blocks to school.

On public transportation, strangers may spontaneously but gently touch small children and even set them on their laps. While this may be disconcerting to non-Argentines, it's not necessarily inappropriate in cultural context.

Many cultural activities are child-oriented, particularly during late July's winter school holidays. Oddly enough, the Friday edition of the financial daily *Ambito Financiero* has the most complete listing of family events.

The northern barrios of Recoleta, Palermo, and Belgrano, with their spacious parks and playgrounds, are particularly good for children. Palermo's zoo is a favorite.

Women Travelers

Like other Latin American societies, Argentina has a strong *machista* (chauvinist) element. Argentine women are traditionally mothers, homemakers, and children's caregivers, while men are providers and decision-makers, but there are increasing numbers of professional and other working women.

Many Argentine men view women—both foreign and Argentine—as sexually available. Harassment often takes the form of *piropos,* sexist comments that are often innocuous, even poetic, but are just as likely to be vulgar. It is best to ignore the comments, which are obvious by tone of voice even if you don't understand them. If the offender is persistent, seek refuge in a café or *confitería.* Some women have suggested wearing a bogus wedding ring, but truly persistent suitors might see this as a challenge.

Despite problems, women have acquired political prominence. The most prominent and notorious, of course, was Evita Perón, but her rise was an unconventional one. The highest-profile females in current politics are Cristina Fernández, a Senator from Santa Cruz province who is also the wife of President Néstor Kirchner, and populist politician Elisa Carrió, a vociferous anti-corruption campaigner and former presidential candidate who, unfortunately, seems better at identifying problems than at offering solutions.

Gay and Lesbian Travelers

Like other Latin American countries, Argentina is culturally Catholic, but Buenos Aires has an active, visible gay scene focused around San Telmo, Barrio Norte, Recoleta, and Palermo Viejo. There are, however, gay-friendly venues throughout the city and even in the Paraná delta.

Demonstrative contact, such as kissing between males (on the cheek, at least) and holding hands for females, does not have the same connotation as it might in North America or some European countries. This does not mean that homosexuals can always behave as they wish in public—the police, never the most enlightened sector of society, have beaten and jailed individuals who have offended their sense of propriety. If in doubt, be circumspect.

The capital's leading homosexual organization is La Boca's Comunidad Homosexual Argentina (CHA, Tomás Liberti 1080, tel. 011/4361-6352, www.cha.org.ar). Early November's Marcha de Orgullo Gay (Gay Pride Parade) goes from the Casa Rosada to Congreso.

Travelers with Disabilities

For people with disabilities, Buenos Aires can a problematical city. The capital's narrow, uneven sidewalks, not to mention fast-moving traffic, are unkind to people with disabilities, especially those who need wheelchairs. On the other hand, the city is fast installing ramps at intersections.

Public transportation can rarely accommodate passengers with disabilities, though the capital's newer Subte stations have elevators and others are being retrofitted. Avis has introduced rental vehicles that feature hand controls.

Few older buildings are specifically equipped, many of them are low and can often accommodate people who have disabilities. Newer hotels are often high-rises, and disabled access is obligatory.

Health and Safety

Midlatitude Buenos Aires and vicinity offer no major health risks beyond those associated with any large city; public health standards are good and tap water is potable. In some parts of northernmost subtropical Argentina, though, there's a small risk of malaria or similar tropical diseases.

A good general source on foreign health matters is Dr. Richard Dawood's *Travelers' Health* (New York: Random House, 1994), a small encyclopedia on the topic. Dr. Stuart R. Rose's *International Travel Health Guide* (Northampton, MA: Travel Medicine Inc., 2001) is regionally focused. Try also Dirk G. Schroeder's *Staying Healthy in Asia, Africa and Latin America* (Emeryville, CA: Avalon Travel Publishing, 2000).

For up-to-date information on health issues in Chile and elsewhere in the Southern Cone, see the U.S. Centers for Disease Control (CDC) Temperate South America regional page (www.cdc.gov/travel/temsam.htm), which covers Chile, Argentina, Uruguay, and the Falkland Islands. Another good source is the United Kingdom's Department of Health website (www.doh.gov.uk), though it's less country-specific than it once was.

BEFORE YOU GO

Theoretically, no vaccinations are obligatory for entry to Argentina, but if you are coming from a tropical country where yellow fever is endemic, authorities might ask for a vaccination certificate.

Traveling to Argentina or elsewhere without adequate medical insurance is risky. Before leaving your home country, obtain medical insurance that includes evacuation in case of serious emergency. Foreign health insurance may not be accepted in Argentina, so you may be required to pay out of your own pocket for later reimbursement. Often, however, private providers accept international credit cards in return for services.

Numerous carriers provide medical and evacuation coverage; an extensive list, including Internet links, is available at the U.S. State Department's website (www.travel.state.gov/ Publications/medical.html).

GENERAL HEALTH MAINTENANCE

Common-sense precautions can reduce the possibility of illness considerably. Washing hands frequently with soap and water, and drinking only bottled, boiled, or carbonated water will all help diminish the likelihood of contagion for short-term visitors—though Argentine tap water is potable almost everywhere.

Where purified water is impossible to obtain, such as back-country streams where there may be livestock or problems with human waste, pass drinking water through a one-micron filter and further purify it with iodine drops or tablets (but avoid prolonged consumption of iodine-purified water). Non-pasteurized dairy products, such as goat cheese, can be problematic and are best avoided.

FOOD OR WATERBORNE DISEASES

While relatively few visitors to Argentina run into problems of this sort, contaminated food and drink are not unheard of. In many cases, it's simply exposure to different sorts of bugs to which your body soon becomes accustomed, but if symptoms persist the problem may be more serious.

Traveler's Diarrhea

Colloquially known as *turista* in Latin America, the classic traveler's diarrhea (TD) usually lasts only a few days and almost always less than a week. Besides "the runs," symptoms include nausea, vomiting, bloating, and general weakness. The usual cause is the notorious *Escherichia coli* (more commonly called *E. coli*) bacterium from contaminated food or water; in some cases *E. coli* infections can be fatal.

Fluids, including fruit juices, and small amounts of bland foods, such as freshly cooked rice or soda crackers, may help relieve symptoms and aid you in regaining your strength. Dehydration is a serious problem, especially for children, who may need to be treated with an oral rehydration solution (ORS) of carbohydrates and salt.

Over-the-counter remedies, like Pepto-Bismol, Lomotil, and Imodium, may relieve symptoms but can also cause problems. Prescription drugs, such as doxycycline and trimethoprim/sulfamethoxazole, can also shorten the cycle. These may not, however, be suitable for children, and it's better for everyone to avoid them if at all possible.

Continuing and worsening symptoms, including bloody stools, may mean dysentery, a much more serious ailment that requires a physician's attention.

Dysentery

Bacterial dysentery, resembling an intense form of TD, responds well to antibiotics, but amoebic dysentery is far more serious, sometimes leading to intestinal perforation, peritonitis, and liver abscesses. Like diarrhea, its symptoms include soft and even bloody stools, but some people may be asymptomatic even as they pass on *Entamoeba hystolica* through unsanitary toilet and food preparation practices. Metronidazole, known by the brand names Flagyl or Protostat, is an effective treatment, but a physician's diagnosis is advisable.

Cholera

Resulting from poor hygiene, inadequate sewage disposal, and contaminated food, contemporary cholera is less devastating than its historic antecedents, which produced rapid dehydration, watery diarrhea, and imminent death without almost equally rapid rehydration. While today's cholera strains are highly infectious, most carriers do not even come down with symptoms. Existing vaccinations are ineffective, so international health authorities now recommend against them.

Treatment can only relieve symptoms. On average, about five percent of victims die, but those who recover are immune. While not a common problem in Argentina, it's not unheard of either, especially in northern subtropical areas.

Hepatitis A

Usually passed by fecal-oral contact under conditions of poor hygiene and overcrowding, hepatitis A is a virus. The traditional gamma globulin prophylaxis has limited efficacy and wears off in just a few months. New hepatitis A vaccines, though, are more effective and last longer.

Typhoid

Typhoid is a serious disease common under unsanitary conditions, but the recommended vaccination is an effective prophylaxis.

INSECT-BORNE DISEASES

Argentina is not quite malaria-free but there's no danger in or around Buenos Aires; a few other insect-borne diseases may be present if not exactly prevalent.

Dengue Fever

Like malaria, dengue is a mosquito-borne disease of the lowland tropics, but it's less common than malaria and rarely fatal. Often debilitating in the short term, its symptoms include fever, headache, severe joint pain, and skin rashes. While most people recover fairly quickly, there is no treatment. Uncommon but often fatal, the more severe dengue hemorrhagic fever sometimes occurs in children, particularly those who have suffered from the disease previously.

Eradicated in Argentina in 1963, the mosquito vector *Aedes egypti* is once again present as far south as Buenos Aires. There were several hundred confirmed dengue cases in lowland subtropical areas of Salta province in 1997, and authorities believe outbreaks are possible in Buenos Aires. The best prophylaxis is to avoid mosquito bites by covering exposed parts of the body with insect repellent or appropriate clothing.

Chagas' Disease

Also known as South American trypanosomiasis, Chagas' disease is most common in Brazil but affects about 18 million people between Mexico and Argentina; 50,000 people die from it every year. Not a tropical disease per se, it has a discontinuous distribution—Panama and Costa Rica, for instance, are Chagas'-free.

Since it is spread by the bite of the conenose or assassin bug, which lives in adobe structures and feeds at night, avoid such structures (these still exist in the countryside); if it's impossible to do so, sleep away from the walls. Insect repellents carrying deet offer some protection. Chickens, dogs, and opossums may carry the disease.

Chagas' initial form is a swollen bite, which may be accompanied by a fever that soon subsides. In the long run, though, it may cause heart damage leading to sudden death, intestinal constipation, and difficulty in swallowing; there is no cure. Charles Darwin may have been a chronic Chagas' sufferer.

HANTAVIRUS

Hantavirus is an uncommon but deadly disease contracted by breathing, touching, or ingesting feces or urine of the long-tailed rat. Primarily a rural phenomenon and most prevalent in the southern Patagonian area, the virus thrives in enclosed areas; avoid places frequented by rodents (particularly abandoned buildings). The disease normally loses potency when exposed to sunlight or fresh air, but a few hikers and farm workers have apparently contracted the disease in open spaces.

It is not a serious problem in urban Buenos Aires, but in July 2002 a veterinarian contracted the disease near the provincial capital of La Plata and later died.

RABIES

Rabies, a virus transmitted through bites or scratches by domestic animals (like dogs and cats) and wild mammals (like bats), is a concern; many domestic animals in Argentina go unvaccinated, especially in rural areas. Human prophylactic vaccination is possible, but may be incompatible with malaria medication.

Untreated rabies can cause an agonizingly painful death. In case of an animal bite or scratch, immediately clean the affected area with soap and running water, and then with antiseptic substances like iodine or 40 percent-plus alcohol. If possible, try to capture the animal for diagnosis, but not at the risk of further bites; in areas where rabies is endemic, painful post-exposure vaccination may be unavoidable.

SNAKEBITES

The federal capital does not have poisonous snakes, but the aggressive and highly venomous *yarará* (*Bothrops neuwiedi*) is a pit viper found in parts of Buenos Aires province and elsewhere in the country. The timid but even more venomous coral snake (*Micrurus coralinus*) is found is humid areas, such as the Paraná delta.

The *yarará*, whose venom paralyzes the nervous system, is responsible for most Argentine snakebite incidents, but such cases are not common. Death is not instantaneous and antivenins are available, but the wisest tactic is to be alert and avoid confrontation. If bitten, get to medical facilities as quickly as possible, but avoid excessive movement, which helps the venom circulate.

SEXUALLY TRANSMITTED DISEASES

While AIDS is by far the most hazardous of sexually transmitted diseases (STDs) and certainly gets the most press, other STDs are far more prevalent and also serious if left untreated. All are spread by unprotected sexual conduct; the use of latex condoms can greatly reduce the possibility of contracting sexually transmitted diseases, but not necessarily eliminate it.

Most STDs, including gonorrhea, chlamydia, and syphilis, are treatable with antibiotics, but some strains have developed immunity to penicillin and alternative treatments. If taking antibiotics, be sure to complete the prescribed course, since an interrupted treatment may not kill the infection and could even help it develop immunity.

The most common of STDs is **gonorrhea,** characterized by a burning sensation during urination and penile or vaginal discharge; it may cause infertility. **Chlamydia** has milder symptoms but similar complications. **Syphilis,** the only major disease that apparently spread to Europe from its American origins in the aftermath of the Spanish invasion, begins with ulcer and rash symptoms that soon disappear; long-term complications, however, can include cardiovascular problems and even mental derangement. **Herpes,** a virus that causes small but irritating ulcers in the genital area, has no effective treatment. It is likely to recur, easily spread when active, and can contribute to cervical cancer. **Hepatitis B,** though not exclusively a sexually transmitted disease, can spread through the mixing of bodily fluids, such as saliva, semen, and menstrual and vaginal secretions. It can also spread through insufficiently sanitary medical procedures, inadequately sterilized or shared syringes, unsterile body piercing, and similar circumstances. Like Hepatitis A, it can lead to liver damage but is more serious; vaccination is advisable for high-risk individuals but is expensive.

HIV/AIDS

As in most countries, HIV/AIDS (AIDS is *SIDA* in Spanish) is an issue of increasing concern. According to Argentina's Health Ministry, there are around 25,000 full-blown AIDS cases and some 130,000 HIV-infected individuals, but concerns are that the figure may be substantially higher—many carriers are probably unaware that they are infected.

HIV/AIDS is not exclusively a sexually transmitted disease (intravenous drug users, who can get it by sharing needles, constitute about 40 percent of cases here), but unprotected sexual activity is a common means of transmission; the use of latex condoms can reduce the possibility of infection.

Buenos Aires has several AIDS support and information organizations, among them Cooperación, Información y Ayuda al Enfermo de SIDA (Coinsida, Finocchieto 74, Constitución, tel. 011/4304-6664) and Línea SIDA, (Zuviría 64, Parque Chacabuco, tel. 011/4922-1617).

SUNBURN

Buenos Aires and vicinity lie within temperate latitudes comparable to those in the northern hemisphere. Sunburn here is not quite the serious problem it is in subtropical northern Argentina, where nearly vertical solar rays are far more intense. In southernmost Patagonia and Tierra del Fuego, ozone-destroying aerosols have permitted the entry of ultraviolet radiation, causing skin problems for people and even for livestock, such as cattle and sheep.

Still, sun worshippers in Argentina put themselves at risk even when the sun fails to break through the clouds. If you dress for the beach, use a heavy sun block; on city streets, walk in the shade whenever possible.

TOBACCO

Almost 40 percent of Argentines between the ages of 16 and 64 smoke, including nearly half the males; tobacco is the direct cause of 39,000 deaths per annum. According to one survey, 3 out of every 10 Argentine *cardiologists* smoke, and few of them make any recommendation against smoking to their own patients.

Still, there is widespread recognition that the habit is unhealthy, and effective smoking restrictions are in force on public transportation and in a few other environments. Health Minister Ginés GonzálezGarcía has made smoke-free workplaces a priority, and the recent Italian example of a widespread and seriously enforced public smoking ban has made such an impression that anti-tobacco legislation is likely.

Enforcement, though, is another issue entirely, as police routinely ignore even traffic-law violations, such as failure to observe pedestrian right-of-way and obligatory helmets for motorcyclists. If faced with second-hand smoke in one of the few places where it's now expressly prohibited, such as buses or taxis, appeal to courtesy with a white lie, such as *"Soy asmático"* (I'm asthmatic).

The Unión Antitabáquica Argentina (Moreno 431, tel. 011/4343-3553, www.uata.org.ar, 9 A.M.–1 P.M. weekdays) lobbies for clean indoor air. Sin Pucho (Tucumán 3527, tel. 011/4862-6913, sinpucho@infovia.com.ar) is an ex-smokers' support group.

LOCAL DOCTORS

At present, thanks to devaluation of the peso, quality medical care is so cheap that in some cases it could justify a trip to Buenos Aires. Many if not most doctors speak English, some very fluently.

Public hospitals include the Hospital Rivadavia (Avenida Las Heras 2670, Recoleta, tel. 011/4809-2002), and the Hospital Municipal Juan Fernández (Cerviño 3356, tel. 011/4808-2600). Visitors considering elective medical care, though, should choose private hospitals and clinics, especially since the economic crisis has strained the resources of public institutions.

The Hospital Británico (Perdriel 74, Barracas, tel. 011/4304-1082) is a highly regarded private hospital.

One of the city's best private clinics is Belgrano's Clínica Fleni (Montañeses 2325, tel. 011/5777-3200, www.fleni.org.ar), whose focus is pediatrics and neurology. It also has outstanding specialists in orthopedics. (Soccer star Diego Maradona did his detox here, and Argentine presidents have had arthroscopies here.)

Another exceptional institution is the Fundación Favaloro (Avenida Belgrano 1746, Monserrat, tel. 011/4378-1200, www.fundacionfavaloro.org), whose specialty is cardiology.

The Instituto Oftalmológico Stefani (Juncal 2345, tel. 011/4826-7028) specializes in Lasik eye surgery.

PHARMACIES

Pharmacies serve an important public health role, but also carry certain risks. Pharmacists may provide drugs on the basis of symptoms that they may not completely comprehend, especially if there is a language barrier; while the cumulative societal impact may be positive, individual recommendations may be erroneous.

Note that many medications available by prescription only in North America or Europe may be sold over the counter in Argentine pharmacies. Travelers should be cautious about self-medication even when such drugs are available; check expiration dates, as many expired drugs are not cleared off the shelf.

In large cities and even some smaller towns, pharmacies remain open all night for emergency prescription service on a rotating basis. The *farmacia de turno* and its address will usually be posted in the window of other pharmacies, or advertised in the newspaper.

CRIME

Even though many Argentines believe assaults, rapes, homicide, and crimes against property are increasing, by almost any international standard Buenos Aires is a safe city. Because *porteños* keep late hours, there are plenty of people on the street at most times—rarely will you find yourself walking alone down a dark alleyway.

Still, certain precautions almost go without saying—most crimes are crimes of opportunity. Never leave luggage unattended, store valuables in a hotel safe, keep a close watch on your belongings at sidewalk cafés, and keep a passport photocopy that shows your date of entry into the country. Do not carry large amounts of cash (money belts or leg pouches are good alternatives for hiding cash and documents), do leave valuable jewelry at home, and do keep conspicuous items, such as photographic equipment, out of sight when possible. Do not assume that any area is totally secure.

If you should be accosted by anyone with a firearm or other weapon, do not resist. Although guns are relatively uncommon—knives are the weapons of choice—and truly violent crime against tourists is unusual, the consequences of a misjudgment can be lethal.

Certain barrios are more crime-prone than

others. Parts of La Boca are inadvisable even during daylight hours, so keep alert as to your surroundings. San Telmo is reasonably secure in daylight hours, but requires caution at night, even though there are many restaurants and clubs in the area.

One disturbing phenomenon is the so-called *secuestro exprés* (express kidnapping), in which criminals hold an individual for a small ransom or, alternatively, force someone to withdraw money from an ATM. Far more common in Buenos Aires province than in the capital, such crimes have *not* targeted tourists—rather, they appear to concentrate on individuals whose movements are familiar to the kidnapper.

More common are crimes of distraction, in which a crook bumps a victim and spills a substance like ice cream or mustard; while the *mostacero* (mustard scammer) apologizes profusely and "helps" clean up the mess, an accomplice surreptitiously lifts valuable items. Pickpocketing occurs on crowded public transportation; carry wallets and other items of value in a front trouser pocket or, even better, an interior jacket pocket.

Money

While traveling in Argentina, it makes sense to have a variety of money alternatives. International credit cards are widely accepted, and foreign ATM cards work almost everywhere. Because ATMs are open 24/7, many visitors prefer this alternative, but it makes sense to have a cash reserve in U.S. dollars (still preferable to euros despite the dollar's weakness).

Argentine banknotes

Travelers' checks may be the safest way to carry money, since they're refundable in case of loss or theft, but changing them outside Buenos Aires is a nightmarish experience even when stability reigns.

Prices throughout this book are given in U.S. dollars because of the Argentine peso's instability, but normally travelers will be paying in pesos. Nevertheless, merchants and services will often accept dollars at the prevailing exchange rate or sometimes at an even better rate.

If carrying an emergency cash reserve, use an inconspicuous leg pouch or money belt (not the bulky kind that fits around the waist, which thieves or robbers easily recognize, but a zippered leather belt that looks like any other).

CURRENCY

Throughout the 1990s, money was a simple matter. The Argentine peso was at par with the U.S. dollar, which circulated almost interchangeably alongside it, but the economic collapse of 2001–2002 has complicated matters. Many merchants still accept cash dollars, but exchange rates vary and any change will come in pesos.

Banknotes exist in denominations of 2, 5, 10, 20, 50, and 100 pesos. Coins exist in denominations of 1, 5, 10, 25, and 50 centavos (cents), but 1-centavo coins are rare and most businesses generally round off prices to the nearest 5 or 10 centavos.

Counterfeiting of both U.S. and foreign currency appears to be increasing. Merchants will often refuse any U.S. banknote with the smallest tear or writing on it, but they will accept any peso note that is not flagrantly *trucho* (bogus). On any banknote, look for the conspicuous watermark with the initials of the historical figure depicted on it—J.S.M for José de San Martín on the five-peso note, for instance.

EXCHANGE RATES

Following the debt default of early 2002, caretaker president Eduardo Duhalde's government devalued the peso from 1 to 1.4 pesos per dollar but, when that proved unsustainable, it floated the currency. After falling to nearly four pesos to the dollar late that year, it recovered to less than three pesos per dollar by early 2005. There are so many uncertainties in the Argentine economy, though, that the exchange rate remains a wild card.

Travelers with euros or British pounds, which have gained strongly against the dollar, will find that their money goes much farther at present. For the most up-to-date exchange rates, consult the business section of your daily newspaper or an online currency converter, such as www.oanda.com.

In Buenos Aires, the best sources on exchange rate trends are the financial dailies *Ambito Financiero* and *Buenos Aires Económico*.

CHANGING MONEY

During the 1990s (when the peso was at par with the dollar) changing money was a nonissue, as the two were virtually interchangeable. The early 2002 peso float, though, made banks, *casas de cambio* (exchange houses), and surreptitious exchanges relevant again. However, the situation has fortunately stabilized after more than a year of chaotic banking restrictions.

ATMs, abundant and becoming universal except in a few remote areas, match the best bank rates and are accessible 24/7. Unfortunately, they generally dispense large banknotes, often of 100 pesos and rarely smaller than 50 pesos.

One way around this problem is to punch in an odd amount, such as 290 pesos, in order to ensure getting some smaller notes.

TRAVELERS' CHECKS AND REFUNDS

Despite the safeguards they offer, travelers' checks have many drawbacks in Argentina. In addition to the time-consuming bureaucracy of changing them at banks and exchange houses, they often carry a substantial penalty in terms of commission—up to 3 percent or even more in many cases. Businesses other than exchange houses rarely accept them under any circumstances and, in out-of-the-way places, nobody will. Travelers' checks, unfortunately, should be a last-resort means of carrying and changing money here; cash (despite its shortcomings) and ATM cards are better options.

BANK TRANSFERS

Many Argentine exchange houses, post offices, and other businesses are affiliated with Western Union, making it relatively straightforward to send money from overseas. For a list of Western Union affiliates in Argentina, see their website (www.westernunion.com).

The American Express Money Gram is another alternative. Amex has a large office in Retiro and affiliates throughout the country.

In an emergency, it is possible to forward money to U.S. citizens via the U.S. embassy in Buenos Aires by establishing a Department of State trust account through its Overseas Citizens Services (Washington, D.C. 20520, tel. 202/647-5225); there is a US$20 service charge for setting up the account. It is possible to arrange this as a wire or overnight mail transfer through Western Union (tel. 800/325-6000 in the United States); for details, see the State Department's website (www.travel.state.gov).

CREDIT AND DEBIT CARDS

Credit cards have been common currency for many years and, in the aftermath of the recent peso crisis, when Argentines could not withdraw their savings, their use became even more widespread. Visa and MasterCard are most widely accepted, but there are inconsistencies—a significant number of businesses prefer American Express, sometimes to the exclusion of the others, or even Diner's Club. Debit cards are also widely accepted, at least those with Visa or MasterCard affiliation.

There may be drawbacks to using credit cards, however. During the 1990s boom years, Argentine merchants generally refrained from the *recargo,* a surcharge on credit card purchases because of slow bank payments. Many have reinstituted the *recargo,* which can be up to 10 percent, to cut their losses due to the peso's loss of value between the customer's payment and the bank's reimbursement. Note that hotels in particular may offer equivalent discounts for payments in cash.

Fluctuating exchange rates may also affect the charge that eventually appears on your overseas account. If the rate has changed in the interim between your payment in Buenos Aires and its posting to the home account, it may be either greater or smaller in terms of dollars (or other foreign currency), depending on the peso's strength.

In general, *propinas* (gratuities) are *not* added to charges for restaurant meals. Keep some cash, either dollars or pesos, for tips.

To deal with lost or stolen cards, the major international credit card companies have local representatives: American Express (Arenales 707, Retiro, tel. 011/4310-3000); Diner's Club (Avenida Santa Fe 1148, Retiro, tel. 011/4814-5627); MasterCard (Perú 143, Monserrat, tel. 011/4331-2088 or 0800/555-0507); and Visa (Avenida Corrientes 1437, 3rd fl., tel. 011/4379-3300).

COSTS

For most of the 1990s, Argentina was South America's most expensive country, so much so that even North Americans and Europeans found it costly. Wealthy Argentines, for their part, partied in Miami, Madrid, Rome, and other inexpensive destinations.

This anomaly was a function of former Economy Minister Domingo Cavallo's fixed exchange rate, which reduced previous hyperinflation to near zero. Cavallo's "convertibility" policy, however, also froze prices at a relatively high but unsustainable level that eventually made Argentine exports noncompetitive and brought the 2002 default.

Since the February 2002 float, followed by banking restrictions that limited the amount of money in circulation, Argentina has been a bargain for visitors who bring dollars or other hard currency. According to the Economist Intelligence Unit, Buenos Aires fell from being the 22nd most expensive city in the world to the 120th (of 131 surveyed). While a strengthening peso and renewed inflation have made things more expensive, by European or North American standards it's still economical, if not truly cheap.

Much, though, depends on the traveler's expectations. There are suitable services for everyone from barebones budget backpackers to pampered international business travelers. Budget travelers will find hotel rooms for US$10 pp or even less and some excellent values for only a little more money. Even hotels and resorts of international stature, like the Hyatt, Four Seasons, and Sheraton chains, had to lower their rates during the crisis. With the recovery, though, strong demand has meant rising prices at the upper end of the spectrum.

Likewise, meals can go for a couple dollars or even less at the simplest *comedores,* but restaurants with sophisticated international cuisine can charge a lot more; even the latter, however, often serve moderately priced lunchtime specials. Still, it's possible to eat exceptional food for half or less of what comparable meals would cost in Europe or North America.

Even now, shoestring travelers can get along on US$20 per day or so for accommodations and food. For US$50 pp per day, it's possible to live very comfortably and eat well, and a budget of US$100 is extravagant. It's worth

Know Buenos Aires

adding, though, that the volatility of Argentina's economy—hyperinflation was a recurrent phenomenon in the last half of the 20th century—makes it impossible to guarantee that prices will not rise.

TAXES

Argentina imposes a 21 percent *impuesto al valor agregado* (IVA, value added tax or VAT) on all goods and services, though this is normally included in the advertised price; if in doubt, ask for clarification (*"¿Incluye los impuestos?"*). Tax evasion is a national sport, however, and hotel owners will often ignore the tax for payments in cash.

Foreign visitors making purchases intended for export can often get a legal IVA rebate upon leaving the country.

TIPPING

In restaurants with table service, a 10 percent gratuity is customary, but in smaller family-run eateries, the practice is rare. Taxi drivers are customarily not tipped, but rounding off the fare to the next-highest convenient number is appropriate. Where there is no meter, this is not an issue.

BARGAINING

Bargaining is not the way of life in Argentina that it is in some other Latin American countries, but in flea markets or crafts markets the vendor may start at a higher price than he or she expects to receive—avoid insultingly low offers or such a high offer that the vendor will think you a fool. Depending on your language and bargaining skills, you should be able to achieve a compromise that satisfies everybody.

Even in some upscale Buenos Aires shops, prices for items like leather jackets may be open to negotiation.

STUDENT DISCOUNTS

Student discounts are relatively few, and prices are so low for most services that it's rarely worth arguing the point. In the case of foreign travel, however, students may be eligible for discount international airfares; consult student-oriented travel agencies and see the Getting There and Getting Around entries for details.

Tourist Information

MAPS

The Automóvil Club Argentino (ACA, Argentine Automobile Club, Avenida del Libertador 1850, Palermo, tel. 011/4808-4000, www.aca.org.ar) publishes the country's most comprehensive series of maps, including the city road map *Carta Vial de Buenos Aires y Alrededores*. It also publishes excellent highway maps, including major city plans, of all Argentine provinces. Members of overseas automobile clubs like the AAA in the United States and the AA in Britain can buy these maps at discount prices.

For getting around town, though, street atlases, such as the annually updated *Guía Lumi* and *Guía T*, are the most useful resources, as they also have detailed bus itineraries and other information.

For topographic maps, visit the Instituto Geográfico Militar (Avenida Cabildo 301, Palermo, tel. 011/4576-5576, www.igm.gov.ar).

TOURIST OFFICES

The Secretaría Nacional de Turismo (Avenida Santa Fe 883, Retiro, tel. 011/4312-2232 or 0800/555-0016, www.turismo.gov.ar) is open 9 A.M.–5 P.M. weekdays only; there's a branch at Aeropuerto Internacional Ministro Pistarini (aka Ezeiza, tel. 011/4480-0224), and another at Aeroparque Jorge Newbery (tel. 011/4773-9891). Both airport branches are open 8 A.M.–8 P.M. daily.

The municipal Subsecretaría de Turismo

maintains information kiosks, all of which distribute maps and brochures and usually have English-speaking staff, at several locations: in the Microcentro (Florida and Diagonal Roque Sáenz Peña, 9 A.M.–6 P.M. weekdays and 10 A.M.–3 P.M. weekends except May–September, when it's open weekdays only); at Puerto Madero's Dique 4 (tel. 011/4313-0187, 11 A.M.–7 P.M. daily); at the Retiro bus terminal (tel. 011/4311-0528, 7:30 A.M.–1 P.M. daily except Sunday); in Recoleta (Avenida Quintana and Roberto M. Ortiz, 10:30 A.M.–6:30 P.M. weekdays and 11 A.M.–7 P.M. weekends); and in San Telmo (Defensa 1250, open noon–6 P.M. weekdays, 10 A.M.–7 P.M. weekends).

In addition, to help tourists who are crime victims, the Policía Federal operates a Comisaría de Turismo (Avenida Corrientes 436, tel. 0800/999-5000 or 011/4346-5748), whose staff can handle English, French, German, Italian, Japanese, Portuguese, and Ukrainian.

FILM AND PHOTOGRAPHY

Color print film is widely available, color slide film less so. In any event, it tends to be cheaper in North America and Europe than in Argentina, so it's best to bring as much as possible. If purchasing film in Argentina, check the expiration date to make sure it's current, especially in out-of-the-way places. In the capital and larger tourist centers, competent print-film processing is readily available and moderately priced. However, it's better to hold slide film until your return to your home country if possible (but store it under cool, dark, and dry conditions) or to visit a specialist, such as Kinefot (Talcahuano 250, tel. 011/4374-7445). For prints, try Le Lab (Viamonte 624, tel. 011/4322-2785).

Environmental conditions can affect the quality of your photographs and the type of film you should use. Bright sun can wash out photographs; in these circumstances, it's best to use a relatively slow film, around ASA 64 or 100, and a polarizing filter to reduce glare. A polarizing filter also improves contrast, dramatizing the sky and the clouds, but can result in a dark foreground if you're not careful.

In the basement of Retiro's Galería Buenos Aires, Gerardo Föhse (Florida 835, Local 37, tel. 011/4311-1139) can do basic camera repairs. Dependable José Norres (Lavalle 1569, 4th fl., Oficina 403, tel. 011/4373-0963) can perform more complex repairs except on some of the latest electronic equipment, and service is quick.

PHOTOGRAPHIC ETIQUETTE—AND A WARNING

Most Argentines, especially *porteños*, are not exactly camera-shy, but do be cautious about photographing political protests—the police are notorious for cataloging dissidents, so protestors may be wary of people with cameras. Likewise, avoid taking photographs in the vicinity of military installations, although "The Sentry Will Shoot" signs are mostly a thing of past.

Generally, if a person's presence in a photograph is incidental, as in a townscape, it's unnecessary to ask permission, but avoid the in-your-face approach. If in doubt, ask; if rejected, don't insist. If you're purchasing something from a market vendor, he or she will almost certainly agree to a photographic request.

There is one absolute no-no, however—without explicit permission, do not even think about photographing Israeli or Jewish community sites anywhere in Argentina. Since car-bomb attacks on Retiro's Israeli Embassy in 1992 and Once's Jewish cultural center in 1994, federal police are stationed outside all of these sites. They will politely or, if necessary, not so politely discourage would-be photographers.

Communications and Media

Buenos Aires is a modern city, and as such the communications infrastructure is similar to what you'd expect in other large cities around the developed world.

POSTAL SERVICES

The privatized Correo Argentino, the Argentine post office, has meant more reliable service than in the past, but recent disagreements have brought government intervention. Domestic services are generally cheap, international services more expensive. Major international couriers provide fast, reliable services at premium prices.

The landmark Correo Central (Sarmiento 189, 9 A.M.–7:30 P.M. weekdays) is worth a visit in its own right, but there are many other branch offices. The main building occupies an entire block bounded by Sarmiento, Avenida L.N. Alem, Avenida Corrientes, and Bouchard.

General delivery at Argentine post offices is *lista de correos,* literally a list arranged in alphabetical order. There is a small charge for each item addressed to you.

Note that in Spanish-language street addresses the number follows, rather than precedes, the name; the U.S. address "1343 Washington Avenue," for example, would read, "Avenida Washington 1343" in Argentina. Argentines and other Spanish speakers normally omit the word *calle* (street) from addresses; whereas an English speaker might write, "499 Jones Street," an Argentine would simply use "Jones 499," for example. It is not unusual for street addresses to lack a number, as indicated by *s/n (sin número,* without a number), especially in small provincial towns.

International parcels that weigh in excess of one kilogram must leave from the Correo Internacional (Antártida Argentina, tel. 011/4316-7777, 11 A.M.–5 P.M. weekdays only), near the Retiro train station.

Private couriers include DHL International

(Moreno 927, Monserrat, tel. 011/4630-1110) and the Microcentro's Federal Express (Maipú 753, tel. 011/4393-6054).

TELEPHONE AND FAX

Argentina has two major telephone companies, Telecom (north of Avenida Córdoba) and Telefónica (south of Avenida Córdoba). The country code is 54; the *característica* (area code) for the Capital Federal and Gran Buenos Aires is 11, but there is a bewildering number of area codes for individual cities, smaller cities and towns, and rural areas. All telephone numbers in the Capital Federal and Gran Buenos Aires have eight digits, while those in other provincial cities and rural areas vary. When calling out of the area code, it's necessary to dial zero first.

Cellular phone numbers in Buenos Aires all have eight digits and the prefix 15. Certain toll-free and other specialty numbers have six or seven digits with a three-digit prefix.

Public telephones are abundant; some of them operate with coins only, but most also accept magnetic phone cards or rechargeable-account cards. The basic local phone rate is 25 centavos (about US$.09) for five minutes or so; domestic long distance is considerably more expensive. Phone cards are convenient for in-country calls but less useful for more expensive overseas calls.

For long distance and overseas calls and fax services, it's simplest to use *locutorios* (call centers), which are abundant in both Buenos Aires and the provinces. Prices are increasingly competitive, and now tend to be much cheaper than placing *cobro revertido* (collect) or *tarjeta de crédito* (credit card) calls to the United States or any other country. Calls are more expensive during peak hours, 8 A.M.–8 P.M. weekdays and 8 A.M.–1 P.M. Saturdays.

Cellular Phone Rental

Opening a cell phone account without a permanent Argentine address is something of a nuisance, but rental phones are available from Nolitel (tel. 011/4311-3500, www.nolitel-group.com). Many upscale hotels include cell phones in their rates, but guests are liable for the calls.

INTERNET ACCESS

In the last few years, public Internet access has become so ubiquitous that no single locale really needs mentioning. Many *locutorios* offer access, but there are also numerous Internet cafés with broadband. Some Internet service providers, most notably AOL, Compuserve, and Earthlink, have local dial-up numbers in Argentina, but these often collect a surcharge for modem access.

Internet services are also so cheap that, if price trends continue, providers will be paying customers to use their services. Rarely does access cost more than US$1 per hour, and it's often even cheaper.

MEDIA
Newspapers and Magazines

Historically, freedom of the press has been tenuous, as Argentine governments have controlled the supply of newsprint and withheld official advertising from newspapers and magazines that have published items not to their liking. Nevertheless, since the end of the 1976–1983 dictatorship, the trend has been largely positive for liberty of expression. Many of the newspapers and periodicals below have websites listed in the Internet Resources section.

Though it's the Spanish-speaking world's largest-circulation daily, the middle-of-the-road tabloid *Clarín* (www.clarin.com.ar) is more sensitive to hard economic times than papers with a steadier niche clientele. Part of a consortium that includes TV and radio outlets, it also publishes the sports daily *¡Ole!*.

According to Anglo-Argentine journalist Andrew Graham-Yooll, you're not really dead until your obituary appears in the center-right *La Nación* (www.lanacion.com.ar)—a remark that reflects the social standing of the capital's

most venerable daily, dating from 1870. With a circulation of nearly 200,000—twice that on Sundays when it has an exceptional cultural section—the paper was the creation of Bartolomé Mitre, who later became president.

Página 12 (www.pagina12web.com.ar) is the tabloid voice of Argentina's intellectual left and, while its outspokenness is admirable, it would benefit from more rigorous editing—many articles are far too long and indulge in hyper-analysis. Political columnist Horacio Verbitsky is one of the country's most famous and capable journalists, however.

Crónica, with a weekday circulation of 400,000 but far fewer on weekends, is a crime-and-celebrities tabloid. *Diario Popular* is somewhat less sensationalist, but in the same vein.

The capital has three financial newspapers, which publish weekdays only: the morning *Ambito Financiero* (www.ambitoweb.com), which also publishes an outstanding arts and entertainment section, the afternoon *El Cronista Comercial* (www.cronista.com), and *Buenos Aires Económico* (www.infobae.com).

Many *porteños* get their daily newspapers and magazines at corner kiosks.

THE PORTEÑO BOOKSHELF

In the 19th century, even as the free-roaming gaucho was becoming a wage laborer on the *estancias* of the pampas, Argentine literature enshrined his most positive qualities in José Hernández's epic poem *Martín Fierro* (1872 and 1879), available in many editions and in English translation. This *gauchesco* (gauchesque) tradition has never completely disappeared, and it is most memorable in Ricardo Güiraldes's novel *Don Segundo Sombra* (1926). Güiraldes's romanticized fiction is also available in many editions and has been translated into English and many other languages.

Born of U.S.-immigrant parents in Buenos Aires province, William Henry Hudson (1841–1922) left for London at the age of 33, but his memoir *Long Ago and Far Away* (1922) has been a staple of Argentine public education. An accomplished amateur field naturalist, he also wrote *Idle Days in Patagonia* (1893) about his explorations in search of birds, plus short stories and even a novel, *Green Mansions* (1904), set in Venezuela's rain forests. Argentines, who often translate forenames into Spanish, know him as Guillermo Enrique Hudson.

A more critical assessment of Argentina and its rural heritage came from the educator and politician Domingo F. Sarmiento (1811–1888). His *Life in the Argentine Republic in the Days of the Tyrants* (1845), an eloquent tirade against rural caudillos that betrays his provincial background, has overcome its polemical origins to become a staple of Latin American history courses in English-speaking countries.

No Argentine author has ever won a Nobel Prize for Literature, but three have won the Premio Cervantes, the Spanish-speaking world's most important literary honor: essayist, poet, and short-story writer Jorge Luis Borges (1979), and novelists Ernesto Sábato (1984) and Adolfo Bioy Casares (1990). Other noteworthy Argentine writers include César Aira, Roberto Arlt, Julio Cortázar, Victoria Ocampo, Manuel Puig, and Osvaldo Soriano, much of whose work is available in English translation. (Publication dates here indicate the Spanish-language original unless otherwise noted.)

Globally, the most prominent is Borges (1899–1986), often mentioned but never chosen for the Nobel. Ironically enough for a classically educated and urbane figure who loathed Perón and Peronism, his short stories, poetry, and essays often focus on urban lowlifes and rural themes, including gaucho violence. Borges never wrote a novel; his most frequently read works are collections, such as *Labyrinths* (1970, in English), many of whose stories can seem obscure and even surrealistic.

Sábato (born 1911) acquired some renown in the English-speaking world as the coordinator of *Nunca Más,* an official account of the 1976–1983 military dictatorship's brutalities. Born in Buenos Aires province but a long resident in the capital, his best work may be the engrossing psychological novel *On Heroes and Tombs* (1961; New York: Ballantine, 1991), which credibly depicts places and examines people in the city; its subsection "Report on the Blind," capable of standing alone, is truly extraordinary. Sábato's novella *The Tunnel* (1950; New York: Ballantine, 1988), about artistic obsession, is equally absorbing but less conspicuously *porteño* in its approach.

Borges's close friend Bioy Casares (1914–1999) collaborated with the older man on detective stories under the pseudonym Honorario Bustos Domecq, but his own fantastical novella *The Invention of Morel* (Austin: University of Texas Press, 1985) is a purposefully disorienting work that director Eliseo Subiela transformed into the award-winning film *Man Facing Southeast*. Bioy's *Diary of the War of the Pig* (New York: McGraw Hill, 1972) takes place in the barrio of Palermo, mostly within the area popularly referred to as "Villa

Freud." His *The Dream of Heroes* (New York: Dutton, 1987) paints a surrealistic portrait of the late 1920s, a time when Carnaval flourished in Buenos Aires.

Though he died young and unsuccessful, Robert Arlt (1900–1942) had a lasting impact on Argentine and especially *porteño* literature in depicting corruption from the scammer's point of view, in such novels as *The Seven Madmen* (London and New York: Serpent's Tail Publishing, 1998).

Son of a diplomatic family, the Belgian-born Cortázar (1914–1984) was a short story writer, experimental novelist, and committed leftist who chose Parisian exile after losing his university post in a Peronist purge. Michelangelo Antonioni turned one of Cortázar's short stories into the famous 1960s film *Blow-Up,* but the author is also known for his novels *Hopscotch* (1963; New York: Random House, 1966), the story of a failed Francophile poet in Buenos Aires, and *62: A Model Kit* (1968; New York: Random House, 1972).

Manuel Puig (1932–1990) authored a series of novels concerning popular culture, and specifically the cinema, including *Betrayed by Rita Hayworth* (1968), the detective novel *The Buenos Aires Affair* (New York: Dutton, 1968), and *Kiss of the Spider Woman* (New York: Vintage, 1991), which Brazilian director Héctor Babenco made into an award-winning English-language film with William Hurt and Raúl Juliá. Puig wrote *Eternal Curse on the Reader of These Pages* (New York: Random House, 1982), about an amnesiac victim of the 1976–1983 dictatorship, in English and later translated it into Spanish.

Journalist/novelist Osvaldo Soriano (1943–1997) wrote satirical novels, such as *A Funny Dirty Little War* (Columbia, Louisiana, and London: Readers International, 1989), depicting the consequences of national upheaval in a small community, and *Winter Quarters* (same publisher and year). His *Shadows* (New York: Knopf, 1993), which takes its Spanish title *Una Sombra Ya Pronto Serás* from a classic tango lyric, became a surrealistically disorienting road movie under director Héctor Olivera.

Essayist Victoria Ocampo (1891–1979), whose poetess sister Silvina (1909–1994) was Bioy Casares's wife, founded the literary magazine *Sur;* some of her essays appear in Doris Meyer's biography *Victoria Ocampo: Against the Wind and the Tide* (Austin: University of Texas Press, 1990). One of her collaborators at *Sur,* which also became a prestigious publishing house and brought figures like Aldous Huxley, D.H. Lawrence, and even Jack Kerouac to the attention of Spanish-speaking readers, was Borges.

Tomás Eloy Martínez (born 1934) is author of several novels dealing with the Argentine condition through fictionalized biography, most notably *The Perón Novel* (New York: Pantheon Books, 1988)—based partly on his own extensive interviews with the late caudillo. *Santa Evita* (New York: Knopf, 1996), by contrast, can only be called post-biographical, as it traces the odyssey of Evita's embalmed body to Italy, Spain, and back to Buenos Aires.

Novelist Federico Andahazi (born 1963), also a psychiatrist, outraged industrialist heiress Amalia Fortabat when an independent jury awarded him her self-anointed literary prize for *The Anatomist* (New York: Doubleday, 1998), a sexually explicit (but hardly erotic) tale set in medieval Italy.

Sometimes called an heir to Borges, César Aira (born 1949) writes seemingly obscure novels, such as *The Hare* (Serpent's Tail Publishing, 1998), about an English naturalist's search for a rare rodent. Set on the indigenous frontier in the 19th century, it manages to tie together several apparently loose and disparate ends.

With a circulation of only about 15,000, Graham-Yooll's own *Buenos Aires Herald* is an English-language daily whose niche market correlates highly with hotel occupancy. It stresses commerce and finance but also produces intelligent analyses of political and economic developments; its Sunday edition includes material from the *The New York Times* and Britain's *Guardian Weekly*.

The German-language *Argentinisches Tageblatt* (www.tageblatt.com.ar) began as a daily in 1889, but is now a Saturday weekly with a circulation of about 10,000.

Noticias is the *porteño* counterpart to English-language weeklies like *Time* and *Newsweek*. *Trespuntos*, though, is more critical and innovative. *La Maga* (www.lamaga.com.ar) is an arts-oriented monthly.

Radio and Television

What was once a state broadcast monopoly is now more diverse, thanks to privatization and the advent of cable, but conglomerates like the Clarín and El Cronista groups now control much of the content. Both radio and TV tend to stress entertainment at the expense of journalism. TV news coverage, however, can be surprisingly good, and there is even a 24-hour tango channel on cable.

Radio Rivadavia, Argentina's most popular station (AM 630), plays popular music and also hosts talk programs. Radio Mitre (AM 790) is the voice of the Clarín group. FM Tango 92.7 plays all tango all the time, and Radio Folclorísimo (AM 1410) plays folk music 24/7.

LIBRARIES

The Biblioteca Nacional (National Library, Agüero 2502, Recoleta, tel. 011/4808-6000, www.bibnal.edu.ar, 9 A.M.–9 P.M. weekdays, noon–7 P.M. weekends) offers guided tours at 3 P.M. daily except Sunday, from March to mid-December only. It also holds frequent special exhibitions, lectures, literary events, and free concerts.

The United States Information Agency's Biblioteca Lincoln is at the Instituto Cultural Argentino-Norteamericano (Maipú 672, tel. 011/4322-3855 or 011/4322-4557).

BOOKSTORES

Buenos Aires has countless general-interest bookstores, as well as specialist shops that deal with academic and rare books, and others with English-language materials. (For details, see the *Shopping* chapter.)

Weights and Measures

TIME

Argentina is three hours behind GMT for most of the year and does not observe daylight savings time (summer time). Because of a drought-induced energy shortage, Uruguay has recently begun observing daylight savings time all year.

ELECTRICITY

Throughout the country, nearly all outlets are 220 volts and 50 cycles, so converters are necessary for North American appliances, such as computers and electric razors. Plugs have recently changed to a pair of flat diagonal prongs; appliances using two rounded prongs still exist, and adapters are easy to find. Adequately powered converters are harder to find, so it's better to bring one from overseas.

MEASUREMENTS

The metric system is official, but Argentines use a variety of vernacular measures in everyday life. Rural folk often use the Spanish *legua* (league) of about five kilometers as a measure of distance, and the *quintal* of 46 kilos is also widely used, especially in wholesale markets and agricultural statistics.

Spanish Phrasebook

Spanish is Argentina's official language, but the stereotypical *porteño* intonation—equivalent to a Bronx accent in New York—is unmistakably different from any other variant. Argentine Spanish in general is distinctive, often Italian-inflected, most notable for pronouncing the "ll" diphthong and "y" as "zh." "Llegar" (to arrive), for example, is pronounced "zhe-gar," while "yo" (I) is pronounced "zho."

Another distinguishing feature is the use of the familiar pronoun "vos" instead of "tu." Verb forms of the *voseo* differ from those of the *tuteo,* although Argentines will always understand speakers who use "tu."

At tourist offices, airlines, travel agencies, and upscale hotels, English is often spoken. In the provinces, it's less common, though its use is spreading, especially in the travel and tourism sector.

Visitors spending any length of time in Buenos Aires, especially students and business people, might look for Tino Rodríguez's *Primer Diccionario de Sinónimos del Lunfardo* (Buenos Aires: Editorial Atlántida, 1987), which defines *porteño* street slang. Note that some usage requires *great* caution for those unaware of *every* slang meaning.

PRONUNCIATION GUIDE

Spanish is a more phonetic language than English, but there are still occasional variations in pronunciation, especially in Argentina.

Consonants

c—as 'c' in "cat," before 'a,' 'o,' or 'u'; like 's' before 'e' or 'i'

d—as 'd' in "dog," except between vowels; then, like 'th' in "that"

g—before 'e' or 'i,' like the 'ch' in Scottish "loch"; elsewhere like 'g' in "get"

h—always silent

j—like the English 'h' in "hotel," but stronger

ll—like the 'z' in "azure"

ñ—like the 'ni' in "onion"

r—always pronounced as strong 'r'

rr—trilled 'r'

v—similar to the 'b' in "boy" (not as English 'v')

y—like 'll,' it sounds like the 'z' in azure. When standing alone, it's pronounced like the 'e' in "me."

z—like 's' in "same"

b, f, k, l, m, n, p, q, s, t, w, x as in English

Vowels

a—as in "father," but shorter

e—as in "hen"

i—as in "machine"

o—as in "phone"

u—usually as in "rule"; when it follows a 'q,' the 'u' is silent; when it follows an 'h' or 'g,' it's pronounced like 'w,' except when it comes between 'g' and 'e' or 'i,' when it's also silent (unless it has an umlaut, when it is again pronounced as the English 'w')

Stress

Native English speakers frequently make errors of pronunciation by ignoring stress. All Spanish vowels—a, e, i, o, and u—may carry accents that determine which syllable of a word gets emphasis. Often, stress seems unnatural to nonnative speakers—the surname Chávez, for instance, is stressed on the first syllable—but failure to observe this rule may mean that native speakers may not understand you.

NUMBERS

0—*cero*

1—*uno* (masculine)

1—*una* (feminine)

2—*dos*

3—*tres*

4—*cuatro*

5—*cinco*

6—*seis*

7—*siete*

8—*ocho*
9—*nueve*
10—*diez*
11—*once*
12—*doce*
13—*trece*
14—*catorce*
15—*quince*
16—*diez y seis*
17—*diez y siete*
18—*diez y ocho*
19—*diez y nueve*
20—*veinte*
21—*veinte y uno*
30—*treinta*
40—*cuarenta*
50—*cincuenta*
60—*sesenta*
70—*setenta*
80—*ochenta*
90—*noventa*
100—*cien*
101—*ciento y uno*
200—*doscientos*
1,000—*mil*
10,000—*diez mil*
1,000,000—*un millón*

DAYS OF THE WEEK

Sunday—*domingo*
Monday—*lunes*
Tuesday—*martes*
Wednesday—*miércoles*
Thursday—*jueves*
Friday—*viernes*
Saturday—*sábado*

TIME

While Argentines normally use the 12-hour clock (A.M. and P.M.), they sometimes use the 24-hour clock, usually associated with plane or bus schedules. Under the 24-hour clock, for example, *las diez de la noche* (10 P.M.) would be *las 22 horas* (2200 hours).

What time is it?—*¿Qué hora es?*

It's one o'clock—*Es la una.*
It's two o'clock—*Son las dos.*
At two o'clock—*A las dos.*
It's ten to three—*Son tres menos diez.*
It's ten past three—*Son tres y diez.*
It's three fifteen—*Son las tres y cuarto.*
It's two forty-five—*Son tres menos cuarto.*
It's two thirty—*Son las dos y media.*
It's six A.M.—*Son las seis de la mañana.*
It's six P.M.—*Son las seis de la tarde.*
It's ten P.M.—*Son las diez de la noche.*
Today—*hoy*
Tomorrow—*mañana*
Morning—*la mañana*
Tomorrow morning—*mañana por la mañana*
Yesterday—*ayer*
Week—*la semana*
Month—*mes*
Year—*año*
Last night—*anoche*
The next day—*el día siguiente*

USEFUL WORDS AND PHRASES

Argentines and other Spanish-speaking people consider formalities important. Whenever approaching anyone for information or some other reason, do not forget the appropriate salutation—good morning, good evening, etc. Standing alone, the greeting "*hola*" (hello) can sound brusque.

Note that most of the words below are fairly standard, common to all Spanish-speaking countries. Many, however, have more idiomatic Argentine equivalents; refer to the glossary for these.

Hello.—*Hola.*
Good morning.—*Buenos días.*
Good afternoon.—*Buenas tardes.*
Good evening.—*Buenas noches.*
How are you?—*¿Cómo está?*
Fine.—*Muy bien.*
And you?—*¿Y usted?*
So-so.—*Más o menos.*
Thank you.—*Gracias.*
Thank you very much.—*Muchas gracias.*
You're very kind.—*Muy amable.*

You're welcome.—*De nada*. (Literally, It's nothing.)
Yes—*sí*
No—*no*
I don't know.—*No sé*.
It's fine; okay.—*Está bien*.
Good; okay.—*Bueno*.
Please—*por favor*
Pleased to meet you.—*Mucho gusto*.
Excuse me (physical).—*Perdóneme*.
Excuse me (speech).—*Discúlpeme*.
I'm sorry.—*Lo siento*.
Goodbye.—*Adiós*.
See you later.—*Hasta luego*. (Literally, Until later.)
More—*más*
Less—*menos*
Better—*mejor*
Much, a lot—*mucho*
A little—*un poco*
Large—*grande*
Small—*pequeño, chico*
Quick, fast—*rápido*
Slowly—*despacio*
Bad—*malo*
Difficult—*difícil*
Easy—*fácil*
He/She/It is gone; as in "She left," "He's gone."—*Ya se fue*.
I don't speak Spanish well.—*No hablo bien el español*.
I don't understand.—*No entiendo*.
How do you say...in Spanish?—*¿Cómo se dice...en español?*
Do you understand English?—*¿Entiende el inglés?*
Is English spoken here? (Does anyone here speak English?)—*¿Se habla inglés aquí?*

TERMS OF ADDRESS

When in doubt, use the formal *usted* (you) as a form of address. If you wish to dispense with formality and feel that the desire is mutual, you can say *Me puedes tutear* (you can call me "tu") even though Argentines use the slightly different verb forms that correlate with the familiar pronoun "vos."

I—*yo*
You (formal)—*usted*
You (familiar)—*vos*
He/him—*él*
She/her—*ella*
We/us—*nosotros*
You (plural)—*ustedes*
They/them (all males or mixed gender)—*ellos*
They/them (all females)—*ellas*
Mr., sir—*señor*
Mrs., madam—*señora*
Miss, young lady—*señorita*
Wife—*esposa*
Husband—*marido* or *esposo*
Friend—*amigo* (male), *amiga* (female)
Sweetheart—*novio* (male), *novia* (female)
Son, daughter—*hijo, hija*
Brother, sister—*hermano, hermana*
Father, mother—*padre, madre*
Grandfather, grandmother—*abuelo, abuela*

GETTING AROUND

Where is...?—*¿Dónde está...?*
How far is it to...?—*¿A cuanto está...?*
from...to...—*de...a...*
Highway—*la carretera*
Road—*el camino*
Street—*la calle*
Block—*la cuadra*
Kilometer—*kilómetro*
North—*norte*
South—*sur*
West—*oeste; poniente*
East—*este; oriente*
Straight ahead—*al derecho; adelante*
To the right—*a la derecha*
To the left—*a la izquierda*

ACCOMMODATIONS

Is there a room?—*¿Hay habitación?*
May I (we) see it?—*¿Puedo (podemos) verla?*
What is the rate?—*¿Cuál es el precio?*
Is that your best rate?—*¿Es su mejor precio?*
Is there something cheaper?—*¿Hay algo más económico?*

Single room—*un sencillo*
Double room—*un doble*
Room for a couple—*matrimonial*
Key—*llave*
With private bath—*con baño privado*
With shared bath—*con baño general; con baño compartido*
Hot water—*agua caliente*
Cold water—*agua fría*
Shower—*ducha*
Electric shower—*ducha eléctrica*
Towel—*toalla*
Soap—*jabón*
Toilet paper—*papel higiénico*
Air conditioning—*aire acondicionado*
Fan—*ventilador*
Blanket—*frazada; manta*
Sheets—*sábanas*

PUBLIC TRANSPORT

Bus stop—*la parada*
Bus terminal—*terminal de buses*
Airport—*el aeropuerto*
Launch—*lancha*
Dock—*muelle*
I want a ticket to…—*Quiero un pasaje a…*
I want to get off at…—*Quiero bajar en…*
Here, please.—*Aquí, por favor.*
Where is this bus going?—*¿Adónde va este autobús?*
Roundtrip—*ida y vuelta*
What do I owe?—*¿Cuánto le debo?*

FOOD

Menu—*la carta, el menú*
Glass—*taza*
Fork—*tenedor*
Knife—*cuchillo*
Spoon—*cuchara*
Napkin—*servilleta*
Soft drink—*agua fresca*
Coffee—*café*
Cream—*crema*
Tea—*té*
Sugar—*azúcar*
Drinking water—*agua pura, agua potable*

Bottled carbonated water—*agua mineral con gas*
Bottled uncarbonated water—*agua sin gas*
Beer—*cerveza*
Wine—*vino*
Milk—*leche*
Juice—*jugo*
Eggs—*huevos*
Bread—*pan*
Watermelon—*sandía*
Banana—*banana*
Apple—*manzana*
Orange—*naranja*
Peach—*durazno*
Pineapple—*ananá*
Meat (without)—*carne (sin)*
Beef—*carne de res*
Chicken—*pollo; gallina*
Fish—*pescado*
Shellfish—*mariscos*
Shrimp—*camarones*
Fried—*frito*
Roasted—*asado*
Barbecued—*a la parrilla*
Breakfast—*desayuno*
Lunch—*almuerzo*
Dinner, or a late-night snack—*cena*
The check, or bill—*la cuenta*

MAKING PURCHASES

I need…—*Necesito…*
I want…—*Deseo…* or *Quiero…*
I would like…(more polite)—*Quisiera…*
How much does it cost?—*¿Cuánto cuesta?*
What's the exchange rate?—*¿Cuál es el tipo de cambio?*
May I see…?—*¿Puedo ver…?*
This one—*ésta/ésto*
Expensive—*caro*
Cheap—*barato*
Cheaper—*más barato*
Too much—*demasiado*

HEALTH

Help me, please.—*Ayúdeme, por favor.*

I am ill.—*Estoy enfermo.*
It hurts.—*Me duele.*
Pain—*dolor*
Fever—*fiebre*
Stomach ache—*dolor de estómago*
Vomiting—*vomitar*

Diarrhea—*diarrea*
Drugstore—*farmacia*
Medicine—*medicina*
Pill, tablet—*pastilla*
Birth control pills—*pastillas anticonceptivas*
Condom—*condón, preservativo*

Glossary

aduana—customs

aduana paralela—parallel customs, corrupt customs officials

albergue juvenil—youth hostel, though the English word "hostel" is now in common usage as well

albergue transitorio—a by-the-hour-hotel, frequently used by young and not-so-young couples in search of privacy

anexo—telephone extension

arrabales—geographically and socially peripheral parts of the city, identified with immigrants and the rise of the tango

asambleas populares—neighborhood assemblies of protestors and activists frustrated with Argentine institutions

avenida—avenue

balneario—bathing or beach resort

barrancas—high ground on the original banks of the Río de Plata, now far inland in San Telmo, Belgrano, and other parts of Buenos Aires because of continual landfill

barras bravas—soccer hooligans, violent gangs affiliated with soccer teams

barrio—neighborhood

boleadoras—rounded stones tied together with a leather thong and used for hunting by indigenous people of La Pampa

bono—bond, a provincial letter of credit serving as a parallel currency equivalent to the peso

bronca—a singularly *porteño* combination of aggravation and frustration; there is no precise English equivalent; the closest meaning is wrath or, in Britain, aggro (the latter according to *Buenos Aires Herald* editor Andrew Graham-Yooll)

cabildo—colonial governing council

caipirinha—a popular drink made with *cachaça* (Brazilian liquor made from distilled sugarcane juice), lime, and sugar

cajero automático—automatic teller machine (ATM)

camioneta—pickup truck

candombe—music and dance of Afro-Argentine *porteños,* of whom few remain

característica—telephone area code

carne—beef; other kinds of meat are *carne blanca* (literally, white meat)

cartelera—discount ticket agency

casa chorizo—sausage house, a narrow residence on a deep lot

casa de cambio—money-exchange facility, often just *cambio*

casco—big house of an *estancia*

casilla—post office box

caudillo—in early independence times, a provincial warlord, though the term is often used for any populist leader, such as Juan Domingo Perón

cerro—hill

chamamé—accordion-based folk music of the northeastern Argentine littoral

chopp—draft beer

ciruja—literally surgeon, a scavenger who picks recyclables from the garbage on Buenos Aires streets; synonymous with *cartonero*

cobro revertido—collect or reverse-charge telephone call

cocoliche—pidgin blend of Italian and Spanish spoken by Mediterranean European immigrants

coima—bribe

colectivo—a city bus

comedor—simple eatery or dining room

confitería—a restaurant/café with a menu of *minutas* (short orders)

conventillo—tenement, often an abandoned mansion taken over by squatters

corralito—unpopular banking restriction imposed by the Argentine government during the 2001–2002 debt default and devaluation

costanera—any road along a seashore, lakeshore, or riverside

criollo—in colonial times, an Argentine-born Spaniard; in the present, normally a descriptive term meaning traditionally Argentine

desaparecido—disappeared one, victim of the 1976–1983 military dictatorship

descamisados—shirtless ones, working-class followers of Juan and Evita Perón

dique—deep-water basin dredged in Buenos Aires harbor

doble tracción—four-wheel drive, also known as *cuatro por cuatro* (the latter written as 4X4)

edificio—building

escrache—public demonstration, originally identifying human-rights violators at their residences, but since extended to perceived corrupt officials and institutions

estancia—cattle or sheep ranch controlling large expanses of land, often with an absentee owner, a dominant manager, and resident employees

estatuas vivas—living statues, mimes in touristed areas of Buenos Aires

estero—estuary

farmacia de turno—pharmacy remaining open all night for emergencies, on a rotating basis

feria—outdoor crafts or antiques fair; alternately, an outdoor bookstall

fichas—tokens, formerly used on the Buenos Aires subway

filete—traditional art of *porteño* sign painters, in a calligraphic style

fileteador—*filete* artist

gasoil—diesel fuel

gauchesco—adjective describing romantic art or literature about (not by) gauchos

golfo—gulf

golpe de estado—coup d'etat

hipódromo—horserace track

hospedaje—family-run lodging

indígena—indigenous person

indigenista—adjective describing romantically pro-indigenous literature, music, and art

infracción—traffic violation

isla—island

islote—islet

istmo—isthmus

IVA—*impuesto de valor agregado,* or value added tax (VAT)

lago—lake

laguna—lagoon

latifundio—large landholding, usually an *estancia*

local—numbered office or locale, at a given street address

locutorio—telephone call center

lunfardo—*porteño* street slang that developed in working-class immigrant barrios like La Boca but is now more widely used in Argentine Spanish, though not in formal situations

machista—male chauvinist

malevo—street bully

media pensión—half board (rates include breakfast and either lunch or dinner) at a hotel or guesthouse

menú—menu; also, a fixed-price meal

mestizo—individual of mixed indigenous and Spanish ancestry

milonga—informal neighborhood dance club, which often includes tango as a participatory rather than spectator activity

minuta—a short-order meal, such as pasta

mirador—overlook or viewpoint

museo—museum

ñoqui—ghost employee, collecting a state salary despite performing little or no work; literally, gnocchi

palacete—mansion

pampa—broad, flat expanse in and around Buenos Aires

pampero—southwesterly cold front

parada—bus stop

parque nacional—national park

partido—administrative subdivision of an Argentine province, equivalent to a county

paseaperros—professional dog walker

payador—spontaneous gaucho singer

peaje—tollbooth

peatonal—pedestrian mall

pensión—family-run accommodation

pensión completa—full board, at a hotel or guesthouse

picante—spicy-hot; the Argentine tolerance for spicy food is very low, however, and most visitors may find foods labeled *picante* to be relatively bland

piquete—protestors' roadblock

piropo—sexist remark, ranging from humorous and innocuous to truly vulgar; also, on *filete,* an aphorism

playa—beach

polideportivo—sports club

porteño—native or resident of Buenos Aires

propina—tip, as at a restaurant

puente—bridge

puerto—port

Pullman—first-class bus, with reclining seats and luggage storage underneath

pulpería—general store, usually in a rural area

quinta—country estate

radiotaxi—a taxi that is available by appointment rather than hailed on the street

recargo—surcharge on credit card purchases

remis—meterless *radiotaxi* charging a fixed rate within a given zone

residencial—permanent budget accommodations, often also called hotel

restó—self-styled trendy restaurant, whose food may or may not match its aspirations

río—river

rotisería—delicatessen

ruta—route or highway

saladero—meat-salting plant of late colonial and early republican times

s/n—*sin número,* a street address without a number

sudestada—cold wind out of the southeast

tango canción—tango song, with music and lyrics expressing nostalgia

tanguero—tango dancer

tarifa mostrador—hotel rack rate

tenedor libre—literally free fork, all-you-can-eat restaurant

toldo—tent of animal skins, inhabited by mobile indigenous people of the pampas in pre-Columbian times

trasnoche—late-night cinema showing

trucho—bogus

turco—Argentine of Middle Eastern descent (literally, Turk)

villa miseria—urban shantytown

viveza criolla—artful deception, ranging from small-scale cheating to audacious chutzpah

Suggested Reading

ARCHAEOLOGY, ETHNOGRAPHY, AND ETHNOHISTORY

Schávelzon, Daniel. *Historia del Comer y del Beber en Buenos Aires.* Buenos Aires: Aguilar, 2000. Urban archaeologist Schávelzon chronicles the evolution of the *porteño* diet through salvage excavations in the city, finding among other surprises that beef consumption was not always so great as some have assumed.

GUIDEBOOKS AND TRAVELOGUES

Darwin, Charles. *Voyage of the Beagle* (many editions). Perhaps the greatest travel book ever written, Darwin's narrative of his 19th-century journey brims with insights on the people, places, and even politics he observed while collecting the plants and animals that led to his revolutionary theories. The great scientist observed the city of Buenos Aires, the surrounding pampas, and parts of neighboring Uruguay, and met key figures in the country's history, including the dictator Rosas.

France, Miranda. *Bad Times in Buenos Aires.* Hopewell, NJ: Ecco Press, 1998. A timeless title, perhaps, but it refers to the author's sardonic analysis of her early 1990s experiences.

Green, Toby. *Saddled with Darwin.* London: Phoenix, 1999. An audacious if uneven account of a young, talented writer's attempt to retrace the hoofprints—not the footsteps—of Darwin's travels through Uruguay, Argentina, and Chile. Self-effacing but still serious, the author manages to compare his own experience with Darwin's, reflect on contemporary distortions of the great scientist's theories, and stay almost completely off the gringo trail.

Guevara, Ernesto. *The Motorcycle Diaries: A Journey around South America.* New York and London: Verso, 1995. Translated by Ann Wright, recently brought to the big screen by Brazilian director Walter Salles, this travelogue follows an Argentine drifter's progress from Buenos Aires across the Andes and up the Chilean coast by motorcycle and, when it broke down, by any means necessary. The author is better known by his nickname "Che," a common Argentine interjection.

Head, Francis Bond. *Journeys across the Pampas & among the Andes.* Carbondale, IL: Southern Illinois University Press, 1967. Nearly a decade before Darwin, in the early years of Argentine independence, "Galloping Head" rode across the pampas and over the Andes into Chile. Originally published in 1826, some of Head's observations on the gaucho's abilities and adaptability resemble Darwin's, but Head detested Buenos Aires itself.

Naipaul, V.S. *The Return of Eva Perón.* New York: Knopf, 1980. The great but controversial British Nobel Prize–winning author's acerbic observations on Argentine society, in the context of his visit during the vicious 1976–1983 dictatorship.

Petrina, Alberto, ed. *Buenos Aires: Guía de Arquitectura.* Buenos Aires and Seville: Municipalidad de la Ciudad de Buenos Aires and Junta de Andalucía, 1994. An outstanding architectural guide, embellished with architectural sketches and photographs, with eight suggested walking tours.

Symmes, Patrick. *Chasing Che: A Motorcycle Journey in Search of the Guevara Legend.* New York: Vintage, 2000. In a brilliantly conceived trip, Symmes follows the tiremarks of Che's legendary trip from Buenos Aires through Argentina and Chile in the early 1950s. At the same time, he encounters a different series of misfortunes than the guerrilla icon.

HISTORY

Andrews, George Reid. *The Afro-Argentines of Buenos Aires, 1800–1900.* Madison: University of Wisconsin Press, 1980. Groundbreaking research on the supposed disappearance of the capital's Afro-Argentine community, which once comprised nearly a third of its total population.

Crow, John A. *The Epic of Latin America,* 3rd ed. Berkeley: University of California Press, 1980. A comprehensive but immensely readable history of the region, told more through narrative than analysis. Several chapters deal with Argentina.

Cutolo, Vicente Osvaldo. *Buenos Aires: Historia de las Calles y Sus Nombres.* Buenos Aires: Editorial Elche, 1988. This weighty two-volume set details the history not just of nearly every city street, but also the stories behind the street names.

Dujovne Ortiz, Alicia. *Eva Perón.* New York: St. Martin's Press, 1996. Filled with controversial assertions, this nevertheless absorbing biography is most eloquent in describing a poor provincial girl's transformation into a powerful international figure through relentless and bitterly ruthless ambition, blended with genuine concern for the truly destitute. Shawn Fields's translation into English, unfortunately, is awkward.

Goñi, Uki. *The Real Odessa.* New York and London: Granta, 2002. Remarkable account of the controversial links between Juan Perón's government and the shadowy organization that spirited Nazi war criminals into Argentina. Employing a variety of archival sources on a topic that most often relies on rumor, Goñi implicates the Vatican and its Argentine branch as go-betweens in negotiations with the Nazi regime's remnants.

Guy, Donna J. *Sex and Danger in Buenos Aires.* Lincoln: University of Nebraska Press, 1991. An academic account of immigration's seamier side, relating it to sexual imbalance in the population, homosexuality, prostitution, the rise of the tango, and even Peronism.

Lynch, John. *Spanish-American Revolutions, 1808–1826,* 2nd ed. New York: W. W. Norton, 1986. Comprehensive account of the Spanish-American independence movements.

Moya, José C. *Cousins and Strangers: Spanish Immigrants in Buenos Aires, 1850–1930.* Berkeley: University of California Press, 1998. An account of the capital's (and the country's) ambivalent relationship with immigrants often disparaged as *Gallegos* (Galicians).

Parry, J. H. *The Discovery of South America.* London: Paul Elek, 1979. Well-illustrated history of early voyages to and overland explorations of the continent.

Rock, David. *Argentina 1516–1987: From Spanish Colonization to the Falklands War and Alfonsín.* London: I.B. Taurus, 1987. Comprehensive narrative and analysis of Argentine history prior to Carlos Menem's presidency.

Rock, David. *Authoritarian Argentina: The Nationalist Movement, Its History and Its Impact.* Berkeley: University of California Press, 1993. Building on his earlier work, the author examines the durability of right-wing nationalism that led to the 1976–1983 Dirty War, even as comparable nationalist regimes were failing in Spain, Portugal, Mexico, and other countries.

Scobie, James R. *Buenos Aires: From Plaza to Suburb, 1870–1910.* New York: Oxford University Press, 1974. Classic account of the city's explosive late-19th-century growth and the transition from "Gran Aldea" to "Paris of the South."

Shumway, Norman. *The Invention of Argentina.* Berkeley: University of California Press, 1991. An intellectual history of Argentina's founding myths, and the degree to which elitist debate excluded entire sectors of society from participation, leading to frequent ungovernability.

Slatta, Richard. *Cowboys of the Americas.* New Haven and London: Yale University Press, 1990. Spectacularly illustrated comparative account of New World horsemen, including both Argentine gauchos and Chilean *huasos.*

Vidal, Emeric Essex. *Buenos Aires and Montevideo in a Series of Picturesque Illustrations Taken on the Spot.* Buenos Aires: Mitchell's English Book-Store, 1944. Originally published in London in 1820, this British naval officer's remarkable travelogue literally paints a picture—with full-color illustrations to complement his text descriptions—of Buenos Aires in the early independence years.

GOVERNMENT AND POLITICS

Castañeda, Jorge G. *Utopia Unarmed: The Latin American Left After the Cold War.* New York: Knopf, 1993. A former academic, now a Mexican presidential candidate, makes Argentina the starting point in his analysis of the democratization in Latin America's revolutionary left, with a particularly good analysis of the Montoneros urban guerrilla movement.

Caviedes, César. *The Southern Cone: Realities of the Authoritarian State.* Totowa, NJ: Rowman & Allanheld, 1984. Comparative study of the military dictatorships of Chile, Argentina, Uruguay, and Brazil of the 1970s and 1980s.

Verbitsky, Horacio. *The Flight: Confessions of an Argentine Dirty Warrior.* New York: The New Press, 1996. Based on interviews with Francisco Scilingo, a self-confessed torturer and murderer who shoved political prisoners out of airplanes over the South Atlantic, this tells of the worst excesses of the 1976–1983 military dictatorship. Convicted in 2005 in Spain, Scilingo was the first Argentine officer to break the silence over human-rights violations.

LITERATURE AND LITERARY CRITICISM

Martínez, Tomás Eloy. *The Perón Novel.* New York: Pantheon Books, 1988. Based on the author's own lengthy interviews with the exiled caudillo, for which fiction seemed the appropriate outlet. According to Jorge Castañeda, "Whether Perón ever actually uttered these words is in the last analysis irrelevant: he could have, he would have, and he probably did."

Martínez, Tomás Eloy. *Santa Evita.* New York: Knopf, 1996. One of Argentina's leading contemporary writers tackles the Evita myth in a fictional version of her post-mortem odyssey from Argentina to Italy, Spain, and back to Buenos Aires.

Meyer, Doris. *Victoria Ocampo: Against the Wind and the Tide.* Austin: University of Texas Press, 1990. Biography of the woman who led the Argentine equivalent of Britain's Bloomsbury Group, through her literary magazine *Sur* and friendships with Jorge Luis Borges, Adolfo Bioy Casares (married to her sister Silvina, also a writer), and international figures, such as Andre Malraux, José Ortega y Gasset, and Rabindranath Tagore. The volume includes 15 of Victoria's own essays.

Wilson, Jason. *Buenos Aires: A Cultural and Literary Companion.* New York: Interlink, 2000. Part of the Cities of the Imagination series, this is a breathlessly thorough summary of what *porteño* authors as well as other Argentine and foreign authors have written about the capital. It's particularly good at conveying what untranslated Argentine authors have written about the city.

Wilson, Jason. *Traveller's Literary Companion: South & Central America, Including Mexico.* Lincolnwood, IL: Passport Books, 1995. An edited collection of excerpts from literature—including fiction, poetry, and essays—that illuminates aspects of the countries from the Río Grande to the tip of Tierra del Fuego, including Argentina (Buenos Aires in particular) and Uruguay.

Vásquez Montalbán, Manuel. *The Buenos Aires Quintet.* London: Serpent's Tail, 2005. Before his death in late 2003, the Spanish novelist sent his fictional Barcelona detective Pepe Carvalho south to sample the food and unravel a lingering mystery from the Dirty War dictatorship of 1976–1983.

Woodall, James. *Borges: A Life.* New York: Basic Books, 1997. An analytical—in the Freudian sense—biography of Argentina's most prominent literary figure. Originally appeared in Britain under the title *The Man in the Mirror of the Book* (London: Hodder & Stoughton, 1996).

ENVIRONMENT AND NATURAL HISTORY

Hudson, William Henry. *The Bird Biographies of W.H. Hudson.* Santa Barbara, CA: Capra Press, 1988. A partial reprint, with illustrations, of the romantic naturalist's detailed description of the birds he knew growing up in Buenos Aires province.

Internet Resources

The following list of general-interest sites does not include private tour operators (which are covered in this chapter), museums (covered in detail in the *Sights* chapter), or services like hotels and restaurants (covered in the *Accommodations* and *Food and Drink* chapters).

Aerolíneas Argentinas
www.aerolineas.com.ar
This is the homepage for Argentina's improving flagship airline.

Aeropuertos Argentinos 2000
www.aa2000.com.ar
The site for the private concessionaire operating most of Argentina's international and domestic airports, including Buenos Aires's Ezeiza and Aeroparque. In English and Spanish.

Ambitoweb
www.ambitoweb.com
Online version of *porteño* financial daily *Ambito Financiero.*

AmeriSpan
www.amerispan.com
Information on language instruction throughout the Americas, including Argentina.

Apertura
www.apertura.com
Business-oriented Buenos Aires magazine.

Argentina Travel Net
www.argentinatravelnet.com
Portal for Argentine travel sites, though not nearly all of the links are closely related to travel. In Spanish and English.

Asociación Argentina de Albergues de la Juventud (AAAJ)
www.hostelling-aaaj.org.ar
Argentine hostelling organization, with a limited number of facilities throughout the country.

Asociación de Alberguistas del Uruguay
www.hosteluruguay.org
Uruguayan Hostelling International affiliate, with a wide network of hostels around the country.

Asociación de Fútbol Argentina
www.afa.org.ar
Argentina's professional soccer league. In English and Spanish.

Asociación Ornitológica del Plata
www.avesargentinas.org.ar
Buenos Aires–based bird-watching and conservation organization.

Automóvil Club Argentino (ACA)
www.aca.org.ar
Argentine automobile association, useful for information and up-to-date road maps. Offers discounts for members of affiliated clubs, such as AAA in the United States and the AA in Britain.

Buenos Aires Herald
www.buenosairesherald.com
Abbreviated version of the capital's venerable English-language daily.

Buenos Aires Milonga
www.buenosairesmilonga.com
The most up-to-date site for those who want to participate in, not just watch, tango.

B y T Argentina
www.bytargentina.com/ecentro.htm
Short-term apartment rentals and other information on Buenos Aires, in English and Spanish.

Caballito
www.caballitoenlinea.com.ar
Portal website to an interesting but little-touristed residential barrio.

Centers for Disease Control
www.cdc.gov
U.S.-government page with travel health advisories.

CIA Factbook
www.odci.gov/cia/publications/factbook/geos/ar.html
The world's most notorious spooks offer a handy public service in their annual encyclopedia of the world's countries, which appears in its entirety online.

Ciudad Autónoma de Buenos Aires
www.buenosaires.gov.ar
Comprehensive city-government site, which includes tourist information, in Spanish only.

Clarín
www.clarin.com
Outstanding online version of the capital's tabloid daily, the Spanish-speaking world's largest circulation newspaper.

Currency Converter
www.oanda.com
Present and historic exchange-rate information.

Department of State
www.travel.state.gov
Travel information and advisories from the U.S. government; its warnings often err on the side of extreme caution.

Dirección General de Patrimonio
www.dgpatrimonio.buenosaires.gov.ar
Within the city-government site, this separate page is a comprehensive guide to historical resources, both archaeological and contemporary.

Dirección Provincial de Turismo
www.vivalaspampas.com
Buenos Aires provincial tourism office, based in the capital city of La Plata.

Feria del Libro
www.el-libro.com.ar
Buenos Aires's heavily attended annual book fair.

Festival del Tango
www.tangodata.com.ar
Information on the capital's increasingly popular series of autumn (March–April) tango events.

Fondo Nacional de las Artes
www.fnartes.gov.ar
Official federal government site with information on performing arts, architecture, cinema, and related fields.

Gay in Buenos Aires
www.gayinbuenosaires.com.ar
Portal to articles and services of interest to homosexual residents and visitors.

Hostelling International Argentina
www.hostels.org.ar
Argentine Hostelling International affiliate, with information on travel and activities throughout the country.

Instituto Geográfico Militar
www.igm.gov.ar
Military geographical institute, preparing and selling maps of the country.

Instituto Nacional de Estadísticas y Censos (INDEC)
www.indec.mecon.ar
Homepage for the Argentine federal government's statistical agency.

La Maga
www.lamaga.com.ar
Website of the arts- and literature-oriented magazine.

La Nación
www.lanacion.com.ar
Major *porteño* daily, with an excellent Sunday cultural section.

La Plata
www.laplata.gov.ar/index.htm
Portal website of the capital city of Buenos Aires province.

Latin American Network Information Center (LANIC)
www.lanic.utexas.edu
Organized by the University of Texas, this site has a huge collection of quality links to Argentina and other Latin American countries.

Lujanet
www.lujanet.com.ar
Portal for Luján, the historical and pilgrimage center of Buenos Aires province.

Mercado
www.mercado.com.ar
Business-oriented Buenos Aires weekly magazine.

Mercopress News Agency
www.falkland-malvinas.com
Montevideo-based Internet news agency covering politics and business in the Mercosur common market countries of Argentina, Brazil, Uruguay, and Paraguay, as well as Chile and the Falkland/Malvinas Islands. In English and Spanish.

Metrovías
www.metrovias.com.ar
Details on Buenos Aires's subway system.

Ministerio de Relaciones Exteriores
www.mrecic.gov.ar/consulares/pag-con.html
Argentine Foreign Ministry, with information on visas and consulates, in English and Spanish.

Páginas Amarillas
www.paginasamarillas.com.ar
Yellow Pages for all of Argentina.

Página 12
www.pagina12.com.ar
Outspoken left-of-center daily, which has shifted away from reporting and toward opinion, but features some of the country's best writers.

PalermOnline
www.palermonline.com.ar
Portal to sights and services in one of the city's liveliest barrios, Palermo.

Puerto de Tigre
www.puertodetigre.com
The suburban gateway to the popular Paraná delta.

San Antonio de Areco
www.arecoturismo.com.ar
The country's symbolic gaucho capital, in Buenos Aires province.

Secretaría Nacional de Turismo
www.turismo.gov.ar
National tourism authority, with information in Spanish and English.

UkiNet
www.ukinet.com
Freelance writer Uki Goñi's human-rights-oriented website, with an archive of his best work from Britain's *Guardian* and other sources.

Usenet Discussion Groups

Rec.travel.latin-america
Regional forum dealing with all Latin American countries, with a steady number of postings on Argentina.

Soc.culture.argentina
No-holds-barred forum that touches on many issues other than travel.

Index

Architectural Highlights

Walking Tours

Acknowledgments

Similar to my efforts in writing about Guatemala, Chile, Argentina, and Patagonia, this book owes its existence in its present form to numerous individuals in North America, Buenos Aires, Montevideo, and elsewhere. Once again, praise to Bill Newlin and his Emeryville staff at Avalon Travel Publishing for continuing author-friendly contracts even as other guidebook publishers are ruthlessly eliminating them.

After more than 25 years' experience in Argentina and Buenos Aires, more than half that as a guidebook writer, I owe enormous unpayable debts to friends, acquaintances, and officials throughout the country. My apologies to anyone I may have overlooked or perhaps deleted because of an errant keystroke.

In Buenos Aires and vicinity, thanks to Diego Allolio; Joaquín Allolio; Sebastián Letemendia; Mario Banchik of Librerías Turísticas; Pablo Blay and Mariana Travacio; Mirta S. Capurro and Mónica Kapusta of the municipal Subsecretaría de Turismo; Diego Curubeto; Pablo Fisch and Silvina Garay of Hostelling International; Andrew Graham-Yooll and Dereck Foster of the *Buenos Aires Herald;* Jorge Helft and Marion Eppinger for keeping me up-to-date on Argentine art; Harry S. Ingham; Dori Lieberman; Juan Massolo; Manuel Massolo; Enrique Meyer of the Secretaría de Turismo de la Nación; Ernesto Semán; and Cristián Soler of Tigre.

In Montevideo, thanks to Manuel Pérez Bravo of Hotel Mediterráneo; Andrés Linardi of Librería Linardi y Risso; José García Briones of Hotel Solís; and Mónica de Mello of Hostelling International. Special mention to Lauro Arias of the Asociación de Exportadores de Vino for helping introduce me to Uruguayan wines.

Stateside, thanks to Leandro Fernández Suárez of the Argentine consulate in Los Angeles; and Patricio Rubalcaba and Misty Pinson of LanChile, Miami.

And finally, thanks to my wife María Laura Massolo; my daughter Clio Bernhardson-Massolo; the memory of my late Alaskan Malamute Gardel; and Gardel's adoptive Akita brother Sandro, who reminds me when I need to take a nap.

PERU

ECUADOR

CHILE

BOLIVIA

BRAZIL

ARGENTINA

EXPLORING THE *South* OF THE WORLD

INTRODUCING LANVACATIONS
Uniquely Crafted Adventures

LAN Airlines Alliance now offers LANVACATIONS, an array of packages for a complete travel experience. You can create a vacation tailored exactly to your specifications, whether you are traveling alone or in a small group, and whether you choose from the modules outlined in our programs or create unique itinerary crafted around your individual interests and desire for adventure. So while you enjoy unforgettable cultural and natural adventures you can relax knowing you will experience travel at its most perfect form.

LAN Airlines Alliance's 75 years of experience will stand behind your trip. Enjoy the complete experience of travel with LANVACATIONS.

LANVACATIONS ★

For reservations and information, please call LANVACATIONS
at 1 800 435 3593 or visit us at www.lanvacations.com

U.S.~Metric Conversion

1 inch = 2.54 centimeters (cm)
1 foot = .304 meters (m)
1 yard = 0.914 meters
1 mile = 1.6093 kilometers (km)
1 km = .6214 miles
1 fathom = 1.8288 m
1 chain = 20.1168 m
1 furlong = 201.168 m
1 acre = .4047 hectares
1 sq km = 100 hectares
1 sq mile = 2.59 square km
1 ounce = 28.35 grams
1 pound = .4536 kilograms
1 short ton = .90718 metric ton
1 short ton = 2000 pounds
1 long ton = 1.016 metric tons
1 long ton = 2240 pounds
1 metric ton = 1000 kilograms
1 quart = .94635 liters
1 US gallon = 3.7854 liters
1 Imperial gallon = 4.5459 liters
1 nautical mile = 1.852 km

To compute Celsius temperatures, subtract 32 from Fahrenheit and divide by 1.8. To go the other way, multiply Celsius by 1.8 and add 32.

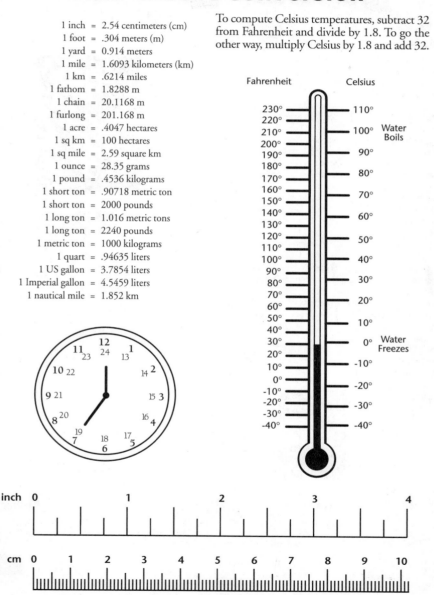

Keeping Current

Although we strive to produce the most up-to-date guidebook humanly possible, change is unavoidable. Between the time this book goes to print and the moment you read it, a handful of the businesses noted in these pages will undoubtedly change prices, move, or even close their doors forever. Other worthy attractions will open for the first time. If you have a favorite gem you'd like to see included in the next edition, or see anything that needs updating, clarification, or correction, please drop us a line. Send your comments via email to atpfeedback@avalonpub.com, or use the address below.

Moon Handbooks Buenos Aires
Avalon Travel Publishing
1400 65th Street, Suite 250
Emeryville, CA 94608, USA
www.moon.com

Editor: Kay Elliott
Series Manager: Kevin McLain
Acquisitions Manager: Rebecca K. Browning
Copy Editor: Kim Marks
Graphics Coordinator: Stefano Boni
Production Coordinators: Darren Alessi, Tamara Gronet
Cover Designer: Kari Gim
Interior Designer: Amber Pirker
Map Editor: Kevin Anglin
Cartographer: Kat Kalamaras
Cartographic Manager: Mike Morgenfeld
Indexer: Rachel Kuhn

ISBN-10: 1-56691-886-3
ISBN-13: 978-1-56691-886-2
ISSN: 1543-6500

Printing History
1st Edition–2003
2nd Edition–November 2005
5 4 3 2 1

Text © 2005 by Wayne Bernhardson.
Maps © 2005 by Avalon Travel Publishing, Inc.
All rights reserved.

Avalon Travel Publishing
An Imprint of
Avalon Publishing Group, Inc.

AVALON
publishing group incorporated

Some photos and illustrations are used by permission and are the property of the original copyright owners.

Front cover photo: © Sinan Anadol

Printed in Canada by Transcontinental